Brothers in Arms

BROTHERS IN ARMS

One Legendary Tank Regiment's Bloody War from D-Day to VE-Day

James Holland

Atlantic Monthly Press
New York

First Published in Great Britain in 2021 by Bantam Press,
an imprint of Transworld Publishers

Published simultaneously in Canada
Printed in the United States of America

First Grove Atlantic hardcover edition: November 2021

Typeset in 11.25/14 pt Minion Pro by Jouve (UK), Milton Keynes

Library of Congress Cataloging-in-Publication data is available for this title.

ISBN 978-0-8021-5908-3
eISBN 978-0-8021-5909-0

Atlantic Monthly Press
an imprint of Grove Atlantic
154 West 14th Street New York, NY 10011

Distributed by Publishers Group West

groveatlantic.com

21 22 23 24 25   10 9 8 7 6 5 4 3 2 1

For David Christopherson

Contents

Note on the Text

Reading the names and numbers of military units can often be confusing, and it can be hard to keep track of who is who. In an effort to make it more obvious, I have listed German units as they would be spelled in the vernacular, so that, for example, the 6th Paratroop Regiment has become 6. Fallschirmjäger Regiment, and 'battalion' has been written 'Bataillon' – not to be pretentious, but simply in the hope that this will help distinguish Allied and German units more easily.

The spelling of many place names has subtly changed since 1944–5; for consistency, I have used the spellings used on British-issued military maps of the time. Geel, for example, is spelled without an 'h' today, but was known as 'Gheel' to the British in 1944 and so this is the spelling I have used.

This book is something of a snapshot of the Sherwood Rangers, not a comprehensive history of the regiment, and so follows just a handful of those who served during the final eleven months of the Second World War. As a result, many who deserve to have their exploits written about or even mentioned in passing do not feature. I hope it will be read in the spirit in which it has been written.

James Holland, June 2021

Jig Gold Beach, 7 June 1944

List of Maps and
Aerial Photographs

Stanley Christopherson (*right*) leans on the bonnet of a jeep as he discusses the situation at Rauray ridge on 29 June 1944 with Lieutenant-Colonel Anderson of the 24th Lancers (*centre*) and Brigadier Cracroft (*second from right*)

Note on Maps and Aerial Photographs

While researching this book, I drew heavily on contemporary aerial photographs and wartime maps (including some used at the time by Stanley Christopherson). These were augmented by liberal use of Google Earth images. For this reason, we are using annotated versions of these various photographs, maps and images in place of a number of the more usual drawn maps used in books of this kind. I have also placed all these various images together at the front of the book rather than integrating them into the text so that readers can more easily locate them. I hope they are as much help to readers as they were to me when piecing together many of the Sherwood Rangers' battles in these last eleven months of the war in Europe.

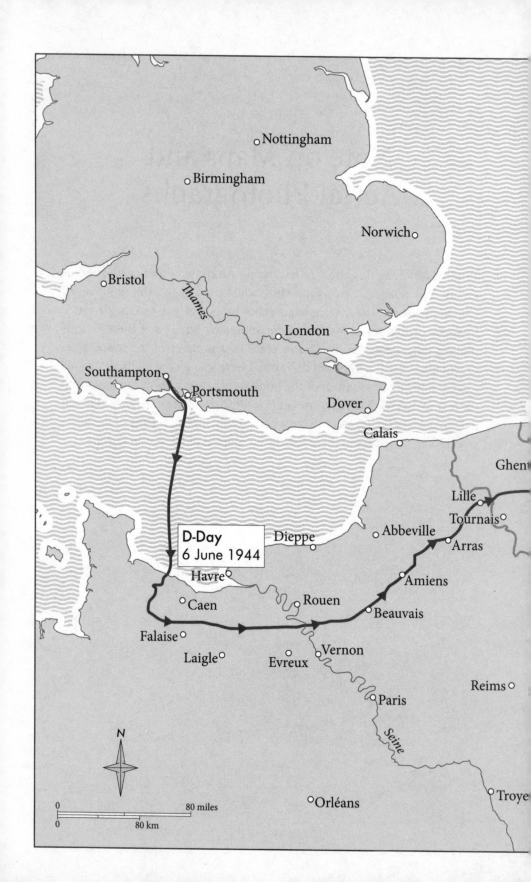

Nottingham

Birmingham

Norwich

Bristol

Thames

London

Southampton

Portsmouth

Dover

Calais

Ghen

Lille

Tournais

D-Day
6 June 1944

Dieppe

Abbeville

Arras

Havre

Amiens

Caen

Rouen

Beauvais

Falaise

Laigle

Evreux

Vernon

Reims

Paris

Seine

N

0   80 miles

0   80 km

Orléans

Troye

THE SHERWOOD RANGERS' ROUTE ACROSS NORTH-WEST EUROPE

End of war for SRY, 5 May 1945

Bremervörde

Hamburg

Bremen

Verden

Amsterdam

Lingen

Bassum

Diepholz

The Hague

Rotterdam

Hengeloo

Arnhem

Hanover

Nijmegen

Maas

Münster

Brunswick

Goch

Rees

Eindhoven

Wesel

ntwerp

Dortmund

Bourg-Leopold

Brussels

Düsseldorf

Heinsberg

Louvain

Geilenkirchen

Maastricht

Cologne

Kassel

Weser

Liège

Aachen

Rhine

Frankfurt

Luxembourg

Strasbourg

UTAH

OMAHA

17 July '44

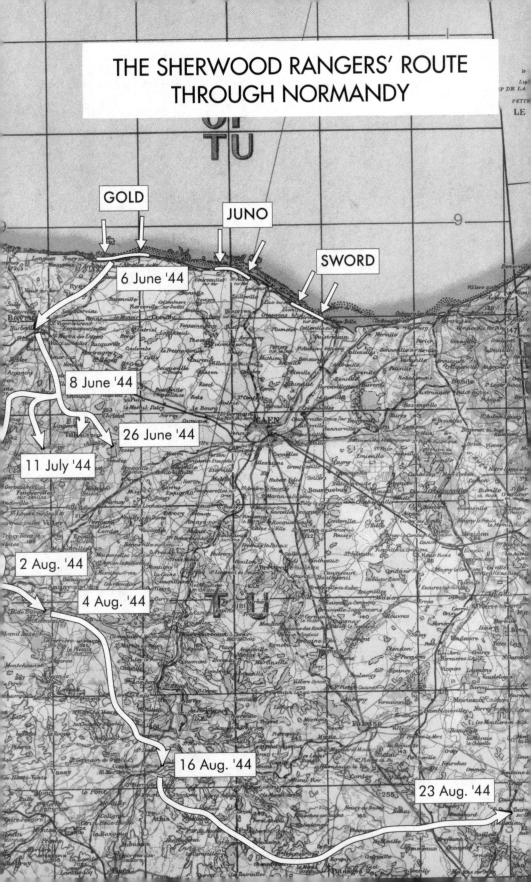

THE SHERWOOD RANGERS' ROUTE
THROUGH NORMANDY

GOLD

JUNO

SWORD

6 June '44

8 June '44

26 June '44

11 July '44

2 Aug. '44

4 Aug. '44

16 Aug. '44

23 Aug. '44

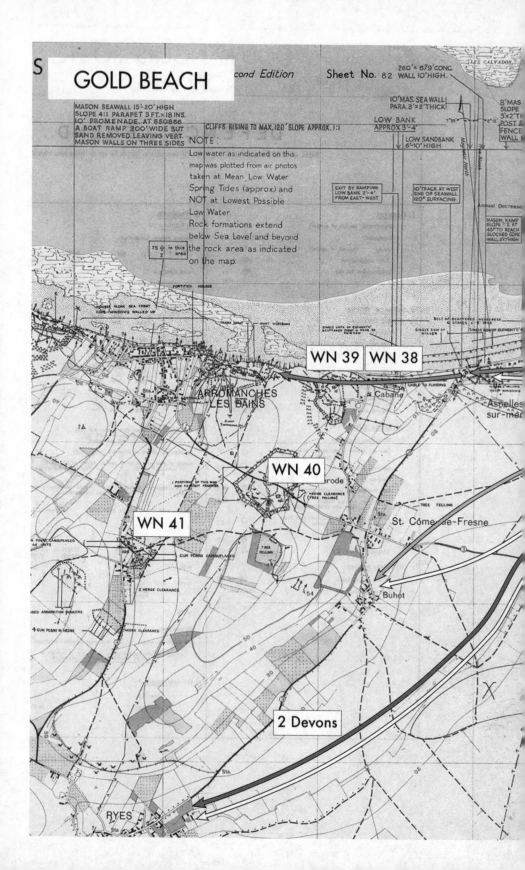

GOLD BEACH

Second Edition   Sheet No. 82   260'× 679' CONC. WALL 10' HIGH.

MASON SEAWALL 15'-20' HIGH
SLOPE 4:1 PARAPET 3 FT.× 18 INS.
10' PROMENADE. AT 850866
A BOAT RAMP 200' WIDE BUT
SAND REMOVED LEAVING VERT.
MASON WALLS ON THREE SIDES

CLIFFS RISING TO MAX. 120' SLOPE APPROX. 1:1

10' MAS. SEA WALL
PARA. 3'× 2' THICK

8' MAS
SLOPE
3'× 2' TH
POST &
FENCE
WALL

LOW BANK
APPROX 3'-4'

LOW SANDBANK
6'-10' HIGH

NOTE:
Low water as indicated on this
map was plotted from air photos
taken at Mean Low Water
Spring Tides (approx) and
NOT at Lowest Possible
Low Water.
Rock formations extend
below Sea Level and beyond
the rock area as indicated
on the map.

EXIT BY RAMPING
LOW BANK 2'-4'
FROM EAST-WEST

10' TRACK AT WEST
END OF SEAWALL
120" SURFACING

MASON, RAMP
SLOPE 1:2 AT
45° TO BEACH
BLOCKED CONC
WALL 5'0" HIGH

Annual Decrease

75 ill in this
2'   area

FORTIFIED HOUSES

WN 39   WN 38

ARROMANCHES
LES BAINS

Cabane

Asnelles
sur-mer

WN 40

WN 41

St. Côme-de-Fresne

Buhot

54

2 Devons

RYES

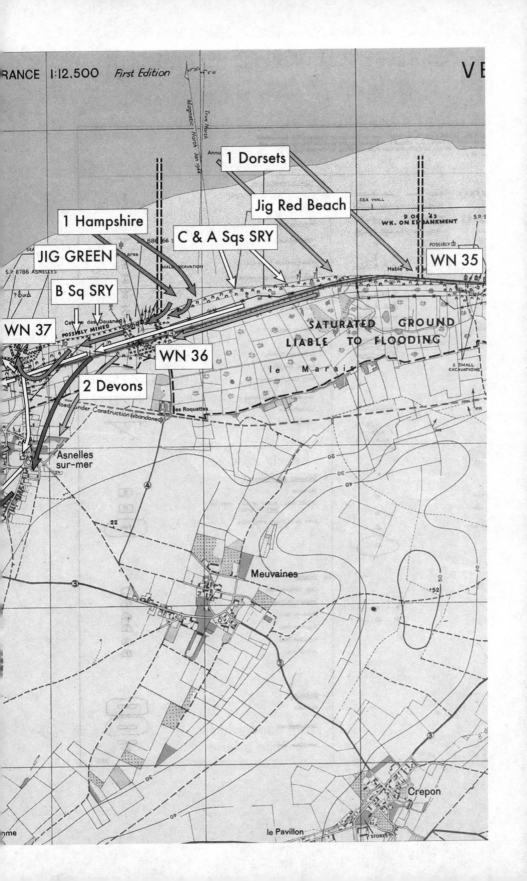

GOLD BEACH, JIG RED SECTOR

N

Waves breaking over
beach obstacles

Swamped landing craft

Water breaking over
beach obstacles

LCT

Shell crater

Tanks and vehicles
coming ashore

Jig Red Beach

Landing craft

LCT pushed
sideways by wind

Trucks

Tanks

Tanks

GOLD BEACH AND ASNELLES, 10.30 A.M. D-DAY

N

3 x SRY tanks

Lead tank

Shell craters

Trench along hedgeline

Trench

Shell craters

Shadows of sun
from east

Knocked-out tank -
probably B Sq SRY

GOLD BEACH AND ASNELLES, 11.30 A.M. D-DAY

Le Hamel

Mines

Anti-tank ditch

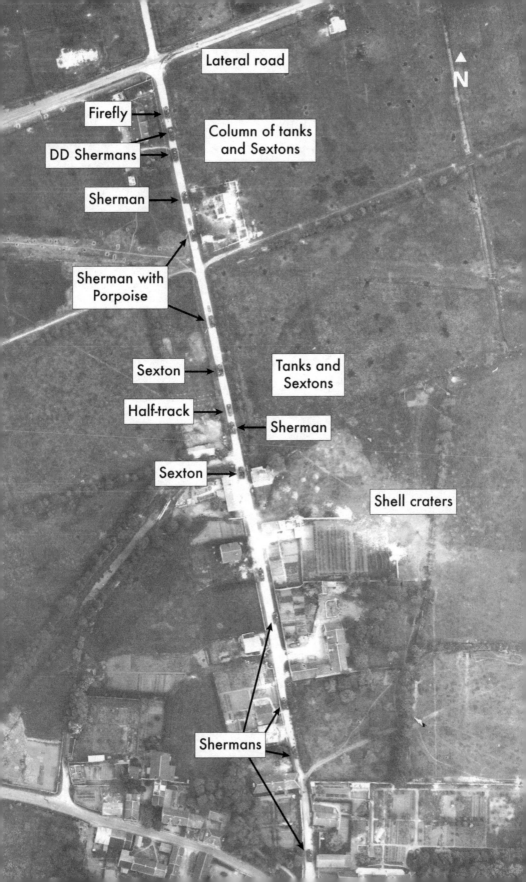

Lateral road

N

Firefly

DD Shermans

Column of tanks
and Sextons

Sherman

Sherman with
Porpoise

Sexton

Tanks and
Sextons

Half-track

Sherman

Sexton

Shell craters

Shermans

Crépon

Meuvaines

Tanks and vehicles

Tanks and vehicles

Lateral road

Waterlogged area

WN 36

Jig Green

Jig Red

LCT

GOLD BEACH AND ASNELLES/LE HAMEL,
1.00 P.M. D-DAY

Ryes

N

Tanks and vehicles

Asnelles

Anti-tank ditch

WN 37

Monty Horley's
tank

knocked-out and
bogged tanks

Breakers over beach obstacles

Monty Horley' tank

Blockhouse with 77mm gun

WN 37

Trench

Shell crater

Tanks and Sextons heading into Asnelles

Flail tank

Knocked-out SRY DDs
and AVREs

Flail tank

Knocked-out
AVREs

Lateral road

SSW

GOLD BEACH JIG GREEN SECTOR,
2.00 P.M. D-DAY

POINT 103, SAINT-PIERRE AND FONTENAY

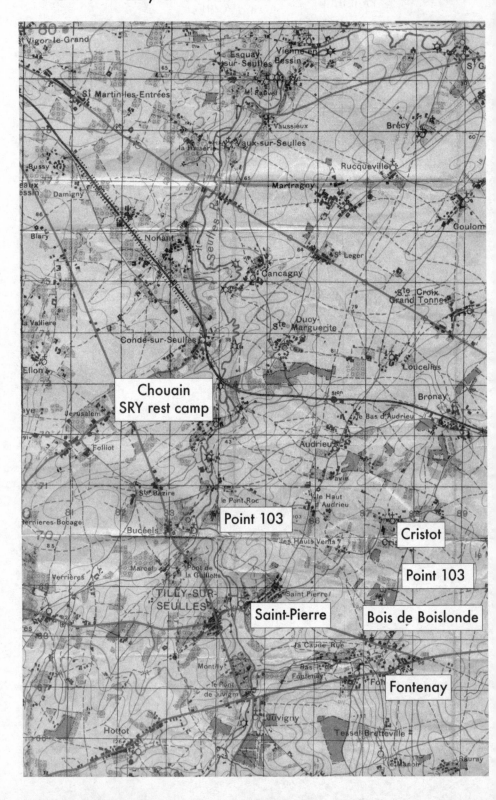

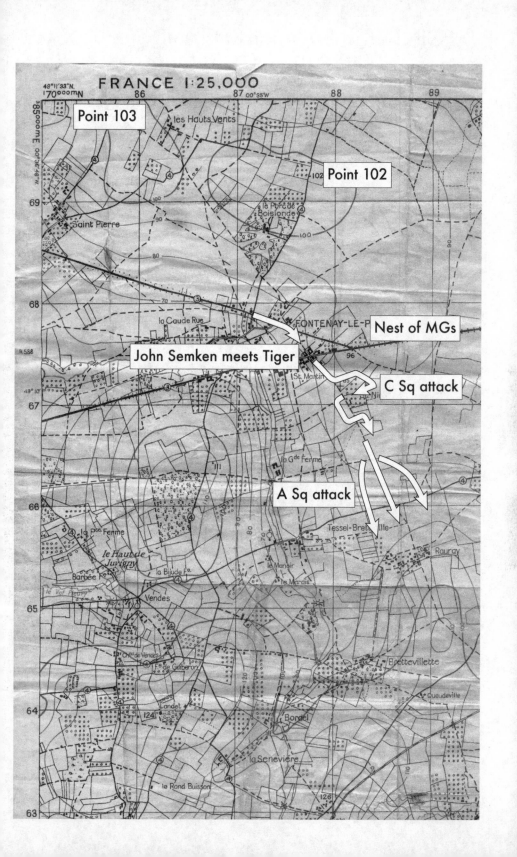

FRANCE 1:25,000

Point 103

Point 102

Nest of MGs

John Semken meets Tiger

C Sq attack

A Sq attack

KEY
1. Keith Douglas killed and buried
2. Peter Pepler killed and buried

Route to Point 103

Vehicle tracks

Le Haut d'Audrie

Lane

Point 103

2.

1.

POINT 103

Château d'Audrieu

Woods where Canadians executed by 12. SS

Audrieu

Cratering in fields

Cristot

SAINT-PIERRE

Keith Douglas and
John Bethell-Fox
escape from river

Tilly-sur-Seulles

Stephen Mitchell tank
knocked out in this tree
and hedge-lined field

River Seulles

Vehicle and tank tracks

To Point 103

B & C squadrons leagurered

Orchards

Road to Audrieu and Point 103

HQ SRY

Manoir from which HQ SRY attacked

Road to Fontenay

146th Brigade attack
25 June

Op MARTLET
25 June 1944

N

Road
Saint-Pierre–Fontenay

'Barracuda'

BOIS DE BOISLONDE AND FONTENAY

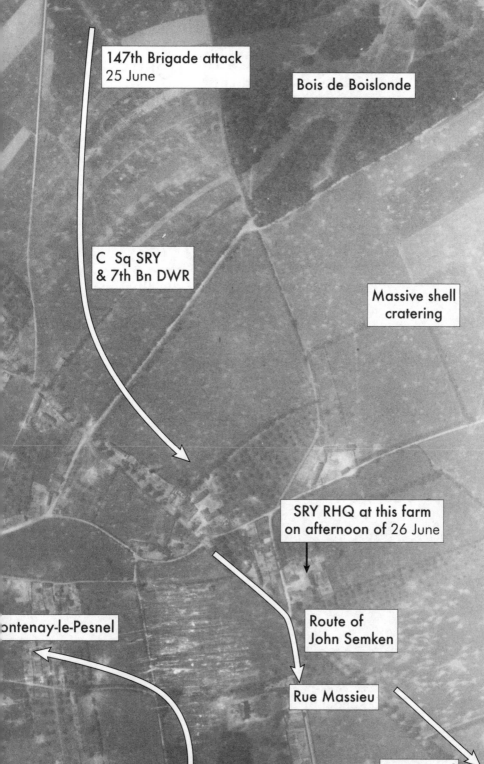

147th Brigade attack
25 June

Bois de Boislonde

C Sq SRY
& 7th Bn DWR

Massive shell
cratering

SRY RHQ at this farm
on afternoon of 26 June

ontenay-le-Pesnel

Route of
John Semken

Rue Massieu

To 'nest' of
Spandaus

Route of Tiger

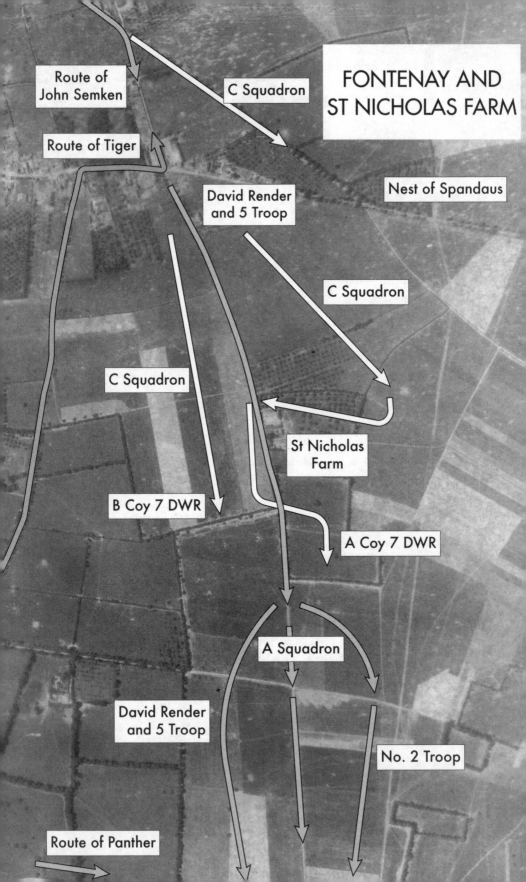

Route of
John Semken

C Squadron

Route of Tiger

FONTENAY AND
ST NICHOLAS FARM

David Render
and 5 Troop

Nest of Spandaus

C Squadron

C Squadron

St Nicholas
Farm

B Coy 7 DWR

A Coy 7 DWR

A Squadron

David Render
and 5 Troop

No. 2 Troop

Route of Panther

An anti-tank platoon of the 11th DLI pauses by the
Panther that was knocked out by Neville Fearn and
George Dring near Rauray on 26 June 1944

A Sherman of the 24th Lancers near Rauray

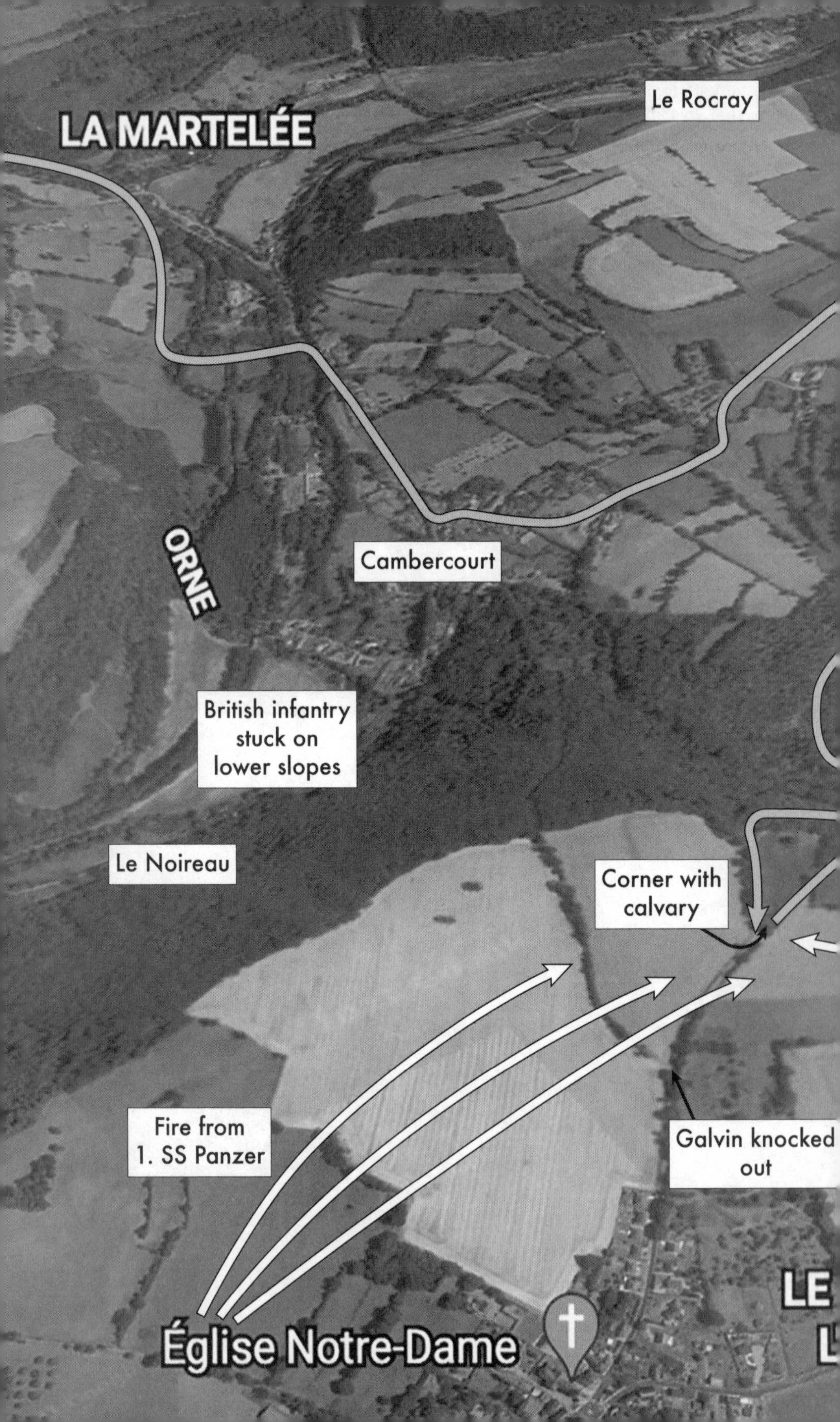

LA MARTELÉE

Le Rocray

ORNE

Cambercourt

British infantry
stuck on
lower slopes

Le Noireau

Corner with
calvary

Fire from
1. SS Panzer

Galvin knocked
out

LE

L

Église Notre-Dame

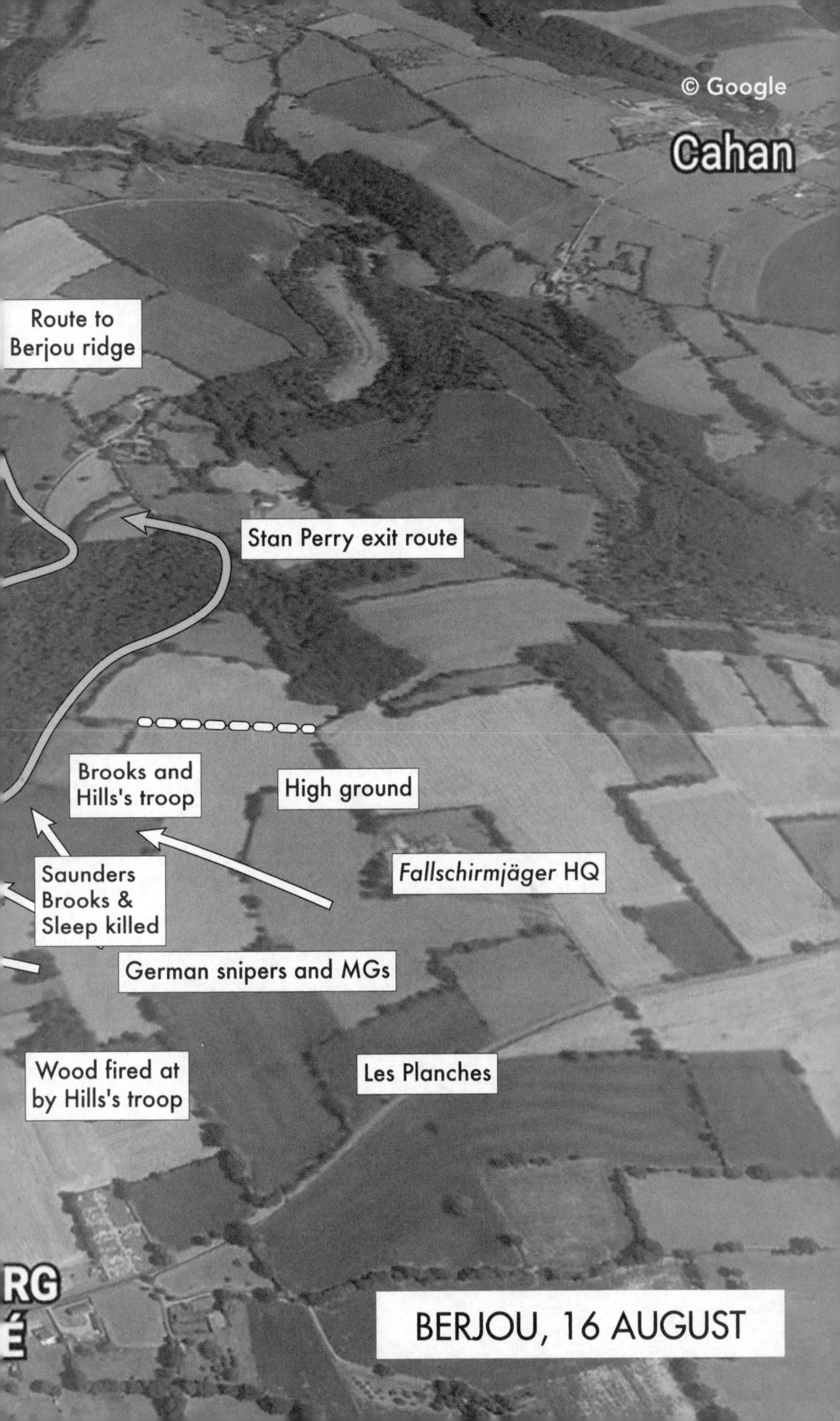

© Google

Cahan

Route to
Berjou ridge

Stan Perry exit route

Brooks and
Hills's troop

High ground

Saunders
Brooks &
Sleep killed

Fallschirmjäger HQ

German snipers and MGs

Wood fired at
by Hills's troop

Les Planches

RG
É

BERJOU, 16 AUGUST

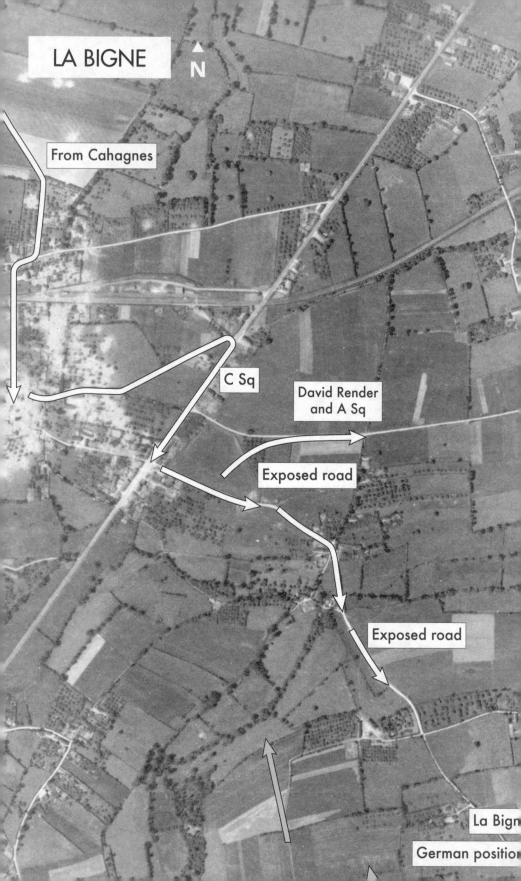

LA BIGNE

N

From Cahagnes

C Sq

David Render
and A Sq

Exposed road

Exposed road

La Bign

German position

T-146960

Two Sherwood Rangers crewmen preparing food beside their tank

A five-man Sherman crew from A Squadron

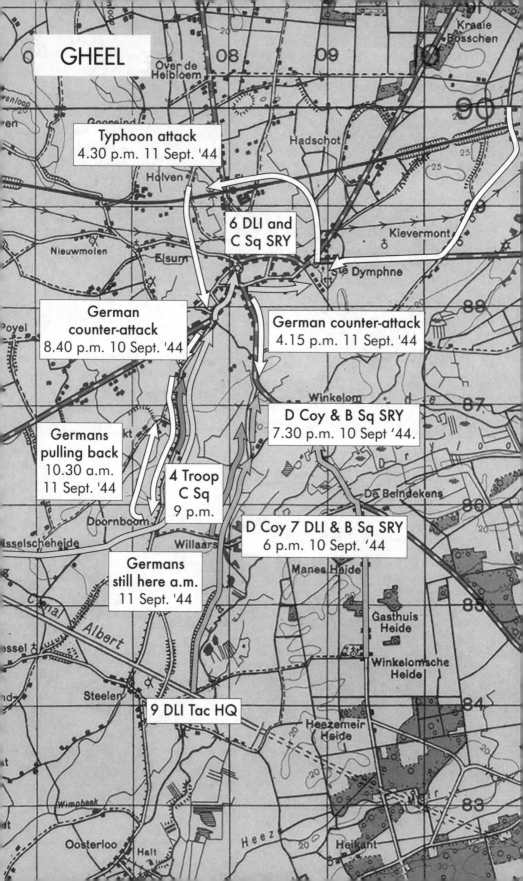

GHEEL

Kraaie Bosschen

Typhoon attack
4.30 p.m. 11 Sept. '44

6 DLI and
C Sq SRY

Kievermont

Dymphne

German
counter-attack
8.40 p.m. 10 Sept. '44

German counter-attack
4.15 p.m. 11 Sept. '44

Winkelom

D Coy & B Sq SRY
7.30 p.m. 10 Sept '44.

Germans
pulling back
10.30 a.m.
11 Sept. '44

4 Troop
C Sq
9 p.m.

De Beindekens

D Coy 7 DLI & B Sq SRY
6 p.m. 10 Sept. '44

Germans
still here a.m.
11 Sept. '44

Manes Heide

Gasthuis
Heide

Winkelomsche
Heide

9 DLI Tac HQ

Heezemeir
Heide

Steelen

Oosterloo

Heikant

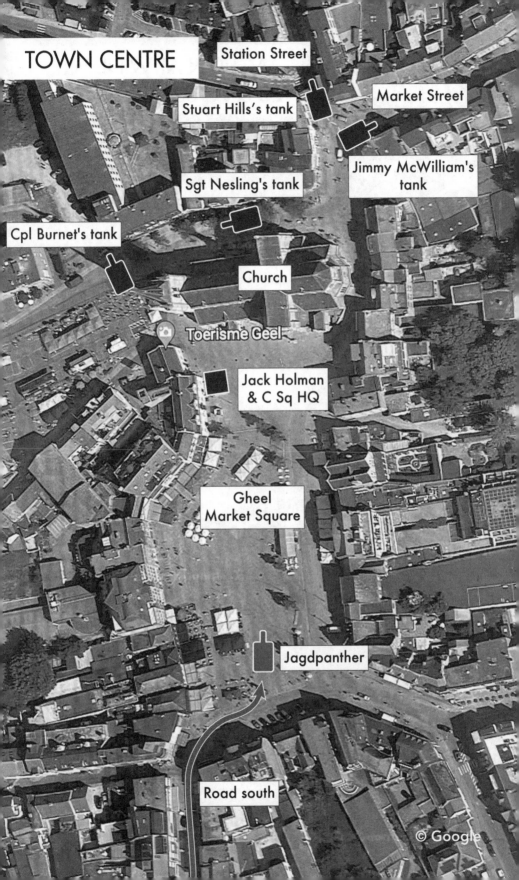

TOWN CENTRE

Station Street

Stuart Hills's tank

Market Street

Jimmy McWilliam's tank

Sgt Nesling's tank

Cpl Burnet's tank

Church

Toerisme Geel

Jack Holman & C Sq HQ

Gheel Market Square

Jagdpanther

Road south

© Google

ACTION AT WINDMILL,
23 & 25 SEPTEMBER 1944

Route of Harry Heenan
25 September 1944

US 82nd
Airborne troops

© Google

Site of windmill

88mm

Site of former orchard

German positions

David Render hit
25 September 1944

Hauptwä

Hidden dyke
where Hills gets stuck

23 September 1944
Route of Hills and Nesling

Ruskamp Tandarts

Grondig Geniethen

German positions

Peter Mellowe

Sgt O'Pray

Tommy Spoors

De Enk

Route through woods

LOCHEM ROAD BLOCK,
23 SEPTEMBER 1944

© Google

The whitewash has already started to streak and
wash away as this Sherwood Ranger Sherman
struggles in the snow during BLACKCOCK

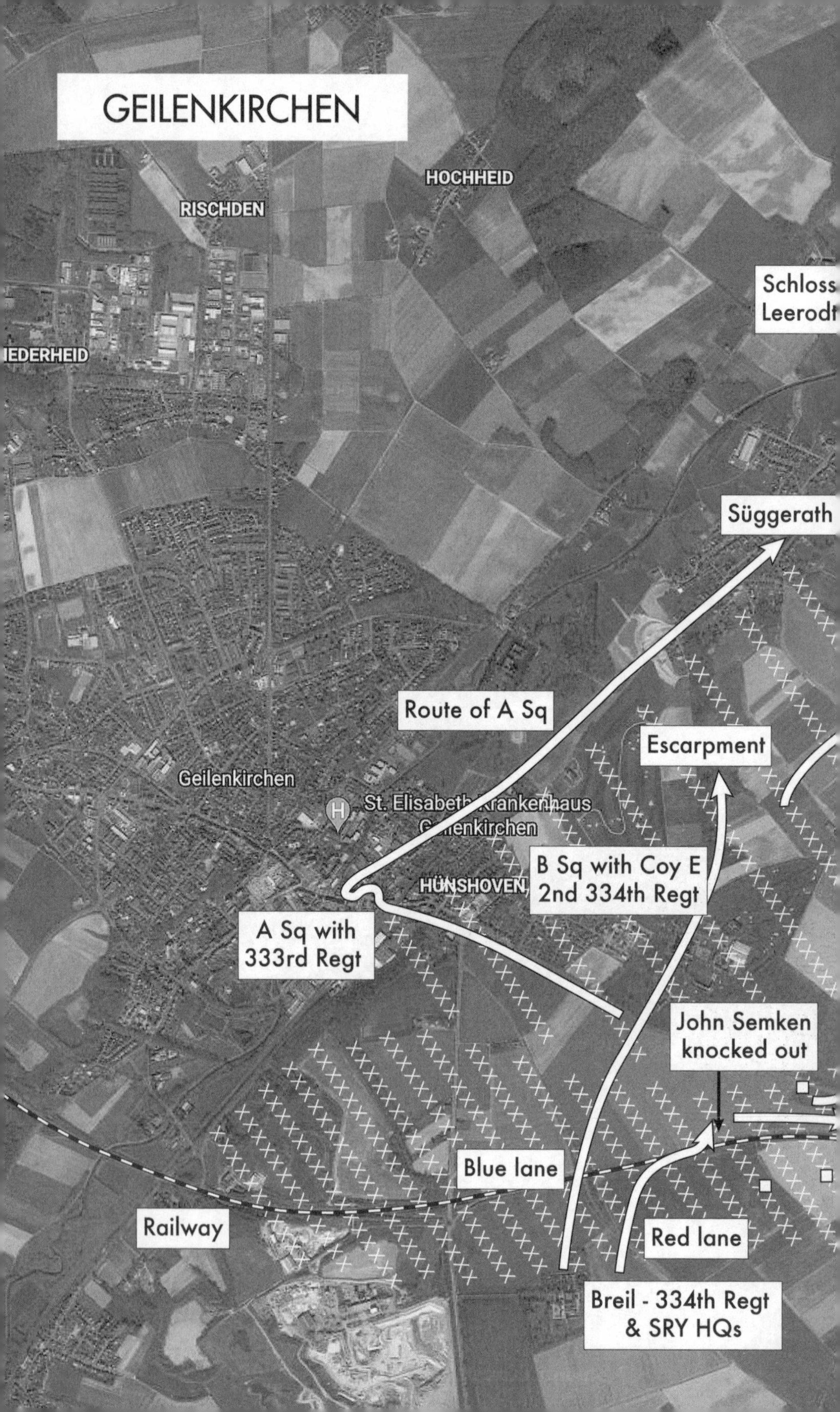

GEILENKIRCHEN

RISCHDEN

HOCHHEID

IEDERHEID

Schloss Leerodt

Süggerath

Route of A Sq

Escarpment

Geilenkirchen

St. Elisabeth Krankenhaus Geilenkirchen

B Sq with Coy E 2nd 334th Regt

HÜNSHOVEN

A Sq with 333rd Regt

John Semken knocked out

Blue lane

Railway

Red lane

Breil - 334th Regt & SRY HQs

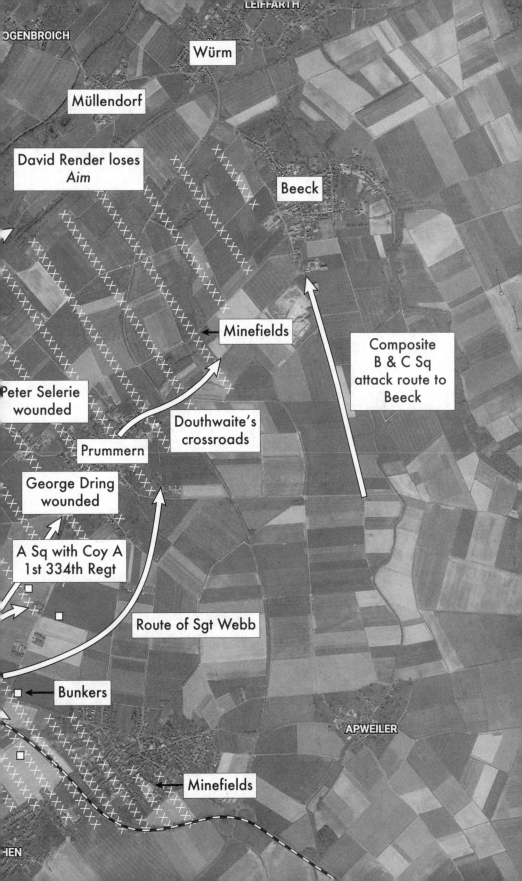

LEIFFARTH

OGENBROICH

Würm

Müllendorf

David Render loses *Aim*

Beeck

Minefields

Composite
B & C Sq
attack route to
Beeck

Peter Selerie
wounded

Prummern

Douthwaite's
crossroads

George Dring
wounded

A Sq with Coy A
1st 334th Regt

Route of Sgt Webb

Bunkers

APWEILER

Minefields

HEN

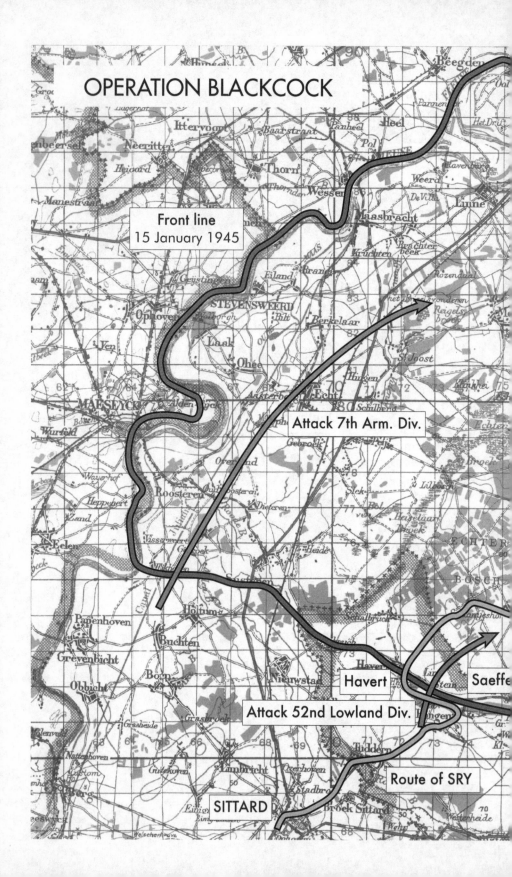

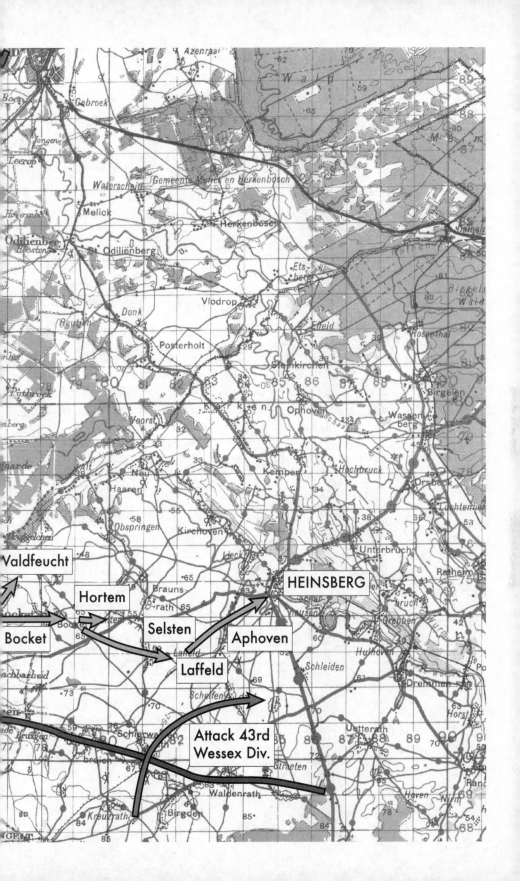

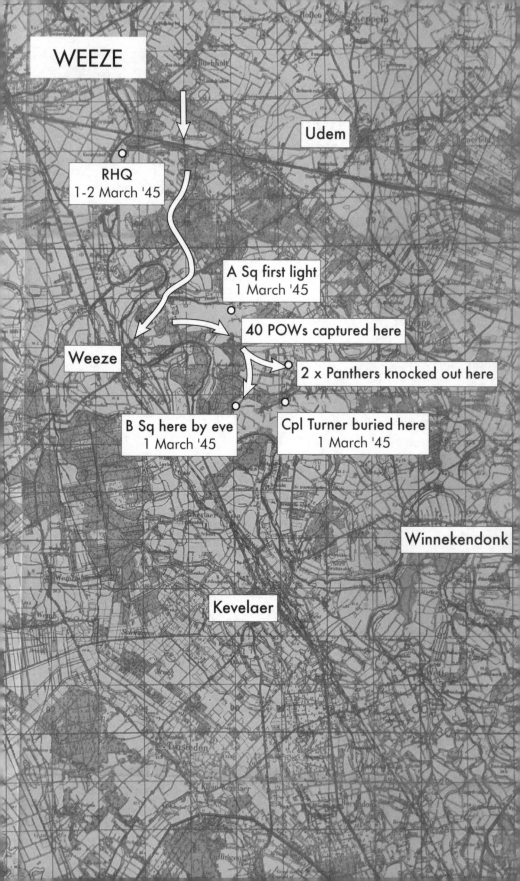

WEEZE

Udem

RHQ
1-2 March '45

A Sq first light
1 March '45

40 POWs captured here

Weeze

2 x Panthers knocked out here

B Sq here by eve
1 March '45

Cpl Turner buried here
1 March '45

Winnekendonk

Kevelaer

Sherwood Rangers in Issum, 6 March 1945

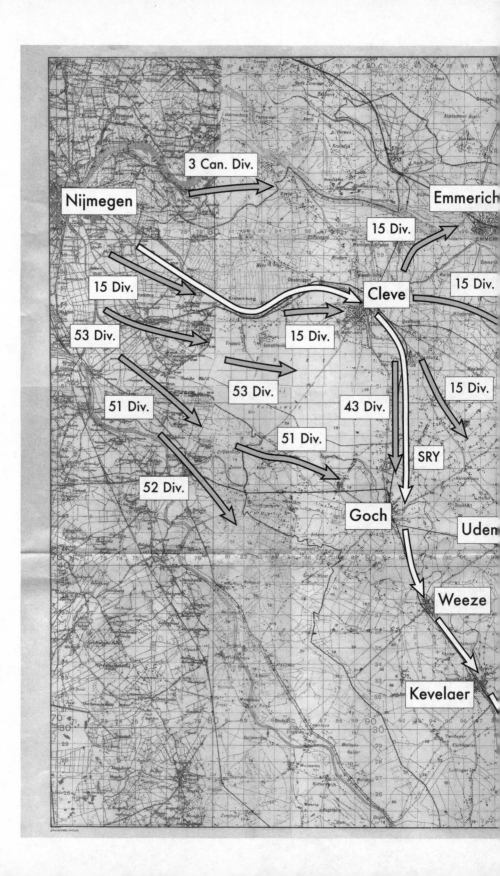

Nijmegen

3 Can. Div.

Emmerich

15 Div.

15 Div.

15 Div.

Cleve

15 Div.

53 Div.

15 Div.

15 Div.

53 Div.

43 Div.

51 Div.

51 Div.

SRY

52 Div.

Goch

Udem

Weeze

Kevelaer

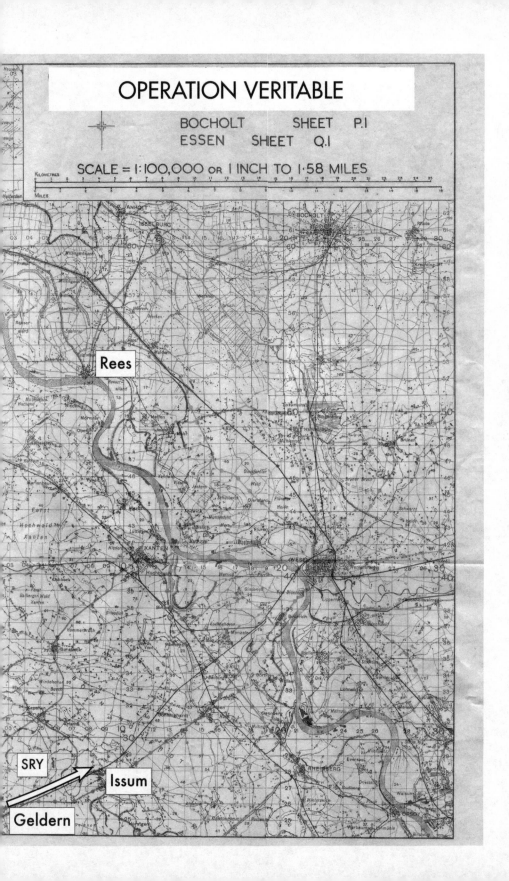

OPERATION VERITABLE

BOCHOLT   SHEET   P.1
ESSEN   SHEET   Q.1

SCALE = 1:100,000 or 1 INCH TO 1·58 MILES

DINXPERLO, MARCH 1945

Bridgehead established by Mellowes' troop and 7th Argyll & Sutherland Highlanders

Second bridge

First bridge

River Aa

Dennis Elmore hit

Route of Denis Elmore

German defences

Crossroads

Orchard

Route of
Peter Mellowes' troop

Stuhr

NEAR BREMEN,
19 APRIL 1945

N

Ernie Leppard's Firefly crew in Issum

Principal Personalities

(Ranks as at end of war)

Lieutenant-Colonel Stanley Christopherson, DSO,*[1] MC,* Silver Star, TD
Commanding officer of the Sherwood Rangers from 15 June 1944 to the war's end

Major Anthony Cotterell
Official war correspondent for British Army

Trooper Stan Cox
A Squadron

Corporal John Cropper
Radio operator/loader, B Squadron 24th Lancers, later 4 Troop, B Squadron

Captain Keith Douglas
Second-in-command, A Squadron

Sergeant George Dring, MM*
No. 4 Troop sergeant, A Squadron

Major Micky Gold, MC, TD
Commander, B Squadron

Lieutenant Harry Heenan
No. 2 Troop leader, A Squadron

Captain Stuart Hills, MC
No. 4 Troop leader, C Squadron, later Intelligence Officer, then commander, Recce Troop

Major Jack Holman, MC
Second-in-command, then squadron leader, C Squadron

Captain Frenchie Houghton
Adjutant, Regimental HQ

Squadron Sergeant-Major Henry Hutchinson, MM
Squadron Sergeant-Major, A Squadron

Trooper Bert Jenkins
Gunner, B Squadron

Myrtle Kellett
Widow of Colonel Flash Kellett, MC, MP, and Head of the Sherwood Rangers Regimental Welfare Association

Sergeant Johnny Lanes
Troop sergeant, A Squadron

Major the Lord Robin Leigh
Second-in-command, Sherwood Rangers Yeomanry

Trooper Ernie Leppard
Radio operator/loader, 5 Troop, B Squadron

Captain Peter Mellowes, MC
4 Troop leader, then second-in-command, A Squadron

---

[1] The asterisk denotes a bar – in other words, a second award of the same medal.

Lieutenant Stan Perry
2 Troop leader, C Squadron

Trooper Arthur Reddish
C Squadron, later driver in A1
Echelon

Lieutenant David Render
Troop leader, A Squadron

Major Peter Selerie, Silver Star
Second-in-command, B Squadron,
then commander, C Squadron

Major John Semken, MC
Technical adjutant, then
commander, A Squadron

Captain Rev. Leslie Skinner
Chaplain, 8th Armoured Brigade,
attached Sherwood Rangers
Yeomanry

Captain Eric 'Bill' Wharton, MC
Troop leader, then second-in-
command, B Squadron

John Bethell-Fox

Stanley Christopherson

Anthony Cotterell

John Cropper

Keith Douglas

George Dring

Denis Elmore

Micky Gold

Harry Heenan

Stuart Hills

Jack Holman

Henry Hutchinson

Myrtle Kellett

Johnny Lanes

Rupert Leigh

Ernie Leppard

Peter Mellowes

Stan Perry

Arthur Reddish

David Render

Peter Selerie

John Semken

Leslie Skinner

Bill Wharton

Prologue

S UNDAY MORNING, 25 OCTOBER 1942. The second day of battle along the Alamein Line in Egypt after two of the longest nights 21-year-old Lieutenant John Semken could remember. He had never known such exhaustion, and yet there was very little chance of him or the rest of his troop getting any sleep that day – not while they were sitting behind the Miteiriya Ridge in their tanks and still trying to bludgeon their way through the enemy's lines – lines dense with millions of mines and wire entanglements.

The British Eighth Army had retreated here to the Alamein position at the end of June following the fall of Tobruk. Three hundred miles they had fled, from Libya all the way deep into Egypt until they were just 60 miles from the key city of Alexandria and only 75 or so from Cairo. Tobruk had been a humiliating defeat that should never have happened, and in truth, it was only the heroic hammering of the pursuing Axis armies by the Royal Air Force that had saved Eighth Army from something close to annihilation. Since then, both sides had been furiously laying minefields along the more than 40-mile length of the Alamein Line, for both Axis and British commanders had recognized that it was along this stretch of the Western Desert that the victors of the North African conflict would be decided once and for all. This was because, along more than 1,000 miles of desert coastline, only here was it impossible to outflank an army; and this in turn was because, some 40 miles south of the Mediterranean coast, the desert, largely flat and, to most eyes, featureless, suddenly fell away down a deep escarpment known as the Qattara Depression. A lone vehicle, perhaps, could find a route up from its depths, but not an outflanking army.

For Feldmarschall Erwin Rommel, the victor of Tobruk, and his German–Italian Panzerarmee, the Alamein Line was tantalizingly close to untold riches: Alexandria and Cairo, of course, but also the Suez Canal, the Middle East, oilfields beyond – and, who knew, possibly even a link-up with the armies of the Eastern Front in the Caucasus. Victory at Tobruk had prompted heady dreams indeed. On the other hand, the British now had considerably shorter supply lines, and if they could withstand Rommel's army and then build sufficient weight of force, then fortunes could be emphatically reversed.

Scrappy, bloody fighting through July had ended in stalemate, which meant Rommel's first great chance to take all of Egypt had passed. Then, at the very end of August, had come his attack on the low ridge of Alam Halfa – but here Rommel was facing a new British commander. General Bernard Montgomery had taken over at the helm of Eighth Army in early August and, fighting a purely defensive battle, had stopped the Panzerarmee in its tracks and put paid to Rommel's last hope of a breakthrough. Now, seven weeks on from Alam Halfa, it was time for a retrained, revitalized and strengthened Eighth Army to attack in turn.

All through the long summer months both sides had continued to lay mines, so that vast fields of these deterrents, mostly of the anti-tank variety, lay buried in the sand all along that 40-mile stretch of the line, in an invisible but deadly barrier. To break the Germans and Italians here at the Alamein Line, Eighth Army had somehow to clear paths through these dense fields of mines and also through the wire entanglements before they could burst out the other side, move freely in the desert once more, and use their now greater materiel strength to fold up the Panzerarmee – and then force the shattered remnants to flee all the way back to Tobruk and beyond, over more than 1,000 miles.

So much desert, so much space for manoeuvre; but here, in the eastern lee of the low Miteiriya Ridge, Lieutenant Semken and his fellow tank men of the Nottinghamshire Sherwood Rangers Yeomanry were pegged in on this second morning of the battle, with almost no room for manoeuvre at all and with scant protection. True, the enemy could not see them where they were sheltering – any more than they could see the enemy – but if they stayed where they were, enemy artillery, firing over the shallow ridge, would catch them eventually. On the other hand, to press forward in broad daylight with insufficient space to move meant they would become sitting ducks.

Semken and his fellow officers had been briefed for the great battle just three days earlier. Two days before that, he and the men of C Squadron had been given brand-new American-built Sherman tanks, only recently arrived from the United States. At 30 tons apiece, each with two machine guns and a hefty 75mm main gun, these armoured beasts were a big step forward and the finest tank now serving in Eighth Army. So, a couple of days to familiarize themselves with these new machines and then they were off, trundling through the assembly area immediately behind the forward Alamein positions ready to head straight into battle.

As so often, the plan had sounded straightforward enough on first hearing. Montgomery aimed to punch two holes through the Axis minefields and defences, one in the north of the line and one further to the south. The northern one was to be the main breach; this was also where the enemy defences were strongest, but Monty believed it was best to hit the enemy head-on along a 10-mile stretch. The problem, though, was that it was impossible to expect the engineers to clear a 10-mile gap through the 3 miles or so of minefields. Instead, there were to be two corridors of three lanes, each of which would be just 8 yards across – no wider than a tennis court. The RAF would heavily bomb enemy positions in the days before the battle, which would then open with a barrage of 908 guns at exactly 9.40 p.m. on the night of Friday, 23 October. Fifteen minutes later, infantry and engineers would get going behind a further barrage of shells raining down from their field guns, and then the massed tanks, anti-tank guns and trucks of XXX Corps – the *corps d'esprit*, Monty had called it – would start moving forward down these impossibly narrow 8-yard channels, advancing for 3–5 miles until they were through the sea of mines and out into the wide open desert beyond.

That Friday night, the three squadrons of the Sherwood Rangers – A, B and C, with Headquarters Squadron following – had moved up through the dark to the final assembly areas. At one minute past midnight, and with the air up ahead still crashing and booming with the sounds of artillery battle, they were lined up in their tanks along the final defence line, anxiously awaiting orders to start moving.

To begin with, Semken had thought everything was going according to plan; he'd never seen such incredible organization and on such an immense scale. Although still very young, he had been with the Sherwood Rangers since 1940, having joined them in Palestine when they were still a mounted cavalry regiment, complete with horses. The horses had long gone, but it was only earlier that year – after a time as artillery – that they had finally become mechanized. Rommel's attack at the end of August at Alam Halfa had been the Sherwood Rangers' first action in tanks, so while they were not new to war, they had been most woefully new to mechanized warfare.

Back then, Semken had been the regiment's navigation and intelligence officer and had watched, aghast, as the lead squadrons had charged towards the enemy, reminding him of the Light Brigade at Balaclava – and had been similarly shot to pieces. Cavalry charges, whether by horse or tank, belonged to an earlier age of warfare. It had been a shock for Semken to see for the first time one of their Grant tanks hit and burst into flames, incinerating the occupants; but then, within moments, more were ablaze. In all, seven had been destroyed and a further four knocked out. As lessons went, it had been a harsh one. The Sherwood Rangers still had a lot to learn.

Since then, they had trained hard, and on that opening night of the Alamein battle, Semken, for one, had felt confidence from the enormous scale of the force assembled. This, however, had soon begun to melt away, as the copybook organization of the assembly areas rapidly disintegrated once the mass of British armour began to squeeze into the narrow, poorly lit lanes. The combination of the grinding tracks of the tanks and the weight and volume of the vehicles soon reduced the sand to the consistency of talcum powder. Choking clouds of smoke and dust filled the air as thickly as the worst London smog. Ahead, engineers were valiantly trying to clear lanes as quickly as possible, but they couldn't work swiftly enough. Not until around 4 a.m. did the Sherwood Rangers finally reach the eastern edge of the first enemy minefield. Halfway through, as they edged along the northern end of the long Miteiriya Ridge, they were stopped. They'd reached the end of the cleared lanes. Up ahead muzzle flashes of enemy artillery could be seen, while arcs of tracer criss-crossed the sky.

Minutes passed; then orders arrived over the radio for them to push on regardless, through the uncleared minefields. Engines were fired up again, adding exhaust fumes to the smoke and dust, and off they went, A Squadron in the lighter and older Crusader tanks leading the way. Miraculously, not one tank was hit, and eventually a sapper told them they had in fact made it through to the other side. Relief was short-lived, however, for now they were met by anti-tank and machine-gun fire. Pulling back was not an option, because more armour was pouring through the channel along which they had passed, adding to the congestion. Shells hurtled towards them and although they fired back, within minutes five of A Squadron's nineteen Crusaders had been knocked out and were burning vividly in the last darkness of the night.

Four of B Squadron's tanks were also hit and began flaming, and then a further four and three more Crusaders. One tank was hit but continued to roll forward, fire erupting angrily from its hatches. It finally ground to a halt, engulfed in flames. There was no sign of the crew, who had burned within its steel shell. Fortunately for John Semken and his crewmates, the Shermans of C Squadron had so far avoided the carnage, because unlike A and B Squadrons they were still stretched out behind, nose to tail, in the minefield.

Daylight revealed scenes of devastation, with burnt-out and still burning tanks littering the desert along with the corpses of British, Italian and German troops. Yet the light also showed up German corridors through the minefields, which enabled the Sherwood Rangers to pull back behind the eastern side of the Miteiriya Ridge. Firing continued through that first full day: orders were to hold fast while the sappers improved the existing lanes and more armour was brought up. A German counter-attack was successfully beaten off and seven panzers knocked out in turn. That night, the Sherwood Rangers were ordered to renew their attempt to burst through the enemy defences and out into the open beyond.

They had lined up – tanks as well as the echelon trucks carrying fuel, ammunition and supplies – when the Luftwaffe thundered overhead and dive-bombed them. A number of the 'soft-skins' were hit, their precious cargoes erupting in balls of flames. Twenty trucks were soon blazing. 'It was,' wrote Semken, 'a night of hell.'

By dawn on this second day of the battle, Eighth Army were hardly much further into the enemy positions. Weight of numbers, and the near-constant RAF hammering of the Axis forces, would ensure eventual success; but for those such as the Sherwood Rangers, leading the way and now caught in the very heart of the bloodshed, this was small comfort.

As the fighting ebbed and flowed, the battlefield was never entirely quiet; shelling continued, so that the boom of the guns, the screaming passage of the shells and the subsequent explosions were almost constant, as were sounds of small-arms fire: the *rat-a-tat* of the Italian and British machine guns, the *brrrp* of the German. Mortar shells continued to fall on the desert ground, splattering shards of shrapnel and rock all around.

It was no wonder that by this second morning of the battle, after too long in his tank with no sleep, Semken was so exhausted. Now, though, there was a lull, and from the remnants of A Squadron, waiting near the Shermans of C Squadron, Semken saw his good friend Ronnie Hill clamber out of his Crusader, hurry across the open desert towards him and climb up on to the rear of the tank as Semken sat in the turret.

Although they were now in different squadrons, Semken and Hill were close friends. They had shared a tent with two others, Ken Graves and the Irishman Ronnie Hutton, during their long months from February to June that year training with tanks at Khatatba camp, north of Cairo in the Nile delta. Semken had thought it a vile place. It had been as hot as hell, with an incessant wind that whipped up the sand and got everywhere – in the eyes, up the nose, into food and tea and drink and every nook and cranny. Even in the shade the temperature was regularly over 100°. Despite this, the four of them had all laughed from dawn until dusk, bound by an intense camaraderie and a shared sense of humour centred on numerous in-jokes and phrases. All four were determined to derive fun from every experience, from morning PT to cooking the tedious daily rations. There was feverish debate about the respective merits and vices of Britain and Ireland, there were songs, and there was drinking. They had been the very best times Semken had experienced since joining the army.

Then in June they had been split up among the squadrons and the serious business of fighting had begun. All four had survived Alam Halfa, and in October both Semken and Hill had been given leave and had headed off together for Cairo. Twenty-six years old, with a mop of dark hair and a moustache, Hill was a born optimist; his eyes always twinkled with good humour, and it was never long before his face creased into a smile or broke into laughter. As far as Semken was concerned, he was an ideal close friend with whom to spend some leave.

They stayed at the Continental-Savoy Hotel, one of Cairo's finest – and centrally located, overlooking Opera Square and Ezbekieh Park. With its popular grill-room, terraces, lush gardens and daily concerts, it gave officers on leave such as Semken and Hill a rare taste of luxury after the hardships of the desert. Perhaps even more importantly, the hotel had some 200 rooms with bathrooms and a permanent supply of hot and cold water. The two men got themselves 'really clean', ate sumptuously, went shopping and to the cinema – and even to the opera, to see *Tobias and the Angel*; after all, it was only just across the road from the Continental.

'You would never believe that we were on the eve of a gigantic campaign,' Hill had said to Semken one day as they had been jogging through the city in a gharry. Then he had said, 'I suppose we don't worry because each of us has the firmest conviction in his own survival whatever may happen to the next chap.'

And now, only a week later, here was Hill, clambering on to the back of Semken's Sherman, his face as cheery as ever but their surroundings so markedly different. Cairo and the Continental-Savoy might as well have been a million miles away.

Whether Hill's belief in his own immortality had convinced him it was all right to climb up on to Semken's tank, or whether it had simply seemed like a safe enough pause in the fighting, was unclear – but the two friends had only been chatting a short while when there was a sudden and dramatic whine, an intake of air and then a crash, and Ronnie Hill disappeared. Or rather, he didn't entirely disappear, because he had been blown to bits all over Semken, who was now drenched in blood and gore from his head to his navel. One moment they had been talking, the next Ronnie had been blown to smithereens, those twenty-six years of learning, of knowledge, of fun, of laughter, of emotions and feelings, all gone with the whine and crash of an enemy shell. And Semken had been left standing in his turret, miraculously uninjured and stupefied with shock.

That same day, General Montgomery realized it was time to pause, rethink and come up with a plan B for his battle. It meant a respite of sorts and allowed the battered Sherwood Rangers to be withdrawn to rest and refit. 'I have never known such exhaustion,' wrote Semken. 'I was too tired to feel tired.'

The battle continued, Eighth Army slowly but surely grinding down the enemy. The revised plan, a renewed all-out attack labelled SUPERCHARGE, was launched in the early hours of 2 November; and about half an hour after it began, the Sherwood Rangers and the rest of 8th Armoured Brigade, of which they were part, rumbled clear of the minefields at long last. They pushed on, past the bodies of German and Italian dead, and made contact with their fellow brigade tank regiment, the Staffordshire Yeomanry. Ahead, an ambulance was scuttling about, picking up wounded. As dawn broke, a yellowish fog had descended over the desert battlefield. Spectral enemy tanks appeared and the Sherwood Rangers opened fire, knocking out two.

By that afternoon, SUPERCHARGE had done the trick; the Panzerarmee Afrika was all but broken. 'The enemy line was crumbling,' noted Semken, 'and prisoners were beginning to come in, in large numbers.' By 4 November, the fighting was effectively over. At around 11 a.m. that day, as the Sherwood Rangers rolled on alongside the tanks of the 1st Armoured Division across the Tel el Aqqaqir track and on beyond the German lines, a lone enemy officer could be seen standing near a burning tank, clutching a simple canvas bag. It was General Wilhelm von Thoma, the commander of the Deutsches Afrika Korps. His swift capture moments later signalled the end of the Battle of Alamein, although it was far from the end of the war in North Africa.

Four days later, Anglo-US forces landed in north-west Africa, part of a giant pincer movement to end the war in North Africa for good. While American and British troops advanced from the west into Tunisia, Eighth Army crossed North Africa from the east. John Semken and the men of the Sherwood Rangers continued fighting all the way across the desert, back past Tobruk, through Benghazi and on to Tripoli and then into Tunisia. They were still with 8th Armoured Brigade and Eighth Army when the war in North Africa finally came to an end on 13 May 1943. By that time, the Sherwood Rangers had learned much but also lost many, including two commanding officers and another of John Semken's great mates, Ken Graves, killed at Wadi Zem Zem near Tripoli on 15 January 1943.

A relief, then, to have survived so far; but for Semken and the rest of the Sherwood Rangers, the war still had two whole years to run – and the final eleven months, from the summer of 1944 in Normandy, through the autumn across Belgium and Holland and the winter into Germany, would be as brutal, bitter and destructive as anything they had yet experienced. Statistically, not one of those tank men of the Nottinghamshire Sherwood Rangers Yeomanry fighting in north-west Europe had a chance of getting through those long final months of war unscathed. And all too many would never make it home.

PART I

Summer – Normandy

CHAPTER 1

Passage

T HURSDAY, 1 JUNE 1944. After the blazing heat and azure skies of late May, the weather had become dramatically unsettled on the south coast of England. At B.9 camp near Fawley on the south coast of Hampshire, their final assembly area before embarkation for D-Day, B and C Squadrons of the Sherwood Rangers found themselves joining the Westminster Dragoons and beach demolition units, all fenced in under tight security waiting for the signal to ship out. Vast rows of tents were hidden in the woods and tree-lined fields, and sitting in one of them that evening was 31-year-old Lieutenant Eric 'Bill' Wharton, taking the opportunity to write to his beloved wife, Marion. Sunday, 4 June was her birthday; two days later, 6 June, was their fifth wedding anniversary, although since that wonderful day they had spent just four months together. War had torn them apart. He pined for her, and even more so now that she was pregnant with their first child. She had written to him at the end of April with this terrific news – the happy consequence of a blissful month's leave with her at the start of the year. His good friend and fellow troop leader in B Squadron, Lieutenant Monty Horley, wanted to be a godfather, he had told her happily. So, too, did George Jones, his oldest friend in the regiment; they had been together since Wharton had joined the Sherwood Rangers back in the summer before the war.

Both he and Jones were from modest backgrounds. Bill had left school at fourteen and joined his father's printing business in Retford in north Nottinghamshire. Both had joined the Sherwood Rangers before the war as troopers, but realizing there was an opportunity for advancement, Wharton had worked his way up through the ranks and then, once in the

Middle East, had pressed hard to be given the chance for officer training. Much to his delight, Colonel Flash Kellett, the regiment's commanding officer, had seen his potential and duly packed him off to OCTU – the Officer Cadet Training Unit – along with George Jones. In truth, since then Wharton had thrived, despite the pain of separation from his adored wife. In many ways, mixing with men from different – and often considerably more privileged – backgrounds, as well as the opportunity to travel, to train and to command, had brought him an education he'd never had as a boy. War was a terrible thing, and he desperately longed for it all to be over; and yet it had been the making of him too.

Above him, the sky was overcast and the air cooler than of late. 'It has rained a little this evening,' he wrote to Marion, 'and brings to mind one of those pre-war days when you and I had intended to go to tennis only to change our plans because of a shower and go for a walk in the cool, fresh country around Babworth. As I look up now at the green leaves on the trees swaying in the breeze, I have a sudden pang of longing to be walking there with you.' He found it hard to accept that five long years had passed since they had spent a summer together, and that this year, yet again, he would be missing both her birthday and their wedding anniversary. At least, though, they had spent some precious times together a few months earlier, including a ten-day holiday in Bournemouth. 'I hope to be laughing at life with you again before so very many months,' he added. 'I will go on thinking of you through the coming days and looking forward with so much anticipation to seeing that smile of yours when we next meet.' And with that he wished her goodnight, told her he would love her always, and signed off. It was his last letter before embarkation. The following day, Friday 2 June, the regiment was ordered to start moving out. Despite the turn in the weather, the invasion, at long last, was about to begin.

The Sherwood Rangers were not travelling all together. B and C Squadrons were assembled down on the coast at Calshot, south of Fawley, on Southampton Water, where they were loading up on to their landing craft, while A Squadron and Regimental HQ were embarking across Southampton Water next to the city itself. In all, split over the two embarkation points, there were 688 men in the regiment – 39 officers and 649 other ranks – along with 179 vehicles and 84 tanks: 61 Shermans (19 for each squadron plus 4 for Regimental HQ), a further 11 light 'Stuart' tanks, 6 close support tanks and a final 6 adapted anti-aircraft tanks. There were also a dozen armoured scout cars, 4 tracked universal carriers, 57 trucks,

11 cars, 8 motorcycles and 3 armoured recovery vehicles (ARVs). Moving just one armoured regiment from southern England to Normandy was no small feat of logistics; moving three Allied armies was a staggeringly complex enterprise.

C Squadron had been allocated four LCTs – landing craft, tanks. Before Trooper Arthur Reddish's tank was ordered to reverse on to one of them, he bent down and picked up a pebble from the beach – a last keepsake from England before the great invasion. He wasn't quite sure how he felt. At twenty-two, he was a very young man still, with no wife or girlfriend, only a widowed mother back home in Lancashire, to whom he sent a large part of his army pay. Young he might have been, but he had already tasted plenty of war. Like John Semken, Bill Wharton and many of the Sherwood Rangers Yeomanry, he'd had his fill of the action in North Africa, having joined them before Alamein. He'd survived that battle without a scratch, serving in John Semken's crew, but then had been badly burned at Wadi Zem Zem when his tank was hit; two of his crewmates had died, horribly, and eleven other tanks in the squadron – eleven out of nineteen – had been knocked out in that one engagement alone. It had been the same day Semken's friend Ken Graves had been killed. A dark day for the regiment, though Tripoli, a great prize, had fallen six days later. Even as part of a victorious campaign, a regiment such as the Sherwood Rangers could suffer grievously.

Apart from a month back home at the beginning of the year, the Sherwood Rangers had been Reddish's whole life for the past two years, and his current tank crew had stuck together since training for D-Day had begun back in February. Of that five-man crew, Corporal Doug Footitt, the gunner, and Sam Kirman, the loader and radio operator, were both twenty-five and, like Reddish, who was co-driver and machine-gunner, desert veterans. Their driver, 24-year-old Geoff Storey, had yet to taste battle, as had their fresh-faced tank and troop leader, Lieutenant Stuart Hills; he was just twenty years old and had gone straight from school to officer training at Sandhurst. Reddish wasn't worried about the new boys, though. Hills, he reckoned, had already proved himself a good commander during training and Geoff Storey a reliable driver. Most important of all, they all liked one another and got on well. That was important.

On top of the four LCTs allocated to each of the three tank squadrons, there were yet more for the Regimental HQ and support vehicles. Landing craft of all sizes had been developed by the British and Americans. Realizing early in the war that if they were to win they would need to conduct amphibious operations, they set about producing these enabling vessels to deliver not just men but also vehicles, including tanks, as well as supplies and other forms of immediate fire-power directly on to defended beaches. LCTs were just one of the impressive and varied repertoire of landing craft. Nearly 60 metres long with a bridge at the stern and forward-dropping ramp at the bow, each of them could carry five 30-ton Sherman tanks and still have a draught of just 3 feet. Out at sea, they could manage some 8 knots and had a range, in theory, of up to 1,000 miles, although no one would have wished to cross an ocean in what was effectively a flat-bottomed raft. On a balmy summer's night, however, they were perfectly well equipped to cross the English Channel. Certainly, on that sunny Friday afternoon at Calshot, no one in the Sherwood Rangers was especially worried about the crossing itself. More apprehension was attached to the prospect of pitching their special duplex-drive – 'DD' – Shermans into the sea some 7,000 yards – more than 3 miles – from the coast, and what reception they would get at their still secret destination for the opening of the second front.

The LCTs were lined up on what had been called 'Tank Park Beach' halfway between Calshot and Lepe, facing on to the Solent. Both B and C Squadrons had been equipped with – and especially trained to use – the extraordinary 'swimming' DD tanks which would, for the first time ever in history, deliver armoured support on to the invasion beaches ahead of the attacking infantry. A Squadron, equipped with ordinary Shermans, would land a little later, deposited directly from beached landing craft.

Lieutenant Hills's troop were on serial 2006, along with Captain Bill Enderby – the squadron second-in-command – and his crew, so five tanks in all, each reversing slowly up the ramp, men in front of them guiding the drivers – *left a bit, right a bit, give it some throttle* – to the accompaniment of competitive banter being yelled along the beach. They might be leaving England, but the invasion was not upon them just yet. There were apprehension and nerves, of course, but not yet at fever pitch; still time for light-hearted exchanges. On serial 2006, Hills's tank was the last to load, which meant they would be first off when the invasion was launched.

Once the LCT was loaded, the ramp went up, enclosing them in the long metal tin, engines growled into action, and they slipped back off the beach and out into the Solent, the stretch of water between the coast of southern England and the Isle of Wight. After some manoeuvring, they joined their flotilla, while other groups of landing craft also formed up. For Reddish it all felt rather familiar – just like the last major exercise they had undertaken.

'It was a lovely summer evening,' noted Stuart Hills in a journal he wrote soon afterwards, 'but the excitement was pretty tense at the time.' As a young man who had been training for this moment for almost two years, he felt no sense of sentimentality, just a surge of adrenalin and nervous excitement. But they weren't heading across the sea just yet. The plan was to start assembling out in the Solent, a process that was to take much of the following day.

Unbeknown to the Rangers on that balmy early June evening, however, the meteorologists were starting to worry about a storm hurrying across the Atlantic. Some 25 miles away as the crow flies, in Southwick House near Portsmouth, the senior Allied commanders were facing the grim prospect of postponing the invasion. At 4.15 the following morning, after the latest weather reports, General Dwight D. Eisenhower, the Supreme Allied Commander, agreed to delay for twenty-four hours. A final decision whether to go or not would be made early the following day, Monday, 5 June – the original date for D-Day. That meant all those now embarked on their invasion vessels would have to stay there, cooped up, penned in, waiting. For all those geed up to land at dawn the following day, a huge mental adjustment now had to be made. There was nothing to do, however, except sit it out. Games of cards, mugs of tea, letter-writing, repeated checks of machinery and equipment, attempted snatches of sleep – this was how those already locked into their landing craft had to spend the time.

Most of those who had been in the army for a while were used to hanging around and to plans changing at the last moment; it was an occupational hazard. Even new boys like Stuart Hills managed to take the delay in their stride. In any case, he was a fairly phlegmatic fellow – resilience was something he had had to develop as a boy, and it had stood him in good stead since joining the army.

Not all new subalterns straight out of Sandhurst were given much choice as to the regiment in which they ended up serving, but Hills and his best friend from school, Denis Elmore, had both been offered commissions with the Sherwood Rangers. For Hills there was a family connection: his father had served in the regiment in the last war, but had then made his career in Hong Kong, which was where Hills had been born in 1924. As was the way with many expat children, Hills was sent back to England for his schooling, first to a prep school in Sussex, aged just seven, and then on to Tonbridge. In all that time, he saw his parents together just twice – when they were both back in England on leave in

1933 and 1939 – and his mother during trips back to Hong Kong in 1934 and 1937. School holidays were spent with guardians or friends. It was just the way life was, and children such as Stuart had to sink or swim. Most managed to swim, building up strong foundations of independence and robust self-sufficiency. Bosom pals like Denis Elmore were vitally important, as were the structures of school life – and in Hills's case that meant especially sports. Hills loved sport, and he particularly loved cricket, as did Denis, who was not only a scholar, but also extremely talented at all sports. By the time they were in their last year at Tonbridge, the pair were opening the batting for the 1st XI together. They even had the chance, in that summer of 1942, to play at Lord's, the most famous cricket ground in the world and the spiritual home of the sport.

By this time, Hong Kong had fallen to the Japanese and Hills's parents had been interned in the notorious Stanley camp, so he was even more on his own. Denis had been highly supportive, always managing to cheer up his friend whenever he was feeling low. Fortunately, Hills had hugely enjoyed his years at school, which for him had been as much a home as a place of learning; now, with his phlegmatic – and pragmatic – approach to life, he had been determined to put his best foot forward and, with Denis, had joined the Royal Armoured Corps the moment they left Tonbridge in the summer of 1942. At primary training at Bovington camp in Dorset, Hills and Elmore met Dick Holman, whose elder brother Jack was already in the Sherwood Rangers. The three became close and from Bovington were posted to Sandhurst for their officer training, even though, because of illness, Elmore was a month behind the other two. From there, all three joined the Sherwood Rangers. Hills arrived at Chippenham Park near Newmarket, where they began their training for D-Day, on 19 January 1944.

Denis Elmore and Dick Holman had both been posted to A Squadron, which was commanded by Major Stanley Christopherson, another of the desert veterans. A Squadron were in reserve for the invasion, which meant they would be landed directly on to the beaches about an hour after B and C Squadrons, and so had not undergone DD training. As a result, they were on landing craft alongside Regimental Headquarters, which included the tanks of the commanding officer, Lieutenant-Colonel John D'Arcy Anderson, Major Mike Laycock, the second-in-command, and the adjutant, Bill Wharton's friend Captain George Jones. Jones had only just been pinched from A Squadron to take up the post of adjutant, and Christopherson had been most unimpressed to lose him: a family retainer on the Laycock family estate before the war, Jones had been commissioned through the ranks and had become a trusted troop leader. Many members of the regiment had a particularly close friend – a soulmate – and for Jones it was Lieutenant Neville Fearn, another A Squadron troop leader. That night, Christopherson, Fearn and Jones were all invited by the navy commander of their LCT to join him in the narrow ward room. Food was eaten, and plentiful amounts of alcohol consumed too – in fact, Jones became so drunk that Fearn had to hoist him over his shoulder in a fireman's lift and cross four LCTs to reach their own berth. 'The next morning,' noted Christopherson, 'George, our most efficient adjutant, was somewhat behind schedule, rather to the irritation of Colonel Anderson.'

Christopherson's talisman for the invasion was not a pebble but a single nine of hearts playing card, which he'd accidentally trod on while at the final C.10 camp at Stoneham, just outside Southampton. A proliferation of messages had been distributed from Eisenhower and from General Montgomery, now the overall land commander for the invasion, as well as from Major-General Douglas Graham, the commander of the 50th 'Tyne Tees' Division, of which 8th Armoured Brigade – and within it, the Sherwood Rangers – were a part. Yet, for some reason he couldn't put his finger on, Christopherson never liked being wished luck before going into action. He preferred his nine of hearts, which he'd placed in his wallet, where he intended to keep it until the war was finally over.

Christopherson was thirty-two, so among the older officers, and unlike many of his fellows, had had the chance in his early twenties to spread his wings and have some fun before getting down to the serious matters of adult life and work. A large part of his childhood had been spent in South Africa, where his father was managing director of Consolidated Gold Fields, but he too had been sent to England for his schooling. From Winchester College he was offered a place at Oxford, but instead decided to sail to South Africa before returning, aged twenty-three, to London and a post with a stockbroking firm in the City. Charming, good-humoured, good-looking, sporty, clever and blessed with an eternally optimistic view of life, he made friends wherever he went.

Although not especially militarily minded, he had joined the Inns of Court Regiment in the Territorial Army, which, on the outbreak of war, was immediately split up. Its members had been called up and Christopherson found himself posted to the Sherwood Rangers, back then a county yeomanry regiment full of Nottinghamshire squires, gamekeepers, horsemen and country folk. With them – and their horses – he was posted to Palestine. There, still wearing their leather riding boots and bandoliers, they took part in a sabres-drawn cavalry charge to quell Arab insurrectionists. For the most part, Christopherson thoroughly enjoyed this overseas deployment. He and his fellows had a wonderful time playing lots of cricket, riding, swimming in the sea, going on courses and enjoying jolly tented dinners in the mess and forays to Jerusalem, Tel Aviv and other landmarks – all alongside like-minded souls, many of whom were becoming the very greatest of pals.

One of those was Stephen Mitchell, with whom he was later in Tobruk during the siege of 1941. By that time, they'd had their horses taken away and had been converted to artillery, which was considered extremely infra dig. None the less, Christopherson had seen the bright side and had learned much. By the time the regiment became mechanized in early 1942 he had also recognized the innate seriousness of the business they were now embarked upon, and was determined that both his squadron and the regiment as a whole should become as polished and proficient as possible. The better they became, the better would be their chances of survival – and of winning the war.

If Christopherson had had any lingering doubts about his determination to lick the squadron into as fine a unit as possible, they had been dispelled first at Alam Halfa and then at Alamein, where he had led A Squadron, and with it the regiment, into battle. He'd been lucky to survive, especially having been wounded in the head by shrapnel on the second morning. Fortunately, the injury had not been severe; he'd been back with the squadron within a week and had survived the rest of the North Africa campaign unscathed.

He'd learned much along the way: that tanks were not cavalry, that they needed infantry alongside them to be their eyes and ears on the ground; and that they should work closely with the artillery too. He had also learned the importance of morale and of making sure all his men were properly looked after, and that in a regiment such as the Sherwood Rangers, a territorial yeomanry unit rather than one of the pre-war regular army, there was room for a broad mix of people of different backgrounds and skills: quiet doers, bon viveurs and eccentrics, city dwellers and country folk, fresh-faced boys and hardened veterans. All were to be embraced and all had a role to play. And so, in A Squadron, he now had new troop leaders such as Denis Elmore and Dick Holman, but also vastly experienced non-commissioned officers – NCOs – such as the diminutive Sergeant George Dring and Squadron Sergeant-Major Henry Hutchinson.

George Dring had been brought up in Lincolnshire, one of the prime recruiting areas for the Sherwood Rangers, and had joined the regiment back in 1935 as a farrier for the horses. Now just turned twenty-eight, he was also a celebrated amateur jockey and huntsman – a true countryman. In North Africa, he had realized his skill at reading the lie of the land could be put to very good use even once they'd converted to tanks, and at the Mareth Line in Tunisia he had frequently clambered out to take a 'shufti' and, in effect, stalked enemy targets on foot first before then bringing his tank successfully to bear. A quiet man, with a fair moustache on his top lip, Dring was utterly dependable and already something of a legendary figure within not only A Squadron but the whole regiment.

So too was Squadron Sergeant-Major Henry Hutchinson. Bigger both physically and in personality than Dring, Hutchinson was from Sutton-on-Trent and had joined the Sherwood Rangers back in 1936. The son of a farmer and Shire horse breeder, he too was a natural horseman – and, like Christopherson, also a keen cricketer, and the pair had formed a tight bond both serving together and playing cricket in Palestine in the early part of the war. Efficient, popular among the lads, and with a natural authority and gift of leadership, he had also proved himself to be fearless in battle. At Alamein, Hutchinson had rescued eleven of his wounded colleagues from no-man's-land before being wounded himself, an episode for which he'd won the Military Medal – the equivalent of the Military Cross for non-commissioned troops.

Men like Dring and Hutchinson were the backbone of the squadron, indeed of the regiment, and gave the others confidence. They would, Christopherson knew, go the extra mile if they had to; they would provide inspiration to others when the chips were down or they found themselves in a difficult situation. Such men would be vital once they landed on the continent and the battle began.

Now, though, on the evening of 4 June, Christopherson felt confident enough in their training, which had been thorough, and in the competence of the regiment, which had come such a long way since last they'd left England's shores – on the boat to France with their horses, Sam Browne belts and polished riding boots. There was now plenty of the right experience woven in among those new to combat, and they were supported by an impressively huge Allied war machine that included immense naval forces of nearly 7,000 vessels, including over 1,200 warships, more than 4,100 landing craft and air forces that amounted to over 3,500 aircraft. Some 20,000 American and British airborne troops were to be dropped and landed at either end of a 60-mile invasion front, followed by 135,000 men along five invasion beaches. For sheer scale, there had never been anything like it.

That Sunday evening, the wind began to whip up, just as the meteorologists had predicted. By 10 p.m., it was a howling gale and the rain was lashing down, clattering against the thin metal of the landing craft. Conditions on board the LCTs, even in the lee of the Isle of Wight, were deeply uncomfortable. None the less, in the early hours of Monday, 5 June, Eisenhower made the momentous decision that they should go ahead on the following morning, Tuesday, 6 June 1944. The invasion was on.

There was still a very stiff wind later that Monday evening, by which time the LCTs carrying the Sherwood Rangers were already well out into the Channel. Stanley Christopherson couldn't help but marvel at the parts of the invasion fleet he could see all around him. It was reassuring. Nerves pricked at his stomach and he wondered whether invaders of bygone ages had felt the same; it reminded him of the sensation he always felt before going out to bat in a cricket match. Humiliating though it might be to get out quickly without scoring runs, the potential dangers facing him the far side of the Channel were far, far greater than anything a bowler could fling down at him. Still, it helped to give oneself more comforting points of reference at such a time.

Only once all the craft were out at sea was the cat let out of the bag as to their destination, although the broad outlines of army, corps and division plans had been explained beforehand, as well as a detailed plan for their own brigade, the 8th Armoured. Plans had been pored over, using models – complete with beaches, topography and villages, but all with coded names. Lieutenant John Bethell-Fox, one of Christopherson's troop leaders, had put good money on it being Normandy; he had spent many holidays there as a boy and recognized the shape of the coastline. Out at sea, the commander of the LCT gave each of the five tank commanders a small dispatch case, securely sealed, which contained the latest printed maps with the correct names upon them as well as the latest intelligence on the German defences; Bethell-Fox had predicted correctly. This information had been collected for the most part by repeated photo-reconnaissance flights over much of north-west Europe in the build-up to the invasion; those pictures had then been skilfully interpreted by British and American teams at RAF Medmenham. It meant that their maps were now extraordinarily detailed, showing every bunker, casement and gun position, even machine-gun posts. Beach obstacles were also marked up, and there were helpful boxes overlaid in red ink, bearing such details as 'EXIT BY RAMPING LOW BANK 2' – 4' FROM EAST – WEST'; it was even indicated where there was a post-and-rail fence in a gap where a masonry wall had been broken.

With the airborne troops securing the flanks, the main amphibious invasion force was to land on five beaches, the Americans in the western half of the 60-mile front on beaches now coded 'Utah' and 'Omaha'. Utah was at the eastern base of the Cotentin peninsula; Omaha lay at 90 degrees to Utah, west of the small town of Arromanches-les-Bains in the centre of the invasion front; then came Gold Beach, immediately east of Arromanches, where some of the British would land; the Canadians would then land on Juno, while the remaining British would come ashore on the easternmost invasion beach, named Sword, which extended to the mouth of the River Orne at Ouistreham.

The Sherwood Rangers were to land on 'Jig Green', the westernmost quarter of Gold, in support of the 231st 'Malta' Brigade, one of the two attacking brigades of the Tyne Tees Division, so named because its battalions had spent the first three years of the war until the invasion of Sicily in July 1943 garrisoning the tiny British island of Malta in the centre of the Mediterranean. B Squadron was to support the 1st Battalion, the Hampshire Regiment, and C Squadron the 1st Dorsets, and they were to reach the beach at H minus 5 – five minutes before 'H-Hour', the moment the main invasion was due to land – just ahead of the Armoured Vehicles Royal Engineers (AVREs), specially adapted tanks that would clear the shoreline of mines and other obstacles. The infantry would hit the beaches almost immediately thereafter. On the American beaches this would be 6.30 a.m., but further east, where the tides were slightly different, the landings were due to take place at 7.25 a.m. That meant the Sherwood Rangers would be rolling on to the beaches at 7.20 a.m. It was hoped that heavy bombers forty-five minutes beforehand, as well as the combined weight of fire from offshore warships and then low sweeps by fighter-bombers, would have neutralized many of the enemy defences. Naval divers would also start dismantling mined beach obstacles, which would be under the water at H-Hour; accompanying the tanks would be not only the AVREs but also the 'Crabs' of the Westminster Dragoons – converted tanks with long, rotating metal chains up front that would 'flail' mines ahead of them. Teams of sappers – Royal Engineers – would also be landed to assist the AVREs in clearing lanes off the beach and beyond to the road that ran parallel with the shoreline towards the hamlet of Le Hamel and the village of Asnelles. On paper, at least, it seemed everything had been thoroughly and comprehensively thought through.

With the LCT pitching and smacking down on the water and the tethered tanks groaning at the strain, Christopherson opened his dispatch
case and set about sorting out his maps and connecting the coded names
used in the briefings with the real names that had now been revealed. As
he discovered, it was not an easy task with the LCT bucking and swaying,
and he began to feel decidedly seasick. 'We spent an uneventful but
uncomfortable and sleepless night,' he noted. 'It was cold and the sea was
very choppy and most of us felt sick, in spite of the seasick tablets which
had been issued to us.'

Not far away aboard a different serial of four LCTs were the DD tanks of
B Squadron, commanded by Major John Hanson-Lawson. His second-
in-command was Captain Peter Selerie, another desert veteran. With
dark hair and eyes and a trim moustache, Selerie was a Londoner whose
Italian grandfather and otherwise English father had pursued careers in
the restaurant, pub and wine business. Selerie himself was a rather urbane
figure, extremely articulate, cultured and well read, with a deep love of
history; he could recite large numbers of poems and liked to sprinkle his
conversation with references to the literature and great events of the
past. At twenty-seven, he was a man of polished dignity and dry humour,
one of that band of eccentrics and rather unlikely soldiers that the Sherwood Rangers had always attracted – and also a natural leader who had
proved himself a popular and highly competent officer.

B Squadron were, like C Squadron, equipped with DD tanks. These were
built with a propeller and waterproofed, provided with a large, inflatable
canvas surround which enabled them to swim. Not unsurprisingly, many of
the men doubted a 30-ton tank could actually manage such a thing, but
these adapted versions of the Sherman were surprisingly effective. Managing these vehicles-turned-vessels on the swim to the shore required a
considerable amount of extra training – but since the single most important
facet of the invasion was that it should not fail, such a large use of training
time was surely, in the circumstances, justified. Another aspect of that training was learning how to escape from the tank if the worst came to the worst
and it sank: this involved first training at Fritton Lake in Norfolk then heading to Gosport, across the water from Portsmouth, to use the Davis
Submerged Escape Apparatus in the Royal Navy's escape test tank.

While there were plenty who had deep reservations about being taught
to surface successfully from a tank within a deep container, all did eventually go through this training – except Corporal Derek Lenton, who had

won an MM at Alam Halfa, and who flatly refused. It had been Selerie's job to persuade him to think again, but Lenton had explained that he had a deep-rooted fear of water from when he nearly drowned as a boy. Selerie had reminded him that as an NCO he had a duty to set an example, but Lenton still refused to go through the escape drill. 'I reduced him to the ranks,' noted Selerie, 'and had him posted to HQ Squadron where he became the driver of one of our three-ton echelon trucks.'

Just before they left B.9 camp, however, the squadron had lost one of their drivers to illness and somehow word of this reached Lenton, who, now with the B1 Echelon, the regiment's long-tail supply unit, was not in the same location. By a combination of bluff and ingenuity, he managed to get to Fawley and to camp B.9, blag his way inside and find Hanson-Lawson and Selerie to ask whether he could take the sick man's place. Only if he wore the cumbersome Davis escape apparatus, Selerie told him.

'Yes, sir, I will,' Lenton told them, 'but between you and me, I won't use it.'

And so, he was back, albeit still only as a trooper.

Now, as they progressed out into the Channel, the wind increased and with it the swell. Selerie ordered the crews on his LCT to start their tanks' engines to try to lessen the chances of mechanical failure in the morning, but the fumes this produced in the well deck, combined with the pitching and crashing of the landing craft, only made everyone even more nauseous, so he hastily told them to switch off again.

Heading up on to the deck as dusk fell, Selerie now saw they were losing way and becoming detached from the rest of the flotilla; when he expressed his concern, the commander of the LCT explained he had a fractured fuel pipe going into one of the two diesel engines. This was not a good start to the invasion. Then, at 1 a.m., Selerie was summoned to see the commander, who explained they had now lost all contact with the rest of the invasion force and that they had probably drifted west. Fortunately, they soon saw the silhouette of another vessel and, although it was strictly against instructions, Selerie ordered the LCT commander to flash the Allied recognition signal. This was immediately returned and they realized, to their enormous relief, that they had run into the left, eastern, edge of the US invasion force heading to Omaha Beach.

Their plan now was to continue on the same course but then turn east just as soon as they saw the coast, at which point they would inevitably rejoin their own force heading to Gold Beach. It might make them a little late, but there appeared to be no alternative. Only later, as they forged on, did they realize they were now no longer in the channels that had been swept clear of enemy mines. Sweeping these passages, especially through the dense minefields that had been laid like a protective curtain some 7 miles out to sea, had been a vital part of preparing for the successful arrival of the invasion forces. The commander of the LCT wondered what they should do, but explained that with the shallow draught of the vessel, they had a sporting chance of making it. What, he asked, did Selerie advise?

'If you knew my brigadier,' Selerie told him, thinking of the 8th Armoured commander, 'there is only one answer – we must be there as the first wave of the invasion and in front of the infantry!' And so they pressed on, across the mines. 'There followed a period of considerable suspense,' noted Selerie. 'No-one but the two of us knew the risk we were taking.'

Despite their seasickness, Trooper Arthur Reddish and the men of C Squadron on serial 2006 had managed to snatch a small amount of sleep. Up before dawn, Reddish was relieved to discover the rain had stopped and the wind dropped somewhat, although they were still pitching and yawing on the swell and there was plenty of water sloshing about on the deck. A light breakfast, and then their gear was stowed and the tarpaulins covering the tanks were removed. As the first glimmer of light spread across the sky, Reddish looked out and, seeing the sea thick with warships and landing craft, felt his morale lift. Now just 7 miles from shore and safely through the channels cleared of mines, and with France now a distant dark mass up ahead, they pressed on, working their way through the escorts and mine-sweepers until they were in the very van of the invasion fleet. Alongside them were not only the other LCTs but also fire-supporting landing craft with artillery on board and even rockets.

Bombers roared over, as planned, and soon after their bombs began to paste the coast, the deep rumble just audible on the breeze. And then the warships opened fire, the shells screaming overhead; and finally the RAF Typhoon fighter-bombers hurtled over, low and fast, and began diving on targets on the shore. It was now between five and ten past seven in the morning of Tuesday, 6 June.

It was D-Day.

CHAPTER 2

Rough Landings

L IEUTENANT STUART HILLS WAS cold, wet and short of sleep, and there was a nauseous sensation grinding in his belly. His morale had sunk pretty low a few hours earlier, but as the light had crept over the sea, so he had seen the vast invasion fleet and, like Arthur Reddish, had found his spirits rising a little. Nearly all the DD-carrying LCTs had reached their launch point, 7,000 yards from the shore, by 6.55 a.m. Furthermore, with the bombers thundering overhead and then the warships opening fire, there was no longer any need for radio silence, and word reached them that the plan had changed. Because of the rough seas, the two deputy SOAGs – senior officers, assault group – Lieutenant-Commander Robert Alexander and Commander Hugh Wheeler, had wondered whether it was too rough to launch the DD tanks. After all, if waves and spray were regularly crashing over the sides of the LCTs, there was every reason to fear that the DD Shermans, with their shallow canvas surrounds, would quickly get swamped. And then they would sink.

Instead, Alexander and Wheeler proposed to the two squadron leaders, Stephen Mitchell of C and John Hanson-Lawson of B, that the LCTs bring them in right to the shore – or as close as they could, because the 15th LCT Flotilla consisted of Mk III LCTs, which were not best suited to landing on the very shallow Normandy beaches; a newer variety, the Mk IV, was better designed for this type of shore landing, which was why they were carrying A Squadron and other armour that was to be landed directly on to the shore. There was a further consequence of making this decision, however. The naval planners had recognized that conditions might not be suitable for launching DD tanks so far out; but in moving closer to the shore, the nearly 60-metre-long LCTs could cause terrible congestion and get in the way of the assault wave of infantry. That meant they would have to move back in the landing pecking order, no longer first ashore but following on after the assault engineers and infantry. It meant they would no longer be spearheading the invasion on the Jig sector of Gold Beach but heading to the shore a while later.

That was disappointing; but it was insanity to try to launch 4 miles out in these conditions, so really, the decision was a straightforward one. Both squadron leaders agreed immediately they should launch as close to the shore as possible; after all, it was better to be a little late to the beach than never reach it at all. On board their LCT, Stuart Hills and the C Squadron second-in-command, Bill Enderby, were relieved by the news; they had already realized the severe swell was going to cause major difficulties.

And so the LCTs pressed forward, spray continuing to lash over the decks as the flat-bottomed craft rose and fell and bucked and swayed. The salty smell of the sea, mixed with the stench of oil, fumes, vomit and cordite, added to the nausea of the tank crews, made worse by rising apprehension – and noise, immense noise, that seemed to make the very air shudder. Behind the LCTs, supporting the assault on Gold Beach, were the big warships, four cruisers and a gunship, their heavy guns pounding enemy strongpoints on the coast, their jagged outlines dark against the morning sky, flashes of orange and smudges of dark smoke marking the gunfire. Ahead of the cruisers were thirteen destroyers, also offering fire support and able to operate far closer to the shore. There were fire-supporting landing craft as well, including converted LCTs carrying a mass of 29-pound high-explosive warhead rockets; each could fire between 800 and 1,000 in clusters of around thirty, their salvoes tearing the air apart with a sound like that of ripping calico. Reassuring though it was to be approaching the shore amid this immense weight of fire, for each man the assault would still be a leap into the unknown.

The LCTs now wheeled around, moving back and clear of the LCAs – landing craft, assault – of the infantry. Deep in the bellies of the main decks of their LCTs, the tank crews had little idea of this manoeuvring – the rolling and crashing of the vessel was disorientating enough as it was. From his craft, Stuart Hills saw shells screaming over and hitting the shore. Encouragingly, there appeared to be little return fire. Then suddenly, a little after 7 a.m., the RAF Typhoons were roaring over, low, dropping bombs and firing cannons at targets on the shore.

The LCTs with the two squadrons of Sherwood Rangers on board circled, then moved back into the line. As they were doing so, Hills saw other LCTs carrying what looked to him like Crabs, the mine-clearing tanks, passing them; these were the AVREs and flails of the Westminster Dragoons, due to go in ahead of the infantry. Once the assault wave had passed through, slowly, the LCTs drew closer to the shore. It was now time for all the crews hastily to prepare for action; personal kit was stowed away in a canvas container behind the turret, while everything on the tank that needed lashing down was firmly secured. The steel hawsers securing the tanks to the deck were released and the chocks pulled away. While Geoff Storey, Hills's driver, took up his position, the rest of the crew sat outside on the top of the tank. Arthur Reddish, the crew's cynic, had named the tank *Bardin Collos*, which he claimed was an Arabic phrase suggesting it was bound to become a casualty before long; certainly, the thought of plunging the beast into the swell, even comparatively close to the shore as they now were, seemed an astonishing act of faith. Sea spray continued to lash over the sides of the landing craft.

At around 7.45 a.m., they were just 700 yards from the shore and suddenly Captain Enderby gave the order for them to launch. With the engine of their tank now running, Hills listened in to the regiment's radio net and tried to hear what was going on, but some other unit was using the same frequency. Then he heard Major Mitchell, his squadron leader, yell, 'Get off the fucking air, I'm trying to fight a battle!'

Overwhelming noise: from five DD Shermans, their throaty engines running and resounding around the confines of the LCT, still rising and pitching on the swell; from the warships' guns booming and the shells whistling through the air; from whizzing, screaming rockets from nearby specially adapted LCTs; from the fighter-bombers; and now from the enemy, whose shells and mortars were exploding in rising spumes. There was also drifting smoke and the thick exhaust fumes from the Shermans. The Sherwood Rangers were new to amphibious operations, and while they had exited from landing craft many times before during training, this was very different.

As the ramp lowered, it was about 7.50 a.m. Ahead was Gold Beach; but unbeknown to the Sherwood Rangers crews about to launch, the invasion here had already drifted eastwards. Hills, peering towards the shore, saw two Crabs on the beach but already burning angrily – these had been among the first to launch, part of six teams from the 82nd Assault Squadron, Royal Engineers, whose job it was to try to clear separate lanes from the beach to the lateral road a short way beyond the dunes. Hills wondered briefly and with mounting apprehension whether the same fate awaited them – until the intricate operation of exiting the LCT safely occupied all his concentration and thoughts. And launching a 30-ton tank into the swell certainly required the greatest of concentration. It had to be driven very gingerly; then, once it was safely in the water, the propellers had to be engaged. The drill was for the LCT to engage slow reverse, but it would still be very easy for the ramp of the LCT to knock them and puncture or damage the screen, as the rough seas made complete control impossible; a sudden wave could easily make the LCT pitch and yaw just at the moment of launching. A wave, hitting them at the wrong moment, could equally easily flood the DD. And 30 tons of steel would sink very quickly.

Bill Enderby now ordered them to go; but just as they started to move forward, it was clear that one of the chains holding the ramp in place had become loose, and until it was tightened they risked tipping to one side as they inched on to the ramp. Tightening the chain took another five minutes. With the LCT stopped, too, they were now a sitting target. Increased enemy fire was hitting the water, the shells screaming towards them. Hills was conscious of other LCTs going past, including others from C Squadron that continued closer to the shore. B Squadron tanks were launching from an LCT away to his right.

Then a shell whammed into the water directly in front of them, another to the side of the ramp, followed by a third on the right. Bill Enderby was wounded by shrapnel, as was Sergeant Albert 'Sid' Sidaway.

'Go, go, go!' shouted Hills over the crew intercom, and with a gentle squeeze of the throttle, Geoff Storey rolled the tank forward on to the ramp and engaged the propellers – and then they were in the water.

Despite the noise, the spray and roll of the swell, Hills managed to keep his grip on the back of the tank, gingerly peering over the screen to watch the shore. It was clear, though, that the screen around them was struggling with the pressure of the swell. They'd gone around 100 yards when Geoff cried, 'We're taking on water, fast!'

Reddish clambered inside and switched on the bilge pump, but to no avail; it seemed likely that shrapnel from one of the shells had damaged the hull underneath the tank and it had been holed. A Sherman with a leak was not going to stay afloat, that was plain as day, so Hills called for them to abandon it immediately. As Storey and Reddish scrabbled frantically to get clear, fortunately Doug Footitt had the presence of mind to

pull the ripcord on the inflatable dinghy. Although Reddish found himself in the water, he and Storey managed to haul themselves aboard in the
nick of time, just as *Bardin Collos* slipped beneath the waves, and with it
all their personal kit and keepsakes. Even in this moment of high drama,
Hills couldn't help wondering what Neptune would think about suddenly
seeing a tank on the sea bottom. Reddish's naming of the tank had become
something of a self-fulfilling prophecy.

The rest of the tanks in their serial appeared to be faring better,
although the men and their DDs were experiencing mixed fortunes. The
various LCT commanders were making different decisions as to just how
far they should venture towards the shore, although landing them directly on to the beaches from these Mk III LCTs was not really an
option – those due to be landing 'dry-shod' were in the Mk IV version,
which was designed for the purpose. The last thing anyone needed was
lots of Mk III LCTs stuck on the shoreline, unable to be swiftly reused
and adding to congestion.

The second captain in C Squadron was Jack Holman, the elder brother
of Hills's and Denis Elmore's friend Dick Holman. Slight of build, with
dark hair, pale blue eyes and a trim moustache, Holman had film-star
good looks and made a point of showing an outward face of serene com-
posure, no matter what he felt inside, determined always to set an example
to his men. On his LCT, the commander had told them they were going
all the way despite it being a Mk III – sometimes the lesser of two evils
was the right option – and so they were ordered to deflate the screens
around their DDs. Despite having trained relentlessly, Holman was
keenly aware that on this morning of the great invasion they faced
considerable dangers: first, simply getting ashore in these swimming
tanks that seemed to defy logic, and then second, getting safely off the
beach. 'The relief we felt,' he noted, 'when we heard we were not to swim,
would have to be experienced to be realised.'

However, no sooner had they deflated than word arrived that they
would be swimming after all, albeit only from a short distance out. There
was then a race against time to replace all the swimming apparatus that
had just been removed, but by working at fever pitch they managed to get
most of the tanks ready. Two, though, had developed air leaks in the
screens which meant they could not be inflated, including the DD due to
be first off. Swift decision-making was needed, and so they lowered the
ramp and nudged the first tank off and into the sea. 'It was goodbye to all
kit, hordes of cigarettes and other attractive stores,' noted Holman, but

there simply hadn't been the time to remove them. 'The tank disappeared with a storm of bubbles.'

Holman's tank and three others on his LCT managed to get off without a hitch; by this time, they were only a few hundred yards from the beach, but the task was still incredibly challenging. The swell was severe, the tidal currents were strong, and as they neared the extreme low-tide edge of the beach they were confronted by a mass of beach obstacles. There were half-buried logs pointing upwards at a low angle, many with mines on top; there were steel 'hedgehogs' – three girders crossed at right-angles; and there were 'Belgian gates', upright metal frames 2–3 metres high. Even those obstacles without explosives could cause fatal damage to the DDs – and the landing craft. On top of that, guns and mortars from the German defences were continuing to fire out to sea. From the landing beaches, the coastline to the west rapidly climbed to sheer cliffs. On top were two *Widerstandsneste* – defensive strongpoints – WN 38 and WN 39. Both had 75mm guns facing down towards Gold Beach.

A further strongpoint, WN 37, had been built around an abandoned sanatorium in Le Hamel, which stood on the sea wall at the western edge of Jig Green. There was also a concrete casement with the embrasure enfiladed down the beach and lateral road which housed a 77mm anti-tank gun. This could fire in a cone along the beach and a little way inland. Some thousand yards to the east was the next strongpoint, WN 36, which included concrete pillboxes and a casement with guns facing seawards. These had all been successfully identified as targets before the invasion, the planners recognizing there would be a lot of enemy fire pouring on to the beaches and out to sea if they were not neutralized beforehand. Unfortunately, while the bombing had created huge numbers of shell-holes, it had failed to destroy the enemy strongpoints. Now the guns of the naval warships were hammering them relentlessly, but while that ensured the men inside the bunkers and casements would be keeping their heads down, few incoming shells were actually hitting their targets. And in between being shelled themselves, the defenders would be firing back at the assault forces.

For men like Jack Holman, struggling in their DD tanks, even a short passage to the shore was extremely hazardous and disorientating. Out at sea, each tank was rolling on the swell, water smacking against the sides of the screen around it. Visibility was poor and dodging the beach obstacles proved extremely difficult because of the sluggish response of the DD's controls and the challenges of trying to see what was ahead with a screen all around. Only the tank commander, perched precariously on the back of the tank, could see anything at all, and to do so meant exposing his head above the parapet and relaying instructions to the driver via the tank intercom. Jack Holman was acutely aware of his extreme vulnerability and felt rather like a coconut at a coconut shy – 'only one wished one were as small as a coconut'.

Stephen Mitchell's LCT, meanwhile, had knocked into another landing craft during the crossing – an occupational hazard in so crowded an invasion force – and the damage prevented the ramp from working out at sea. The only alternative was to take the tanks all the way to the beach, trying to weave a channel through the obstacles. The planners had known this wouldn't be easy, which was why the DD tanks had been proposed and developed in the first place. Considerably smaller and more manoeuvrable than LCTs, these swimming tanks would offer much smaller targets and be better able to weave through the obstacles. None the less, it had also been supposed that, in June, the invasion would be launched in balmy calm weather.

In all, five of C Squadron's tanks ended up at the bottom of the sea, while B Squadron lost three. One of those was Bill Wharton's DD, which launched into the water only to sink like a stone – as a 30-ton tank could easily do if there was a fault in the screen or a wave crashed over the top. Because he was on the back of his tank, he managed to swim clear, but tragically, Troopers Hewlitt, Green and Jackson went down with the tank; their Davis Escape Apparatus had not helped Wharton's crew. Trooper Lowe had managed to swim clear only to be machine-gunned in the water. Wharton himself was hauled back on to the LCT. He had so very nearly widowed his wife and left his unborn daughter fatherless.

On a different LCT was his friend Lieutenant Monty Horley. Horley's co-driver and second gunner was 21-year-old Bert Jenkins, a Londoner from Brixton and the son of a musician in the BBC Band. Bert himself was a keen musician who played the French horn; he'd joined the Royal Armoured Corps as a boy soldier aged sixteen, simply because he'd heard it had a big band. In between military training, that had been his life in the army – until at the end of 1941 he was posted overseas, eventually reaching Egypt and, from Port Tewfik on the Suez Canal, finding himself sent out to Khatatba camp. Eventually, he was told to deliver a new Grant tank to the Sherwood Rangers, not realizing he was going to be staying with them. Posted to B Squadron, he then fought with them all the way through the rest of the North African campaign.

Now, two years on, his long journey through the war had brought him to the edge of a ramp on an LCT some 700 yards out from the Normandy shoreline. 'The damned sea,' said Jenkins, 'it was really rough. And then we had to go down that ramp to get into the sea. Our driver, he was so careful, we hardly knew we were moving.'

Once successfully in the water, they began moving to the shore, weaving their way through the beach obstacles and then on to the beach itself. Jenkins reckoned they reached the beach around 7.30 a.m.; actually it was probably a little later, around 7.45–7.50 a.m. – so, a little late, but not too much. Another B Squadron tank heading to Jig Green was that of Sergeant Bill Digby. Their LCT had been on the western edge of the flotilla with nothing to be seen on their right. They had launched a few hundred yards from the shore and shortly afterwards found that one of the steel struts holding up the screen had begun to collapse. With the tank still swimming and rolling on the swell, Digby had managed to clamber to the front and to force the strut back into place; and they made it safely to the beach.

Monty Horley and his crew had now reached Jig Green. While the DD was swimming, the tracks were still going round, so that as soon as it hit the sand, they gripped and took a firm hold. The trouble was, with the propellers still running, their speed was extremely slow, but stopping to disengage them immediately would make them a sitting duck; so they wove their way through a channel that had already been cleared by engineers of the 73rd Field Company, R, and only then, near the very top of the beach, paused to disengage the propellers and deflate the screen.

Moments after they had disengaged the propellers something hit them – Jenkins wasn't sure what exactly – and suddenly the canvas screen went up in flames all around them. *Christ,* Jenkins thought, *we're going to be fried in here. We're finished.* But they weren't, because the flames rapidly burned through the rubber pipes, at which point the screen collapsed and the flames died.

All of them managed to get out and Jenkins found himself crouching beside Horley and Trooper Jesse Worboyes – he had no idea where the other two had got to – when a machine gun raked them. 'I ducked to the ground and scrambled round the back of the tank and hid by the propellers,' said Jenkins, 'and when things had calmed down, I looked around and the other two were lying down dead where we'd just been standing. It was terrible.' Terrified, he remained where he was, lying there, unable to think what he should do. 'There was not a thing around on our right at all,' he said. 'Nothing. I didn't hear anything from left either.'

The shock he was feeling was one reason why he could see nothing; clearly, at that moment, he was unable to digest what was going on around him. There were, in fact, other Sherwood Rangers DDs, along with some AVREs – a number now knocked out – a little further up Jig Green. Bill Digby's DD arrived at much the same time. Once on firm sand, they stopped almost immediately, disengaged the propellers and collapsed the screen. In the operator's seat, Lance-Corporal Philip Foster was using his periscope, which gave him only a very narrow slit of visibility – but he could still see Le Hamel at the western edge of Jig Green. Right on the sea wall, looking down the beach, was a casement housing its 77mm anti-tank gun. Behind it loomed the sanatorium, a complex of buildings perched at the edge of the shore and dominating the skyline. Shells were screaming over from the guns up on the hill beyond towards Arromanches, but from Foster's very narrow perspective, Le Hamel appeared deserted.

Over the net, they heard Monty Horley tell them his own tank was on fire; then silence. Suddenly, the 77mm gun in the casement opened fire and a moment later they were hit by one of the rounds. With the tank still pointing towards the shore, the shell ploughed through the 3-inch steel of the turret, severing both of Sergeant Digby's legs on its passage. Digby, who had been standing in the turret, collapsed on to the floor with nothing left of his legs but a few bloody strands of flesh. Foster had also been hit, in the foot, and now saw blood welling up through a hole in his boot. Digby pleaded for morphine, which Foster was able to give him, while the driver frantically tried to move away. With now no visibility behind him at all, he reversed to the edge of the sea where the tank promptly got stuck. With Digby legless and draining blood, and with Troopers Arthur Bond and Fred Potts in the turret also wounded, it was imperative to get out quickly and try and get help. This was far from easy, but somehow they managed it, the walking wounded carrying Digby up to the dunes where they sheltered by a knocked-out tank, hoping medical aid would come to their rescue.

But, as Bert Jenkins was also discovering, there were few others to be seen, and Digby urged Philip Foster to shoot him and put him out of his misery. The whole point of the Sherwood Rangers landing first on the beach was to offer vital fire support for the infantry. It was, however, a symbiotic relationship: the tanks needed the infantry as their eyes and ears on the ground. When the two were separated, neither could work very effectively. Had D-Day dawned clear and summery on a sea of calm, it might have been so very different, but the assaulting troops were landing amid mounting mayhem. The swell, the surf, the low cloud and the poor visibility were extremely disorientating, an effect made considerably worse by the strong tidal currents and wind from the west. The broad, flat sides of the landing craft were effectively acting as sails, and many of the invasion flotillas were being driven eastwards. B Squadron was supposed to be supporting the leading two companies of the infantry of the 1st Hampshires, while C Squadron was to perform the same role for the 1st Dorsets. Both tanks and infantry had been due to land on the eastern half of Jig Green, but A Company of the Hampshires had landed where A Company of the Dorsets had been due to come in, and the rest of the assaulting infantry was coming ashore on Jig Red – a delineation which began some 300 yards to the east of the WN 36 strongpoint. A Company of the Hampshires landed initially to little opposition, realized they were too far east, and so began moving diagonally across the beach, directly towards WN 36, where they suffered badly. The Hampshires' battalion commander was twice wounded, while their A Company commander and second-in-command were both killed. Vital leadership, and with it cohesion, were suddenly and dramatically absent. Machine-gun fire was coming not just from WN 36 but also from WN 37 at Le Hamel, from where the 77mm in its enfiladed casement was also now wreaking havoc.

B Squadron had lost three tanks in the run-in and a further two on the beach, but the rest landed more or less where they should have done. There was little these could do for those wounded and abandoned, however. Bert Jenkins remained crouching next to his dead comrades behind his knocked-out tank, while poor Bill Digby lay sheltering with his crew, his legs little more than stumps, waiting for a medic to rescue him. Much of C Squadron appear to have landed somewhere on Jig Red, which was another reason why Bert Jenkins barely saw another soul. It was easy to see why this happened. Coxswains on the LCTs, while well trained, lacked experience of operating in such rough conditions at sea – and under enemy fire. Once some of the landing craft started drifting eastwards, there was an understandable sheep mentality of following the mass. On one level, it didn't really matter, because although the entire beach was under fire from the guns on the cliffs to the west, the three strongpoints on Gold Jig itself were widely spaced apart with few troops in between. What's more, beyond WN 36 there was a kink inland, and a little further on, the coast curved slightly – but significantly – to the right, which meant that those on the upper end of the beach were clear from the arc of fire from WN 37 at Le Hamel.

However, what the enemy defences lacked in manpower was compensated for by thousands of mines and coils of wire stretching all along the coast and separating the beach from the lateral road a short way inland. Beyond that, especially behind the Jig Red stretch of the beach, the fields were waterlogged by German flooding. As a consequence, those landing on Jig Red were doing so in the face of little opposition, but not without rapidly mounting problems, because while the naval frogmen and Royal Engineers had been valiantly trying to clear channels through the obstacles where they were supposed to be, they had not done so where most of the assaulting troops were actually now coming ashore. This meant that landing craft were now arriving on parts of the beach where there were no lanes. It was possible to dodge the beach obstacles, but only with difficulty, and many were suffering damage. The inevitable consequence was that congestion soon built up. The timetable was slipping – as was any sense of coordination.

In the surf, and amid the thousands of beach obstacles, the carefully orchestrated and rehearsed plan was being torn to shreds.

CHAPTER 3

Off the Beaches

I T IS IMPOSSIBLE TO overstress the difficulty of mounting such an amphibious assault: the rough winds, the tides and currents, the relentless noise, the deafening, ground-shaking explosions, the fizz of sniper bullets, the scythe-like machine-gun fire, shells whistling through the sky, the confusion of units that have lost cohesion, the stench of smoke, cordite, burning; and, of course, fear and the lack of clear visibility or a wider picture of what on earth was going on.

Actual timings on D-Day are impossible to work out precisely. While those involved might have had a clear notion of the time before the invasion actually began, once enemy fire was raining down, landing craft and DD tanks were surging towards the shore and then arriving on the beaches themselves, very, very few men were looking at their watches. The sense of time also became distorted; what might have seemed like ten minutes in their mind's eye a day or two later could well have been an hour, and vice versa. The war diaries of all the units taking part are littered with generalities, rough timings and mixed-up map references; after all, the adjutants and intelligence officers writing them in the days that followed very often hadn't themselves witnessed much that had gone on, and there was no benefit to anyone in recording for posterity a day of confusion and misplaced or late landings. All that mattered was what was achieved at the end of the day and the state of the unit involved.

What can be said is that the six lanes between the beach and the lateral road due to be opened by teams of the 82nd Assault Squadron, Royal Engineers, were not swiftly cleared as planned, which added considerably to the congestion and difficulties. The first team near Le Hamel were unable to get ashore, so only two lanes were opened on Jig Green – and belatedly – while the rest were on Jig Red. Here, lanes were opened by Teams 4 and 5, the first of them some 700 yards from the eastern side of WN 36, which rapidly became the main landing zone for Jig Gold. All of the teams had lost AVREs – to mines, enemy fire or because they had become bogged down in the sand – and, to make matters worse, the commander of 82nd Assault Squadron was killed in the turret of his AVRE soon after getting ashore. The loss of senior commanders in the infantry was made worse by much of the Malta Brigade's HQ signals team and equipment ending up in deep water too far from the beach.

As a result of these difficulties, those few tanks and assault vehicles that had landed on Jig Green were isolated, cut adrift from the infantry and getting hammered from the strongpoint at Le Hamel, although the two dozen and more lying knocked out or stricken did, at least, offer some cover for those from B Squadron that were still in one piece. The tanks coming ashore further east on Jig Red were considerably safer, but because of the waterlogged fields there and the many obstacles still on the beach, congestion was immense – even more so as it became rapidly clear that because of the currents and the wind, the tide was rising considerably faster than the planners had anticipated.

Where exactly most of C Squadron came ashore is not clear, but it seems most had already drifted eastwards before launching. Jack Holman, for one, appears to have landed on Jig Red, and admitted they had all become rather spread out. 'Opposition,' he noted, 'was remarkably light,' which certainly suggests he came ashore somewhere east of WN 36. So, too, did Stephen Mitchell and his LCT, arriving after the initial first waves of infantry.

Fast approaching the beaches on Jig Red were the landing craft of 8th Armoured Brigade HQ, including tanks of a 'protection troop' from the 24th Lancers, one of the brigade's three armoured regiments. On one of the landing craft was Captain Rev. Leslie Skinner, a padre in the Royal Army Chaplains' Department. Skinner, a Yorkshireman, was thirty-two years old, with humorous eyes, dark hair and a neat moustache. He had joined the Methodist Church and had been sent out to India on his first official appointment. Soon after his arrival, however, he had become ill, resulting in acute deafness and a passage back home. At the outbreak of war he had been serving a ministry in Derbyshire, but had joined the Chaplains' Department and by successfully disguising his hearing problems had managed to get sent back out to India, from where he had moved on to Iran, Iraq and Egypt.

Eventually, however, he had been caught out and once again sent back to England. Skinner, however, was nothing if not determined, and had managed to blag his way to another active posting – this time as senior chaplain to 8th Armoured, but attached specifically to the Sherwood Rangers. Now, on this morning of D-Day, he was aboard an LCT along with 8th Armoured's brigade major, Lawrence Biddle, who had served with the Sherwood Rangers in North Africa. And, like just about everyone else, the Reverend Skinner was cold, wet and feeling seasick.

They were approaching the eastern end of Jig Green at around half-past eight.[1] On the run-in they had come under fire – targeted by the enemy guns on the cliffs overlooking the Gold Beach assault. Then Lawrence Biddle had asked for volunteers to help roll out the coconut matting once the ramp had gone down; this was supposed to help give the vehicles purchase on the otherwise soft sand and clay patches to be found on the Jig Red part of the beach. Having put his hand up, Skinner took his place with the others behind the roll – at which point the landing craft beached and promptly hit a mine. The blast knocked Skinner backwards on to a Bren carrier, blew off the leg of one of the men next to him and wounded the other. Winded and badly bruised on his side, Skinner managed to stagger back to his feet, but the ramps had become jammed by the blast. While some of the men were frantically trying to free the doors, he helped a medic give morphine to the wounded and patch them up as best they could. Finally, the ramp went down and, though his side was hurting like hell, he helped roll out the matting. The trouble was, the water was about 6 feet deep, the swell and the surf were still considerable and the matting wouldn't sink.

They had landed close to WN 36, which by now had been overrun by the Hampshires, although further along, Le Hamel and the guns on the cliffs beyond were still causing problems. 'Shellfire pretty hot,' noted Skinner. 'Infantry carriers/jeeps baling but left us to matting as tanks revved up. Washed aside but made it to beach.' Ashore, chaos reigned. Several bulldozers had already made it off the beach, and the sappers were desperately trying to clear a route through the wire and mines to the

[1] In his war diary, Skinner says 'stand to' was at 0700 and that they beached at 0725. After the war, Skinner explained that the timings in his diary were for the lead squadrons, not his own landing time.

lateral road. Shell-holes and craters peppered the landscape. The road leading from the beach behind WN 36 had been cratered and was, for the time being, impassable, which meant clearing another route around it. One bulldozer tried to push through but hit a mine. Skinner then spent an hour with some sappers helping to smash the remains of a pillbox. 'Heavy work with pickaxe and chest hurting like hell,' he scribbled in his diary later. 'Finally got half-track in queue. Another standstill.' Gridlock gripped the assault; without accompanying armour and fire support, the infantry could do little. Certainly, no one was clearing Le Hamel just yet.

The intention had been that A Squadron would land at H plus 90 alongside the third infantry battalion of the Malta Brigade, the 2nd Devons. This would have brought them ashore by 8.55 a.m., assuming all had gone to plan; but the congestion had delayed them. Earlier, at H-Hour, Stanley Christopherson had been listening on the radio set in his own tank aboard its LCT to see how B and C Squadrons were faring. With the mass of conflicting radio traffic as well as the atmospherics, the reception had been piecemeal and cluttered with static and other voices, but – like Stuart Hills around the same time – he had clearly heard his great friend Stephen Mitchell cursing others using his net. 'He certainly appeared most irritated,' noted Christopherson, 'but it was good to hear his voice, which meant he was safe for the time being.'

Finally, it was their turn to land. A mile from the shore they mounted their tanks and switched on the engines. A mass of landing craft were now converging on Jig Red and there was chaos as they all jostled their way through the beach obstacles, some of which were now submerged under the rising tide. Trying to avoid each other and the obstacles was extremely difficult, and Christopherson's LCT did ram an iron stake, which, fortunately, was not capped by a mine. None the less, they had to reverse and extricate themselves, all with the wind still howling and the currents playing havoc. Soon they found themselves pointing back in the direction of England; Christopherson couldn't help wishing they could keep going in that direction.

Eventually, however, they righted themselves, and 100 yards out the LCT commander ordered 'full speed ahead' and drove towards the beach. They slid on to the sand, the ramp was released with a crash and one by one the tanks slowly made their way down, through the few feet of water and on to the beach. It was now after 9 a.m., but A Squadron tanks were still coming ashore at around 10 a.m.; an official photographer captured the moment that *Aberdeen* exited its LCT, close to high tide with virtually no room on the beach left at all. One of the other problems was that the tide was coming in more quickly than normal because of the storm and also further up the beach, causing even greater congestion.

One of the first people Christopherson saw was Bill Enderby, the senior commander on Stuart Hills's LCT, who had made it to the shore despite a broken arm. Having had it dressed, he was one of the walking wounded about to be shipped back to hospital in England; a new second-in-command of C Squadron was needed already. That they had met at all suggested that they were close to where Enderby had landed – on Jig Red, rather than Jig Green.

Around the same time, Regimental HQ was also landing, with its four Shermans. The CO's was called *Robin Hood*, while that of Lieutenant Denis Markins, the signals officer at RHQ, was *Maid Marion*. The remaining two, those of the second-in-command and adjutant, were, inevitably, called *Little John* and *Friar Tuck*. All four were immediately ushered off the beach and soon found themselves crossing one of the cleared lanes and moving on to the lateral road, joining the exodus of vehicles now rapidly pouring off the Jig Red sector of the beach.

By this time, Peter Selerie had also made it to Jig Green. Because of the casualties already taken on the western half of Jig, the naval beach master, Lieutenant-Commander Brian Whinney, had made the decision quite early to suspend further landings there because of the still active gun casement at Le Hamel – the strongpoint that had knocked out Monty Horley's and Bill Digby's DDs. Selerie, and the four other tank crews on his LCT, did not know this, however.

In fact, because of the problems with their LCT's engines, they had been playing catch-up all morning. Fortunately, the commander of the LCT had heard over his radio of the decision to bring the tanks right in to the shore, a decision Selerie was mightily relieved about and which he considered a 'splendid Nelson touch'. By the time they were finally approaching Jig Green, though, it was well into the morning and the tide was in, covering most of the obstacles. For the most part, the only indication of where these defences were was the surf breaking over them. Selerie's troop were not without their own fire support, however. Rocket-firing landing craft were hosing the Le Hamel strongpoint, as also were naval guns, and even self-propelled tracked field guns still to disembark. Enemy shells were whistling towards them, too – a sound, Selerie realized, he had not heard since the fighting in Tunisia of May 1943.

Some 200 yards from the shore, the LCT commander dropped his anchor, which meant they would have to swim the last bit after all. All the tanks managed to launch safely; as they neared the beach, Selerie saw a number of tanks ahead of them had bogged down, so over the net told the others to engage first gear once their tracks took hold on the sand, and to advance very slowly. By doing so, they all managed to clear the beach and head towards the dunes beyond; the misfortunes of others offered a certain amount of cover as by now there were a number of tanks and AVREs littering the shoreline.

Selerie thought the situation seemed a bit of a shambles. There were no infantry anywhere, and knocked-out flail tanks where he'd assumed there would be a cleared lane to the lateral road. They were also still under enemy shell-fire. There were, though, some sappers on the ground who courageously began to clear a lane manually. Trying to give themselves as much cover as possible in a tank on an open beach, Selerie and his crew gave suppressing fire towards Le Hamel. One tank in his troop had its gun martlet hit by an anti-tank round, but they all continued counter-firing and for a while the enemy gun appeared to have been silenced. This gave a troop of B Squadron tanks the chance to get clear of Jig Green, move down the lateral road and turn towards Asnelles; an American P-38 Lightning photo-reconnaissance aircraft was overhead around 10.40 a.m. and took pictures of four DD Shermans crawling carefully through the village, which appeared to be otherwise unoccupied. This was most likely Lieutenant Colin Thomson's troop. Yet although these tanks had managed to get past the Le Hamel blockhouse anti-tank gun, it was soon firing again, threatening the safe passage of vehicles along the lateral road.

The strength of the much-vaunted German Atlantic Wall lay right on its very crust. Preparations for a second line of defence were being prepared, but on D-Day were still far from complete; so, once that outer crust was broken, the invading forces could expect to face far less opposition. Breaking through that crust, however – the entire sea defences along this stretch of the coast – represented a huge challenge. WN 36 had fallen, and so too had WN 35, further east, but both the 77mm gun and other defences in Le Hamel were still doggedly holding out, as were the strongpoints further west on the high ground that overlooked much of Gold Beach.

It was now vital to get many of the rapidly increasing number of vehicles clear of the beaches. Although there was a road off Jig Red that ran left and south towards the village of Meuvaines, the D-Day objectives were to push further west and south-west, to take Asnelles, Ryes and Bayeux. Progress, though, was being blocked by the strongpoints at Le

Hamel and up on the cliffs. Knocking out the extremely troublesome anti-tank gun that was watching every movement along Jig Green and the lateral road was clearly now an urgent imperative, because although four B Squadron tanks had sneaked past nothing much else had managed to do so.

Some time a little after 11 a.m., Captain Arthur Warburton, a forward observation officer – FOO – of the Essex Yeomanry, 8th Armoured Brigade's artillery regiment, was pushing down the lateral road when, some 300 yards from the crossroads, his tank was hit by the 77mm at Le Hamel. Fortunately, he and his crew survived the strike, and Warburton now called out over the net to Sergeant Bob Palmer, commander of a Sexton moving down a short distance behind. The 25-pounder field artillery gun mounted on its Sherman chassis was supposed to lob shells in an arc over distances as long as 8 miles; it was not designed as a high-velocity anti-tank gun operating in clear view of its target over open sites. Yet Warburton now asked Palmer to use it in just that way. Palmer was perhaps 400 yards or so from the casement; jumping down from his Sexton near the No. 2 Team exit from Jig Green, he hurried over to the line of trees that hid him from view of the casement and peered through his field glasses to have a look at the troublesome gun emplacement. Seeing a large mushroom of concrete housing the anti-tank gun, he realized immediately that the only chance of destroying the gun was to get a bull-seye through the aperture, which, with a Sexton, meant getting as close as possible and firing that lucky shot before they were hit themselves. Back in his Sexton, he decided that speed of manoeuvre was key. Hurtling forward down the road at nearly 30 mph, he drew up some 40 yards from the crossroads, turned the Sexton 45 degrees and opened fire. The first shell was a bit high and to the left, but the second was a direct hit. And with that, the gun was at last silenced.

That single strike changed the fortunes of those on Gold Beach, because even though the rest of the strongpoint at Le Hamel and the defences on the cliffs to the west had not been subdued, traffic on the lateral road could no longer be threatened by that 77mm gun. As for those guns on the cliffs to the west, they were mostly still firing down the beach at the larger targets of the landing craft still approaching the shore. While the infantry were now moving inland and west over the waterlogged fields, motorized traffic could start to push south and south-west through Asnelles, bypassing the rest of the Le Hamel strongpoint for the time being. Getting the ever-increasing mass of vehicles off the beaches as quickly as possible was not just a matter of easing congestion but also, importantly, one of widening the bridgehead and getting inland, as it was feared the enemy might try to counter-attack from the south. Strength in depth was the best antidote to any such counter-thrust.

American photo-reconnaissance aircraft were busy overhead again from around 11.30 a.m., and the photographs they took showed vividly what was going on below. At one part of Jig Red, lanes had been cleared between the shore and the lateral road, and around these the beach was thick with landing craft and teeming with men and vehicles. Further along, on Jig Green, the remains of knocked-out and bogged-down tanks and AVREs littered the shore; even Monty Horley's DD Sherman could be seen close to the Le Hamel casement.

The roads to the south, however, were heavy with British traffic, demonstrating just how valuable Sergeant Palmer's aperture shot had been and how quickly it had eased up congestion on Jig Red. Advancing towards the village of Asnelles were the Sherman DD tanks of the Rangers' B or C Squadron, as well as Churchills towing trailers known as 'porpoises' and the Sextons of the Essex Yeomanry. While the detritus on the beaches, the cratering and smoke, the wrecked vehicles and landing craft all spoke of the difficulties the invaders had experienced, it is remarkable just how many men and how much machinery had been got ashore in such a comparatively short space of time – having already faced both appalling conditions and a determined enemy. The photographs, if nothing else, provided a vivid demonstration of the Allies' materiel strength.

Meanwhile, the infantry, including the Dorsets and Devons, had begun to move cross-country. While armoured columns managed to pass through Asnelles without much incident, the infantry were delayed at the eastern edge of the village by enemy-held trenches and snipers; but then, having cleared the village, they were able to push on to Le Buhot and Ryes, some 3 miles inland, this time with the support of Stanley Christopherson's A Squadron and assorted AVREs and Sextons. Apart from a brief period in northern Tunisia, this was the first time the Sherwood Rangers had fought through villages and enclosed country. 'And it was not altogether pleasant,' Christopherson noted with his usual understatement. He was immediately aware that the field of visibility while passing through narrow lanes or along hedgerows was often extremely limited in a way that it had not been in the desert. Sniping had already begun and word spread rapidly. Operating the tank with hatches down and with periscopes was next to impossible, especially without infantry alongside, which meant the tank commander needed his head out of the turret – and that made him horribly vulnerable.

The threat from Le Hamel was still considerable, moreover. Dominating this small coastal outpost was the sanatorium complex, taken over by the defenders and used by snipers, machine-gun teams and as an OP – observation post – while the casement that housed the 77mm gun that had caused such havoc earlier had a further 50mm gun facing west, in the opposite direction, and some mobile anti-tank guns as well. There were few other buildings, and the entire strongpoint was defended not only by the usual belt of mines and wire but also by a significant anti-tank ditch. The only way in was via the lateral road. Given all the Allied naval fire-power out at sea, and the visibility of the sanatorium as such an obvious and dominating landmark, it is surprising that it hadn't been levelled early in the day, but by late morning it was still standing and still covered by the strongpoints – and guns – on the cliffs between Jig and the town of Arromanches-les-Bains.

The threat from the casement, along with the other guns at Le Hamel, had hampered operations on Jig Green all morning. Owen Evers, another desert veteran and driver of *Maid Marion* in Regimental HQ, was following the CO's tank and moving along the lateral road westwards in the direction of Le Hamel when a shell landed close beside the colonel's Sherman, presumably fired from the guns further west on the cliffs. Although the Sherman stopped, damage appeared to be slight, and Evers saw Lieutenant-Colonel D'Arcy Anderson jump down on to the ground, wearing only a tin hat for safety. The colonel had only gone a few paces when he was hit by a sniper and fell to the ground.

'If you want to win a Military Cross,' Evers told Lieutenant Denis Markins, 'you've only to jump out and rescue the CO.'

Markins suggested Evers might want to win the medal instead. But Evers wasn't interested in winning medals. He was only interested in keeping his head down and surviving the war. As it was, two infantry lads pulled Anderson clear of the road and into the safety of a culvert beside it. Then Evers and their Regimental HQ tanks sped on forward. It was the last any of them saw of the CO. Stanley Christopherson was placed temporarily in charge until the regiment's second-in-command, Major Mike Laycock, could get ashore. Not that a commanding officer could do a great deal with the regiment both strung out along the beach and now starting to push inland. Photo-reconnaissance aircraft of the US Ninth Air Force were over again at around 1 p.m., and their pictures clearly showed yet more vehicles moving inland – but also two troops of tanks, spaced apart, heading west to assault Le Hamel; almost certainly these were from B Squadron of the Sherwood Rangers.

Peter Selerie and his troop had been held up getting off the beach – the lane off Jig Green was already littered with knocked-out tanks and AVREs, four of them in all – but some time after 1 p.m. were advancing down past the crossroads from which the road led to Asnelles and towards Le Hamel itself. To their right, perched next to the sea wall, were the buildings of the sanatorium complex. While on this approach road they encountered a Churchill Mk III AVRE – a Churchill tank equipped not with a main gun but with a 290mm spigot mortar. The men had swiftly renamed it the 'flying dustbin' because of the size of mortar it fired. Selerie had paused to speak to the AVRE commander, Sergeant Bert Scaife, who was by this time the only survivor of his team of five AVREs from the 82nd Assault Squadron.

Selerie told him they would head towards the large, multi-storeyed buildings of the sanatorium; Scaife's AVRE could throw an impressive amount of high explosive, but it lacked any kind of velocity or range, so had to get close to its target to be effective. Selerie now offered to give him cover while the AVRE trundled down the road to the sanatorium. All four tanks poured machine-gun fire and shells from their main 75mm gun, which helped Scaife get his Churchill to within 50 yards of its target. Selerie watched Scaife's AVRE fire and saw the flying dustbin hit the building just above the front door; part of it collapsed like a deck of cards. Defenders, weapons and rubble collapsed amid clouds of dust, and soon after that more defenders emerged with their hands in the air. Scaife then manoeuvred his way to the rear of the casement overlooking the beach. With another AVRE petard to the rear, the casement was completely knocked out for good.

With Jig Green finally clear, Bert Jenkins was picked up. Ever since the first moments of the landings, he'd remained where he was, taking cover at the rear of his tank, the bodies of Worboyes and Horley lying a few yards away. He'd seen the tide go out and come back in again, and during all that time no one had ventured along to his end of the western side of Jig Green. 'It wasn't until later in the day that I heard others come, but they had been way down the beach. Everybody was way down.' Then, in the afternoon, once the enemy casement near him had been knocked out, he was found and taken to an aid post. 'And I was given something to drink and a blanket, because I was all wet and covered in sand', said Jenkins, 'and I was put with a lot of other blokes who'd also lost their way.'

Meanwhile, Stuart Hills and his crew, having escaped their sinking tank, had had something of a grandstand view of the day's events, albeit from out at sea. With no paddles except their hands, they had been unable to prevent their dinghy from drifting eastwards too. 'The dinghy,' noted Arthur Reddish, 'proved impossible to navigate.' Helpless in the tiny craft, they watched aircraft thunder over, heard more shells screaming through the air, witnessed two LCTs get hit and be tossed about by the waves, saw tanks and AVREs burning on the shore. Suddenly, a shell whistled in towards them, exploding a short distance ahead. This was followed by another behind. They all feared they had been bracketed – identified by an enemy gun, which was firing a shot, watching where it landed, and then adjusting until it hit the target; fortunately, in the nick of time, an LCG – landing craft, gun – sped over, hauled them aboard and moved clear just as another shell landed virtually on top of the abandoned dinghy. These landing craft were bristling with cannons and could get far closer to the shore than any warship, even a destroyer.

Taken below deck, they were plied with whisky and chocolate; once restored, they went back on deck to watch the action as the LCG hurried back and forth providing fire support on the shore. In the afternoon, Hills saw infantry directly beneath the sea wall in front of the sanatorium – these were men from the Hampshires still trying to subdue Le Hamel. As the LCG opened fire, Hills also witnessed Scaife's AVRE and two of Peter Selerie's Sherman DDs attacking the big building.

Hills and his crew were still on the LCG that evening, and wondering whether they might ever get off again. By that time, Le Hamel had been completely knocked out; fighting alongside the Hampshires had been Shermans of Lieutenant Colin Thomson's troop in B Squadron. His troop sergeant, Bill Bracegirdle, won an immediate Military Medal for his part in the fighting that afternoon, for despite his own tank being hit, he and his crew continued firing, knocking out one 50mm anti-tank gun and then, after his own gun was put out of action, remaining where they were to direct the fire of another B Squadron tank on to further enemy positions. Thomson's and Selerie's troops then pressed on with the Hampshires to help clear WN 39, the strongpoint on the top of the hill to the west. When these guns were also finally overrun, the threat to the Jig sector of Gold Beach was largely over; at one of the captured guns, 124 empty shell cases were found.

The regiment's three sabre squadrons – the fighting squadrons, A, B and C – now came together at Le Buhot, to which Stanley Christopherson and his A Squadron had returned after the capture of the village of Ryes earlier in the afternoon. Up to this point, B and C Squadrons had been under command 1st Hampshires and 1st Dorsets, which meant that from a command perspective they had been temporarily cut adrift from the regiment and by turn 8th Armoured Brigade's command. Now, the three sabre squadrons all came back under RHQ.

Le Buhot was a small hamlet that stood amid lush, rolling Normandy farmland halfway between Ryes and Asnelles. In the absence of any kind of enemy strength in depth, now the crust of the defences had been smashed there were rapid gains to be made. At any rate, by around 4 p.m. the Sherwood Rangers had regained some cohesion and were ready for the next phase of operations to support another of 50th Division's infantry brigades, the 56th, which had landed that afternoon and was now clear of the beaches. Being 'in direct support' meant that while they were now, as the phrase suggested, supporting the infantry, they remained under command of 8th Armoured Brigade rather than being directly commanded by the units they were supporting. This was a subtle but very important distinction, designed to ensure that infantry commanders insufficiently expert in handling armour – or artillery for that matter – did not issue unreasonable orders. Being 'in support' rather than 'under command' was designed to encourage more effective collaboration between the infantry and their supporting armour.

Now, at Le Buhot, Stanley Christopherson and his squadron were preparing to link up with the infantry of the 56th Brigade's 2nd Essex Battalion. A signal had reached Christopherson that he was to meet Lieutenant-Colonel John Higson, the commander of the 2nd Essex, at a specific rendezvous, but on arriving he could find no trace of him. There were, however, a few Essex men there, who told him their CO was several miles further down the road.

Christopherson wondered how he was ever going to catch up with Higson in his Sherman on narrow roads now thick with traffic. Fortunately, the solution suddenly and rather magically presented itself when he spotted a fully saddled horse standing patiently outside a house in Le Buhot. Christopherson had set off for war back in 1939 as a mounted cavalryman, and now here he was, returning to the saddle on this first day of the liberation of north-west Europe. 'Never in my wildest dreams,' he noted, 'did I ever anticipate that D-Day would find me dashing along the lanes of Normandy endeavouring, not very successfully, to control a very frightened horse with one hand, gripping a map case in the other, and wearing a tin hat and black overalls.'

Colonel Higson was understandably somewhat startled when Christopherson rather breathlessly appeared, but it meant they were able to coordinate their advance on Bayeux. Apart from reports of sniping, there had been little sign of the enemy, and they managed to reach the south-east outskirts of the city by evening and to see off some light opposition near the city's railway station. Patrols then got across the River Aure and pushed on to the village of Saint-Loup-Hors and over the next stream, the River Drôme, to the south-west of the city, to occupy the slightly higher ground there. Bayeux was there for the taking, and Christopherson urged Colonel Higson to attack and take it that night. He was not to be persuaded, however.

None the less, D-Day had been a success, not just at Gold Beach but along the entire length of the invasion front. The weather had been overcome, as had the Atlantic Wall. US and British airborne troops had secured the flanks, and troops were ashore and consolidating their bridgeheads along all five of the invasion beaches. From Jig Gold, the Sherwood Rangers had certainly played their part. Now, from around 10 p.m., the three sabre squadrons leaguered up for the night. That meant forming the tanks into a protective box, then carrying out basic maintenance, replenishing ammunition and fuel, getting a meal, and then trying to catch some much-needed sleep.

Padre Leslie Skinner had spent much of the day tending to the wounded at Jig Red, but after seeing forty-three men on to an LST – the larger, 100-metre-long landing ship, tank – had made radio contact with Dr Charles Young, the regiment's doctor, or MO – medical officer – to ask him to check the wounded men before it sailed. Young had been with the regiment in the desert and was a popular figure; for some reason no one seems able to explain, he was affectionately known as 'Hylda', a nickname he appears to have arrived with when he joined the Sherwood Rangers and which by all accounts he didn't mind a bit. The troopers also knew him as 'Bum Shandy' because of his trick of rooting out shirkers by threatening them with an anal examination. This wheeze worked very well even if he did cop an unfortunate nickname as a consequence.

At any rate, the doctor had found Skinner at around 3.30 p.m. and checked each of the wounded in turn; there was only one he thought might not make the journey back across the Channel. Skinner then quickly dashed off a letter to his wife, Etta, which the skipper of the LST promised to post in England, then set off to catch up with the regiment. He eventually found Regimental HQ in a field near the church at Sommervieu, where he finally got his head down at 11.30 p.m. His D-Day, however, was not over yet. At a quarter past midnight, they were ordered to move a little closer to Bayeux and so off they went again, eventually leaguering up in an orchard. 'Bed on ground about 01.30,' scribbled Skinner in his diary, 'dead beat. Fell asleep beside a half-track, indescribably filthy.' So far, just on this one day, the regiment had suffered forty casualties, including a number who were missing, presumed dead or wounded.

It was a lot, and a bleak warning of what was to come.

CHAPTER 4

Point 103

B Y THE TIME THE Sherwood Rangers' B Squadron had leaguered up
for the night of D-Day at the edge of Bayeux, they had just five tanks
remaining, but by morning had been joined by a further seven. 'It was
heartening,' noted Peter Selerie, who was rather in awe of the work by the
beach recovery teams and by their own fitters, men from the LAD – light
aid detachment – attached to the regiment. As soon as the beaches had
been secured, the LAD had begun the work of pulling out bogged-down
tanks and repairing others that had suffered battle damage. Not only had
many been put back into running order, they and their crews had rejoined
the squadron. Given everything else that was going on in this first twenty-
four hours of the invasion, it was little short of a miracle. It meant that of
the nineteen tanks in the squadron, irrecoverable losses on D-Day had
been three sunk in the sea and four knocked out for good. Those were
considerable, but would soon be made good with the flow of replacement
tanks already heading across the Channel, part of a constant ferrying of
supplies that it was hoped would ensure the Allies won the battle of the
build-up; having won a tentative toehold on D-Day, the challenge now
was to establish overwhelming materiel dominance before the enemy
could organize themselves into a coordinated and decisive counter-
attack. The long tail of the Allied war machine – its ability to supply the
fighting element at the front – was a part of modern warfare at which it
had already excelled in North Africa, Sicily and southern Italy.

The sooner the five Allied invasion beaches could join into one single
bridgehead, the harder it would be for the Germans to knock them back
into the sea. Captured ground was to be swiftly consolidated and ever

more men and supplies from southern England poured in. The further inland the Allies were, the further a German counter-attack would have to push them back and the more difficult the enemy's task would be. Broadly speaking, D-Day had gone very well. Airborne troops had secured their objectives, holding key ground, destroying bridges and protecting the flanks. All five invasion beaches had seen their allotted forces land and secure a bridgehead. As a proportion of casualties to men landed, the Canadians had suffered the worst but had also made the greatest inroads, while the Americans at Omaha had experienced terrible casualties initially but had managed to take the most challenging of all the invasion beaches. The American 4th Division at Utah had faced the lightest of opposition. The main city of Caen, a D-Day objective for the British troops landing at Sword, the most easterly beach, had not been captured, but it was hoped that Bayeux, of less strategic importance but still a major thoroughfare, would be swiftly taken that morning of 7 June.

With the confusion and difficulties of the amphibious invasion behind them, the Sherwood Rangers were able to operate alongside the infantry and move into Bayeux in a two-pronged attack. Once again with the 2nd Essex, A Squadron moved in from the south, while the twelve remaining Shermans of B Squadron came in from the north. The town was eerily quiet to begin with, and entering it was a nerve-wracking experience, especially for the tank commanders who had to have their heads out of the turrets to be able to see anything in the narrow medieval streets. As it was, one driver in B Squadron misjudged a corner and knocked down part of a house in the process. It was very easily done.

Fortunately, Bayeux had been largely abandoned by the enemy, except for a few snipers and a machine-gun post hidden in a house in the south of the town. A return shot from one of Stanley Christopherson's A Squadron Shermans set the house on fire. Soon afterwards, Christopherson was astonished to hear the clanging bells of a fire-engine and then to see it hurtle past. 'Regardless of the machine-gun fire,' he wrote, 'they held up the battle, entered the house, extinguished the fire and brought out the German machine-gun section.'

And with that, Bayeux was in the hands of the Allies. Moving across the city from the north, Peter Selerie was among those who saw growing numbers of civilians take to the streets to cheer the Allied troops. Slowing as they drove down a narrow street, he saw a girl throw some flowers to him. Selerie reached out but failed to catch them. Other civilians emerged to offer cider and food; the town, largely untouched, was the first in France to be liberated.

Beyond Bayeux, the tanks parted company with 56th Brigade. Before the invasion, 8th Armoured Brigade had been asked to prepare plans for a mobile armoured group to hurry south and capture the small market town of Villers-Bocage immediately after their D-Day objectives had been taken. This town lay some 15 miles south-west of Caen and was a key road crossing. Since, in the pre-invasion plan, Caen was to have been taken on D-Day, reaching and capturing Villers-Bocage, ideally on D plus 1, would ensure a vital nodal point was then denied to the enemy. In effect, it was to be a blocking position to baulk an enemy counter-attack, and then a place from which the follow-up armoured divisions could push through and exploit their opportunity.

Although Caen had still not been taken, the principle behind the original plan remained; the quick capture of Villers-Bocage would certainly make taking Caen that much more straightforward and still offered opportunities for further drives south. However, orders for the armoured column were not issued until 11 p.m. on 7 June; it was to be ready to push south from Bayeux to Villers-Bocage the following morning, D plus 2, Thursday, 8 June. Brigadier Hugh Cracroft, 8th Armoured Brigade's commander, had also prepared some 'intermediate' objectives, the first of which was a low ridge overlooking the Seulles river valley, marked on the map as Point 103.

The armoured force set out early on the 8th in two columns, with 4/7th Dragoon Guards[1] leading the left-hand route and the 24th Lancers the right-hand route; the Sherwood Rangers were to follow. All were up early – around 4 a.m. On the go like this, each crew received ration packs and the men were responsible for feeding themselves. Breakfast always included tea – usually tea leaves, tinned condensed milk and sugar all brewed together. Primus stoves were issued to each of the crews, but very often water would be boiled over a tin filled with soil and soaked in petrol; it burned longer than one might think and could heat up the tea in pretty quick order too. Tea aside, breakfast would be a snatched mouthful – some chocolate or boiled sweets, or perhaps a

[1] The 4th/7th Dragoon Guards were created in India in 1922 with the merging of the 4th (Royal Irish) Dragoon Guards and the 7th (Princess Royal's) Dragoon Guards. In 1936 they became the 4/7th Royal Dragoon Guards, but remained more widely known as the 4/7th Dragoon Guards, or even 4/7th DG.

biscuit. Normandy was rich and fertile farmland, but on this first morning inland there had been little opportunity to barter or scavenge any
fresh eggs, milk or other produce.

Engines were run up in the dark, the electric starter motor wheezing
before the Chrysler multibank erupted into life in a cloud of choking
smoke and exhaust fumes. When they did finally rumble forward,
most crewmen were feeling their fair share of nerves. Experienced in
combat though the hard core of the regiment was, this countryside
was unfamiliar terrain. Gentle, rolling hills and valleys, a patchwork
of small fields and farmsteads and a seemingly endless number of villages, nearly all surrounded by orchards. Little woods and copses dotted
the landscape, while the roads – most just grit rather than tarmac – were
almost all lined with dense hedgerows grown up from earlier boundary
mounds and earthen walls. In Normandy, this kind of countryside was
known as *bocage*, and was especially dense in the western half of the
region. While it quickly gave way to wide, open and sweeping arable
farmland just a few miles to the east towards Caen, this stretch, between
Bayeux and the little town of Tilly-sur-Seulles, was unmistakably *bocage*
country.

Some of the Sherwood Rangers crews had already experienced sniping and anti-tank gunfire as they'd pushed southwards. On D-Day
afternoon, outside Le Buhot, Jack Holman's tank had been hit and his
driver, Trooper Arthur Lacey, badly wounded in the arm. Holman
managed to pull him clear and take him to the side of the road, only for
them to be targeted by a sniper. These risks made any advance a tense
experience, but there was no avoiding the roads; even tracked tanks
needed these arteries to get from A to B, and so they were effectively
canalized and the lead tanks in the column left at the mercy of a lurking
enemy anti-tank gun. That same afternoon, as A Squadron was advancing towards Bayeux, Mike Howden's tank in A Squadron was in the
lead. Howden suffered from a bit of a stammer, and soon after joining
the Sherwood Rangers had come on the net and announced, 'Sorry, but
my m-m-m-microphone is d-d-d-dis' – his mic was not working. This
had caused much hilarity and ever since then he had been widely – and
affectionately – known as 'Dis-Mike', a nickname he took in his quiet
stride.

His gunner was nineteen-year-old Stan Cox, from Didcot near Oxford;
he'd joined the regiment back in January straight from the 55th Royal
Armoured Corps Training Regiment, and unlike Howden, who was a

desert veteran, was entirely new to combat. All the crew were inside the tank except Howden, whose head was out above the turret, while Cox sat at his gunner's position: a small round seat just to the right of the main gun, peering through the periscope.

Suddenly, Howden spotted movement in one of the nearby trees. A sniper, maybe? He wasn't taking any chances, so said to Cox, 'Give them a burst of machine-gun fire.'

Cox quickly traversed the gun and trained it on the trees – but then, instead of pressing the trigger button for the coaxial machine gun, hit the main 75mm gun instead, which fired with a huge boom, sending the breech recoiling. It was a good shot, though, as it smashed the trunk about halfway up and the tree toppled over – and with it the sniper.

'B-b-b-bugger, Cox,' Howden said, 'that was a b-b-b-bit b-b-b-bloody drastic!'

On this third day of the invasion, snipers picked off two tank commanders of the 24th Lancers, whose leading tanks then came under attack from anti-tank guns hidden in the village of Putot-en-Bessin, away to their left as they moved south from Loucelles. The road here wove through slightly more open country, largely devoid of trees, and the enemy gunners had clear sight of them from their hidden positions in Putot. These gunners were from the 12. SS Panzer-Division 'Hitler Jugend', who had started reaching the front on the night of D-Day and who had been fighting mostly Canadians pressing inland from Juno Beach ever since. Having been ordered to throw the Allies back into the sea, the 12. SS men had hit something of a Canadian brick wall. They had also executed a number of prisoners they'd taken, in the wooded grounds of the Château Audrieu.

There had only been one panzer – armoured – division in Normandy on D-Day, although the Allies knew there were some ten mobile divisions spread throughout France and the Low Countries, most or all of which, it was assumed, would be sent as quickly as possible to the Normandy front. While the German divisions protecting the Atlantic Wall were of poor quality, badly equipped and trained, it was recognized that the mobile divisions were of a different calibre altogether. Some of these units were army and as such, part of the German armed forces, or Wehrmacht; others were Waffen-SS, the front-line component of the Nazi party's military wing. Whether Wehrmacht or SS, however, these panzer and panzer-grenadier divisions were the best-equipped units the German army had, with the latest weaponry – and were also, for the most part, decently trained and highly motivated. These men were largely German, rather than men wearing German uniforms, as was the case with a lot of the lesser infantry units, which had conscripted men from captured territories in Eastern Europe and the Soviet Union; they were also highly disciplined and could be relied upon to keep fighting no matter how many casualties they suffered. The 12. SS were brutally violent and the first panzer division to move up to the front. Even after getting a bloody nose at the hands of the Canadians the day before, on D plus 1, they were still a formidable opponent, and although the 24th Lancers managed to destroy a couple of self-propelled guns and two anti-tank guns, and capture some seventy-five prisoners, they also had several tanks knocked out along with nine killed and six wounded.

Without infantry to help them, the Lancers' tanks could not get into Putot, and so by late afternoon they had pulled back to Loucelles, while the Sherwood Rangers, keeping well clear of Putot and even Audrieu, advanced over a railway line and across wide, open fields a little way to the west; aerial photographs showed their route all too clearly. Effectively, they had reached Point 103 by outflanking the villages and roads that led up to this ridgeline. Here, at the crest, a sunken track lined by beech trees offered good cover as well as commanding views down towards Tilly in the Seulles valley and, on its eastern edge, Saint-Pierre; the two villages were almost one, separated only by the River Seulles itself. A dead-straight Roman road then linked Saint-Pierre to Fontenay-le-Pesnel, a couple of miles to the east. Beyond, to the south, the ground rose once again to another ridgeline. So long as the British held the ridge around Point 103, they would be able to see any enemy trying to push north from Tilly. Conversely, if they wanted to get the ridge beyond, they would have to advance in full view of any enemy troops dug in there. On reaching Point 103, though, it was not clear whether the enemy held the ridge to the south. Intelligence suggested the Panzer-Lehr-Division was heading towards them with the same brief as that of the 12. SS – to knock the Allies back into the sea. But how near they were was unclear that late afternoon.

Since it was A Squadron who had reached Point 103 first, Christopherson asked one of his troop leaders, Lieutenant John Bethell-Fox, to take his tank down towards the River Seulles and recce Tilly and Saint-Pierre. Bethell-Fox was a fluent French speaker, so well placed to question some of the locals. Trundling down the road, he reached Saint-Pierre but initially found this small village of narrow lanes and stone houses deserted; it seemed the locals had either fled or hidden in their cellars. Eventually, though, Bethell-Fox found one elderly Frenchman who told him he'd seen a foot patrol of a dozen Germans who were similarly questioning locals about the whereabouts of the British. It was clearly time for him to beat a retreat – and quickly, for suddenly he heard the sound of tanks not far away.

At that moment, Bethell-Fox was unaware that he had narrowly avoided bumping into leading troops from the Panzer-Lehr-Division, commanded by a former Afrika Korps commander, Generalleutnant Fritz Bayerlein, one of the few senior German commanders in the west with considerable experience of fighting the British. His division, formed from a cadre of battle-hardened and highly experienced veterans and training instructors, was one of the very best in the entire German army. They were also at full strength with just under 15,000 men, and well equipped too, although they had suffered badly from Allied fighter-bombers during their hurried advance from Le Mans, where they'd been based on 6 June. Bayerlein had been furious; he understood the need to reach the front quickly, but had also witnessed enough of Allied air power to know that travelling by day would expose them horribly, and so it had proved. By the time the division reached the ridge to the south of the Seulles valley, they had lost a staggering 84 half-tracks, prime movers and self-propelled guns out of 700, 103 trucks – 10 per cent of the total – and five tanks. These were grievous losses for a division before even reaching the front.

None the less, their arrival meant there would be no easy passage to Villers-Bocage for 8th Armoured Brigade. While the Panzer-Lehr's strength had been dented, they were still a formidable outfit, and as hardened and tough an enemy as any the Sherwood Rangers had yet confronted during the war. A baptism of fire awaited them in their first major battle in Normandy.

Padre Leslie Skinner believed very strongly that his role was twofold. Of course, he was expected to hold services for the men and to provide solace and spiritual care and guidance; but it was also his task to record the losses and report these returns. And this was a part of his job that he was determined to oversee as effectively and wholeheartedly as he could. As far as was humanly possible, he would make sure he accounted for every single loss in the regiment. It would be his business to account for the wounded and missing, and to recover and bury each and every man who was killed while serving with the Sherwood Rangers. If that meant extracting a mere burned crisp from a brewed-up tank, then so be it. Everyone lost would get a proper burial, so that their families could be told and so that there would be a grave to visit once the war was finally over. This, he believed, was his profound duty as a Christian.

So it was that on the 7th, having been up at 4.30 a.m. and finding he wasn't needed at the regimental aid post, he borrowed a motorcycle and headed back to Gold Beach to check on the casualties from the previous day and to try to find news of the missing. Bill Digby, who had lost his legs at Jig Green, had been recovered but was not expected to survive his catastrophic injuries; and he could find no news at all of Lieutenant Stuart Hills and his crew, who were sadly assumed to have all drowned. Better news was that the brigade Forward Delivery Squadron – FDS – was also now ashore with ten fresh tanks.

Heading back south in the afternoon, Skinner found the regiment outside Bayeux, and finally managed to get a wash for the first time since coming ashore. He eventually got his head down some time after midnight, but like the rest of the regiment was up again before dawn – this time at 4.15 a.m. – and joined Regimental HQ as they moved on south towards Point 103. 'Wretched tank country,' he noted. 'Occasional shelling and mortar fire from enemy. Many isolated enemy infantry positions and snipers.' These shots were coming from the 12. SS and also disparate packets of troops falling back from the coast; at this stage of the invasion it was very difficult to know for sure what ground had been taken and cleared, and what still contained pockets of resistance.

Around half-past nine that morning, he was with the medical units of the regimental aid post – RAP – waiting in a wood while the sabre squadrons pressed forward. Suddenly, two high-explosive shells whistled into the wood near the entrance gap, wounding one man. Skinner and Sergeant James Loades both discovered small shrapnel punctures in their tin helmets, while Dr Young's half-track had its radiator smashed. This then had to be towed further into the wood to a point from which the RAP could continue to function.

Later that evening, Lieutenant Laurence Verner was brought in, having been shot in the chest by a sniper. He was in a bad way, and although Dr Young managed to patch him up it was clear he needed to be taken to one of the newly established field hospitals as quickly as possible. After helping to place him in a truck, Skinner went with him, holding on to a blood drip with one hand and gripping on to the rear door and bumper with the other as they bounced their way over roads made rougher by the earlier passage of tanks and other vehicles. By the time they reached the 75th Field Ambulance Unit in a field near Longues-sur-Mer, Skinner had severe cramps in his arms and legs, and by the time they had unloaded Verner, night had fallen. 'Journey back in dark nightmare,' he scribbled. 'Doctor had moved again. Found him by 0130 by which time feeling tired and somewhat faint.' He finally got his head down at 2 a.m., but with shelling somewhere close by disturbing the still of the night, what sleep he did get was fitful, to say the least. Two and a half hours later, he was up again for another day. That night, Bill Digby died; Lieutenant Verner would go the same way later on the fourth day of the invasion.

Heading to join 8th Armoured Brigade, and eventually the Sherwood Rangers, on 8 June was the war reporter Major Anthony Cotterell. Journalists, film cameramen and photographers were by now a familiar presence in modern warfare, their task to feed news and images from the front line to eager civilian audiences back home. They were also there to keep the soldiers at the front up to speed with what was going on in the wider war; most troops relied on forces newspapers and radio reports to keep them abreast of what was happening either side of them. It was important to maintain morale, especially so when so much was being asked of them.

Cotterell was twenty-seven at this point; at the start of the war he had been a journalist for the *Daily Express*, back then the most accessible and widely read newspaper in Britain. Much to his annoyance, he was conscripted in March 1940 and posted to the Royal Fusiliers, which meant putting his pen aside and pursuing a conventional career as an infantry officer. This he endured for a little over a year until in June 1941 he was recruited to ABCA – the embryonic Army Bureau of Current Affairs, which had been newly set up within the War Office specifically to keep the troops informed of what was going on in the war. Cotterell set to the task with no small amount of zeal, writing a fortnightly news pamphlet called *WAR*. The booklet went down rather well, as it was full of personal stories of people he had met and exciting accounts of their bomber missions and various other aspects of military life. By 1943, he was not only *WAR*'s chief editor, but also its star reporter.

Cotterell had become rather obsessed with airborne forces and had himself completed a parachute training course. He had hoped to accompany the 6th Airborne Division into Normandy on D-Day, but permission had been refused. Instead, he got himself attached to 8th Armoured Brigade, coming ashore on D-Day with an allocated seat in one of the brigade's pool of headquarters tanks. Finding the tank and its commander, Corporal Cook, had been something of a problem, however. Having landed separately on Gold Beach, he had lost them entirely and ended up near Crépon, a village inland from Gold King, where 69th Brigade had come ashore. On D plus 1, he had cadged a ride on an RAF truck, passing scenes of fighting, seeing dead Germans with their faces blasted off and peppered with bullets, and getting held up as flame-throwing Crocodiles blasted an enemy strongpoint in their way. By nightfall, he'd still not found a single vehicle sporting a yellow square with a red fox's mask, the symbol of 8th Armoured Brigade. The following morning, however, during a pause on the road after some tanks up ahead had accidentally bashed a house and knocked over a telegraph pole, he at last spotted a chap he'd met on the steamer coming over before they'd been transferred to different landing craft. This fellow was in a new tank and also heading for 8th Armoured Brigade HQ; so, after hailing him down, Cotterell grabbed his kit and clambered up to sit behind the turret alongside a mass of stowage that included water cans, compo ration boxes and a No. 18 radio set. Eventually, they pulled into a newly wrecked cornfield, three sides of whose hedgerowed boundary were a mass of tanks, trucks and other vehicles. This, it seemed, was 8th Armoured Brigade HQ. Even better, Corporal Cook and his crew – and tank – were there.

Cook was only nineteen, dark-haired and quick to smile, and greeted Cotterell warmly, helping him put his kit on the back of the Sherman. He then told the reporter he would be taking the co-driver's position. This didn't mean he would be driving the tank at any time; rather, he would be up front, ahead of the turret, on the right-hand side, manning a .30 calibre Browning machine gun and offering an extra set of eyes. The crew all called this position 'lap-gunner', and it came with a simple cushioned seat that could be raised if he needed to have his head sticking out, or lowered to submerge himself entirely in the belly of the tank and use a periscope instead. The trouble with the periscope was that it offered an incredibly narrow view and the thick glass was disorientating to look through. To his right was a radio set, along with more ammunition for both the machine gun and the main gun, while next to him on the left was the gearbox and then the driver. Behind was the perforated steel cage that housed the turret and the three other crewmen. Although the Sherman was more spacious inside than most tanks, that was not saying much. There were any number of hard-edged objects on which to knock one's head or shoulder – and, of course, the tank was a moving ammunition store. Getting in and out was not remotely straightforward: for Cotterell, it involved pushing head and shoulders up through the really very small hatch, then manoeuvring his feet on to the seat and pulling himself up; to get off the tank, he would have to slide off the front or side. For the three in the turret, there was just one escape route: through the turret hatch, which was round and split into two halves. These, when lowered, came together in the centre; when open, they stood splayed rather like butterfly wings – albeit rigid wings made of steel.

Inside the tank it was dark, especially if all the hatches were down, which was why the interior was painted white. On a good day, the Sherman smelled of fuel, oil, rubber and canvas; once moving or firing, however, the inside was quickly filled with choking fumes and smoke, even though there was an extractor fan. On a bad day – which meant, in effect, any long day – food, sweat and piss could all be added to the cocktail. There was nothing very comfortable at all about the inside of a tank.

The lad next to Cotterell, the driver, was called Cherry, another youngster – so named, Cotterell assumed, because of his rosy cheeks; he never got around to actually asking whether it really was his surname. Hogg – another teenager – was the radio operator and loader, while the gunner was Jack Collin, a desert veteran in his early twenties. At twenty-seven, Cotterell must have seemed ancient to these boys – and a commissioned officer, too, whereas Cook was only an NCO; and a corporal at that, just two ranks from the bottom.

Soon after Cotterell's arrival they were ordered to move to Point 103 to join the Sherwood Rangers Yeomanry, who would be their hosts for Cotterell's entire assignment. This, he vaguely assumed, would last a couple of weeks – assuming he was not killed or wounded, which was a distinct possibility. Half an hour later, the crew were debating the chances of them being sniped – or rather, of Cook being sniped – since the line of traffic on the road had come to a halt. Over the tank intercom, Cotterell heard one of the lads mention that if Cookie did get sniped he'd quite like his watch.

'I'll haunt you forever if you pinch my watch,' Cook replied. 'With my dying breath I'm going to spit on my cigarettes, eat my money, tear up my watch. You won't get nothing.' He then suggested that since they'd stopped, they might as well have a brew. That meant making some tea.

'Want me to get out and be sniped, I suppose,' said Cherry.

'Man, there's no snipers,' Cook replied. 'I've had my head out the last half hour.' Up ahead, some SP – self-propelled – guns were firing, then some planes swooped overhead. It wasn't clear to them whether the hold-up was caused by congestion or the enemy. A corporal in the neighbouring tank said, 'It's always the bloody same. Right up in the front and don't know what the hell's happening. Some day the war will be over and we'll go on.'

'Yeah, waiting for some sucker to turn up and tell us where to go,' muttered someone else. In fact, they were all part of 50th Division's movement of artillery, infantry and more tanks to support 8th Armoured Brigade, but they were being held up by heavy fighting in and around Audrieu as the 12. SS continued to drive forward in the direction of Bayeux. It meant the only way to gain access to the Sherwood Rangers on Point 103 was by continuing to sweep further south and west across fields.

As a result of this confusion in a rather disjointed front line, it wasn't until after 8 p.m. that Cotterell and his temporary hosts finally got moving. By that time, they'd not only had several mugs of tea but also a supper of stew, sultana pudding, more tea and biscuits. Their column had been held up by fighting a little to the north-east of Point 103, at Sainte-Croix-Grand-Tonne, close to the village of Loucelles, where the 24th Lancers were in action that day.

The trouble was, 8th Armoured Brigade's drive south had not got any further than the ridge of Point 103. Not only was the Panzer-Lehr now reaching Tilly, the 12. SS had pushed a wedge towards Bayeux and much of the left-hand flank was in enemy hands, so that the front line ran not west–east, but almost north–south from Point 103 to the village of Loucelles; Audrieu, for example, less than a mile to the north of Point 103, was still in enemy hands. It meant that the Sherwood Rangers were now rather isolated and still without infantry or much artillery support, although a company of the Cheshires, a machine-gun battalion, had joined them and so too had some anti-tank gunners. None the less, Stanley Christopherson was not the only one to feel rather naked and alone without any infantry protection; without doubt, they were in a very vulnerable position indeed. It was vital, though, they held that piece of high ground, because once the artillery arrived in numbers, observers would need it to direct fire down into the valley and beyond.

The following day, Friday 9 June, dawned grey and misty with thin but persistent drizzle, and as dawn crept over them it was hard to see anything much – the valley below was shrouded in rainy low cloud. John Bethell-Fox tried to peer through his binoculars but could see little. Somewhere up ahead they could hear the sound of tanks – that low rumble and the squeak of the tracks. 'But with this blasted drizzle we could not see a thing,' noted Bethell-Fox. 'My field glasses with soaking lenses were more than useless.' Eventually, he did spot some tanks down by the Seulles river in the valley; he was certain they were German, but Major Mike Laycock, the acting CO, had information that other British tanks were moving up, and no one wanted to risk opening fire on their own side.

Bethell-Fox was once again sent to investigate, this time accompanied by Captain Keith Douglas, Christopherson's second-in-command in A Squadron, who volunteered to keep him company. Bethell-Fox and Douglas were very close – soulmates within the squadron – having forged their friendship in North Africa. Douglas was a highly talented poet and artist, and had already written not only some of the finest poetry yet to emerge from the war but also a vivid and superbly written account of the regiment for which he had been given a publishing deal back in March. He'd changed the names, but had made no attempt to disguise his very real friends and comrades in the Sherwood Rangers: Bethell-Fox had become 'Raoul', while the former commander, 'Flash' Kellett, was 'Piccadilly Jim'; Christopherson had been renamed 'Edward'. Douglas had been quite hard on some of his colleagues. 'Edward' was depicted as an easygoing charmer but lacking any depth or intellectual substance, which was not the case: Douglas had failed to appreciate the happy-go-lucky and optimistic surface Christopherson liked to present. He was a positive fellow, but he also understood the importance of showing an upbeat and outwardly unfazed appearance in front of his men, recognizing that commanders needed to lead from the front and do their best to maintain the all-important morale at all times, no matter what they might be feeling inside. Douglas himself, more prone to mood swings and less able to hide his feelings, had failed to understand that. Christopherson had agreed to read the manuscript before publication and even to write a foreword. In fact, despite what he might have thought a hurtful depiction of himself, his only objection to the original text was Douglas's description of his dancing as 'deplorable': as Christopherson pointed out, he'd never seen him dance. 'I considered myself well above the average,' noted Christopherson, 'and as a result of my protest he agreed to alter the text.' It says much about Christopherson's sangfroid that this was all he was prepared to object to. The book was still to be given a publication date when they set sail for France, however.

Douglas had been a complete misfit when he had first joined the regiment. Born to comfortably middle-class parents, he had had a tumultuous childhood. His mother suffered from acute ill-health and his father's chicken-farm business collapsed. Completely broke, Douglas senior then moved the family from Kent to Wales – and soon after that divorced his wife, about which the young Keith was deeply upset. Fortunately, he won a scholarship to Christ's Hospital school, which took him away from home; but he grew up harbouring deep resentments. He railed against conformity, thought many of his fellow officers were insular, narrow-minded, boorishly unsophisticated and snobbish, and instinctively disliked the rules and restrictions of army life. Yet he was also kind-hearted, and lively company. As time went on, so he embraced the camaraderie of squadron and regimental life, so that many of the chips that had weighed on his shoulders when he joined the Sherwood Rangers had gradually slipped away.

He had become Christopherson's second-in-command in North Africa and remained so after that campaign, and as such was one of the more senior officers in the regiment. He'd also developed some strong friendships – with 'Johnny' Bethell-Fox for one, and also with Jack Holman, who had invited him back to the family home in Cornwall during their leave in England. With a book deal for his North Africa memoir and with a collection of his poems due to be published later in the year, he had a bit of money at last and had grown in confidence. On D-Day, he'd stopped his tank to help his friend Jack Holman and the wounded Trooper Lacey; no one could ever doubt his personal courage. Christopherson, in fact, thought he could be recklessly brave at times. At any rate, Douglas now offered to accompany Bethell-Fox down the hill towards Tilly to find out exactly whose tanks were moving about down there in the valley.

Using the north side of the village of Saint-Pierre as cover, they took their tanks into an orchard near the river; from here, Bethell-Fox and Douglas clambered down and went forward on foot, grenades in their belts and Douglas clutching a German submachine gun he'd picked up on D-Day. Crawling along the river-bank, they'd only gone a few yards when a burst of machine-gun fire rang out and bullets scythed through the branches and foliage directly above them. 'With common accord,' noted Bethell-Fox, 'we turned around, sprinted and dived into the river with bullets flying after us.' While they now knew beyond any doubt that it was the enemy who were rumbling along the road between Tilly and Fontenay-le-Pesnel, they wondered how on earth they were going to get back to their tanks. Douglas suggested they should swim 100 yards upstream, where, out of sight, they could then crawl out and make a dash for it.

What was now absolutely clear was that, even if they did manage to get safely back to Point 103, the situation for the Sherwood Rangers was considerably more perilous than it had been the previous evening, with the 12. SS at their rear and now the Panzer-Lehr in front of them. That Friday promised to be a tough day for the regiment. And so it was.

CHAPTER 5

Felled in the Field

D ESPITE THE DANGEROUS SITUATION in which they found themselves, both John Bethell-Fox and Keith Douglas managed to get
back safely to their Shermans, where they dropped into the turrets and
set off again; but as they climbed back up the slopes, Bethell-Fox saw
tracer fire hurtling over the top of Douglas's tank, which was about 200
yards ahead of him. Shells, too, began whistling over and crashing around
them, and also towards the rest of A Squadron further up the ridge. Since
Douglas and Bethell-Fox had been away, the squadron had moved down
a few hundred yards from the sunken track that marked Point 103 and
were now arrayed along three sides of a long, rectangular field lined with
trees and hedgerows. This move forward of a quarter of a mile or so had
been ordered so that the tanks could keep the enemy engaged in the valley
below while the infantry and anti-tank guns, now arriving behind them,
began digging in on the crest around Point 103 and towards Cristot.

The trouble was, although the hedgerows and trees offered a bit of
cover, they didn't provide much protection, especially now the squadron
were on the exposed slopes below the crest. What's more, either side of
them were open fields with no cover at all, which meant they were now
rather fenced in. All the Germans had to do was keep firing shells and
mortars in their direction and the chances were some would hit their
mark, either directly or from the blast.

As Bethell-Fox neared the field, he ordered his driver to head through
a gap in the trees, swing sharp right and then pull up alongside Stanley
Christopherson's tank. Douglas, meanwhile, had come to a halt inside
the field too, away to the left, and Bethell-Fox watched him jump down

and start running towards Christopherson, who was now sheltering in a ditch at the foot of the hedge line. At the same time, two further tanks, including Mike Howden's, were hurriedly running along the edge of the field but, for some reason, on the exposed side of the hedge and treeline. A moment later, both were hit. In fact, Mike Howden had been moving his tank from out of the woods and trying to engage the enemy below, because from behind the trees it was almost impossible to get a clear shot down into the villages.

They had been lucky: it was probably only a 50mm round that had hit them right on the front, where the armour plate was thickest. Even so, the tank was stopped dead.

'I think we'd better get out,' Howden told the crew. Everyone managed to clamber out without being hit after Stan Cox, as gunner, had righted the turret to twelve o'clock – straight ahead – so that the driver and co-driver could get out of their hatches at the front. Cox was last out and was sliding down the back of the tank when he realized he still had his headphones on. 'I stopped to take them off and throw them back in the turret,' said Cox, 'and I jumped off the back and as I jumped, he hit us on the left-hand side, and I caught the blast and bits of shrapnel.'

For a while, he lay there, fully conscious, aware he'd been hit, but curiously numb; he couldn't feel a thing. The rest of the crew had run to the woods but hurried back and dragged him clear – and just in time, because soon after that the tank brewed up, either from another hit or from the ammunition inside catching fire. Huge angry flames shot out from the open hatches and thick, black, oily smoke billowed into the sky.

'A burning tank is amazing to watch,' wrote Bethell-Fox, who saw both tanks get hit. 'It looks as if it is burning fiercely and must burn itself out at any moment, but it will go on burning fiercely.' Bethell-Fox had jumped down from his tank and joined Christopherson in the ditch at the foot of the hedgerow. Not only were tanks firing from the villages, mortars were starting to rain down upon them too. Mike Howden appeared to be in a state of shock. 'Mike's stammer prevented any kind of speech for half an hour,' wrote Christopherson, 'and his complexion, which at the best of times is devoid of colour, was even whiter than snow.' Christopherson thought the situation had become 'most uncomfortable', which was something of an understatement. Their own tanks were firing away but the hedgerows and trees were offering minimal cover, while mortar shells lobbed towards them made them feel even more exposed. Bethell-Fox scurried back to his tank only to discover it had also been hit; two of his crew were badly wounded and his driver in deep shock. Setting off again on foot, he managed to scrounge some self-heating tins of soup, blankets and morphine, and then did his best to look after them. 'I am glad to say,' he wrote, 'that I was able to make things more pleasant for these poor beggars. They just lay there, bleeding and silent.' Presently, a jeep arrived; the wounded men were strapped on to stretchers on the back, after which it drove off to collect Stan Cox too, before safely speeding away first to the RAP and then to a field hospital.

Bethell-Fox now reported back again to Christopherson, who was still in the ditch with more mortars crashing around him.

'John,' he said, as Bethell-Fox crouched down beside him. 'I have some bad news for you.'

Bethell-Fox looked at him silently, waiting.

'Keith has been killed,' Christopherson told him. Bethell-Fox was stunned. 'I stared at him,' he wrote, 'and I felt hot tears running down my cheek.' It seemed Douglas had been killed by an air burst as he'd been moving from his tank.

That day, Lieutenant Peter Pepler, a troop leader in B Squadron, was also killed; he and Laurence Verner had both joined the regiment just a few weeks earlier on the same day in May. Another tank in Bethell-Fox's troop was also knocked out while trying to shoot a Panther tank. This enemy panzer was moving back and forth along a sunken lane in the valley, pausing, firing, then moving again. Eventually, however, Sergeant George Dring had got out of his tank and stalked the Panther on foot until he was satisfied he'd worked out its movements. Back in the tank, he hit it five times in quick succession. And silenced the beast.

By exposing themselves below the crest of Point 103, the Sherwood Rangers had enabled the British to establish themselves firmly on the ridge, the Essex Yeomanry and the infantry of the 8th DLI – Durham Light Infantry – arriving via the western route across the fields to the north. Brigadier Cracroft, the 8th Armoured Brigade commander, had also arrived, and while the Sherwood Rangers were still engaging the Panzer-Lehr in Tilly, he set off with the COs of the 24th Lancers and the 8th DLI to see whether it was possible to mount an attack down towards Saint-Pierre.

The situation was still confused, because the front line still ran south–north rather than west–east, between Point 103 and the village of Loucelles, where the 24th Lancers had been fighting the 12. SS the previous day. Incredible as it seemed, Audrieu, scarcely a mile to the north of Point 103, was still in enemy hands, as was Cristot a similar distance to the east on the ridge. At any rate, late in the afternoon Brigadier Cracroft was sufficiently concerned about the situation on the ridge that he ordered the 4/7th Dragoons and 1st Dorsets up to Point 103, with instructions to bypass and ignore the enemy in Audrieu if necessary; his prime concern was holding on to the high ground along the ridge, and rightly so.

It was along with this column that Anthony Cotterell and his allotted crew moved up to Point 103, the Dorset men following behind and keeping a lookout for snipers. Everyone was a bit jittery about being sniped. By the time they reached the beech-lined track of Point 103, most of the Sherwood Rangers were still caught up in the fight a little further on, down the ridge towards the valley. When the crew took cover in a farmyard until it became possible finally to join the regiment, Cotterell took the opportunity to get out of the tank and look around. The occupants of the farm had sensibly left their home – the sole occupiers were now a turkey and its young in the scullery.

Some infantry were now moving up and pushing down the far side of the ridge towards the sound of battle; this was the 8th DLI moving in to attack Saint-Pierre along with the 24th Lancers. Cotterell followed them a short way. All around the fields were already pockmarked with chalky round shell craters. A German panzer burned fiercely in a field, its ammunition exploding in an impressive but sobering fireworks display.

Joining the Sherwood Rangers that day was their first replacement officer since D-Day, Lieutenant Stan Perry, twenty years old and beginning a career in an armoured regiment after a circuitous route in the army that had included a stint attached to the Suffolk Regiment and another with the SAS. A working-class boy, brought up in Bury St Edmunds in Suffolk – later to become surrounded by airfields of the US Eighth Air Force – his father worked in the Tate & Lyle sugarbeet factory. Both his parents were deeply religious and teetotal, but no puritans; Perry and his elder sister had a very easy-going and happy childhood. A keen and talented rugby player, Perry played as much as he could but still found the time to win a scholarship to read Mathematics at Emmanuel College, Cambridge. But it was 1941, Britain was at war and Perry believed he should do his bit, even though he had some precocious concerns about the morality of war. And so, much to his father's disappointment, he chose to join up, volunteering at seventeen along with a local friend of his. Cycling to the RAF recruitment office in Cambridge, they were persuaded by the officer in charge, a retired cavalryman, to try instead the Young Soldiers Regiment at Bovington, suggesting that if they did, they might well end up as officers.

Sure enough, after basic training at Bovington, and a promotion to 'unpaid lance-corporal', Perry was put forward for officer selection, passed the pre-OCTU – officer cadet training unit – test and was posted to Sandhurst. He was thrilled. 'I came from a fairly humble background,' he said. 'Sandhurst, well, that was for upper-class public school boys.' And he rather enjoyed it – not least because his physical training instructor was Matt Busby, who although a professional soccer star,[1] encouraged Perry with his rugby and also boxing. 'He used to take us out on a six-and-a-half mile run every morning,' said Perry. 'He would lead and would turn round and say, "I'll sweat the beer out of you idle boogers!"' Perry passed out of Sandhurst in July 1942 at a parade at which the King himself was present.

Perry had been attached to the 142nd (Suffolk) Regiment, RAC, but after Sandhurst was posted to Catterick in North Yorkshire and, instead of joining his parent regiment, ended up as Motor Transport Officer to the garrison. He was not pleased. 'I joined up to drive a tank,' he said, 'not a bloody desk.' A rugby friend of his suggested he try for the SAS instead, which by 1943 had made a considerable name for itself in North Africa with its daring feats behind enemy lines. Incredibly, Perry was sent all the way to Alexandria in Egypt for an interview, duly accepted, then promptly sent all the way back home to England again. Unfortunately for him, this happened just as the North African campaign had come to an end and the future of the SAS was rather uncertain.

Back in England in the summer of 1943, he heard nothing more for a few months; then finally he got a posting. By this time, it had been decided to expand the SAS and use them in the planned invasion of France the following summer, and so that autumn Perry was finally posted to Ringway near Manchester for his parachute training, where he did more than forty jumps, and from there to Scotland to join 1 SAS, which from early 1944 was training for the invasion of France. Unfortunately, once in Ayrshire, he

---

[1] Later Sir Matt Busby, legendary manager of Manchester United.

soon fell foul of Johnny Cooper, one of the SAS originals and now commissioned. Matters came to a head when Perry became so riled he thumped Cooper. By this time it was May 1944 and the invasion just around the corner. It was Blair 'Paddy' Mayne, commander of 1 SAS, who saved Perry's bacon. 'He said, "I'll give you two choices,"' Perry recalled. '"Find another regiment or go for a court martial for striking a superior officer." So I chose to look for another regiment.'

Since his training had originally been in tanks, he got in touch with Stuart Hills, one of his classmates at Sandhurst. Hills reckoned the Sherwood Rangers were still looking for a few more officers. Perry wrote to them, was accepted, but then got sucked into DD training in Portsmouth, and by the time he had completed it, the Sherwood Rangers were already loaded and at sea. He finally arrived in Normandy on D plus 3, and once offloaded was sent straight to the 4/7th Dragoon Guards. They told him he was in the wrong place and where to find the Sherwood Rangers – and, on presenting himself at long last, he was sent to see John Semken, who had literally just taken over as second-in-command of A Squadron.

Later that afternoon, a large German column was spotted leaving Tilly and heading north-west out of the town towards Bayeux. It was now they who were in the main firing line, however; Peter Selerie moved a troop of B Squadron tanks so they were lined up with their main guns at maximum elevation and then began the process of bracketing. 'In the end we managed to register on the road,' he wrote, 'and with three other tank guns suitably zeroed on the target, we wrought considerable havoc with our 75mm HE rounds.' Soon the SP guns of the Essex Yeomanry, now in position on the northern reverse slopes of the crest, joined them, and together they stopped the enemy in their tracks. Such was the advantage of holding the high ground, showing exactly why Brigadier Cracroft had been so determined to hang on to it.

Enemy mortaring and shelling continued into the evening, but the attack into Saint-Pierre by the 24th Lancers and 8th DLI eased the threat considerably and allowed the Sherwood Rangers to hand over their positions on the forward slopes to the 4/7th Dragoon Guards, about which Stanley Christopherson, for one, was delighted; they were all exhausted after such a punishing day. They were now ordered to pull back a couple of miles and join the A1 Echelon for supplies of fuel, ammunition and food.

That same Friday, Padre Skinner had once again returned to the beaches and been relieved to find Stuart Hills and his crew safe and sound. They were awaiting a new tank and expecting to rejoin the regiment any day. In the evening, he was back at Regimental HQ, where he learned the news about Peter Pepler and Keith Douglas. Skinner could not help remembering a conversation he had had with Douglas one Sunday in May following a village church service at Sway, where A Squadron and RHQ had been based. The two had gone for a long walk in the New Forest and Douglas had expressed his conviction that he was unlikely to return from Europe. 'He was not morbid about it,' Skinner recalled – and actually, Douglas also talked at length about his future plans for when the war was over. Only later did he once again mention his feeling that he was unlikely to survive. His nagging gut feeling had tragically been proved right.

As soon as he heard the news, Skinner firmly intended to retrieve both dead men right away, but Mike Laycock, the acting CO, refused to allow him to do so. 'Bed by 0300,' jotted Skinner, 'after few sharp words with CO about not being allowed forward to recover bodies of Douglas and Pepler.'

John Bethell-Fox, meanwhile, had spent the rest of the day feeling stunned, angry and revengeful. He got his head down later that night in Douglas's sleeping bag and fell asleep almost immediately, exhausted in both body and mind. 'To all purposes, he has vanished from our sight,' he wrote of Douglas soon after. 'He was there one moment and gone the next . . . as long as I live and I hope after, I shall feel him with me, alive and watching.'

CHAPTER 6

Tragedy at Tilly

S ATURDAY, 10 JUNE WAS only the fifth day of the invasion, but the Sherwood Rangers had barely pulled out of the line before they were urgently sent back again up to Point 103. Everyone was utterly exhausted. None of them had got much sleep since joining their LCTs on the evening of 2 June, and they were getting even less now they were in the thick of the action; the tank crews were lucky if they managed three hours a night, and even that was disturbed by shell-fire and uncomfortable conditions.

A rule of thumb in warfare is not to attack unless you have a three-to-one advantage in men and materiel. Unfortunately, at this early stage of the campaign, that wasn't the case for Brigadier Cracroft, even now that some of 50th Division's infantry had joined them; rather, they were facing the Panzer-Lehr head-on, and no longer just the vanguard but pretty much the entire division. Early on the 10th, the 8th DLI, who had taken Saint-Pierre the previous evening, were counter-attacked and almost pushed back out of the village entirely. With the help of the 24th Lancers they managed to retake much of it, but not the southern and western part around the church or the bridge that led across the Seulles to Tilly. Furthermore, the old main Roman road that led east to Fontenay-le-Pesnel and eventually to Caen was still in enemy hands, while the ground to the east of Point 103 was still held by the enemy; that morning, the Germans tried to attack the ridge from the small village of Cristot, only a mile or so due east of Point 103. This attempt was driven off by a combined counter-attack from the 4/7th Dragoons and 1st Dorsets, but Brigadier Cracroft urgently needed his third tank unit. It was to be another long day for the Sherwood Rangers.

For infantry and armour alike, this kind of warfare was incredibly dangerous. Here, in this otherwise sleepy rural backwater, there were wide open fields with almost no cover, rolling over gentle slopes with wide views. But there were also plenty of woods, sunken, hedge-lined lanes and, around the villages, orchards. Saint-Pierre was built around two main but parallel roads that curved and sashayed down towards the river. Between them and all around them were orchards, for this was the country of cider and calvados, two apple-based drinks made by every self-respecting farmer in the region. Hedges, woods, orchards and narrow, sunken roads – these were perfect places to lie in wait for any unsuspecting enemy troops, which made this part of the world comparatively easy to defend but very difficult in which to attack, as both sides were discovering.

There was also a feeling among the Sherwood Rangers that a lot of what they had learned in North Africa was not really applicable here. With Keith Douglas killed, John Semken had been moved to A Squadron as Christopherson's second-in-command. He'd been technical adjutant since the end of the campaign in North Africa, which meant he was responsible for the supply and maintenance of all the vehicles of the regiment – all 200 of them. 'I was,' he said, 'queen bee of all the regimental fitters.' Now, overnight, he had become Christopherson's senior officer in the squadron.

Semken had been worrying about how they were going to fight since the moment he came ashore at around midday on D-Day. As he looked around at the lines of tanks and guns and trucks beetling off the beach and on to the lateral road, it had occurred to him that no one had given much thought about how to fight inland. 'For five months,' he said, 'our sleeping and waking thoughts had been preoccupied with how the hell we were going to get ashore, and what the hell was going to happen if we couldn't. And now it was all over and we hadn't really thought about what happened next.'

After reaching Point 103 once more and filling the gap vacated by the 4/7th Dragoons, later that afternoon the Rangers were given new orders. A Squadron was to move south-east towards Point 102, which was a slight rise about 2 miles due east of Saint-Pierre and a mile south of the village of Cristot. Their task was to cover the Dorsets and 4/7th Dragoons, while B Squadron was sent down to Saint-Pierre to relieve the 24th Lancers, who had lost twelve tanks that day. Already, Semken, on this his first day in combat in Normandy, had the distinct feeling no one was really sure what they were doing. In the vast open spaces of the North African desert, they'd been able to operate together meaningfully as a regiment, and on one radio net. But the Normandy countryside was too close for that, with too many voices competing for air times, and at the same time the different squadrons were being given different roles. That Saturday, 10 June, was a case in point. A Squadron was sent south-east along the ridgeline to support the infantry as the enemy counter-attacked from Cristot, while C Squadron were ordered off on armoured patrols south-west of Point 103 towards the Seulles as it wiggled north from Tilly, and B Squadron were sent down to Saint-Pierre. 'The result was complete chaos,' said Semken, 'because you never knew where other people were and you didn't know where they were facing.' He reckoned that since each squadron was operating pretty much independently, it would be much more sensible for each to have its own net.

C Squadron's armoured patrols had done well, however, not only making contact with elements of the Panzer-Lehr north-west of Tilly but also relaying targets back to the increasingly plentiful artillery now behind the crest of the ridge. Also that afternoon, an American jeep drove up to 8th Armoured Brigade's field HQ. Having explained he was a liaison officer of the US 166th Medium Artillery Regiment, the American officer wondered whether the brigadier could do with some heavy fire support. Cracroft was delighted and eagerly gave him a host of targets beyond the range of the Essex Yeomanry. By evening, all enemy thrusts had been checked; yet while a concerted German counter-attack might have been halted for the time being, pushing the enemy back out of the Seulles valley and off the ridge was quite another matter, such were the challenges of going on the offensive in this close countryside.

It was Peter Selerie who located B Squadron's temporary headquarters in Saint-Pierre. Entering the village from the road that led down from Point 103, he had passed a large orchard on his right, an open field on his left and then, at a crossroads, on the right-hand side, had spotted a small farm and farmyard enclosed by a stone wall. No one felt very comfortable spending the night in the tight, enclosed environment of a village like Saint-Pierre, but this farmhouse seemed as good a place as any, with some protection from the wall and easy access to the roads. The rest of the squadron leaguered up for the night in the orchard to the rear, with the Durhams furiously digging in around them. Meanwhile, A and C Squadrons, now also ordered down to the village, were moving into the orchards at the northern edges.

This move forward, and the comparative calm up at Point 103, had finally given the padre his chance to get forward and bury those killed the previous day, although there was still the odd bullet zipping and hissing altogether too close for comfort as he carried out his grim work. He found Keith Douglas without so much as a scratch on him; he must have been killed by the concussive blast. Peter Pepler was also on the ground where he'd been killed, the fatal damage caused only too visibly by machine-gun bullets that had hit his head. Another body, that of Trooper John Simpson of the 24th Lancers, was also buried in the soft, chalky soil. Skinner took the dog-tags from each and carefully noted the grave sites with a map reference. Once the battle had passed and a cemetery had been sited, all would be dug up again and reburied.

Suddenly, most of the regiment was concentrated horribly close together, but the brigadier was determined that Saint-Pierre should not be taken back again. Christopherson, for one, spent a sleepless night waiting for an expected counter-attack, hearing persistent mortar and shell-fire whistling and exploding on and off throughout the hours of darkness. There was also a tank still burning in the fields between Saint-Pierre and Cristot that flickered and lit up the sky, a ghastly reminder of the fragility of their continued existence. Fortunately, no assault came; as they would soon learn, the Germans were not fans of night-time attacks.

The next morning, Sunday, 11 June, Regimental HQ joined them in Saint-Pierre and took over the farmhouse from B Squadron, Peter Selerie backing out his tank into the neighbouring orchard while *Robin Hood*, now Mike Laycock's tank, moved in. Arriving from the beaches to join the rest of the regiment for the first time was Captain Patrick McCraith, commander of the Recce Troop. He had reached Point 103 the previous evening and moved down with his smaller but faster M3 Stuart tanks at first light. McCraith had seen the padre as he reached the orchard and asked him how to find RHQ. Skinner told him and he hurried off in a Dingo scout car, reaching the farmyard just in time to join the morning 'O' group. 'O' stood for 'orders' – this was an on-the-spot conference for the officers of both the Sherwood Rangers and the Durhams to discuss plans for the day. Christopherson's A Squadron were to move back up to the ridge to keep watch on the main road to Fontenay in case the enemy tried to attack from the east, while Stephen Mitchell's C Squadron were to head south through the village with a company of 8th DLI, cross over to Tilly and try to push up on to the ridge beyond – a tall order with the Panzer-Lehr well set the far side of the River Seulles. B Squadron were to stay where they were in reserve. In fact, that same morning, Major-General Douglas Graham, the 50th Tyne Tees Division commander, reached Point 103 and, after talking the situation through with Brigadier Cracroft, agreed that in view of the weight of enemy strength immediately in front of them, there was absolutely no chance of pushing through to Villers-Bocage.

There was no disgrace in this at all; such a strike had always been an opportunistic idea, and the situation had dramatically changed since it had first been proposed. If the enemy were reluctant to withdraw, it was far better to grind them down and consolidate what gains had been made. Every day following the invasion, Allied materiel strength grew and the bridgehead was strengthened. And so the task of pushing them back into the sea became harder. The Sherwood Rangers, along with their fellow armoured regiments in 8th Armoured Brigade, were very much at the sharp end in confronting one of Germany's best panzer divisions and parts of another. Consolidating their own position and preventing the enemy from taking further ground was no small achievement.

General Graham now threw the 4/7th Dragoons and 1st Dorsets in an attack to take Cristot and so ease pressure on the ridge from the south-south-east. At the same time, Stephen Mitchell's C Squadron had their orders to clear the rest of Saint-Pierre and beyond, if possible. Both the assault on Cristot and C Squadron's push were timed for around 11 a.m. The second of Mitchell's tanks was just rumbling down the main village road and passing the farmhouse where RHQ was based when suddenly a flurry of mortars whooshed in, showering those outside in the yard with shrapnel and blast. Bill Wharton's great friend George Jones, the adjutant, was killed, as was Lieutenant Laurence Head, the intelligence officer. So too was Mike Laycock, the acting commanding officer and a legend within the regiment. Brother of the founder of the Commandos, Bob Laycock, he had gone to war with the Sherwood Rangers back in 1939 and been the first man in the regiment to win a Military Cross. It was a huge shock for the regiment, and left them without a commander. Stanley Christopherson heard the news on the regimental net from John Hanson-Lawson, the B Squadron leader. Patrick McCraith, the Recce Troop leader, and Sergeant Bernard Towers, the signals sergeant, had also been badly wounded. 'This was indeed,' noted Christopherson, 'a shattering blow.'

There was barely time to digest what had happened. At RHQ, Padre Skinner helped move the wounded to Dr Young's new RAP at the north end of the orchard. Every time anyone moved in the yard, more mortars and firing hurtled towards them. Someone in Recce Troop suggested there were German observers in a classic French country house a couple of hundred yards to the south on the parallel rue de Cristot. Set in its own grounds, with a high-pitched roof of grey slate and a third storey of dormer windows, it was an obvious OP with views to the northern half of the village and all the way up to Point 103, for although to its south were thick, mature limes and beeches, to the north was yet another lower-lying orchard.

When this suggestion was relayed to Stephen Mitchell, he ordered the house to be destroyed. While it was a shame to have to blast such a lovely building, it was considerably more of a tragedy to let men get killed because of it. No one was feeling sentimental about French houses that morning.

Things moved quickly at RHQ. *Robin Hood* pulled away and Peter Selerie shifted his own tank 15 yards to the edge of the farmyard to try to get a clear shot at the villa. Hurriedly, John Hanson-Lawson pulled out maps and orders from the CO's stricken tank and stood beside it quickly scanning the threads of command. In his haste to fire before more rounds hit RHQ, Selerie's tank smashed an apple tree in front of them instead. This spun round and collapsed, crashing on to *Robin Hood*, its branches whipping the B Squadron leader. 'Hanson-Lawson only scratched but very angry,' scribbled Skinner. 'We all gathered he wanted Peter to be quickly somewhere else. Peter obliged. Moved again and in three shots demolished whatever there was in the proposed target. Mortar shelling ceased thereafter.' Everyone but Hanson-Lawson thought the incident funny – a much-needed moment of levity amid the tragedy.

Lieutenant Ian Greenaway also now attacked the house, blasting the roof, while Tim Olphert's troop pushed on down the rue de Cristot to reach the main Roman road between Tilly and Caen. Olphert's leading tank misjudged the turn towards Tilly and got stuck in a ditch, while the second was immediately knocked out by an enemy shell. It was hard for crews to keep calm in such circumstances: the CO dead, enemy all over the place, too many voices on the net, infantry yelling from outside the tank and visibility limited by trees, hedges, houses, the unfamiliarity of the terrain and, of course, smoke. Tank commanders had to try to listen to instructions on the net while also still talking on the intercom to their own crew. It was a lot to process, especially when at any single moment they might be hit themselves by a life-threatening missile; there had been too many burning tanks around them the past few days. Also on the road was a carrier, a small tracked infantry and ammunition vehicle, still working but with just one man still alive of its crew of Durhams. Lance-Corporal Tippett jumped out of his ditched tank and offered to drive it clear, while Mitchell ordered Greenaway's troop to move straight over the road, through the small orchard and on to the comparative cover of a hedge a further 200 yards beyond. Mitchell then directed his third troop to guard the main road while he and the rest of his headquarters troop rattled across to join Greenaway.

All was quiet for a while as the rest of Saint-Pierre was cleared by the infantry. Enemy shelling and fire were still coming over from Tilly, however, and then, later in the afternoon, a strong enemy attack began from the east of their position; the earlier British assault on Cristot had already been halted. Two Shermans covering the road came under attack from an enemy StuG – a high-velocity SP anti-tank gun. 'We all tried to knock it out,' wrote Mitchell, 'but unfortunately they were both brewed up and had a very unpleasant time on the ground as we had attracted enemy artillery.'

Suddenly, they all felt rather pinned down and couldn't get a clear shot at the StuG. Mitchell tried calling up the infantry but most were still in a farm a couple of hundred yards behind them. Over the net, frantic chatter now came in of an enemy thrust from the south-east across the open ground between Cristot and Saint-Pierre. From the turret of his Sherman, Mitchell had a clear view of several enemy panzers – although it seemed that because of the trees and buildings he was the only one in his squadron who could see them. Swiftly rotating the turret, he directed his gunner, who hit one enemy tank four times in swift succession and forced another to withdraw. Moments later, however, Mitchell's tank was hit twice in its turn and although it didn't brew up, he and his crew hurriedly bailed out in case it did. A short while later it was still intact and so his crew tried to get it going again – but without success; so Mitchell grabbed his dispatch case and codes, and together they hurried back across the road and joined a platoon of frightened Durhams who thought they were cut off.

Meanwhile, earlier that day, a German thrust had been attempted towards the western side of Point 103. The enemy had been using the meandering River Seulles as it wound northwards to try to infiltrate across into the British positions, but Stanley Christopherson's A Squadron had seen it coming and stopped it dead. Soon after, with the immediate threat passed, Christopherson had handed over A Squadron to John Semken and then hurried down to Saint-Pierre; within the regiment, Stephen Mitchell was next in line in terms of seniority, but no one had heard anything from him after his tank had been knocked out. After Mitchell, it was Christopherson, so he took temporary command of the regiment.

With the 4/7th Dragoon Guards, Dorsets and Essex Yeomanry back at Point 103, A Squadron moved down to Saint-Pierre too, only for the Germans to put in their assault from the south-east towards the ridge. Stanley Christopherson, hearing this news over the net from Saint-Pierre, worried the Germans were going to move around their flank and attack their echelons behind the crest, but the defenders on Point 103 were doing well: a number of enemy tanks had been hit and infantry mown down, and the attack was once again halted – fortunately, before a single echelon vehicle was hit. Brigadier Cracroft was not so fortunate, however. Returning from a conference with the newly arrived 7th Armoured Division coming up on their western flank, he reached his HQ at Point 103 in the middle of more heavy shelling and was wounded in the head. So too was Lawrence Biddle, the brigade major who'd served with the Sherwood Rangers. Biddle and Christopherson had been pre-war friends in London and had initially joined the Inns of Court Regiment together before being transferred to the SRY.

By early evening, the fighting at last died down. The British attacks had stalled, but so too had those of the Panzer-Lehr. It was stalemate, underlining once again the extreme difficulty of attacking in this very cramped countryside. As dusk began to fall, with the 4/7th Dragoon Guards and Essex Yeomanry back on Point 103, Stanley Christopherson ordered the entire regiment to leaguer, and then he and Padre Skinner held a brief burial service in the orchard, a sombre affair which was further clouded for Christopherson by the lack of news of Stephen Mitchell, his greatest friend in the regiment. Since abandoning his tank, he seemed to have vanished: nothing more had been heard of him or his crew.

Nor was the day's fighting entirely over. As the last tanks squeaked and rumbled back to the orchard, with darkness now rapidly falling, the air was suddenly and dramatically torn apart by machine-gun fire, mortars and shell-fire from the direction of Tilly. At the time, Christopherson was having a discussion on the back of his tank with John Hanson-Lawson and the now forgiven Peter Selerie, half a bottle of whisky perched beside them. 'I suggested that we should adjourn to our tanks,' he noted, 'until I recalled them when things were quieter.'

Not long after, between bursts of mortar fire, Christopherson heard scrabbling on the back of his tank and seized his revolver, thinking it might be a German sniper who had infiltrated their lines. Peering cautiously over his turret he saw Peter Selerie, his arm outstretched, poised to snatch the half-bottle of whisky. Seeing Stanley, he immediately pulled back his arm.

'Did I leave my map case on the back of the tank?' he asked, his face a picture of innocence.

'I don't think so, Peter,' Christopherson replied, 'but do take the bottle of whiskey.'

Selerie thanked him, grabbed it and scuttled off back to his own tank, dodging the mortar shells falling in the orchard. Christopherson now brought the regiment out of leaguer and ordered it to counter-fire. The next hour or so was uncomfortable; although they held Saint-Pierre, both the tanks and the Durham infantrymen were out on a limb and very exposed. Eventually, however, things quietened down again, and Christopherson came over the net to order them to cease firing. All counter-attacks had now been checked; Point 103 was secure and so too Saint-Pierre. And then, just after midnight, Stephen Mitchell and his crew reappeared, much to the relief of all – not least Christopherson.

No one slept much that night, however, disturbed as they all were by the continual shelling and the tension about their situation. Padre Skinner had his hands full helping at the RAP with the casualties, including Tim Olphert, who had suffered a head wound; Lawrence Biddle and the brigadier were also there. Casualties had been comparatively light, in the circumstances, but half the regiment's tanks had gone since D-Day and the Durhams had suffered considerably. 'RAP still busy until 0330,' Skinner recorded in his diary. 'Slept for ¾ hour on floor of farm shed in which RAP was, beside wounded DLI offr lying on stretcher waiting for return of half-tracks to complete evacuations. Floor very hard.'

A lot was being expected of these men, and the battle against the Panzer-Lehr was still far from over.

CHAPTER 7

A Brief Discourse on
How the Regiment Worked

JOINING THE ORCHARD LEAGUER that Sunday evening was nineteen-year-old Lieutenant David Render, new to A Squadron, new to the Sherwood Rangers and new to war. None the less, he had had his own fair share of bewildering and life-threatening experiences since D-Day. Less than a week earlier, he'd been at a Royal Armoured Corps holding camp at Reeth in north Yorkshire, having recently completed his officer training at Sandhurst. At Reeth, he'd been undergoing long-distance treks designed to keep the newly commissioned officers active; then out of the blue he had been singled out and told to report to Portsmouth.

He travelled south on 6 June, completely unaware the invasion had begun. After a long and frustrating train journey he eventually reached Portsmouth the following day, where he was met by a captain who drove him in a jeep a short distance to a field at the edge of the city. There, sixteen Cromwell tanks were lined up. Lolling nearby were a bunch of uninterested young troopers. Render was told he was now in temporary charge of both the men and the tanks.

'Right,' said the captain as he pulled up beside the Cromwells. 'Waterproof them. You've got thirty-two men here, two men to a tank.'

Render pointed out that he had no idea how to waterproof a tank.

'Well,' replied the captain, pointing to one of the tanks, 'we've done one over there. You can look at that and do the same. There's Denso tape and putty so get on with it. You've got two days.' And then he drove off. There was no mention of going to Normandy.

Render was a bit thrown by this, but organized the men and got them to work as best he could. The following morning, 8 June, the captain reappeared and told them it was time to go; he didn't explain where to. Render's protest that it hadn't been two days and they hadn't finished was brushed aside and off they went, two men per tank, straight to the docks and on to a waiting LST. They had barely loaded the last of the Cromwells when the LST was pulling away and they were heading out to sea. Render had been utterly flummoxed to learn they were bound for Normandy and the front. Clearly, he, the men and the Cromwells were all urgently needed over there, but everything had happened so fast he had barely had time to consider that he was now heading to war. 'We never knew what the hell was going on,' he said. 'No idea at all.' He was still in charge of – and responsible for – all the troopers and tanks on the LST, and now had to deal as well with a truculent LST crew who had clearly already made several trips back and forth since D-Day and weren't much inclined to humour a fresh-faced teenage officer asking for food and bedding for his men. It was not a particularly auspicious start to Render's first command.

From Totteridge in North London, Render was the son of a builder. His father was sufficiently successful to send his two sons to public school, but David Render had hated it, especially when, at the start of the war, the school had been evacuated to Westward Ho! in Devon. Back for the holidays, he had had a huge row with his parents, refused to go back and instead had gone to a polytechnic college in London. That had been the summer of 1940, and he and his friends had joined the Local Defence Volunteers – soon renamed the Home Guard – manning road blocks two nights a week and watching the Battle of Britain being fought out in the skies above the capital. By this time, his elder brother, who had joined up in 1939, had been taken prisoner in France and had been consigned to a POW camp in Germany.

On his eighteenth birthday, in September 1942, Render had volunteered to join up with eight of his mates; he opted for the Royal Armoured Corps because he'd always liked vehicles and had thought to himself that he wasn't much keen on walking – his feet, he reckoned, were better suited to pressing pedals. Having joined the ranks and been posted to Bovington, he and a friend had then realized they were eligible for officer training, so applied, passed, and were sent to Sandhurst.

However suddenly and dramatically Render's fortunes had now changed, well over a year and a half had passed between joining the army and finding himself in an LST heading for Normandy, and only a few days earlier in Reeth he had been cursing and wondering whether he would ever see any action. Training was pretty thorough for young subalterns such as himself, even in the middle of a war when there was an imperative to process new officers quickly. He knew how to perform all the roles in any tank, was trained in most small arms, was physically extremely fit and had been taught many of the tactical lessons learned the hard way by the men of the RAC who had already taken an active part in the war.

Even so, training was one thing and reality was another – and that reality came crashing down on him when they finally reached Gold Beach on D plus 4, Saturday, 10 June. As they approached the shore, Render was shocked to see a number of dead RAF personnel floating face-down in the water. The LST just barged straight through them – and moments later the doors on the bow were opening and the skipper was yelling at him.

'Get those fucking things off here,' he shouted, 'because I don't like them.' As he was shouting, a German Me109 fighter roared over, spraying bullets; luckily, no one on the LST was hit. Render now ordered the first two men in the leading Cromwell to move off. They inched forward, but as the Cromwell left the ramp it immediately sank like a rock into the sea with the two men on it. Neither reappeared. Render could barely believe what had happened; the LST was so close to the shore. 'I'd just been talking to them,' he said, 'and there were all these other dead bodies floating all over the place. I'd never seen dead people before.' Appalled, he worried that it was somehow his fault that two of the men in his charge were now dead as well.

The skipper of the LST yelled at him some more, then began frantically repositioning the vessel; but as they reversed, the chain on the Kedge anchor snapped, whipped back and sheared off the railings and part of the superstructure down the starboard side. They were, though, now clear and able to make a second attempt to ground the LST a little further along the beach. This time, the ramp was lowered on to hard sand; there was a heart-stopping moment as the second tank edged forward, but it made it ashore without further drama, as did all the remaining Cromwells.

From the beach they were directed to a large field, now a vehicle park of trucks, half-tracks, other tanks and jeeps. No one seemed to know who the now fifteen Cromwells were for. Later that afternoon, a truck appeared and picked up all the men, replacements for some armoured regiment or other, but Render was left behind, his brief time in charge of the men and tanks over. No explanation was given as to why they had been whisked off without him. As dusk fell, he settled down with his bedroll and wondered whether he'd been forgotten.

The following morning, Sunday, 11 June, he was taking an early walk along the beach and had stopped to talk to someone when he suddenly saw spurts of sand kicked up and a moment later a Messerschmitt roared over at almost zero feet followed by a Spitfire, followed by another Me109 and then a further tail-chasing Spitfire, all with guns blazing. They were gone before he had a chance to react, but he quickly realized the spurts of sand had been the overspill of the bullets fired by the fighters. 'It suddenly dawned on me,' he said, 'that I'd seen all those dead blokes, lost a tank, and now this. It was a sharp learning curve.'

Render returned to the vehicle park, by this point really beginning to despair; he'd not even had the chance to tell his parents he was heading to Normandy. Then, as evening fell, a dispatch rider drove up, asked him his name and then told him to grab his kit and get on the pillion seat. Off they went, along many of the roads the Sherwood Rangers had already travelled a few days earlier, winding their way in the evening sunshine along lanes, past newly created ammunition dumps, through villages, bypassing Bayeux and finally driving on up to Point 103 and beyond, down to the edge of Saint-Pierre and into the orchard where A Squadron of the Sherwood Rangers, a regiment of which Render had never even heard before this moment, were now leaguering.

He was immediately taken to see John Semken, the acting squadron leader now that Christopherson had taken charge of the regiment. It was a hell of a day to join the Sherwood Rangers. News had arrived that Lieutenant Verner had died of his wounds: that was a troop leader gone, along with the A Squadron second-in-command, Keith Douglas, two days earlier. With Mike Laycock and half of RHQ wiped out too, that night the regiment had its third CO since landing on D-Day. Much of Saint-Pierre was already destroyed and around them in the fields were burnt-out and still burning wrecks, the dead and all too many signs of the bitter fighting.

Semken, however, greeted the new arrival warmly – the first genuinely friendly face Render had seen since leaving north Yorkshire. With his gentle, lean features and dark eyes and hair, Semken looked even younger than his twenty-three years, despite all he'd seen in the war so far. He explained to Render that he would be given a day's instruction from one of the squadron's officers then would take over 5 Troop. He didn't mention Render's predecessor, Lieutenant Verner, or that he'd been killed by a sniper.

Along with Stan Perry, Render was one of the first replacement officers to reach the Sherwood Rangers after D-Day. The extraordinary rotation of personnel through the regiment, which would continue right through to the end of the war in Europe, had begun.

On Monday, 12 June, US troops from Omaha and Utah beaches finally joined hands near the hinge town of Carentan. With this linking-up, the Allied bridgehead was now continuous along a 60-mile front from the base of the Cotentin peninsula in the west to the River Orne and the high ground beyond in the east. American troops were battling up the Cotentin and pressing south towards Caumont and Saint-Lô, while the British and Canadians were also pressing southwards around Caen. The outcome of the campaign was still not secure, but things were looking very promising for the Allies – even though the Germans were showing no sign of a hasty retreat any time soon.

That Monday was a little less frenetic for the Sherwood Rangers. As the Allied planners had expected, German armoured units were being sent as quickly as possible not just to Normandy to meet the invasion, but in particular towards Caen, which was at the eastern end of the Allied front and so closest to the rest of France – and through France to Germany. This was the hinge on which the Allies wanted to pivot eastwards, and so it was understandable that the Germans would want to focus their efforts there and attempt to use this eastern half of the front as a base from which to launch a coordinated counter-attack. There were by this point three panzer divisions in Normandy: 21. Panzer, which had been the only one in the area on D-Day, and now 12. SS and the Panzer-Lehr as well. All three had been flung straight into the battle, with the Sherwood Rangers and their fellows in 8th Armoured Brigade and 50th Division taking the brunt. Both 12. SS and Panzer-Lehr had been ordered on to the offensive the moment they arrived, which was bad news for them but good for the British and Canadians they were coming up against. Ideally, any formation arriving into a new area needed time for all its moving parts to arrive – 15,000 men and their vehicles could not possibly move as one – and then have a chance to get a sense of how the land lay. Yet instead, the various divisional units were being flung into the battle, piecemeal, as soon as they reached the front. Both 12. SS and the Panzer-Lehr had found themselves hurled against Cristot and the ridge around Point 103 right away. The heavy and relentless fighting since the morning of the 9th had been testimony to that.

More panzer divisions were on their way, but from further afield and battling against bombed bridges, daylight Allied fighter-bombers and French Resistance sabotage operations, all of which were delaying them very effectively; already, less than a week after the invasion, it was clear the Allies were winning the battle of the build-up of men and materiel. Meanwhile, in the middle of the Allied bridgehead, opposition had been pretty slight, allowing the US 1st Infantry Division to scythe south 20 miles and take the town of Caumont. This had left a big hole in the German defences between that town and the Panzer-Lehr around Tilly, and it was through this gap that the British 7th Armoured Division, the 'Desert Rats', were now ordered to try to drive a wedge, the idea being that they would then fold in around the Germans and take Caen from the rear. It was what 8th Armoured Brigade had been originally asked to do on D plus 1, but while they now had their hands full, there was an opportunity for 7th Armoured to exploit this gap on their western and right-hand flank. British commanders, from General Montgomery, the overall Allied land commander, to General Miles Dempsey, British Second Army commander, were aware this was a fleeting opportunity – but it was also one worth taking, because the potential rewards were so obviously huge. It remained, though, a long shot, as the further 7th Armoured pushed, the longer their own line of supply would become and the deeper they would be into enemy territory.

At any rate, the Desert Rats began their advance that Monday, 12 June, while the task of those troops still on and around Point 103 was to keep the Panzer-Lehr both busy and distracted. The Sherwood Rangers were given a holding role, with A Squadron moving back up to the ridge and the 24th Lancers taking over the drive south towards Tilly.

This was David Render's first day in action, and he was under the instruction of Lieutenant Neville Fearn, another desert veteran, and one who seemed as welcoming and genuinely warm as John Semken. His first contacts with the crew didn't go quite so smoothly. Having been allocated his tank, called *Aim*, that morning, while they were waiting to move, Render had gathered his crew and told them to 'T and A' the sights – test and adjust them. This, he had been taught at Sandhurst, was standard daily routine, and absolutely vital because it was the means of aligning the gunner's optics with the main gun. It was a simple enough procedure. Two pieces of string, or even grass, were made into a cross-wire on the muzzle of the 75mm and held in position by grease. Then, from inside the turret, one looked down the barrel from the breech at some landmark, such as a specific tree, building or church spire some distance away. Then one looked through the gunsight at the same point; if all was well, the two views would be aligned, or, at least, not too much out of kilter, although during the rigours of daily action they could go a little awry – which was precisely why daily checks and adjustments were needed.

The sergeant of the troop Render was due to take over after his day's instruction, Leslie Jackson, was on hand when he met the crew of *Aim*. Forty years old – more than twice Render's age – and from Retford in Nottinghamshire, Jackson was a pre-war Sherwood Ranger, married with a family, and, after long years fighting in the Middle East and North Africa, clearly had no truck whatsoever with some fresh-faced boy straight from England; and frankly, it was easy to understand why. Render, on the other hand, thought it important to establish some kind of authority straight away, and so gave the order to test the sights.

'You can piss off,' said Sid Martin, the gunner, another older man who had been a miner before the war.

'No, I'm not pissing off,' Render replied, 'and I want to see your sights T'd and A'd.'

'Do what you like,' muttered the gunner.

'Well, if that's the relationship we're going to have, it's not much cop, is it?' said Render.

'I don't give a monkey's,' came the reply.

Conscious Sergeant Jackson was doing or saying nothing to support him, Render felt he had no choice but to do the test himself, and was horrified to discover that the sights and gun were massively out of alignment, so much so they could not have possibly hit anything they'd taken aim at.

Soon after that they moved off. Unbeknown to the tank men, the Panzer-Lehr and 12. SS had been ordered to continue to attack and had overnight sent armour forward from Fontenay. To the west of Point 102 was a rectangular-shaped wood angled as though facing towards the ridge and Point 103, while the fields immediately around it were also thickly hedged and tree-lined. Some panzers and grenadiers – infantry – had managed to work their way into these woods and hedges. A Squadron were ordered to clear them out again.

By this time, the sun had risen and it promised to be a warm and sunny day. Render rolled up his battledress sleeves, which immediately prompted a rebuke from his instructor. Lesson No. 1 was to always protect the skin from unnecessary burns. Lesson No. 2 was to keep looking through his binoculars. Lesson No. 3: 'Don't get out of the tank and go swanning about. You get killed doing that.' Fearn was clearly thinking of Keith Douglas. Lesson No. 4 was not to close the turret hatches down, because then the tank and crew were virtually blind. No. 5 was never to wear a helmet – it was an easy target for snipers and got in the way. No. 6 was to put it instead on the machine-gun bracket on the turret with goggles on the rim. 'The German snipers often think it's your head,' Fearn said, 'and shoot it instead.' Finally, Lesson No. 7: 'Don't *ever* raise your voice excitedly over the radio net.' It was all rather bewildering, but Render recognized he was being given sound advice and determined to follow it religiously.

He survived this first day, even though the squadron found themselves on the move and in a firefight with the enemy, which entailed moving, pausing behind cover, firing and moving again. Fortunately, A Squadron seemed to outgun the enemy considerably, and eventually the Germans withdrew – but as they were retreating out of sight down a sunken lane, the squadron sergeant-major, Henry Hutchinson, had his tank attacked by a lone grenadier leaping out and firing a panzerfaust at almost point-blank.

The panzerfaust was a single-charge tube with propellant that fired a high-explosive warhead. It was no good at long range, but at anything up to around 30 yards it could penetrate more than 5.5 inches of armour – which was way more than the thickest part of a Sherman tank. The problem for its operator, of course, was that tanks rarely operated alone, and so the moment he'd fired one charge he was then likely to be in severe peril himself. So while it wasn't quite a kamikaze weapon, it wasn't far off. Certainly, it needed extreme discipline or fanaticism – or both – to be effectively operated. In any event, on this occasion the warhead tore through the steel of the front side of the tank, killing the driver, Trooper Claude Turner, and badly wounding the legs of the co-driver, Trooper Hackett. The rest of the crew escaped unhurt but Hutchinson, one of the most battle-hardened and respected men in the entire regiment, was understandably badly shaken by this attack. The panzerfaust was a weapon with which they would all become horribly familiar in the long weeks and months that followed.

Stan Perry, meanwhile, had been posted from A Squadron to C, to take over Tim Olphert's 4 Troop. This was his first day in action, but although still only twenty years old, Perry was not overly daunted; he was certainly a little more worldly than some, and with it, more self-assured than most. 'The first thing one had to do,' he said, 'was to get confidence and relation-ship with the crew.' As soon as he was with them, he noticed a couple of the older lads spoke in back slang. This involved taking the consonant from the front of a word, putting it at the end and then adding 'ay' – so 'talk' became 'alktay' and 'back' 'ackbay'. To the uninitiated, it sounded like gibberish; but it enabled the men to talk about Perry behind his back. By the time Perry went into action the following day, he'd been with his crew for a couple of days. He'd always had an ear for languages and could speak French and some German. At any rate, he quickly twigged the back-slang code but said nothing until they went into action. 'And then I spoke to them in back slang,' he said, 'and they were absolutely aghast. That was quite fun.' It also won him over to the crew. 'It began an understanding and a relationship with them,' added Perry.

By the evening of Tuesday, 13 June, John Semken felt physically and mentally drained. Like the rest of them, he'd been on the go constantly since leaving England, with nothing more than snatched moments of sleep. From Mill Hill, in north London, Semken had started the war as a very young articled clerk in a law firm, and had assumed his working life would be that of a lawyer, following in the footsteps of his father. Then war had come and he'd found himself joining the Sherwood Rangers in the Middle East, then fighting across North Africa in a tank. Now here he was in Normandy, suddenly given the responsibility of a hundred or so men and a squadron of tanks to command. He was still only twenty-three.

Stanley Christopherson had been told the regiment would be going into action again the following day, and so he called together the senior commanders for an O group.

'Well, chaps,' he told them, 'we have just got to do another Balaclava charge and then we will pull out.'

No one said a word. Semken could barely stand, he was so tired. Seeing this, Christopherson then said, 'All right, we are pulling out tonight as soon as it's dark. Go back to your squadrons and get ready.'

It was a brave decision for a new acting regimental commander, but once he had dismissed them he got on to Brigade HQ and persuaded them his boys needed to pull out right away. It seems they recognized the urgency of Christopherson's request, because they agreed – although in truth, the decision was made easier by the news that evening that 7th Armoured Division's thrust had been halted at Villers-Bocage.

John Semken, meanwhile, had gone back to their leaguer. 'Everybody was asleep,' he recalled. 'I got on the air and couldn't raise anybody in the whole squadron.' He had to shake one of his own crew awake and then send him round with a hammer to bang on the tanks to wake them all. Eventually, they got going, but although it was only a few miles, to fields around Monceaux-en-Bessin south of Bayeux, they still had to drive across fields and down winding, narrow roads, in the dark, with little more than slits in the headlights to light the way, and this demanded high levels of concentration – which was in rather short supply after a week of battle. 'Nightmare drive in the dark and dusk to new positions near our B echelon SE of Bayeux,' scribbled Padre Skinner. 'Arrived 0230 dead tired. Dropped down under greatcoat on bare ground to sleep.' Nearby, a battery of 105mm guns was firing all night, the boom sending throbbing pulses through the ground where the men lay. Despite this, the exhausted Skinner slept right through it all for fourteen hours. He was not alone. Neither John Semken nor any of his crew heard a single gun fire all through the rest of the night or throughout the next morning.

Not until four-thirty in the afternoon did Skinner finally rise; he then spent a leisurely hour getting some food, and a further hour washing, shaving and putting on some fresh clothes before writing to his wife, Etta. These hours of rest over, however, he returned to work, making up the casualty lists of all fifty-four men killed or wounded since D-Day, writing up where each of those killed in the field was buried – six of them by himself, in graves he had dug. Personal effects of the dead had to be sorted, packaged up and taken to B3 Echelon at the edge of Bayeux. Then there were the next-of-kin letters to write, a task that also fell to the relevant squadron leaders and Stanley Christopherson, still acting CO. It was a grim business.

Although an armoured regiment such as the Sherwood Rangers had a war establishment of some 700 men in all, less than half of them actually served in tanks. The main fighting components were the three sabre squadrons, A, B and C, each divided into five troops of three tanks with four more tanks in squadron headquarters. This amounted to 95 men per squadron, of which, at this time, 15 would be in each troop, five per tank. In all, a squadron had 158 men; those not in tanks were in the administrative troop and siphoned off into the supply echelons. Each squadron had an attached ARV – an armoured recovery vehicle with a winch, tow chain and other equipment for pulling out a bogged or stricken 30-ton Sherman tank – along with a Scout wheeled armoured car, five 15-cwt trucks, twelve 3-ton trucks and a single universal carrier tracked vehicle. Then there was Regimental HQ, which had a further four tanks, and Headquarters Squadron, which had no tanks, but four four-wheel-drive cars, eight 15-cwt trucks, two 3-ton lorries, at least one universal carrier and three motorcycles.

Although these support vehicles, and the drivers, clerks and cooks who manned them, were attached to specific units within the regiment, almost none of them would be up front with the armour. Instead, they were designated to the various echelons, the support team. It was a bit like a modern professional sports team: there might be eleven men on the pitch, but there will be double that number behind the scenes supporting them. In the case of the Sherwood Rangers, the echelons came under the command of Major Roger Sutton-Nelthorpe, one of the few officers still in the regiment, like Stanley Christopherson and Stephen Mitchell, who had headed off to the Middle East back in early 1940. This meant that, apart from the CO, Sutton-Nelthorpe commanded by far and away the most men in the regiment – an establishment of 203, but in reality, a further 189 as well – 63 from each of the three squadrons; for although these 'administrative troops' were directly supplying the needs of one of the three squadrons, they were all part of the regiment's echelons.

The echelons – two of them – were further divided. A Echelon tended to be closer to the action and was responsible for delivering the most pressing supplies, namely food, fuel and rations, and was divided again into A1 and A2. A1 Echelon was under command of the squadron leader and consisted of two equal parts – one kept forward with one full day's resupply of fuel, ammunition, water and rations, and the other back with HQ Squadron. A2 Echelon remained under HQ Squadron and carried all personal possessions and equipment not needed in action.

Sutton-Nelthorpe had brought both A2 and B Echelons right up to the northern, reverse, slopes of Point 103 on 11 June. B Echelon oversaw the less pressing supplies – tentage, many of the clerks, and clothing, and was usually further back; over the past few days, B Echelon had been just to the south of Bayeux, about 7 miles away. Frankly, there was no need for them to be closer, and it helped no one if they were near the front, both getting in the way and putting themselves unnecessarily in the firing line. B Echelon too was divided, into 1, 2 and 3 sections, each with areas of particular responsibility.

While each regiment had its own fitters, electricians and carpenters within the echelons, they were also allocated a light aid detachment or LAD. These were part of the Royal Electrical and Mechanical Engineers – better known by their acronym, the REME (pronounced 'reemee'). Each LAD would be around twenty to twenty-five men strong and would include a mobile workshop, a mobile winch, and a plethora of tools and stands with which to carry out a really remarkable amount of field repairs.

Very often a tank knocked out during a day's fighting would be recovered by night, taken back to the LAD's mobile workshop and up and running again the following day. Even completely burnt-out tanks were recovered and stripped of anything that could be used again before being scrapped.

Maintenance of the front was a very big aspect of the Allied war effort. Back in 1942, after the loss of Tobruk in June and the retreat back to the Alamein Line, the new British Commander-in-Chief Middle East, General Sir Harold Alexander, had made it clear to all serving under him that there would be no more retreats, a tenet eagerly adopted by his Eighth Army commander, General Sir Bernard Montgomery. This principle had held sway ever since and become very much part of the British way of war. Any territory taken, no matter how easily or hard fought for, should be held and not relinquished. To do so was a waste of young lives and spilled blood, not to mention time and resources. It was also incredibly bad for the morale of an army made up mostly of conscripts and men who would far rather be safe at home.

The consequence of this policy, however, was a mindset that minimized risk as much as possible and in which offensive operations were only to be undertaken once sufficient strength had been built up. It was no good capturing a town, hill, swathe of desert or piece of Normandy countryside if it was swiftly lost again and then had to be fought over a second time. Of course, there had been setbacks; but there had been very few retreats since the summer of 1942, and certainly none of any major significance. Not only was it important to build up overwhelming strength, it was also vital to ensure that once an attack went in, it could be maintained. This was one of the main reasons why the Allies had developed such a long tail. In Second Army, for example, some 43 per cent of its troops were service corps, while only 14 per cent were infantry and just 8 per cent were armour – and that 8 per cent included all the 'administrative' troops in an armoured regiment. What that meant was that, in all the three armoured regiments of 8th Armoured Brigade, fewer than 1,000 men were actually manning and operating tanks. It was hoped that the spear with which Second Army had landed in Normandy had a very sharp and effective point; but it also had a very long shaft.

Three main tanks were being used by the British Second Army now in Normandy. The Churchill was slow, but could climb more steeply than any other tank in the theatre, and had the thickest frontal armour of any currently on the battlefield. The other British-built tank, the Cromwell, some of which David Render had brought over from Portsmouth, was fast, had a comparatively low profile, reasonable armour and a half-decent main gun. Then there was the US-built Sherman, the most widespread Allied tank, used by the Americans, Canadians and British alike. There was also a fourth, the M3 Stuart, a lightly armoured and lightly armed tank which was agile, fast and used mainly in a reconnaissance role. When the first ones arrived in North Africa, they ran so sweetly one man called it a 'Honey' and the nickname stuck; certainly the men of Sherwood Rangers' Recce Troop, who were equipped with these tanks, always referred to them as Honeys.

Armoured regiments were equipped with one or other of the three main tanks, never a mixture. The 8th Armoured Brigade was supplied entirely with Shermans, which were 30 tons apiece and considered 'medium' tanks. Both the Americans and British had, and were developing, heavier tanks with bigger guns and thicker armour, a policy the Germans had already adopted with their 45-ton Panther and 56-ton Tiger. Both used a powerful anti-tank gun, which had greater range and velocity than the 75mm main gun in the Sherman and Cromwell and many of the Churchills. While field guns had great range and could lob a shell in an arc across the sky often to a target unseen by the gunners, an anti-tank gun would operate over open sights, or in plain view, hurtling a shell with enormous velocity over shorter ranges. The Tiger's main gun, for example, the 88mm, could fire its shell at around 2,755 feet per second with an actual range of around 9 miles, although its armour-piercing capabilities tailed off after a mile or so. However, the Germans had very few of these tanks; their most common panzer was the Mk IV, similar in size, armour and gun to the Sherman, and the StuG, which was not, strictly speaking, a tank but a self-propelled gun or 'SP', as it did not have a rotating turret. It was mechanically reliable – which was a lot more than could be said for the Panther or Tiger – had a very low profile, and generally was equipped with a 75mm main gun like the Mk IV and Sherman.

The Sherman did have a number of advantages, however. There were a lot of them and they were, for something as intrinsically complex as a tank, comparatively simple. Mechanically very reliable, they were also easy to repair; an engine could be whipped out and replaced in just two hours by a competent LAD team, while to replace the gearbox, the front underside of the tank was unbolted and the transmission accessed and replaced without too much fuss. It was five-speed – four forward, one reverse – and manual, and had a simple driving system of clutch, stick, throttle and brake based on those of American automobiles, which meant new young drivers quickly got to grips with them; anyone who knew how to drive a car could drive a Sherman. The gearbox even had synchromesh, unlike trucks and other military road vehicles, so that when changing gear the driver simply had to put his foot on the clutch and shift the stick, rather than double declutch. Panther and Tiger transmissions, by contrast, were incredibly complex, broke easily and were extremely difficult to access.

The Sherman also had a very simple track-and-wheel system, with suspension bogeys on the outside of the wheels rather than tucked away behind a mass of interlocking wheels as in the Panther. Furthermore, the Sherman had a number of shared features that were interchangeable across a number of American-built vehicles including armoured fighting vehicles and trucks, such as headlights, headlight guards and other small features like hooks and chain links.

The main gun on the Sherman was very quick-firing – faster than any other on the battlefield – and the turret rotated more quickly than any other tank of the time: both very useful attributes. Another feature, unique to the Sherman, was a stabilizing gyro, which meant it was far better at firing on the move than any other tank in the field. While it was the gunner's job to rotate the turret, the commander had easy access to an override switch on the underside of the turret, so that if he saw something and needed to move the turret quickly, he had that option. In the weeks and months to come, these would all prove invaluable features for the tank crews of the Sherwood Rangers.

Perhaps most importantly, what the Sherman offered was enormous battlefield strength, with tens of thousands of them already built. While production of Tigers would stop in August 1944, by which time just 1,347 had been built, and the total number of Panthers produced would be some 6,000, by the war's end some 49,000 Shermans would have been built, and 74,000 Sherman hulls, the excess 25,000 used in other forms, such as Sextons. And on the battlefield, numbers counted. What's more, the most dangerous time for a tank was when it was stopped and the crew had to get out in a hurry, as Stan Cox had discovered. So far in the fighting in Normandy, most of the casualties to the Sherwood Rangers had occurred outside the tank not in it, and although a number of their tanks had brewed up, most had not erupted into life-threatening flames until after the crew had escaped – or tried to escape. This was because the biggest cause of fire was from exploding ammunition rather than the shell that initially made the impact, and this seldom occurred instantaneously.

Mechanical reliability, then, was a big part of a tank's strength, because fighting across fields, through woods and down narrow lanes required robust tracks, a robust gearbox and a robust engine that would not let its crew down. No one wanted a tank to stop because of mechanical failure. Few tanks – if any – could trump the Sherman for robustness and reliability, and even if it did get hit or lose a track or need an engine replacing, such was its essential simplicity, and such was the efficiency of the long tail of Allied logistics, supply and maintenance, that many could be reintroduced to the battlefield in quick order.

None the less, Americans and British alike had recognized that the Sherman could use a more powerful gun. The US Army had developed a variant with a high-velocity 76mm gun, while the British had adapted a number of Shermans with a 17-pounder anti-tank gun, which, at the time of D-Day, trumped even the much-vaunted German 88mm, with a velocity of around 3,200 feet per second. It was a big beast and required a slightly redesigned turret to accommodate the recoil, which meant sacrificing the co-driver and using that space instead for storage for its bigger shells. The Sherman equipped with this gun was quickly nicknamed the 'Firefly' because of the bright muzzle flash on firing, and by D-Day 342 of them had been issued to the British and Canadians – and some of those had been given to the Sherwood Rangers. The senior commanders of the regiment had not been entirely sure how best to use them, but had decided to keep them together within the squadron headquarters troop; Henry Hutchinson had been operating a Firefly when it was hit by a panzerfaust the previous day. They were just another feature of this new kind of warfare in Normandy to which the regiment had to adapt.

As the Sherwood Rangers rested and refitted after the first week of battle, it was clear that, for all their enormous experience from North Africa, there was a great deal that was new about fighting in Normandy: a quite different landscape, a reinvigorated enemy with improved weaponry, their own new equipment and a new battlefield structure. While in North Africa they had been part of an armoured division; now, in Normandy, 8th Armoured Brigade had been redesignated an 'independent' armoured brigade, which had enormous ramifications for how they were deployed.

During the Second World War, the division, rather than the brigade, was the unit around which the size of armies was judged. In the case of the Allies, there were infantry divisions and armoured divisions, both around 15,000 men strong, give or take. The main fighting component of an infantry division, such as the 50th Tyne Tees, was its three infantry brigades, each with three battalions of 845 men. An armoured division, on the other hand, was an all-arms motorized formation, rather like the German panzer division, and included one armoured brigade of three armoured regiments and one motorized infantry brigade, as well as attached artillery and service troops. By 1944, the British Army had decided that armoured divisions were best used to charge through gaps in the enemy line and operate together in big leaps and bounds. This was known as 'exploiting' or the 'pursuit battle'. Most of the hard slog of fighting – or the 'deliberate battle' – was carried out by infantry divisions, with independent armoured brigades supporting them – as well as attached artillery for a specific operation. As a rule of thumb, each of the three armoured regiments of the 8th Armoured Brigade, for example, would be attached to one of the infantry brigades of the division, while each of the squadrons would be expected to fight alongside one of the infantry battalions. 'The tank colonel works with the infantry brigadier,' noted Stanley Christopherson, 'and the tank squadron leader with the infantry battalion commander.'

This was all well and good, but it meant that commanders in the independent armoured brigades were always outranked by those in the unit they were fighting alongside: the brigadier by the major-general of the division, the lieutenant-colonel of the armoured regiment by the brigadier of the infantry brigade, and the major of the squadron by the lieutenant-colonel of the infantry battalion. That was why, when Christopherson had been all for heading straight into Bayeux on D-Day, he had been overruled by the commander of the Essex battalion. So far, in the battles around Tilly and Point 103, Brigadier Cracroft had had a fairly free hand – until Major-General Graham of 50th Division had arrived and taken charge instead. Suddenly, 8th Armoured Brigade's component parts had been effectively subordinated to the Tyne Tees Division.

As the Sherwood Rangers licked their wounds outside Bayeux, there was much for them to think about. Clearly, the fighting in Normandy was going to be tough. To survive, they would have to learn and adapt very quickly – and that meant every man, from the seasoned trooper to new teenage troop leaders like David Render through to the commander of the regiment – for on 13 June 1944, their first full day out of the line, just who would lead them in the weeks and months to come was yet to be resolved.

CHAPTER 8

Into the Woods

On 13 June, Stuart Hills and his crew finally rejoined C Squadron. Until then, they had been waiting at the Forward Delivery Squadron near Gold Beach – the same place where David Render had been initially sent – for orders and a new tank. As its name suggested, the FDS was effectively the holding park for newly arrived tanks, and Hills's crew was competing with a number of other units and crews who needed replacement tanks. Given the huge logistical challenges facing the Allies in the first few days of the invasion, it perhaps wasn't a surprise that Hills and his men had been twiddling their thumbs for a number of days.

Now, with a brand-new Sherman and news that the Sherwood Rangers had been pulled out of the line, they were finally sent on their way, rumbling past fields pockmarked with shell-holes and littered with dead, bloated cattle, most lying on their backs with their legs comically stuck in the air, but already starting to rot and spreading their all-pervading stench across the countryside. There were also an alarming number of dead soldiers, among the first dead bodies Hills had ever seen. 'It brought it home to me with a trembling horror what I was going to face and perhaps suffer,' he wrote. 'I knew then that more scenes of carnage and devastation would inevitably follow.'

They eventually found the regiment in an orchard. Hills was relieved to be back among his fellows, as was Arthur Reddish, who was delighted to see his pal Ray 'Busty' Meek, who was in a different C Squadron crew.

'You'll get a shock after the desert,' Meek told him. 'We could see the buggers on the desert and they could see us. Here, they could see us but I'll be buggered if we could see them.' Reddish looked around, noting the orchard, the knee-high grass and the thick hedgerows round about. Busty reckoned it was ideal country to defend, but attacking through it had given him the creeps. Later, the entire crew, Hills included, had a chat about the different tactics they would now need to use. They all agreed they'd have to share in keeping a good lookout from now on. Reddish, as co-driver, would watch their right flank, and Doug Footitt, the gunner in the turret, would watch the left. Snipers were clearly going to be a nightmare. Hills would try to keep his head as low out of the turret as possible.

Bill Wharton, meanwhile, had managed to get back to the regiment more quickly than Stuart Hills and had played his part in the fighting around Saint-Pierre. Like everyone else, he had been exhausted by the time they pulled out. 'One of the worst aspects of fighting here,' he wrote to his beloved wife, 'is the long hours of daylight which necessitates reveille at 4.30 and not being able to pull out until about 11.30, after which time there is always a certain amount of work to be done making it always after midnight before we go to bed.'

Nor was there a chance to completely relax even now, for although they were out of the direct line of fire they were still under orders to be at a moment's notice to give support to 7th Armoured Division's drive towards Villers-Bocage and beyond. None the less, Wharton spent 15 June snoozing in the sunshine, washing some clothes and writing to Marion. He now had a new crew. 'There is nothing like active service for really getting to know fellows when you live and eat together. Despite the tight corners we have been in we have been able to laugh it off afterwards and have at times simply roared at our own wit. Maybe it is a form of relief, but anyway, it helps a lot to take away the strain of the fighting.'

They'd been having a laugh out of Trooper Mills, for example, a small, cocky lad from Long Eaton who was Wharton's new gunner. Mills told the others he never smoked except in dire emergency. Around Saint-Pierre, during a brief pause in a particularly harrowing action, they all began smoking furiously, Mills included. 'Now,' added Wharton, 'whenever we hand round the fags we never fail to ask him if the situation is acute enough to warrant him lighting up.' Another of his crew was from Worksop, local to the Sherwood Rangers, and Wharton had been impressed by his cool demeanour at all times. A third was a youngster from London, who was in the printing business, as Wharton himself had been before the war. The driver was a Welshman, who Wharton worried was a 'wee bit nervous' – but he reckoned he was a good fellow and they would all look out for him.

Inevitably, thoughts turned to home whenever he wrote to Marion, and the prospect of their first baby, due at Christmas. 'I do look forward to the time,' he wrote, 'when you and I will be able to step out looking our handsomest.'

That day, Thursday, 15 June, Stanley Christopherson was confirmed as the new commanding officer of the regiment. Stephen Mitchell was the senior major, but had been missing on the fateful Sunday when Stanley had taken temporary command and had expressed no desire to command himself. Christopherson, on the other hand, had immediately gripped the situation, demonstrating decisiveness and authority and, perhaps even more importantly, sound judgement too. He was thrilled and excited by this challenge of command, and deeply honoured – after all, he had joined the Sherwood Rangers back in 1939 as a humble subaltern, and his skill and experience as a soldier had developed and grown alongside those of the regiment as a whole. Determined to meet the challenges of command head-on, he also wanted to introduce a fresh approach to leadership. No one had been much impressed with D'Arcy Anderson, who had been too much of a regular career soldier for the somewhat eccentric tastes of the SRY, and also too aloof. Mike Laycock had been hugely respected as a true Nottinghamshire man; but although Christopherson had liked him enormously and respected his obvious bravery, he was also a somewhat intimidating character; everyone had been keenly aware of his ferocious temper. He had not been known as 'Black Mike' for nothing.

Christopherson was determined to bring a more accessible and kindly approach to command; no matter how he might be feeling inwardly, he would present a face of cheery optimism at all times. He had learned back in the desert that it was important to be constantly learning the lessons of combat, and for all the men, the officers especially, to be open-minded and constantly striving to improve in all they did. Only by doing so would they increase their chances of survival in this incredibly perilous role in which they found themselves.

The losses they had suffered, and Christopherson's elevation, required a bit of a reorganization within the regiment. Since D'Arcy Anderson's wounding and Mike Laycock's stepping up as acting CO, there had been no second-in-command – but one was needed, and Christopherson persuaded Stephen Mitchell to take on the job. This was good for both men, as they were the best of friends within the regiment yet as squadron leaders had seen comparatively little of each other. In the testing times ahead, Mitchell would be a great source of support to the new CO. This meant in turn that there were now vacancies to command A and C Squadrons. Christopherson had no second thoughts about giving A Squadron to John Semken, while Peter Selerie took over C. Stepping into George Jones's shoes as adjutant was Terry Leinster, another pre-war member of the regiment who, like Jones, Wilf Bridgeford – now appointed technical adjutant – and Bill Wharton, had joined as a trooper but had since been commissioned.

That afternoon, Christopherson held an officers' conference, putting his new team in the picture about the wider situation. Unfortunately, 7th Armoured Division's drive had been halted at Villers-Bocage. The leading column, largely made up from the 4th County of London Yeomanry, had reached the town early on the morning of the 13th. However, quite by coincidence, a company of some of the first Tiger tanks to reach Normandy had arrived the previous evening en route to the front; now, seeing a long line of armour halted in the town, they had swiftly moved down a parallel road, blasting the unsuspecting British column. The ensuing battle, in which the British lost something between twenty-three and twenty-seven tanks and the Germans around thirteen to fifteen – including six precious Tigers – ended what slim chance there had been of driving a wedge through the German line and forcing a substantial enemy retreat. It meant a continuation of the grinding attritional fighting that had already begun.

For the Sherwood Rangers, that meant a return to Point 103 the following day; here, from the 17th, they would help defend the eastern side of the Seulles valley as it wiggled northwards from Tilly, and also across the ridge to the village of Cristot, which looked down towards Fontenay-le-Pesnel. There, they would be supporting the newly arrived 49th 'Polar Bears' Infantry Division, which had just landed in Normandy. Christopherson was also able to tell his officers that they had been fighting against the 12. SS, and more specifically the Panzer-Lehr. Before they returned to Point 103, however, they were to head a few miles west to support 69th Brigade. B Squadron was to be in the lead with the rest of the regiment in reserve.

John Hanson-Lawson's squadron were to be operating over ground with which they were completely unfamiliar and in support of troops they had not fought alongside before. Unsurprisingly, maintaining contact with the infantry proved difficult. The tanks were there to provide some heavy on-the-spot fire-power – knocking out enemy mortars and machine-gun posts, spraying hedgerows with machine-gun fire, or blasting observers and snipers from buildings or church spires – but they in turn needed the infantry to be their eyes on the ground, especially in this close *bocage* country where it was easy for the enemy to hide. Bill Wharton's tank was hit at about midday. It was soon blazing fiercely, although fortunately not before he and all his crew had managed to escape without a scratch. He then sent the rest of the crew back to safety with a prisoner – actually, a Frenchman in German uniform, who had emerged from a wood with a white flag. Wharton, meanwhile, stayed behind to bring back another tank that had been hit and was *hors de combat* although still running.

The regiment was back at the ridge around Point 103 on 17 June. That day Stanley Christopherson attended a commanders' conference at 8th Armoured Brigade's field HQ, called by Brigadier Cracroft, who was still on his feet, having had his earlier wounds patched up. Christopherson was not alone in voicing his concerns over how they were to maintain contact and communication with the infantry. Normandy was new to everyone, and they were having to find the answers on the hoof, often at the cost of tanks and men.

Before the invasion there had been little all-arms training, with infantry, armour and artillery rarely all operating together. This might seem like a terrible failing, but Britain was a small place and there were millions of men to train and move about. Training space was at a premium, as was use of the road and rail network. So units tended to train where they were based, except in preparing for the large joint amphibious landing exercises, which were rightly seen as a priority because successfully landing and pushing inland trumped all other considerations.

Culturally, too, the British Army had always tended to work out tactical doctrine on the hoof. This was largely because of the wide and varied nature of the army's commitments, which, because of the empire, stretched all around the globe; what might work for fighting in Europe was very different from what was needed along the North-West Frontier of India and Afghanistan, for example, or in the Middle East, or the Far East. In any case, weaponry and warfare were developing very quickly, and this evolution often required changes in tactical and operational approaches.

Of course, the lessons from fighting in other theatres were absorbed, digested and applied, but this took time; it was not possible, for example, to assimilate the lessons from the fighting in Sicily the previous year with a click of the top brass's fingers. Indeed, some of those lessons were only starting to be applied to training and tactical doctrine from around April – and six weeks or so before D-Day was a little late for widespread absorption into the armies preparing to cross the Channel.

Furthermore, Allied commanders – with General Montgomery at the top of the chain as overall Allied land commander – had expected the Germans to retreat swiftly in phases if the initial landings proved successful. This was an entirely reasonable assumption, based on what the Germans had in fact done in North Africa, Sicily and southern Italy. Certainly, it made very little tactical sense to fight an attritional battle close to the coast, because for as long as they did so the Germans would remain in range of offshore naval guns, which added significantly to the Allies' fire-power.

Now, though, ten days into the battle, the Germans seemed determined not to give ground, and so already a slogging match had developed, particularly in the British and Canadian sector of the front around the key city of Caen. It went against the grain of previous German form as well as military logic; and in consequence, those in the front line, the Sherwood Rangers included, now found themselves having to think quickly on their feet and work out how to fight as effectively as possible in a kind of warfare no one had really expected, on terrain that was completely unfamiliar and for which they were not really prepared. Certainly, the tactics that had served in North Africa, with its wide open spaces, were of little value here in the close country of the *bocage*.

It was, then, perhaps not surprising that in the few days in which 8th Armoured Brigade had been fighting with the infantry, the partnership had not been especially effective. Typically, armour and infantry would start an attack in the place and at the time planned, but the moment the enemy responded everything would go to pot. Infantry would hit the ground and take cover, and the tanks would be left exposed without their vitally important spotters. Although the Sherwood Rangers were operating 'in support' rather than 'under command', the issue of infantry commanders outranking the commanders of the attached armour ensured it was hard for the tank men to assert themselves. This disparity of rank was not because armour was considered less important, but rather because it was considered that an armoured regiment was the largest practicable unit that could support an infantry brigade.

*

Lofty orders had been given to the newly arrived 49th Division: they were to surge southwards, take the village of Fontenay-le-Pesnel and then push on to the small village of Rauray and a low-lying – but significant – ridge beyond. First, however, the British needed to widen and expand what had become a dangerous salient which, on a map, looked rather like a flint arrowhead that extended from the eastern banks of the Seulles as it wiggled north and down from Point 103 to Saint-Pierre. The danger of a salient was that it could be attacked from the sides; and while the River Seulles provided a helpful barrier on the western side, the 12. SS would be able to strike from the east, through Cristot and using the high ground of Point 102 and the wooded area of the Bois de Boislonde.

The first objective, then, was to take and hold both Point 102 and the Boislonde. The attack was to launch on Saturday, 17 June, with the 6th Duke of Wellington's Regiment – DWR – in the lead, supported by the armour of the 24th Lancers. Point 102 was a comparatively low but significant hill that dominated the open farmland between the shattered villages of Cristot and Fontenay. Just to the south of it were orchards and then the wooded parkland of the Boislonde. This had been laid out in a rough square with sections of woodland divided like a loose mosaic by grass pasture. It had become a key part of the battlefield because it offered cover for an attack by the enemy towards the ridge, but equally for the British pressing south towards Fontenay-le-Pesnel, a mile to the south. Unlike the North African desert, the distances here were very short indeed.

The idea was to plaster both objectives with the combined guns of four field regiments – some ninety-six guns in all – and for the 6th DWR, the 24th Lancers and a battery of anti-tank guns to advance behind this barrage. The 6th DWR had spent two years in Iceland before returning to England, and while they were all thoroughly and extensively trained, they were entirely new to combat. Unsurprisingly, although the attack went in on schedule at 2 p.m., the fog of war, not to mention enemy counter-fire and heavy sniping, soon saw all cohesion lost. It didn't help that the radio link to the leading companies was soon down; and although after an hour or so it miraculously sprang back into life, by that time tanks, anti-tank guns and infantry were no longer really operating together.

As it happened, the artillery barrage had proved effective, having smashed nearly all the heavy weapons positions of the III. Bataillon, 26. Panzergrenadier Regiment, men from the 12. SS Division 'Hitler Jugend', who had been dug in around the park. Those who had survived the British artillery onslaught then saw the tanks of the 24th Lancers heading towards them. 'Behind them strolled the infantrymen openly across the terrain,' recorded the 12. SS chief of staff, Hubert Meyer, 'hands in their pockets, cigarettes between their lips.' What followed was rather reminiscent of the Battle of the Somme; certainly, it was a brutal baptism of fire for the 6th DWR. Any remaining insouciance quickly evaporated as the enemy opened fire and the fighting descended, as it soon did, into violent hand-to-hand combat. In all, the 6th DWR lost three officers and fifty other ranks killed, and a further seven officers and over 100 men wounded. Those were big losses for one day's fighting. They had, though, forced the SS men to pull back clear of the Boislonde.

The following day, Sunday, 18 June, it was the Sherwood Rangers' turn to support the infantry. This was a significant date for the men of the DWR: the anniversary of Waterloo, the greatest battle fought by the great general whose name they bore. It was also to be the first day in combat for Stuart Hills – and his driver, Geoff Storey – and the first for Arthur Reddish in this close countryside of Normandy. Reddish was apprehensive, but knew he had to help Storey and try to give him confidence. His own Browning machine gun, shiny and pristine with a sheen of gun oil, was ready; he had a belt of ammunition fixed into the breech, with a box of ammunition belts conveniently placed within easy reach. His Sten submachine gun was at hand, as well as a number of spare magazines, a loaded revolver and a box of hand grenades. He had some creature comforts within reach, too: a Primus stove, a water container and tins of food packed on his right along with a blanket, a towel and a number of spare periscopes, which were easy to slot into the aperture.

Reddish also reminded Storey that his MG only had a limited traverse. 'If you see me firing to the right, for instance,' he told him, 'and I can't quite get to the target, I'll be relying on you to slew the tank a little bit to the right to increase my arc of fire.' He also told him that if he should spot the enemy, he should keep the warning short, sharp and to the point. 'Panzer, eleven o'clock, two hundred yards!' would do it.

He discussed the possibility of a fire in the tank. It didn't pay to dwell, he told Storey, but one also had to be pragmatic. When Reddish's tank had brewed up in the desert, he had been in the turret and had found himself on the turret floor feeling drowsy but no pain; the agony had come after he had managed to get out and the burns were exposed to air. The most important thing was to know exactly how to get out and to ensure there was nothing unnecessary blocking that route. 'Be aware at all times,' Reddish warned him, 'which hatch you'll be exiting from.'

The previous evening, Reddish had caught up with his friend Busty Meek, whose troop was to be in the lead when they pushed into Cristot on their way to attacking Point 102.

'That place really got me down,' Meek told him, recalling that, with others in C Squadron, he had already fought there.

Reddish tried to be positive. This time, they were being supported by artillery and anti-tank guns. 'We've got the full team out tomorrow, Busty,' Reddish had told him, 'and that'll make a difference.'

They were up at 4 a.m., after a night on the ground in sleeping bags under the cover of a tarpaulin pulled out from the side of the tank. Doug Footitt, the crew's corporal, had been up earlier and had prepared some bacon and beans for them all, and some tea to wash it down. Half an hour later, the squadron's tanks wheezed then cracked into life amid a swirl of exhaust, and rumbled and squeaked forward from their leaguer around Point 103 towards the shattered remnants of Cristot, little more than a mile away.

Already, the artillery was shelling the enemy as they passed through Le Haut d'Audrieu and headed down the road towards Cristot, the infantry of the 7th DWR – equally new to battle – moving with them. Suddenly, the infantry went to ground. Reddish, Hills and the rest of the crew were wearing headphones and these, combined with the noise of the engine, masked the whine of incoming shells. 'But infantry body language,' noted Reddish, 'always told a story.'

With a blinding flash, a shell landed right in front of the tank, but although the shrapnel clattered loudly against it, there was no damage except to Reddish's periscope, which was shattered. This he quickly replaced, and on they went. The infantry began getting up again – all except those felled by the shell. The light was improving, but it was a miserable morning of low cloud and drizzle, and Reddish could see little except for the high hedgerows either side and the tanks and men ahead. They rumbled on, more shells and then mortars crashing down nearby. Up ahead was Cristot, some buildings burning. The air was thick with smoke.

A T-junction. 'Follow the tank in front, Geoff,' said Hills over the crew intercom. They headed into the village. Chatter on the squadron net: the lead troop had been fired at by an anti-tank weapon.

Peter Selerie's voice: 'Where's the fire coming from?' An occasional crack and *brrrp* of small-arms fire, the bang of a tank main gun. A number of dead lying in the ruins. Infantry crouching by wrecked build-ings. They steered around a dead German whose body was a mess. An anti-tank shell audibly scythed past them.

'What do you reckon?' asked Storey.

'When you hear the "swish", Reddish replied, 'they're too bloody close!'

More chatter on the net. The leading troop reckoned the fire was com-ing from a belt of trees south of the village.

Selerie: 'Give me a map reference and I'll get our friends on to it.' He meant the Essex Yeomanry in their Sextons.

An infantry officer now signalled to Hills and, following his lead, the troop of three tanks moved into an orchard. The DWR men were in a ditch at the eastern edge of it and pointing towards a hedgerow 100 yards or so beyond. Now all three Shermans opened fire, the main guns boom-ing, machine guns hammering, tearing through the hedge – and then the infantry were up and taking the next field without a fight.

They were now in Cristot. A pause to coordinate the next assault – on Point 102. Stuart Hills was ordered to go and report to Peter Selerie, and while he headed off, having survived his first engagement as a troop leader, his lap-gunner, Arthur Reddish, did what all Tommies did when there was a pause and some otherwise anxious time needed filling. He brewed some tea.

Meanwhile, A Squadron was also moving through Cristot. Not a single house was left undamaged. Tank tracks scoured lines across the sur-rounding fields, which were also scarred by thousands of shell-holes, white circles of blasted chalk and soil. Dead had been left in the village and in the surrounding fields. Bodies very quickly turned waxen once the blood had drained or stopped flowing, so they no longer looked like they had ever been alive at all. After a few days, they began to rot, the skin darkening and putrefying and beginning to emit a sweet, cloying, sickly stench that spread through the air. Already, around Cristot, the air was heavy with this reek from the rotting bodies of men and cattle caught in the vicious fighting.

As in any battle, there was a lot of stopping, waiting, hanging around. Entire hours and mornings could be swallowed up by the discovery of a new enemy position, by waiting for the results of patrols, or by a hold-up in the vanguard that was inexplicable to those further down the line. The plan was for the 7th DWR to push on to Fontenay, and for the 11th Royal Scots Fusiliers then to follow through that evening and take Rauray. It sounded so straightforward; but 7th DWR foot patrols revealed the area was still rife with snipers – and, worse, that Point 102 was still held by the enemy, even though the Boislonde, a mere couple of hundred yards to the south, remained in the hands of the 6th DWR; they had had an uncomfortable night and morning being shelled.

At the edge of Cristot, A Squadron were in yet another orchard, trying to keep out of sight. David Render was peering through his binoculars, trying to understand the lie of the land. He could see the Boislonde and Point 102, and beyond, through the grey drizzle, the roofs of Fontenay, glistening in the rain. To see a little better, he ordered his tank to move on to the exposed forward slope south of the village.

'Hullo, 5 Able to 4 Able,' he now heard over the net. It was Leslie Jackson talking to George Dring. 'I don't think much of that, do you?' For an old-timer like Jackson, young, inexperienced, over-confident teenage troop leaders were a liability until they'd earned their spurs. His suspicions of Lieutenant Render now appeared to have been justified.

'Able 4 to 5 Able,' Dring replied. 'Naw do I, but he'll learn.'

Hearing this, Render realized he'd made a potentially fatal mistake and, hurriedly turning *Aim* around, scuttled back up the slope. Lesson No. 8: never, ever advance on a forward slope without proper investigation. 'I got away with that one,' he noted, 'but never repeated it.'

Plans were being prepared for an attack in the early afternoon when suddenly the air was ripped apart by the opening of a heavy artillery and mortar barrage on the Boislonde from the enemy. Hastily, plans were changed, and John Semken's A Squadron were ordered to hurry to support the 6th DWR in the wooded parkland, while John Hanson-Lawson's B Squadron were brought up to support the 7th DWR's attack on Point 102. C Squadron was to remain in Cristot, ready to support either attack if needed. Lieutenant Stan Perry's 4 Troop were now dug in, hull down, behind a hedge just to the south of the village. Perry, wondering why they were sitting there doing nothing, spent his time scanning forward with his binoculars. Down below in the valley he could see Fontenay – a few rooftops, a couple of churches.

The enemy shells fell short of C Squadron, however, and through the smoke Perry spotted movement on one of the church steeples of Fontenay. Concluding the steeple was being used by the enemy as an OP, he ordered his entire troop to open fire at it. He did feel a bit bad about targeting a church, but he was certain it was being used by an artillery observer. 'Perhaps,' he said, 'that salved my conscience a bit.'

The enemy barrage – or 'stonk', as it was known – was much nearer the bone for the men of A Squadron. Shells screamed over, blasting the ground and the trees of the wood. Barely had the shelling begun when one of David Render's crew said, 'Thou fookin' boogers!'

Render then saw a tracked Bren carrier emerge from the wood and charge back across the open field towards them. It sped on past without stopping, followed shortly after by another. Moments later, they saw infantry running out of the woods and across the open field too. Render tried to stop them but they kept on, hurrying past towards the village and the rear areas beyond.

Render now called up John Semken on the net and asked what was going on. Semken wasn't sure and asked him if he'd seen any enemy tanks. No, Render told him. As ordered, Semken now led his squadron down towards the Boislonde, as men, carriers and half-tracks continued to hurry past them back towards Le Haut d'Audrieu. Semken could get no sense from anyone. 'Every passing group shouted to us that "they were coming" and that they themselves were "the last one out",' he said. 'We just waited with our fingers on the trigger, and nothing happened. And we went on waiting – and no Germans came.'

The Germans had been there, however, and the 6th DWR had been caught by a violently pressed counter-attack by the III. Bataillon, 26. Panzergrenadier Regiment that had seen more than sixty more men killed or wounded. What had stopped the SS men from pressing home their attack was the screaming in of British artillery, called up by the infantry as they had begun to cut and run. Unfortunately for John Semken's men, they were caught at the edge of the Boislonde just as their own side's shells started exploding. 'Being shelled among trees is no joke,' said Semken, 'because it produces an air-burst effect and your tank turret provides no real protection.' For the first time ever, Semken actually shut down the lid and crouched in the turret, desperately hoping for the best. That afternoon, he lost two of his officers. Denis Elmore, Stuart Hills's great friend, was hit in the face by shrapnel and invalided out, while John Bethell-Fox, in one of the squadron's Fireflies, had his jaw smashed by a misfire from the 17-pounder. When Padre Skinner saw him at the RAP, Bethell-Fox was unable even to swear. That was two troop leaders gone, plus two troop sergeants – and tank commanders – Rush and Harding, who were also wounded.

Semken's men were now holding the northern part of the Boislonde amid abandoned carriers, discarded ammunition and other debris – and without any infantry, all of whom were dead, wounded, missing or had scarpered. It was an extremely dangerous situation for them. Peter Selerie's tanks were ordered from Cristot to support Semken's squadron. Stuart Hills was shocked by the carnage he saw in the village. 'A handcart stood in the middle of the village,' he wrote, 'piled high with bodies, and the German soldier who had been pulling it was half-standing, dead in the shafts.' As they headed south towards the wooded parkland, Hills ordered his troop to move swiftly over the open ground, throwing caution to the wind. 'Because I was ignorant,' noted Hills, 'it didn't worry me much.' His crew, however, were considerably alarmed by what they considered recklessness. None the less, they reached the Boislonde unscathed and only there, at the end of the bombardment, were they hit. Corporal Cyril Greenwood, now commanding Tim Olphert's old tank, was wounded, so Hills handed over command of his tank to Doug Footitt and hurried over to Greenwood's.

Fortunately, the intense barrage from the British artillery had stopped the SS men in their tracks. Already badly hammered since their arrival in Normandy, the III./26 Panzergrenadier Regiment simply could not afford to press home their attack and risk further catastrophic casualties. With the British barrage over, David Render opened the hatch and tentatively peered out. All around him were smoking fragments of metal shrapnel, the ground cratered, trees shattered by blast. Twice more that afternoon, the enemy tried to push forward; but each time the Sherwood Rangers, supported by artillery and the machine-gun companies of the Kensington Regiment, managed to repulse them. Stanley Christopherson spent his time shuttling between his squadrons; David Render never saw him but did hear him on the net, his voice always calm, directing the squadrons and the Recce Troop, making sure there were no gaps in the line, and later cajoling and encouraging the infantry of the 7th DWR as they began sending patrols into the Boislonde. 'Christopherson brought his command influence to bear,' wrote Render. 'His presence did much to restore their confidence and ours and demonstrated how firm leadership can prevent panic and restore a situation.'

A tense stand-off now fell on the Boislonde, with the Sherwood Rangers holding the northern part and the SS men still clinging to the southern sections. Sergeant George Dring was peering through his binoculars when he spotted a tank moving up from beyond the park and announced his discovery over the net.

'Aren't you under a misapprehension about the target?' Peter Selerie cut in. 'Surely it is a cow? Over.'

'I've never seen a cow with a turret on it before,' Dring replied. 'Out.'

Meanwhile, the delayed assault on Point 102 finally went in at 3.15 p.m., with B Squadron supporting the 7th DWR in their first action. With the enemy counter-attack on the Boislonde baulked and the Germans on Point 102 isolated, the attack was a success; the high point was in British hands less than half an hour after it began, although even this swift victory cost the 7th Battalion more than eighty casualties.

Later, a further attempted enemy counter-attack was again stopped by Allied artillery, and although B Squadron stayed in the line, at dusk A and C Squadrons were pulled back to leaguer for the night as the 7th DWR dug in along a line that ran from Point 102 through to the northern half of the Boislonde. Stuart Hills, for one, had been rather shaken by his first experience of battle: the confusion, the limited visibility, the extreme violence and the carnage he had witnessed were all enough to shock anyone. Fighting in Normandy was proving a horrible, brutal and attritional affair, and while Allied artillery and fire-power were clearly superior to those of the enemy, it was the infantry and the armour that would have to take this already shattered land – inch by inch, yard by yard. And at the cost of all too many lives.

CHAPTER 9

On the Hoof

PADRE SKINNER HAD LEARNED to trust the normally sound judgement of Doctor Charles 'Hylda' Young, but at 10.30 p.m. that Sunday evening the regiment's MO had suddenly decided that he didn't like the current location of the RAP, close as it was to B Squadron's leaguer near Point 102, and so insisted they find somewhere else. While they swanned around in the dark looking for a new place for the RAP where they might get their heads down, they were twice shot at – probably from their own side – before finally the doc decided upon a farmyard not far from where they'd been based earlier. Skinner thought it a terrible place to have chosen; since Mike Laycock and RHQ had been hit in Saint-Pierre, he'd not been at all keen on farmyards. Fortunately, his worst fears had not come to pass. 'Apart from one odd burst shell fire that brewed up an infantry ammo-truck in field behind,' he noted, 'we were OK.' The following morning, however, Monday, 19 June, they moved out only for the farm to be heavily shelled a mere half an hour later.

It was an absolutely filthy day. Rain sheeted down and the wind was up too; so much for midsummer. Despite the foul weather, Skinner spent much of the day looking for Trooper Bert Lywood and Sergeant Bill Bartle. Both men were in the Recce Troop, and Bartle had been with the regiment since the start of the war. A bit older than most, he wore a thick moustache and invariably had a foul-smelling pipe in his mouth. 'We called him "Old Bill Bartle", because of his striking similarity to the caricature of "Old Bill" of the 1914–18 war,' noted Stanley Christopherson. 'Nothing ever ruffled him and he was loved by all.' It seemed Bartle had been at the edge of the Boislonde the previous day and had left his Honey tank to head out on a foot patrol, taking with him a pea-lead – a field telephone wire so he could call back to the troop. Nothing had been seen of him since. Trooper Lywood had been giving him cover with a Bren when he'd been shot and killed.

Skinner found Lywood, but his body was too exposed and he couldn't reach him to bury him. But of Bill Bartle there remained no sign. Not a trace. Most likely, he had been obliterated by a shell. The following day, with the wind and rain still raging, Skinner went forward again, and this time managed to reach Lywood and had begun digging a grave when he was called back by Christopherson, who lightly ticked him off for being too far forward and unnecessarily exposing himself to danger.

The bad weather brought something of an impasse along the Tilly–Fontenay front. Shelling, mortaring and sniping continued, but Christopherson was able to leave just one squadron in the line alongside the infantry, who had been greatly reinforced and were now dug in on Point 102 and through to the southern edge of the Boislonde, the 7th DWR having captured the southern sections on the 20th. This meant the squadrons were rotated so that each was given a rest of sorts. The plan was still to push on to Fontenay and then strike on up to the Rauray ridge beyond, which, although comparatively low-lying, none the less commanded sweeping views not only back towards the Seulles valley but also north-east towards Caen. Capturing it would not only deny the Germans northwards-looking observation but also give the British a similarly strong piece of high ground for further operations southwards towards the next valley, that of the River Odon.

But there was nothing doing with the rain slashing down and gale-force winds blowing. 'CO and Sqn Ldrs attended another conference at 147 Bde HQ,' noted Terry Leinster, the adjutant, in the regimental war diary. 'Seemingly all Inf Brigadiers appear the same (with the exception of 231 and 69 Bdes). They all appear to be middle aged, rather grim, considerably slow in their thoughts and without any sense of humour.' At this conference, the attack on Fontenay was postponed for another twenty-four hours. The following day, 21 June – midsummer day – it was postponed again. That day, the 24th Lancers relieved the SRY on Point 102, which meant the entire regiment was briefly pulled out of the front line. Once again, the chance to pause, rest, take a deep breath, had not come soon enough.

Everyone was sick of this corner of Normandy. The countryside around Point 103 and Cristot, down to Point 102 and the Boislonde, had been driven over so many times every man knew every square inch of it. Stanley Christopherson had been particularly sickened by the sight of a dead German in one of the narrow rides through the Boislonde. The body had protruded over the edge of the track, and every time a tank passed by his arm was further crushed until nothing remained but a congealed mess of flesh and bone.

On Thursday, 22 June, the storm finally subsided. It had been the intention of General Montgomery and his Second Army commander, General Dempsey, to launch the first major Allied assault on 18 June; but persistently indifferent weather had held up the build-up of men and materiel, and then, on the 19th, the storm had arrived. Two vast floating harbours had been designed, constructed and successfully towed across the Channel, and were almost completed and open for full business at the moment the storm struck. These Mulberries, as they had been named, were now being subjected to gale-force winds and 10-foot waves. Unfortunately, Mulberry A, the American one at Port-en-Bessin, was wrecked, while the 'Gooseberry' – the breakwater – off Utah Beach was also largely destroyed. Mulberry B, at Arromanches, just to the west of Gold Beach, fared much better, but for three days all unloading had to be suspended, and by the time the wind finally died down on 22 June, some 800 vessels, mostly landing craft, had been lost. It was the most terrible bad luck for the Allies and had significant consequences for the troops now battling their way inland.

As a direct consequence of the storm, General Montgomery reckoned they were five or six days behind schedule, which amounted to at least three divisions' worth of troops – an entire corps. It was, however, a matter of urgency for the British to launch a major attack soon, because Ultra decrypts of German radio traffic, picked up and deciphered at the Government Code and Cipher School at Bletchley Park, had revealed that some seven panzer divisions were about to reach the British and Canadian sector around Caen, and that once they were in the line they would be thrown together to mount a coordinated counter-attack. It was imperative that Dempsey's men launched their own assault first to throw the newly arriving panzer divisions off balance.

Dempsey and Montgomery had intended to launch such an attack with no fewer than three corps, but that was no longer possible. Instead, Dempsey decided to attack to the west of Caen in two phases. The recently arrived VIII Corps would provide the main assault, code-named EPSOM, which would launch on 26 June, while on the right XXX Corps would attack a day earlier to clear Fontenay-le-Pesnel and take the Rauray ridge beyond. In other words, the XXX Corps plan was exactly the same as the one given to 49th Division, which had been launched on 17 June – only now it was called Operation MARTLET and was part of something altogether much bigger.

At least the lull had given Stanley Christopherson the chance to rotate his squadrons in and out of the line; it was not the same as a complete rest, but better than nothing. He was spending much of his own time attending one planning conference after another and various intelligence briefings. The general picture was good, he was told. Six German divisions had been destroyed – albeit mostly low-grade coastal ones – and two more badly mauled. He was also informed that along the whole front, the Allies outnumbered the enemy two to one. That, though, was not a big enough advantage for a breakthrough. Christopherson was also concerned about his officers. He felt happy that Selerie, Hanson-Lawson and Semken were all up to the job, but worried about how he might replace them should they become casualties themselves. Jack Holman was a possibility, but the other officers were either a bit young or lacking experience for such a job, especially now that the squadrons were largely operating independently from one another.

With this in mind, on 23 June he drove over to 29th Armoured Brigade HQ, having heard that Major Henri Le Grand, a Belgian officer who had served with the Sherwood Rangers in North Africa, was anxious to return. Christopherson's charm offensive on the brigadier got nowhere, however. Next, he visited his old friend Major Micky Gold, who had been with the Sherwood Rangers for much of the North African campaign but who had since been posted to the 23rd Hussars. 'I had a few words with Michael,' wrote Christopherson, 'who threatened that he would desert and return to the regiment if division [actually brigade] did not agree.' As it happened, Gold's CO did agree to a transfer after EPSOM, although on the proviso that officer casualties were not too great and that he could still spare him.

In fact, it was Micky Gold's sudden arrival in Normandy a few days earlier that had prompted Christopherson's visit to 29th Brigade HQ. Having landed on the 18th, he had somehow managed to tune into the Sherwood Rangers' net. 'The first we heard of him,' wrote Stephen Mitchell, 'was when he came up on our wireless when things were rather sticky and wished us all the best, which really helped us quite a lot.' Gold was a larger-than-life character – a charmer, smooth of tongue, who never took life too seriously and who could be maddeningly infuriating, but who was the life and soul wherever he went. He was also a fearless and inspirational officer who had repeatedly proved his worth in North Africa. Certainly, Bill Wharton had been delighted to see him when he'd subsequently appeared alive and well among them – a welcome blast of fresh air amid the wind, rain and carnage. 'It was grand seeing the old boy again,' he wrote to his wife, 'and his puckish grin. He was in great form and we were soon laughing together as of yore.' When John Hanson-Lawson came up and found them both howling with laughter, he accused Wharton of being drunk. In fact, Wharton hadn't had a drink since a few surreptitious swigs of whisky on D-Day.

A couple of replacement officers did arrive on the 24th, although these were second lieutenants fresh from England – so David Render was no longer the new boy. One was twenty-year-old Lieutenant Harry Heenan, who had arrived in gloriously hot summer sunshine the previous day; it had been as though the great storm had never happened. On his landing craft, he had managed to write a quick note to his parents, unable to keep the massive scale of what he was witnessing to himself. 'There are hundreds and hundreds of ships,' he wrote, 'from battleships to squirts our size, in all directions. The sky is full of balloons. It really is an amazing sight.' They were not to worry about him, he added, signing off breathlessly.

Born and brought up in Yorkshire, Harry had been sent to Douai College in Berkshire, although he had left before the sixth form as his father did not believe in higher education. Instead, Heenan had begun working for the Westminster Bank in London. With aspirations as a writer, he had entered a writing competition organized by the bank and, much to his delight, his essay had won. A devout Catholic whose faith played a profound part in his young life, he accepted the war was a matter of moral necessity and so when war broke out had volunteered, joining the Royal Armoured Corps and subsequently gaining a commission. This had all rather interrupted any nascent literary career, and he now found himself in Normandy and joining the Sherwood Rangers – although while at the FDS he had managed to go to Mass at the local French church. Finally reaching the Sherwood Rangers on D plus eighteen, he was sent to John Semken's A Squadron, which most needed replacements after the recent losses of John Bethell-Fox and Denis Elmore.

The first two and a half weeks of battle had shown the men of the Sherwood Rangers that many of the tactics they'd learned in North Africa now had to be discarded. Implementing such changes on the hoof was no easy matter, but the lull prompted by the storm had given them a chance to gather their thoughts and begin analysing what they had experienced so far. The burden of responsibility for this, of course, fell on the more senior commanders – Stanley Christopherson, Stephen Mitchell and the squadron leaders – and on the more experienced men like George Dring and Henry Hutchinson.

The Sherwood Rangers had left England back in 1939 with the class structure still firmly in place in the regiment as outside it, and with clear dividing lines between officers and other ranks. To a certain extent, those barriers still existed; but they had become less rigid as the regiment became increasingly collegiate. In the tanks themselves, there was little standing on ceremony and Christian names were used. Men like Bill Wharton could rise through the ranks and were accepted by their fellow officers as equals. And ideas were listened to as well. Already, Stanley Christopherson had imposed a firm but more open style of leadership. From early on in his career with the Sherwood Rangers, he had understood that only by maintaining a constant desire to improve and evolve would he and his men have any chance of surviving. Never had this been more the case than now, as they faced brutally tough challenges. Opposing them were two of Germany's best trained and motivated divisions, both, at this early stage of the battle, still flush with men and weaponry. They were operating in terrain that was unfamiliar and for which they had little training, and alongside infantry that was entirely new to combat and over whom they had absolutely no control whatsoever.

This flexible approach to tactics was also embraced by John Semken, who, like Christopherson, had realized the battlefront was no place for complacency. One of the principles he rammed home to all his crews was the need to fire first and keep firing. The Sherman might have thinner armour than a Panther or Tiger, or even the British Churchill, but its main 75mm gun was incredibly quick-firing for a tank. When called upon, the key was to fire one round after another in rapid succession. 'It was absolutely vital that you should shoot the first time you see any sort of target,' said Semken, 'shoot, shoot, and keep shooting, because it may not do him any damage, but it discourages him.' The enemy – whether in the form of a hidden anti-tank gun, another tank or SP gun, or infantry and mortar teams lurking behind a hedge – was less likely to be firing back if shells were hurtling towards him. British tank men were well served with supplies of ammunition, and no one was going to be chastised for firing too many rounds; it was far better to fire a lot of rounds and then have to pull back to get more ammo than to be cautious and end up being knocked out. The war correspondent Anthony Cotterell had been astonished to learn that 8th Armoured Brigade had fired the best part of a million rounds of machine-gun bullets in five days' operating around Cristot and the Boislonde. Shoot first and ask questions later was very definitely the mantra.

Semken also implemented a change in the way the squadron's 17-pounder Fireflies were used, something that Christopherson was quick to adopt throughout the regiment. 'I found they were being used as a squadron leader's bodyguard,' said Semken. 'These four 17-pounders were just sort of sitting behind me collecting the shells but not really doing any good.' He now distributed them to four of the five troops, so that instead of three tanks per troop there were four. He proposed the three ordinary Shermans should lead the way and then, if there was a target that warranted the extra fire-power and velocity of the mighty 17-pounder gun, the Firefly would be hurried forward.

The problem with the Firefly was twofold. First, its muzzle flash was so bright it rather drew attention to itself. 'You'd have to be terribly careful to see that there were no infantry in front of you or near you when this bloody thing fired,' said Semken, 'and if you put it through a hedge and fired, well, there wasn't any hedge.' Second, the barrel was really a bit too long for the hull and turret design of the tank, which made it unwieldy when moving over anything other than flat, even ground. There was a support bar attached to the forward part of the hull, but in order to traverse this had to be disconnected, and that was the last thing anyone wanted to do in the heat of battle. Yet there was no denying it was a very powerful and accurate gun. Semken's system was a better way of adding fire-power to each troop and ensured the Firefly was properly employed rather than wasted.

Semken also recognized that the tank commander was the key member of the crew. 'The tank commander controls everything, directs everything,' he said. 'Those chaps below, in the turret and hull, they don't know what's going on at all. They don't know where they are or where they are going.' This was in part because the tank commander, with his head exposed above the turret, was the only one who could really see anything, but it was also because most troopers simply wanted to do what they had to do to get through the war; although there were still some from the pre-war Yeomanry serving, most of the men in the Sherwood Rangers now were conscripts who didn't want to be there, would never have been in uniform had it not been for the war, and had no desire to take on any kind of leadership role with the massive hike in personal risk that involved. And who could blame them?

It did mean, though, that new officers, such as David Render or Harry Heenan, had to be brought up to speed very quickly and learn fast, or their chances of survival would be severely limited. If the rest of the crew were largely blind, then the tank commanders, and especially the troop leaders, had to keep an eagle eye out at all times. That meant being glued to binoculars and also being able to read maps and the landscape around them properly. Semken was particularly adept at translating what he was looking at on a map into actual terrain. Over the squadron net, he would warn of upcoming features, whether it was a wood or a dip in the land. It was something that had impressed David Render. 'Hearing him talking to us calmly over the net,' recalled Render, 'made a huge difference and did much to boost the confidence of a young officer.'

Another change of practice agreed by the senior officers of the regiment concerned how they used their radios. Each tank was equipped with an intercom system so that each member of the crew could speak to the others over the roar of the engine and the noise of the guns, despite being in different parts of the tank. Each man had a set of lightweight headphones and a throat microphone, plugged into a jack near their station. Tank-to-tank communication was by a No. 19 set, which had a range of around 25 miles. The problem was that an entire armoured regiment using one net caused mayhem because inevitably people would be talking over each other at the same time, and the airwaves soon clogged up. In North Africa, when the three squadrons had tended to operate closely together, it just about worked so long as only the commander and squadron leaders did most of the talking.

In the close country of Normandy, where the three squadrons tended to have quite different roles and were out of sight of one another, it didn't work at all. For the most part, Christopherson had two squadrons in action and one in reserve. The reserve squadron could remain on the regimental net and simply listen, while one of the squadrons might be on the regimental A net and the other on the B net. 'Of course,' said Semken, 'you didn't know what the other squadron was doing but that didn't matter because you were often doing quite a different operation.'

That was fine for most of the individual tanks and, for much of the time, even the troop leaders, but the squadron leaders had to listen into

the A net at all times, which was more difficult if they were mainly operating on the B net. The radio really was the god of the battlefield. It was
how tanks, troops, squadron and regiment all communicated with one
another when in action. However, although the No. 19 set was a highly
sophisticated piece of equipment for the day, it was far from perfect,
could be capricious, and required both skill and immaculate radio discipline for it to be used effectively.

It was possible, for example, to listen to both the A and the B net at the
same time, but an operator could only be on one net to transmit – and in
the heat of battle, it was all too easy to forget to switch off transmit: usually
the offender was alerted by a more senior officer bawling at him to get off
air. For squadron leaders in battle, listening to both nets all of the time was
mentally exhausting. Careful judgement was also required, because one
troop might be reporting in followed by a second. The squadron leader
had to know when both troops were describing the same thing – the
amount of enemy behind a certain hedge, for example – and when they
were talking about something quite different. That was not always straightforward and another reason why clear, precise radio talk was so very
important.

It was also why a really first-class and highly proficient radio operator
was so prized. Netting in was done together the moment the regiment
was roused in the morning, when RHQ would transmit the Net Identification Signal, or tuning call, with all operators tuning in to the right
control – which in itself was quite a procedure and required very delicate
tuning to what was a very, very fine degree until the dial could be locked.
In theory, there was only one net a day, but the No. 19 set was notorious
for wandering and so very often – perhaps two or three times a day –
there would be 'check nets' in which the fine-tuning and locking the dial
had to be carried out again.

Clearly, radio nets could easily be flooded with chatter if discipline was
not used at all times. Those speaking needed to remain calm and clear,
and use as few words as possible – something else that was far from easy
in the heat of battle. Yet such discipline really could be the difference
between life and death: it was no good hearing garbled and excitable – and
incoherent – speech from too many people in the heat of an engagement.
A misunderstood instruction or observation could be fatal.

Radio communications, then, were challenging enough just between
troops, squadrons and regiment; but for successful operations, the tank
men also needed to be able to communicate with the infantry and

attached arms. This was largely done through the squadron command vehicle and RHQ, which was not ideal. Until a better means of infantry-armour communication could be found, the Sherwood Rangers were going to continue having difficulties working with the troops on the ground. It was simply another challenge of fighting in this difficult close country.

Leslie Skinner had still not found a trace of Bill Bartle, although he had continued searching despite the gentle ticking-off from Stanley Christopherson for putting himself unnecessarily at risk. Tracking down casualties had continued to take up a large part of his time, although chasing up the welfare of those recently wounded had given him the opportunity to nip into Bayeux. There, he bought a small Camembert cheese and also a length of dark green silk – Sherwood Rangers green – which could be cut into scarves. With the amount of neck-craning tank commanders needed to do, and the rubbing of the mic harness, this gesture had gone down well, as silk prevented chafing.

On 22 June he was back at the Boislonde. He could still see Trooper Lywood lying dead and out of reach, which bothered him greatly. Then, on the way back up towards Cristot, he was stopped by a DWR officer who asked him to bury a couple of tank men who were dead in a ditch near Cristot and getting a bit high. Skinner agreed and followed him to the spot. There he found two men from the 4/7th Dragoon Guards, fellow tankers in the 8th Armoured Brigade. They stank appallingly and were already crawling with maggots. 'Scrounged some blankets and started to tie them up,' noted Skinner. 'DWs officer went away to be sick and not return until I had finished.' Fortunately, some of the men had already dug graves, so Skinner read the funeral service and then was violently sick himself.

Later, he went back to the Boislonde in a Dingo with a member of Bill Bartle's crew and finally recovered Trooper Lywood. While he was there, however, he cautiously pushed forward on foot to have another look for Bartle, was shot at in the lower part of the wooded parkland, and then crept forward using the hedgerows until he was only 200–300 yards from Fontenay. But there was no sign. He was back at Regimental HQ at Chouain around 10.30 p.m. 'I hate posting anyone "Missing",' he scribbled. 'Always so distressing for families.'

The following day, Skinner heard from Ian McKay, the Recce Troop leader, and Bartle's commander, that apparently an SRY man had been buried by the infantry near Point 102, but on investigation, the padre learned it wasn't true, so Bartle remained missing. Stanley Christopherson persuaded him to agree to a posting of 'missing believed killed'. Defeated, he returned to his tent at Chouain to write casualty letters. There had been a lot to do – seventy-six casualties in all since D-Day, of which eighteen had been killed, Bartle included; condolence letter-writing was a grim task, but the time simply had to be found.

News also had to be given to the Regimental Welfare Association back in England. This had been set up early in the war specifically for the veterans and families of the Sherwood Rangers by Myrtle Kellett, the wife of the Rangers' CO at the time, Lieutenant-Colonel Edward 'Flash' Kellett, who had taken over in the summer of 1940 when the regiment was in Palestine. Myrtle was quite a beauty, something of a society figure and well connected. Her husband, a former Irish Guardsman, had been MP for Aston, in Birmingham, and had moved to the Sherwood Rangers in 1932 after leaving the army to pursue his career in politics full-time. He and Myrtle were also serious adventurers, travelling extensively in many of the more remote corners of the globe; they once spent an entire winter in Afghanistan. Kellett had unquestionably laid the foundations of the regiment it had since become, drawing in a range of highly talented and bright young officers around him in the opening months of the war – men like Christopherson, Mitchell and Gold – and creating the spirit that encouraged men like Bill Wharton to rise through the ranks. He knew Churchill personally and used his influence to push the Sherwood Rangers whenever he could; it was Kellett who had ensured they became mechanized. Between his taking command and that happening in early 1942, he packed off the men on a variety of training courses that would prepare them for an armoured role; he also personally cherry-picked all new officers and made sure they were already trained in armour. The regiment's rapid evolution into a highly successful armoured unit, as well as the eccentric blend of characters and lack of stuffiness that marked it out, most definitely remained a lasting legacy of Kellett's influence.

When Kellett was killed in Tunisia in early 1943, Myrtle had agreed to continue her good work. Its purpose was twofold. First, and perhaps most importantly, it served to help the families of the men serving with the regiment. With no welfare state or social care, many faced a dramatic loss of income with their husbands away. Army pay was niggardly – just 3 shillings a day, so at 20 shillings to the pound £1 1s a week at the start of the war for a private soldier, although it did go up the further he rose through the ranks, and a sergeant would be getting over £3 a week. The army calculated a soldier was saving himself at least 35 shillings a week because he was given food and lodging – although a hole in the ground in Normandy was hardly lavish accommodation. A miner, for example, was getting between £3 8s and £4 2s a week in 1940, and well over £5 a week by 1944. By D-Day, army pay had risen to 5 shillings a day, but that was only for those already with three years' service.[1] Married soldiers with children got an extra 10 shillings, which by D-Day had been raised by a further 10 shillings a week.

This was little more than peanuts, and the miserly pay rises had not remotely kept pace with inflation, which in Britain had risen to between 14 per cent and 25 per cent – food prices had risen by 17 per cent since the start of the war. For unmarried soldiers, this was manageable, because there was little to spend their pay on anyway, and the army did at least feed them and house them – if a tank could be considered housing. Army pay became more of an issue if a soldier was married, and especially if he and his wife had children, because many families simply could not support themselves on the measly army pay. A war service grant was available if, after paying rent and other household bills – including food costs – a wife at home was left with less than 36 shillings a week. Early in the war, it had not been uncommon for a soldier's peacetime employer to top up his salary, but five years on this was pretty rare. A soldier permanently disabled in battle was eligible for 40 shillings a week, plus an additional 10 shillings for his wife and 7 shillings and sixpence for each of his children. Widows of those killed were given 32 shillings a week plus 11 shillings for each child, but for many this was considerably less than they might have expected had their husbands died while in normal full-time employment in peacetime.

Supporting families of soldiers with financial troubles was, then, one of the primary roles of Myrtle Kellett's Regimental Welfare Association. Those who were a little bit better off were encouraged to contribute to the pot, which was then used to help soldiers and soldiers' families who were in difficulty. In effect, it acted like a soldiers' charity – but purely for those who had served or who were serving with the Sherwood Rangers.

Yet another important role of the RWA was to keep families up to date with what their menfolk were doing. Letters from all those in the ranks were censored, and no one was supposed to write about where he was or

---

[1] For comparison, 5 shillings a day amounted to just under £10 in 2017 values.

what he was doing in any detail. With this in mind, senior officers wrote long letters to Myrtle, which then formed the basis of a newsletter that could be sent to the families. All of them knew her well, and both Christopherson and Mitchell had bent over backwards to see her on their return from North Africa. In fact, Christopherson was rather smitten with her; and with her striking good looks, charm and taste for adventure, it was easy to understand why. She was unquestionably the Mother of the Regiment – and a rather glamorous one at that.

At any rate, with the new CO up to his eyeballs with planning conferences for MARTLET, it was his second-in-command, Stephen Mitchell, who wrote to her during the lull on 22 June with a list of casualties to date. He hoped all their relatives had been notified and assured her Stanley was writing to them all with as much detail as possible. 'I don't think at the moment there is very much hope for Sgt Bartle,' he added, 'but I don't think this should be passed on until we can find out more.' Myrtle, too, would be writing to the relatives, as well as overseeing the return of personal effects. Mitchell was, he admitted, worried about the shortage of officers, and did not hide the difficulties they had faced so far. 'Most of the fighting has been at close ranges and not at all like the old desert days when one could see what was happening all around,' he wrote. 'We work very closely with the infantry and that in itself is very difficult as their line of country isn't ours.' He signed off promising to get himself 'thoroughly into the welfare picture' and to keep in close touch with her. There was no escaping the sombre tone, however. The losses suffered already, the weather, the huge responsibility on his and Stanley's shoulders; it was hardly surprising he was feeling a bit blue. And then there was Operation MARTLET – a major attack right into the jaws of the enemy. Really, there wasn't much cause for cheer.

CHAPTER 10

Fontenay

THE WAR REPORTER ANTHONY Cotterell had spent the past fortnight based at 8th Armoured Brigade headquarters with his adopted tank crew, beetling between the brigade's three tank regiments, talking to the commanders and learning about life in the front line. It was Operation MARTLET, however, that he was especially keen to report upon, because it was the first major British offensive operation since D-Day, precursor to the larger EPSOM battle that was due to begin a day later. And he was going to be in the thick of it, because his tank had been placed in John Hanson-Lawson's B Squadron.

Early in the evening of Saturday, 24 June, Stanley Christopherson called a regimental orders group of his senior officers for the final briefing, to which Cotterell was invited. Regimental HQ was still based in fields near the village of Chouain, a mile or so to the north of Point 103. Speaking from the rear of a Bedford 3-ton lorry that doubled up as the regimental office, with maps spread out on a collection of ammunition boxes, the CO talked them all through the plan of attack. 'He was a creditably bemedaled young man,' noted Cotterell, despite being several years younger than Christopherson, 'with a twinkling personality and an attractive air of unassuming expertness.'

The 49th Division, Christopherson explained, would be attacking on a two-brigade front. On the right would be the 148th Brigade, with a start line to the east of the northern edge of Saint-Pierre. The 24th Lancers would be providing the armoured support for them. On the left would be 147th Brigade, which were to be supported by the Sherwood Rangers, with their start line from the Bois de Boislonde. An infantry division had three brigades, each made up of three infantry battalions, just as an armoured brigade had three armoured regiments. The infantry battalion was just under 850 men strong, including four rifle companies each with a fighting strength of around 127 troops. It was standard practice to attack with two of the three fighting units, keeping a third in reserve, and this would apply for MARTLET. It was also usual to keep 10 per cent of any fighting unit 'left out of battle' – or 'LOB'. This was a safety net so that if the company or battalion should suffer severe losses, there would still be a cadre of men left with which to re-form the unit. It did mean, though, that a divisional assault such as this one would begin with three out of four companies up front, from two out of three battalions from two out of three brigades, less 10 per cent and other casualties not yet made up. In other words, a brigade assault amounted to only around 650–680 infantry.

On the other hand, these poor souls who would be taking the ultimate leap of faith and advancing across this now battered and desolate corner of Normandy were being supported by considerable fire-power. Since the main EPSOM assault was not due to launch for a further twenty-four hours, 49th Division was able to borrow some artillery. In all, eleven British, two Canadian and one US field artillery regiments would be supporting the attack, each with twenty-four guns, which meant 336 in all. Two anti-tank brigades had also been brought up, each of forty-eight tracked and mobile guns – mostly M10 Wolverines, which had a Sherman chassis and were mounted with a big high-velocity anti-tank gun. They lacked much armour so were not used in the van, but were fast and agile. And as if that wasn't enough, the eastern flank of the attack would be protected by armoured reconnaissance troops.

The 146th Brigade and 24th Lancers were to clear the western half of Fontenay and then push forward to a wood called Le Haut Juvigny. This objective had been marked by a line drawn on the map, which for the purposes of the battle plan had been code-named 'Walrus'. The 147th Brigade, meanwhile, were to clear the eastern half of Fontenay and reach the road that ran roughly west–east from Juvigny and was now code-named 'Barracuda'. From there, they were to push on across the open and gently rising ground just to the north of Rauray, a mile or so south of Fontenay. This line was code-named 'Albacore'.

The battle would begin, Christopherson told them, with an artillery barrage at 3.45 a.m. B Squadron, supporting the Royal Scots Fusiliers, would start moving at 4.15 a.m. C Squadron were to support the Duke of Wellington's, while A Squadron would be waiting in reserve.

With the O group over, it was now up to the squadron leaders to brief their own officers and NCOs. Anthony Cotterell joined John Hanson-Lawson at B Squadron's leaguer. Tanks stood dark and solid and still. The mood was quiet. Sombre. Hanson-Lawson told them that the open ground between Fontenay and the Boislonde would most likely be mined. He'd asked for mine-clearing AVREs, but they hadn't been available. As a result, only one troop was going to advance initially. Hanson-Lawson was sorry, but it had to be done. Tanks were needed to blow holes through the hedgerows for the infantry to pass through; there was no alternative.

'There are German OPs in the churches,' he added, 'so we'll have to knock the church towers to pieces. There are three of them. It's not a nice thing to do, but there you are.' He warned them things could get pretty hot and that they'd have to sleep in their tanks. He wondered aloud whether they should send out a picquet – a forward guard – but then decided against it. 'OK, boys,' he said, finishing up – then, trying to add a note of optimism: 'I think the whole thing's a piece of cake.'

At 8.30 p.m. the crews started up their tanks amid the usual clouds of oily exhaust and then moved out, all nineteen of them, plus Cotterell's tank, two half-tracks with medical teams and the squadron leader's scout car. From Chouain, the route led them across open fields now scarred with endless track marks, up on to the track that ran along Point 103 and then on, down towards Point 102 and the Bois de Boislonde. At 8.50 p.m., they drove past a notice that said 'No vehicles to pass this point'. On, past infantry digging in, past freshly dug graves and shattered cottages. Some artillery – their own – opened fire, and the column paused, before eventually getting going again a quarter of an hour later. Signallers were laying wire along a lane, one man climbing a broken telegraph pole. Up the lane, then into a field. This was to be their leaguer for the night, directly to the north of Point 102. 'We came to a halt straddled across a shallow ditch,' wrote Cotterell, 'just next to a burnt-out German armoured car number 934966. The ditch around it was littered with bits of British and German uniforms, empty cigarette packets, grenades, rounds of ammunition, and a letter addressed to SS Mann Alfred Arndt.' Cotterell noticed it had been posted in Germany on 19 June.

'Funny to think there might be enemy patrols looking at us now,' said someone.

'Which is the way back to the beach?' asked Cherry, the driver.

Moments later, three German fighter planes roared over low, machine guns spitting. They didn't hit anything.

They cooked up a meal, then at 11 p.m. were ordered into a tight leaguer, so that their guns all faced outwards. At 11.45 p.m., Major Hanson-Lawson called a final O group. Everyone was to stay in their tank. Any sign of trouble, use the Sten gun, not the tank MGs. 'Remember,' he added, 'in a few hours there will be hundreds of infantry everywhere. They will be forming up in the field just behind. There's already a company out cleaning up as far as the minefields. So, for God's sake be careful who you're shooting.' A sergeant then reported a discovery of a mine in their field. Cotterell followed Hanson-Lawson to investigate, but neither had a torch. Without much further poking around, Hanson-Lawson decided it wasn't a mine. Then he ordered everyone back to their tanks.

Cotterell discovered that a tank was an awful place in which to try to kip. His own seat was like a padded cocktail bar stool with no place to rest his head. It was impossible to recline. If he lolled his head to the right, he hit the radio, and to the left there was nothing. If he tried to rest his head in his hands, he clunked against the machine gun. He noticed that Cherry, next to him in the driver's seat, fell asleep almost immediately, despite the discomfort. But sleep eluded Cotterell. He was too uncomfortable. He was too keyed up.

The guns opened up at 3.45 a.m. sharp. Cotterell had never heard noise like it. 'Not just one noise,' he wrote, 'but noise in several moods, some shattering, some whining, some staccato, from vicious whine to tube train roar.' He watched tracer slashing across the sky and Very lights – flares – rising and bursting over the German lines. At 4.50 a.m. they started up and moved out, the barrage still going on and shells whining overhead. Something was burning behind some trees away to their left. Headphones and microphone on. The tank vibrating from the roar of the guns.

Hanson-Lawson's voice: 'X-ray nine for Christ's sake keep near your set. I've been trying to get you for fifteen very vital minutes.' X-Ray nine was Jimmy McWilliam, one of Hanson-Lawson's two captains and the infantry liaison officer for the attack – a scheme hastily introduced to try to keep the infantry and tanks cooperating more effectively. Then Cotterell heard Hanson-Lawson say, 'It's the same old story. Infantry Sunray just gone off.'

As the sun began to rise Fontenay remained swathed in mist, made considerably worse by the number of shells fired and the ensuing smoke.

Cotterell listened, transfixed by the radio chatter, as they halted and waited for news of what was going on up ahead. The lead troop were waiting for their infantry guide, but there was no sign of him.

'Hello X-ray eleven,' Hanson-Lawson said to the lead troop leader, 'we are all behind you. Stick it, old man, stick it. You are doing damn well. I'm still trying to get through on the other line.'

'This bloody smoke,' said McWilliam. 'I'm in a pretty thick fog. I've lost touch with everyone. I don't know how long it will last. Over.'

'Hello X-ray nine,' Hanson-Lawson answered. 'Same old story. Communications collapsed completely. The only thing is to prepare to stay there.'

More chatter about the smoke. Couldn't see anything. Useless without a guide. Where were the infantry? Unfortunately, in the smoke, as thick as the worst London smog, the leading troop had lost all contact with the infantry they were supporting. Meanwhile, the battalion commander of the Scots Fusiliers had also lost touch with his two leading companies. Battle was often immensely confusing and disorientating. Hanson-Lawson called up Christopherson to put him in the picture – or rather, the lack of one. 'X-ray two,' he added, 'has been talking a Sunday on my level. He is exceedingly confused. And we all are.' The fog of war.

Progress was slow. At 6 a.m., a number of explosions burst close by Cotterell's tank – so close, he had to brace himself to stop being hurled against the side of the tank. Three-quarters of an hour later, the forward troop was being told to find a static position. The battalion commander was still out of touch, so the second-in-command was hurrying back to talk to the brigadier in person. There was a rumour the enemy were massing for a counter-attack. The smoke continued to sit heavily and shroud Fontenay.

Five minutes later, the situation seemed to be improving – for no obvious reason. The rest of B Squadron were lined up behind a hedge until, around 7.30 a.m., they finally began to move forward, albeit very slowly. By 8.15 a.m. they were inching around the south-western part of the Bois de Boislonde and into a field overlooking Fontenay – not that they could see it. A pause, then on they went again, slowly rumbling forward, tracks squeaking. Some 300 yards on, they halted by an apple tree. Finally, the village began to emerge through the smoke, glorious sunshine bursting through the haze. Debate over which hedge to blast for the infantry. Then further chat about enemy OPs. Hanson-Lawson wanted permission from Christopherson to blast the three church steeples in Fontenay. The latest barrage stopped – the infantry now creeping into the village. A Firefly next to Cotterell's tank opened fire. A dozen rounds and one of the church steeples was hit. Now Corporal Cook was ordered to fire at the left-hand church steeple. It was 8.50 a.m.

'Load H.E.,' he said over the intercom. 'Electric pylon, one o'clock. Steeple with smoke coming from it. Quick, chaps, get your do on it before it's covered in smoke.'

'Fifteen hundred,' said Jack Collin, the gunner.

Cook: 'Better make it two thousand.'

The gun boomed, the noise immense but bearable. The tank rocked backwards with the recoil then forwards again.

'You missed it, cock. Load H.E.'

Collin: 'Too much range.'

'Down to fifteen hundred,' said Cook.

The stench of cordite, the propellant, filled the tank and the empty shell case clattered on to the floor of the turret. The smoke made the nostrils smart and stuck toxically at the back of the throat. The turret had a solid floor but the cylindrical cage was made up of a thick mesh, so smoke and stench wafted through the entire tank.

Cook: 'Wait a minute. I think it's gone all right. All right, have a dabble. No, wait a minute, it hasn't gone. Cover nest again.'

A voice on the net: 'Infantry situation is going well.'

'Very glad to hear it.'

Cook, still peering through his binoculars, head out of the turret: 'Bring him down again. Another two hundred.' Boom, and the tank rocked again. 'That was right. You want to come left a bit.'

'No more H.E. left in the turret,' said Hogg, the operator.

'OK, could you whip the reserves up, Major?' said Cook. Cotterell found it no easy task to unclip and extricate these from under his feet.

Soon after, an enemy tank was spotted in trees near the village. Straining his eyes, Cotterell thought he saw something. They fired at it. Adjustments called out from Cook. The tank scurried through the trees. It was blasted to hell, not just by them but other B Squadron tanks as well. Suddenly, it blew up. Cotterell, in his lap-gunner position, machine-gunned the spot, then his Browning jammed. It wasn't a tank, it was a StuG self-propelled gun, and while first it burned gently, then the ammunition began exploding and flames spurted out as high as the trees.

One of the B Squadron tanks was hit, but the crew got out safely. Christopherson wanted to know how it was hit.

'Larwood did it with a very fast one,' replied Hanson-Lawson. The

Sherwood Rangers did like their cricketing references. Cricket and horses.[1]

Christopherson: 'OK, we'll get down to recover it.'

Shell, mortar and machine-gun fire was now nearly constant. Occasionally an explosion nearby and the clatter of shrapnel on the outside of the tank. By 10 a.m. the smoke was starting to clear properly, and Cotterell saw the battered remains of the village. Occasional rifle bullets fizzed and zipped nearby.

At 11 a.m. it seemed safe enough for Cotterell to clamber out and scurry over to talk to John Hanson-Lawson, only for several shells to burst overhead. A Firefly fired in response, the blast knocking Cotterell over. He got back to his feet, his eardrums pounding but otherwise unhurt.

The fighting wore on. Confused and not really going according to plan – a plan that had looked so straightforward the previous evening with its lines and division of labour, but one that, of course, could not account for so many unknowables, from the density of the smoke to the response of the enemy. By 9.15 a.m., the 146th Brigade and the 24th Lancers had captured Bas de Fontenay, the western part of the village, and were approaching the road that marked the Barracuda line objective; but the main part of the village, where 147th Brigade were attacking with B Squadron, was more firmly held by the 26. Panzergrenadier Regiment of the 12. SS. In the plan, the 7th DWR, with C Squadron supporting them, were to pass through the infantry of the Royal Scots Fusiliers once they had captured Fontenay and then press on to the Albacore objective line just short of Rauray. It had been repeatedly stressed that it was imperative to complete all phases of the attack, with objectives secured, by midnight, so as to give significant help to the main EPSOM attack a little to the east the following day. It had been hoped the 7th DWR would be pushing through Fontenay by around midday, but with the Royal Scots Fusiliers barely beyond the northern edge of the village, they had remained where they were. Why they weren't pushed forward immediately to add a bit of heft to the RSF's effort is not clear. It wasn't clear to the men of C Squadron either, who had spent the morning hanging around Point 102, waiting, drinking tea and smoking.

On hearing the news that the attack in Fontenay had ground to a halt, Leslie Skinner had scrounged a couple of pints of rum from Dr Young's

---

[1] Harold Larwood was a very quick bowler who played cricket for Nottinghamshire (hence his popularity with the Sherwood Rangers) and England.

half-track and, grabbing half a dozen water bottles, had filled them all fifty–fifty water and rum, then set off forward to see if he could provide a welcome pick-me-up to the troops. Having spotted Ronnie Hutton in his Dingo, he gave him one of the bottles. 'He smiled his usual kindly smile,' noted Skinner, 'obviously just to please the padre. When he got the taste his face was a picture.'

The padre continued on down through the Boislonde and beyond, where he found several B Squadron tanks and pockets of infantry. All were most grateful for the drink he had brought. Suddenly, there was a burst of machine-gun fire and Skinner dived into a slit trench on top of a startled Scots Fusilier, who was getting his first taste of combat. Skinner tried to reassure him the firing was high above their heads, at which the young man cursed and, picking up a ration-box lid, lifted it above the ground. A burst of MG fire cut it in two. 'It shook me,' admitted Skinner. 'Didn't know which of us was most frightened. When firing stopped, I moved out. He, poor devil, had to stay.'

Skinner would have done better, in fact, to stay where he was. A little while later he was helping to bring in a wounded Royal Scots soldier on a stretcher and approaching their RAP when a mortar shell exploded about 20 yards away. A piece of fizzing shrapnel struck him on his cap badge, and while the metal badge almost certainly saved his life, he received a bad gash and was knocked out. He was sent first to the advanced dressing station, then to the casualty clearing station. The padre had become the Sherwood Rangers' latest casualty.

Meanwhile, B Squadron were still battling hard in support of the infantry at Fontenay. They weren't moving too much, and shells, mortars and small-arms fire continued relentlessly. Just after 12.30 p.m., machine guns began hammering furiously, German ones with their rapid cyclic fire from the village, and the steady Brens and Brownings from the hedgerows on the village's northern edge. Anthony Cotterell opened fire with his Browning on a party of around fifty German grenadiers who unwisely began moving into a cornfield across their front. 'I operated my Browning with no real feeling,' wrote Cotterell, 'until they started firing back, at which my feelings underwent a sudden development.' There was also tank fire coming from a triangular wood just beyond the village to their left. Anthony Cotterell's tank turned and fired towards the wood but apparently without effect. Away to their right, a Sherman burned. Tiger and Panther tanks were also reported to be now in the village, and so they moved back from their rather exposed position to behind a hedge. Next to them, though, was a dead cow, bloated, on its back, its legs sticking up. The stink was appalling – so bad that they moved a further 50 yards only to find themselves beside two dead Tommies. With them was an abandoned Bren machine gun, so Cook jumped out and took it.

On the net, a B Squadron tank commander sounded agitated. He was in the village and being fired on. Another also reported from the village but wasn't really very sure where he was. Hanson-Lawson came on the net and helped the lost tank commander orientate himself, then told him to blast a particular house. Meanwhile, figures had been seen moving in a cornfield and, having decided they were German, not French civilians, a number of tanks opened fire, including Cotterell's. One of the tanks in the village reported that he had now successfully destroyed the house he'd been asked to hit.

Hanson-Lawson then moved forward to speak to the commander of the Royal Scots. As they were talking, they were mortared and several men wounded, although Hanson-Lawson was unscathed.

At 2.30 p.m., Cotterell heard Stanley Christopherson's voice again.

'Hallo, X-ray, I am right in saying we are not on the south road yet?'

'Hallo, X-ray, yes.'

Mid-afternoon. Around 3.15 p.m. Cotterell's tank was ordered to support X-ray Five as it entered the village. As they neared the houses, a jeep was blown up. Progress was faltering. Shattered shell-blasted trees. Two stretcher-bearers hurrying back anxiously. Now they were moving along a hedge. Infantry were digging in. Nearby, a British tank burned next to a blackened, brewed-up Panzer IV. Every building had been smashed or damaged. Across a road, infantry were working their way through one house, looking for snipers. The house pummelled earlier by one of the B Squadron tanks blazed furiously. Not a single civilian could be seen. In odd momentary lulls there was deathly silence.

Some time near 5 p.m., they were called back to refuel and rearm. So back they went, across the fields, down a track and on, past the Bois de Boislonde, until they reached the A1 Echelon waiting for them. Hanson-Lawson went on the net and told them they would not be going back into action that day, although they would remain at immediate readiness to do so should they be called upon. Two tanks had been knocked out, which was not so very bad considering the intensity of the fighting.

As B Squadron pulled back, so orders were now issued to 7th DWR to enter the fray at last – a decision that, frankly, should have been made hours earlier. Zero hour for their attack was to be 6.45 p.m., but

Lieutenant-Colonel John Wilsey, commander of the 7th DWR, could not make contact with a number of supporting arms – a situation made worse when his intelligence officer was shot and wounded by a sniper. It was at moments like this that Second Army's considerable fire support worked against them. Moving forward with C Squadron of the Sherwood Rangers was straightforward, but coordinating their attack with the two anti-tank batteries, the machine-gun companies, reconnaissance troops and artillery was altogether more complicated and time-consuming. Had the 7th DWR been more experienced, perhaps they would have simply hurried down and rushed Fontenay, but they lacked the necessary confidence for such tactical flexibility. If infantry were going to advance into the jaws of death, their commander wanted to know there was plentiful fire-power to support them. Almost inevitably, zero hour kept slipping, until it was finally agreed the attack would go in at 9 p.m.

Stuart Hills and his crew had assumed they would not be needed after all that day, but around 7 p.m. he had been called to a conference and told they would be going in with the infantry – not with a mass of artillery, but silently and making the most of the fading light.

'Prepare for action, chaps,' he told his troop on his return, 'we're going in as soon as it gets dark.'

'What's the form, then?' asked Sam Kirman, the operator.

'Brace yourselves for a shock,' Hills told them, then explained the plan. 'And our troops will be in the lead with our tank in front.'

This prompted a lot of cursing. Arthur Reddish couldn't understand how a squadron of tanks and a battalion of infantry could do a job that a force three times larger had failed to pull off.

'Well, thank Christ I've made my will,' said Kirman.

After a good moan, however, the crew calmed down and made ready. Tracer rounds were placed in the MG ammunition to aid firing in the fading light. Inside the tank, it was almost pitch dark already; the periscopes were useless. Reddish would travel with his seat raised and half out of the hatch. At 9 p.m. they started up the engines, then rumbled off. Reddish thought it really might be for the very last time; he didn't feel at all confident about the attack – nor did his pal, Busty Meek, with whom he'd had a quick word. Meek's crew had been just as stroppy about the plan.

They trundled forward at 9.15 p.m., Hills's tank leading, infantry on their right. As they neared the village, suddenly an enemy machine gun opened fire from the upper storey of one of the houses, the infantry scattered and bullets pinged around the edge of the tank. Reddish was about to fire when two infantrymen ran crouching right in front of him. 'Get behind us!' he yelled. Very quickly, Doug Footitt, the gunner, found the enemy MG, spraying it with bullets and following up with two quick rounds which set the building on fire.

They worked their way into the village, something that had been impossible earlier; it seemed the German armour had also pulled back for the night as B Squadron had done. Opposition was surprisingly light. Fontenay itself was now a shattered wreck of burning houses, blackened, smouldering armour, dead soldiers, smoke and dust. Over the net came orders for Hills's troop to support a Churchill Mk III AVRE with a bunker-busting 'flying dustbin' petard. It had been ordered forward to destroy a chateau that the SS had apparently been using as a headquarters. There was no infantry available, so Hills ordered the machine-gunners like Reddish to sit half out of their tanks, each with a Sten gun ready to take on any lone enemy armed with panzerfausts.

Following the Churchill, they rumbled forward, slowly and deliberately, everyone taut and alert. No firing came, however, nor did any enemy appear. Halting before the chateau, Hills and Reddish saw one of the crew get out of the Churchill, put the mortar in the petard and then get back into the tank. Moments later, it fired: there was an immense crash, a crumbling of bricks and masonry and an immense amount of dust. The chateau collapsed. 'It all seemed so simple,' noted Reddish.

Also now part of C Squadron were Anthony Cotterell and his adopted tank crew, who had been transferred when B Squadron had pulled out. Cotterell, it seemed, was a glutton for punishment. They'd struggled to find their new hosts, however, only catching up with them in the dusk when they reached the village, having accidentally squelched over a dead cow en route. There, they eventually stopped at a road junction where there was a small shrine with a crucifix and joined a troop of C Squadron. Soon after, the tank in front hit a mine with a blinding white flash. The tank jolted, rolled on a few yards then stopped. Incredibly, after a brief inspection by the crew, they got back in and continued, the tank having apparently suffered no lasting damage. A traffic jam ensued in the village. Cotterell got out and found Lieutenant-Colonel Wilsey, the 7th DWR's CO. He'd lost all contact with his infantry.

'It's impossible country to fight in,' he complained. 'They march up, they lie down and you've lost them.' As if to prove the point, moments later a section of ten men approached up the road, then got into the ditch alongside it and disappeared from sight. 'Indeed,' noted Cotterell, 'in this country of high lanes and many hedges, corn fields and ill-defined front lines, it was almost impossibly difficult to maintain coherent formations.'

Up ahead, two houses burned, lighting up the sky. Mortars continued to explode in desultory fashion. Occasionally, tracer criss-crossed the sky. It was around midnight, and Fontenay was finally in British hands.

Tomorrow, though, the battle would continue. Rauray and the ridge beyond remained their objective. And to get there, the Sherwood Rangers would have to fight a duel with the Panther and Tiger tanks of the 12. SS.

CHAPTER 11

Tiger, Tiger, Burning Bright

M ONDAY, 26 JUNE. TROOPER Arthur Reddish was woken with a gentle dig in the ribs and handed a mug of hot, sweet tea and a bacon sandwich. It was 4 a.m. and they were not far from the main road from Tilly that ran across the top of Fontenay. A short distance away, Anthony Cotterell was also waking, although for his breakfast in the early half-light he was given tinned pork stew, which he found a bit hard to stomach at that time of day. The mug of tea, such an important part of the British soldier's daily fluid intake, went down much better. They spotted some infantry nearby looking on enviously and so passed around a few mugs to them too. It was raining. Again. As dawn began to break, the village and surrounding countryside were shrouded in a low mist. Visibility was poor and everything was wet: the ground, the grass, the surface of their tanks.

The plan for the day was for 146th Brigade on their right to advance from the south-west of the village. They had reached the Walrus objective line, which bordered the northern edge of Tessel Wood. This wood stood about half a mile south of the village and was of similar size to the Bois de Boislonde. The task for them on this second day of MARTLET was to push on through to the final phase of the battle plan, the Albacore line on the western edge of the Rauray ridge. The 24th Lancers and 4/7th Dragoon Guards would give fire support to the infantry, who now had far fewer artillery to help them because at around 6 a.m. Operation EPSOM was being launched a few miles to the east.

Meanwhile, Peter Selerie's C Squadron, including Stuart Hills's troop and Anthony Cotterell's adopted crew, were to support the 7th DWR as they took a leap towards Rauray from the eastern end of the village. The ground to Rauray sloped gently over largely wide, open fields, up to the small village and the low ridge just beyond it. It wasn't a big climb by any stretch of the imagination, but the ridge was none the less a dominating position. Rauray itself was little more than a mile or so away from the edge of Fontenay, but in between the two villages there was comparatively little cover, while a few hundred yards south of the main road to Caen stood St Nicholas Farm, which, like almost all farms hereabouts, was surrounded by a dense orchard. Both apple trees and extensive farm buildings offered obvious cover for the enemy, and sure enough, an infantry patrol sent out in the early hours of the morning reported enemy infantry and panzers at the farm. In fact, it was held by a combination of the 26. Panzergrenadier Regiment and 12. Pionier-Bataillon of combat engineers, both from the 12. SS. The plan for the 7th DWR and C Squadron was first, at around 6 a.m., to clear a triangular wood just to the east of Fontenay, in which there were enemy mortars and a 'nest of Spandaus' – the Allied nickname for German machine guns – and then to storm St Nicholas Farm. Advancing over open ground towards an enemy well hidden by trees and buildings was asking for trouble, however, which was why the support of two field regiments of 25-pounders and a further medium regiment of 155mm guns was extremely welcome news. Infantry and armour were to advance behind the barrage and storm the farm.

As Anthony Cotterell's tank moved forward from its night position, Cherry, the driver, said, 'D'y'see what we went over then?'

'Yes, here's another one,' said Cook from the turret. Cotterell realized they'd run over two dead bodies. A few prisoners escorted by Tommies came down the road, looking impossibly young but weary. They paused near the edge of the village and Cotterell got out to talk to an infantry officer who was stooping by a low wall talking to an artillery observer officer. Suddenly, several mortars fell nearby.

'I reckon they are the people at the farm,' said the artillery officer, 'and I can't get on to the FOO.' The FOO was the artillery forward observation officer, who was up front with the infantry and a radio set, calling out targets for the gunners a mile or so further back.

Cotterell clambered back into the tank, noticing as he did so a white rabbit appear and suddenly turn from the corner that led to St Nicholas Farm and Rauray and hop off up the road. On the net he heard chatter from the western attack of 146th Brigade. Tigers had been reported and the infantry wanted the armour to fire at them. In fact, the western attack was struggling to make much headway. The enemy, with a number of panzers, had been in and around the Tessel Wood, and fierce fighting was taking place at close quarters.

By 6 a.m., C Squadron were lined up along the dead straight road from Tilly and Saint-Pierre, which just to the east of Fontenay was tree-lined. Ahead of Anthony Cotterell's tank was a field 500 yards or so wide, and beyond that was the triangular wood that was hiding a nest of German machine guns. The job for Selerie's men was to give fire support as the infantry, crawling along the ditches at the side of the road, moved up towards the wood. Enemy machine-gun fire was *brrrp*ing and rattling from the wood. 'Sitting there in the tank one didn't half feel a target,' wrote Cotterell. 'Enemy machine-gun fire, or enemy fire of any kind, always seems so much more vehemently determined than the fire put down by your own side.'

A haystack in a field was flaming. There was a lot of smoke.

'Can you see the infantry crawling across the field?' said Cherry.

'Must be bloody awful in that wet grass,' Cook replied.

Their tank remained where it was. Cherry asked Corporal Cook whether he could have a little nap. Cotterell was astonished by Cherry's ability to detach himself from the firing and fighting going on beyond the road in the neighbouring field. Soon after, the wood was cleared; now the 7th DWR could use it for launching their assault on St Nicholas Farm, no more than 700 yards away to the south. The difference between the distances involved in this close fighting in Normandy and back in North Africa really could not have been greater.

The infantry now formed up for the attack on St Nicholas Farm – only for news to arrive that the promised artillery would not be able to help them after all. The amount of Allied artillery was considerable, and far outweighed that available to the Germans. However, it couldn't be everywhere all the time. The 49th Division's attached artillery was supporting 146th Brigade's attack that morning; some field artillery from the EPSOM attack had been promised to support 147th Brigade, but word now came through that it was still needed for EPSOM after all. This was quite a blow, because getting the infantry – not to mention tanks – across that open ground in broad daylight would be difficult, to say the least. Everyone was aware of what had happened in the last war, when far too many young men had been cut to pieces as they'd advanced across no-man's-land.

The 143rd Field Artillery – the Kent Yeomanry – were brought forward in their Sextons, so the attack was not to be entirely without fire support. And C Squadron of the Sherwood Rangers were still on hand, too. All these changes took time to sort out, though, and so it was not until 9.30 a.m. that the infantry began leaving their slit-trenches and advancing over the open ground. Anthony Cotterell's tank was now in an orchard between the two roads that converged before heading to Caen. Suddenly, enemy fire burst out and the infantry went to ground. A Sherman was hit and caught fire; Cotterell heard on the net that one of the crew was badly burned. A deafening explosion just above them made Cotterell jerk in his seat, banging his head against the hull. Cook ordered Cherry to reverse a few yards behind the flimsy cover of a tree. The house at the corner of the orchard was ablaze. Then six Luftwaffe aircraft roared over at low level. Those infantry not in the advancing companies were dug in around the orchard's edge. On the net there were now reports of Tiger tanks, but the tank that now appeared down the road from Rauray was not one of these but a Panzer IV. Up close, they were quite different, the Tiger being substantially larger; but from a distance, it was easy enough to confuse the two. Cotterell's tank opened fire at the enemy panzer, but it was actually Lance-Corporal Dodd of C Company, the 7th DWR, who stood up when the tank was almost upon them and fired a PIAT. This was a hand-held spigot mortar a bit similar to an American bazooka or German panzerfaust. At any rate, he hit it at very close range, which was when any such devices were at their most effective. And Dodd lived to tell the tale, which was frequently not the case when using such weapons.

Cotterell's tank continued to fire at the Mk IV, until the crew suddenly twigged that it had already been knocked out. It was now about 1.30 p.m., and at last the rain had stopped and the sun come out. The morning had disappeared amid the faltering fighting. Soon afterwards, the two leading infantry companies were called back, having suffered a number of casualties and their attack having failed to take St Nicholas Farm. A little to the west, 146th Brigade's attack had also stalled – a reminder of just how difficult it was to advance successfully in this Normandy countryside, when the defenders could always remain largely hidden and when the attackers had to get up and advance in plain view. A new plan was needed.

When news reached him of the failed attack on St Nicholas Farm, Stanley Christopherson ordered both A and B Squadrons down from the Point 102 area north of the Bois de Boislonde to Fontenay, while hurrying down there himself in his own tank, *Robin Hood*. Fontenay looked even more wrecked now, with its burnt-out houses and rubble strewn across its streets. He found the CO of the 7th DWR, Colonel John Wilsey, at his headquarters in a farm on the corner where the road from Cristot met the main road from Tilly on the northern edge of the village, along with the OP officer from the divisional artillery. Christopherson pointed out that St Nicholas Farm had to be taken, come what might; otherwise they would never get to the Rauray ridge. It was especially important they got a move on because the armour and infantry of the western assault was still bogged down in the woods and thick hedgerows there, facing panzers from both 12. SS and the Panzer-Lehr. The 24th Lancers and 4/7th Dragoon Guards, moreover, were discovering their room for manoeuvre limited by an impassable stream to their left, which ran north to south and separated the two halves of the British attack.

'The Inf had had a rather sticky time,' noted Christopherson with his usual understatement, 'and were not at all enthusiastic about giving us any support.' However, they thrashed out a plan. C Squadron would lead the attack, with two companies of the 7th DWR in support and the divisional artillery firing heavy concentrations on all suspected enemy strongpoints, the farm included. The infantry would follow the tanks for the first 1,000 yards, then dig in; A Squadron would then push through C Squadron and continue on up to Rauray. The assault would begin at three-thirty that afternoon.

The artillery opened up right on time, shells screaming over in a flurry and detonating amid columns of earth and grit and smoke. St Nicholas Farm was targeted, but so too were a number of small copses and thick hedge lines. Behind this, Peter Selerie led his squadron into attack, all of them hoping the artillery had done its work. The 700 yards to the farm was no great distance, but it would be all too far if the enemy still had hidden anti-tank weapons trained on them. Selerie had split the squadron into two, with half crossing fields to the left of the road to Rauray, the other half to the right. Anthony Cotterell's tank had just begun to take its place in the column when it was recalled to Brigade HQ: his time with the Sherwood Rangers was suddenly over. At least he'd seen plenty during his fortnight in Normandy – certainly enough with which to write up a major two-part report for *WAR*.

Stuart Hills's tank and troop were in the middle of the left-hand formation, the same side of the road as the farm. To begin with the advance went well, and the left-hand group were moving wide to pass the farm when Arthur Reddish suddenly saw two flashes to his right at about three o'clock. Two Shermans burst into flames.

'Where's the fire coming from?' Selerie called, over the squadron net.

Nobody knew, but it had not been the farm. A brief debate. Then Selerie ordered the right-hand group to swing into the orchard around the farm and at least clear it and hold it for the infantry following behind. Selerie manoeuvred his own tank into the lead then swung right.

'Now there's a sight for sore eyes,' said Sam Kirman, the operator. 'Old Pete leading his gallant lads into action!' Everyone laughed; a welcome release of tension. However, Selerie now waved on Hills to take the lead.

'I knew it was too bloody good to last,' said Kirman. It was, though, the right thing to do; it made no sense for Selerie to be the point man. The lead tank was in the most dangerous position, and the squadron leader was the most valuable officer. Anyone operating a tank was at extreme risk when in combat, but there was no need for Selerie to add to his own risk unnecessarily. What's more, it was important he could see as many of his tanks for as much time as possible, and he could not do that while in the lead.

So it was left to Stuart Hills's crew to take the leap of faith and burst through the hedgerow surrounding the orchard and St Nicholas Farm, both Reddish and Footitt firing their Brownings as they did so. The orchard was thick with trees, and long grass had grown up between them; Reddish reckoned it was like entering a green cave. But there were no enemy tanks or guns that he could see. *Thank God.* As they pushed on they saw the farmhouse, and Reddish gave that a hosing of machine-gun fire too. Two more Shermans were alongside them now, machine guns blazing, and then the rest. The noise was immense – like the Grand Fleet in action, Reddish thought. They now burst out of the orchard with the farmhouse and outbuildings on their left, straight across the road and into a field bordered to the south and west by a thin hedge. Too thin for the enemy to be dug in there, Reddish thought to himself, and felt himself relax a bit. Time to change the belt in the Browning. The breech had become so hot it had begun to fire single shots of its own accord. Grabbing a towel, he wiped the sweat from his face and neck; it was warm in there, but fear and adrenalin had played their part too.

Geoff Storey drove them forward towards the hedge that faced south towards Rauray, dodging numerous dead cattle, legs in the air, the sweet, cloying and invasive stench of their already rotting bodies inescapable.

Rauray was barely a mile away. Reddish peered up ahead towards the village. A few hundred yards in front of them was a crossroads and further on, away to the left, what appeared to be a wood, although it was actually a small, heavily tree-lined field. There was another wood just to the left of Rauray, too, jutting out perhaps 200 yards from the edge of the village. And then he saw it – a Panzer IV, just emerging from the wood.

'Enemy hornet!' he called out over the intercom. 'Eleven o'clock. One thousand five hundred yards!'

Hills responded quickly. 'Gunner, traverse left, steady, on. Enemy tank. AP. One thousand five hundred yards. Fire when ready!'

Peering through their binoculars, Hills and Reddish both saw the first shot bounce short of the tank before hitting it. A gush of blue exhaust and the panzer jolted into reverse, then stalled. Reddish and Storey laughed as they imagined the driver panicking. Footitt fired again, another armour-piercing round, and hit it more squarely this time, although at that range it didn't penetrate. Moments later, the panzer lurched off again, reversing back among the trees.

With St Nicholas Farm captured and the infantry now digging in, it was finally time for A Squadron to enter the fray. One of the difficulties facing the MARTLET operation was space and room for manoeuvre, especially in the wreckage of Fontenay, so it was not until C Squadron had moved out that A Squadron headed down towards the village. This was to be Harry Heenan's first action, although he was still an officer under observation in 2 Troop and so commanding only his own crew. But it was David Render's 5 Troop who were now ordered by John Semken to push through Fontenay and wait for the rest of the squadron in a hedge-lined field just off the road leading south to Rauray. Leading the way, Render took his tank down the main road east from Tilly; turning on to rue Massieu, he saw Stanley Christopherson in the turret of *Robin Hood*, parked up at the side of the road, headphones over his black tanker's beret, obviously talking to someone. Render passed him, rumbled over the crossroads at the end of the street and led his tanks into a small, triangular, hedge-lined field on the right of the road. Having manoeuvred out into an extended line, his tanks all facing southwards towards St Nicholas Farm and Rauray beyond, Render radioed to Semken that he was in position. It was now around 5 p.m.

Soon after this, Lieutenant Neville Fearn arrived. Render now dismounted, hurried over and climbed on the back of Fearn's Sherman. As he did so, he spotted the head of a tank commander speeding towards the village from the south-west. For an instant he assumed it must be a C Squadron tank, but then he realized the man was wearing a black side-cap, and so that he must be German. It looked as though he was heading straight for them – but then, and apparently without seeing Fearn, Render or the rest of 5 Troop, the panzer turned into the rue Massieu.

'Shit!' said Render to Fearn. 'It's a bloody Jerry!'

And not just any Jerry tank, but a Tiger – all 56 tons of it now heading towards the rest of A Squadron. Tigers, with up to 120mm frontal armour and the high-velocity 88mm gun, could make short work of a Sherman in a one-to-one duel, so it looked bad for Stanley Christopherson, who was still talking to Brigade HQ at the far end of the road as John Semken turned into the rue Massieu. Fortunately for Christopherson, Semken had just passed his CO when the Tiger turned into the same road but from the far end. Semken's Sherman and the Tiger now faced one another, around 120 yards apart. For a split second, Semken stared at it, stunned, then said to his gunner, Henry Simons, 'Fire, it's a Hun!'

Semken always insisted they move with an AP round 'up the spout' – in the barrel, ready to fire – and so Simons now pressed down on the foot firing button, the gun boomed, the tank rocked and the shell hurtled towards the Tiger at more than 2,000 feet per second and at point-blank range. 'And the road was filled with smoke from the tracer,' said Semken. 'Couldn't see a damn thing. So we kept firing.' Round after round was pushed into the breech, empty cases clattering on to the turret floor as each shell slammed into the Tiger. And with each shot, Simons very slightly adjusted the lay of the gun. Within little more than half a minute they had fired ten rounds – and then Semken heard over the net that the enemy crew were bailing out.

Seeing what was about to happen, David Render had sped back to his own tank and ordered the crew to start it up and hurry back to the road, hoping he might shoot the Tiger up the backside, which was one of its more vulnerable parts. By the time he had manoeuvred into the road, however, it was all over. 'The smoke slowly dissipated,' said Semken, 'and we saw this Tiger looking at us. And there was a faint trail of smoke coming out of the bloody thing and its gun was pointing straight at me. And, of course, if there was a round up the spout and it cooked off, it would have gone through me.' Quickly, he ordered his driver to move round it and warned those following behind they all needed to get out of there as quickly as possible.

The Tiger was from the 2. Kompanie, SS-Panzerabteilung 101. This unit was commanded by Michael Wittmann, who had been largely responsible for destroying the leading tanks of the City of London Yeomanry at Villers-Bocage almost two weeks before. It had since been attached to the 12. SS, although what this lone tank was doing entering Fontenay on its own, without any kind of support, is not clear. Perhaps it was trying to ape Wittmann's actions on 13 June. It seems Semken's first shot had hit the gun mantlet and metal splinters had entered the driver's hatch, which was open. With his driver wounded and red-hot splinters hitting the inside of the tank, and further rounds slamming into it one after the other in quick succession, the commander ordered the crew to bail out. They were swiftly captured and with them their tank.

While for them the war was over, it most certainly was not for John Semken and the rest of A Squadron. Semken had never been a fan of what were known as 'Balaclava charges' – not since seeing B Squadron get shot to pieces at Alam Halfa back on 1 September 1942. Yet here there was no real alternative. Rauray had to be taken. First, however, the 7th DWR were to push forward some 500 yards and dig in, while the 11th Durhams also moved up from Fontenay. Once the 7th DWR were in position, Semken's tanks were to lead the attack with the DLI following closely behind, the infantry once again providing eyes on the ground and ensuring there were no enemy troops lurking with panzerfausts. It was around 6 p.m. when the 7th DWR began moving forward; they encountered a number of enemy rearguards – German infantry given the specific task of slowing down the British as much as possible – and it was not until 7.30 p.m. that they had cleared the ground and dug in with clear fields of fire up towards the ridge.

By then it was a glorious evening, the sun lowering in the sky and casting a golden glow across the fields of corn that ran all the way to Rauray and the ridge beyond.

'All stations,' said Semken over the squadron net. 'All stations. Advance.' He had arranged his squadron in a three-pronged attack. Out to the right, passing straight across open fields, was David Render's 5 Troop. To the left was 2 Troop, among them Harry Heenan in what was about to be his first significant taste of combat. In the centre was Semken himself, and for this particular attack he had brought his Fireflies together as a 'Praetorian Guard'. Behind, waiting to move up when needed, were the remaining three troops, following 250 yards behind. Each tank was to keep well apart from its neighbour so there could be no chance of an overlapping double target for any lurking enemy anti-tank gun lying in wait.

Semken might have cited the Charge of the Light Brigade, but this was to be no dramatic surge forward, rather a steady advance with plenty of pausing to douse hedgerows and to allow the Durhams following behind to keep pace. Shermans could speed at 30 mph if they really needed to, but the role of the independent armoured brigades was to work closely with the infantry, which generally meant moving at walking pace. Indeed, it was with this role in mind that the Churchill tank had been designed and built. Yet it had not been built in enough numbers to fulfil that role, and so the ubiquitous Sherman had been given the task instead. And the Sherman certainly did have some considerable advantages. As Semken had discovered earlier that afternoon when confronted by the Tiger, no tank could challenge the Sherman for rapidity of fire – twenty rounds a minute if needed, which amounted to one shot every three seconds. That was a hell of a rate of fire.

As Semken's HQ troop headed down the road to Rauray, Render's and Heenan's troops found themselves moving along thick hedgerows on their outer flank. An enemy machine gun opened up, spitting bullets at twenty-three per second. The infantry dropped to the ground and imme- diately the Brownings responded, tearing apart the air – a slower, steadier rate of fire, but deafeningly loud as bullets raked the hedge lines in long bursts. No one was conserving ammo. Main guns boomed, tanks rocking with the recoil, HE rounds bursting and shattering chunks of hedge, bits of wood and soil spewing high into the air. From their turrets, Render and his fellow commanders peered forward, straining for movement. The air thick with smoke, cordite. The stench sharp on the throat, sting- ing the eyes.

Then calm again as Render halted the fire. Infantry back on their feet. A few enemy dead sprawled from the hedgerow. The Durhams moved forward, pig-stick bayonets on their rifles, clearing the foxholes and scrapes in the ground at the foot of the hedge. Germans were pulled clear and forced to their feet. One looked shell-shocked. Another angry and defiant. Render looked down at him – a young lad, face filthy, refusing to raise his hands as he was roughly searched. He looked up at Render, eye- ing him with utter contempt. Then a mortar shell landed fairly near and the infantry once again went to ground. But not the young SS grenadier, even though more mortars were falling. 'He laughed at those who had taken cover,' noted Render, 'and I can still remember the startled look of momentary surprise on his face as a shell splinter struck him square on the forehead and he crumpled dead on the ground.'

They moved on. Semken's voice came clear over the net, controlling each troop to take them forward a bound at a time, ensuring each tank maintained a distance of 100–150 yards from the next. It was now nearly 9 p.m.

At Rauray, headquarters of the 12. Panzerregiment of the 12. SS 'Hitler Jugend' Panzer-Division, the commander, Sturmbannführer Max Wünsche, a highly decorated Knight's Cross winner and veteran of the Eastern Front, was having a terrible time – as was Standartenführer Kurt Meyer, the divisional commander. On the night of D-Day, as the division had begun reaching Normandy, it had been some 20,000 strong, flush with weaponry and *esprit de corps*; now, nearly three weeks on, having been in action constantly, it was badly depleted with almost no replacements and covering more of the front than it could reasonably cope with. Earlier that morning, Meyer and Wünsche had stood in Rauray watching their panzers moving forward to meet the British assaults as the British barrages for EPSOM and for the assault through Tessel Wood opened up. At that point, Meyer had issued Wünsche with clear orders: (1) stop the British attack dead in the Tessel area immediately; (2) hold Rauray, the cornerstone of the division, at all costs. Meyer told Wünsche that he was responsible for Rauray.

Wünsche's panzers had done a good job of halting the British around Tessel, but had suffered a number of losses and had had their hands full for much of the day dealing with 146th Brigade and the armour of the 24th Lancers and 4/7th Dragoon Guards. To the east, the rest of the division had then had to contend with the EPSOM attack. More panzer divisions were approaching and arriving at the Normandy front, but it was 12. SS, even with the Panzer-Lehr to their left, that faced the main brunt of the twin British assaults of MARTLET and EPSOM. So depleted were the 12. SS that Wünsche had been given command of a hastily cobbled together *Kampfgruppe* – battlegroup – of grenadiers from the III./ 26. Panzergrenadier Regiment combined with his own remaining panzers plus some of Wittmann's Tigers. Now British tanks were advancing towards Wünsche's headquarters at Rauray. Neither Wünsche nor his senior panzer commanders had expected this further attack so late in the day. Outposts of grenadiers had been overrun, but most of the infantry were dug in around Rauray while his panzers were returning from the Tessel area. Others were emerging from the regiment maintenance area just to the south of the village.

Now, at around 9 p.m., the summer evening still quite light, the panzers began to take on the advancing Shermans of A Squadron. David Render heard a crack and a round hit the ground uncomfortably close. Germans used a propellant that had a lower flash than that of the Allies, so it was often extremely difficult to spot them. Frantic peering through his binoculars didn't help; he saw nothing. Across in the fields on the far side of the road, 2 Troop had begun returning fire. Then suddenly Render spotted a glint of sunlight on metal at the edge of the village and realized he was looking at a panzer.

'AP. Traverse right,' he ordered. 'Eight hundred yards. Enemy hornet dug into the right side of prominent building.'

His gunner traversed – but too far. Render called out an urgent correction as Corporal Johnny Lanes in the Sherman closest to his opened fire as well. Render was expecting his gunner to call out 'On!' once he'd locked on to the target, but it didn't come. With frustration, Render hauled his gunner out of his seat and sat in his place, using the power-assisted traverse control handle to bring the gun on to the target. A press on the firing button and the shell hurtled forward. Then he quickly swapped places again, pushing himself back up through the open turret, and called out an adjustment as the shot had fallen short. With the second shell they hit, and again with the third and fourth. *Shoot, shoot, and keep shooting.* Semken's mantra.

'Next thing was that German tanks started to appear,' said Semken. Wünsche had amassed a mixed force of Panzer IVs and several Tigers and Panthers and moved them forward to engage the Sherwood Rangers. There was no one in the regiment with better eyesight or a greater ability to read the land than George Dring, the sergeant in Dick Holman's 4 Troop, who first spotted a Panzer IV and shot it through the driver's visor from just 200 yards. The tank brewed up almost immediately with the crew only just managing to escape in time. Soon after, he spotted a Tiger at 1,000 yards. While Dring's gunner, Harry Hodkin, was hurriedly traversing, the Tiger fired a shot at them but missed; perhaps it was the sunlight, or perhaps it was simply fatigue, but the German aim that evening was proving poor. Before the giant panzer could attempt another shot, Dring then pumped five rounds at it, the last of which smashed the driver's periscope. Much to his delight, he saw the enemy crew bail out. 'We knocked out one of them, and then we knocked out another of them. And another,' said Semken. 'Our tails were well up.'

Suddenly, a Panther tank, No. 204 from the 12. Panzerregiment, emerged from the trees that lined the road to the west. It was returning from the fighting around Tessel, but now cut across Render's troop at 90 degrees to A Squadron's advance. It was too close for anyone in 5 Troop to get off a decent shot, but Semken's cohort were a little further back, and at 80 yards Neville Fearn fired and punched a hole straight through the vertical plate above the rear drive sprocket. A moment later, George Dring hit it a second time, his third panzer of the day. The Panther stopped dead in its tracks, right by the crossroads, and again the crew bailed out. Two were cut down by the hail of machine guns from the advancing Shermans.

Dring's field day continued as he spotted a second Tiger emerging from the north-west of Rauray village. He fired six shots in quick succession; two missed, the third hit and caused no damage, but the fourth was right on target. Over the net, Fearn told him he thought he'd missed and hit a brick wall behind.

'You don't see a brick wall spark like that,' Dring replied. Moments later the Tiger started to smoke. Others had also fired at it, and five rounds in all tore holes through the rear of the Tiger while another smashed the engine hatch to the rear. There was no question that the backside of the Tiger was its weak spot; but even so these crippling strikes, from 1,400 yards' distance, were remarkable shooting, especially with a 75mm gun.

As the A Squadron men pressed on, they began to overrun the infantry dug in to the front of Rauray. Semken ordered 5 Troop to clear the orchards and hedgerows to the west of the village. Here was a network of interconnecting trenches, foxholes and mortar pits between the hedgerows and trees. Render's men had to depress the coaxial Browning machine gun next to the main gun as low as it would go to hose the enemy positions. Johnny Lanes's Sherman was up alongside Render's, and the troop leader turned back to see where Sergeant Jackson had got to when suddenly a grenadier tried to climb up the front of *Aim*. It all happened very quickly, the SS man gripping a stick grenade in one hand and struggling to haul himself up with the other. Without thinking, Render grabbed his submachine gun, a German MP40 he had picked up earlier during the fighting around Point 102. As he drew it to his shoulder, his attacker was on the front of the tank with one hand on the top of the driver's hatch, his other still clutching the grenade. Render opened fire, blowing the attacker clear of the tank.

Around the same time 1 Troop, which had been moved up by Semken, was also clearing enemy positions as the light finally began to fade. Having doused the enemy with machine-gun fire and HE, Lieutenant Ronnie

Grellis began hurling grenades. To his mounting frustration, the enemy would not surrender, even though they had been severely shot up and were cowering in their foxholes. Clambering down, he then captured them on foot at the point of his revolver. Listening to all this was Stanley Christopherson back at Fontenay, as well as the rest of A Squadron. As so often happened in the heat of the moment, his operator had forgotten to switch the radio set from the external net to the intercom. 'As a result,' wrote Christopherson of this exchange of Grellis's, 'the whole regiment heard the most thrilling and enthralling conversation between him and his crew and appreciated the shouts of encouragement from his crew as he dealt with the German infantry.'

Soon after, Sergeant Dring claimed yet another panzer. 'To the east of Rauray,' ran a report written just after, 'he took on a Mk IV at 1,200 yards, fired two HE ranging rounds and then one AP through the tracks, which went in and finished it.'

It was now finally beginning to get dark and, with the infantry some way behind, there was no time to push on into the shattered roads of Rauray itself. Incredibly, not one tank in A Squadron had been knocked out. In part this was due to the uncoordinated nature of the German defence, but also Semken had been right about one thing: the enemy rarely shot back – and certainly not accurately – when they were being shot at themselves. Concentrated high-velocity fire from the Fireflies and almost constant firing from the rest of the squadron's Shermans had forced the enemy tank commanders to keep their heads down – literally. But closing the hatches had badly affected their visibility and with it their aim. The Sherman's superior rate of fire had, in this instance, won the day in a rare tank-on-tank duel. The result proved, emphatically, that when used correctly, the US-designed and built Sherman could be a match for any tank on the battlefield.

John Semken's tactics had been spot on – this was one Balaclava charge that had paid off.

CHAPTER 12

Faces Gone, Faces New

'AFTER ANOTHER LONG, TIRING day among the fun and games, we have today been out of it for maintenance and rest,' Bill Wharton wrote to his wife, Marion, on 28 June. 'Yesterday was the most miserable time since we landed.' After the astonishing successes of Monday, 26 June, the 11th Durhams had arrived and taken over the positions held by the SS grenadiers just to the north of Rauray, digging in there for the night. As John Semken's men had pulled back to rearm and refuel, John Hanson-Lawson's B Squadron had arrived to take over the support of the DLI.

The tank crews were up and at battle positions by 4.30 a.m. that Tuesday, 27 June. After the brilliant sunshine of the previous evening, the morning had dawned cold, grey and wet, the rain sheeting down once more. After an O group with the commander of the Durhams, John Hanson-Lawson sent out two troops with some foot patrols from the Durhams to investigate the situation in Rauray. As the Shermans moved down through the east of the village and headed south, a hidden anti-tank gun opened fire. All three tanks in the troop were hit and knocked out. Lieutenant Ray Scott, in the lead troop, was killed along with one of his crew, and so too were the other two tank commanders, Sergeants Lionel Biddell and George Green, both desert veterans. Two of Biddell's crew and one of Green's were also killed. All the survivors were wounded. That was the entire troop wiped out in a few moments of ghastly violence.

One moment they had been alive and well, the next moment they were gone.

With the rest of the regiment in leaguer to the north of Fontenay, B

Squadron had to put their losses to one side and soldier on alongside the Durhams. It took all morning to clear the village. John Hanson-Lawson had stalked a Panzer IV which appeared to be knocked out only for it to open fire at close range. Hanson-Lawson's tank was hit in the flank and started to burn. While the driver and co-driver managed to get out, Hanson-Lawson and his signals sergeant, Bill Crookes, struggled to free themselves as the flames quickly whipped up inside. Seeing this, Bill Wharton jumped down from his own tank, ran through the rain and helped rescue the men, dragging them clear to safety. All had suffered burns to the head and hands. The entire crew were then brought back down to the farmhouse in Fontenay, where Christopherson now had the RHQ. 'Sgt Crookes was in a bad condition,' noted Christopherson, 'but when I spoke to him he smiled and told me that he suffered no pain.' Crookes died shortly afterwards from his burns and loss of blood. Christopherson was very upset about his death; when he had first joined the regiment back in 1939, Crookes had been his troop farrier. Bill Wharton was also distraught – not only over the loss of Crookes but also over the deaths of Sergeants Biddell and Green, both of whom had been his very good friends since before the war. 'My spirits reach zero,' he wrote, 'when I contemplate the loss of such splendid men. It seems so unfair that the best have to go.' The loss of Hanson-Lawson from active service was a considerable blow, too, although he looked sure to survive. Christopherson had known him in civilian life in London before the war. Now the regiment was short a squadron leader.

Rauray was finally captured a little after midday, by which time A Squadron was back, in reserve behind what was left of B Squadron. The village had not only been Max Wünsche's headquarters, but also the site of their panzer maintenance detachment, the equivalent of the British LAD. A number of panzers were discovered in and around the village, abandoned because of mechanical failure or lack of fuel. The Sherwood Rangers quickly made plans to use them. 'We got them going,' said John Semken, who examined one of the Tigers, 'and I asked whether I could have one of these because I'd like to have a tank that I could shove through a hedge knowing that nothing could penetrate from the other side.' In no time they had painted out the black crosses and instead added the red fox's head on yellow, which was the emblem of 8th Armoured Brigade, and '996', which was the Sherwood Rangers' number. A British Army film unit shot footage of the colonel riding in a captured Tiger, being driven by men of A Squadron. Sadly for them all, this was as close as the panzers got to becoming part of the Sherwood Rangers' arsenal. Permission to use them was denied, and a day later tank transporters arrived, loaded them up and whisked them back off to England for detailed examination.

Bill Wharton made no mention in his letter to Marion of his heroics or the bitter fighting in and around Rauray, although he admitted to his wife that for 'sheer misery' the day had been hard to beat. By evening, the squadron had just two officers still standing, of which Wharton was one, and only seven of their nineteen tanks. As dusk fell, they pulled back to leaguer for the night. The plan was for the 4/7th Dragoon Guards to press on south the following day. 'We did receive a farewell gesture from our friends in the shape of a few air bursts over our heads as we pulled out,' wrote Wharton, 'but except for the odd piece of shrapnel among the kit, no damage was done. Wet through to the skin, I soon remedied that state of affairs by stripping and washing, having a good stiff tot of rum and then, placing my bed under a tarpaulin, I laid me down to rest and dream of you.'

For the next few days, the Sherwood Rangers remained in the line but in a holding role rather than in any major assaults. On the 28th, the 4/7th Dragoon Guards pushed forward with the infantry towards Brettevillette, a small hamlet built around a manor farm to the south, and although they had not captured it the Rauray ridge was now firmly secured. The whole area was a wreck. 'I must say that good old Catholic is rather in the background just now,' Harry Heenan wrote in a letter home. 'The only France I have seen lately is a muddy, blown up France with dead Germans and dead cows lying all over the place.'

Overall, the situation along the front was reasonably good. The Americans had cleared the whole of the Cotentin peninsula and captured the port of Cherbourg the previous day, 27 June, while MARTLET had finally taken its prime objective and EPSOM had punched a corridor 4 miles wide and 5 miles deep across the River Odon, already known by the British as the 'Scottish Corridor' after the 15th Scottish Division that had been in the vanguard of VIII Corps' advance. There had been lofty hopes in London and Washington that EPSOM would bring about a major breakthrough and force the Germans into headlong retreat, but after the great storm and the slowdown in delivery of men and materiel, Montgomery had approached the offensive with a more realistic set of expectations. General Dempsey, the Second Army commander, had thought a breakthrough possible but unlikely. Both men had hoped, however, that the battle would draw in as many freshly arriving German panzer divisions as possible and force arriving units to be flung in piecemeal as they reached the front, where they could be chewed up by the Allies' superior fire-power. They hoped this would prevent the coordinated counter-thrust that was the enemy's last realistic chance of throwing the Allies back into the sea.

Although by the evening of the 28th EPSOM had begun to run out of steam, that hope had been fulfilled. In all, the British now faced seven of the ten panzer divisions available to the Germans in the west, as 9. SS Panzer, 2. Panzer, 2. SS Panzer and 10. SS Panzer had all begun reaching the front. Ultra decrypts of German Enigma radio traffic revealed that II. SS Panzerkorps, which included 9. SS, 2. SS and 2. Panzer divisions, had been ordered to counter-attack at the western base of the British bulge in the line created by EPSOM. With this in mind, the VIII Corps troops in the corridor, along with 49th Division on their right, were now ordered to reinforce those gains and hold firm. So long as they were able to stand their ground, Dempsey reckoned there would be a wonderful opportunity to grind down the enemy. This was because the Germans always counter-attacked. It was a part of their doctrinal DNA. Behind it was a sound principle: to let the enemy come on, then, once he had overextended and exhausted himself, to punch back as strongly as possible.

The trouble with counter-attacking, however, was that to do so they had to emerge from their dugouts, foxholes and places of camouflage and move over open ground, just as the British had to do when they attacked. And by 1944 the Allies had realized that this Pavlovian response played to their own strengths – above all, industrial levels of fire-power. Ranged against this German counter-thrust was the full weight of British artillery, supported by offshore naval guns, which were still within range, and close air support from the Second Tactical Air Force – fighter-bombers and low-level twin-engine 'medium' bombers to bomb, strafe and harry.

On Thursday, 29 June, the II. SS Panzerkorps flung themselves straight into the battle, over ground with which they were unfamiliar and against an enemy they had yet to confront – and a very different one from that they had faced on the Eastern Front. Down came the full force of artillery, air and naval power, and stopped the attack in its tracks. 'It was impossible to gain ground against this superior firepower,' noted Kurt Meyer, the commander of the already badly mauled 12. SS, 'not to mention the absolute air supremacy.'

The Sherwood Rangers had been pulled back out of the fray on 29 June, the day Sergeant Jim Christie of the No. 5 Army Film and Photo Section arrived to take photographs of the men and knocked-out enemy tanks still strewn about the scenes of recent fighting. Christie took a series of photos of the Panther knocked out by Neville Fearn and George Dring, as well as of Stanley Christopherson, wearing black tanker's overalls, leaning over the bonnet of a mud-spattered jeep and talking to Lieutenant-Colonel Anderson of the 24th Lancers and Brigadier Cracroft.

Christie also took a number of pictures of George Dring and his crew, the panzer killers, with their tank, *Akilla*. The tracks and suspension bogeys were thick with mud and grass. Two appliqué armour plates had been welded on to the sides, to give added protection to the turret and the lap-gunner. The dull olive-drab paint was scratched and muddied from driving through hedges, while both forward of and behind the turret were a mass of camouflage netting and a huge amount of stowage – canvas tarpaulins covering bedding, haversacks and the crew's personal kit. The crew themselves looked exactly what they were: a bunch of scruffy young lads, confident in their own skin. The self-effacing Dring, with his blond moustache and field glasses around his neck, looked a little embarrassed by the fuss, as did Spike Bennett, the operator. But Harry Hodkin, the gunner, whose firing actually destroyed two Tigers, one Panther and two Mk IVs, had his tanker's beret perched casually on the back of his head and was smoking, grinning straight at Christie. He was loving it. Blondie Denton, the youngest in the crew and the lap-gunner, stood at the back not quite sure where he should be looking, while Sid Gould, the driver and the oldest man in the crew, smiled cheerfully enough from his perch at the edge of the sloping front. A moment captured in time.

And no doubt all forgotten about by the following day, 30 June, when they were holding a part of the front to the east of Fontenay and Cristot, which was effectively the western hinge of the German counter-thrust. The enemy were no more successful that day either, although the strength of the German attack had prompted Dempsey to pull men back off Hill 112, a key bit of high ground south of the River Odon. While it was never good to relinquish any kind of high ground, the risk of the men stranded there becoming cut off was considerable – and it would almost certainly have happened, as the full weight of 10. SS and the newly arrived 1. SS was hurled against them. A cardinal point of British doctrine, as laid down in the Western Desert in August 1942, was never again to suffer a major reverse on the battlefield. By 1 July, the twin operations of EPSOM and MARTLET had seen that principle borne out. As the new month dawned, Germany had lost its last conceivable chance of kicking the Allies out of Normandy – and with it the battle there.

How long it would now take, and how this already brutal campaign would play out, were still very unclear. The Allies, however, were determined to continue to bludgeon their way forward by any means necessary. On 30 June, A Squadron were back at St Nicholas Farm, where they spotted some ten German tanks – from 9. SS Panzer-Division – a little way to the east, heading towards the base of the Scottish Corridor. They were too far away to engage, but that evening Semken's men had a grandstand view of RAF Bomber Command's attack on Villers-Bocage. Some 256 heavy bombers had been sent to bomb this small town, whose confluence of roads was crucial to the manoeuvre of enemy panzer divisions now at the front.

The low roar of the bombers could be heard before they were seen, and grew louder and louder until the aircraft were flying directly over the battlefield. Bomber Command flew almost all its missions both at night and from 18,000 feet and more, but here, to ensure greater accuracy, they were attacking in the evening light and from just 4,000 feet up. David Render, for one, watched with awe. 'The large number of lumbering aircraft came in low over our heads,' he wrote, 'with their bomb-bay doors open and we could clearly see the bombs slung inside their fuselages.' Barely a house was left standing in the town, and Render and his fellows, although some miles away, found themselves covered in brick and masonry dust drifting back over them from the devastation.

On 2 July, Peter Selerie's C Squadron were supporting just one company of the 10th Durhams as they pushed south from Rauray towards Bretteville, to see whether it was enemy held. It soon became clear the enemy was indeed there, not just among the farm buildings but in hedgerows extending to the west, and one platoon of Durhams got pinned down. Stuart Hills's troop were sent to help give them cover and get them out again. Moving forward across fields, they suddenly spotted exhaust smoke from the far side of one of the hedges, which suggested an enemy panzer or SP gun. After blasting the hedge they hurriedly tried to move themselves into a better position that gave them a little more protection, but in doing so Hills's tank became bogged down, something that could happen only too easily after all the rain that had fallen the previous month. Since they were operating under radio silence, Hills ordered Arthur Reddish to organize a tow from one of the other tanks. Clambering out of his forward hatch, Reddish headed to Sergeant Kirby Tribe's tank, but as he neared it, tucked himself into the side of a hedge;

experience had taught him to always keep out of sight as far as possible. Not far from Tribe's tank he was stopped in his tracks by a burst of automatic fire that fizzed and spat all too close for comfort. He couldn't work out where it had come from, though, so after a brief pause he moved forward again. Another burst of fire, again a little ahead of him.

'Red, you bloody fool!' Tribe shouted when he saw him. 'Get back to your tank!' It turned out Tribe didn't have a tow rope in any case. Cautiously, Reddish picked his way back to discover that John Saunders, the commander of the third tank in the troop, had twigged what had happened and had hurried over to pull Hills's tank out – and thankfully all was well. By laying down smoke and blasting the enemy positions, the Durhams managed to extricate themselves.

That night, C Squadron remained at Rauray to support the infantry and the A1 Echelon trucks were brought up to replenish them with food, fuel and ammunition, staying behind some cover 400 yards or so from the village while each tank in turn rumbled over. Reddish decided to walk, and passed the Durhams' headquarters where he spotted a German prisoner. To his surprise, the German waved at him cheerily.

'Who's that chap?' Reddish asked one of the Durhams.

'We found him camouflaged in a tree in the middle of our lines,' he was told. 'He's the fellow who fired at one of your tankies.' The man had been given some chocolate and cigarettes and had told his captors that he'd been ordered to keep the Tommies clear of the very hedge Reddish had tried to walk down. Reddish gave him a wave in return. 'And it was returned,' he wrote, 'with a grin.'

That same evening, Stanley Christopherson came up to see Peter Selerie and the rest of the squadron. While on his rounds he saw a black rabbit suddenly appear at his feet, then duck into the hedgerow beside him. On a whim, Christopherson decided to try to catch it; rabbits were a welcome variation to the normal rations. Plunging into the hedge, he eventually managed to trap it in the thick base of the hedge – but in the process tumbled through to the other side and landed, hot and sweating, almost on top of a private in the Durhams who had been asleep in a foxhole. Christopherson muttered his apologies for waking him and walked away with as much dignity as he could muster – which was not very much.

Still clutching the rabbit in his arms, he wandered over to C Squadron's leaguer and asked after Selerie – who, he learned, was having a nap in the squadron scout car after an exhausting day in combat. These Dingos, with the driver's seat removed, were the most comfortable vehicle in the armoury in which to sleep safely while at the front, and a well-earned perk for the squadron leader. Reaching the Dingo, Christopherson opened the sliding roof and saw Selerie stretched out and fast asleep. 'Obviously,' noted Christopherson, 'he was dog-tired and, fascinated, I listened to the usual whistling which emanates from the open mouth of a deep sleeper, and vaguely wondered what he was dreaming about.' Exhausted Selerie might have been, but Christopherson was not going to pass up such a golden opportunity. Gently, he placed the rabbit on Selerie's chest. For a short while, the rabbit sat there, twitching its nose and gazing at the face in front of it. Gradually, Selerie began to wake, then suddenly opened his eyes in shock. Rubbing them in disbelief but finding the rabbit still there, he lunged for it, at which it hopped off and retreated to the end of the scout car. Only then did Selerie notice Christopherson, laughing beside the Dingo. Trying to get up and salute all at the same time, Selerie spluttered his apologies, but Christopherson gently pushed him back down again. 'In fifteen seconds,' he noted, 'he was once again unconscious.'

By this time, Padre Skinner was in a military ward of the civilian Meanwood Park Hospital in Leeds. All those with head wounds were evacuated to Britain once stable enough to travel. Really, the standard of medical care was exemplary for the time. Skinner had been patched up, X-rayed, operated on and later X-rayed again. His head hurt like hell, and more than a week on from his wounding he was still suffering appalling spells of acute dizziness. Old bruising marks on his skull were puzzling the doctors; Skinner thought them possibly the result of a football injury some years earlier. By Tuesday, 4 July, however, he was feeling well enough to get up. Reading the latest edition of *Lilliput* magazine, he was startled to read an article by Keith Douglas. 'Shook me a bit,' he noted in his diary.

The following day, he was discharged and sent home to Hartlepool and a welcome reunion with his wife, Etta. His local doctor X-rayed his head yet again and, satisfied he was healing well, Skinner wrote both to the Chaplains' Department and to Stanley Christopherson, asking to return to the Sherwood Rangers as soon as possible and pleading with Stanley to keep the post open for him.

Meanwhile, the regiment were at last out of the line and back among the lush orchards of Chouain to the south of Bayeux. 'The relief was enormous,' noted Arthur Reddish. 'We were virtually sleepwalking through our duties.' All the B as well as A Echelon vehicles were brought up too, so for the first time since long before the invasion, the entire regiment was finally assembled together. It was a chance for all the exhausted tank crews to get clean, pick up some fresh clothes, eat properly and, of course, get some sleep. 'Yesterday we pulled out for the rest we so much require and looked forward to after nine days at the front,' wrote Bill Wharton to his wife, Marion. He was one of two officers – Johnny Mann was the other – picked out by Stanley Christopherson as particularly deserving cases and told to head on to the British Army rest camp on the coast. 'The time is now 11.30, the following morning,' added Wharton, 'and we have just put in our first appearance of the day at the mess, having had a beautiful ten hours' sleep.' A cinema had been set up at the camp, as well as cricket and football grounds. He was just happy to be alive and to be able to walk peacefully along cliffs that just a few weeks earlier had been part of Hitler's Atlantic Wall defences. And the weather was, for once, fine and sunny. 'I just wish I was walking on this summer's day with you,' he added.

There was less opportunity to rest for Christopherson and Stephen Mitchell, however, who yet again had a raft of condolence letters to write, new replacement officers and men to welcome, and reports and conferences with those higher up the chain to attend about what lay next in store. A renewed effort to capture Caen was brewing, and there was to be a further thrust beyond the Odon to recapture Hill 112. It was always the high ground that had to be prised from the enemy – and that ground was always most fiercely defended.

Stephen Mitchell took the opportunity of the pause to write to Myrtle Kellett with the sad news of the latest round of casualties as well as a more lengthy report on the regiment's activities since all the way back in February – which Myrtle then used as the basis of the latest Regimental Welfare Association report, distributed to the wider families of those serving. 'Stan is doing very well as C.O.,' he told her. 'My one worry is that he will go swanning off to see various people, to do recces and all that sort of thing so that I never know where he is or what he's doing. But,' he added, 'he produces the goods.' He also wanted to make sure she had all the next-of-kin details for the many replacement officers and troopers who had reached the regiment since D-Day. 'The sun is shining at last today,' he wrote on 6 July, 'and we are drying out nicely. It does make such a difference altho' we cursed it in no uncertain terms in the Middle East.'

Among the officers now arriving was Micky Gold, who had managed to get his much desired release from the 23rd Hussars and returned to take command of B Squadron. Having just turned thirty-six, Gold was a little older than most of the Rangers, but still darkly handsome and the kind of bon viveur who had an uncanny knack of drawing people to him. He also had a well-earned reputation as a charismatic, cool-headed and unquestionably courageous commander from his time in North Africa, all of which made him an invaluable addition to both squadron and regiment.

The son of the eminent Olympic oarsman Sir Harcourt 'Tarka' Gold, the first person to be knighted for services to rowing, Gold was an Old Etonian who had known both Christopherson and Mitchell before the war, when, like Stanley, he'd been working in the City as a stockbroker. He had set off for Palestine with the Sherwood Rangers back in early 1940 with just three possessions: a battered copy of *Winnie the Pooh*, a Bible and his hunting horn, all of which had now followed him to Normandy. Along with self-confidence and a determination always to find whatever fun there was to be had, he also brought with him a welcome amount of valuable combat experience. On one occasion in Tunisia, he had had a gut feeling that he needed to move his troop in the middle of the night, which at the time had prompted much cursing; yet by morning, their original leaguer had been shelled and obliterated. A sixth sense like that was only developed by front-line experience.

Gold was thrilled to be back, although horrified by the losses, especially those of four pre-war veterans. Sergeants like Green, Digby, Biddell and Crookes were the backbone of the squadron. 'We were all close friends,' wrote Gold, 'a friendship proven of daily companionship, dangers shared, difficulties overcome.' They were irreplaceable – and yet they had to be replaced, and were. Corporals were promoted and new troopers filled the gaps. Within a matter of days the troop that had been wiped out had sprung up anew, as if by magic.

Another officer to arrive was Major Geoffrey Makins, a regular who had moved from the Royal Dragoons. Makins was an experienced officer, having served through much of the North African campaign and also in Sicily. He'd twice been wounded, had an MC to his name, and was by all accounts utterly charming: an inspiring and selfless young commander. It was for all these reasons that he'd been singled out to go to the Staff College, a sure sign of future promise. A car accident had delayed his completion of the course, but he had then been posted as a staff officer at Canadian Second Army Headquarters. He now needed some further experience as a squadron leader; clearly, he was being earmarked for command of a regiment of his own a little further down the line.

It was an army decision to post him to the Sherwood Rangers, and one in which Stanley Christopherson had absolutely no say, although frankly, they were lucky to get someone of his obvious experience and calibre. Micky Gold had returned on the same day and was senior in age and service to everyone else, so he could not be the one to make way, while Peter Selerie, at twenty-six, was also older and had served for longer than John Semken, who was still only twenty-three. Makins himself was twenty-eight. So, despite his superb leadership since taking over A Squadron, it was Semken who had to step aside for Makins. David Render, for one, was utterly shocked and horrified, but it was just the way things were and was absolutely no reflection on Semken – who reverted to the rank of captain and became squadron second-in-command.

While the Sherwood Rangers were out of the line, the Canadians and British made a further attempt to take the city of Caen. The attack was preceded by heavy RAF bombardment on the evening of 7 July, laying waste to the northern edge of the city where it was believed the enemy were dug in, a raid that was seen, albeit at a distance, by the Sherwood Rangers at Chouain. For Harry Heenan, who had survived his baptism of fire and who had now witnessed the brutality of war at first hand, the arrival of the heavy bombers was one of the best sights he'd seen in Normandy. After all, if they could smash the enemy, the Rangers in their tanks wouldn't have to. 'There was the effort against Villers Bocage and then last night a terrific do north of Caen,' he wrote in a letter home to his friend John. 'Someone suddenly notices these sods drifting in, and then everyone grabs their glasses – and we have super glasses on the tanks – and we just stand back and cheer.' He had watched the sky begin to be smudged by bursts of anti-aircraft fire and then in had come the Lancasters and Halifaxes, quite low, swerving and weaving. Overhead, large numbers of fighter aircraft were swirling about, protecting the bombers below them. 'The whole thing,' he added, 'is a superb spectacle.' The attack on Caen itself began the following day.

While they might have been spared that particular battle, they all knew they'd soon be heading back into action; relief at finding themselves out of the line was all too quickly replaced by the thought of future operations. It was a dull weight that bore down upon the crews once more. The situation might have been broadly good for the Allies in Normandy, but no one thought the Germans were remotely beaten yet; and although EPSOM and MARTLET had, in many ways, been a success, the stubborn refusal of the Germans to retreat in bounds as they had in North Africa and Italy showed that Normandy was going to be different – a bitter, bloody, grinding and attritional slog in which infantry and independent armoured brigades like the 8th would bear the brunt of the fighting. Bare statistics from the action to date suggested that the chances of any tank crewman getting through unscathed were very small indeed, and while new officers like David Render, Stuart Hills, Stan Perry and Harry Heenan had felt growing confidence in what they were doing, there was no question they faced appalling odds and diminishing returns. This was something every man, no matter what his role in the crew, had to reconcile himself with and try, as best he could, to put out of mind. It was not easy.

Harry Heenan managed to use the brief respite to attend Mass at a nearby church. His French was just about good enough, he wrote in a letter to his friend John, for him to ask, 'A quelle heure dit M. le Cure le Masse?' As he was leaving one particular service, a small French boy impulsively clutched his hand. 'I was most terribly affected,' wrote Heenan.

After a couple of days out of the line, Arthur Reddish and his mates heard rumours they would soon be back with the 50th Tyne Tees Division and the 231st Malta Brigade, with whom they had landed on D-Day. The rumours were well founded; Stanley Christopherson had been told this would be the case on 7 July when he had gone to visit the brigade. More planning conferences followed for what was being called Operation MAORI II, a thrust south-west from Tilly-sur-Seulles to the village of Hottot-les-Bagues. This was to support Operation JUPITER to regain Hill 112, so reluctantly relinquished at the end of the EPSOM operation, which would be launched hot on the heels of the assault on Caen. The attack on Hottot was also intended to continue the chewing up of the Panzer-Lehr, who were still holding the line south of Tilly. There was to be no relaxing of the pressure against the Germans: the British and Canadians were attacking in a series of thrusts along a 15-mile front.

All seven panzer divisions in Normandy were now ranged against the British and Canadians. Nowhere, anywhere in the war, was there such a density of German armour; and while Montgomery and Dempsey had considerably more artillery, as well as support from offshore warships and command of the skies, the opposition, under orders from Hitler not to cede a single yard, was still considerable. The series of thrusts now planned would lead to gains of a mile or two, nothing more; they were more reminiscent of the Western Front in the last war than the battle of manoeuvre that had been such a feature of the current conflict, and the XXX Corps drive to Hottot represented only a demoralizingly small bite southwards. 'Another conference at 231 Bde HQ,' wrote Terry Leinster in the regimental war diary on 8 July. The three squadrons were to support different battalions: A Squadron the Devons, B the Hampshires, C the 10th DLI of the 49th 'Polar Bears' Division – a different brigade and division altogether. After the conference, the squadron leaders were hustled off with their respective battalion commanders to look at the ground over which they would be attacking. 'The country is incredibly enclosed and difficult for tank manoeuvring and fighting,' Leinster added solemnly.

As part of the changes to the regiment, Doug Footitt had been promoted and given his own tank to command. Stuart Hills had also had a quiet word with Arthur Reddish and Sam Kirman, both of whom had more than enough experience to command. He wanted to recommend them both for promotion.

'Not for me, thanks,' Reddish told him. 'I'd prefer to be a member of a good crew than have a tank of my own.' Kirman said much the same. Both were all too well aware that their chances of survival would diminish exponentially the moment they took command of a tank; but more than that, Reddish felt he had found his niche as a co-driver and lap-gunner. Hills understood. 'We shook hands on it,' noted Reddish. Nor would Hills be with them for the coming battle; he had been told by Christopherson that he would be the liaison officer between the regiment and 50th Division. In part this was a rest for Hills, but it was also to give him a bit of broader experience and a chance to see things from the perspective of the infantry and at division level. In his place was the newly arrived Lieutenant Frank Galvin, along with Trooper Dickie Dexter as gunner.

'The awful day came,' wrote Reddish, 'and we were briefed for action.' Afterwards, he caught up with Doug Footitt, now commanding his own tank.

'I'm not looking forward to this lot, Red,' Footitt told him. Reddish shook his hand and wished him luck.

It was now 9 July 1944. The Sherwood Rangers had suffered eighty-eight casualties since D-Day, of which more than forty were dead. That represented almost two-fifths of the men serving in the regiment's tanks. In just over a month.

CHAPTER 13

Exhaustion

E ARLY MORNING, TUESDAY, 11 July 1944. As the sun rose, the men of the Sherwood Rangers were met with a vision of endless shades of green. Here was a rolling landscape of lush pasture and innumerable orchards, lined with thick, fecund hedgerows, not yet obviously past their midsummer best. And woods. Normandy was ripe with woodland. The intricate web of roads, most lacking tarmac and made instead of grit and earth, wound their way across this landscape, linking *manoir* to hamlet, hamlet to village, village to town. Some, dead straight, had been originally laid out by the Romans; others wound their way along natural folds in the land or along the numerous rivers and streams.

At first glance, this pastoral scene was as beautiful as ever; yet scrutinized from the air or through binoculars, the mortal hurt already rained down upon this formerly quiet corner of France was plain to see. Tank tracks, and truck and jeep tyre marks, now scored the fields, so that from above it seemed the countryside had been overrun by traffic. Rural farmland that had been crossed for millennia by little more than horse, cart and the two feet given to man had suddenly been flooded by machinery, belching exhaust and smoke and firing hot missiles of destruction. Tanks were there in Normandy to destroy and to help preserve the young lives of the forward troops; buildings, whether humble or sacred, found to be in the path of this typhoon of steel, or to be sheltering enemy observers and snipers, were pulverized, sometimes with regret but usually without remorse.

Yet the most damage was caused by aerial bombardment and by artillery. The village of Tilly-sur-Seulles, which a month before had been a thriving place largely untroubled for centuries, now had just one house still standing intact. Hottot-les-Bagues, the objective for MAORI II, had been similarly untouched but now lay absolutely shattered, its houses broken and crushed, a place of rubble, dust and shattered glass. All around these villages, those otherwise lush pastures and orchards were scarred by a staggering number of shell craters, the orchards marked by blasted trees. Not a single field between Tilly and Hottot had escaped, and in the orchards and meadows there was also death. Dead cows, dead soldiers, and the air ripe with their pungent decay.

That month of fighting had seen the 50th Tyne Tees Division caught up in a bitter battle of attrition with the Panzer-Lehr in which the front line had barely shifted. By the second week of July, however, the German division had been moved to the west of Saint-Lô, where they now faced the Americans. In their place were the 276. Infanterie-Division, who had finally made it to Normandy from the south of France, and while they were not in the same league of combat effectiveness as the Panzer-Lehr, they were at least fresh. What's more, on their flank was 2. Panzer-Division. At Hottot, meanwhile, patrols had identified the enemy as the II. Bataillon, 986. Regiment, supported by panzers camouflaged and dug in at Le Cordillon, a manor house surrounded by a sizeable wood – renamed 'Hammer Wood' after its shape – just to the west of the village.

From their orchard near Chouain, the Sherwood Rangers had moved a mile or so west to Folliot the previous day, 10 July. As usual at the front, they were up at 4.30 a.m. and moved out a little over an hour later. Up to the start line, a mark of coloured crayon drawn on the map. Artillery a mile or so further back, mortar teams dug in along hedgerows and the heavy Vickers machine guns of the Cheshire Battalion dug in among the pastures at the flanks of the attack. At 6.45 a.m., the infantry ready, the Hampshires in the lead, B Squadron of the SRY poised alongside, engines ticking over. Devons and A Squadron alongside on their left – and on *their* left, 10th DLI of 70th Brigade, to which C Squadron were attached. Quiet, pre-battle calm.

Seven o'clock. A deafening roar as the artillery opened fire, along with the crackle of Vickers machine guns and the whine of mortars. The ground shaking, Hottot and the surrounding fields, woods and orchards disappearing behind thick smoke as explosion after explosion rippled over this blighted countryside. Now counter-battery fire coming back from the German gunners. Shells hurtling both ways; incoming shells sound different from outgoing. Inside the tanks, the usual giddy sense of disorientation – the narrow prism of visibility, the smoke, the noise, and the calm, methodical voice of the squadron leaders over the net. A battering of the senses, and the stench of smoke, exhaust, oil, rubber, sweat. And that pungent odour of death. Ahead of them, engineers, some on foot, some in AVREs, blasting holes through the hedgerows to let the tanks through, infantry moving forward like spectres through the smoke. And the continual din of guns and explosions.

The advance behind the barrage, then the moment when it lifts; the whizz and whine of mortars, the fizz and *brrrp* of machine guns. Infantry and tanks pressing on, clearing one hedgerow after another, but slowly, field by field, orchard by orchard. Phase 1 of the advance achieved by 9.30 a.m. Then the inevitable counter-attack. Always. Panzers appearing a little after 11 a.m. By 1.15 p.m., four enemy tanks reported as knocked out in Hammer Wood.

David Render remained in the turret, his tin helmet fixed more obviously outside; it was a trick he had been determined to continue employing ever since Neville Fearn had told him about it. The ground sloped up towards Hottot, a tricksy patchwork of fields. Geoffrey Makins might be their squadron leader now, but the influence of John Semken was very much with them as they used four-tank troops for the first time with the addition of one of the squadron's Fireflies. Lance-Corporal James Redfern was commanding the Firefly in Render's troop, and as a squadron they'd agreed that the three Shermans would lead up to the hedgerows with the Firefly operating off to the flank. 'With that bloody great barrel,' said Render, 'it was no good for manoeuvring in that God-awful close country.' Instead, they would make sure it was there, on standby, if they suddenly found themselves confronted by an enemy panzer. 'Redfern's job,' noted Render, 'was to hit it and destroy it with his 17-pounder.' At the close ranges of the fighting in Normandy, the high-velocity 17-pounder could penetrate most enemy armour.

Render reckoned the tactics worked well that day during the fighting for Hottot. As always, Corporal Johnny Lanes was there, right alongside him, but Sergeant Jackson was hanging back. 'He was windy,' said Render, 'and so I had to lead my troop, wherever we went.' In all, the regiment knocked out seven tanks that day, of which A Squadron claimed four, but by five o'clock, although the enemy counter-attack had been stopped dead, their own advance had also run out of steam at the second objective.

Unbeknown to the tank men, the infantry had asked their forward observation officer to call in some close air support. Not long after, rocket-firing Typhoons had roared in and dived down on them, mistaking their Shermans for enemy panzers. Render barely had time to shout a warning and half-close his own hatches before two rockets exploded either side of him, showering his tank with shrapnel. Three more Typhoons dived on them and although no tank was knocked out, a number were hit by the blast. Dickie Holman, who had just turned twenty-one, had all his presents wrapped in a tarpaulin on the back and all were shredded by shrapnel from the attack. 'It was a horrible experience,' wrote Harry Heenan. 'They are a terrifying weapon. I have a piece of shrapnel that exploded about a foot from my head.'

By evening, they were still a little way short of the imaginary line south of Hottot they had hoped to reach. The Devons had lost ten dead in the fighting and fifty-six wounded – a quarter of their two attacking companies. The Hampshires lost their CO, Colonel Howie, killed, and C Company alone suffered 53 casualties – almost half their number.

To the right of the advance, C Squadron had spent much of the day on the start line alongside the Durhams, waiting to be given the order to move. Their objective was a line south of the Roman road between Hottot and Juvigny, but they were not to start until the Malta Brigade had completed the first two phases of the planned attack. Because of the heavy opposition around the village, it wasn't until 4.30 p.m. that they finally got going. Almost immediately, Arthur Reddish saw one man get hit and fall just in front of his tank. He lay there on the ground, smoke coming from his back where white-hot shards of mortar shrapnel had struck him. Reddish opened up with his Browning, spraying a hedgerow ahead of them. An enemy MG replied, but then fell silent. Now they were nearing the road, a farmhouse up ahead, and, some 200 yards or so beyond it on their right, a thick wood. A Crocodile – a flame-throwing Churchill tank – now appeared on their flank as they neared the farmhouse. Reddish had not seen one in action before and was startled by the scale of the 100-yard-long sheet of vivid flame that spat from it, dousing the farm and setting the second floor ablaze. Then he saw movement through the trees beyond and, to his horror, realized it was a horse tethered. Another jet of flame hit the horse, enveloping it in flames. It struggled, then fell. 'The entire scene,' wrote Reddish, 'was sickening to watch.' Beyond the wood the land sloped quite sharply, and the bright flames and ensuing smoke became a magnet for enemy mortars, which began falling in a cluster around them, smashing their periscopes. Lieutenant Galvin moved the troop back, then to one side, then forwards again, continually shifting them away from the mortar concentrations. The infantry began hurriedly digging in along the hedgerows.

It had been another tough day for the regiment. Ronnie Grellis, who had single-handedly captured a trench of SS men at Rauray, had part of his jaw shot away by a sniper. Geoffrey Makins, Semken's replacement, was badly wounded in the stomach and face while out of his tank – another victim of mortar shrapnel – in his first action with the regiment. Mike Howden was also wounded in the head, although not too seriously. A further eight others were wounded, and another tank commander killed – Doug Footitt. Stuart Hills's crew, Arthur Reddish included, were distraught at his loss. 'It was really very sad,' Hills wrote in a letter to his parents, 'as we had become good pals and somehow he was not at all happy when he left my crew to command a tank of his own.'

That night, the Devons pleaded with A Squadron to remain with them, so two troops, David Render's included, stayed forward through the hours of darkness. It was something they all hated, as it meant almost no sleep – someone had to be on prowler guard at all times – and this after the usual night-time maintenance routine: refuelling, rearming, cleaning the gun and the Brownings, checking the tracks, topping up the engine oil, getting something to eat and trying to calm down after a day of near-constant adrenalin-charged tension.

The following day, Wednesday, 12 July, the attack continued, and finally A and B Squadrons climbed up the ridge and took Hottot – or, rather, the rubble that was all that remained of it. Later in the day, both were pulled back to Chouain while C Squadron remained a second night with the infantry, during which they opened fire on a German patrol; several enemy dead were discovered the following morning. They, too, were pulled out later that afternoon. 'Hottot,' wrote Harry Heenan, 'was one of those nasty little two-day affairs with limited objectives.' Such was the battle of attrition in Normandy.

The regiment remained based in Chouain until 17 July. They had now lost forty tank commanders since D-Day, more than two squadrons' worth, and six at Hottot alone. Immediately, though, Stanley Christopherson was whisked off to Brigade HQ on 13 July for a commanders' conference to discuss – yet again – armour–infantry cooperation, which continued to be problematic. None the less, reports from 231st and 70th Brigades had been hugely appreciative. 'Both these brigades,' noted

Christopherson proudly, 'stated quite firmly that the 8th Armoured Brigade and especially the Sherwood Rangers, had given them better support than other armour with which they had fought.'

The issue now was how to transport infantry right up to the firing line alongside the armour. Britain had plenty of tracked universal carriers and also US-built half-tracks, but these didn't have much protection and would necessarily have to be abandoned at some point and hidden out of the way while the men proceeded on foot, so were not an ideal solution. So discussions began about whether the tanks should start carrying the leading infantry platoons into battle. It wasn't particularly safe cramming lots of infantry on the outside of a tank – but then again, going into battle was inherently dangerous, so that was hardly an argument against, and they would obviously get down the moment the firing started. It would mean, however, that in future the infantry would at least pass the start line and move in to attack with the armour.

There was no getting round the fragility of the human body, and men could not be blamed for hitting the ground once enemy mortars, artillery and machine guns opened up. Furthermore, any battle was incredibly messy and confusing. Artillery was the chief cause of the fog of war, but the British also tended to create a lot of smoke deliberately, firing smoke shells to mask their advance, and effectively too – although never effectively enough for those doing the attacking. Smoke did tend to subdue SPs and panzers, however, which were understandably reluctant to stray too far when they could see nothing. Like everything in battle, though, the advantages of lots of smoke came with disadvantages, too – chiefly the loss of visibility to one's own side as well as the enemy.

The next day, Friday, 14 July, Christopherson held a squadron leaders' conference of his own, at which the acting 8th Armoured commander, Colonel Tony Wingfield, also looked in. Gathered around Christopherson in his orchard RHQ were the young men with the responsibility of finding the most effective way to operate in this markedly different theatre of war – including John Semken, swiftly reinstated as commander of A Squadron. As Christopherson had concluded back during their early days in tanks in North Africa, the best chances of survival were to be found in getting smart and really thinking through and analysing what was happening to them. This was exactly the spirit he was fostering within the regiment now – one where ideas and opinions were listened to and, if valid, acted upon, and swiftly. For nearly six weeks they had been operating on the hoof, without more than a couple of days' break at any one time, but Colonel Wingfield had assured him the regiment would now be given a decent rest. None the less, already a raft of new tactics had begun to be adopted. Semken's suggestion of spreading the Fireflies among the troops was now agreed upon; in fact, other armoured regiments were concurrently drawing the same conclusions.

There were still some concerns about the Sherman. 'The high silhouette,' said Peter Selerie, 'was a very great disadvantage. The German tanks with their low silhouette didn't stand out like a sore thumb in the way that the Sherman did.' Selerie was not entirely correct about that. The Panzer IV was only two inches lower than the Sherman, and Tigers and Panthers were significantly taller: only the StuG self-propelled gun had a substantially lower profile. Undeniably, though, the Sherman had a very distinct profile and was also 10 inches higher off the ground than either the British Cromwell or the Churchill. Very often perceptions were more important than reality, and Selerie was no doubt reflecting a consensus view.

All recognized, however, that the Sherman's 75mm did have some important advantages, despite an inferior velocity compared with the Firefly gun, or those of the German Panther and Tiger. Not only was the gun-stabilizing gyro an excellent addition, its rate of fire was exceptional. The crews also began to really rate the HE rounds. 'It was a marvellous thing,' said Semken. 'You could put a round through each window and one through the roof and you could knock the ceiling down, you could set the whole place on fire.' This was very useful when dealing with snipers, OPs and machine-gun nests. They had also learned that it was possible to adjust the fuse to give the explosive charge a very slight delay. 'The result,' said Semken, 'was that if you hit a wall, it would enter before it exploded. You really could have a wonderful time with high explosives from the 75mm.'

Furthermore, the Sherman was extremely manoeuvrable, and so long as a troop worked together and saw an enemy panzer before it saw them, the chances were it could best the enemy tank. The key, they had realized, was to pummel the panzer with three or four rapidly fired rounds from each tank. 'Which is very discouraging to him,' said John Semken, 'because you'd be surprised but as soon as someone is hit, never mind if they're not penetrated, they stop shooting.' This was not least because the enemy would be covered in smoke, and the sound of the striking shells would terrify the enemy crew and force them to close their hatches. After these few rounds, the Shermans would hurriedly change position and repeat. So far in the campaign, more often than not the German crew, ears ringing from the intense noise of being repeatedly hit and having suffered some kind of damage to their panzer, would bail out. Now, though, the Sherwood Rangers troop leaders each had a Firefly they could call upon. One shot from the 17-pounder tended to do the trick. And using the 17-pounder also had an important psychological effect; it told the enemy that the British now had a tank armed with a big, powerful, high-velocity gun.

Even so, tank-on-tank action was still comparatively rare. A greater danger came from hidden anti-tank guns, panzerfausts and even snipers. On pulling out of Hottot, David Render had discovered two neat bullet holes in his helmet fixed to the turret. It was a sniper who had shot away half of Ronnie Grellis's jaw; and a sniper who had killed Laurence Verner. And these threats led directly to the issue of exhaustion.

A lot was expected of all these young men, but especially of the tank commanders and the troop and squadron leaders. 'The driver suffers the greatest physical strain,' noted one report, 'but the tank commander is subject to the greatest nervous strain resulting from constant tension, especially in combat.' Absolutely. Sticking the most vulnerable part of one's body above the protection of the steel hull and concentrating, concentrating, concentrating constantly, was utterly exhausting, mentally and physically. Tanks were designed to bring a degree of flexible firepower and crew protection to the battlefield, yet the needs of the crew manning them had not yet caught up with the technology – except, perhaps, for a padded seat and head rest above the optics.

Visibility was always a problem in a tank, yet poor visibility was the price paid for the strength of its defences. Dust, grit and mud continually got in the eyes and at the back of the throat. When it was dry, the amount of dust whipped up was extraordinary. You really needed goggles, but these were never quite good enough, and although essential for the driver and lap-gunner if their heads were out of the hatches, commanders rarely used them. And when it was wet, the dust would turn into mud and grit, all of which got spat up at the crew.

Then there were the fumes. The noxious smoke and exhaust produced by the tank were fairly effectively sucked out of the turret and hull, but still repeatedly swirled around the inside, where, like the dust, they got into the back of the throat and the lungs. On a warm day it would also be blisteringly hot inside, the sun and the heat from the guns baking the steel like an oven. An American report recommended ten hours as the absolute maximum a crew should spend in a tank, but many days in combat were inevitably much longer than that – especially in summer, when the hours of daylight were at their greatest. At the front, most crews in the Sherwood Rangers were doing well to get four hours' sleep in twenty-four.

Up at 4 a.m., or a little after. A mug of tea, some breakfast. Make sure the tank is ready. Stow personal kit away. Wait to move. Into action at, say, 6 a.m., maybe 7. Then in combat all day. Of course, there were always lulls – but for the tank commander, especially, there was little respite. A tank with hatches down was a blind beast, and it was more dangerous to be blind than for the commander to have his head out of the turret. Yet the commander had to be alert all the time. Watching, directing, giving orders and listening to others on the net at the same time, alert to the faintest movement ahead and on his flanks. Decisions had to be made constantly. And that was just the tank commander; for the troop leader, and especially for the squadron leader, it was much worse. So much responsibility rested on their young shoulders. A moment's lapse in con-centration, a moment when they stopped looking, or failed to process information correctly – that moment could be the difference between their men living and dying. 'The tank commander spends at least twelve hours a day standing,' said John Semken. 'It really is exhausting.' As dusk fell, they would usually – but not always – be pulled back. On alert until dark. Then O groups for the tank commanders and maintenance tasks for the crew. Some supper. A tarpaulin pulled out from the side of the tank, bedroll out. Fully clothed. Filthy, smelly. Sleep at midnight, maybe 1 a.m. Then repeat. And all the time men were being wounded and killed, the troops and squadrons shifting in shape like desert sands. That, too, played on the nerves, as did the sheer fear of upcoming action. One tried not to think too hard about it, but it was difficult not to.

Stan Perry quickly imposed a strict new rule in his troop. 'As soon as the troop moved off,' he said, 'I would call a halt and dismount. And I expected my tank crew and my troop tanks to bale out immediately, no matter where they were or what the ground was like.' He believed it was an important and potentially life-saving exercise. If hit, they had perhaps twenty or thirty seconds to get out before the tank brewed up. 'And I thought it was important we had routines and quick reactions. You didn't mess about.' He developed a system whereby the gunner would put his shoulders under the tank commander's backside and give him a shove to hurry him out of the turret, then the operator got his shoulders under the gunner and pushed him up, and finally the gunner reached down and pulled up the operator. 'So we went out in a quick stream.' The driver and lap-gunner would similarly practise getting out of their hatches. A drill practised repeatedly could be carried out even in the panic of a flaming tank. That was Perry's hope, at any rate.

Yet more officers and troopers arrived. Slight anxiety followed the arrival of new subalterns. Most were incredibly young and not all had even trained on Shermans. Much of what they had been taught in their officer training had to be unlearned because it was not applicable to the rapidly changing tactics needed in Normandy. Christopherson and Mitchell, and their squadron leaders, had to hope the new boys could learn quickly and that they were not too wet behind the ears. David Render, all at sea when he'd first arrived, had managed to wise up very swiftly and was already an old hand. He felt Sergeant Jackson was still reluctant to put his head above the parapet, but Render had got the measure of his own crew, whose bolshy insubordination had long since disappeared. Stan Perry had never had such problems. With the new arrivals, it really was a question of pot luck whether they would cut the mustard or not. If they didn't, the chances were they wouldn't last long.

Christopherson also set up a cadre class for potential NCOs in an effort to get more troopers to step up to becoming potential tank commanders. New replacement tanks also arrived from the FDS, and repaired tanks were brought back into the ranks. Tanks were still being named, now beginning with a letter that corresponded to the squadron to which they belonged. Harry Heenan's was called *Alpha*; Stan Perry had inherited *Caligula*. 'There was a bit of a classical theme going on,' he said. 'I suppose from one of the better-read senior officers.' Perry had been very tickled by the name of George Dring's tank, now the most celebrated in the regiment, let alone A Squadron. The idea of naming tanks using the first letter of the relevant squadron had been introduced by Lieutenant-Colonel D'Arcy Anderson; apparently, Dring had not known what to call his tank and so Stanley Christopherson, then his squadron leader, had suggested 'Achilles' after the mythical Greek hero and warrior. 'George had never heard of Achilles,' said Perry, 'but accepted the suggestion from his superior officer and had it painted on as he thought it should be spelled. And so it was called "Akilla".' Somehow, that seemed more appropriate.

*

In the early hours of 16 July, two random enemy shells hit the Rangers' leaguer at Chouain, landing near A and B Squadrons. Bill Wharton was woken by the first explosion – as indeed they all were – and then heard Trooper Morris, the operator in his crew, calling out and telling them he was going to take cover in their tank. Suddenly another shell screamed in. 'No matter how much I tell these boys to stay put until a lull,' wrote Wharton, 'always the odd one loses his nerve and all too often becomes a casualty. He was hit in both legs, the Achilles tendon severed in each case.' Wharton hurriedly bandaged up Morris, reassuring him he had got a good 'Blighty' wound – one that would send him home – and then looked around for other casualties. He soon discovered Sergeant Bert Hardy, who had been on leave for a fortnight and had just returned that day. A big piece of shrapnel had torn open his back and one look was enough for Wharton to realize the poor fellow was not going to pull through. And so it proved. Wharton helped stretcher the wounded to the MDS – main dressing station – but Hardy died a couple of hours later. Micky Gold had lost his fourth troop sergeant that month.

That same morning Wharton went with Gold to an open-air church service at Second Army HQ and was thrilled to be standing within spitting distance of General Montgomery himself. Afterwards, Gold whisked him off to Bayeux. The city was one of the few centres in Normandy that had largely avoided serious damage, and was bursting with liberated life once more. Gold took Wharton to meet his latest girlfriend, who lived with her parents in a street near the centre. They were welcomed in and sat in a lovely garden surrounded by high stone walls, drinking coffee and tots of rum. The garden was also abundant in strawberries, gooseberries and redcurrants, to which Wharton was encouraged to help himself. After a while they went off to lunch at a bar in the town where all the war correspondents liked to congregate. Gold was in his element, introducing Wharton to Bob Cooper of *The Times*, charming the waitresses and showering attention on his French girlfriend, who was only twenty years old and engaged to a schoolteacher. 'But M is trying to talk her out of it,' Wharton wrote to his wife, 'the rogue.'

After such an awful start to the day, Wharton had thoroughly enjoyed the rest of it. He'd even had a couple of hours' late siesta and had woken to discover the NAAFI supplies had arrived and been passed around. The NAAFI – Navy, Army and Air Force Institutes, pronounced 'Naffy' – had been set up back in 1920 to provide recreational supplies to the British armed forces but had really come into its own during the current war, providing canteens and bars for the troops, and selling various home comforts at knock-down prices. Wharton received a bottle of English beer, seventy cigarettes, a bar of soap and a new razor blade. 'I feel like a millionaire!' he told his wife.

Their official time of rest and recuperation was over the following day, however, with a move to Caumont in the centre of the Allied line. This was 12 miles from Chouain and had been captured early in the campaign by the US 1st Infantry Division and held by them ever since. Harry Heenan, for one, enjoyed the journey, and seeing the entire regiment lined up on the move, a column over a mile long, roaring along the lanes of Normandy. 'And all the people and lesser mortals such as artillery and infantry turn out to wave you on,' he wrote in a letter to his parents. 'Everyone is stacked up with ammo and all the worldly possessions of the crew are piled on the back.'

At Caumont they took over the positions of the 2nd Battalion of the US 67th Armored Regiment, commanded by Colonel J. Davis Wynne, who, on meeting Stanley Christopherson, immediately recognized the Sherwood Rangers' shoulder flash and shook his hand warmly. It turned out he'd been their instructor for the American M3 Stuart tank – the 'Honey' – in Palestine when the regiment had become mechanized more than two years earlier.

They had moved because both the British and the Americans were preparing for major offensives. The Americans had not only cleared the entire Cotentin peninsula but had almost captured Saint-Lô too. General Omar Bradley, commander of the US First Army, was preparing to launch a major offensive from the north-west of Saint-Lô, code-named COBRA and scheduled to launch on 24 July. In the meantime, on 18 July, General Dempsey's Second Army launched Operation GOODWOOD to the east of Caen, which was preceded by heavy RAF bombing of the German positions on the Bourguébus ridge to the south-east of the city. By this time, Hill 112 had also been recaptured and British forces were continuing to push the front to the south-west of Caen. It was hoped – or rather, expected – that either GOODWOOD or COBRA would see the German line crack at long last. And by now, with V-1 flying bombs raining down on London and the Soviets making great strides on the Eastern Front, there was considerable political pressure on Montgomery to break out of Normandy quickly.

The Sherwood Rangers would be in action again before long, but for the time being they had no direct part in either operation. Instead, their role was to hold the line and support the infantry who were a mile or so south of Caumont, facing the 2. Panzer-Division and dug in around a big wood called the Bois de Buissard. This lay south-west of the road from Caumont halfway to the small town of Cahagnes, still firmly held by the enemy. On their second day at Caumont, Christopherson received a request from the infantry for a squadron of tanks – 'to give it moral support, as it was felt rather lonely in the wood,' he noted, 'to which I had to agree'.

He decided the squadrons should toss for it. Micky Gold appointed Bill Wharton as his coin caller. Wharton was feeling rather pleased with himself as he'd just been promoted to acting captain, but called poorly and so it was B Squadron who had to pack up and head down to the woods. Gold was not overly pleased, not least because he'd already found a delightful farmhouse in which to base squadron HQ. 'However, in position,' wrote Wharton, 'he has again found himself a farm building and is enjoying home comforts once more.' On their first night, Gold, Wharton and Colin Thomson sat up with an old gramophone playing and a bottle each of whisky and gin. The MO, 'Hylda' Young, and Stanley Christopherson both dropped by and shared a drink or two. Micky Gold had an extraordinary gift for making the absolute best of any situation in which he found himself.

The following day, Wharton found time to write to his wife. 'Yesterday was a sunny day, which made me think of summer back home with you,' he wrote. 'Do you realise, my dear, that our last summer together was 1939! We married, I haven't played tennis since then, haven't seen you in shorts, we haven't swum or sunbathed together or picked strawberries. What a lot we have to make up for, darling.'

What a long war it had been already.

CHAPTER 14

Back into Action

O N 17 JULY, FELDMARSCHALL Erwin Rommel, the German commander in Normandy, had been severely wounded when his car
was shot up by Spitfires, and three days later an assassination attempt on
Hitler was made at his east Prussian headquarters. Both events had a direct effect on the German defence of Normandy: the loss of Rommel
brought in a new commander at a critical moment, while the Führer's
anger and increased paranoia following his survival meant German commanders were even less likely than before to question his decisions and
orders. Although German forces in Normandy were close to breaking
point and badly needed to pull back, buy some time and reorganize
themselves, Hitler would countenance no such move. They were to continue to fight for every yard, and to the last man if necessary.

Meanwhile, the Allies continued to do all they could to smash the German defences and create a decisive breakthrough. The next operation for
the British was GOODWOOD, launched on 18 July. Over the next five
days, in the largest single armoured thrust the British had yet attempted
in the war, they managed to push the Germans back 7 miles, badly
chewed up yet more enemy troops, and enabled Montgomery to get British and Canadian troops on to the key Bourguébus ridge, a particularly
valuable bit of high land to the south-east of Caen. GOODWOOD didn't
bring about the dramatic breakthrough that Eisenhower had hoped for,
but it had kept most of the panzer divisions in the British and Canadian
half of the front, and that augured well for the big American assault,
Operation COBRA, due to launch on 24 July. In the meantime, Saint-Lô
had finally fallen to General Bradley's men on the 19th, and preparations

for the biggest US operation of the campaign so far were going well, despite the return of poor weather, with what to those on the ground felt like biblical levels of rain.

Such downpours were just about the only thing troubling the Sherwood Rangers, who were experiencing the quietest section of the entire front. 'A quiet day,' wrote Terry Leinster on 20 July. 'The country is very pleasant and the farms practically undamaged. It is hard to believe, even in the area of B Squadron, which is forward, that the German line is so close.' The 12th KRRC – the King's Royal Rifle Corps, attached to 8th Armoured Brigade – were sending out night patrols, and the Essex Yeomanry were occasionally shooting at enemy guns and mortar positions, but that was about the limit of the action. 'I have my ears cocked,' wrote Bill Wharton, 'for that peculiar sound which I have learned to pick out as being a near one. The enemy does this sort of thing throughout the day and sometimes night, firing a few rounds at a time so as not to give away his own position and generally making a nuisance of himself.' Nothing landed close enough to cause B Squadron any damage, although early on the 22nd six shells landed in the B3 Echelon area. But German artillery was learning that whatever they sent over, the Allied gunners would reply with considerably more. In a quiet sector such as this around Caumont, neither side showed much inclination to rock the status quo.

Stephen Mitchell was happy to report to Myrtle Kellett back home in England that the men had inherited a number of American foxholes and slit-trenches, which they had since enlarged and in which most were sleeping by night – having driven their tanks over them first for extra protection. If the odd enemy shell whistled over, they barely batted an eyelid. The men, he reported, had also made friends with the local farmers, and there wasn't a crew who hadn't supplemented their rations handsomely with eggs, meat, fresh butter and milk. They'd also been sending men away to the nearest bath unit, usually set up in fields, but first the dust and then the mud had been so bad that they were coming back every bit as filthy as when they'd left.

Arthur Reddish was certainly enjoying the respite. He'd caught up with an old friend from home who was in the 15th Scottish Division, which had moved up on their right – and, with his squadron pal Busty Meek, had made friends with a local French family. He and Meek had been ambling through a hamlet near Caumont when a young girl had come out and offered them both glasses of cider. Her father then invited them inside and gave them calvados, the local apple brandy. Both Reddish and Meek were touched by the family's kindness and charmed by the girl, so when she asked if she could see their tanks, they readily agreed. 'She was a beautiful little lass,' noted Reddish, 'and the crews just loved her.' Reddish had been struck by the obvious poverty of the family and so had organized a whip-round for some spare rations. He and Busty had soon gathered a sack of tinned food which they took back to the girl's parents. When they handed them over, the little girl's mother burst into tears.

Later, the two men were invited to supper. For both of them, the chance to get away from their tanks and from living in a hole in the ground and, for just a few hours, to experience something close to domestic normality really lifted their spirits. Afterwards, the girl drew back a curtain in the corner of the room revealing a Calvary scene, with Christ on the cross. Solemnly, she knelt and prayed for them, then gave them each a religious token. Reddish placed his underneath the field dressing he always carried, and vowed to himself he would keep it there for as long as he remained in the army.

B Squadron stayed up with the infantry near their wood on the road to Cahagnes. Bill Wharton was still thrilled about his promotion and glad that so many NCOs, of which he had once been one, had congratulated him and appeared genuinely pleased for him. His advancement meant a social lift, too, and he was now enjoying the evening tête-à-têtes at Micky Gold's farmhouse HQ. Gold had brought a number of home comforts to their new digs, adding an array of cases and a tin trunk, as well as his slippers, scarlet pyjamas, aftershave and other creature comforts. He had also managed to get hold of Trooper Arthur Leadbetter, Donny Player's former batman – an officer's soldier-servant. Player had been at the beating heart of the pre-war and desert war regiment, and had taken over as CO from Flash Kellett towards the back end of 1942. His family, who owned the Players tobacco company, were fabulously well off, and so when Donny had gone to war he had taken his valet, Leadbetter, with him for the ride. Player had been killed in April 1943, towards the end of the Tunisian campaign, but Leadbetter had survived and remained with the regiment. Now Gold had nabbed the former valet for himself. 'This chap looks after him like a mother!' wrote Wharton. 'He reclines on his bed while Arthur plays the gramophone and Colin and I do the work.' He often wondered why he liked Micky so much – but of course, it was because Gold was a bon viveur and enormously good fun to be around. And there was no denying that Gold did have style.

They were drinking every night and eating royally well, the rations

liberally bolstered with local food bartered from the farmers. Occasionally, a few shells would scream over, but otherwise not much was
happening. 'Another quiet day,' recorded Terry Leinster on 21 July.
'Another very quiet day,' he wrote on the 24th, and a day later, 'No activity
other than intermittent shell and small arms fire from both sides.' No one
in the Sherwood Rangers was complaining.

Meanwhile, in London, Myrtle Kellett continued to oversee the Regimental Welfare Association with vigour. V-1 flying bombs – 'doodlebugs'
as they were known – were by now falling regularly on London, although
Myrtle refused to be cowed by these latest attacks and absolutely forbade
her only child, Diana, either to fall flat on the ground should they hear
the engine of a doodlebug cut out, or even to run to a shelter. 'People like
us don't,' she told her firmly.

Undaunted, Myrtle remained in London, living at Gloucester Place
after the home she had bought with Flash, near Paddington, had first
been commandeered by the War Office and then flattened by the Luftwaffe during the Blitz. It was at Gloucester Place that Captain Leslie
Skinner, now recovered, visited her on 20 July. Despite regular letters
from Stephen Mitchell and even Stanley Christopherson, she was keen to
hear from him all that the regiment had been up to. They also talked
about the casualties so far, including the circumstances in which they
had happened, and she made Skinner promise to keep her as well
informed as possible in the future.

The following day, Skinner headed to Chippenham Park outside Newmarket in Cambridgeshire, as per his orders. The SRY had been based
here earlier in the year on their return to England; on his arrival now, he
discovered no fewer than seven padres already waiting to be posted. It
was by no means guaranteed that he would be sent straight back to the
Sherwood Rangers; but he managed to persuade the commanding officer
there that the regiment was waiting for him in Normandy and that he
needed to get back immediately. 'He knew I was pulling a fast one,' noted
Skinner, 'but agreed to send me on the Transit Unit for Armoured Corps
troops at Lewes in Sussex on the south coast, though he pointed out he
could give me no authority but he was prepared to give me a warrant.'
Skinner duly made his way to Lewes, taking off his RAChD – Royal Army
Chaplains' Department – shoulder flash and becoming instead plain
'Captain Skinner' of the Sherwood Rangers Yeomanry and 8th Armoured
Brigade. Much to his relief, the ruse worked; no one batted an eye.

On 24 July, he landed at Arromanches and came ashore from the Mulberry harbour. After a fair amount of fruitless travel, frustrating delays in various holding units and an FDS, he eventually arrived at B3 echelon late on the 25th. The rest of the regiment, Roger Sutton-Nelthorpe told him, was 5 miles up the road. Early the next morning, 26 July, he managed to borrow a motorcycle and headed up to the B1 echelon, where he was delighted to catch up with his old friend Dr 'Hylda' Young. Pleased though he was to see Young and the CO and other old friends, there was more sombre news waiting for him too. 'Long list of casualties in my absence,' he noted, 'with numerous burial details etc to check.' While he'd been away there had been 93 casualties in all, including 22 killed in action, a further six who had died of wounds and five missing.

By this time, Operation COBRA had been launched, although only the day before, on 25 July – bad weather had prompted General Bradley to call a day's postponement. Initially, it looked like COBRA had failed to deliver the intended knock-out blow, despite 72,000 bombs being dropped on the Panzer-Lehr and despite the enormous build-up of American forces. As the day progressed, however, it gradually became clear that the combination of American artillery, infantry mounted on tanks and other armoured fighting vehicles, and rampaging fighter-bombers providing coordinated close air support via direct VHF radio link to the ground was proving too much for the crippled German forces. By the following morning, 27 July, the Germans were in full retreat in the US half of the line, the air forces were having a field day as suddenly the enemy were being caught out in the open during daylight hours, and the armour and infantry were surging south in pursuit. After long weeks of grinding attrition, the breakthrough had finally happened. The endgame in Normandy had begun.

That same day, 27 July, acting on a plan put to him by General Dempsey, Montgomery issued a new directive for a major drive south from Caumont – exactly where the Sherwood Rangers were based and unquestionably the quietest part of the entire front since the invasion. There was certainly an argument for continuing to push due south from Bourguébus ridge south-east of Caen, taken during GOODWOOD, as from that stretch of high ground the old Roman road ran straight to Falaise; another strong thrust there might fold up the Germans in a massive pocket. On the other hand, a major drive south from Caumont also had plenty in its favour and would enable the British and Americans, side by side, to swing south and then east in a giant sweep, which would break the hinge of the German line in the west. What's more, it would give the Canadians, still in the Caen area, a greater chance to recover from their recent efforts before being flung into another major action.

This new plan was to be called Operation BLUECOAT, and would be given to XXX Corps on the right and VIII Corps – which had been involved in both EPSOM and GOODWOOD – on the left. Although the Sherwood Rangers had fought mostly in the *bocage*, most of Second Army had so far been fighting over the wider, more open landscape immediately around Caen. BLUECOAT, however, would see two separate thrusts driving south through rolling hills and the dense *bocage* of what was known as 'la Suisse Normande'. Here, there was one ridgeline after another, most running roughly east–west, so against the planned line of advance. Yet more hedgerows, yet more orchards and yet more woodland. On the other hand, 2. Panzer had been shifted east, and ranged against them were only two infantry divisions and a few elements of 10. Panzer. It was not only the quietest part of the line but also arguably the weakest.

Monty had at first thought BLUECOAT should be launched on 2 August, but by the evening of 27 July, with the Americans now dramatically charging southwards, it was hastily brought forward. It was now due to begin on Sunday, 30 July.

Stanley Christopherson now had to deal with not only a new offensive but also new commanders. Brigadier Errol Prior-Palmer, an Irishman and regular cavalryman, now took over 8th Armoured, and arrived with a reputation as a stickler for smartness and saluting, which was not really the Sherwood Rangers way. For BLUECOAT, they would be supporting the 43rd Wessex Division, commanded by Major-General Ivo Thomas – whom Christopherson and the Sherwood Rangers immediately renamed 'Von Thoma' after the German general captured at Alamein. Like Prior-Palmer, Thomas came with a slightly terrifying reputation as a hard and relentless driver of his men. A sense of humour and a love of the ridiculous were what kept Christopherson sane; and, as he soon discovered, Thomas was utterly devoid of either, although after the brutal fighting his division had suffered on Hill 112 earlier that month, there was certainly little for him to smile about. Small and wiry, with piercing eyes, a long nose and a bristling moustache, General Thomas was as hard as nails and struck Christopherson as the kind of person who relished both fighting and its accompanying discomfort. The two men could not have been more different.

BLUECOAT was an altogether bigger operation than anything the Sherwood Rangers had been a part of so far, and as a consequence Christopherson had been given the Essex Yeomanry, a squadron of Westminster Dragoons flails – their old friends from D-Day – and also a squadron of flame-throwing Crocodiles. As usual, each squadron would be operating independently and attached to a different Wessex Division infantry battalion. Because BLUECOAT had been brought forward by three days, Saturday, 29 July, had been a day of frantic planning. Their start line was to the east of Caumont; first up from here would be A Squadron with the 5th Dorsets, who were to capture the village of Briquessard before the Wessex Division pushed on down to take Cahagnes, then Jurques and then Ondefontaine. Montgomery had made it clear to Dempsey that the days of slow attrition were over. In the attack, 'all caution to be thrown overboard, every risk to be taken, and all troops to be told to put everything into it'.

Getting ready for BLUECOAT was an extraordinary feat of logistics and organization. The whole of VIII Corps had had to be moved across to the west of Caumont, in secrecy and at breakneck speed, in a little under forty hours. Tens of thousands of men, thousands of vehicles, stores, ammunition and other supplies all moved across the network of narrow roads and lanes under the noses of the enemy without their discovering what was afoot; operationally, Second Army was an incredibly slick outfit by late July 1944.

Not that the Sherwood Rangers needed to concern themselves much with this, as they were already in situ. On the morning of the 29th, John Semken had been to see the 5th Dorsets, newly arrived in the area the previous evening. As had already happened time and again, he was outranked by the lieutenant-colonel commanding the infantry, who began telling him how things were to be done rather than listening to what Semken was trying to tell him. A Squadron was to slot into the 5th Dorsets' plan and that was that. Later, Semken sent David Render up to see them as his troop would be accompanying them to their first objective – a wood just to the north of the village of Briquessard. Once this had been cleared, the main divisional assault would begin with the Somerset Light Infantry – SLI – taking Briquessard itself, and the 5th Dorsets, with A Squadron supporting them, taking Le Mesnil Levreau, a farmstead three-quarters of a mile to the west. Together, they were then to clear a small stream, which although dry was an obvious defence line for the enemy. With the infantry and tanks creating a bridgehead across this dried river-bed, the next infantry battalion, with C Squadron's help, would pass through and push on to the small town of Cahagnes a mile or so further on to the south.

This area, which had been the front line for weeks, was expected to be mined, and held by enemy troops with mortars, plenty of machine guns and panzerfausts, and artillery support further back. Since BLUECOAT demanded speed, smashing this crust swiftly was vital.

Render had every bit as frustrating a time with the Dorsets as Semken had done and became riled by Major Brian Favelle, the C Company commander of the 5th Dorsets, who insisted Render's troop lead ahead of the infantry. The 5th Dorsets had had a torrid time on Hill 112, and it was understandable they would regard tanks as less vulnerable than infantry. It was, however, missing the point that tanks operating in such close country needed the eyes of the infantry to guide them and pick out targets, and that only with the infantry leading could they most effectively provide that fire support. Clearly, Major Favelle viewed the tanks primarily as a means of protecting his men, rather than his men as providing protection for the armour so that both could use their combined firepower to the greatest effect. It was a subtle but important distinction; but because there was no accepted doctrine on this point before D-Day, the Sherwood Rangers repeatedly found themselves outranked in the ongoing debate.

Render left his meeting with Favelle without the matter being resolved; it hardly helped that he was still only nineteen. Yet although a teenager, he was already something of an old hand in A Squadron – so much so that he was even given a new subaltern, Lieutenant David Alderson, to instruct, just as Neville Fearn had instructed him seven weeks earlier.

Meanwhile, that evening of the 29th, Bill Wharton found time to write one last letter to his wife. He had greatly enjoyed his ten days at the farmhouse, playing host to a number of visitors, the CO included, who had brought with him a box of American cigars. 'An hour ago,' he wrote, 'we had what will probably be our last dinner there and which consisted of two chops each, baked and new potatoes, peas, followed by plums and cream. M. has been in great form (how he loves comfort and how he always has it under all conditions!).' On the eve of battle, he was feeling understandably wistful and yearned to see his beloved wife. 'Darling,' he wrote, 'we have come far along our road and I am looking forward to continuing it with you. The pity is we are missing so much. Often, I want you so very much and I know at those times we could be delightfully happy if we could be together – so much in love. It is so hard to have to wait to love you.'

RAF Bomber Command were once again brought in to provide some heavy muscle with which to kick off BLUECOAT. Harry Heenan, waiting ready with his troop at the start line to the north of the road due east of Caumont, watched them come over. A misty start to the day badly affected visibility, so that only 377 heavy bombers out of the 692 sent could actually drop their loads, and only two of the six targets were hit. None the less, for those on the ground, whether watching or on the receiving end, the bombardment was still of an overwhelming scale. 'They sailed over us as we waited to go,' wrote Heenan, 'suddenly appearing as ghostly shapes among the low scudding cloud, with bomb doors open and great bombs inside. You could see the clouds being torn apart by the great blast bombs exploding just over the hill.'

Arthur Reddish thought it an incredible sight. 'We felt the earth shake,' he noted. 'Dust and smoke rose over the target area. It was awesome – and a little frightening – to see such a display of explosive power. The effect on our opposite numbers could only be imagined.' David Render had been so close the planes had thundered over his head at what had felt like little more than tree-top height. Cahagnes, their target, was only a couple of miles to the south. 'When the bombs hit the ground,' recorded Render, 'they were so near ahead of us that the tanks shook and we became covered in dust. That was precision bombing all right!'

The timing of BLUECOAT's launch on the ground was dictated by the RAF's strategic bombers, which had come over from around seven-thirty that Sunday morning. David Render's wood clearing with the 5th Dorsets was due to launch at 8 a.m., with the main assault following two hours later. It was still rather misty as Render led his troop off towards the trees. As it happened, he had got his way; the infantry had set off first and C Company, in avoiding a marked minefield, had run into an unmarked one. Major Favelle had been one of the first victims, losing a foot as he'd trodden on a vicious anti-personnel Schü-mine. As Render rumbled down a lane, he saw the major strapped to a stretcher rigged to a jeep heading in the opposite direction.

If working out the respective roles of tank and infantry was one of the key issues of cooperation between the two, the other was communication.

C Company had been on the left-hand flank, with B Company making straight for Le Mesnil Levreau. However, C Company, thrown by the unmarked minefield, were no longer advancing along the agreed route, and in the morning mist and smoke – again, the all too literal fog of war – Render and his troop lost all sight of the infantry. There was no radio contact with the Dorsets, and so they continued on their way through the lonely wood. 'Very unhealthy,' he noted, 'but as there were no Germans around either, I just pressed on ahead.' Suddenly, they were out of the wood and almost in someone's back garden at the northern edge of Briquessard, which was the Somerset Light Infantry's objective, not that of the 5th Dorsets. The infantry attack on the village had not even started yet.

On they went down a little track and then growled into the village square, lined on two sides by terraced houses and facing a green. Suddenly there was a loud whoosh and a thump and a large hole appeared in the sloping ground in front of them. A moment later, a second whoosh and the roof of one of the terraced houses to their right disintegrated. Render had seen a flash of movement in the house on the opposite side of the village green. Quickly turning the turret, he gave the order to fire, flinging several rounds into the building and watching as stone, masonry, debris and bodies were hurled into the air. With that, the enemy missiles stopped.

Now all was quiet once more, and as the rest of the troop joined him in the village, it seemed the enemy had cut and run. Render now clambered down and with his German submachine gun cocked and ready, wandered over to the house he had destroyed where he found the bodies of half a dozen or more German troops. Something else caught his eye, however: a long tube with a trigger mechanism, far larger than the more common and disposable panzerfaust. Render picked it up and tied it to the back of the tank, not realizing he was the first person to capture a panzerschreck, an anti-tank rocket launcher based on the American bazooka. He'd been lucky the men firing it had been such poor shots. Before they moved on, Render spotted a number of larger anti-tank Teller mines lying unhidden on the road ahead. Picking them up and casually throwing them to the side, he then got back into his turret.

With Briquessard empty, Render reported in to John Semken and waited for the rest of A Squadron to arrive. The mist had burned off and was now giving way to a glorious summer's day. When Semken and the others joined them, Render was ordered to push on south out of the village towards Cahagnes, completely unaware that to the west, the 5th

Dorsets had not yet even crossed the road from Caumont towards their objective of Le Mesnil Levreau. It was equally clear the Germans had no idea that British tanks had punched such a deep hole into their lines, because as Render led his troop south, an entire platoon of more than thirty enemy infantry were moving calmly across an open field. Render's machine-gunners opened up, mowing down fifteen and swiftly taking the rest prisoner. It was now the afternoon and A Squadron were ordered to hold firm where they were, while either side of them the infantry slowly inched forward. It had been a good day for A Squadron, but BLUECOAT still had a long way to go.

The rest of the battle would not be so easy.

CHAPTER 15

Bloody Ridge

'N EWS THAT 24TH LANCERS being withdrawn from Bgde,' noted
Padre Skinner on 30 July, 'to be broken up to supply replacement
manpower.' In fact, the decision had been made a week earlier and they
weren't the only ones; the 27th Independent Armoured Brigade had been
entirely broken up following GOODWOOD and the 13/18th Hussars
hurriedly moved across to 8th Armoured in time for BLUECOAT. What
remained of the 24th Lancers were to be distributed across the rest of the
brigade.

The same fate might so easily have befallen the Sherwood Rangers, as
Stanley Christopherson was all too aware, not least because the SRY was
the junior regiment in the brigade. Precedence was based on age and status; the 4/7th Dragoon Guards had been the senior regiment, then the 24th
Lancers because they were regular army, not Territorial Army like the
Sherwood Rangers. But in the end, such decisions came down to numbers,
and the 24th Lancers had suffered more. Christopherson felt desperately
sorry for Lieutenant-Colonel William Anderson, the CO of the 24th Lancers, whom he had got to know well; but, unlike the Germans, the British
liked to operate at full strength. Harsh though it was, the 24th Lancers' loss
was the Sherwood Rangers' gain, even though they kept the blue symbols
on their turrets as junior regiment, 4/7th DG kept the red as senior, and
13/18th Hussars took on the yellow of the second regiment.

At the time BLUECOAT was launched there were four German corps
facing the British and Canadians, and although the mighty panzer divisions had been seriously depleted, more and more infantry divisions had
been brought in. The 276. Infanterie-Division, now facing the Sherwood

Rangers, had a hard cadre of Eastern Front veterans, and although they lacked transport, the Germans hastily reinforced this part of the front with elements of 10. SS Panzer, while even a part of 21. Panzer was due to be swiftly moved across to confront this new threat.

And once again, the Sherwood Rangers were advancing with infantry with whom they had not yet fought. It was unavoidable, given the levels of casualties among front-line infantry units after four days or so of action. This in turn meant a constant rotation of brigades. Had the Germans retreated in stages, as they had elsewhere in North Africa, Sicily and Italy, and as they had been expected to do, then there would have been longer pauses in the fighting, the armoured divisions would have been thrust through to exploit more swiftly, and the strain on the infantry would have been less constant. This would have allowed the independent armoured brigades more of an opportunity to stick with one infantry division and get to know them accordingly.

It was notable, for example, that in VIII Corps, advancing on the right flank of the BLUECOAT operation, 15th Scottish Division were supported by 6th Guards Brigade, with whom they had actually trained before D-Day. Thus their staffs and senior officers were singing from the same hymn sheet and working in partnership, rather than the infantry pulling rank. Perhaps unsurprisingly, the forces on VIII Corps' front, where they were further away from the enemy's armoured reinforcements moving from the east, managed to drive a much deeper thrust southwards than did XXX Corps on the left. A less heavy-hitting enemy, combined with greater infantry–armour cooperation, paid off handsomely.

For the most part, the further west the British advanced, the further the troops progressed, so that while the Sherwood Rangers and the Wessexmen weren't making quite the same progress as VIII Corps on their right flank, they still pushed south quicker than 50th Division and the Desert Rats on their left. It was difficult, scrappy fighting for the Sherwood Rangers, although cooperation with the infantry seemed to improve rapidly following A Squadron's initial difficulties with the 5th Dorsets.

On the second day in action, infantry and tanks together pushed southwards towards Cahagnes. Micky Gold's B Squadron led with the infantry of the 7th Hampshires, and although the opposition was slight, the dense network of small, narrow fields, many waterlogged and nearly all lined with thick hedgerows, and the endless orchards, meant progress was slow. Each field or orchard had to be cleared, all tracks and roads swept of mines, and routes found around craters. For the tank commanders, especially, it meant another long and exhausting day, standing in the turret, watching for any sign of the enemy.

Bill Wharton's troop led the advance into Cahagnes that evening, alongside a section of the Recce Troop, and with dusk falling reported it clear. C Squadron followed, rumbling through the shattered remains of the town. 'Cahagnes was a terrible mess,' wrote Stuart Hills, 'like every other Normandy village we fought through.' Here too the typhoon of steel had swept through, bombs raining down from the sky, then shells from the artillery, leaving almost nothing standing. Stan Perry had a close call. Leading C Squadron through the shattered town with his head out of the turret, his neck caught on a wire strung across the street, a vicious trap set by the retreating enemy. Fortunately, they were not travelling fast, and there was enough slack in the wire for him to bellow to his driver to halt and to get it clear of his head. 'But,' he said, 'it was a bit of a close run.' He could easily have been decapitated. As they continued south, though opposition was slight, progress was slow because of mines, blown roads and pockets of resistance; but by evening they were nearing the village of Jurques, some 4 miles south of Cahagnes.

On Tuesday, 1 August, A Squadron, still on the right, was ordered to capture Point 361 alongside the 5th Wiltshires. This lay on an open ridge south of the wooded slopes of the Bois du Homme to the west of Jurques. Once again, opposition was not particularly strong, and Harry Heenan's troop were the first to reach the top, although they were fortunate to spy a Jagdpanther before they'd been spotted themselves. Clearly, the enemy armour was reaching this potentially valuable bit of high ground at the same time as they were; certainly, the senior German commanders in Normandy had not anticipated such a major attack as BLUECOAT in this sector and were now frantically trying to rush in reinforcements. The speed of the British advance had caught them completely off guard, and here, around Point 361, that worked very much to the advantage of John Semken's men.

None of the Sherwood Rangers had seen a Jagdpanther before – a self-propelled gun with a giant 88mm fixed on to the chassis of a Panther – but A Squadron swiftly pummelled it with rounds before it could manoeuvre, and in so doing knocked off one of its tracks. With the beast now immobile, the crew bailed out. George Dring also spied two Tigers moving up, and decided once again to get out and stalk them on foot, guiding his crew towards the first and then smothering it with a combination of HE and armour-piercing rounds. It was the third Tiger he and his Sherman crew had knocked out. He then spotted a second Tiger that had become bogged down – which, in a 56-ton tank after the heavy rain of the previous ten days, was easy enough to do – and a further Tiger that had also become bogged and been abandoned. One Jagdpanther and three Tigers was not at all a bad haul and helped them secure the ridge that evening.

The squadron cleared the rest of this part of the ridge, and on their way down the other side Harry Heenan's troop caught an enemy infantry counter-attack just as it was beginning. 'So we pulled off the road and took up positions and blew them to hell,' he wrote. 'I got an entire platoon of about thirty blokes.' While mopping up afterwards, Heenan stopped his tank to pick up a badly wounded Tommy. Mortars were raining down so it was a brave thing to do. He patched up the man as best he could, gave him a shot of morphine and, with the help of another infantryman, managed to hoist him on to the back of the tank. Soon after that, they overran some German troops and took them prisoner. 'Finally departed as a convoy,' Heenan wrote, 'consisting of 1 Sherman tank with a wounded bloke, 1 infanteer, and two Jerries on the back, followed by two Jerries with a wheelbarrow containing the near dead remains of a third.'

By that evening the regiment had covered nearly 7 miles in the past forty-eight hours. By last light, C Squadron were formed up in a large field just off the road, the men carrying out their nightly checks and mainten-ance and getting some food. Suddenly, at around 11 p.m., several German planes flew over very low, dropping flares. 'We felt quite naked,' noted Stu-art Hills, 'for everything was lit up like daylight.' It was a heart-stopping moment; everyone froze, waiting for the enemy shells to rain down. All along the road were infantry vehicles – carriers, trucks, artillery – and men, all of them sitting ducks. The planes circled and dropped a number of bombs, but fortunately none hit anything – at least as far as Hills could see.

Not far behind this column was Padre Skinner. 'Towards evening,' he noted, 'news of breakthrough and Boche on the run.' Despite the ineffect-ive air attack, it did seem the road heading south was open. A slightly breathless excitement gripped the 43rd Division command, and new orders now arrived from General Thomas. Both Montgomery and Demp-sey had urged speed, and for caution to be thrown to the wind, so that was exactly what Thomas now insisted they do. There was to be no pause; instead, they were to press on through Jurques and then to Ondefontaine, 5 miles to the south-east.

It was always a good idea to exploit success, yet although opposition had been slight so far, both the tank crews and the infantry were already exhausted. After long weeks of the cloud and rain that had blighted the campaign so far, blazing heat had borne down on them all day from an azure blue sky. The infantry had been on their feet or in vehicles non-stop since the 30th, while the tank crews had been wedged into their tanks by day and sleeping in them at night; the A1 Echelon had been coming up each night for refuelling and rearming. Long days, then, made worse by the heat, the choking dust whipped up by this mass of armour and vehicles, and by even less sleep than usual when in the firing line.

No matter. Orders were orders, and having believed their work was done for the day, tank men and infantry alike spent the next hour packing up once more and getting ready to move out. Around midnight they were off, C Squadron with the 7th Hampshires leading and B Squadron with the 4th Dorsets following. This time the infantry of the leading companies were crammed on to the tanks, their route lit partially by the moon but also by searchlights that had been brought up for use as floodlights. 'Von Thoma' was confident they could race to Mont Pinçon, the highest point in Normandy, 8 miles to the south-east, that very day if they got their skates on. It was a tough night for everyone. Some men and crews struggled to stay awake; others felt continually on edge, waiting for the first major pocket of resistance or ambush or mine, their apprehension made worse by fatigue.

None the less, Peter Selerie and the leading tanks of C Squadron reached the edge of Jurques from the north-west around 5 a.m., as dawn was breaking. Getting through the village, however, was no easy matter, not because of enemy resistance but because the place had been bombed, leaving not a single house standing, and numerous detours had to be made around craters. The retreating enemy had also laced the place with mines. 'The place had been bombed earlier,' recalled Arthur Reddish, 'and smoke and dust still hung around.' Several buildings were on fire, and Reddish thought the village had a terrible, dismal feel about it. A number of vehicles, carts and bicycles lay abandoned in the road, as though the enemy had cut and run. If there were any civilians left in this obliterated village, there was certainly no sign of them.

Twice they were held up for over an hour while the sappers cleared a path. And then the enemy shelling began. To the south, the countryside climbed, and it was clear the Germans had abandoned Jurques and sensibly pulled back to this high ground. The road to Ondefontaine ran east from the village, then curved south-east and climbed through farmland and orchards up to the long, dominating, wooded ridge of the Bois du

Homme. This ran for at least 20 miles, roughly west–east, and was an incredibly strong natural defensive position: high ground, allowing eyes on anything that moved to the north, and wooded too, offering the defenders all the cover they could possibly want. General Thomas had hoped to sweep on over this horrible ridge, but the shelling of the village suggested the Germans had finally regained some kind of balance and that the 5-mile advance to Ondefontaine was going to be tough. Before it lay the farming hamlet of La Bigne, a mile and a half south-east of Jurques. Clearly, there were enemy troops here, looking down on the long column's every move.

If Peter Selerie had a sinking feeling as he ordered his squadron to push forward to La Bigne, he gave no sign of it, instead urging them on with his usual cheerful confidence. Such was the British strength, they would eventually overcome the German defences here; but on this morning, it was impossible to know at what cost. And, as was always the way in Normandy, it was the infantry and the armour that had to take that leap of faith and push forward into the line of fire. That required immense courage because, as every infantryman and every tank crewman knew, each step forward, each yard, could be their last. That road to La Bigne was horrible: narrow, exposed and with little cover.

Lieutenant Frank Galvin, who had temporarily taken Hills's troop at Hottot but now commanded 1 Troop, was in the lead, with Hills's 4 Troop following. Unloading their infantry, they decided to make a dash for the dead straight Roman road, heading at speed up the northern route that wound out of the village, then turning south. Where they met the road to La Bigne, they were held up again by mines, both at the junction and in the fields either side. Mines were the bane of quick movement. Sappers had to be brought forward and the entire column ground to a halt until some kind of passage had been cleared. Knowing this, the enemy had the place zeroed, which led to the infantry hitting the ground, leaving the armour and engineers exposed. Smoke shells would be fired in response, the tanks would also open fire, and the Essex Yeomanry would be called up – but all that took time. Certainly, shelling now increased, although so far, thankfully, no tank had been hit. It was now well into the morning, and the sun was up again and blazing down on them. The entire column was strung out: C Squadron in the lead, followed by carriers, half-tracks, armoured cars and a battery of the Essex Yeomanry, then B Squadron and more of the same.

Eventually, with a path cleared through the mines, C Squadron advanced up the road towards La Bigne, Stuart Hills in the lead, the infantry now on foot and tentatively walking alongside. They crossed the River Odon, here just a tiny stream, and began climbing the winding road up the hill towards the farmstead of La Bigne. This stood on a kink in the road that continued on up to the next ridge; and, like most farmsteads in Normandy, it was surrounded by thick hedges, trees and orchards. Half a mile further on was another farm, again protected by a thick orchard that ran along the ridgeline and across the path of the road, with hedgerows extending beyond and clear views down on to anything moving up the road out of Jurques.

Suddenly, machine-gun fire ripped through the air and mortars began crashing around them. Infantry hit the ground, Brens and their own mortars replying. Hills pushed on, reaching a right-hand bend in the road, only to be confronted by three Mk IV tanks just a few hundred yards ahead.

'Gunner, traverse right,' Hills ordered. Voice trying to remain calm. 'Steady, on.' Then the order to Dickie Dexter to fire. They hit the first panzer, then hurriedly fired several smoke shells before manoeuvring off the road and playing 'cowboys and Indians' in the orchards with the other two. Captain Jack Holman, the squadron second-in-command, along with Captain Arthur Warburton, the FOO from the Essex Yeomanry, moved their tanks into the orchard just to the right of the La Bigne road junction. From there, Holman provided covering fire while Warburton directed the Essex Sextons towards the enemy positions. In moments, shells were screaming down on La Bigne, smoke, dust and grit rolled and swirled over the ridge, and Lieutenant Galvin's troop moved up to a small cutting a short distance from the hamlet, which offered a limited amount of cover. They manoeuvred themselves into a hull-down position with only their turrets visible – and not a moment too soon, because two StuGs were now seen moving along the ridge to the south. Galvin's tanks fired round after round of HE and the StuGs halted immediately, although it seemed they had not been hit.

The noise was immense as shells, small-arms fire and mortars tore apart the summer air. Behind them, stretching up the Roman road, through Jurques and beyond, the column was still strung out. Suddenly, Lieutenant Galvin's tank was hit by one of the StuGs, albeit not seriously. Then, moments later, the enemy SP was hit in turn by Sergeant Whittaker and brewed up. The second SP was so pummelled its crew were spotted hurriedly bailing out. However, even though these two mobile guns had been knocked out, the enemy's shelling was intensifying. Several carriers back on the road were hit, and then three tanks, two in C Squadron and one in B, were hit in quick succession, two brewing up. Lieutenant Donald Campbell, a close friend of Stuart Hills's, was killed, along with his crew – one of the first to be incinerated in their tank. Other crew members managed to escape, only to be killed as they bailed out. One of the burning tanks, the second in C Squadron to be hit, was commanded by Lieutenant Alan Birkett. Trying to escape when his tank brewed up on the road to La Bigne, he was hit in the stomach and fell back into the turret, trapping his gunner and operator, Troopers Fred Heslewood and Leslie Watson. They eventually managed to escape, although by this time they were on fire. The driver and lap-gunner had also bailed out and safely scampered clear, but Birkett's tank now began to roll backwards down the road towards a group of infantry carriers and vehicles. Seeing this, Sergeant Guy Sanders, already with a Military Medal to his name, calmly ran up to it, jumped on the hull, stretched his arms down into the driver's compartment and, despite the flames swirling in the turret, pulled the steering levers so that the tank slewed off the road and into a ditch at the side, before safely jumping clear again. His quick thinking and selfless courage had prevented a greater tragedy.

Despite continued small-arms fire and heavy mortaring, the weight of fire from the tanks and the 25-pounders gradually wore down the enemy defence, and a little after midday La Bigne was in British hands. Peter Selerie now drove up in his scout car for a conference with the infantry beside a hedge on the far side of the hamlet. 'There followed a particularly sanguinary encounter,' he noted. 'We had just about decided about the next bound forward when a mortar bomb landed in the middle of us.' The infantry officer was killed; so were Selerie's driver, Trooper Rob Howie, and an officer from the Essex Yeomanry. Selerie's operator was wounded, and so too was Selerie himself, hit in the shoulder and back by shrapnel. Only Jack Holman emerged unscathed. Selerie was hurriedly put on to a stretcher. At one point, the enemy fire became so intense that his bearers put him down while they dived into a ditch at the edge of the field. 'Some five years as a cavalry officer had given me a splendid vocabulary which I proceeded to use at the top of my voice!' he wrote. 'They returned rather sheepishly and I was carried to the jeep.'

Stuart Hills and his troop were in an orchard that straddled the road, awaiting orders and unaware of the calamity that had struck the squadron. With mortars continuing to crash down nearby, they all had their hatches down when suddenly there was a knocking on the side of the tank and shouting from outside. Cautiously, Hills and Arthur Reddish opened their hatches. It was Jack Mitchell, one of the pre-war men, and a radio operator in the troop as well as the squadron football captain.

'What's wrong with everybody?' he said. 'Come outside. Bugger the bloody mortars. I'm not scared of the bastards!'

At the same time, Hills was summoned on the net to an O group in La Bigne. As he cautiously clambered down, he suggested to Mitchell that he should return to his own tank.

'Not me,' Mitchell replied. 'I'm not afraid of the bloody mortars.'

Hills scampered off to find Holman, from whom he learned the terrible news – Birkett and his friend Campbell had been killed, along with two men from each of their crews – as also had Rob Howie, one of the great characters of the squadron; and Peter Selerie was badly wounded. Holman was now acting squadron leader. Another mortar bomb fell nearby, slightly wounding Sergeant Sanders.

The battle was quietening down, however – one of those lulls that tended to happen. Arthur Reddish decided to clamber out and go and see his pal Busty Meek. It was a foolhardy thing to do, but he was exhausted and aching from too long in the tank, which now stank badly of fuel, fumes, sweat and piss. Suddenly, he heard an incoming shell and had a sixth sense it was heading right for him. It seemed to take for ever to land, screaming in a long crescendo. Diving to the ground, he waited – and then it crashed in, little more than 20 yards away, a large piece of shrapnel clanging against the nearest tank. Getting to his feet, he spotted a massive piece of shrapnel nearby then hot-footed it back to his tank.

Hills was also now hurrying back. On his way, he saw Jack Mitchell lying beside his tank, a cigarette still in his mouth. Quite dead. Back in his own tank, he discovered a badly shaken up Reddish. Wearily, he thought about the two dead men, Mitchell and Howie. He couldn't wait for the padre to come up, so asked for volunteers from his crew to help him bury them. No one wanted to – they were too shaken up and too exhausted. Hills didn't press the point. Instead, he grabbed a shovel and headed off on his own, burying the two men under some trees near the banks of the River Odon.

The fighting ran out of steam that afternoon as they pressed on further, a few hundred yards south of La Bigne, and came up against further resistance from the ridge beyond. It took time to move artillery into position, work out targets, fire and then move forward again. Mortars and small-arms fire and occasional shelling continued. General Thomas now ordered a renewed attack under cover of darkness in the early hours of the following morning, Thursday, 3 August. This was abruptly halted by extensive mines and continued mortaring and small-arms fire. In Stuart

Hills's tank, everyone was grumbling as they stuttered forward, stopped, fired, inched forward, then stopped again. 'To say we were tired,' noted Arthur Reddish, 'was the understatement of the decade.' They'd been on the go for seventy hours, barely able to leave their tanks. Calls of nature had been answered within the tanks, into empty shell cases. Meals had also been prepared inside, which only added to the noxious stench. They were filthy, had had no sleep for three nights and three days – except the odd snatched cat-nap – and not much more before that.

Still the attack was pushed forward again as another hot day spread across the Suisse Normande. The problem now was the lack of access roads up to the ridge. It was simply such a dominating feature, thickly wooded, from which the enemy could remain hidden and enjoy the benefit of height. From the single road leading to Ondefontaine through the Bois du Homme to the numerous tracks between farmsteads, the Germans had every route zeroed and also mined. Sappers would be sent forward to clear the mines, but would then come under fire from machine guns and mortars. Montgomery and Dempsey wanted a speedy advance, but they didn't want all their men slaughtered in the process. The alternative was to pound the enemy positions with ever more artillery and air power, have the sappers clear mines and a route through, and then advance again with armour and infantry. But that took time.

A Squadron was now brought up to the hamlet of Montpied, just to the north of La Bigne and overlooking the narrow River Odon. They were to make themselves as inconspicuous as possible and provide fire support for C and B Squadrons, still slowly pushing along the road with the infantry. David Render's troop moved along a track looking down towards the wooded Odon valley, beyond which the ground rose again: one of the many folds in the gradually rising land up to the ridge of the Bois du Homme. He knew a lot more about reading the lie of the land than when he'd first reached Normandy, and so quickly moved his tanks below the skyline on to the forward slope and ordered his tank commanders to keep their eyes glued to their field glasses. Not long afterwards, he was amazed to see what looked like an entire company of German infantry marching across in front of a wood not much more than a few hundred yards away. Immediately, he ordered the troop to open fire, first with their Brownings and then with HE fired into the trees above them to cause an airburst effect of shrapnel and lethal splinters of wood. It was a slaughter, and underlined the dangers of moving in a narrow line under the noses of enemy guns. Render, however, was furious that David Alderson, the new boy under his instruction, had not fired from his tank, chastising him over the net for refusing to fire whenever he was ordered to do so.

Alderson replied that he hadn't done so because it seemed unsporting to mow men down like that in cold blood. 'I think I went a bit too far,' said Render, 'when I quoted the statistics of his chances of survival and that he would shorten them considerably if he didn't learn to follow instructions.' So many of the Sherwood Rangers would never have been in uniform but for the war; and even those who had been part of the pre-war yeomanry had been part-time soldiers. War, though, had toughened them, and quickly. None of them wanted to kill their fellow men or destroy villages or smash church steeples – but these acts of brutal violence were necessary if they were to win. If they were to have any chance of saving their men and themselves. War was making hardened killers of these otherwise gentle, humour-loving folk.

That evening, A Squadron moved up, through C and B Squadrons, to take the lead alongside the 5th Dorsets. It was once again 5 Troop's turn to lead, which meant Render's own tank being point once again. Other troops took it in strict turn to be lead tank, but Render still had issues with Sergeant Jackson and felt it was unfair on Johnny Lanes, the other tank commander, to expect him to take the lead more than his fair share of times. 'As a consequence,' he wrote, 'I always put *Aim* at the front of the troop and each time I did it when leading the whole squadron it became a little harder.' It was terrifying, because everyone in the tank knew they were first in line to hit a mine, be shot at by a panzerfaust or get blasted by an anti-tank round. Nerves were taut, hearts beating furiously, senses attuned to the slightest movement. Fear gripped each man; and yet somehow they had to keep going, conspicuous and feeling incredibly vulnerable despite the tank's bulk. Thoughts of burning tanks and bodies riddled with bullets had to be put to the back of the mind, even though it was hard to blot them out.

The plan was for Render to advance several hundred yards ahead of Johnny Lanes, who would cover him from a static position; then he would move forward and Jackson would follow behind in the Firefly. Then the process would be repeated. It was dusk as they got moving, climbing past pockmarked farmland towards the thick, rising forest, the infantry alongside. Render had gone about 400 yards when an anti-tank shell swished past like a thunderbolt from somewhere in the woods to their right.

'What the fuck was that?' Render cried out before swiftly calling,

'Anti-tank! Reverse!' Lurching backwards off the road, they were able to take a hull-down position while Johnny Lanes's tank fired several rounds of HE towards where the shot had come from. Render now called out directions while in his headphones he heard John Semken feeding them back to the battery of Essex Yeomanry Sextons following behind. Their response was impressively swift. Within a minute or so, the first 25-pounder ranging shot was whining over.

'Right fifty, add two hundred,' Semken called to them. 'Fire for effect.' Moments later, the first salvo screamed over, and thirty seconds later came the next. Further artillery was then directed on to the woods. Another troop passed them and pressed on, inching up the road, clear of the fields and into the wood; but hidden guns and yet more mines along the road meant Ondefontaine was not captured that night.

The next day it was C Squadron who were to take the lead again, along with the 7th Hampshires, moving off at dawn. This time it was Hills's troop on point and their turn to feel the raw fear of being the lone tank in front. Two hundred yards on, they reached their first mines, which then had to be cleared. Another delay. Then on again, turning a bend in the road only to be met with a felled tree that was liberally booby-trapped. Yet further delay as the sappers hurried forward. Eventually, they moved off again and, having successfully pushed through the first stretch of the forest, they emerged to see open farmland gently sloping away on their right and steeply rising and thickly wooded slopes on their left. On they went, rumbling forward. It was quiet. Too quiet. Nervous crew chatter about what the enemy was up to.

'We must be on their blind side,' said Sam Kirman.

A long, straight road now led to the village of Ondefontaine, a mile further on. They reached a crossroads and turned left into the village, which they now saw nestled beneath the highest point of the wood ridge. Ahead was the church. A white sheet was thrust out from a farmhouse window, then another. Reddish felt sweat run down his face; he was tense, on edge. They all were. Where were the enemy? A platoon of infantry scuttled past and took cover beside a stone house next to a junction opposite the church. Now Geoff Storey inched the tank forward – and immediately two anti-tank rounds swished past and crashed into the church wall.

'Reverse!' Hills shouted. Clearly, the enemy were lying in wait in the southern half of the village. That it was not more firmly held at the northern half suggested that only a skeleton force remained and that the bulk of them had now fallen back off the ridge to the next line of hills. Sergeant

Sanders tried to get his tank round the church from the back, but came up against the same obstacle: a sighted anti-tank gun pointing down the road. An infantry officer now approached Hills and ordered him across the junction, but Hills pointed out they would be no use to anyone brewed up. Shortly after, Jack Holman arrived and joined them.

'Why don't we pull back a little,' suggested Hills, 'and let Arthur's boys have a go? Then we'll all go in.' He meant Captain Arthur Warburton, the FOO of the Essex Yeomanry. This seemed a sensible solution.

'Well done, Stuart,' said Reddish as Hills got back into the tank; he'd heard the entire conversation.

They pulled back. The infantry officer came up to Hills's tank.

'There's a German operating a radio in yon steeple,' he said, pointing to the church. 'Would you put a solid shot through it, old man?' Hills agreed. Dick Dexter's first shot was wide but the second went straight through it.

'That'll do!' said the officer happily.

Inside the tank, the tension had lifted palpably.

'Look at Dexter smirking,' said Sam Kirman. 'But he won't be going to heaven after desecrating a church steeple.'

'I'd give him a fifty–fifty chance, Sam,' said Reddish. 'After all, his first shot missed. The poor bloke's heart wasn't in it.'

'Wasn't it, by Christ,' said Kirman. 'I was watching the bastard. He had a wicked glint in his eye.' Dexter, with unusual reticence, said nothing to this banter.

Soon after that, shells came screaming in. Ondefontaine disappeared amid swirling clouds of smoke, dust and debris. Reddish didn't like to see the homes of ordinary folk being destroyed, but he was so tired he was past caring. Eventually the stonk ended and they moved forward, firing HE and dousing everything in their path with machine-gun fire. They moved through the village and on into a field and there, at the far end, hidden in a hedgerow, was an abandoned assault gun. One enemy soldier lay dead alongside, a neat hole through his helmet.

'Any sign of the enemy?' someone shouted.

'Only dead ones,' came the reply.

A halt was ordered and they cut their engines. As Reddish clambered from his tank, he paused, and listened. He couldn't hear anything. No birdsong, no mortar fire. The battle was, for the moment, over.

CHAPTER 16

Letters Home

I T WASN'T QUITE THE end of the fighting at Ondefontaine; the village had to be completely cleared. Stan Perry's troop, following behind the others, had seen a Frenchman on the far side of the village, and Perry had asked him – in his passable French – whether there were any Germans left in the village. The man told him he thought they had all gone, but he pointed out one house where there might still be some inside. Perry dismounted, Colt .45 in hand, and took his gunner with him armed with a Sten. Having stationed his gunner by the front door, he kicked it open, thought he saw a fleeting glimpse of movement inside and fired. 'There was a big bang and a whir,' said Perry, 'and I'd shot a grandfather clock.'

They went in, but the place was empty, though there was an uncorked and full bottle of wine on the table with a glass beside it. The gunner made for it, but Perry pulled him back. Sure enough, there was a trail of fuse leading to a mine. The bottle had been booby-trapped. Armed with his SAS training, Perry was able to dismantle it safely, discovering a spring underneath the bottle that would have triggered the fuse.

The Bois du Homme and the ridge extending eastwards also had to be cleared. B Squadron and the 4th Dorsets had had a torrid time that same day, 4 August. Bill Wharton had been given the job of contacting the infantry early that morning. It had rained heavily overnight and was still pouring by the time he was up and about, so he was soon soaked as he searched for the Dorsets, wandering through the trees, crops and thick bracken. On more than one occasion he worried he had crossed over into enemy lines. Eventually, he found the infantry, and their attack went in early that afternoon, at around 1.30 p.m., but made no headway at all. The Dorsets suffered badly, and were shelled heavily throughout the night too, although the squadron, hunkering down in the woods, took no further casualties.

'I am a bit vague recalling how long we have been engaged on this operation but I believe today is the seventh day,' wrote Bill Wharton in a hastily scribbled letter on the 5th. 'We have moved several miles and one day in particular we killed and captured a lot of Germans in some very close fighting.' For Wharton, as for so many of them, humour was an important part of staying sane. Like a lot of soldiers, his driver was an incurable looter. Just at the start of BLUECOAT, the corporal had returned to the tank after a forage clutching a huge doll with blonde ringlets dressed in a flowing crinoline dress. They named her 'Marguerite' and she now accompanied them wherever they went, riding inside the tank when in action and outside at other times. 'We have great fun asking over the intercom how she is going,' wrote Wharton, 'especially if we have been firing or a leaving barrage has been brought down on us. It must be admitted that she takes it calmly, barely turning a blonde hair.'

Like everyone else, though, he felt shattered; it wasn't just the physical exhaustion but the mental strain that was beginning to take its toll, and that really did bear down particularly hard on a troop and tank commander. The battle for France, he told Marion, seemed to consist of pushing through one field after another, each of which could be hiding a gun, or a tank, or some such. He also felt he was doing more leading than any other officer in the squadron. 'The thing is that now I am captain I shouldn't be troop leading but we lose these guys as fast as they come up or they are inexperienced (some are windy) and so I continue to go out in front,' he wrote. 'I sometimes wonder if I am running my luck too far.'

He wasn't the only one having such thoughts. At Ondefontaine, 'Hylda' Young had reached the men in his half-track and was horrified by their condition. All had eyes reddened by dust and sunken from exhaustion. Young drove straight to Brigade HQ, insisted on seeing the Brigadier and told him the regiment had to be rested if it were to continue as a fighting unit. It did the trick. That night, C Squadron leaguered up in an orchard near the village, the men sleeping outside their tanks for the first time in a week. 'It was marvellous to wake up hearing the birds singing,' noted Arthur Reddish. 'There hadn't been the slightest enemy shelling in the night.'

BLUECOAT was not over yet, however. On the 5th, there was more clearing of the ridge to the east to be done, while A Squadron pushed on towards Mont Pinçon, the original XXX Corps objective where the 4/7th Dragoon Guards and 13/18th Hussars were still battling to clear the heights. This, like Ondefontaine, was another high wooded ridge that dominated the surrounding countryside for miles in all directions.

On Sunday, 6 August, news reached Colonel Christopherson that 8th Armoured Brigade were to support the Wessexmen almost immediately in an operation to cross the River Noireau, some 15 miles to the south. This was being called BLACKWATER, and was due to begin the following morning. It was, however, dependent on the complete capture of Mont Pinçon first. This was not finally in their hands until the 7th, by which time the Germans had launched their ill-conceived counter-attack west towards the town of Mortain.

Events had been moving fast during BLUECOAT. The Americans had continued driving southwards with Third Army under General George S. Patton now in theatre and unleashed. US troops had pushed into Brittany and then also wheeled eastwards far to the south. First Army had eventually met stiffer opposition, but the badly mauled German forces now in Normandy had been squeezed into the south, and with Patton's Third Army sweeping east were in danger of becoming entirely encircled. It was at this moment that Hitler had ordered Operation LÜTTICH, a counter-thrust to the west coast near Avranches. Not a single German commander in Normandy thought this was a good idea; they had been urging the Führer to allow them to retreat back to the River Seine while they still had the chance. Hitler was not to be swayed, however, and after the assassination attempt back on 20 July, no one was willing to put his neck on the line and refuse a direct order from the commander-in-chief.

BLUECOAT itself had proved a great success, with VIII Corps driving a wedge some 20 miles south and, in the process, drawing in and chewing up two panzer divisions – 2. and 21. Panzer – precious armour that now would not be capable of taking part in LÜTTICH. The Wessexmen's thrust towards Mont Pinçon had been considerably more successful than the slower advance of 7th Armoured and 50th Divisions. The latter's performance, indeed, adjudged lacklustre by General Dempsey, had cost the jobs of General Bucknall, XXX Corps commander, and Major-General Erskine, CO of the Desert Rats. Both were sacked for being too slow and lacking the vigour he had demanded. No such complaint could be directed at General Thomas, however; he might have been nicknamed 'Von Thoma' by the Rangers, but to his own men he was 'Butcher'.

Mont Pinçon finally fell on 7 August, the same day the Canadians

launched Operation TOTALIZE, a drive south from Caen to Falaise. The
end in Normandy was now in sight – although even on the 7th, B Squadron
and the 4th Dorsets continued clearing the Bois du Homme east of Ondefontaine. Then a cause for cheer: BLACKWATER was postponed and news
arrived that the regiment would be pulled back for a four-day rest to Coulvain, a village a mile or two north of Jurques. Back they went, down the
dusty roads, past the burnt-out hulks of tanks lost earlier in the fighting,
past numerous recently dug graves, through a landscape shattered by war:
fields cratered by shelling and mortars, houses smashed and reduced to rubble, a summer scene pungent with death.

Stanley Christopherson was pleased with the way in which cooperation
with the infantry had improved as BLUECOAT had continued; the ruf-
fles facing John Semken at the outset had soon been forgotten, and
especially so as the different units had got used to one another. Carrying
infantry on the backs of tanks had made a great difference, and was an
innovation that would continue. Christopherson had also been expecting more casualties, given the lengthy nature of the battle. Even so, B and
C Squadrons, especially, had suffered. C Squadron had lost eight men
killed, including two troop leaders, as well as their commander badly
wounded. Lieutenant Campbell had been a good friend of Stuart Hills,
while 'Jock' Howie had been a hugely popular character within the squadron. So too was Peter Selerie. 'Nothing ever got Peter down,' noted
Christopherson. 'In battle he showed no fear, and he proved a most able
squadron leader who we all missed when he had to be evacuated.' Selerie
was one of the great characters of the regiment, slightly round of face,
somewhat eccentric, and the embodiment of the unique and individual-
istic nature of the Sherwood Rangers. 'He was inclined to be somewhat
pedantic in speech,' wrote Christopherson, 'and was prone to using long
and ponderous words, even when reporting over the wireless. Instead of
saying, "In the wood to my left front, three enemy tanks moving left to
right, am engaging," he would monopolize the air by reporting, "I can
without question discern three moving objects in yonder wood, which
give me an unquestionable impression of resembling three Tigers, which
appear to portray hostile inclinations. It is my intention to offer immediate engagement" – much to the frantic impatience of other tank stations
with important messages for transmission.' He would be missed. Fortunately, his wounds were not life-threatening.

The distressing task of recovering bodies was left to the padre. Initially,

Christopherson had refused to let Skinner attempt to reach the burnt-out hulks of Campbell's and Birkett's tanks, so it wasn't until Friday, 4 August, by which time the front had moved on up to Ondefontaine, that he had been able to get to them. He learned that two of the men killed, Troopers Heslewood and Watson, who had bailed out burning, had later died of their wounds: they had been taken to the Dorsets' RAP and buried there. Reluctantly, he had moved on to the two tanks. Entering Birkett's first, he found nothing inside but a blackened and charred mess. 'Dorsets MO says other members of crew consumed by fire having been KIA,' he scribbled in his diary. 'Searched ash and found remains of pelvic bones.' At Campbell's tank, the three men in the turret were still there but unidentifiable and firmly welded together. Skinner clambered into that narrow, confined chamber, which reeked of burned remains and death. Everything was covered in soot, the corpses brittle and carbonized. He tried to prise the three men apart. 'Managed with difficulty to identify Lt. Campbell,' he added. 'Unable to remove bodies after long struggle – nasty business.' That was putting it mildly. Back outside the tank, he vomited. Not until the 7th was he able to get all three bodies out of the tank and identify them separately as Campbell, Corporal Ronald Ramswell and Trooper Ronald Schofield. He then buried them near the railway crossing at Jurques, close to where they'd been hit five days earlier. 'Awful business,' he noted, 'dreadfully sick – glad it is done now.' What a good man Skinner was.

At Coulvain, the regiment was once again brought up to strength and Jack Holman was confirmed as the new commander of C Squadron. There was a touch of the dandy about Holman, and not just because of his dashing good looks. Like Selerie and Stanley Christopherson, he was invariably smiling and cheerful, but had his affectations, from using a cigarette-holder to referring to everyone as 'old boy'. A bit of cheery insouciance was no bad thing, however. 'His completely unflappable manner was a great help,' wrote Stuart Hills, 'and he had the habit of making even the most dangerous situation into something of a joke.' Stan Perry rather enjoyed the flamboyancy of both Selerie and Jack Holman; one time when it was raining, he had seen Holman standing in the turret with an umbrella above his head. It had made him laugh.

Men from the disbanded 24th Lancers had joined the Sherwood Rangers and been posted to Micky Gold's B Squadron. Lieutenants Harry Cowan and Arthur Cameron were good friends, and once they'd heard the devastating news that the regiment was to be disbanded, they had called together the men of their respective troops and put it to a vote to ask for a transfer together to the Sherwood Rangers. 'The main thing that swayed everyone,' said Corporal John Cropper, 'was the fact that the SRY weren't as full of bull as some of the armoured units.' Their wish was duly granted and so they had joined the Rangers at Ondefontaine on 4 August, having merely changed cap badges and shoulder flashes. Cropper and his crew moved wholesale to 4 Troop under Harry Cowan.

John Cropper, now aged twenty-six, had been a policeman in Milnrow near Liverpool when war had broken out back in 1939 and could have remained in that role for the duration; after all, the police played an invaluable role and he'd been busy during the Battle of Britain and the Blitz investigating suspected fifth columnists, helping to maintain civil order and guarding downed enemy aircrew, along with a host of normal police duties. Yet he'd asked to swap dark blue for khaki, and had finally been allowed to do so in July 1943. Initially he'd joined the King's Own Yorkshire Light Infantry, but despite his police training had struggled to master their quick marching drills, and so had transferred to the Royal Armoured Corps. By June 1944 he was a reinforcement in the 8th Armoured Brigade's FDS, and sailed for Normandy a few days after D-Day. After three more days stuck at the FDS, he had finally been posted to B Squadron in the 24th Lancers as an operator on 14 June. For the next few weeks he had been in the thick of the action at Cristot, the Bois de Boislonde and Fontenay, and in the fight for Tessel Wood.

These had been brutal battles for the Lancers, just as they had for the Sherwood Rangers. In June alone, the 24th Lancers had lost 27 officers and 115 other ranks, almost a third of their fighting strength and two-thirds of their officer numbers. Some thirty-eight tanks had also been destroyed in that time. Cropper had been promoted and given command of his own tank; while many others, such as Arthur Reddish, had turned down that role, Cropper was one of the older ones, had a keen sense of responsibility, and rather relished the opportunity to lead and command.

The rest at Coulvain gave Cropper and his fellows a chance to get to know some of their fellows in the Sherwood Rangers and for all of them to recharge batteries. 'The occasional rests are very highly organized,' Harry Heenan wrote to a friend. 'As soon as we come out we have beer, baths (no, not brothels!) ENSA shows, pictures and all the lot laid on.' The comic singer George Formby even appeared and played for them.

Most men used these rest periods to write letters back home. These were then collected up and brought to Regimental HQ, where those by other ranks were given censorship checks by a couple of allocated officers. Then an RHQ clerk sorted them and arranged for them to be put on a ship back to Britain within forty-eight hours at most, so that they would be with families or friends within a matter of days.

Officers' letters were not checked, but for them too the rules were strict: there was to be no mention of locations, and no reference to specific events except in the vaguest of terms for at least a fortnight after they occurred. Harry Heenan, who was a devout Catholic, liked to present an extremely confident and gung-ho front in his letters. 'It is plain that Jerry has had it,' he wrote during the rest at Coulvain. 'Over a period of weeks, we have just about torn the guts out of his armies here and I reckon he will be lucky if he gets much away.' None the less, he did admit to feeling very tired and reckoned the only reason A Squadron was doing so well was John Semken, who he thought was a 'bloody marvellous bloke'. Heenan struggled in the heat and had been plagued by horseflies, which seemed to be everywhere and which added to the discomfort of life in the front line. Like Stan Perry's driver and many others, Heenan had also built up a collection of booty, including a large swastika flag, a camera, binoculars and some German writing paper he'd discovered in a knocked-out panzer; he, however, was determined to parcel up his loot and send it back home quickly in case his tank got brewed up. 'When a tank blows up,' he wrote, the bravado slipping a little, 'the turret is blown clean off. When I see the pictures in the magazines of blown up and burnt-out Jerry equipment, I wonder what people would think of precisely similar photos of Shermans and Churchills, which I have seen looking pretty horrible.'

The new commander of XXX Corps, Lieutenant-General Brian Horrocks, visited the regiment and made a great fuss of them. Horrocks had commanded a corps at Alamein, and although badly wounded in Tunisia, he was well known to those who had been in North Africa; a popular figure, he was nothing like as remote as many senior generals. It was noticeable that he had made the effort to visit the Rangers as a regiment within two weeks of taking over the corps; they'd not seen Bucknall, his predecessor, once. Certainly, Stanley Christopherson was thrilled by Horrocks's compliments for the regiment, which he felt had been sincere rather than just pep-talk hyperbole. It counted for a lot when they were battling so hard and sacrificing so much.

*

The rest at Coulvain also gave the men a chance to get clean and put on fresh clothes. For much of the time they looked a rather rag-tag bunch, which was in many ways a hangover from the Eighth Army days in North Africa, where a more relaxed approach to soldierly appearance took root at an early stage; later, indeed, it was positively endorsed by General Montgomery, trying to show a sense of commonality with his increasingly civilian army by creating the image of a beret-wearing commander. Now, in Normandy, he continued in this vein, with corduroy trousers and pullovers and an informal insouciance. Inevitably, it rubbed off. Tank men, rather like fighter pilots, were allowed to get away with a casual flamboyance that generally speaking was not shared by their peers in the infantry.

For the Sherwood Rangers, it began with the tanks themselves: Shermans covered in netting, foliage and large amounts of stowage, and given curious names like *Akilla*. Denim battledress of one-piece and two-piece overalls had been introduced for tank crews – and others – but the Sherwood Rangers mostly wore the standard two-piece serge battledress of trousers and jacket, plus black beret. It was common practice to wear scarves – often of silk – because of the constant need to swivel one's neck; this helped avoid chafing. Stanley Christopherson had a set of black overalls he often wore, which had zips at the bottom of the legs, as well as a pair of American brown paratrooper's jump boots. Many found the standard issue black leather-soled hobnailed boots impractical to wear in a tank, and so an assortment of footwear was worn – from suede crepe-soled desert boots to plimsolls and Commando-issue rubber-soled boots. Stan Perry tended to wear his Denison smock, which he'd been given during his SAS training, while Sergeant Nev Hinitt had a short US combat jacket, the ubiquitous M41. Certainly, personal comfort and pragmatism outweighed any notions of uniformity.

They all shaved regularly – even in the Sherwood Rangers, that was accepted as an essential daily requirement – but that and vigorous teeth-brushing was as far as personal hygiene went. 'Personal ablutions were limited,' admitted Stan Perry, 'and most preferred "shit, shave and shampoo" in leaguer to avoid the risk of morning frustration by an early call to deploy.' Only out of the line would there be a regular change of underclothes, and while in combat most men spent all day and every day in the same clothing, under- and outerwear alike. Stan Perry did better than most, however. 'I was extremely lucky that my wireless operator insisted that it was his duty to do my washing,' he noted. 'He even owned a small flat iron heated on a Primus stove.'

Most people tried to time the call of nature to when they were leaguered up for the night, and this meant wandering off with a shovel and
finding a quiet place to squat. Personal inhibitions soon went by the way-
side; they had to. Going for a pee could be done at one of the many times
a tank came to a halt, but there were days when on the road or in battle
when there wasn't much if any opportunity to get out of the tank. Such
situations called for an empty shell case and some nifty manoeuvring
around the cramped surroundings of the tank. 'Peeing wasn't too much
of a problem,' said John Cropper, 'but if it was the other you had to be
very careful because if the tank rocked or hit a bump you were in serious
danger of giving yourself an unwanted re-bore!' Stan Perry tried his level
best to avoid conducting bodily functions in the tank. 'In extremis we
used a 75mm shell case,' he noted, 'which was a good "pissoir".' Certainly,
the inside of a Sherman could become pretty ripe.

Crews also carried an assortment of weapons. Each tank man was issued
with a pistol – usually a standard-issue service revolver, although some had
US .45 calibre Colts and even German handguns. Many mistrusted the
Sten, which had a reputation for firing too easily – for example, if dropped
or put down too hurriedly. David Render had picked up a German MP40
submachine gun, known by the Allies as a 'Schmeisser', for which he was
rather ribbed by his friend Heenan. Others, Stan Perry among them, had
American Thomsons. There were also mountings for an extra machine
gun on the turret cupola, but few in the Sherwood Rangers chose to have
these because to operate them, the commander had to be even further out
of the turret – and if he was firing a machine gun, he couldn't be concentrating much on what was up ahead and around them. Perry also picked up
a German MG42 and had it fixed to his turret, but not for long. 'The big
snag,' he said, 'was that if you fired it everybody thought you were a bloody
German. So I got rid of that pretty quickly.'

It wasn't just the men who got a spruce-up – for the tanks, too, Coulvain
offered a chance for maintenance and cleaning. Yet even this much-
needed time out of the line, with a bit of rest and relaxation, was not
enough for all the men. One of those who'd got beyond that point was
Dick Dexter in Stuart Hills's crew. On reaching Coulvain, he'd refused
point blank to leave the tank. Instead, he just sat there, at his gunner's
position, barely saying a word.

'He's become armour conscious,' said Sam Kirman. 'He doesn't feel
safe unless he's got a couple of inches of armour wrapped around him.'

They'd all noticed Dick had become increasingly taciturn over the past few days; it was, of course, combat fatigue. Eventually, he was coaxed out and taken away in an ambulance. So that was another of their crew gone. Stuart Hills himself was also starting to struggle, the endless casualties chipping away at his confidence; he'd been particularly hard hit by Campbell's death, and it hadn't helped having to bury Howie and Mitchell single-handedly. He wondered, like Bill Wharton, when his luck might run out. He could clearly visualize the distress his death would cause his family and friends, and couldn't shift it from his mind. He also worried about his parents, both still prisoners of the Japanese, of whom he'd heard nothing. Hills was still only twenty years old.

Bill Wharton and his friend Colin Thomson had been drinking a lot of whisky since coming out of the line, although he was trying to keep a bit back for moments of stress in the future. He was also worrying about Micky Gold, who had lost much of his joie de vivre since their last battles. The easy bonhomie of those days near Caumont had vanished. 'He has not been so intimate with Colin or me of late,' wrote Wharton, 'although that is nothing to go by as he was ever subject to many moods.'

Perhaps Gold simply needed a day with his French girlfriend. At any rate, he persuaded Christopherson to accompany him to Bayeux for the day, where once again the family welcomed him with open arms, treated him like a long-lost son, and insisted both he and Christopherson join them for lunch. Stanley watched in awe of the obvious affection they felt for his friend, and wondered how on earth Micky could have made such firm friends in such a short space of time. A feast was laid on, both Angele, Micky's girlfriend, and her equally attractive sister Marie hanging off Gold's every word. 'Michael, speaking French fluently,' noted Christopherson, 'was in great form and kept the whole family in fits of laughter.' Micky Gold's dark mood seemed to have abated. Afterwards, they went shopping and Micky bought the girls straw hats. Then, after bidding them farewell with kisses and embraces, they drove back to Coulvain. And back to the war.

CHAPTER 17

The Noireau

H ARRY HEENAN WAS RIGHT that the Germans were beaten – in Normandy, at any rate. Their counter-attack towards Mortain and Avranches had been a predictable failure, and they were now reeling from the overwhelming weight of the combined Allied armies. Even a Polish armoured division had now entered the fray, joining the Canadians as they pressed on southwards. Operation TRACTABLE, the final drive towards Falaise, was launched on 14 August, while the US Third Army had taken Alençon, far to the south, on the 12th. The remnants of the two German armies were now being pressed on almost all sides in what was becoming known as the 'Falaise pocket'. Their only chance of escape was due east before the pocket was closed.

The role of 8th Armoured Brigade, alongside the 43rd Wessex Division, was to push on south to try to close the western end of the pocket. On 14 August, they took a large stride southwards some 16 miles towards the River Noireau. Their task was to swiftly secure crossings over the river. On that first day back in action, John Semken's men, along with the 5th Dorsets, captured the village of Proussy and took more than 100 prisoners. B Squadron, meanwhile, with the 7th Hampshires, cleared Les Haies, although not before a German rearguard had knocked out two tanks and damaged two more.

A key high point overlooking the Noireau valley was captured later in the day by C Squadron and the 4th Dorsets, along with a further 100 or so prisoners. Yet despite this significant bound and the clearing of the high ground north of the Noireau, General Thomas, taking a leaf out of Dempsey's book, summarily sacked Brigadier Norman Leslie, the commander of 130th Infantry Brigade. John Semken had been at the scene when Leslie was sacked, and was utterly appalled. 'General Thomas was a lump of shit,' said Semken. 'He was absolutely hated. This permeated the whole division.' Stanley Christopherson was saddened by what happened, as he liked and rather respected Leslie. 'I felt sorry for him,' wrote Christopherson, 'as the original orders were not clear and I felt somewhat apprehensive myself as the Sherwood Rangers were supporting Leslie's brigade.' Christopherson survived the cull, but one of the infantry battalion commanders was also axed, like Leslie, for being too slow. Colonel Basil Coad, commander of the 5th Dorsets, was promoted in Leslie's stead. Although only thirty-seven at the time, he was a popular and avuncular figure, known to all as 'Daddy Coad'. Christopherson, though, had never seen a man in such a dither. 'All the brigade and battalion commanders in 43 Division were somewhat fearful of Von Thoma,' he noted, 'who at the same time infuriated them as he insisted on fighting their battles and would not leave them alone after the final operation orders had been issued.'

Now that it was mid-August, the nights were drawing in a little, which meant slightly shorter days and heading to leaguer a little earlier than they had done back in June. Usually, the echelon trucks would already be there, waiting for them, with fuel, ammunition, food and other supplies. Most crews and troops had fairly set routines. In Stan Perry's troop, as soon as they reached leaguer, the driver and lap-gunner would fuel up. 'And quite often,' said Perry, 'that would be jerry cans and sometimes we would even have to form a little chain, so then we all had to muck in.' The Sherman absorbed 40 four-and-a-half-gallon jerry cans, and each can had to be manhandled from a truck then lifted on to the engine decks and poured in – which in itself took time.

The gunner and operator, meanwhile, would load up with ammunition and check everything inside the turret was properly housed so it didn't roll about. Each shell and belt of bullets had to be carefully passed up and stowed. Mechanical checks would also be carried out. Perry would help with these, unless he was called to an O group. Only once these tasks were done – and they could easily take an hour or more – would they have a meal. Perry's gunner was the cook in his tank; his party piece was to put hard tack biscuits in a sack and then get the driver to run the tank over it to crush them up nicely. 'And then he would mix it with some tinned pork and vegetables and make what he called chapattis, which he'd then fry over the Primus.' With all the tasks complete and food eaten and cleared up, at last they could consider sleep, usually on the ground next to the tank. 'I was a bit flash,' admitted Perry. 'I had a sleeping bag.'

On this particular night, 15 August, C Squadron had pulled into leaguer and begun their nightly routine after a rough couple of days, for although they'd suffered few casualties it had been exhausting and the country had become increasingly difficult, with narrow, winding and dusty roads, and everyone on constant edge about possible snipers, enemy troops with panzerfausts and hidden anti-tank guns. Now they were on a kind of plateau of rolling farmland overlooking the Noireau valley. This plunged quite steeply in places and much of it was thickly wooded too. Suddenly, a runner arrived from RHQ, which was leaguering next to them, summoning him to see the colonel.

Perry hurried to the collection of trucks, scout cars and tanks that formed RHQ and reported to Stanley Christopherson. 'I think every single member of the regiment that I ever met would have done anything for him,' said Perry. 'He had a facility for knowing people and befriending people, whatever their rank, whatever their style. He was a wonder at regimental commander, he really was. And so if Stanley said jump up in the air three times, you jumped up in the air three times. We had that regard for him as our commander.'

On finding the colonel, he was told he was needed for a special mission. Their objectives were the village of Berjou and the high ground around a feature on the map marked as Point 337, both of which were the far side of the River Noireau. The original plan had been to cross that night, but the Germans had destroyed all the bridges, and the steep valley sides and dense woodland meant there were very few crossing places for armour or indeed any other vehicles. They had, though, identified a possible fording point just north of the village of Cambercourt. Here, beneath where they were now leaguering, the slopes were gentler – and, even better, there was a track through a wooded gorge that led directly down to the river.

Christopherson told Perry that he remembered he had had training in the SAS.

'You're used to doing a little night job,' Christopherson said to him. 'Will you go and have a look and tell me whether it's crossable?'

Of course, Perry replied. Christopherson had asked very politely, but it was an order all the same. An infantryman went with him, and also a sapper with a mine detector. Off they set, crawling through the trees and then, out in the open, along hedgerows. Suddenly, they saw lights and realized they were the glowing cigarettes of troops dug in and protecting the river-bank. 'And with a bit of careful listening we realised it was a German machine-gun post dug in,' said Perry. 'The infantryman was very keen on having a go at it, and I said, not bloody likely – that'll tell everybody we're here.'

So they skirted around the group, made it to the river's edge and had a good look, their eyes now accustomed to the dark and the moon giving them enough light to see. Perry found a place where cattle had been watering so there wasn't much of a river-bank, and the stream here looked to be no more than 3 or 4 feet deep. The sandy bottom was a bit of a concern, but there was no alternative that he could see in the moonlight.

They headed back, lobbing several grenades at the enemy machine-gun post on the way to knock it out, then hurried back up the slopes to their lines, where Perry reported to Christopherson. By this time, it was early in the morning, so he shuffled off back to his tank, got into his sleeping bag and swiftly went to sleep.

Only an hour or so later, he was shaken awake by a runner summoning him to see Jack Holman. It was now 3 a.m. on Wednesday, 16 August. Holman wanted him to lead the crossing of the Noireau as he'd already recced the site. 'And I want you over the river by dawn,' Holman told him. Hurrying back to his troop, he got them all up. Cursing in the dark, bleary-eyed. Into the tanks, start up, rumble forward, Holman on the net cursing them already for being too slow. Rumble down through the trees to the open ground ahead of the river. Sappers busy clearing mines. Perry saw a dead engineer, blown up. It hardly made him feel sanguine. Hold up near the river-bank. Stop, get out, and talk to the sapper officer.

'Oh, you won't be able to get over here for another hour or two,' he told Perry. 'We're still working.'

Back in his tank, Perry had Holman on the net telling him to get moving. Mines or no mines. Behind him were Frank Galvin's 1 Troop, then Stuart Hills's 4 Troop. 'We were the only three complete troops in C Squadron,' noted Perry, 'after the fighting of the previous few days.' In the original plan, the infantry had been due to cross with them, riding on the tanks, but the Duke of Cornwall's Light Infantry – DCLI – had already managed to cross on foot, wading through the narrow river. The Sherwood Rangers hadn't worked with the DCLI before. Taking a deep breath, Perry told his troop they would have to risk it. 'Stay in my tracks,' he told them. 'If I get blown up, you'll know that I've cleared the way for you. But absolutely stay in my tracks.'

Nerve-wracking, yes, but Perry reckoned it was better to face the chance of getting the front of his tank blown off than to get a bollocking from Jack Holman. And he recognized the commanders higher up the chain thought this was important. To his relief, he made it across without hitting any mines. On the other side, the ground climbed immediately into close country thick with hedgerows and small fields. A road led to the small village of Cambercourt, whose main feature was a cheese factory. Beyond, as the ground rose steeply, a thick belt of woodland covered the slopes to the top of the ridge. Berjou, their objective, was up at the top, a little further on, beyond the wall of woods. The road that led there wound its way eastwards before dog-legging back and wiggling its way through the wood and on to the plateau of the ridge beyond. All the way, the road was lined either by dense hedgerows or woodland. It was a nightmarish stretch of countryside for tank crews, ideal for any enemy equipped with machine guns, mortars, sniper rifles and panzerfausts.

The right-hand side of the road into and out of Cambercourt was by now held by the infantry. Perry had been told he would have a platoon of them watching out for snipers and lurking panzerfausts. Already, some 600 mines had been cleared that morning from this short stretch of road up to and beyond Cambercourt, an incredible number. But as he rumbled towards the village, he was accosted by an infantry major and ordered to help his troops winkle out some enemy who appeared to be dug in on their right. Perry, conscious his orders were to get straight up the hill, demurred. 'This chap threatened to put me under open arrest for not obeying his orders,' said Perry. 'So I called Jack and he said, do as you're told. Head for the top of the hill. You're covering the Berjou road. Don't go swanning off anywhere else.' So far since D-Day, such friction seemed only ever to happen when the Sherwood Rangers were operating with an infantry unit for the first time, as was the case this morning. The officer was having none of it – until Perry put him on the radio to Holman. At that point the infantry officer stormed off and Perry went on his way, the rest of C Squadron following his lead.

They were winding their way up out of Cambercourt, along the high-hedged road, when they heard a loud bang and suddenly the radio aerial slithered like a whip over the turret and disappeared, hit by a panzerfaust round. It could so easily have been very much worse – but now, while their own intercom still worked, Perry had no radio contact with the rest of the troop or with anyone else in the squadron or even the regiment – a significant problem, given that he was leading, and also because tanks were more effective when working together. On balance, he thought he should continue on his way but lay off the track in case of mines. This meant working his way into the fields and through the trees, but he reckoned it would be safer; he just hoped the lads behind would follow even though they could no longer hear him.

Once they reached the woods there was no choice but to move back on to the road, as it was cut into the steep sides of the hill and the only bit of level ground there was. Thick woodland loomed above and below them.

Visibility in this close country was still difficult. Small arms were chattering and mortars falling and exploding as the infantry further down the slopes tried to push up on to the ridge. Eventually they emerged, climbing out of the treeline and on to the open farmland of the high ground around Berjou. Perry's tank was now entirely alone, with no infantry protection and out of contact with the rest of his troop who had fallen some distance behind. Thick hedgerows lined the road, while fields rose gently away to their right and more steeply to their left, climbing perhaps 100 feet or more to another line of trees and yet more hedgerows. They were perilously exposed.

Perry scanned carefully for panzerfausts but didn't spot the second warhead fired directly at them. Suddenly, there was another loud crash and the lap-gunner cursed that his trousers had been burned. It seemed a panzerfaust had been fired and punched a glob of steel through the front glacis and straight between the legs of Perry's co-driver. It was something of a miracle that, apart from his singed trousers, no one was hurt and that nothing especially critical had been hit.

Perry now saw a junction up ahead and, aware these were good places for hidden anti-tank guns, moved off the road again and into a field, rejoining it near a roadside Calvary shrine. Here, a track cut away to their left from the cross, back towards the woods behind them. His gunner, a fervent Catholic, asked if he could get out and offer a prayer. 'I drew the line at him dismounting,' said Perry, 'but I did stop to let him say a prayer.'

They rumbled on a short distance, but still he couldn't see the other two tanks in his troop, which meant his tank was the only one up on the ridge, and already attracting a barrage of mortar and small-arms fire. Bullets and shrapnel clattered against the hull. 'It was getting pretty hairy,' admitted Perry, who decided it would be prudent to half-close the twin lids on his turret. As he put out his left arm to pull back one of the covers, he felt a stab of pain and thought he'd been stung by a bee or wasp. But his arm flopped down his side and then he saw he'd been shot – a sniper bullet had hit him in the arm but had been stopped by the bone. It hurt a bit but wasn't bleeding too badly, and Perry had enough of his wits about him still to order his gunners to spray the line of trees away to their left on the sky-line with their machine guns and blast it with HE. 'And the first one we did,' said Perry, 'a figure dropped out of it, and I think that was the sniper who got me.'

Despite his wound – and very nearly being drilled in the head – he ordered his tank to press on. Berjou was only a little further down the road. He had no idea where the tanks following him were, and without his radio could do nothing to call them up. His arm hurt all right, but he reckoned it was going to hurt whether he was there on the ridge or back at the RAP. His operator made a splint for him and forward they went towards Berjou.

The enemy, a mixed bunch from the 3. Fallschirmjäger – Parachute – Division and the 1. SS Panzer-Division 'Leibstandarte SS Adolf Hitler', were demonstrating just how effective they could be with a handful of machine guns, mortars and panzerfausts in this countryside of woods, dense hedges and lines of trees. Perry's tank had not progressed much further when they were hit by a third panzerfaust warhead, this time in the track drive sprocket on the driver's side. This meant they could now only drive on one track, damage that would have been enough to prompt most crews to bail out. 'But I had a very good driver,' said Perry, 'and by inching forward then braking a bit, and then inching forward a bit more, he could drag the dead track and still move a bit.' A little while later, the wireless operator managed to rig up a secondary aerial so that, although they still couldn't make contact with the other two tanks in his troop, Perry was able to speak to Jack Holman – who told them to try to get back to the river.

Tank warfare could be confusing at the very best of times, but for Perry at this moment, cut adrift from both the rest of his troop and the squad-ron, the situation was particularly alarming. He was wounded, so too was his tank, and travelling on one track the couple of miles back to the river was a torturous prospect. They managed to turn the tank round and head back down the track past the Calvary shrine, a route which, for the most part, kept them clear of the enemy on the higher ground to the left of the road. 'We went back cross-country again,' he said. 'I was supposed to take the road but I was always a bit wary of roads.'

Out of contact with the rest of his troop – or any other, for that matter – Perry was unaware that his troop sergeant's tank had already been knocked out on the way up, which had held up both Corporal Brooks, following third in his troop, and the subsequent troop of Lieutenant Frank Galvin. And it was Hills's troop that was next – his tank had been the seventh to ford the Noireau. The plan had been for Stan Perry's troop to get up on to the ridge, then turn left into the field that led up towards a farm and the highest point round about. It was from further up this hill that he'd been sniped. Galvin and his troop were to do the same and secure this dominating high ground, and then Hills and his troop would thunder straight on into Berjou, confident that Perry and Galvin had him covered. Infantry were to provide support on the ground.

Every part of the plan was going to pot, however. The infantry were still battling it out on the lower slopes where the tanks simply could not go, while their artillery had hammered the woods running up to the ridge but had not directed fire on to this hill beyond – which was not at all obvious from aerial photographs and even maps, which were in short supply. Yet it was here, the objective of Perry's and Galvin's troops, that the 3. Fallschirmjäger men had concentrated – and for obvious reasons. The hill dominated the farmland around it, and offered an ideal OP from which to watch the road below – which, after all, was the only one that climbed up from Cambercourt and the River Noireau. It made it a simple target to zero.

Corporal Arthur Brooks had eventually emerged from the woods to find no sight or sound of his troop leader. Greeted with a flurry of mortars and MG bullets spattering around him and clattering against the tank, he had ordered his driver to cut back along the lane from the Calvary shrine in an attempt to tuck himself behind the hedge alongside the track. This, though, left him open to attack by panzerfaust, not least because there was a sunken lane that led from the hill down to the far end of the track that the *Fallschirmjäger* could use. With mortars and machine-gun fire continuing to drop and rattle around him, he was now frantically asking for urgent support over the net. And well he might – he was a sitting duck.

Already, it was late morning. Actions like this always sucked up time. Brooks didn't know what had happened to Perry, but for himself he did know that being alone and isolated up there was not good. Clearly, he needed reinforcing, and quickly, so it was agreed that Lieutenant Galvin would push forward with his troop and try to take the high ground in short order before Hills then moved up and into the village. They had to hope Brooks could fend off the enemy until Galvin's troop could come to his aid.

While Galvin now emerged with his troop from the woods and out on to the road, Hills's three tanks waited out of sight among the trees further back below the ridge. For Hills, the start of the journey had not been half as bad as he'd feared, except for the odd shell and mortars landing close by. The troop had had no trouble at all as they'd climbed the road and entered the wood. In fact, the only trouble at this stage was with Arthur Reddish – who had smashed his right forefinger when the blast of a nearby shell had slammed his open hatch on to it just as he'd been trying to fix it into its locking ring. He was in agony but able to carry on for the moment.

For the time being, Hills and his troop now waited in the woods for the signal from Galvin that they were clear to storm the village. Time ticked by and no news came. They tried to raise him on the radio but got no response, either from him or from the other two tank commanders in his troop. This was because they were all on the 'B' net – the shorter-range net for the troop – rather than on the 'A' net for the entire regiment. Brooks, isolated and in desperate need of help, had switched his radio to 'A', which was why Hills could hear him. Hills now called up Jack Holman, who was similarly in the dark back down near the river, trying to get the infantry to play ball; the DCLI men were still clearing the woods and the slopes where the tanks were not able to venture.

Inwardly cursing Galvin, Hills eventually decided he should press on. He wondered where on earth they were – and cursed the lack of infantry too. Some had now reached Brooks, however, having scrambled up through the steep wooded slopes behind him – but they amounted to just a handful, a platoon, nothing more. Once again, going into action with an unfamiliar infantry battalion had led to poor cooperation and, as a consequence, the C Squadron men were now facing the enemy almost alone.

As Hills's troop rumbled forward and emerged from the woods, it was clear the plan was continuing to fall apart badly. There was still no word from Galvin. Now, as Hills's tanks pushed out into the open farmland, mortars and small-arms fire crashed around them. Rather than head into the village, he ordered his troop to turn left, towards where Brooks was valiantly trying to hold on. Hills tried to keep his head down as much as possible and told his crew to keep swivelling their periscopes, watching out for panzerfausts – and within moments a fizz of a sniper's bullet whipped past his head, just inches away.

Mortars continued to crunch around them and shells too, seemingly from a wood on the far side of the village, where there were men from 1. SS Panzer equipped with a Nebelwerfer – a six-barrelled rapid-firing mortar whose shells screamed with a particularly chilling moan, from which they'd got their nickname 'moaning Minnies'. None the less, Hills's three tanks managed to manoeuvre around the fields, so that they were out of sight of the crest of the hill and the farm, and link up with Brooks, who was also carrying wounded men from Perry's second tank on board. Hills now ordered him to try to move back to the road and head back down to the river, while he radioed for the Essex Yeomanry to shell the likely enemy gunners. He then moved forward and all three tanks opened fire on a thick copse just 100 yards or so ahead of them. With shells crashing around them, mortars bursting and clattering against the hulls, and smoke drifting over the battlefield, all they could do was fire HE and spray the trees and hedgerows with their Brownings and hope for the best.

'The next five minutes,' noted Reddish, 'were horrendous.' First came word of Frank Galvin. It seemed he and his troop had not turned up on to the hill but instead had pushed on towards Berjou and been hit around a bend in the road just before the village – by what was not clear, but his tank had been brewed up and the entire crew killed in the inferno. Moments after this news reached them, Corporal Brooks's tank was hit as he returned towards the woods, the blast blowing him clear of the turret. Seeing this, Sergeant Guy Sanders, one of Galvin's troop who had dealt with Lieutenant Birkett's burning tank just two weeks earlier, jumped down to help the wounded corporal. It was an act of immense bravery – but as he did so a renewed flurry of mortars crashed down, and both Sanders and Brooks were cut down and killed. Around the same time, Sergeant Sleep, in Galvin's third tank, was drilled in the head by a sniper's bullet.

Eight men in the squadron now dead and seven wounded. Six of those casualties were tank commanders, four of whom had been killed, including one of the squadron's legends, Sergeant Guy Sanders, MM.

Hills sat in his commander's seat while this carnage unfolded, aware that he was every bit as vulnerable. Minutes passed. More infantry appeared and then shells from the Essex Yeomanry began to crackle through the air; the wood beyond disappeared amid a swathe of explosions, dust and smoke. If there were enemy tanks, none were seen; the greatest danger in this countryside and from these German rearguards was from the ambush, and that moment had now passed. The danger had not gone but it had lessened. Hills did not know this, however. 'Those taking part in a battle never know what is in front of them or what is going to happen,' noted Hills. 'And it is the uncertainty and ignorance that jars the nerves and causes that well-known sinking feeling in the upper half of one's abdomen – the point being that one can never tell when, or from where, the fatal shot will come, and one is always expecting it.'

That was very much how John Cropper in B Squadron was also feeling as his tank pushed on up through the woods. He had no idea what had been going on up ahead and he and his crew were all on edge, nerves taut, expecting a German with a panzerfaust to jump out at any moment. Suddenly, there was a thunderous roar overhead. 'I frantically spun around in the turret to see what it was,' he said. 'Everybody was scared to death.' It was a German fighter plane, so low it was barely above the trees – and it was followed by an RAF fighter, blazing away.

Such was the tension in the tank, an argument now broke out between two of his crew, over music of all things. 'Our nerves were shot,' admitted Cropper. 'Within seconds they were literally screaming at each other – I had to be very firm with them to break it up.' By the time they emerged on to the higher ground, the situation had improved greatly, with weight of fire telling against the enemy.

Already, Hills's troop, with the infantry behind and around them, had pushed forward across the fields, clearing the hedgerows as they went. Cropper's crew weren't the only ones scared; Reddish could barely contain his fear. Next to him, Geoff Storey, the driver, admitted he was scared too. How could they not be after what they'd witnessed earlier?

At a crossroads of hedgerows, Hills ordered Storey to put his foot down and they burst straight through into the next field, surprising a number of German paratroopers on the other side. They captured about sixty, the infantry rounding them up. 'All they had,' noted Reddish, 'were rifles and the odd light machine-gun. Perhaps they'd run out of panzerfausts.' Hills now moved his troop into the lee of a small hill and directed Captain Arthur Warburton and the ever-dependable Essex Yeomanry to pummel possible enemy positions. Shells whooshed over, and during this rain of fire one massive explosion occurred, sending a rolling angry ball of flame erupting into the sky. They must have got lucky and hit an ammunition dump.

The fighting had taken all day and it was getting dark by the time Lieutenant-Colonel George Taylor, the commander of the DCLI, appeared and proposed an assault on the village. But with dusk falling, Hills had only four tanks available and Jack Holman now called him back to leaguer. Their hellish day was over.

The following morning, Arthur Reddish woke to the sound of birdsong. For a moment, he listened, happy – then, with a jolt, he remembered the previous day's events. So many of his friends had gone. Brooky – Corporal Brooks – had been promoted the same time he and Sam Kirman had declined the chance to command their own tanks. Bill Sleep had been with the regiment since the start of the war and had been a good NCO, popular with the lads. Guy Sanders was a hero to many in the squadron: fearless and loved by all. Frank Galvin had been a good fellow and his crew all friends of Reddish. It was hard to comprehend they were all gone.

The campaign in Normandy was so nearly over, the Germans on the run. The crossing of the Noireau was but one day in many of bitter, costly fighting; but for those involved, it had been a hellish place that Wednesday, 16 August. And it was a harbinger, if ever one was needed, of the long, hard battles the Sherwood Rangers Yeomanry still faced in the days, weeks and months to come.

PART II

Autumn – Belgium
and the Netherlands

CHAPTER 18

The Chase

BERJOU WAS CAPTURED THE next day, 17 August, with B Squadron pushing on through and taking the village of Honorine-la-Chardonne, a couple of miles to the south. A firm bridgehead over the Noireau had been established and 'Von Thoma' seemed pleased; at any rate, he did not sack any more commanders. Stanley Christopherson could breathe a sigh of relief. RHQ was established in a farmhouse at the edge of Berjou. It was a glorious late summer's day, the sun strong, the light golden. That evening, Christopherson took a walk to the end of the village and marvelled at the view of the surrounding countryside with its hills and endless patchwork of fields and woods. Ahead of him were the steep sides of the narrow valley leading down the Noireau, and beyond, to the north, the rolling country of southern Normandy over which they'd passed during the previous few days. 'From there,' he wrote, 'I could fully appreciate why the mortar and shell-fire had been so accurate. The Germans could see every movement we made.'

The padre, Leslie Skinner, had had a lot of catching up to do that day. On his way to the ridge he passed an orchard and, seeing a tree of ripening apples, decided to stop to gather some. When he reached it, two Germans, armed to the hilt, emerged from a slit-trench and surrendered to the unarmed chaplain. Having offloaded his prisoners, he reached the newly established RHQ at lunchtime only to learn of the terrible losses for C Squadron, so retraced his steps back to the previous day's start line to bury the dead. He found Brooks, Sleep and Sanders, and dug and marked their graves, but Galvin's tank was still burning. All around it was an absolute shambles, with plenty of German dead lying round about in addition to the charred wreck of the Sherman. 'Fearful job,' he noted, 'picking up bits and pieces and re-assembling for identification and putting in blankets for burial.' Jack Holman offered him some men to help, but Skinner refused; he didn't want those who had to fight to witness what he was seeing. 'This was more than normally sick-making,' he noted. 'Really ill – vomiting.' All were buried in the hastily established Wessex Division cemetery at the crossroads on the edge of the village.

Some much needed comic relief was found at C Squadron's leaguer, however. One of the troopers had gone off with a spade to answer the call of nature and, having pulled down his trousers and squatted down, found himself facing a German soldier armed with grenades and an automatic rifle. Both quickly jumped up, the German to surrender, the trooper to protect his modesty. 'The sight of the heroic trooper,' wrote Skinner, 'clutching his trousers with one hand, and marching his still-armed prisoner down the hill to captivity was quite a sight.'

It was only a brief moment of cheer, however. Dead Germans lay all around RHQ, and Skinner could not sit back and let them remain there. These too were young men who needed decent burial, especially with the sun beating down. He had just finished this latest round of burials and was being sick yet again in the ditch when Brigadier Prior-Palmer stopped by and told him to 'take it easy'. Skinner appreciated the sentiment, but felt very profoundly that it was his duty to see these men buried. 'Horribly sick again before going to bed,' he scribbled, 'and again during the night, several times.'

Stan Perry had joined the growing ranks of the Sherwood Rangers who had returned to England. Having been helped to clamber from his tank, he'd been taken to the RAP where 'Hylda' Young had patched him up, and from there had been sent to a field hospital and then put on a ship for home. At Portsmouth he transferred to a hospital train which, after getting going, then came to a halt at a level crossing. He was among the walking wounded and, spotting a pub tantalizingly open, asked a medic how long it would be before they moved. A couple of hours at least, came the reply.

So he nipped off to the pub and ordered himself a pint, his first in many a long week. When he went to pay for it, the landlord told him firmly he wouldn't be accepting his money. 'And all of a sudden,' said Perry, 'there were five pints of beer lined up.' He'd enjoyed a couple of them when a man came in with a large basket full of all manner of goodies, from bars of chocolate to fruit, and handed it over to him. Would he take it back on to the train and share it with the rest of the lads? Soon after, a nurse hurried in and told him he needed to get back on board as they were about to leave. 'I've had to search some places for my patients,' she told him, 'but never in a public bar.' Restored and feeling nicely appreciated, Perry was soon on his way to Baguley, a military hospital built in the grounds of the Baguley Sanatorium in Manchester. There he was finally operated on to remove the bullet still in his arm and to set the broken bone.

The Normandy campaign came to an end on 19 August when Polish and US troops met up and closed the Falaise pocket, within which the bulk of the German forces in Normandy had been almost entirely encircled. Most had remained trapped there: barely two dozen tanks and 50,000 men out of two armies got away, hurrying to flee back across the River Seine; at least 300,000 were killed, wounded or taken prisoner in Normandy. Now there was not a single panzer division – the cream of the German army – that could still function effectively as a fighting unit. Nearly 2,500 German tanks and other armoured fighting vehicles had been destroyed in Normandy and well over 300,000 men killed, wounded or captured. It was a colossal Allied victory.

On 15 August a second Allied invasion force had landed in southern France. Operation DRAGOON had seen the US Seventh Army set ashore some 151,000 American and French troops, which were to sweep northwards and help clear southern France of the occupying Germans. Meanwhile, the plan for Eisenhower's forces in the west was now for the US Third and First Armies to sweep east and north-east across France while the British and Canadians pressed north-east. The first objective was to liberate all of France, after which Allied forces would push on into Belgium, Holland and Germany itself. The immediate task was crossing the River Seine, behind which the shattered remnants of the German forces in Normandy had retreated.

The Sherwood Rangers were out of the action as the battle for Normandy ended, spending a couple of quiet days at Honorine-la-Chardonne – happily, a village largely undamaged and sweet-smelling; at least until the wind changed and suddenly the all-pervasive stench of rotting dead cattle returned.

On Sunday, 20 August, Padre Skinner held a church service for the regiment and was pleased that some 250 turned out; perhaps, though, it was not surprising that so many of those who had survived would want to offer up a prayer. During the ten weeks since D-Day the Sherwood Rangers had lost 44 officers and 175 other ranks. Since there were only 36 officers in the regiment at any one time, that meant, statistically, no officer had a chance of surviving unscathed. Those still alive might be grateful, but most were wondering how much longer it would all go on. What chance did they have of surviving until the war was finally over? Every man had to try his hardest to shut out such thoughts, but it was never easy. All of them had seen too much already.

Stuart Hills was certainly struggling to process what had happened. 'The shock of death,' he wrote, 'is, I suppose, something that every man in action very soon gets hardened to and reactions are less painful than death under peaceful surroundings, but the effect that our six commander losses caused that day was something that not only affected me but the squadron's spirit as a whole.' Friendships in war were formed more quickly than in peacetime, and were often deeper too. Bonds forged by the shared experience of war were intense, and to be chatting and laughing with a friend one moment and then to see him killed and his spirit violently shattered for ever was hard – all the more because one knew one might so very easily share the same fate.

That same Sunday afternoon, Skinner was visited by John Semken, and the two of them had a long talk. Semken had lent the padre a book of devotional readings and prayers, and they chatted about faith and mysticism; Skinner was happy to do so, conscious that spiritual guidance came in many different forms. Semken was battling on, but increasingly gripped by a sense of fatalism. 'The casualty levels were terrible. Unceasing,' he said. 'It was crazy, really. I always used to say that we were living on borrowed time.'

New officers and reinforcements arrived and troops were hastily reorganized. Sam Kirman was promoted to signals sergeant. Arthur Reddish was able to congratulate him before heading off to see the MO about his crushed finger at the urging of his pal Busty Meek. It looked terrible; 'Hylda' Young took one glance at it and sent him down the line to one of the field hospitals, where he was given emergency surgery. For some reason, no anaesthetics were available for him; instead, he was given a large tot of rum. 'The finger was opened, drained and the nail removed,' noted Reddish. 'It was a bizarre experience.' Now only Geoff Storey remained with Stuart Hills from the crew that had found itself bobbing about in a raft on D-Day.

Stephen Mitchell agreed to take back command of C Squadron, which, so badly mauled, needed his quiet and senior authority, and Jack Holman returned to his position as second-in-command. Taking over as second-in-command of the regiment was Major the Lord Rupert Leigh. His arrival was an inauspicious one. Stanley Christopherson had been walking around the Regimental Headquarters tanks when he spotted a very short, round-faced man struggling to free himself from a barbed-wire fence on which he'd managed to catch himself. Christopherson hurried over to help him; once free, Leigh saluted smartly and announced himself. Aged thirty-six and the 4th Baron Leigh of Stoneleigh, he had commanded the Royal Gloucester Hussars, which had remained stationed in England. Bored and determined to play a more useful role in the war, he had applied to join a regiment in the field and been posted to the Sherwood Rangers. Christopherson immediately dubbed him 'the Baron'. 'He spoke very little,' he noted, 'but possessed a subtle wit, which he showed on many occasions and when something amused him he displayed his mirth with a most delightful giggle which shook the whole of his frame.'

An expected move was cancelled and instead, at around midnight on 22 August, orders arrived for them to head east early the following morning, in what would be their largest bound since arriving in France. They moved out at 6.50 a.m., when, with British double summertime in force, it was still dark. Never before had the regiment moved at such speed; with no mines to stop them or German ambushes anywhere, the roads were wonderfully clear – until they neared the tiny village of Chambois and had to cross the River Dives. A few days earlier, this had been where the last German troops had desperately tried to escape the closing Falaise pocket. Caught in an horrific bottleneck, they had been hammered by a combination of Allied artillery and fighter-bombers.

Shocking scenes of destruction greeted the Sherwood Rangers as they crawled through the partially cleared remnants of the fleeing and defeated German armies. 'The sight is horrible,' wrote Harry Heenan the following day. 'Hundreds and hundreds of dead and mangled horses, stacks of German bodies, Tigers, Panthers and Mk IVs, big guns, little guns, cook lorries, moaning Minnies and the whole darned lot. You can see places where we have chased an individual truck across fields and fields and then finally blown it to bits.'

It had rained overnight and into the morning, so the roads, already churned up by the mass of vehicles that had been using them in recent

days, had become seas of mud. Before that, though, the weather had been
hot, blazing down on the carnage. The result now was ghastly: bodies
swollen, blackened and rotting, millions of flies and a stench so powerful
it made everyone gag. It would be cleared up in due course, but hadn't
been yet. Unavoidably halted in the middle of this slaughter, Stanley
Christopherson saw the Baron clamber down from his tank and walk
over to *Robin Hood*. It was Leigh's first experience of a battlefield, and the
first time in the couple of days since his arrival that Christopherson had
seen him with anything other than a ruddy complexion. He had gone
quite yellow and was puffing furiously on his pipe in an attempt to hide
the stench and prevent himself from vomiting.

'A bit of a mess,' he said.

'Yes, the air force got them fair and square,' replied Christopherson,
having clambered down too. He was puffing every bit as hard on his own
pipe and hoping Leigh wouldn't notice how close he was to throwing up
himself.

'Is it generally as bad as this?'

'I have not seen much worse than this,' said Christopherson, noticing
the remains of a horse that had been blown to bits just a few yards from
his own tank.

Fortunately, they soon got moving again and managed to get clear of
this apocalyptic scene. Ahead, they met more clear, open highways, and
passed through cheering crowds at Gacé, Touquettes and Saint-Evroult-
Notre-Dame-du-Bois, before finally leaguering in beautifully untouched
and unspoiled countryside about 3 miles east of the town of L'Aigle in the
département of Orne. They had moved some 60 miles in a single day,
which just went to show how fast Allied armoured regiments could travel
when not confronted by endless mines, guns and lurking enemy equipped
with panzerfausts.

Here in the fields and orchards near L'Aigle the regiment would remain
for the next few days, partly to give the men a much-needed rest, but also
to attend to the tanks and vehicles; urgent maintenance was needed. For
the exhausted men, this was the first time since D-Day they really were
clear of the sound of guns, the stench of death, and the threat of random
enemy shelling, the remaining German troops having hurriedly headed
north and east back across the Seine. 'Whenever we came out of action
for several days, a feeling of exuberance existed among us,' noted Stuart
Hills. 'We did not bubble like an effervescent schoolboy, but we knew that
for a short spell the numbness would disappear from our minds and

bodies, and that for a change, instead of being automatons of destruction we could be human beings.' The chance to catch up on sleep, to wash and get clean again, to put on fresh uniforms – these were small comforts but seemed the heights of luxury after what they had been through. Soon, too, the men were bartering for food with the farmers – eggs, milk, and fresh meat and fruit made a welcome change from the usual rations. In Hills's troop there was a trooper called John Bennett who was a dab hand with the piano accordion, and in the evening they took to sitting around a fire, drinking NAAFI ration beer and local cider and having a sing-song – bawdy tunes, comic songs or well-known numbers of the day. Hills wasn't musical himself and didn't have much of a voice, but he recognized these were moments of timeless significance that really did bring men together. Music, he thought, was wonderful for morale.

Drink definitely helped, too. During their last leave, Harry Heenan had got hold of a bottle of Cointreau and two of brandy, which he and his fellows had swiftly seen off. It was his twenty-first birthday on 25 August and he thoroughly enjoyed his day. 'We were by the grace of God static,' he wrote to his parents, 'and had a real party in the evening, with the big nazi flag as table cloth and we all got slightly tight.' That might have been something of an understatement as he reckoned he'd drunk a lot of 'champagne cider' and at least half a bottle of whisky. Bill Wharton was also drinking considerably more than he would usually have done; like Heenan, he was normally fairly temperate. On 27 August, Wharton was suffering from a sore head, having had too much cider and calvados the previous evening at the farm where they were camped. 'The farmhouse is more the manor,' he wrote, 'a huge place of some four storeys high which at the moment is a rabbit warren teeming with refugees.' Wharton was impressed by the hospitality of the owners towards their fellow citizens in need, and by their willingness to open their arms to their liberators. He and Colin Thomson had been invited to a dance in the village, which they had both enjoyed, and on arriving back at the house found seven of the lads from B Squadron sitting around a huge table with a number of French refugees as well as family members all having dinner.

Wharton and Thomson were ushered in, given glasses of cider and calvados – which explained Wharton's hangover at the time of writing – and engaged in conversation about the Soviet Union. Their French host wondered whether they would all soon be at war with Russia once the Nazis had been drummed out. Were they, he wondered, frightened of the Soviets? As veterans of the famous Eighth Army, Wharton and Thomson both replied that they were not afraid of anyone. 'Which, of course,' Wharton wrote, 'is a lie, for my experience has taught me that everyone is frightened of the other fellow and it is only pride and an unwillingness to show that you are scared that keeps you going.' As for fighting the Russians, they told the Frenchman there was not a hope. They'd had more than enough fighting already these past five years.

The rest periods always ended too soon. 'The end never seemed far off,' wrote Hills, 'and on one awful day the word would come round to pack up and we would be on our way again' – grumbling and cursing as they did so. This time, notice was given suddenly just after midday on Sunday, 27 August; seventy minutes later they were moving out, a great cacophony of engines and squeaking tank tracks – although without Micky Gold. Stanley Christopherson had given him a pass to go on a 'recce' to see his old regiment, the 23rd Hussars, and he had disappeared off in a jeep with Squadron Sergeant-Major Edwin Biddle and his rather straight-faced batman, Nicholas Rugman. When the orders arrived for the regiment to get moving, there was still no sign of Gold and his entourage.

The war could not wait for them, however. The Sherwood Rangers were expected at the Seine that evening, and once again they sped through the towns and villages they passed. Film footage was taken showing the regiment hurtling through one village, civilians out on the streets, waving and cheering them on, the Recce Troop leading the way ahead of Shermans piled high with stowage and camouflage webbing – and a Firefly, its turret rotated so the long barrel pointed backwards.

Four Allied armies were now sweeping east and north-east: the Canadian First Army closest to the coast; then the British Second Army with XXX Corps, including 8th Armoured Brigade and the Sherwood Rangers, on the British southern flank; then the US First Army; and finally US Third Army. Paris fell on 25 August, to French troops of the 2nd Armoured Division and Americans of the 5th Infantry Division; it was one of the first places where the River Seine was crossed. The Germans had been so utterly smashed in Normandy that there had been little resistance in between, although a defence of sorts was being made on the northern banks of the river. One of the biggest challenges was the lack of bridges, all of which had been destroyed by the Allies before D-Day to hamper the Germans' movement. Their destruction had been very effective in slowing the German response to the Normandy invasion, but it was now far easier for them to cross the river, with their meagre forces, than it was for the Allies, with their vast numbers of troops and vehicles and their huge arsenals.

The Sherwood Rangers, however, were heading not to Paris but to Vernon, 40 miles west of the capital. The regiment romped nearly 70 miles that afternoon, although it had to leave Stuart Hills and Dick Holman behind as their tanks broke down en route; they spent a very comfortable and pleasant night in a hotel in Evreux, although C Squadron was still so short of officers that Hills had to leave his tank and crew behind and hurry up to Vernon early the following morning.

A Squadron were the first of the Sherwood Rangers to cross the Seine, early that day on a new Class 40 pontoon Bailey bridge that had been hastily completed during the night and was code-named GOLIATH; the infantry had already gone across in boats and on a lighter Class 9 pontoon Bailey bridge built alongside and predictably named DAVID. On the far side, however, there were steep wooded slopes, not so very different from those around the Noireau, and the enemy, elements of 150. Grenadier Regiment, were showing some resistance with machine-gun and mortar fire.

David Render's 5 Troop were to be first across the 100-yard-wide bridge, which had yet to be tested and which bowed significantly in the middle from the fast-flowing current. None of his crew liked the look of it much, and so Render decided they should all sit on the back of the tank rather than inside in case the worst happened and they tipped into the water. His driver wasn't particularly happy about being the only one inside and, having inched on to the bridge, then put his foot down, speeding over as quickly as possible, the bridge creaking and groaning and Render and the rest of the crew clinging on for their dear lives. Sappers shouted at them to slow down, and once safely on the other side Render bawled at his driver while the rest of the crew muttered that he was a 'fookin' twat' for driving so recklessly. 'I don't think it bothered him in the least,' wrote Render, 'he was just glad to be back on firm land.'

John Semken followed not long after in a Firefly, and the squadron pushed on into the thick woods beyond, where they met up with the 7th Somerset Light Infantry and a distressed battalion commander who had lost one of his companies during fighting in the forested bridgehead. The tanks offered to push on and try to locate the missing company, but the thick woods were a mass of tracks and it was an easy place to become disorientated; David Render could readily see how an entire company might have gone missing.

They had not gone far when Render heard the whine of a tank turret moving, and a moment later spotted a Panther just as its muzzle flashed and a shell whistled past and hit a tree behind. With a shell already up the spout, his gunner quickly fired back, hitting the panzer but without causing any obvious damage. Instead, the Panther hastily reversed with a puff of oily exhaust. Close woodland like this was not the place for a Panther with its long-barrelled gun.

They never did find the missing company of Somersets; it later transpired they had pushed too far, become cut off and then been captured. The decision to send in this company had been made by General Thomas, not by the battalion commander, who had been worried about the inexperience of this particular company commander. Despite having given rise to the loss himself by his needless micro-managing, when Thomas heard what had happened he summarily fired the Somersets' CO.

The following day, having helped expand the bridgehead at Vernon, they pushed on a further 20 miles. Micky Gold had reappeared in the afternoon and, rather than concocting some implausible lie, had confessed all to Stanley Christopherson. It seemed he had never had any intention of visiting the 23rd Hussars. Rather, after they'd driven only a short way, he told both Biddle and Rugman they were actually going to go to Paris, a journey of about 80 miles. The ever debonair and cosmopolitan Gold simply wanted to see the newly liberated capital – a city he knew well – for himself. Great moments in history were occurring and he wanted to witness them in person.

They reached the city without a hiccup, reckoning they were among the first – if not *the* first – British troops in Paris since the liberation two days earlier. Parking up outside a café, they went and sat down, ordered wine and were soon invited over for a meal by some grateful Parisians. As they ate and drank they could still hear machine-gun and rifle fire in the distance. Satisfied he'd now witnessed the freed Paris at first hand, Gold told Biddle and Rugman it was time to head back to their camp near L'Aigle. Arriving there later that evening after their eventful day trip, they found only the squadron clerk, sitting alone and forlorn on an old ammunition box, waiting for them.

Gold and his fellows eventually caught up with the rest of the regiment the next afternoon, as B Squadron was pushing out of the bridgehead over the Seine. 'When Michael reported to me,' noted Christopherson, 'he still appeared to be reliving his hectic hours in Paris and was in no mood to attend an orders group.' Gold was not remotely contrite; rather, he told Stanley that, as representatives of B Squadron, they had raised the prestige of the squadron and the regiment by having been the first British fighting troops in the French capital. What's more, the story had rapidly evolved in the retelling. It was not a café they had been to, but the Ritz, where a disabled Tiger tank had stood outside. They hadn't drunk wine, but champagne, and rather than being invited to share a meal by a few Frenchmen, had been mobbed by grateful Parisians who partied with them long into the night. Had General 'von Thoma' been in charge, Gold would have been sacked; but the Sherwood Rangers always liked a bit of spirit, and Christopherson gave his old friend nothing more than a mild ticking off. In truth, he had found the whole episode hilarious.

The regiment was back together for the next stride, due north towards Amiens. With the Canadians still clearing the coast and the Americans pressing north-east and eastwards, British Second Army were hurrying to clear northern France and then push on into Belgium. On 29 August, the Sherwood Rangers were hastily formed into an armoured regimental group along with the mobile Essex Yeomanry and a company of motorized infantry from the 12th KRRC. Both Chris Sedgwick of the Essex Yeomanry and Derek Colls of the 12th KRRC were under Christopherson's command and travelled with his Regimental Headquarters. This was an all-arms combination, commanded by men who knew and liked each other, and was able to function with speed and highly effective coordination. It was also assembled quickly and efficiently. A rearguard at Ecos was swept aside, while B Squadron together with the mounted KRRC blew away further resistance at Saint-Rémy – and without a single casualty.

The weather took a turn for the worse, but Harry Heenan, for one, was grateful that the days were starting to draw in. 'We can't start before about seven in the morning,' he wrote, 'and have to stop fighting or whatever is happening by about 9 at night, so we get more sleep than in the light days when we went to bed at 0100 and got up again at 0430.' He was now feeling sharp, keenly alive and flushed with the excitement brought by victory and the heady chase across northern France.

On they went, the narrow valleys and *bocage* of Normandy left behind and replaced by wide, open and undulating farmland. Now they could adopt the old desert formation of one squadron up front leading, RHQ close behind and a squadron on each flank. They covered another 30 miles on the 29th and over 50 on the 30th. Such distances took their toll on the tanks, however, whose rubber-padded tracks took a beating on the rough roads. In B Squadron, John Cropper and his crew were forced to hand over their tank to an officer whose own tank was out of action; they followed in one of the trucks for a day while the officer's tank was being repaired. 'We did a lot of truck bashing on that trip,' said Cropper.

Six A Squadron tanks became bogged down trying to cross the Thérain river and had to be rescued by the LAD, but still they forged on, meeting no organized resistance. On, past Amiens.

On 1 September they crossed the River Somme, the next major obstacle, and just to the north met some resistance near Flesselles. Here, Sergeant Leslie Cribben and Trooper John Sharpe of the Recce Troop were killed when their Honey light tank was hit by a Panzer IV. At the next town, Naours, they ran into a large number of German infantry; fortunately, they had no supporting fire, and so were quickly overcome and the survivors rounded up.

Heenan was leading the squadron – and regiment – as they thundered towards Doullens, which lay in the shallow valley of the River Authie. The road north into the town was a long, straight one that ran past an eighteenth-century star-shaped fort to the left. Heenan crested the brow and surged on down the hill into the town – only to see a 75mm anti-tank gun positioned and waiting on the bridge, now just a few hundred yards away.

A flash, a crash, and suddenly a shell hit a glancing blow on the turret, gouging a groove and missing Heenan's head by very little. Slamming on the brakes, his driver frantically put the Sherman into reverse, nearly crashing into the tank that followed and causing a pile-up. Dismounting, John Semken now ordered David Render's 5 Troop to work around the citadel and manoeuvre into the town from the flank.

Render quickly found a track around the fort, which seemed to have an odd-looking aircraft of some kind on a ramp on the top of the fortifications; only later did he learn this was a launch site for the V-1 flying bombs still raining down on London. Pushing on round the fort, he broke on to a road that led back into the town, only to be accosted by a woman who, in broken English, and pointing frantically towards a large wooden barn, urged him, 'Good men. Don't shoot.' Dismounting, and, this time, with Sergeant Jackson beside him, Render approached the barn, gripping his captured German Luger pistol. In the barn were around twenty Germans, their rifles stacked against the wall. Ordering them out on to the road, and with Brownings trained on them, Render and Jackson disarmed them and searched them for papers. Then, in his best pidgin German, Render ordered them to head south and surrender to the first British troops they saw.

Off they went, while Render and his troop mounted up again and got ready to move on into the town. Suddenly, Johnny Lanes called out that the prisoners were not heading south but running north towards their own lines. Without hesitation, Render ordered his men to open fire, cutting them down like hay. The troop hurried on, hearing tank gunfire, and as the bridge came into sight they saw the German crew dead on the ground around it and the Pak 40 knocked out. While Render's 5 Troop had been heading around the citadel and capturing Germans, Sergeant George Dring had stalked the anti-tank gun on foot and directed *Akilla* through some trees to deliver a fatal volley.

A Squadron now pressed on into the town together with a company of the KRRC, destroying several more guns and capturing more than 100 enemy troops. 'I had a lucky escape,' wrote Heenan of his Doullens experience, 'and also a triumph when I knocked one and possibly two out.' With the town in their hands, they realized the importance of the V-1 site, reported it to the higher command, then pressed on again – David Render, for one, happy to have done something to directly help his family back in London. Despite this battle for the town, the regiment still surged a further 50 miles that day. Later, Harry Heenan ribbed his great friend David Render about his late arrival at the bridge – the banter of two young men flush with confidence. These were giddy times, as daily they took giant strides across France in much the same way the Germans had done as the British and French retreated back in 1940. How the tide had turned.

CHAPTER 19

Talking with the Enemy

TIME AND AGAIN, STANLEY Christopherson had to refuse permission to Leslie Skinner to go and find the regiment's dead. On Saturday, 2 September, the padre wanted to recover the bodies of Sergeant Cribben and Trooper Sharpe, who had been killed at Flesselles, but the colonel stopped him; odd pockets of German troops were still round about and it was an unnecessary risk. Eventually, though, later in the afternoon, he relented – although not before telling Skinner he was a damned fool and insisting that if he saw no British troops in the village he was to leave their vehicle well out of sight and approach cautiously on foot.

As the padre neared the village it seemed ominously quiet, and so, as instructed, he asked the driver to wait while he clambered down and walked on. Sure enough, the knocked-out remains of Cribben's Honey light tank stood abandoned near the railway station. He soon discovered that while the wounded had been picked up and taken to a field hospital, the two dead men had been laid out in the parsonage next to the church and were about to be buried by the priest and some locals. The graves had already been dug – right under the noses of the Germans: a lone panzer stood a little way down the road, the crew watching.

Despite their presence, Skinner helped with the burial of the two men. The village priest worried there were no coffins for them, but a farmer brought in some hessian and Skinner stitched Cribben and Sharpe into makeshift bags, made out their name details and ensured the right marking of the crosses, then watched from the parsonage as the priest led a modest funeral procession down the road to the graveyard. The Germans continued to look on but without interfering. Having seen the two men safely committed, Skinner hurried back to the edge of the village where he found the driver and truck. 'With rifle at the ready,' scribbled Skinner, 'he was more than glad to see me. It must have been a long hour and a half.' Safely back in the truck, they hurriedly set off northwards to catch up with Regimental Headquarters.

The Sherwood Rangers sped on, past Arras and over the battlegrounds of the last war. 'I saw the Great War cemeteries,' wrote Harry Heenan, 'and the great Canadian Memorial at Vimy Ridge. It was very moving to think of the men who fought over these great battlefields of the Somme and the Marne.'

Bill Wharton was also struck by all he'd witnessed. 'I cannot begin to describe the terrific incidents of the last three weeks or so,' he wrote to his wife, 'during which time we have travelled right through France and into Belgium. The scenes of welcome in Northern France have been absolutely terrific.' Heenan was every bit as thrilled by such scenes. 'The tanks get covered in flowers and tricoleurs and Union Jacks and we all wear little rosettes permanently now,' he wrote. 'They give us hens and eggs and wine and we give them chocolate and cigarettes and bully beef, which they like. You have to shake hands with everyone, in fact, they form a queue to get at you and you have boys and girls running around kissing you frantically.'

At one point, Wharton's troop was leading as they entered a village, which meant his was the first tank in. Fired on by a panzer that fortunately missed, Wharton's tank rapidly fired back, and the enemy tank scuttled away. Pausing in the centre of the village, Wharton jumped down and was mobbed and kissed by ageing grey-bearded men – 'so no shy young maidens,' he assured his wife. They then moved to the edge of the village to keep a watch on the flank as the rest of the squadron thundered through. Wharton was invited to lunch first in one house and then another, was plied with wine and spirits, and ended up feeling a little half-cut. It was as well they were ordered to move out again before he was given any more. 'In fact,' added Wharton, 'in recent days I have had most of my meals in different people's houses and for the last three nights have slept in a bed.'

The chase continued, up past Lille, in the north of France. On 3 September, the fifth anniversary of Britain's entry into the war, they covered a further 65 miles, and on the 4th they crossed over into Belgium. Here, Stanley Christopherson called an O group for his squadron leaders. John Semken and A Squadron were to press on to the town of Oudenaarde,

Micky Gold and B Squadron to Kherkove, both to capture separate bridges across the River Scheldt and to prevent any kind of counter-attack southwards. That evening, Stanley Christopherson and his armoured regimental group headquarters reached the town of Renaix to a rapturous reception and set themselves up outside the dye works on the edge of town. They had now travelled 250 miles in nine days – including an entire day off, 2 September, for maintenance. This was further and faster than the Germans had advanced during their lightning march through France back in May 1940.

The chase was not without incident. Pockets of enemy would be over-run, and from time to time they would be shot at. As always, the troop leading the squadron took the greatest risk, and so this responsibility would pass to different troops in turn. During one leap forward, 4 Troop in B Squadron pulled over to the side of the road after a morning in the lead. Once the rest of the squadron had passed them, they moved on again – but no sooner had they done so than John Cropper, whose tank was now at the rear, spotted some farm buildings and veered off the road towards them.

'Where the hell do you think you're going?' Lieutenant Cowan yelled at him. Cropper pointed to the farm and the other two tanks in the troop followed. It was not the enemy that he'd spotted, however; rather, he was hoping the farm might yield up some chickens and eggs. Soon the men of 4 Troop had taken over the farm and were running around chasing chickens. 'One chap was trying to bring them down with a Sten gun,' said Cropper. 'He missed with every shot.'

Before long, mortars began to rain down, fortunately not very heavily, and so they beat a retreat and hurried to catch up with the rest of the squadron. Cropper's tank rejoined the road with the gunner, Ted King, on the back of the tank cooking a captured chicken in a pan over a Primus. When, a little later, they came under fire and were involved in a brief action, King had to come back into the turret and take up his position as gunner. 'So the stove, pan and chicken,' said Cropper, 'were passed down to the co-driver and as we went into action he sat in the front of the tank with his chicken cooking away at his feet.'

Events were moving every bit as fast elsewhere across the front. The US First Army drove through Mons in Belgium, creating a big gap in the German lines, while Third Army liberated Verdun in north-eastern France on 3 September, the same day British troops entered Brussels. Antwerp was then liberated on the 4th. These were staggering gains; the

Guards Armoured Division, for example, had travelled some 330 miles from the Noireau area in Normandy in just over four days to enter Brussels. Most Belgians were not even aware Allied troops were in Belgium, let alone the capital, until suddenly Shermans and Cromwells were rolling down the city's streets.

Yet the great chase was finally starting to run out of steam. It was to the huge credit of the Allied logistical chain, as well as the mechanical reliability of their tanks, armour and other motor transport, that so much ground had been covered in such a very short time – certainly, there was no way German tanks would have withstood such punishment – yet none the less, the Allies were reaching their culmination point: the moment their lines of supply became so overextended they could no longer operate effectively. The Allied advance was literally running short of fuel – most of which was still coming in through Normandy – and many other supplies besides.

What's more, German resistance was increasing as the Allies began to run into those parts of the enemy armed forces that had not been in Normandy. Much of the German Fifteenth Army, for example, had been spared, and the Belgian and Dutch coast, including the estuary of the River Scheldt, which led to Antwerp, remained in enemy hands. The British inland were also ahead of the Canadians who were clearing the Channel ports in northern France, so that much of the left – coastal – flank remained in enemy hands. The Sherwood Rangers and their battlegroup were pushing towards Ghent in the north, and on 5 September C Squadron had got to within 15 miles of the city while A Squadron captured more than a hundred prisoners at Oudenaarde.

That same day, B Squadron had moved back to Renaix and then been ordered to investigate a village south-east of the town. Bill Wharton was leading a patrol of tanks and infantry when they were met by local Belgian resistance fighters who told them the small village of Pierre was occupied by around 1,200 German troops who had captured and shot a number of the local Maquis and made it clear they had no intention of surrendering, despite now being effectively surrounded.

Wharton set off towards the village; as he neared it he was shot at by an anti-tank gun, which fortunately missed. Hastily pulling clear, he paused while the Maquis brought him the priest of the neighbouring village; then, having spoken to the priest and fashioned a large white flag, he entered the village, hoping the gesture of truce would be observed. It was a courageous act on his part and one that could very easily have ended badly.

However, the Germans observed the truce and, on meeting the first enemy troops, Wharton demanded to see their commander. He was duly taken to see the colonel, who told him he had considerable troops and arms at his disposal and had no intention of surrendering – especially not to an officer of junior rank.

Hurrying back to his tank, Wharton contacted RHQ and spoke to Stanley Christopherson. Although the German colonel had refused to surrender, Wharton had sensed a chink in his resolve. Perhaps if Stanley came down, he suggested, his superior rank might do the trick. Christopherson agreed, and after grabbing Stephen Mitchell, who spoke German, and Chris Sedgwick of the Essex Yeomanry, drove over to Pierre, where they found Wharton talking to the local resistance, who were demanding at least two Germans for every one of the four of their number who had been shot. It was not clear whether these resisters were going to prove more of a hindrance or a help, but they did suggest that Christopherson and his party enter the village in an old Renault they had somehow kept – and kept going – rather than a military vehicle. The amply cushioned priest, who had clearly not suffered much from wartime rationing and food shortages, agreed to accompany them.

The Renault arrived and Christopherson, Mitchell and Bill Wharton all clambered in, with the outsize priest perched on the bonnet clutching the flag of truce. 'Not surprisingly,' wrote Christopherson, 'it took a long time to get the car started.' Eventually, however, after a long push by the Maquis and other locals who had suddenly appeared, it burst into life with a bang, lurching forward so that the fat priest nearly toppled off the bonnet. A couple of hundred yards further on it stopped again, and the pushing procedure had to be repeated, the Belgians each offering different advice to the hapless driver. Eventually they got going again, and roared into Pierre in a cloud of dust. 'I shall never forget,' wrote Christopherson, 'the most remarkable spectacle of the worthy priest balancing, with great difficulty, his fat bottom on the bonnet of the car, vigorously waving the huge white flag, which was a sheet fixed to a pole, and clutching his large black straw hat.' It was hardly the entrance of mighty conquering warriors.

Clambering from the car, Christopherson, Mitchell and Wharton were escorted past numerous anti-tank guns and troops to see the garrison commander, whose headquarters were in the village inn. On entering the bar, Christopherson demanded to see the colonel and was told he was in conference in one of the upstairs rooms. 'I told the orderly to lead the way and we followed,' noted Christopherson. 'He pointed to the room and I gave an imperious knock on the door, which I opened without waiting for a reply.' Inside, the colonel was addressing some twenty of his officers, all of whom turned to look at the new arrivals with utter disdain.

'I am Colonel Christopherson,' Stanley told him, trying not to show a hint of the apprehension he felt. 'I presume you are the commander of this garrison. If so, kindly clear the room so that we can discuss terms of surrender.'

Christopherson was quite pleased with the tone in which he conveyed this message, although he was irritated that beside him, Stephen Mitchell kept nervously tugging at his moustache; it rather threatened to undermine his own assured authority. The colonel – short, dapper and wearing an Iron Cross first class – bowed.

'I should be obliged if you would allow me five more minutes with my officers, alone,' he replied, 'then I should be pleased to hear what you say.'

Christopherson agreed, and the trio left the room and headed back downstairs. There they found a Belgian officer who had been captured by the Germans and was being guarded. Both the Belgian and the guard were dumbstruck to see the three British officers, but once he had recovered from his shock, the Belgian lieutenant told them the garrison was indeed well equipped and strong in numbers, and contained a number of fanatics. He also told them the Germans had captured four British tank crew.

Around ten minutes later they were called back up. As they climbed the stairs, Christopherson told Mitchell to try very hard not to tweak his moustache. 'Stephen scowled,' noted Christopherson, 'and murmured something about me being irritated at not having a moustache to pull to conceal my own nervousness.'

German officers were leaving as they went back into the room. Only the colonel remained and his adjutant, who wore a black uniform and had a scarred face. 'His adjutant was a typical Hun,' wrote Christopherson, 'and was continually clicking his heels.' He was rather taken by the adjutant's very smart black leather jacket. They spoke in German, Mitchell doing an admirable job of translating and managing to leave his moustache alone.

'No organized German resistance now remains in France or Belgium,' Christopherson told the colonel. 'My regiment, consisting of tanks, infantry and guns is outside this village waiting to attack. I can summon air support within half an hour, you are completely cut off and without contact with your higher formation. I demand the surrender of your garrison.' The bit about air support was not strictly true, but he felt there was no point in undercooking his position.

The German colonel accepted the situation for them was bleak. 'But I have under my command a garrison strong in men, guns and ammunition,' he replied. 'It is my wish, and the wish of my officers, to fight and to delay your advance. It would be dishonourable for me as a German officer to surrender so large a garrison without fighting.'

This slightly unnerved Christopherson – and also Mitchell, who became so discombobulated he could no longer translate properly. Christopherson hastily suggested they speak French instead, at which point the adjutant's face lit up as he announced that he could speak it fluently. Since Mitchell spoke French better than German, the negotiations were able to continue more freely. Christopherson pointed out that while he understood the colonel's concerns about honour, the consequence of fighting would be untold casualties and yet more bereaved families in Germany.

This seemed to hit home, and Christopherson now winked reassuringly at Mitchell. Although he was confident that if it came to force they could prevail, he was determined to do his best to avoid casualties, among both his own men and the civilian population, and also to spare the village, which was currently untouched. Yet although the German colonel was wavering, the loss of honour entailed in surrendering seemed to weigh heavily upon him. It took a further hour of persuasion, threats and appeals to his humanity before, finally, he conceded. He would surrender – so long as he could do so at the head of his men, and so long as Christopherson gave a sworn and written assurance that none of his men would be handed over to the Maquis. Christopherson agreed, and arranged to meet him at six that evening at the edge of the village where the road crossed the railway line. He also promised to send Dr Young to attend the colonel's wounded.

After a series of formal bows, the three Sherwood Rangers officers departed, found the fat priest anxiously waiting by the car and rejoined their contingent, who had waited for them at the edge of the village in increasing anxiety that some disaster had befallen them. The entire afternoon had had a rather surreal air to it, and now the negotiation party were back among their own, Christopherson ordered up the rest of B Squadron and a company of the KRRC, while Chris Sedgwick brought up some Sextons ready to respond should the Germans renege on their pledges.

Six o'clock came and went, and half an hour later Christopherson and his fellows began looking at one another with mounting concern. Then a burst of German machine-gun fire ripped across the evening air. Their first thought was that the Germans were attempting a breakout. At much the same moment, Dr Young appeared with his ambulance to collect the wounded, as promised. Christopherson told him to head into the village but very cautiously. At the inn, Young was met by the black-jacketed adjutant, who professed ignorance about any shooting. The doctor suggested to the adjutant that he should return to Colonel Christopherson in the ambulance with the driver while he attended the wounded. Just as the adjutant was getting into the ambulance, more firing rang out, accompanied by the explosion of mortar shells. At this, Young dashed back to the ambulance and the German adjutant back into the inn.

On reaching his own lines once more, Young told Christopherson he'd not seen any other Germans in the village. 'I forthwith called for Bill Wharton's troop,' noted Christopherson, 'and we entered the village, expecting to be shot up at any moment.' Instead, they were met by the German adjutant, who frantically waved them down. It seemed the Germans had left the village at the opposite end to the one agreed and had been fired on by a patrol of Green Howards. Hurrying on through, Christopherson and Wharton saw Germans taking cover either side of the road. Rolling straight through, they reached the Green Howards, told them to cease fire and then found the colonel, looking rather shaken by the entire experience and clutching the bridle of a magnificent white horse. Christopherson asked him why he was marching out in the opposite direction to that agreed. A brief consultation of the map showed that the railway, which looped all around the village, actually crossed roads leaving Pierre in two places, not one. They had been marching towards the wrong crossing.

So there had been no perfidy on the part of the Germans after all; and with this confusion cleared up, the German colonel asked permission to address his men and then to give orders for them to break arms before marching off to captivity. Christopherson agreed and watched as the German garrison were brought to attention. The colonel then explained to his men that they had agreed an honourable surrender and then bade them farewell. An NCO barked the order for the men to break arms, and they promptly began crashing their rifles and weapons on to the ground and breaking the butts. After this, each man raised his right hand and shouted 'Sieg Heil!' three times. Christopherson was rather impressed. 'The colonel then turned to me,' he wrote, 'handed over his pistol and signalled his orderly to hand over his white charger.' And with that, the surrender was complete. A difficult and potentially costly battle had been avoided, despite moments of both extreme apprehension and also comedy.

Despite the pleas of the local Maquis, Stanley Christopherson kept his word and refused to hand over any of the German prisoners, although he agreed to write a report for the resistance men, which included their witness statements and would be available once the war was over for any war crimes investigation. Then, after a day of rest and maintenance, they were off again, this time to Brussels. Christopherson did not relish the thought of sending an entire regimental battlegroup through the city, so as they approached he sent Micky Gold on ahead to recce a route through, arranging to meet him at the city's edge.

He'd picked Gold because of his fluent French. 'But in the haste of the moment,' he noted, 'forgot his amazing capacity for making friends and his fatal charm to members of the opposite sex.' Sure enough, there was no sign of Gold at the agreed rendezvous, so Stanley, in a jeep and with Stephen Mitchell beside him, went ahead and led their column into the city. Although Brussels had been liberated several days earlier, the party had by no means ended and they were mobbed by cheering crowds, their jeep swamped with flowers, food and wine. Progress was slow, but eventually they made their way through and continued to Aarschot, a small town to the north-east of the city.

Here they paused for further much-needed maintenance, the squadrons leaguering in the surrounding villages. Some of the original tanks that had landed on D-Day had covered more than 2,000 miles since then, and most needed repairs and overhauls of some kind. There was also another chance for most of the men to sleep under cover. 'Once again,' wrote Bill Wharton, 'the majority of the boys have found themselves homes in the village and daily we have a crowd of visitors to see us.' The Sherwood Rangers had arrived at the right time for fruit, and were showered with a glut of grapes, plums, apples and pears. 'I must have eaten pounds and pounds' worth of plums, grapes and peaches during the last few days,' wrote Harry Heenan. 'We have a great pile of large peaches on board now.' In return, the men enjoyed handing over bars of chocolate to the children, most of whom had not seen any in more than four years. Their tanks had also been transformed by endless graffiti written in chalk. 'We also have the names of half the towns of France and Belgium,' added

Heenan, 'with the dates scrawled on our sides by the people as we pass through.'

Micky Gold finally reappeared the following morning, 8 September, apologizing profusely to Christopherson and explaining he had badly lost his way. Why, or with whom, he did not specify, but he was soon forgiven and in no time had managed to find himself a billet that included a suite of rooms and a Belgian household happy to run around at his beck and call. He also suggested to Christopherson that they take a jeep and head back to Brussels for dinner. Stanley pointed out that none of them had any Belgian money, but this objection was brushed aside. So, off they set, with Arthur Warburton of the Essex Yeomanry in tow, driving right into the heart of the city and parking outside the Carlton, one of the finest restaurants in Brussels.

As they entered, Gold stood aside to allow two very striking Belgian girls and their escorts to pass, bowing and giving them a winning smile as they did so. Moments later, he was talking happily to them and within minutes Gold, Christopherson and Warburton were all invited to join their party for dinner. 'The food was superb,' noted Christopherson, 'the wine excellent, and we had a most delightful evening.' Nor did it end there, for afterwards they were invited to join the girls back at their house, where they all drank champagne. At around 2 a.m., they finally left – only for Warburton to claim he had left his gloves behind. 'It took him 20 minutes to find his gloves,' wrote Christopherson, 'assisted by one of our beautiful hostesses.'

How far away the war seemed that night, or even the following morning, in the regiment's peaceful surroundings near Aarschot. The sun shone down in the last hint of a fading summer, but with an autumnal sharpness in the air that reminded Bill Wharton they were now in the second week of September. His birthday was fast approaching; in just under two weeks, he would be thirty-two. 'I reckon that is just about too old for campaigning, don't you?' he asked in a letter to Marion. 'Besides, I want to get home to my wife and daughter instead of gadding about the continent.'

He was unaware, of course, that in the days to follow the Sherwood Rangers were about to face some of their darkest moments.

CHAPTER 20

Surrounded

T HE BATTLE FOR GHEEL was a terrible one for all those involved – the
151st 'Durham' Brigade, the German defenders, the Sherwood
Rangers and all the various other units involved. For three weeks the
Germans had been on the run, beaten, the Allies striding in giant leaps as
they forged their way through France and into Belgium. Stuart Hills was
not alone in feeling a little blasé and believing the worst was now behind
them. On 10 and 11 September 1944 any such hope was to be proved
cruelly and tragically misplaced. Few remember this battle now; like so
much of the fighting that followed Normandy, it has been swallowed up
by a wider narrative that lacks much detail or understanding, in which
the Allies pressed relentlessly on, inching incrementally into Germany.
Yes, there were some large-scale operations, such as the Battle for Arnhem or the Battle of the Bulge, that are generally remembered as setbacks
rather than triumphs, as though the wind had firmly been taken out of
Allied sails after the stunning victory in Normandy; but eventually, the
narrative runs, sheer weight of numbers prevailed, not least because of
the vast scale of the battle along the Eastern Front, and in the end Nazi
Germany was crushed.

This narrative is one that does a great disservice to all those Allied
troops who slogged their way towards the eventual German surrender in
May 1945. It ignores the difficulties of the terrain, the worsening weather,
the continued pointless but incredibly effective defence of the Germans.
And it ignores the immense sacrifice made by so many young men in the
last eight months of the war. Right up to the very end, the fighting was
relentlessly brutal and extremely violent, and those in the front line faced

great danger and utterly appalling odds against getting through unscathed. Proportionally, the Sherwood Rangers more than played their part in these last battles of the war in Europe, and that was especially true of the tank, troop and squadron leaders. Just as they had throughout the Normandy campaign, they continued to shoulder extraordinary responsibility and risk.

A young squadron or troop leader had to learn very swiftly to multi-task in battle or suffer the consequences. Shells might be raining down, both from bigger guns and from the ubiquitous and deadly mortars. Machine-gun fire would be rattling, while the ever-present threat from snipers and panzerfausts meant keeping an eagle eye out at all times. While all this was going on, he would have to communicate with his crew over the intercom while also listening to the wider nets of the other tanks in his troops as well as the rest of the squadron. He had to concentrate at all times, his senses keenly attuned to all that was going on around him. And on top of all this, he had to make sure he kept his head – for most, protected by nothing other than the black wool of his beret – above the turret almost all of the time. Further challenging him would be the fog of war: smoke, rain, mist – or on clear days, the sun in his eyes. Frequently, these young men would have to make instantaneous decisions without any pause for consideration or analysis – decisions upon which lives depended. A pause, a moment's doubt, could be fatal. So, too, a lapse in concentration. So much was laid on these young men's shoulders. David Render would not turn twenty until 18 September; Harry Heenan had only just turned twenty-one on 25 August. 'They always think I am terribly young to be an officer,' wrote Harry Heenan after he'd been to a dinner organized by the mayor in Aarschot, 'and will hardly believe I am 21.' Stuart Hills was still twenty years old; John Semken only three years older. They were little more than boys, really.

Nor was the war standing still in terms of technology and tactics. Normandy had forced the Sherwood Rangers rapidly to work out new methods of operating and fighting, but those hills and folds and tiny fields of dense *bocage* had gone. Now they were operating in land that was as flat as a board, like much of the desert; but unlike Egypt and Libya, here it was criss-crossed with canals and dykes running among fields and woods and villages and towns. And as well as adapting quickly to this new environment, they had also to adapt to an entirely new concept: shortages. In Normandy, they had at least had very short lines of supply. Increasingly vast supply dumps were never more than a few miles behind the front line. Forward delivery squadrons, too, were never far away, so new tanks could swiftly be brought up to the front. All this had now changed. Their lines of supply were horribly stretched, and even with maintenance days the tanks had taken huge punishment in travelling great distances. Even the astonishing mechanical reliability of the Sherman had proved fallible after covering more than 300 miles in a fortnight. Now, just as the Sherwood Rangers were being ordered back into the fight, they were not even close to full establishment. Ammunition and fuel were also running low.

It could not be helped, however. The chase might have ended, but there was still a lot of work to do. With the Germans only now regaining some kind of balance, and with the cream of their armoured forces destroyed, a swift end to the war in the west seemed tantalizingly close, especially since it wasn't only in the west that the Wehrmacht had been given a mauling. The great Red Army offensive that summer, Operation BAGRATION, had smashed a giant hole along the Eastern Front that had destroyed much of the German Heeresgruppe Mitte – Army Group Centre – and pushed the front westwards to within touching distance of Warsaw. Yet despite this shrinking of the Reich, the challenge for the western Allies was how to get across the Siegfried Line, the major German defences along the country's western border, and the mighty River Rhine, which protected the frontier. Much of this borderland was lined with dense forests and rivers. Geography was not going to help a swift strike into Germany.

What's more, the weather was noticeably worsening again and the days dramatically shortening as they neared the autumn equinox. 'I am afraid that if the weather stays like this,' wrote Harry Heenan perceptively, 'tearing wind and driving sheets of rain, we are not going to get this business finished til next year. It only wants good weather, an armoured push into Germany and the dreaded Typhoons roaring over the skies of the homeland to finish it off.'

As it happened, the recently promoted Field Marshal Montgomery was of much the same mind, and, conscious that time was of the essence, he proposed making a dash through Holland, crossing the Rhine at Wesel, then turning east above the Siegfried Line. This, he suggested to Eisenhower, should now become the main Allied effort. There were some logical reasons for this approach. In Holland, the Rhine was considerably narrower than it became as it wound its way south, while the northern German–Dutch border was not protected by the extensive defences of the Siegfried Line, or Westwall, as it was also known. Patton's Third Army, for example, now approaching Strasbourg in eastern France and nearing the mighty Rhine, was already some 450 miles from the supply bases still in Normandy. That was a very long supply line indeed.

An Allied strike into Germany through what was effectively the back door, therefore, had some merit. Montgomery's first proposal was Operation COMET, but was swiftly increased in scale for a crossing over the Rhine at Arnhem, to the north of the Siegfried Line defences, where the river was significantly narrower. The plan was to use the Anglo-US Allied Airborne Army: British airborne troops would secure the bridge at Arnhem, while American paratroopers would secure crossings over other significant rivers such as the Waal at Nijmegen, just 10 miles to the south of Arnhem. While airborne troops captured and kept open these vital bridges, the British XXX Corps would steam hell for leather some 60 miles, blazing a corridor through which ever more troops could flow. This way, Germany's two great barriers, the Siegfried Line and the River Rhine, could be overcome and the path to Berlin blown wide open. This was to be called Operation MARKET GARDEN. There was absolutely no question that such an operation faced major challenges, but with a highly trained and motivated Allied Airborne Army sitting back in England waiting to be deployed, and with the enormous benefits such a strike would create if successful, it was, on balance, worth the punt.

First, though, a firm start line for XXX Corps' drive had to be established from the Escaut in northern Belgium, a river straightened into a canal, which ran in a roughly semi-circular arc and which, at its closest, was 15 miles south of Eindhoven, one of the crossing points for XXX Corps' planned drive to Arnhem. To reach the Escaut, however, the British first needed to get across the Albert canal, another significant obstacle, which, at its furthest point, ran west to south-east 15 miles to the south of the Escaut.

This was an obstacle the Germans had no intention of tamely giving up. Commanding all troops in the west was Feldmarschall Walter Model, the commander-in-chief of Heeresgruppe B, which included 15. Armee along the Belgian and Dutch coast and 7. Armee, desperately trying to rebuild after its almost complete destruction in Normandy and now facing the Americans to the south and east. On 5 September, Model had summoned Generaloberst Kurt Student, commander of the *Fallschirmjäger* forces, and told him to build as a matter of urgency what was to be designated the 1. Fallschirmjäger Armee. His mission was to collect all available units, put them together in double-quick time, and plug the 60-mile gap between 15. Armee and 7. Armee. His first priority was to get a force together that was capable of holding the Albert canal at all costs for as long as possible – not least to buy time to build up the rest of his new army.

His task was made no easier by some 65,000 Dutch Nazis fleeing Holland for Germany and clogging up railway lines and roads; yet within a matter of days he had organized a mass of Luftwaffe airfield defence, training and occupation units which, along with the 719. Infanterie Division, extended down to the Albert canal. Forming behind this were further units, a mish-mash of armour and SP guns and artillery, but also *Fallschirmjäger*. Although these paratroopers were not the uniformly elite units they had been during the Blitzkrieg years and, like all units of the Wehrmacht, had suffered from drastic cuts to training, they still had a cadre of highly competent and experienced men and collectively were certainly a cut above the rest.

While the Germans had been hurriedly shoving these forces forward, the British had made a bridgehead across the Albert canal at Beringen, 30 miles south-west of Eindhoven in Holland, and then a second breach just to the south of Gheel, a small market town a little way to the northwest. It was to support the crossing here that the Sherwood Rangers were now sent.

The 50th Tyne Tees Division, the regiment's old friends from D-Day, had been ordered by General Dempsey to get across the Albert canal swiftly at Gheel. In the early hours of 8 September, infantry of 69th Brigade managed a crossing at a place called Het Punt, to the south-west of the town, but now General Graham, the Tyne Tees Division commander, ordered his 151st 'Durham' Brigade to make a second crossing at the village of Steelen, a mile and a half to the south-east. The Gheel area was held by a German battlegroup of some 3,500 men called Kampfgruppe Dreyer, after its commander, Oberstleutnant Georg Dreyer: a mixture of infantry and Flieger regiments, which were Luftwaffe airfield defence troops and for the most part undertrained and understrength. For all that, though, they had a handful of mortars and several 88mm anti-tank guns, and were supported by three batteries of field guns – some thirty-six in all, as well as small arms and an increasing number of panzerfausts. Certainly, they were a considerably more coherent and threatening force than anything the Sherwood Rangers had seen since Normandy.

Not until Class 40 Bailey bridges had been secured over the canal could any armour be brought up. The first bridge was opened at Het Punt

George Dring and his crew astride their tank, *Akilla*, near Rauray, where they helped knock out five enemy tanks on 26 June: a Tiger, two Panthers and two Panzer IVs. *From left to right*: Dring, Harry Hodkin (gunner), Blondie Denton – standing (lap-gunner), Spike Bennett (operator) and Sid Gould (driver).

Right: John Semken in North Africa and (*far right*) his great friend Ronnie Hill, with whom he shared his leave in Cairo before the Battle of Alamein.

Below: Some of the legends of the Sherwood Rangers, following their Military Medal inauguration after returning from North Africa. *From left to right*: Cpl Derek Lenton, MQMS John Scott, Sgt Erny Thwaites, SSM Henry Hutchinson, Sgt Guy Sanders, Sgt George Dring and Sgt James Loades.

Below: B Squadron at B.9 camp near Fawley in May 1944, just before D-Day. The officers and senior sergeants are in the third row.

Bottom left: Shermans lined up in southern England before loading for D-Day.

Bottom right: Waterproofing a tank on board a landing craft.

Sgt Bill Digby, fatally wounded on Jig Green on D-Day.

An A Squadron Sherman driving off an LCT on to Jig Red on D-Day.

Sgt William Bracegirdle, who won an MM for his actions on D-Day.

Sherwood Rangers DD Shermans passing through Bayeux on 7 June.

Shermans advancing inland.

The Sherwood Rangers found themselves stuck around Point 103, Saint-Pierre and Fontenay for much of June and saw bitter fighting. Dead cattle such as these (*above left*) were a common sight, while a knocked-out Pak 40 anti-tank gun and Panther (*above*) mark the road into Fontenay from Saint-Pierre. On the same road, but looking west, Charles Renney's knocked-out B Squadron Sherman lies abandoned (*left*).

Below left: A 24th Lancers Sherman heads south towards Rauray past the Panther that was knocked out by Neville Fearn and George Dring on 26 June, while (*right*) Stanley Christopherson sits beside the 88mm gun of a Tiger captured intact at Rauray.

Left: John Hanson-Lawson, commander of B Squadron, rescued by Bill Wharton at Rauray.

Right: B Troop of the Essex Yeomanry with their Sexton, a Sherman chassis mounted with a 25-pounder field gun. The Essexmen were invaluable friends to the Sherwood Rangers.

Above: John Semken and Stanley Christopherson (*left*) in conversation on the eve of BLUECOAT. *Above right*: Semken in the turret of his Sherman at the start of BLUECOAT.

Left: A Squadron tanks move up towards Ondefontaine on 4 August, while Tommies clamber over a captured Jagdpanther (*below left*), an increasingly common foe for the Sherwood Rangers. An assault gun rather than a tank, it had an 88mm gun built on a Panther chassis.

Below: The indefatigable Padre Leslie Skinner (*right*) conducts yet another burial service in the field.

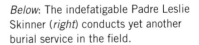

Frank Galvin (*left*), a troop commander in C Squadron. *Above,* sappers clear mines, a constant hindrance. Laid in their millions by the Germans, these simple devices could bring a column to a halt and clearing them sucked up huge amounts of time.

Above: John Cropper's crew next to his tank, *Blue Light Special*, during a pause in the fighting, while (*below*) a C Squadron crew pose with their Firefly and its powerful 17-pounder gun.

John Semken (*top left*), during a pause in the charge through France and Belgium. The Sherwood Rangers faced a bloody battle at Gheel. Among those with Stuart Hills and Jack Holman desperately holding the centre of town were Cpl Cyril Burnet and his Firefly crew (*left*), in a photo taken during the battle, and Sgt Stan Nesling (*above, far left*), with his crew.

Above: Lt Ted Cooke's troop was wiped out at Gheel by hidden Jagdpanthers near St Dimpna's Church as they advanced across this open field. One Jagdpanther (*right*) was destroyed by Cyril Burnet's Firefly as it tried to infiltrate the market square, while another was knocked out near the edge of town (*below*).

Left: Johnny Mann, killed at Gheel. Sgt George Stanton, (*right*), in his ARV, heroically resupplied the C Squadron trapped in Gheel on the night of 10–11 September.

The Sherwood Rangers moved to the Nijmegen sector after Gheel. *Above left*: Here, a Stuart of the Recce Troop moves through Beek, with paratroopers of the 82nd 'All American' Airborne Division. The trooper here is using a British Bren light machine-gun. *Above right*: Also near Beek, Stanley Christopherson and Jack Holman (in the duffel coat) consult astride *Bramley*, which actually belonged to the Essex Yeomanry.

Below: Sgt Nelson and his crew pose with their Stuart on 23 September; two days earlier they had been the first British troops into Germany.

Geilenkirchen was an awful battle for all involved, as winter had set in and the ground had turned to a glutinous quagmire of mud. *Top*: C Squadron Shermans move out of Prummern with men of the 334th Infantry, while (*right*) a US Dodge struggles through the mire. Cpl George Ward's C Squadron (*below left*) crew move through Prummern. Losses at Geilenkirchen were terrible, although the seemingly untouchable Jack Holman and his crew (*below right*) were among those to emerge intact the other side of the battle.

After Geilenkirchen, the Sherwood Rangers paused to rebuild and recover. *Top left*, Jack Holman and Jimmy McWilliam, his hand wounded at Gheel now gloved, pose for the camera, while (*top right*) A Squadron officers opt for a formal portrait: *clockwise from top left*, Dick Holman, David Render, Ronnie Hutton and John Semken.

Left: There was also an investiture ceremony on 30 November. Stanley Christopherson has a DSO pinned to his chest by Field Marshal Montgomery; afterwards he joined his fellow officers at Brunssum (*below*). John Semken is standing left, Stanley Christopherson is next to him, while Jack Holman stands in the middle and Stuart Hills to his right.

The rain turned to ice and snow by the end of the year, bringing more misery and fresh challenges. *Above*: the ever-cheerful Stanley Christopherson stands alongside fellow senior officers before BLACKCOCK, the attack to reduce the Roer triangle. The snow meant hurriedly whitewashing tanks (*right*), although BLACKCOCK was briefly threatened by yet more rain – and mud – before the freeze returned (*below*).

Below left: Johnny Lanes' Firefly, hull down near Heinsberg, while SRY tanks with 52nd Lowland Division infantry move through Havert (*below right*).

Left: General Horrocks, commander of XXX Corps, with Monty (*centre*) and Major-General Ivo Thomas of the 43rd Wessex Division. No one liked Thomas much; he had a reputation as a brutal driver of his men. He was also utterly humourless, a serious crime in the eyes of Stanley Christopherson and the Sherwood Rangers. They knew him as 'von Thoma' after he German general captured at Alamein.

Above: Sid Collis and crew of 4 Troop, B Squadron, in their winter 'Pixie' suits. The next major operation was the assault across the Reichswald. Tanks line up for PEPPERPOT (*right*) on 8 February 1945 – David Render is standing on the back of his tank, *Aim*, on the right. Flooding of the Rhine caused terrible problems during VERITABLE, as Stanley Christopherson's photos (*below left and right*), show all too clearly.

Operation VERITABLE was another grinding, attritional battle in which weather, flooding and other conditions added considerably to the challenges. *Above*: British vehicles drive through a flooded Kranenburg on 12 February, while (*above right*) following the capture of Cleve, Sherwood Rangers tanks move forward with infantry south of the city. In mid-February, the regiment moved back to Cleve and RHQ managed to find a house still intact (*right*). Stanley Christopherson is on the right, holding his dog, Beek, with Chris Sedgwick of the Essex Yeomanry next to him, Bill Enderby behind and Neville Fearn partly hidden on the step.

Above: crew members of C Squadron.

Left: John Cropper's Firefly, *Blue Light Special II*, rumbles forward.

Above: Issum, like so many towns that found themselves in the front line, was badly knocked about; its church steeple was just one of so many that were blasted by Allied gunners.

Above: Stanley Christopherson with an American soldier in Issum. The Americans, who linked up with the British in the town, were accidentally shot at and placated with gifts of tank Pixie suits.

Above left: The Sherwood Rangers crossed the mighty Rhine on 26 March. Most of the tanks were ferried over and are pictured waiting their turn (*above right*). Stanley Christopherson, standing in his scout car, was one of the first in the regiment to cross using the light pontoon bridge codenamed GRAVESEND.

Right: Tanks gather on the far side to help establish a firm bridgehead.

Above: A remarkable set of photographs of Peter Mellowes' troop as they emerged from the wood at De Enk and attempted to outflank the Lochem road block. In the first, Mellowes leads his troop, while in the third, Sgt Alf O'Pray (*left*) moves forward. Moments later, O'Pray's tank is hit and Mellowes frantically tries to pull back.

Above: Nev Hinitt, who along with his brother, Arthur, was a stalwart of the Recce Troop. Stuart Hills had coveted command of the Recce Troop and here (*above right*) stands behind the crew of his Stuart light tank, or 'Honey' as they were known to the British.

Right: Bill Enderby and his crew. Enderby returned to the regiment in February to take command of A Squadron, much to David Render's chagrin.

Above left: Lt Ray Gaiger (*centre*), with Hugh McDonald (*left*), who had to be restrained from flying punches at some German prisoners after B Squadron were ambushed near Löningen. Diehards with panzerfausts, like this German soldier (*above right*), were a threat right to the end of the war.

Above: Sherman Rangers and infantry move into Bremen, the war now so nearly at an end.

Right: David Render, (*third from right*), with fellow A Squadron men after the city's capture.

Below left: David Christopherson in Karlshöfen in October 2020, the place where his father was told the Sherwood Rangers' long war was over. The grave of Lt Rhys Thomas (*below right*), killed at Cleve in his first action, aged just nineteen. The regiment's casualties during these last eleven months of war were absolutely appalling.

mid-morning on 9 September, shortly followed by the second at Steelen. Early on the 10th, Stanley Christopherson was ordered to send the regiment up to support 231st Malta Brigade; but when he reached the canal he was told that the Durham Brigade had already been counter-attacked once, that the bridgehead was far from secure and that they were needed instead to help the Durhams drive through to take Gheel.

A plan was swiftly drawn up. C Squadron would advance out of the small bridgehead with the 6th DLI, head through the village of Doornboom and make straight for Gheel. B Squadron, meanwhile, and the 9th Durhams were to take the village of Winkelom and then attack the town from the south-east. The usual artillery stonk would soften up the enemy and pave the way.

With the Baron still away on staff business in Brussels and Stephen Mitchell reinstated as second-in-command of the regiment, Jack Holman was back commanding C Squadron. The Sherwood Rangers had been hurried forward that morning, C Squadron in the lead, only to learn that orders had changed, but without any new ones except to head towards Gheel. 'Information was extraordinarily lacking,' noted Holman, 'and we were led to believe that there were few enemy troops in the area – the old story which always proved so fatal.' As a result, they crossed the Het Punt Bailey bridge with very little idea of what was expected of them or what enemy they were facing. At Doornboom, they met the 6th DLI and Holman ordered two troops forward towards Gheel under Stuart Hills and Lieutenant Ted Cooke. His only other troop, just two tanks strong under Captain Johnny Mann, would be kept back at Doornboom along with his own squadron HQ.

Stuart Hills was sanguine enough – there had been not even the faintest hint of trouble during the crossing – and by late morning they had linked up with the infantry and been told the plan. Both Hills's tank crew and his troop looked very different from those who had landed in Normandy. Arthur Reddish had still not returned; Geoff Storey had been posted to a newer, less experienced crew; and Sam Kirman had gone to RHQ as the second-in-command's signals sergeant. In their place, Hills now had Bob Ingall as his driver and Corporal Jim Darrington as his operator, with Bill Cousins still in place as gunner. The lap-gunner position was empty because not enough replacements had reached them. His other two tanks were both Fireflies because there weren't enough Shermans, and were commanded by Sergeant Stan Nesling and Corporal Cyril Burnet. Since Fireflies didn't have a second machine gun anyway, it meant the troop was three Brownings down and lacking a bit of their usual fire-power.

The artillery began their barrage over Gheel at 2 p.m. that Sunday, 10 September. Civilians in the town had been out at church but now, with shells screaming over, hurried back home. A number of houses were hit, but as far as Hills was concerned the shelling seemed pretty feeble – certainly compared with the kind of artillery support they'd enjoyed in the past. Nor did the infantry appear very numerous. He reckoned he couldn't see more than about thirty of them. There were, in fact, considerably more than that, but D Company of the 6th Durhams were certainly under strength – the whole of 50th Division was by now short of numbers – and attacking with only two platoons forward and one in reserve. Realistically, that meant about sixty men or so.

Round about Gheel the land was flat, a patchwork of small fields. Farm-steads and small settlements stood up against the skyline, as did the town itself, dominated by the large church of St Amand at its heart and, away to the east, the equally tall church of St Dimpna. The advance towards Gheel had barely gone a few hundred yards when enemy machine guns opened up from dug-in positions near the hamlet of Stokt. German machine guns, with their incredible rate of fire, could be devastatingly effective, especially in an initial engagement, and Hills saw a number of Durhams cut down either side of him. His three tanks still had three Brownings, however, and they now sprayed the enemy positions and blasted them with HE. 'But the Boche continued to sit in his slit trench and return it,' he wrote just a few days later. 'At one stage I got so close to their trenches that it necessitated backing my tank in order to depress the gun sufficiently to fire point blank with H.E. and it certainly shook them. We then ran the trenches over and the infantry poked them out at the point of the bayonet.' He spotted several white flags raised but he was in no mood to be clambering out of his tank. Instead they pressed on, joining the main road from Het Punt that led straight into the town. There, at the junction, he paused and spoke to a subaltern in the Durhams, the only officer he'd seen, suggesting his men follow close behind the leading Sherman and that he'd put a round of HE into every house to try to limit Spandau fire. Lieutenant Ted Cooke, meanwhile, with his troop, cut across fields to the south and headed towards the eastern edge of the town.

As Hills's troop rumbled into Gheel they spotted a towed 88mm gun, which they immediately shot up and knocked out, then overran a further four light anti-aircraft guns. In each case the crews simply scarpered as soon as they saw the tanks approaching. He also spotted other, smaller, guns that had been similarly abandoned. They then headed on towards the market square, pausing to blast every single house. Hills had hardened since D-Day; by now he had seen too many of his fellows killed and wounded, too many blackened, burning Shermans, and self-preservation and the preservation of his own side trumped all other considerations. Several houses were already burning from the earlier barrage. This quiet little town, subjected to Nazi occupation for more than four years, now found itself on the front line.

Hills's approach seemed to do the trick, because before they'd gone far Germans began surrendering in droves, Hills taking a very nice gold watch for himself from one prisoner, while civilians emerged and began cheering. As the tanks paused, a number of locals clambered up on to them, their joy at being liberated apparently greater than their concern at the destruction of their home town. Hills reckoned he'd fired between fifty and sixty HE rounds to get in, the Fireflies just four apiece. Leaving a section of ten men to deal with the POWs, Hills now pressed straight on up the main road called the Pas and into the large rectangular market square, with its tall church of St Amand at the far end. Just as they arrived, a Volkswagen *Schwimmwagen* – a small, amphibious off-road vehicle – tore into the square: it was promptly raked by Cyril Burnet's Browning even though he was carrying civilians on the back of his Firefly at the time. The three officers leaped out and ran for their lives, only to be cornered and captured by the Belgian resistance a few moments later.

Gheel was now in British hands. Stuart Hills, who had got used to seeing the Germans on the run and beaten, had expected nothing less. Even so, he was not so complacent as to take any chances and sensibly refused to let Stan Nesling press on any further, even though his troop sergeant was straining at the leash to do so. Hills now called up Holman, who told him he would head up with the squadron troop and HQ right away. Hills then clambered down and set off on a tentative foot patrol. From the north-east corner of the square, Stationstraat led all the way down to a railway line and level crossing. Guarding it was a gun, pointing in their direction, and a five-man crew. 'Needless to say,' noted Hills, 'we moved no further.'

Instead, he positioned the three tanks so they could guard the entries into the square, and a few moments later Jack Holman arrived in his scout car and set up his HQ in the town hall at the north-west corner of the square. 'Everything had gone so rapidly that it seemed too good to be true,' he noted. 'Perhaps our jubilation was somewhat excessive, not to mention premature.'

He was certainly right about the latter point, for although the 6th Durhams and C Squadron now held the market square, the battle for Gheel was far from over. To the south-east, the 9th Durhams, supported by Micky Gold's equally understrength B Squadron, had managed to push close to Winkelom but had faced heavier opposition from the outset. Artillery fire, mortars and smoke canisters had been brought down on the village and the junction to the north-west from which the road led into Gheel; the Durhams had suffered, and their leading platoon commander in B Company had been killed. They finally got into Winkelom around 6.45 p.m., but by then enemy fire had increased, not just from artillery, mortars and small arms, but also from large tanks that were now being reported.

In fact, they were not tanks but SP guns – and among the biggest the Germans had: a company of Jagdpanthers of 1. Schwere Panzerjäger Bataillon 559. These had been kept in reserve by the German LXXXVIII Korps commander, General Hans-Wolfgang Reinhard, ready to confront the British attack at either Gheel or Beringen. Earlier that day, Oberst Dreyer had assured Reinhard he had the situation under control, but a sixth sense had told the corps commander his battlegroup in Gheel might need help; and so, at 1 p.m., an hour before the British attack began, he had ordered his Jagdpanthers forward. Like the Sherwood Rangers, they were short of numbers, with only seven available, but with their Panther chassis, thick armour and 88mm anti-tank guns, they posed a significant threat.

Because SP guns had no rotating turret – being mobile anti-tank guns rather than the more manoeuvrable and tactically flexible tanks – the key to their effective use was to find somewhere as hidden as possible where they could lie up with as much of their hulls protected as possible. There were plenty of hedgerows to the east of Gheel and around St Dimpna's Church, and it was behind these that two of them had manoeuvred themselves. Crossing a flat, open field to the south of the church at around 5 p.m., Ted Cooke's unsuspecting troop were sitting ducks. They'd simply not seen the Jagdpanthers. One tank was knocked out, and then the other two were caught out in the open. None of them stood a chance against those big 88s. Cooke was among those killed in the rapid slaughter. He had only joined the regiment after Berjou, but had quickly become firm friends with Stuart Hills, and the two of them had had a day out in Brussels together only a couple of days earlier. From Gloucestershire, Cooke was only twenty-one but had recently married; now, suddenly, his wife had been cruelly widowed.

While a pair of Jagdpanthers remained near the church to guard the eastern exit from the town and also to fire south towards the British at Winkelom, the remaining five now moved on around the northern edge of the town. Spotting one of them, Stuart Hills opened fire, but it disappeared on its way. These Jagdpanthers now cut south to join up with the Luftwaffe infantry getting ready to the west of the town to counter-attack south towards Doornboom. These infantry only learned that Gheel was occupied when the Jagdpanthers turned up at around 5.30 p.m. and told them. Oberst Dreyer had earlier devised a complicated counter-attack that involved his various Flieger regiments attacking at once in three directions – due south, from the east and from the west – towards Doornboom. Now, however, aware the British were in the town, he ordered his central thrust, with the Jagdpanthers in support, to wheel round and head back into Gheel instead.

As it happened, the fading light, inexperience, and the age-old problem of newly arrived armour attempting to cooperate with infantry all contributed to the German counter-attack splintering in growing confusion, with most of the troops continuing on their way south as had been originally planned. At the same time, the 8th DLI, the third British infantry battalion in the brigade, should have been heading north down the Doornboom road to reinforce the beleaguered troops in Gheel. Largely because the Bailey bridge at Steelen had been hit and knocked out, however, they did not get going until around 8 p.m., and as they headed down the road, the lead company ran straight into the advancing Germans and were swiftly overrun.

Johnny Mann and Sergeant Teddy Cawston were commanding the only two C Squadron tanks still south of the Doornboom crossroads. Pushing forwards towards the village that evening, they soon ran into the German advance south of Gheel. Mann was shot in the head and fell back into the turret, dead; then the tank was hit by one of the Jagdpanthers and brewed up almost instantly. Troopers Ernest Winchester, John Saunders and William Reid were all killed. A burning tank was always a terrible sight to witness, especially in the gathering dusk. A round from an 88mm, fired at comparatively short range and with immense velocity, was the enemy weapon most likely to destroy a tank more or less immediately. If a shell penetrated, it was not just the armour-piercing solid shot that entered the tank at nearly 2,000 mph, but splinters of white-hot metal – spawling – too. Enormous amounts of kinetic energy hit the inside of the tank, creating a powerful blast effect. If the spawling or shot penetrated one of the shells lined up around the edge of the turret, and next to the driver's and lap-gunner's heads, then their explosive charges could detonate, which would in turn detonate others. If the hatches were down, the pressure could burst the turret into the air like a champagne cork, despite its weight of nearly 10 tons. The effect on the men inside barely bore thinking about. If the hatches were open, as they usually were – and as they were on Johnny Mann's tank – the fire and explosions would be largely contained within the tank itself, with bizarre but morbidly perfect smoke rings puffing up into the sky. Before long, the flames would become angrier, rising up out of the hatches and belching thick, black, oily smoke across the battlefield and high into the sky for all to see. Any other tank man seeing this would know that he, too, was only a split second from suffering a similar fate. There was something especially grotesque about being burned alive. It didn't do to dwell, but it was hard not to sometimes.

Stanley Christopherson still had A Squadron south of the canal, waiting in reserve, and was forward himself with Brigadier Desmond Gordon of the Durhams, who earlier had moved his tactical HQ across the canal at Het Punt and was planning to transfer his caravan and trucks to a new location on the road to Doornboom. At around 8 p.m., Christopherson was discussing the plan of action with him as 69th Brigade were due to move up on their left, when Gordon's intelligence officer appeared. 'I think I should tell you sir, that there are two enemy tanks in a sunken lane 300 yards to our left flank,' he said. 'If you watch carefully, you can see them and it is quite easy to hear them.'

'For God's sake,' said Gordon, turning to Christopherson, 'bring your tanks up quickly.' Stanley immediately ordered A Squadron to get across the bridge and be ready to go into action if necessary.

Meanwhile, in Gheel itself, the three tanks of Hills's troop, plus that of Captain Jimmy McWilliam and Jack Holman's scout car, and a handful of infantry from the 6th Durhams, were all that held the town. Stuart Hills was not alone in feeling quite terrified. 'Night was falling and it was very disturbing to think that we were surrounded and a very small force at that,' he wrote. 'The infantry were thin on the ground and as darkness fell sent us the most pessimistic reports.' To make matters worse, they were now very low on ammunition.

At around half-past ten that night, one lone Jagdpanther crept into the town, having peeled off from the others to the south and worked its way up the Pas using much the same route as Hills and his troop had done earlier that afternoon. To enter the market square it had to take a sharp turn to the right, and because it had no turret it could not rotate its gun. Instead, it aimed directly at Jimmy McWilliam's tank, which was in the far right-hand corner. Fortunately, when it fired, it missed. Corporal Cyril Burnet now fired back at almost point-blank range, and his Firefly's big 17-pounder drilled the Jagdpanther. It brewed up immediately: Hills felt the blast 100 yards away. It was noticeable that no one in the Sherwood Rangers was keen to criticize the Firefly any more, now they were used to them and knew how to work with them more effectively. The dead Jagd-panther did little to ease anyone's nerves, however. Sitting there in the square, they all felt as though there were enemy snipers with panzerfausts lurking in every shadow, and that any moment more troops and more Jagdpanthers might appear. Hills remained standing in his turret, staring out, listening keenly to the sounds of battle to the south and south-east, and hoping they might somehow survive. It was going to be a long night.

Meanwhile, in the area around Winkelom, the 9th Durhams and B Squadron found they were being attacked from the north and the north-west, even as darkness fell. All afternoon it had been stop and start. They had moved forward, fired, then faced off a counter-attack and advanced again. Another day in which time had been sucked away amid confusion, smoke and gradually strengthening opposition. At least, that was how it seemed to the B Squadron men.

Nor was there any sign of things quietening down now that darkness had fallen, which was unusual as the Germans rarely fought at night. Lieu-tenant Harry Cowan's 4 Troop were advancing slowly down a rough road towards Gheel from Winkelom. Third in line was Corporal John Cropper, perched in his turret and peering through his night-vision binoculars; they weren't very effective but were better than nothing, given the lack of moonlight. Every nerve in his body seemed strained and he was strug-gling not to misread every shape ahead as the lurking enemy. The sounds of battle seemed magnified by the night air. The constant whine of shells, the *blap, blap, blap* of mortars and cracks of rifle fire mixed with the *brrrp* and *tat-tat-tat* of machine guns. 'The flashes of guns,' he wrote, 'also sup-plied a large flickering circle of illumination which silhouetted trees, hedgerows, buildings and the procession of tanks.'

Cropper had one earpiece of his headset over one ear, but was keeping the other ear uncovered in an effort still to hear the noises around him; he hoped that if he failed to see something he might at least hear it. Soon, the battle began to grow in intensity as the enemy first pushed south towards Doornboom then swivelled eastwards to face the threat from B Squadron and the 9th Durhams. Suddenly, Cropper heard a flurry of shells scream over. They exploded nearby. On the net, Lieutenant Harry Cowan urgently ordered them off the road and then instructed them to sweep into line abreast to face this threat. This, however, meant heading out into open fields – fields already soft from the plentiful rain that had fallen in recent days. Cropper's tank was still manoeuvring when the right track hit soft ground and sank down.

'Hold it, Ritchie,' Cropper called to his driver. He'd never been one for formal drill commands, not least because he considered himself only a part-time soldier. 'Go easy or we'll dig in.'

It was already too late, however. The right track began to spin; they were stuck. Immediately, Cropper tried to call up Sergeant Carr, whose tank Four Charlie was the closest, but couldn't raise him. Cursing inwardly, Cropper realized he was going to have to get out and try and run over to Carr's tank.

'Listen lads,' he said to his crew. 'I'm going to see if I can find Four Charlie to give us a tow. I'll get the hawser off and lay it out first and if he's got one we'll lay his out too and join them together. That will keep him off the soft ground. Keep the gun pointed towards the enemy and keep a good look-out.' He warned them to remember he was out there and not to shoot anyone until they were absolutely certain it wasn't him.

After clambering down and unshackling the hawser, he set off to try and find Four Charlie, which had disappeared into the darkness. Several shells screamed in and he flung himself on to the ground. They crashed nearby without touching him, so he clambered to his feet and set off again. Ahead, a dark shape loomed and after straining his eyes and moving forward a few steps more he saw it was a Sherman. He began shouting and waving his arms. Another salvo of shells whistled in and he flung himself down once more, although in the light of their explosion he clearly saw the silhouette of Sergeant Carr in the turret of his tank. Cropper yelled again, and as he neared, saw Carr turn and call out, 'Oh, my God, a Jerry!' followed by 'Traverse right!'

'No, no, no!' shouted Cropper. 'Don't shoot, sergeant, it's me, Corporal Cropper!' Frantically, he ran and managed to reach the edge of the tank before the barrel could depress sufficiently. Only then did Carr hear him and lean over to listen as Cropper, between gasps for breath, explained his predicament. Carr duly brought his tank over, pulled out his own hawser and before long managed to haul the stranded tank clear. At last Cropper was able to clamber back into his turret. 'It was like going back to a home fireside,' noted Cropper, 'after being out in a wild raging storm.' Only once he'd recounted his near-death experience at the hands of Four Charlie's guns did Keith Cornish tell him that Carr was almost stone deaf.

It was now around 11 p.m. They got going again, soon after pulling in line with Lieutenant Cowan's tank along a hedgerow – and then realized there was no sign of Carr's tank. Although they were some 50 yards apart, the sky flickered with crackling flares, and in the flashes of explosions they could spot one another quite easily. Firing continued and they returned fire as well, then moved position several times. They wondered what had happened to Four Charlie, then Cropper forgot about them until some time later he heard the familiar rattle and squeak of tank tracks coming from their rear left. Cropper peered into the inky darkness with his night glasses and after a brief heart-stopping moment saw the familiar profile of a Sherman pull up beside the hedge a little way away. Then it suddenly moved off again, crashed through the hedge and continued on its way.

'Baker Four.' Cowan calling on the net. 'Which of my babies is advancing? Baker Four, over.' No one answered. Silence.

'It's Four Charlie,' Cropper muttered over his crew intercom. 'He's not answering. Keith said he was deaf but his operator's not deaf, or is he?'

'Old Harry's never on net,' replied Cornish.

Cowan: 'Baker Four to babies. Report signals. Baker Four, over.'

Both Cropper and Haydn Thomas in Able Four responded, but still there was nothing from Sergeant Carr. The spectral Sherman now turned left up ahead of them and across their front, after which it disappeared from view. Soon after that, around 11.30 p.m., Harry Cowan's tank was hit by a Jagdpanther. The driver, Wally Blaxall, and lap-gunner, Raffles Lake, were killed, Blaxall immediately. The men in the turret bailed out, but Cowan, who had been hit in the leg by the blast, was unconscious by the time he was found by his radio operator, Trooper Edwin Riches. Picking up the wounded lieutenant, Riches carried him to Baker Four, put him on the back, and Cropper and his crew drove him to the aid post.

By the time Cropper's crew had made their way back and rejoined Sergeant Roberts, there was still no sign of Carr and Four Charlie. B Squadron's fortunes were about to turn even worse, however. A heavy mist now fell over the battlefield, adding to the confusion. Sergeant Ronnie Wilson's tank in 2 Troop was also hit and three of the crew, Wilson included, were killed. Sergeant Bill Pollard, also in 2 Troop, clambered out of his tank for a foot recce only to encounter a German soldier emerging from the mist – whom he shot dead with his revolver. Around this same time, Micky Gold was hit in the left eye by a glancing blow from a sniper's bullet and had to be evacuated; Edwin Riches saw him being brought in to the aid post to see 'Hylda' Young in the early hours. 'He looked so miserable and dejected and spoke in a weak small voice,' wrote Bill Wharton, 'poor old boy!'

Eventually, the fighting died down. Cropper must have dozed off, because the next thing he knew dawn was breaking. Peering out of his tank, he saw the hedge he'd been using as cover was thin and offered almost no protection at all, but the flat battlefield south of Gheel still lay shrouded in mist. He waved to his friend 'Robbo' Roberts in Able Four, who waved back. It seemed they were the only survivors of 4 Troop; of Sergeant Carr's tank, there was still not a sign.

CHAPTER 21

Gheel and Garden

A s THE SUN ROSE over Gheel, Stuart Hills, Jack Holman and the rest of the small cadre of C Squadron had somehow survived the night. Hills had not slept a wink; he reckoned it had been the worst and longest night of his life, but he was still alive to see this Monday morning, 11 September. At least they now had plenty of ammunition once more, thanks to the impressive actions of Sergeant George Stanton.

Stanton, the C Squadron mechanical sergeant, had first performed heroically the previous afternoon in hurrying up to the field south of St Dimpna's Church to rescue a number of Lieutenant Cooke's troop. This was all the more courageous as his transport was an ARV – an armoured recovery vehicle: essentially, a Sherman without a turret, but with a boom, jib and winch instead. These ARVs were vital pieces of equipment and ensured that almost all knocked-out tanks, except those that had completely brewed up, were whisked off the battlefield as soon as darkness fell, and towed back to their own lines to be repaired and put back into action. Stanton and his men had carried out their recovery of men in broad daylight, however.

Later that evening, Jack Holman, still in Gheel, realized his squadron's situation was potentially catastrophic unless ammunition could be brought up, and so radioed back for help. Sergeant Stanton immediately volunteered to make a dash for it and bring a resupply. Since much of his recovery work was done at night he was well used to operating in the darkness; but on the other hand, none of them had much idea what the enemy strength was to the south of Gheel, so this mission very likely meant passing through enemy lines, and as such entailed a huge risk. After waiting for the fighting to die down, and hoping the enemy were getting some kip, Stanton set off on his own, hurtling north with his foot firmly on the throttle. Despite being shot at by both machine guns and captured 6-pounders, Stanton sped towards the town and made it safely to the beleaguered C Squadron men. The combination of speed, the dark, chutzpah and a healthy dollop of luck got him there in one piece. By making this brave dash, he unquestionably saved C Squadron from certain annihilation.

Overnight, both sides had gathered further reinforcements. General Graham had ordered 69th Brigade up; they had moved up along the main road to Gheel from Het Punt and had also taken over the Durhams' positions south of Doornboom. A company of the 2nd Cheshires' heavy machine-gun battalion had also crossed over into the bridgehead. General Reinhard had wanted to pull back, as his infantry had suffered badly during the fighting of the previous day and night, while his Jagdpanther force had lost two tanks and was simply not big enough to make a decisive difference. His army commander, however, Feldmarschall Kurt Student, refused to sanction a retreat and instead ordered forward the II. Bataillon of the 6. Fallschirmjäger Regiment, who despite having suffered badly in Normandy were as good an outfit as any in the Wehrmacht. Whether they would arrive in time to make a difference, however, was a moot point, because although two Jagdpanthers were still hull down near Doornboom, and several others were protecting St Dimpna and the south-eastern part of Gheel, the British were closing in around them. It was now the Jagdpanther force and Luftwaffe infantry dug in south of Gheel who were dangerously exposed. That didn't mean they were a spent force yet, though.

Across the fields towards Winkelom, dawn had revealed that three B Squadron tanks had been knocked out during the night: Cowan's, Sergeant Wilson's and Sergeant Carr's Charlie Four. John Cropper found out early that morning, when Bill Wharton had called into the aid post to check on Micky Gold – who would soon be heading back to England, his war over. He left a very big hole to fill, not just in B Squadron but in the regiment as a whole.

As ever, in such situations, those still standing had to dust themselves down, take a deep breath and keep going. Colin Thomson took over command of the squadron, and early that morning called the surviving tank commanders over for a hastily convened O group. As they stood there in the mist, dew heavy on the ground and glistening on the metal of his Sherman,

Thomson told them the latest intelligence suggested the Germans had pulled back but left a rearguard in and around Gheel. Their job was to drive those remaining Germans out and link up with the 6th Durhams and C Squadron tanks in Gheel. Bill Wharton's No. 1 Troop was to lead, with Cropper's tank bringing up the rear. Thomson wanted John Cropper to take over his current position once they moved out just before 7 a.m. and then hold it, but in the meantime had a further task for him. The dead were being brought in and laid out in a field next to the road they had swung off the previous night. He was to go down there and try to find their lads. 'If you can,' said Thomson, 'remove their personal possessions from their bodies and one of the identity discs they should have around their necks. Make each set into a separate little bundle and you can hand them to me when you rejoin us, about, say 0900 hours. OK?'

Cropper nodded and set off back to his tank. After moving up, he dismounted and reluctantly headed off to the field of dead. 'I was going somewhere I didn't want to go,' he wrote, 'to do something I didn't want to do, but it was something I had to do.' He found the field. The dead were all laid out, faces waxen, but much to his relief, none too horribly mutilated. Most were infantry, but then he spotted Old Harry – Haydn Thomas, the operator in Carr's tank, who was never on the net. He looked as though he were asleep. 'I touched him,' wrote Cropper. 'He was icy cold, and somewhat rigid.' As ordered, he removed one of the stiff card identity discs, then reluctantly rummaged through his pockets. Finding only a pitifully few small items, he tied these up in a handkerchief, then stood up, looked down and paused a moment. 'I didn't pray,' noted Cropper. 'I didn't think. It wasn't homage really, just a sort of "Cheerio, Harry."' He also found Henry Randle, although there was no sign of Carr and the other two crew members; it seemed they must have been taken prisoner.

Grim though his task was, Cropper was at least spared the start of B Squadron's battle. As the lead troops and the infantry of the 9th Durhams pushed north towards Gheel they ran into several of the Jagdpanthers, which had moved into hull-down positions blocking the path towards the town. Bill Wharton's great friend – and now acting squadron leader – Colin Thomson then had his tank hit. His driver, Les Harris, lost both legs and Thomson himself was wounded.

That left Bill Wharton and Lieutenant Davis as the only officers in the squadron. Since Wharton was senior, he now took over command, hastily moving his remaining tanks clear of the Jagdpanthers and using their far greater manoeuvrability and greater rate of fire to force the enemy guns out of their positions. One Jagdpanther was hit and knocked out by the B Squadron men, while the other moved back towards Gheel.

Sporadic and confused fighting continued to the south of Gheel throughout the morning, all across the fields, roads and sunken lanes south of the town; yet despite repeated efforts, the much-depleted 9th Durhams and B Squadron tanks could not force a way through. At around midday, Stanley Christopherson was once again south of the Doornboom crossroads, seated in the turret of *Robin Hood*, along with Dick Holman's troop from A Squadron, their tanks not only trying to winkle out the Jagdpanthers but also providing indirect fire support. Suddenly, a machine-gunner from the Cheshires, who was dug in close to his tank, called over to him. 'I should just like to confirm, sir,' he said, 'that that there tank is one of yours.' Clambering down, Christopherson hurried over to the machine-gun team and saw, to his horror, a Jagdpanther crawling down a lane towards them. Although *Robin Hood* was currently out of the Jagdpanther's sight, Christopherson did not want to reveal himself by starting up its engine. Dick Holman's troop was a little further away and so he rushed over, finding Holman's tanks hull-down in a sunken lane from where they would soon be able to get a clear shot if the Jagdpanther kept going on its current course. Sergeant Bill Charity was the tank commander of a Firefly in Holman's troop and it was on to the back of this tank that Christopherson now clambered, crouching down behind the turret and telling Charity to get ready.

Then, suddenly, there it was, inching across their eyeline. Charity's gunner fired but the shot was high.

'Reload,' said Charity. 'Drop fifty.'

The Jagdpanther had already stopped and started to move so that the great barrel swung around towards them. Christopherson offered up a silent prayer.

'On,' said the gunner.

'Fire!' called out Charity.

Christopherson put his fingers in his ears as the tank rocked forward and back again from the blast. He then cheered as he saw the armour-piercing shell hit and penetrate the gun mount. Charity then followed up with three more rounds, all of which hit. By now the Jagdpanther was burning; as the crew bailed out they were cut down by machine-gun fire. This SP had belonged to Leutnant Gerhard Kossack, the Jagdpanther company commander.

Not long after this Dick Holman's tank was knocked out, and one of the crew, Herbert Simms, killed, though the other four, Holman included, escaped. They'd been lucky; it was always a matter of capricious chance whether a crew was incinerated, got out safely, or got out and were promptly killed by machine-gun or mortar fire. A second Jagdpanther was later knocked out by a sergeant in the 8th DLI using a PIAT, and then a third was hit and destroyed by a 6-pounder. By early afternoon, south of the town, the British were slowly but surely winning back lost ground and the Germans began falling back behind the railway to the north of the town.

The padre had spent the previous couple of days first with 522 Company, RASC, the Royal Army Service Corps unit supporting the regiment, and then visiting the brigade workshops near Brussels, which were already working around the clock. These and the B3 echelon had all been moved on the 10th, and he had joined RHQ later to learn from Stanley Christopherson that the regiment had had a heavy day and that a bigger show was likely to be launched very soon. In fact, Operation MARKET GARDEN, the ambitious plan to drive a 60-mile passage into Holland and to cross the Rhine at Arnhem, was given the green light by General Eisenhower, the Supreme Allied Commander, that very day. It was due to be launched in a week's time, on 17 September.

First, though, XXX Corps needed to get up to the planned Escaut start line, and that meant clearing Gheel and the land to the north up to the canal. Not for the first time, Skinner was refused permission to go up to the front line, but managed to reach the bridgehead later that day, crossing the Albert canal on the technical adjutant's Dingo. Johnny Mann's Sherman was still burning fiercely, although the fire in Dick Holman's tank was dying down, but he couldn't get near either of them. He did, though, manage to recover three other bodies and give them temporary graves before joining Dr Young at his RAP.

In Gheel itself, Jack Holman's beleaguered band of brothers continued to hold the market square. There were five tanks, along with a number of men rescued overnight from the knocked-out tanks of Lieutenant Cooke's troop near St Dimpna's Church, and George Stanton and his ARV crew manning a machine gun. The infantry had been pulled back overnight to form a perimeter defence around the town – not that Holman had been told this; the C Squadron men felt rather abandoned.

Early in the morning, tragedy struck when Corporal Burnet, who had destroyed the Jagdpanther the previous night, was killed by a sniper bullet in the head; yet again, bad luck had picked Burnet out rather than one of the others, but his death meant yet another tank commander had gone. The town now looked pretty bashed about. A Bren carrier had been knocked out and stood ruined not far from the burnt-out Jagdpanther. Shells were falling intermittently, but still the C Squadron men kept up their vigil at the corners of the square. 'The tank was covered in bricks, plaster and glass,' noted Stuart Hills, 'with dust everywhere.' Everyone in his crew was utterly exhausted but apprehensive and on edge. Nerves taut.

It was in the afternoon that their situation became increasingly desperate. The Germans had only three Jagdpanthers left, and by around 1 p.m. these were all north of the railway; but by this time the II. Bataillon of the 6. Fallschirmjäger Regiment were arriving in Gheel, where they started aggressively infiltrating from all sides. Still protecting the edge of the town were the 6th Durhams. They, too, had suffered badly; on the previous day alone, they had lost one officer dead and six wounded, and a further thirty men killed, sixty-seven wounded and forty-three missing. These were appalling figures, especially since the battalion had been understrength even before the battle for Gheel began.

Small arms, mortars and the occasional shell could be heard all around town, and the enemy were palpably getting closer as the afternoon wore on. Jack Holman began to realize they could not hold the town – not against infantry armed with panzerfausts and without any infantry of their own – so called over Stuart Hills and Jimmy McWilliam to tell them. They then hurried back to their respective tanks, and Hills had clambered into his turret when there was a deafening crash and McWilliam's tank burst into flames on the corner of Nieuwstraat and Stationstraat in the northeast corner of the market square. Hills, who had his back to McWilliam's tank, jolted with the sudden shock and turned to see the crew bailing out – all except the radio operator, Corporal Eric Higgins, who had been killed outright. 'It was a wicked moment,' noted Hills. 'I had no idea where the shot had come from or what it was.' Immediately, he sent a frantic message over the net, his mind reeling.

Just minutes later, his own tank was hit with a violent blast. A sheet of flame rose angrily from the lower right-hand side. Sparks showered high into the air. A fizz and a sting across his forehead and his beret disappeared; a lethal shard of shrapnel had barely grazed him. Luck had smiled on him that moment. More frantic words on the net; at least no one was hurt. Bob Ingall reversed clear into the square; he was sure he'd seen an enemy soldier with a panzerfaust a split second before. He was right: a

panzerfaust had been fired by a *Fallschirmjäger* from a bar on the corner –
by the same man, Fahnenjunker Heinz Köhne, who had done for Jimmy
McWilliam's tank. Stan Nesling also now hurriedly moved his Firefly
back into the square, furiously firing and traversing his machine gun as
he did so, the noise echoing around the confined street.

A handful of Durhams pulled back into the square, reporting that enemy
troops were moving through one house after another. Ammunition was
low. Around 4 p.m., Typhoons appeared in the skies, having been ordered
to help knock out the enemy armour. They spotted no Jagdpanthers but
did shoot up a number of enemy troops near St Dimpna's Church, which
seemed to buy the men in Gheel some time, but around the town the rest
of the 6th Durhams were now pulling back into the bridgehead. With all
the C Squadron tanks now in the square itself, and still watching carefully
for any movement, Hills jumped down to talk to Jack Holman and Jimmy
McWilliam about their plan of escape. 'Jimmy seemed quite cheerful,'
wrote Hills, 'but he was badly burned and his hand and leg looked a mess.
All he could talk about was what he was going to do when he got back to
Glasgow.' Perhaps it was the shock talking.

Two tanks first, then the fitters, infantry and Sherwood Rangers without tanks in the middle, and then the remaining tanks to follow: that was
the order of evacuation. Dusk was falling by the time they made their
move. 'The first withdrawal I have ever been involved in,' noted Stuart
Hills, 'and I hope the last.' Fortunately, it went well, largely because the
enemy held the northern part of the town but no longer had any troops
in the south. Hills, for one, was immensely relieved to still be alive,
although it was something of a miracle that he was. Only once safely back
within the bridgehead did he get out to see the damage to his tank: a hole
right through the entire sprocket assembly into the transmission casing.
This had saved Bob Ingall; but had Arthur Reddish still been in the tank
as lap-gunner he'd have lost his legs and probably his life as well.

For the Sherwood Rangers, the bloody battle for Gheel was all but over.
The next day, the 15th Scottish Division was moved up into the bridgehead
and together they moved back into the town in the evening, with the promise of relief by the County of London Yeomanry. Although the enemy were
swiftly pushed back, the German defence of Gheel and the Albert canal
had bought General Student the time he needed to mass a larger force further to the rear, so that by the middle of the month he had five divisions in
and around the south-eastern half of Holland, of which two, the 7. Fallschirmjäger Division and the division-sized Kampfgruppe Walther, were

of a reasonably high standard. The German presence in this part of the world was strengthening by the day.

That Tuesday, 12 September, Leslie Skinner finally managed to get into Johnny Mann's tank, as well as Sergeant Carr's and Lieutenant Cowan's. 'Fearful job searching ash,' he wrote. 'Ghastly – two orderlies helping me had to give up.' Skinner was the last to leave the town, taking with him the injured from the hospital, both walking and on his truck, including some wounded Belgian resistance fighters. This was against regulations, but the Mother Superior pleaded with him to take them as they would all have been shot if the Germans came back. It was a hazardous journey in the dark and they came under fire on the way, but all made it safely back across the canal that night.

The battle for Gheel had been the worst two days for the regiment since Wadi Zem Zem in Libya back in January 1943: forty-six casualties in all, of which half were fatal, including two officers dead. Eleven tanks had been knocked out and two damaged. It was a ghastly reminder that while the end of the war in Europe was unquestionably in sight, the Germans were not beaten yet.

The brigade was due to be playing its part in MARKET GARDEN, although this was to be a supporting role only; the Sherwood Rangers were to be formed into a battlegroup, which Christopherson would command, to play a picketing role. Depending on how the operation went, they would then pass under command of the 82nd 'All American' Airborne Division. It would be the first time they had worked directly alongside US forces.

First, though, the regiment needed urgently to rest, refit and reorganize, and so they were packed off to Bourg-Léopold, barely 14 miles to the east of Gheel and close to the forming-up base for MARKET GARDEN. Their new camp was just outside the town amid a wood still in full leaf; the sun was shining too, giving their few days of rest the feel of an Indian summer. 'It is lovely here, darling,' Bill Wharton wrote to his wife, 'among the fir trees and heather and I feel not a little homesick as such surroundings remind me of autumn days spent walking with you.' He had had high hopes of being home with her and their unborn child by this time, but was now preparing himself mentally for another few months of war.

Harry Heenan was less homesick – or least, he admitted no such feelings in his letters. 'I am sitting at the moment by my bivouac,' he wrote in a letter to his parents. 'My bed, newly arrived, triumphantly erected, and freshly made . . . In the warm and balmy air, with the sun shining brightly,

I am arrayed in gleaming shoes, khaki socks, corduroys (several shades lighter than the Colonel's, which is in the Heenan tradition), clean shirt and a glorious silk scarf.' His complexion, he added, was ruddier than normal, but he was freshly bathed and his clothes clean. And for once, all was quiet around him.

The men were also delighted to have been given a large issue of German loot after capturing an abandoned supply dump. Wines, spirits, cigars and other luxuries had been shared out. His troop had been given a bottle of brandy and some decent Bordeaux, which, to Heenan's horror, the men had poured into one big bottle and then drunk. 'The idea of it!' he wrote.

Brigadier Prior-Palmer had also made the most of this windfall by organizing a cocktail party for all the brigade officers, which went down well. Stanley Christopherson thought it 'most pleasant'. 'We drank a mixture of wines and spirits,' noted Bill Wharton, 'and smoked cigars, most of which had been captured from the Germans. And, of course, I woke up this morning with a headache – it really isn't worth it.'

A number of awards were also announced. John Semken had won a Military Cross, as had Ian Greenaway, who had lost a leg at Saint-Pierre back in June, and also Johnny Mann – sadly, in his case it was a posthumous award. George Dring was given a second Military Medal, and further MMs were announced for Sergeant George Sanders – posthumously – Bill Nelson and Ted Birch. 'All so thoroughly deserved,' noted Stanley Christopherson. Medals were, to a certain extent, a lottery; after all, didn't anyone who went into battle in a tank deserve a gong? But only a certain number were ever awarded, and there was a tacit understanding that an individual award was a reflection on an entire crew, troop or squadron, and that a bundle of medals represented the effort of the entire regiment. Bill Wharton, for example, had been put forward for an MC and it was widely agreed beforehand that he had the best chance of all of getting it for his actions at Rauray. But, somewhere higher up the chain, he had been passed over. If there were any resentments, however, it was over who had been left off the list of candidates, rather than towards anyone who had been picked out for a medal.

These sultry September days at Bourg-Léopold were another rare opportunity to recharge batteries. 'Life is full of little incidents now it gets dark early,' wrote Harry Heenan. 'Upon leaving the mess about 2200 hours, you fall first of all over the tent ropes and then bang slap into the first trench. Resuming your way, blaspheming hideously, you walk into a branch of a tree and the whole thing quivers and water cascades over you.

You eventually reach your bivouac to find that you have lent your torch to someone and can't remember where you put your pyjamas. However, all ends well, and there is almost always bags of sleep going nowadays.'

It was also a time for reflection, not always welcome. Stuart Hills never struggled to sleep after a major action. At Bourg-Léopold, he crashed out the moment he lay down. 'The subsequent awakening, however,' he wrote, 'brought utter dejection: one felt a sense of hopelessness, gloom and depression as one realised that the strains and torment were about to continue.'

Bill Wharton, for his part, had been hit hard by the losses in B Squadron even while the battle around Gheel had raged. It was not very long ago that he, Colin and Micky had been lording it in their farmhouse, drinking and laughing into the night. Now he was the only one left. And so many others had gone too. 'Again, I have had the bitter experience of seeing some of the best boys go,' he wrote to his wife, 'and that feeling of intense loneliness when I was left to carry on.' Now, at the camp, those same feelings of loneliness returned; a bottle of Scotch arrived for Micky Gold, labelled 'Tonic,' which he appropriated and drank. He also mourned Johnny Mann, who had been a close friend, and worried about those who had been wounded, while also envying their escape. At first, he feared Colin Thomson might lose a leg, but the later news had been better. Micky Gold, on the other hand, had lost an eye, which meant that front-line service for him was over; he would not be returning to the Sherwood Rangers. Gold had written to Christopherson, however, and was remarkably upbeat despite having had his left eye removed. He reported that the girlfriends they had met in Brussels had been to visit him, and had brought so much champagne and wine, it was almost flowing from his empty eye socket. Soon, both Gold and Thomson would be flown back to England – 'the lucky guys,' Wharton added.

Plenty of new faces were arriving, both officers and tank crew. An Australian former 24th Lancers officer, Captain Dick Radcliff, joined A Squadron; so, too, did Lieutenant John Holmes, straight from Sandhurst, who was posted to C Squadron. B Squadron also received its share of new boys. 'A new young officer has just arrived at the squadron,' wrote Bill Wharton, 'and the sight of his fresh complexion makes me feel like a greybeard. They keep coming and going while I continue the Old Man River act.'

Among the new troopers arriving at B Squadron was eighteen-year-old Ernie Leppard, from Battersea in south London. Leppard came from a long line of plasterers, the family trade; but he had done well at school and was good at mathematics, and so after leaving at sixteen in 1942 got a job as a clerk for a firm of flour importers. He had also joined the Home Guard – his unit had its HQ at Clapham Junction, the busiest railway station in the country. Leppard had joined a rocket-launcher team based in nearby Battersea Park, overseen by the regular army's Anti-Aircraft Command. 'I think,' said Leppard, 'in twelve months I was on the rockets in Battersea Park, we actually brought down one aircraft. Well, we claimed we brought one down.'

With the coming of winter in 1943, he decided to join up. For some reason, the winters during the war were proving cold and wet, and he didn't fancy another one turning out most nights on Home Guard duty. Along with about forty other recruits, he was sent up to Bradford in Yorkshire, where they were all given a door lock in pieces and told to reassemble it. It was a simple aptitude test, but Leppard was the only one able swiftly to put the mechanism back together, which suggested he had a practical and mechanical mind. As a result, he found himself back south again at Bovington for training with the Royal Armoured Corps.

His training was pretty thorough, covering all skills from driving to gunnery to infantry training as dismounted crew, but Leppard ended up specializing as a radio operator and loader. In early September 1944 he was considered ready for active duty and, with his draft, was sent to Southampton, where in sheeting rain they set sail for Dieppe, now in Allied hands. They landed there on 12 September, the last day of the Sherwood Rangers' battle at Gheel. After a night on a concrete floor at the port, they were trucked up to the 256 FDS, eighteen wireless operators in all. 'I was there twenty-four hours,' said Leppard, 'and then of the eighteen, they lined us up and said, you six go to the 4/7th Dragoons, you six go to the 13/18th Hussars, and you six go to the Sherwood Rangers, who we'd never heard of before.' At the SRY, the six of them were split among the three squadrons. Leppard was posted to B, but to begin with there wasn't a crew for him, so he spent a few days typing for Tony Gauntley and Bill Wharton at the B Squadron office, which was a 1,500 cwt truck.

For all the new arrivals there was, however, a cadre of the old guard still within the regiment. Tony Gauntley, who had been at RHQ, took over B Squadron; Bill Wharton, who had, after all, been with the regiment since the start of the war, was now second-in-command. Jack Holman, who had also been in North Africa, was promoted to major and given C Squadron on a permanent basis, while the newly decorated John Semken remained at A Squadron. These men could pass on their wisdom and experience to the new boys arriving; so, too, could David Render, Stuart Hills and Harry Heenan, now all with considerable experience under their belts; they may have been young men, but they were also old hands, veterans now.

John Semken, despite his youth, still prompted barely disguised devotion from his men. 'Our major, John Semken, the 23 year-old veteran,' wrote Harry Heenan to his friend John on 16 September, 'is a most remarkable bloke. Besides being a brilliant squadron leader, he has a very fine mind. He quite often gets quite temperamental, as life is a terrible strain for him and when we are in the midst of things, he nearly dies of fatigue.' The previous night, Semken, Heenan and other officers had stayed up talking. 'We talked solidly from 1930 hrs to 0200 hrs which is a pretty good session,' Heenan added. 'He thinks I am a good conversationalist, which pleases me because he is absolutely brilliant himself.' David Render was every bit as reverential. 'We worshipped him,' he said, 'and loved him in a way that only soldiers can love one another.'

Operation MARKET GARDEN began on 17 September, with some 19,000 airborne troops landed from 2,083 air transports – the British 1st Airborne Division landing around Arnhem, the US 82nd Airborne around Nijmegen and the US 101st at Eindhoven. This was the 'MARKET' part of the plan; the 'GARDEN' operation, XXX Corps' drive to Arnhem, began at 2 p.m. the same day, preceded by a 350-gun artillery barrage and with a constant air presence of RAF 83 Group Typhoons overhead. On 16 September at Bourg-Léopold General Horrocks had held his briefing for GARDEN, which Stanley Christopherson and his senior officers attended. No one, least of all Horrocks, doubted the challenges of moving more than 20,000 vehicles down what was effectively one road, although confidence was high. Of even greater concern than potential resistance from the enemy, though, were the ever-capricious weather prospects. Christopherson's nose was also slightly put out of joint when, in his opening address, Horrocks gave high praise to the Wessex and Tyne Tees Divisions but failed to mention 8th Armoured Brigade. No doubt it was just an oversight; but it rankled all the same.

Since the Sherwood Rangers were to act as pickets at the end of the line, they did not move out until the rest of the corps had already got going. From the 18th, they were at one hour's notice, and finally were on their way on 19 September at 7 p.m.: the entire regiment, plus A1 and A2 echelons, a battery of the Essex Yeomanry and detachments of the RASC, as well as a battery of mounted light anti-aircraft guns and a company of the 12th KRRC: a grand total of 377 vehicles. 'We travelled,' noted Terry Leinster in the regimental war diary, 'throughout the night.'

CHAPTER 22

Luck

CORPORAL JOHN CROPPER HAD a brand-new Sherman; Four Charlie, or *Pin-Up Girl*, as he had named his first tank, had been sent away for refurbishment. The old tank had been lucky enough and there was always a worry a new one might not be, but there was no denying that after so much punishment, both from being in combat and the wear and tear from the long chase into Belgium, *Pin-Up Girl* had been struggling. Fred Gasson, the gunner, came up with the new name, *Blue Light Special*, which was army slang for a rumour. He'd also managed to pilfer a pot of white paint and a brush, and daubed the name on the tank. Once they'd packed on all their stowage, added some camouflage netting and sat in it and smoked and brewed tea, it quickly became their home from home.

There was nothing like a long journey of 70-odd miles to wear in a new tank – and those 70 miles were going to take quite a while if the first part of their journey was anything to go by. The 20,000 vehicles in XXX Corps were causing no small amount of gridlock along the road to Arnhem, and just a few hours after leaving Bourg-Léopold they ground to a halt and remained stationary for three hours until 5 a.m. Eventually they got going again and reached Eindhoven later in the day. Having not slept a wink they were all dog-tired by the middle of the afternoon. On they went: stop, start, move off, trundle along for a stretch of several miles, stop again. This was a largely flat but occasionally softly undulating landscape of the reclaimed, drained land known as polder, punctuated by brick-built villages and small towns and roads raised above the surrounding farmland by a network of dykes. Sometimes the road wound its way northwards through bare, open land, but often the route was tree-lined.

Debris marked the route – knocked-out and blackened vehicles and signs of battle spoke of a journey north that had been anything but straightforward; not for nothing was it soon nicknamed 'Hell's Highway'.

Although in the van of the Sherwood Rangers' advance, both ahead and behind them Cropper could see a long column of vehicles, and before long the low rumble and rock of the tank made him feel soporific. He wasn't alone: at one point 'Ritchie' Richardson, the driver, actually nodded off. Seeing the rest of the crew were also out for the count, Cropper had to clamber out of the turret and down the front of the tank, lean through the open hatch and shake him awake. It was fortunate they'd been on a straight stretch because all the time the tank had been driving forward.

North of Eindhoven, they had to cross the bridge over the Wilhelmina canal at Son. Here, a pocket of enemy troops had infiltrated back and were seen on the bridge as the lead elements of B Squadron approached. Assuming the Germans were trying to blow it up, B Squadron rushed it, spraying their Brownings and killing the enemy, and got across before any damage could be caused; but it had been a close-run thing. They continued on their way, reaching the River Maas at Grave just a few miles south of Nijmegen; here they made contact with the 82nd Airborne Division.

They had arrived at a critical moment in the MARKET GARDEN battle. That night, tanks from the Guards Armoured Division, from their bridgehead on the northern banks of the River Waal north of Nijmegen, would attempt to push on and reach the final bridge – over the River Rhine at Arnhem. In fact, the lead elements of XXX Corps had had a tough fight to reach Nijmegen in the first place, although they had made up time and reached the city in mid-afternoon the previous day, 19 September. Unfortunately, the long bridge across the Waal had not by then been captured.

The 82nd 'All American' Division was commanded by Major-General Jim Gavin, who, at thirty-seven years old, was the youngest two-star general in the US Army. By this time, he was a veteran of North Africa, Sicily and Normandy, both a fearless commander and hugely competent. However, at Nijmegen, as elsewhere, the very brief seven-day planning window for the operation had simply not been enough. Gavin's men had been given a wide area of operations and the tasks of capturing not only the bridge at Grave as well as that at Nijmegen, but also the Groesbeek Heights, the high ground that overlooked the city to the east and south-east, just a stone's throw from the German border. No attempt was made to drop troops at both ends of the Nijmegen bridge; rather, they were dropped only to the south. And while, unquestionably, the Groesbeek Heights posed a threat, Gavin made securing these a priority over capturing the bridge, which was a cardinal error. If the enemy managed to get a foothold on the heights, then the operation might fail; but if the All Americans did not swiftly take the bridge, then MARKET GARDEN could not possibly succeed. In other words, it was a case of putting the cart before the horse. He did allocate one of his regiments, the 508th Parachute Infantry, to take the bridge on Day 1, but the 508th was led by his least effective regimental commander, Colonel Roy E. Lindquist, who failed to press home an assault with any kind of urgency. By the time the Guards arrived, it was still in German hands.

A plan was hastily put together that would see the Guards Armoured supporting an extremely difficult crossing by men from the 3rd Battalion 504th PIR in boats. However, the boats did not arrive in time and so this attack was not put in until the evening of the 20th – which was when the Sherwood Rangers were moving into position on the Groesbeek Heights. Unfortunately, it was only on the afternoon of the 20th that Allied commanders became aware that the British paratroopers of 1st Airborne Division were already losing their grip at Arnhem; as at Nijmegen, men had been dropped only on one side of the bridge, in this case the north. The British also made a similar mistake to that of the All Americans: too many men were left guarding drop zones for a second follow-up lift rather than heading hell-for-leather to capture both ends of the Arnhem bridge.

The German response had been swift, the paratroopers were too widely spread, and there had been innumerable communications failures; and although the northern end of the bridge was taken, the enemy initially clung to the southern end and then gradually fought back. That evening, 20 September, the British paratroopers clinging on at Arnhem Bridge were finally overwhelmed.

Although the Nijmegen bridge was now in Allied hands, another two days passed before men of XXX Corps reached the Rhine. Much of the corps' punch had been absorbed by sporadic fighting elsewhere and weakened by supply issues along this narrow 60-mile corridor. The Germans were counter-attacking at Eindhoven and making increasingly heavy assaults across the German border to the east of Nijmegen on the Groesbeek Heights. These battles tied up not only much of XXX Corps but also the 82nd Airborne, while at Arnhem the remaining 1st Airborne Division were surrounded and defending an increasingly desperate perimeter to the west of the town at Oosterbeek. Paratroopers were *coup de main* troops, designed to move rapidly, to snatch and grab. Necessarily, they were lightly equipped and armed; and now they found themselves stranded and rapidly running short of supplies.

MARKET GARDEN had always been ambitious, and by the 21st it was clear it had failed, even though the fighting at Arnhem would continue for several days more. For it to succeed, every part of the plan had needed to work, which was a long shot, to say the least. What is remarkable, however, is how close they were to pulling off a miraculous victory. By the evening of the 19th, XXX Corps was just 8 miles from Arnhem – tantalizingly close, with all the bridges either captured or still intact. It was not close enough, however; which is not to say it was not worth the attempt; after all, the Allies had created an entire airborne army, all of whom were volunteers, trained for just such an operation. The Germans, although regaining some of their balance, were none the less still vulnerable to a heavy knock-out punch in Holland, while the alternative – a slog through dense forests and the heavy defences of the Siegfried Line – was hardly very enticing. MARKET GARDEN might have been a long shot, but there was no doubting it could have worked – and it very nearly did.

None the less, it had always been seen as a thunderclap operation, designed to crash through feeble and disjointed German forces still in disarray. Unfortunately, the enemy was no longer in anything like the disorder they had been on 10 September when MARKET GARDEN had been given the green light. The British 21st Army Group – with the help of the two American airborne divisions – was facing not just the 15. Armee to the west, but the 1. Fallschirmjäger Armee as well. Now entering the battle in addition was a newly established corps, Korps Feldt, named after its commander General Kurt Feldt, hastily cobbled together and based around Wehrkreis IV, the local regional recruiting and training organization. This corps and its 406. Landesschützen Division were protecting the German border along the mass of the Reichswald, a dense forest just to the east of the Groesbeek Heights.

And it was to help the 82nd All Americans hold and defend the heights that the Sherwood Rangers were now posted. The Groesbeek Heights were not particularly high, but because of the otherwise largely flat countryside to the north, west and south they were certainly high enough to be of military significance; from this ground, anyone with a pair of binoculars could see a considerable distance. They also dominated a 10-mile stretch of land between the Waal and Maas rivers, and marked the western edge of an increasingly undulating terrain that ran north–south overlooking the River Meuse to the west. The heights also marked a clear pocket of territory between Holland and Germany. This was borderland, and it was inevitable that the Germans would not only defend it tenaciously but do everything they could to push the Allies back off this dominating high ground.

On Thursday, 21 September, Lieutenant David Alderson, who had been given a roasting by David Render at La Bigne for his lack of aggressive spirit, but had survived since then, was now leading his troop from A Squadron near Beek and hoping to be the first British tank on German soil. They were heading down a road, reported to be clear, when they were suddenly hit by a 75mm anti-tank round fired from close range. The AP round killed Alderson's driver, Trooper James, shattered the legs of his operator, Trooper Foley, and wounded the lap-gunner and gunner, Troopers Weston and Connell, with shrapnel. The tank continued to rumble forward but moments later burst into flames, the four survivors, even Foley, frantically bailing out of the moving tank. 'I was perfectly all right,' wrote Alderson in a report the next day, 'but we were machine-gunned as we were jumping off and rockets and mortars started dropping.' Fortunately, there was a deep ditch beside the road, so they dived into that, while the enemy gun fired three shots at George Dring's tank, following behind. All three missed: he swiftly reversed, moved into a better position and took out the enemy gun with a single shot.

The enemy had been dealt with for the moment; but now, a little further on, Alderson's tank rolled off the road and into the ditch. Then ammunition within the tank started exploding and zipping and fizzing all over the place, so that the ditch was no longer any kind of refuge. Alderson picked up Foley and carried him to safety, then went back for the co-driver. Suddenly, there was an almighty explosion and the turret corked into the air, forced clear of the hull and crashing down again beside the burning tank.

Alderson sent his gunner back for help and did his best for Foley, bandaging his shattered knees with the only two field dressings he had. 'He showed great courage,' noted Alderson, 'and kept calling me "Skip," my nickname by the crew.' After what seemed like an eternity, medics turned up in a jeep and, after bandaging the wounded and strapping them in, sped off pell-mell, with Alderson sitting on the bonnet and clinging for dear life.

Back at the squadron, Semken suggested to Alderson that he have a few days' rest. 'But I will not, as it is best to get back in a tank as soon as possible after a brew up while one's nerve is still good,' he wrote, adding, 'I have decided my nerves are OK.' He didn't sound very convinced, though.

Because of that episode, Alderson's tank was not the first into Germany. That honour fell to Sergeant Doug Nelson and his crew in Captain Ian McKay's Recce Troop, who crossed into Germany near the village of Wyler – and, although only operating as a patrol, captured a German prisoner who had been a naval cadet before being shoved into the infantry instead.

The following day, Leslie Skinner also managed to step over into the Reich. 'Not very exciting,' he noted. 'Like looking from one farmer's field into another's – which in fact is all it is.' Meanwhile, John Semken's A Squadron were sent to the southern stretch of the Groesbeek front, to the area around the village of Mook, while C Squadron were posted to the north of the heights and the area around Beek, a village which, in 1944, was half in Holland and half in Germany.

Mainly, they were carrying out patrols and holding the line. There was occasional shelling and mortaring and, for the first time since D-Day, significant numbers of Luftwaffe aircraft overhead. Enemy panzers were becoming rarer, but Germans armed with panzerfausts were all too numerous, becoming an increasing plague to the tank men. Apart from Alderson's tank being knocked out, however, the regiment was suffering more from the weather, which had taken a turn for the worse, than from the enemy. The men were desperately trying to get their hands on warmer clothing. Jack Holman had a wool duffel coat, and Harry Heenan's parents, worrying about their son, offered to send him out a wool-lined leather jerkin. He replied telling them he was reasonably well kitted out. 'I have two P.T. vests, two scarves, some gloves, two sweaters and a cricket shirt,' he wrote to them, 'and I can tell you I will not have any compunction in wearing the whole lot at once.'

The Americans were something of a curiosity to the Sherwood Rangers, who had not had a huge amount to do with their battlefield allies until this point. 'They were the most tremendous chaps,' said John Semken. 'They said, we've come here to kill bloody Krauts, so why don't we get on with it? That was their attitude. They were really, really terrific. We got on very well with them.' Being called the Sherwood Rangers certainly helped win over their new comrades in arms, who thought they must be a special elite armoured unit – first because the name 'Sherwood' was familiar to all those who had seen the massive Hollywood hit film *Robin Hood*, starring Errol Flynn, but also because the US Army had their own Rangers, which were commando special forces. The tank men were happy to play along. They also endeared themselves to the Americans because their tanks held plenty of rations. The 'All Americans' were running short of their own and were getting hungry. 'We used to give them our stuff out of the tank,' said David Render, 'because we always had quite a bit of food we'd keep back.' It was good for the Brits to be the ones handing over the tins and bars of chocolate for a change.

Stanley Christopherson quickly instigated a rotation system with the squadrons: two would operate daily with the Americans while the third rested, which usually meant one based around Beek in the northern part of the sector and another around Mook in the southern. On Saturday, 23 September, it was the turn of C Squadron to be in the northern part. It was a dismal morning as they set off from just to the east of Nijmegen with a battalion of the 508th PIR. That afternoon, men of the US 325th Glider Infantry Regiment were due to land in the open land just to the east of Groesbeek, so their task was to clear the land immediately to the north of the village of Zyfflich, which, as the crow flies, was only around 3 miles north of one of the planned landing zones.

Away to their right, the wooded slopes of the Groesbeek Heights could clearly be seen, but down on this stretch of land, just to the south of a serpentine loop in the Waal, the ground was flat polder country, with each track and road raised high on dykes. It was very different from Normandy; the ground all around them was waterlogged, which meant the tanks had to drive on the raised dykes with almost no room for manoeuvre. Stuart Hills didn't like it one bit. 'It meant that if we were fired on we would quite certainly have had it.' He was not feeling at all confident as he trundled along at walking pace, leading his troop. Down below, on the polders, were the infantry, while the new boy, Lieutenant John Holmes, led a second troop on a roughly parallel road on his left and a third troop was further north, hugging the route of the Waal.

For the most part the country around them was bare, empty farmland, villages and church spires punctuating the skyline. Hills made sure his crew shot at any building along their way and anything that moved; his gunner, Bill Cousins, killed a pig and a number of chickens en route – after all, it was better to blast the first flicker of movement than delay and end up with a panzerfaust hurtling towards them. Fortunately, they saw no enemy at all until they were nearing the village of Leuth, a short distance north of the German border. They were just turning a left-hand bend when they suddenly spotted a number of enemy infantry dug in below the dyke, who quickly scarpered at the sight of a troop of tanks and accompanying American paratroopers. 'It was just a matter of firing at their backsides as they ran,' noted Hills. A little way ahead was an orchard to the right of the road and beyond that a windmill, clearly visible above the trees. Small-arms fire now clattered around their tank from the apple grove, then a figure suddenly got up in front of them with a panzerfaust – but Bill Cousins blasted him before he could fire. Seeing a track on the right that ran along a narrow waterway, Hills turned down it so that he could get off the road and be better placed to fire at the orchard and the buildings around the windmill beyond, and let Corporal Jim Darrington, now commanding his own tank and following, move on along the road.

Moments later there was an explosion as Darrington's tank was hit by a panzerfaust. Hills looked across anxiously; all the crew were safely bailing out. Then another crash, and another, as Darrington's stricken tank was pummelled by an 88 from the orchard and started brewing up. Behind Hills was Sergeant Stan Nesling in his Firefly, and now joining the fray was Sergeant Jones from John Holmes's troop – their route had joined Hills's a quarter of a mile back and, since Darrington's burning Sherman was on the road, Jones followed Hills and Nesling down the track. Around them, the Americans hit the ground and began firing back, while the C Squadron men blasted the orchard with HE and their Brownings. Mortars and artillery shells soon began raining down and, trying to move his position, Hills rolled his tank forward and promptly tipped over the edge of the watercourse, so that he was stuck halfway down the bank and unable to reverse back out. It was now a sitting duck. Machine-gun fire was clanging around them like steel rain, and now the tracer set fire to the stowage on Jones's tank. Nimbly clambering out, Jones managed both to put out the flames and somehow avoid getting shot, before clambering back into the turret to score a bullseye with his next shot, blasting the enemy MG positions with HE.

Hills desperately wanted to call in the fire support of the Essex Yeomanry, but with the road between Eindhoven and Nijmegen temporarily cut, the gunners were short of ammunition. C Squadron and the paratroopers were on their own. Hills knew it was only a matter of time before they were hit, and sure enough another crash smacked into the tank. A flash of orange flame, a shower of sparks, and they were all hurriedly bailing out again and running clear. The second panzerfaust strike on them that month. Spotting the enemy soldier who had fired it, Sergeant Nesling let fly with his 17-pounder, obliterating the man completely. Fortunately for Hills, the panzerfaust had been fired at range; the closer they were, the deadlier the strike. Hills and his crew now dashed from ditch to ditch until they were clear, and, having had to abandon all their personal possessions in their haste to escape the tank, grabbed discarded German items such as blankets and weapons in an effort to make up the losses. It was with no small sense of relief that they safely reached squadron HQ just a short way along the road back to Beek.

The weather brightened in the afternoon, just in time for the 325th GIR landings, which took place as planned, and successfully too. Hills remained with Jack Holman the rest of the day until, as darkness fell, the squadron pulled back having suffered no more losses. It was a day that was to prove typical of the Sherwood Rangers' experience in the Nijmegen sector.

On Sunday, 24 September, some fifty German aircraft came over to bomb Nijmegen, followed by a dozen more. 'But nothing near us,' wrote Padre Skinner in his diary. 'We are a lovely target near only road through forest – as distinct from tracks – but trees are too thick for them to see or do much about it. But we cannot get off the road.' That same day, the celebrated BBC war correspondent Frank Gillard visited the regiment to make a feature on the first British troops in Germany – and Stanley Christopherson was filmed standing on German soil. 'The most cheerful troops that I have encountered were those on the Reich border,' reported Gillard. 'They were the men of a County Yeomanry Regiment, the first troops back from the Middle East to land on D-Day. And they are now the first British troops to enter Germany.'

It poured with rain that Sunday, and although the Sherwood Rangers were not in the midst of a heavy battle, they were still in action, which was always exhausting and tense no matter what happened.

'Well, it is several days since I wrote to you,' scribbled Harry Heenan that same day to his parents, 'and this letter is just a hurried note – there is nothing much to report. As you can imagine, life is pretty strenuous again . . . Anyway, we are sorting out Jerry in no mean style, though resistance is pretty tough again.' His thoughts then turned to home. 'I sometimes imagine myself on King's Cross station, waiting for the train,' he added – the train that would take him back to Yorkshire. 'Gosh, the number of times I have gone up and down that railway! And boy, will I be happy next time I do.'

The following day, Monday, 25 September, the regiment was supporting both the newly arrived 325th GIR, who had taken over the southern Mook sector of the front around Kiekberg wood, and the 508th PIR, who remained in the north. A Squadron were on duty in the northern sector and found themselves sent down to support the very same troops with which C Squadron had been operating two days earlier. Now, though, the Americans were firmly dug in around the bend in the road some 400 yards or so from the orchard, which was still held by the enemy.

Leading A Squadron along this road was David Render's A Troop, while his great friend Harry Heenan was leading his troop on the same parallel route taken by Lieutenant Holmes on the 23rd. Reaching the American positions, Render clambered down to talk to the American company commander. From the American slit-trenches, he peered through his binoculars and saw a Jagdpanzer guarding the road and a number of familiar coal-scuttle helmets moving about. Render was familiar with the Jagdpanzer; it was an SP gun, and, unlike the Jagdpanther, very low in profile and armed with a 75mm anti-tank gun. He'd been told by John Semken that the Americans were pinned down and needed their help, but as far as he could tell a kind of truce had descended in this little corner of the front.

'Wait a minute,' Render said to the American major, 'what are those buggers doing?'

'Yeah, well, they're not shooting at us,' the major replied, 'so we're not shooting at them.'

'Christ,' said Render, 'my major would have my guts for garters if I don't go for them. Let's shoot the bastards.'

The American major was not much impressed by this bravado, and told him flatly that if he and his troop wanted to go up there and take them on then he was welcome to do so. Render would have preferred the help of the infantry, but he knew John Semken would take a very dim view of them sitting around doing nothing with the enemy in plain sight. He peered through his field glasses again. To the right the field looked a bit soggy, but the ground appeared firmer off the road to the left. Quickly, he made a plan of action: he'd turn the bend and fire at the Jagdpanzer with AP, hoping it didn't get him first, trusting in the speed and quicker rate of fire of the Sherman, as well as its stabilizing gyro to maintain his aim. Then he and his next tank, commanded by Corporal Johnny Lanes, would charge the road, closing the distance between them and the enemy, before pulling off the dyke to the left to avoid being skylined on the raised road. They would then blast out the enemy with MG fire and HE from their main guns. His third and fourth members of the troop, one of which was a Firefly, would hang back and give them cover.

With the benefit of surprise and as the first to break the unofficial truce, Render's gunner hit the Jagdpanzer on the charge with his first shot. It brewed up immediately in a ball of flame and thick oily smoke that also provided a bit of cover as Render and Lanes made their charge down the road. A hundred and fifty yards further on, Render gave the orders to slew off the bank, at which point a shell whooshed just over Render's head. A split second later came the enemy gun's retort. Panic. An 88. And there it was, up ahead, hidden in the trees by the side of the road. Nor was the ground to the left dry – it was swampy. Render yelled to his driver, Trooper Dixon, to reverse. The grinding of gears. Tracks sliding. Going nowhere. A second round screamed in, ploughing a furrow into the bank beside them. The shot too short, but the next round – *fucking arseholes, they're going to get me!* Then wham! The next round hit them and Render slumped back into the turret, his vision black. 'Christ!' he said, 'I'm blind!' Others in the crew were yelling at the driver to get them the fuck out of there, and the driver cursing that he was doing his fucking best. Ken Mayo, his operator, now pulled Render's hands from his face, swiftly brushed off the dirt and cleared his eyes. 'Oh, Christ,' said Render, 'I can see!' The dirt, debris and flash of flame from the glancing blow had singed his eyebrows and covered his eyes. Why had the shell not penetrated? Must have been HE not AP. Panic and fear had gripped him. Render pushed himself back up, bracing himself for the fourth round, but suddenly a crash of gunfire rang out and the Pak 43 ahead of them was hit and the men around blasted into the air. 'Wallop!' said Render. 'An HE round right in the middle of this gun and killed the fucking lot.'

Render could scarcely believe it, but then heard Harry Heenan's voice on the net. 'Hello 5,' he said, 'do you feel better now?'

'Harry! Thank Christ for that. I was a dead duck then.'

'I know, but you're all right now. I'll see you . . .'

Then he stopped talking. Render thought nothing more of it; radios could cut out at any moment. Johnny Lanes pulled them out shortly after and, having cleared the rest of the orchard of the enemy, they pulled back, Render still in a state about the near-miss. Christ, he'd been lucky. Perhaps the German anti-tank crew had been inexperienced; perhaps they'd not had any AP rounds. Perhaps it was a bit of both. But thank God for Harry, he thought, who had been on the parallel road, heard the firing, and pulled off down a farm track and drawn up at 90 degrees to the German positions – and then fired through the trees.

When they pulled into leaguer later that evening, Render immediately went off to look for his friend to thank him for saving his life and shake him by the hand. But Harry's dead, he was told. Render was dumbstruck. 'What are you talking about?' he said. 'Harry's not dead. He can't be.'

But he was. He'd been sitting on the edge of the turret talking to Render when he was shot in the thigh and stomach and bled out soon after. 'I have to live with that one,' said Render, who was devastated by the loss, more so than by any other of his comrades who had been killed so far. 'I shall never forget him, of course.' Render's life had been hanging by a thread and yet he'd survived, saved by the quick thinking of his best friend in the regiment – moments before that same friend had been unluckily picked out. There was no rhyme nor reason to it. All that hope, that promise, that youthful vigour and wonder – characteristics that defined this promising young man – had gone; he had been twenty-one, a fully grown man, and yet for all the responsibility he shouldered and for all his undoubted courage, his letters had revealed a heart and soul that had yet to completely shed their youth. His loss was a bitter blow to the squadron, as John Semken admitted in a letter to Heenan's devastated parents; Harry had been their only son. 'He was universally loved and respected throughout the squadron,' wrote Semken, 'particularly by the few hard-headed old warriors who remain.'

No matter how much a man might grieve for a dead friend, the war continued, and the Sherwood Rangers continued to play their part. The cycle of men in and out of the regiment went on. New faces, new crews. As ever, the burden lay most heavily on the troop and squadron leaders. After their tank was knocked out on 23 September, Hills's crew were told to take a rest until a new tank could be brought up – except for Hills himself, who, as troop leader, was put with another crew, and the following day found himself in the Mook area of the front, which meant he was working with new American infantry – the 325th GIR – as well as a new crew. He was up at C Squadron HQ on the Groesbeek Heights when Jack Holman received a call for help. Just off the road between Groesbeek and the village of Wyler, some paratroopers were stuck in woods and needed armoured fire support to help get them out.

Off went Hills with his troop, heading down a tree-lined road that ran from the heights almost due east. From here, the large, looming mass of the Reichswald, the great German border forest, could be seen a few miles ahead, over largely flat, open farmland, dotted with farmsteads and villages. Just up ahead were fields still scattered with wrecked gliders from the landings of the 325th GIR. As he neared the American CP – command post – two shells whooshed in, landing worryingly close.

Hills moved his troop off the road and behind some trees, and headed over on foot to the farmhouse where the Americans had their CP. They were pleased to see him. The wood was only a matter of a few hundred yards away, down a left-turning track, but the Germans were shelling it and making it impossible for the Americans stuck there to get out; there were now a number of wounded down there too. As Hills walked back to his tank, he felt overcome by despair. They would have to head down there without firing for risk of hitting the Americans, and it was clear they'd be under the watch of the enemy the whole time. 'As I walked back,' he wrote, 'I was nearer tears than I have ever been. It seemed such a hopeless task yet refusal to do the job was out of the question.'

Speed seemed to give them their best chance of surviving. They dashed forward, turned left, then right into the wood, shells screaming over. Down to the far side, where Hills fired in every direction to the front, pumping out round after round of HE and spraying the enemy positions with both machine guns while the Americans collected their platoon together.

Pull back into the wood – Americans clambering on to the back – then out again, even while shells were bursting in and around the trees. They made it – a miracle – hearts hammering. Having deposited the men back at the farmhouse, Hills led his troop back up to the heights. He was quite overcome with relief.

But no sooner had they reached C Squadron HQ than they were ordered back down again. The Americans now planned to send a stronger force to take the wood and the German positions beyond. Cursing, back they went, into heavier shelling and mortar fire, Hills's tank blasting at a white farm building that seemed to be the German CP. Back out they came a little while later, although by this time Sergeant Sidney Collis's tank had been hit, first by HE, which had prompted the crew to bail out, and then with an AP round, which had caused it to brew up. Fortunately, Collis and his crew had got out in time. Again and again that day, Hills could have had his tank knocked out, and could have been killed or wounded at any moment. He'd been lucky. He'd been spared. There really was no rhyme or reason to it.

They were in action again on the 28th, back near the windmill. Lieutenant Holmes and his crew knocked out three tanks in a matter of minutes just as dawn was breaking. Enemy shelling was heavy that day, but the American paratroopers stuck it out. Hills witnessed one of their paratroopers still firing even though he'd lost an arm and a leg. 'The 82nd', wrote Hills, 'behaved magnificently.'

This was the pattern of the fighting here in the Nijmegen sector: fending off counter-attacks, increasingly on the attack themselves, wearing down the enemy and pushing them back, often just a few hundred yards at a time. Stanley Christopherson spent much of his time beetling backwards and forwards between the Beek front and Mook, a lot of it with Colonel Charles Billingslea, the commander of the 325th GIR. At 6 feet 6 inches, Billingslea was a giant of a man, but softly spoken, courteous, brave and respected by all. Christopherson liked him enormously. On 2 October, Billingslea planned a major assault to clear the Kiekberg wood between the Heights and the Reichswald down to Middelar on the Maas.

Christopherson was up at Billingslea's forward CP at 5.30 a.m., but before the attack went in, two officers from the Guards Armoured Brigade arrived. They were to be relieving the Sherwood Rangers in a few days, and so Christopherson made the necessary introductions and explained the lie of the land. In order to get a better view, they crawled forward through some trees – and must have been spotted, because moments later shells were whooshing in and crashing around them, shards of wood and steel spraying in all directions and the ground pulsing from the force of the explosions.

Soon after, the barrage stopped, and when Christopherson shook himself down and looked around, he saw that Billingslea's adjutant had been killed and one of the Guards officers was missing. No trace could be found of him, although later they found his compass. 'I had never quite realized,' noted Christopherson, 'that a direct hit from a large shell could remove practically all evidence of a human body.' He was badly shaken by the experience, as he'd been talking to the man just moments before; the officer had been telling him that he was just twenty-one and had only joined his regiment that very day.

Billingslea seemed to have as much of a lucky charm around him as Stanley Christopherson. The whole of his headquarters staff were killed or wounded during the time Stanley was with him, yet neither of them suffered so much as a scratch. Why was that? Why were they spared? One time they were suddenly mortared at the CP; Billingslea jumped into a slit-trench, Christopherson into his scout car. 'When all was quiet,' noted Christopherson, 'we found that all our party had been wounded except for Billingslea and myself.' While he was taking cover in his scout car, Christopherson saw a badly wounded German soldier lying on a stretcher next to the house that was Billingslea's HQ, and thought he should quickly dash out and move him to some kind of safety. But with the mortars raining down, he decided to stay put. When the stonk was over and he clambered out, he saw the German had been killed. He'd been no more than seventeen or eighteen at the most, and with his thick spectacles looked a most unlikely soldier. It was pitiful to see this boy lying there, dead. Christopherson felt a pang of guilt that he might have given the young German a chance of life.

Whether it was fate, God, the gods, luck or simply random chance, Christopherson was still standing after five years of war. So too were Stuart Hills and David Render and Bill Wharton. Statistically, they were an anomaly, and all of them privately wondered how long their luck might last.

PART III

Winter

CHAPTER 23

Revolving Doors

THE SHERWOOD RANGERS WERE relieved by the 4th Coldstreams on 6 October and pulled back to Winssen, about 3 miles due west of Nijmegen, for a rest, although this lasted only two days rather than the four they had been promised. By the 9th, they were back into the line in the Mook sector. The failure of MARKET GARDEN had brought about a major rethink at the highest levels. The lightning strike through the back door into north-west Germany had proved a busted flush, but such a huge effort had been made at significant cost to the 1st Airborne Division and the 1st Polish Independent Parachute Brigade – not to mention the US airborne divisions and Allied air forces – and also to the Allied supply situation. A choice had been made to prioritize MARKET GARDEN over the clearing of the mouths of the Scheldt and now, at the beginning of October, the Allies had control of Antwerp but not the wide river estuary that led to this all-important port. Clearing this soggy, low-lying tract of western Holland, with its myriad waterways and islands, was not going to be easy. The issue was the extreme length of Allied supply lines, most of which still fed through Normandy, combined with shortening days and worsening weather. The Sherwood Rangers were told to get ready for an operation to clear the Reichswald, working alongside the 43rd Wessex Division, but this was then cancelled, and instead both the Wessexmen and 8th Armoured Brigade were put into a defensive holding position. Until the Scheldt was cleared, a task given to the Second Canadian Army, the British invasion of Germany would have to wait.

The Americans also had their supply problems; even the US Seventh Army, which had landed in southern France in the middle of August, was becoming overextended. The difficulties were not helped by the devastated condition of the Channel ports – when they were finally liberated; at this point Dunkirk, for example, was still stubbornly holding out against the Canadians. General Patton's Third Army had tried to bludgeon its way through Metz on the Franco-German border in September but had been unable to take the city. To the south, his men attacked across the Maginot Line, originally built by the French in the 1930s to keep the Germans out, but again could not break through. General Courtney Hodges' First Army, meanwhile, continued attacking through the dense Hürtgen forest, while on 2 October the attack on the German border city of Aachen began. The days of giant leaps and bounds were over; it was back to bloody attrition. A collective air of gloom descended with the growing realization that giddy hopes for a swift end to the war in Europe had been dashed. No one now expected it all to be over by Christmas.

Through the revolving doors of the Sherwood Rangers came some old faces as well as plenty of new ones. Arthur Reddish was back. He'd been stuck in a transit camp in Normandy; then, when it had seemed likely that he might be sent to a different regiment altogether, he had absconded on 10 September with a fellow called Gordon Hatherway, a trooper in the 13/18th Hussars. They'd got themselves to Brussels and once there decided they'd earned themselves a holiday and so spent the next ten days drinking, eating, enjoying the hospitality of friendly Belgians and chatting up the girls. On 25 September, they both reckoned it was time they tried to make their way back to their regiments, keenly aware that after twenty-one days of being absent without leave they would be considered to have deserted, which suddenly seemed a rather serious matter.

Reaching the Sherwood Rangers was easier said than done. Eventually, after a wild goose chase around the newly liberated parts of Holland, they reached Bourg-Léopold and 8th Armoured Brigade's rear HQ, still in the wooded parkland where it had been before MARKET GARDEN.

The following morning, Reddish got a ride back up to the regiment and on arrival decided his best ploy was to pretend he'd done absolutely nothing wrong. RHQ was a collection of army tents in a wood on the Groesbeek Heights; there he found the quartermaster's lorries and drew his kit, which had been kept there since he'd left after the Berjou battle. Suddenly, however, he was being yelled at by the Regimental Sergeant-Major, Arthur 'Brud' Barlow, and told he needed to present himself to the colonel. The Germans chose this moment to lob over some shells; when that had stopped and the dust cleared, Reddish was hauled before Stanley Christopherson, who, not unreasonably, asked him where he'd been.

'I don't know, Colonel,' Reddish replied, a line he was determined to stick to. Of course, it fooled no one, but Christopherson packed him off to see the MO, 'Hylda' Young. Seated before the doctor, Reddish once again claimed he had no idea where he'd been; he simply couldn't remember. Young wasn't taken in either, but couldn't help laughing and diagnosed 'suspected amnesia'.

Back in front of Colonel Christopherson, Reddish handed over the note. Christopherson read it then threw it in the air.

'Look, Trooper,' he said. 'I'm giving you an ultimatum. Either go back in a tank tomorrow or face a court martial.'

'I'll go back in a tank, sir,' Reddish hastily replied. 'This afternoon if you like.'

At this, Christopherson couldn't help smiling too. 'All right, off you go,' he said. 'Report to Major Semken.'

There were other changes. Robin Leigh, the 'Baron', had been away in Brussels on a course and on staff work since first joining the regiment after Berjou, which was why Stephen Mitchell had remained in post for a while. Mitchell had now taken back command of C Squadron from Jack Holman, who had reverted to second-in-command; and Leigh finally took over again as regimental second-in-command. The Baron had also brought with him seven new officers from his old regiment, the Royal Gloucester Hussars, including Frenchie Houghton, who had been his adjutant in the Gloucesters and now took on that role in the SRY as well, with Terry Leinster, who had been in post since June, taking over a troop in B Squadron. Three entire troops from the 49th Royal Tank Regiment also joined the Rangers, including two officers, Lieutenant Harry 'Bing' Crosbie and Lieutenant Peter Mellowes, both twenty-one. Crosbie and Mellowes were great friends, having been at Sandhurst together and then both having joined 49 RTR. Now they continued to stick together like glue, both joining B Squadron in the Sherwood Rangers.

Mellowes was a tall, bespectacled and slightly studious-looking young man, from a quiet and unremarkable middle-class background. He'd joined the local Home Guard with his father back in 1940, then joined up at eighteen in 1942 and been sent to Bovington to join the 48th Training Regiment. With his somewhat sheltered background, he had been an innocent all at sea among the streetwise lads from the East End of London and elsewhere, but had knuckled down and learned quickly; and, having won a stripe as a 'provisional unpaid lance-corporal', had later been earmarked as officer material. Then his army career had very nearly come to a dramatic halt when he'd suffered from gas gangrene in his left hand. He'd been a whisker away from having it amputated, but had been treated in the nick of time, recovered and safely returned to Bovington. He had found the training tough but not oppressive, and had enjoyed the social awakening and being surrounded by lads from all sorts of backgrounds. 'They were a grand lot,' he noted, 'and always ready to help out when one had to bullshit your kit for guard duty.'

From Bovington, he'd been posted to Sandhurst, and then to what was known as a CDL regiment. The abbreviation stood for 'Canal Defence Light'. These secret units consisted of tanks fitted with a powerful searchlight, used to produce artificial moonlight; they could also be flashed rapidly on and off, supposedly to confuse the enemy at night. In reality, however, by 1944 it meant a regiment training and waiting to be shipped into an active theatre. In fact it was 49 RTR, which landed in Normandy on 12 August, still with their outdated Grant tanks, precursors of the Shermans, and attached to 79th Armoured Division. No one seemed to know what to do with them, and although they were gradually re-equipped with Shermans, by the beginning of October they'd still not been pressed into action. It was then, on 7 October, that three complete troops joined the Sherwood Rangers.

Mellowes and Crosbie were welcomed into the SRY, as were all newcomers, but it meant there were suddenly a lot of new faces about the place. It was ever thus. The regiment never stood still, and it was the task of the command, from Christopherson down to squadron level, to welcome the new arrivals and ensure they were absorbed into the regiment as seamlessly as possible.

As for the old hands, many were feeling the strain. Bill Wharton, for one, was not in good spirits just now. During the regiment's brief time out of the line they had been besieged by civilians, many of them refugees, who watched their every move and constantly pestered them for food. Of course, they handed out what they could, but it was a stark reminder of the awful misery and depredations caused by the war. And all his friends had gone. 'Sunday evening,' he wrote to Marion on 9 October, 'and the combination of dark evening, no real friends, and circumstances have brought that browned-off feeling.' By 'circumstances' he meant the relentlessness of what they were experiencing – long periods of combat followed by ever briefer spells of leave, most of which were dominated by tasks: sorting out billets, conferences, condolence letters. There was also a pervasive and growing feeling that more was expected of them than was reasonable. The reduction of their planned leave was a case in point. 'You can imagine our feelings,' he added, 'when we received notice that we are to return to the fun and games tomorrow.' Now, with dusk falling, he had moved into a small room to be alone and write to his wife – the one person he wanted to be with more than any other in the world, but from whom he was so cruelly separated.

His peace was soon disturbed by four noisy officers coming back to the house – three of whom were new to B Squadron. 'Damn them – the young pups,' he wrote. 'I hope we get rid of 'em after this thing is over. Actually, they are all right, being much better than the usual type we get as they have been for some years with a regiment that has recently been disbanded and consequently know their stuff.' These were the 49th RTR men. That they were now with the SRY at all was a stark reminder of the parlous state of British manpower after five long years of a global war – a war that still had some way to run. Britain's population was only around 40 million, half that of Germany, yet the country had been fighting on land, in the air and at sea since September 1939. Really, the drain on personnel was immense. North-west Europe might be the priority battle at present, but British troops were concurrently fighting in the Far East and in Italy as well as manning numerous outposts throughout the world. Manpower was also needed to manufacture vast numbers of ships, tanks and aircraft and to sustain an enormous war industry. Home defence was still important as V-2 rockets rained down on London, while back in August, the Royal Navy had formed the Pacific Fleet. 'I am inclined to agree with you,' Wharton added sadly, 'that the Germans will fight hard on their soil – as indeed, they are doing – and that it will be a matter of months before they are finally beaten.'

Meanwhile, Stuart Hills was about to be given a different role. Christopherson was aware that Hills had seen a huge amount of action since D-Day and that his nerves were just beginning to fray a little. Keeping a watch on the troop and squadron leaders especially was a part of the job Christopherson took very seriously indeed; so too did Leslie Skinner and 'Hylda' Young, and the three of them, as well as Stephen Mitchell, made a point of discussing how their subordinates were getting on. There was some flexibility within the regiment to move people around, and so Christopherson took Hills aside when they were in Winssen and asked him if he fancied joining him at RHQ for a stint as intelligence officer. 'Though not actually bomb happy,' noted Hills, 'I was getting rather tired of tank fighting, which I was beginning to find a great strain.'

So he agreed, and brought his current tank driver, Bill Cousins, with him to drive the Dingo scout car that went with the post; Hills reckoned Cousins needed a rest as much as anyone. As luck would have it, however, on their first night at RHQ – back in the line near Mook – they were heavily shelled. RHQ was a watch tower and Hills was sleeping on the ground floor with Terry Leinster, who had yet to join B Squadron. To begin with the shelling was sporadic, but it increased as the night wore on. The windows above them began splintering, so they moved their camp beds to the other side of the building, only for the shelling to worsen further. After one particularly close volley there were cries and screams, so Hills got up and dashed around to the front of the building to see that Cousins was all right. 'A few more shells landed closer than ever,' noted Hills, 'and seeing no sign of Bill I raced down the steps to the cellar where the Colonel and other officers were and the Colonel made me stay there.' Bill Cousins was brought in soon after, wounded, along with six infantrymen. 'Hylda as usual dealing with the whole lot,' added Hills. Cousins had survived unscathed through most of the North African campaign as well as Normandy, but his war was finished on this first night at RHQ, a posting that was supposed to be a cushy number and a reward for having put himself in the firing line for so long.

The regiment was out of the line, then in the line, then out of it again. Yet more conferences at brigade, not least to discuss the still thorny issue of cooperation between infantry and tanks in forthcoming operations. There were REME maintenance checks of their tanks – the regiment scored highly, which was a feather in their cap – demonstrations of Crocodile flame-throwers, and the usual visits of the mobile bath units and make-shift cinema. There were also rumours of a major offensive through the Reichswald.

This was because of talks on 18 October between Generals Eisenhower, Montgomery and Bradley, the US 12th Army Group commander, to agree next steps. Eisenhower announced they were to pursue a 'broad front' strategy, an approach generally favoured by American commanders, and one that, given the Allies' enormous resources of air power and fire support, had a great deal of merit. In any case, the dashing strike operation to plunge a route into northern Germany had failed, and the Allied armies – American, British, Canadian and French – were now lined up along nearly

400 miles of the German border. A broad front strategy played to Allied strengths and ensured the Germans would need to repel attacks along a front they were increasingly ill-equipped to defend.

Phase one was for Montgomery and Bradley's armies to capture the Rhineland, the western area of the country between Holland and the River Rhine: British Second Army would attack south-eastwards from the Nijmegen area across the Reichswald and take Cleve and Goch, while the American First and Ninth Armies were to assault due east, where they were already involved in bitter fighting both at Aachen and in the Hürtgen forest. At the same time, the US Third Army under Patton was to continue driving on towards the Saar, while even further south the US Seventh and French First Armies would turn towards Germany from Karlsruhe to Mulhouse.

Supplies were the limiting factor. The Allied way of war was to push forward, relentlessly, and always to have enough of everything to ensure that any major attack was successful. Compared with the Germans, they remained awash with supplies, but it was no good comparing themselves with the enemy – after all, fighting with a paucity of supplies had not worked for them. Without this very long tail – this Big War approach – the Allies would not attempt such operations, and quite rightly too. So until the port of Antwerp was open, Second Army could not undertake a strike into the Rhineland.

As a consequence, the second half of October and early November was an odd, in-between time for the Sherwood Rangers and the rest of Dempsey's Second Army, as the Canadians, helped by Royal Marine Commandos and the 52nd Lowland Division, continued slogging their way through the polders along the Scheldt. The battle for the island of Walcheren, the northern mouth of the Scheldt, began on 31 October, but even at the beginning of November Antwerp was still not open for seaborne trade. Even when at the front, they were on the defensive, holding the line only. All the while, though, a more gradual build-up continued, using longer lines of supply; the strength that had been sapped by the monumental effort of the four months of fighting since D-Day was slowly but surely being replenished – not just among the Sherwood Rangers, but across the entire Second Army.

Arthur Reddish had thought the colonel had made a mistake when sending him to see John Semken, but that wasn't the case. Semken had specifically asked for him to be his gunner in his own tank. The two had served together in North Africa, when Semken had been in C Squadron.

Reddish was sorry to bid goodbye to some old mates, but he was good pals with Trooper John Savage, Semken's soldier-servant, whom he knew from the desert days, so that was at least one familiar face. According to Savage, everyone knew just what Reddish had got up to during his brief desertion, and not a man in the regiment believed his cock-and-bull amnesia story. It turned out Reddish had Semken to thank for having got off so lightly, the squadron leader having promised Christopherson he would personally vouch for his future good conduct.

Wednesday, 18 October, was a maintenance day for the regiment.

'I want the inside of this tank as clean as a surgery,' Semken told his crew, 'with all weapons in tip-top shape and the tank engine ready for anything.' After dismissing the rest of the crew, he called Reddish aside. 'Now you're back with me, Red, I expect you to do everything right from now on. You are the squadron leader's gunner and I want you to set an example to the other gunners. Understood?' Reddish promised he wouldn't let him down, and set to immediately, stripping and cleaning the gun. The breech had apparently been proving a bit sticky, and Reddish was able to solve the issue partially himself and then swiftly get the squadron armourer to make it work perfectly.

Ernie Leppard was no longer a regimental clerk but instead the operator in Johnny Taylor's crew in B Squadron. Taylor had only just been made up to be a tank commander. Leppard liked Taylor from the outset, and he also gelled with Bill Kendrick, the driver, and Wally Davis, the lap-gunner. It was Arthur Falconer, the gunner, he didn't warm to – but then again, none of them did. 'He wouldn't pull his weight,' said Leppard, 'and we was all after getting rid of him.' It was essential crew members all knitted well together, because when in action each man had a defined role and was dependent on everyone else to carry out their respective jobs as efficiently and effectively as possible; it was about trust as much as anything. 'If a crew got on, well, they was lifetime friends,' he added. 'And, of course, you had to depend on your life with them.'

The operator's job was not an easy one. He had to listen to orders coming over the net and relay them swiftly, and a good operator would be switching between the A and B nets in case there was important information; Frank Galvin's troop had not been disciplined enough at Berjou and it had cost them dear. 'You had to be nimble with what you were doing,' said Leppard, 'you know, with the different frequencies you were required to go on and you had to change the frequencies every day and you changed the codes every day.' It was also his job to load the gun. In the heat of battle there was a lot for the operator to do, think about and listen to – and often all at once. This strange period, however, was a good time for the crew to get to know one another; foibles could be learned and understood before they got into intense fighting, with all the pressures and tension action brought about. From patrol work around Mook, on 21 October the regiment took over the positions of the 13/18th Hussars on the 'Island' – the narrow strip of polder country between Arnhem and Nijmegen. It wasn't really an island, although this area, 8 miles deep at most and 20 wide, was almost entirely surrounded by the Waal and Lower Rhine. Once again, it was a holding role, guarding against a German strike from the Arnhem area to the north.

As new faces came in, some of the old ones were leaving. One of those was Bill Wharton. The Sherwood Rangers were now suddenly so awash with new officers, Stanley Christopherson chose him to go home for a course at the RAC headquarters at Bovington in Dorset. It all happened very suddenly. One moment, Wharton was trying to adjust to the prospect of long, bleak months to come; the next, he was being told to pack his bags and get back to England. Fortunately, he was able to enjoy a couple of precious days with his beloved wife – reunited at long last – before reporting to Bovington on 25 October. 'It is just so hard to leave you,' he wrote on his first evening there. 'Wish you were with me now – shall have to think about you until I go to sleep. Lots of love, Marion, my darling.' Hard though it was to part from her, at least, for the time being at any rate, he was safe, and no longer in the front line.

That same day, 25 October, Peter Selerie rejoined the regiment, but only after a vigorous and determined campaign, for the powers that be had earmarked him for the embryonic 155th Regiment, RAC, which was still training in England. It says much about Selerie's loyalty – and courage – that he preferred to head straight back to the front and the Sherwood Rangers instead. After being wounded at La Bigne, he'd been evacuated to England, where he'd ended up in a hospital in Leicester. News of the regiment trickled in, not least via the Welfare Association, but also from letters from friends still out at the front. There had been depressing numbers of losses, and from his hospital bed, he found himself writing all too many condolence letters.

As for himself, he was all right. Mortar bomb shrapnel had been removed from his left shoulder, arm and leg, although some remained in his lower back. It didn't bother him, however, and having made a good and swift recovery, all things considered, he was eager to get back to the regiment. To his enormous dismay, however, he was instead posted to the 35th Armoured Brigade near Newmarket – a unit that had not seen action but urgently needed some experienced officers. Distraught, he arrived at Newmarket only to be sent on a tour of RAF stations to lecture about the role of armour and how to improve armour–air cooperation.

He immediately recruited Myrtle Kellett to his cause. 'To my great dismay,' he wrote to her on 28 September from 155th Regiment, 'I find myself posted to the above regiment instead of the SRY.' He told her he had been up to London to lobby friends who might have influence. 'I have written simply frantic notes to Stanley C and Ian Spence.' Spence, briefly CO of the Sherwood Rangers in Tunisia, but now an RAC brigadier in Brussels, managed to pull strings, as did Myrtle Kellett and Stanley Christopherson, so that 35th Armoured Brigade were bombarded with requests to release their new major. It took a little while, but by the end of the second week of October he was on a boat to Dieppe – along with Stephen Mitchell, who was returning from a brief spell of leave. They were then put on to a train. Perhaps understandably, considering the immense damage the Allied air forces had wrought on the European railway network, progress was painfully slow and included a succession of long halts. At one, they stopped by a tented camp alongside the line; so Selerie clambered down and strolled over, and was directed to the officers' mess of the Irish Guards. A smartly dressed mess waiter emerged and Selerie asked him what he might have to drink.

'Sir, you being a cavalry officer,' the mess waiter replied in a pronounced Irish brogue, 'you'll be after having some champagne.'

'After discovering that was Bollinger,' noted Selerie, 'we did a deal on the spot.' It was a close-run thing, however, because just then the train whistled and Selerie had to dash back. The mess waiter flung the case at him as he leaped aboard, Selerie hastily handed over the agreed number of francs, and the train began slowly chugging on its way. It was the only time in his life he had drunk Bollinger from an enamel mug, but he reckoned it tasted like the nectar of the gods.

He was delighted to be back, although ten weeks after he'd been invalided out, the regiment looked quite different. With Stephen Mitchell back at C Squadron, Selerie was given B Squadron to command, taking over from Tony Gauntley, who in turn now shifted over to A Squadron to be John Semken's second-in-command.

*

'The Colonel and Major Gauntley attended a lecture on the Siegfried Line,' noted Stuart Hills, the new guardian of the regimental war diary, on the first day of November. 'Capt Fearn, Major Mitchell MC and Capt Coleman did an indirect shoot with C Sqn which was very satisfactory. There was a Squadron Leaders conference re: discipline and drill.' Three days later, Brigadier Prior-Palmer organized a brigade dance in the miraculously undamaged town hall in Nijmegen, which stood only 4 miles or so from the nearest German positions. It wasn't exactly a three-line whip, but Stanley Christopherson felt honour bound to attend and took with him five other officers, including his old friend Peter Selerie.

Prior-Palmer had attempted to bring up some fifty girls from Brussels, but couldn't get his plan past security concerns. As the dance began, Christopherson found himself standing next to Fearn and Selerie and talking to two Dutch girls, one of whom was extremely good-looking and the other quite the opposite. Fearn wasted no time in whisking off the beauty to dance, leaving Christopherson and Selerie with the other, who was rather large, covered in spots, and spoke no English.

'I think you should dance with this charming girl,' Christopherson suggested to Selerie.

'Sorry, Colonel,' Selerie replied, 'but I can't dance.'

'I am afraid that I shall have to order you to take a lesson from our charming friend.'

'I am sorry, sir,' Selerie insisted, 'in that case I shall have to disobey an unlawful command.'

Christopherson now changed tack. 'If you dance with her,' he said, 'I will give you the next Jeep which is allocated to the Regiment.' This was a sore point for Selerie, who had been very disappointed to rejoin the regiment and discover he no longer had a jeep; he'd recently stolen an abandoned civilian Opel, but it wasn't really cut out for the job.

'Make it a Jeep and two first-class wireless operators for my squadron,' he replied, 'and I will dance.'

'All right,' Christopherson agreed, 'but it's pure blackmail.' Selerie led the girl away, leading her through a very rapid quick-step. Later, Christopherson tried to wriggle out of the deal by claiming that Selerie, having had a few drinks, had bartered them away in return for dancing with the local beauty. Selerie, however, denied this.

A few days later, the Sherwood Rangers heard they were to be leaving the Nijmegen sector and heading south to a different part of the front entirely.

Before they left, Stanley Christopherson visited General Gavin, with whom he had got on extremely well, and presented him with a polished 75mm shell case which had been adorned with a regimental cap badge and an inscription, and had then been fashioned into a cup complete with handles. It was the first time they'd presented such a gift to one of the units with which they had fought, but they had been rather impressed by the 'All American' Division. Certainly, it made a difference when the troops were all volunteers, highly motivated and inculcated with an extremely aggressive fighting spirit. British airborne troops, Commandos and other special forces such as the SAS were cut from a similar cloth. What particularly marked the 82nd Airborne men out to the Sherwood Ranger men was their aggression, and the fact that – unlike conscript infantry divisions – they rarely went to ground the moment enemy fire opened up. This was of huge benefit to the tank men, and made a welcome change after the endless discussions they had had about how best to work with infantry ever since D-Day. The solution seemed plain enough: to operate with better-motivated and more aggressive infantry. 'We unanimously agreed,' noted Christopherson, 'that these American Airborne troops, especially the 82nd Division, were among the best, if not the best, infantry we had yet supported.'

In many ways, Christopherson's approach was the same: to be aggressive. He was not in favour of recklessness, and there was a fine line between the two, but time and again aggressive tactics – such as the fire first and relentlessly policy – had worked, whether in A Squadron's evening assault on Rauray at the end of June or the rescue by Stuart Hills's troop of the Americans in the wood at the end of September. Read the ground, keep alert, keep watching and keep firing: that was the mantra. The enemy rarely fired back if they were being fired at themselves. Christopherson's only quibble about the All Americans was that perhaps they were sometimes just a bit *too* tough. 'I shall never forget seeing a Jeep full of American paratroopers driving along with the head of a German pierced with an iron stake and tied to the front. That spectacle still haunts me.'

The Sherwood Rangers left the Nijmegen sector on 9 November, this time with their tanks on low-loader transports, and headed off on the journey south to take part in Operation CLIPPER, a joint Anglo-US assault on the German border town of Geilenkirchen. That the Sherwood Rangers were heading down there at all was because it wasn't only Montgomery who had been having supply problems; General Bradley had too.

He had had to siphon off units from his First and Ninth Armies to support Patton's drive towards the Saar, which prompted a sudden adjustment of the northern half of the Allied line. The US airborne divisions were to be pulled back out of the British sector and Second Army were to extend their stretch of the front all the way down to Geilenkirchen, about 80 miles to the south of Nijmegen. The new boundary between the British and General Bill Simpson's US Ninth Army would be the River Wurm, just to the south-west of Geilenkirchen.

Geilenkirchen, before the war an unremarkable market town on the German border some 35 miles south-west of Düsseldorf, had become a key anchor point at that stretch of the Westwall; either side of it were some of the strongest parts of the Siegfried Line defences, with immense minefields, anti-tank ditches, concrete emplacements and a host of interconnecting strongpoints. Bradley wanted Ninth Army to push forward to the Rhine at Cologne, yet Simpson recognized that if Geilenkirchen were not taken first, his left flank would be dangerously exposed. On the other hand, if he included the town as an early objective in his drive east, his troops could easily get sucked into taking it at the expense of a swift push to the Rhine.

While Horrocks still had his XXX Corps HQ near Nijmegen, Simpson visited him and asked him to consider helping him take Geilenkirchen. Initially, Horrocks politely refused, pointing out that he had only one division available and that taking the town would require two. A few days later, Horrocks was invited to a fine dinner at Eisenhower's headquarters, which Simpson also attended. It was all very convivial, but over whiskies and cigars afterwards, Eisenhower suddenly turned to his guest. 'Well, Jorrocks,' he asked, using the British general's nickname, 'are you going to take Geilenkirchen for us?'

Horrocks explained again that he only had the 43rd Wessex Division available. 'I couldn't possibly take the town,' he told the Supreme Commander, 'one of the strongest positions on the Westwall, with just that one division.'

At this, Eisenhower turned to Simpson and said, 'Give him one of ours.'

'Sure,' replied Simpson. That division was to be the 84th Infantry, newly arrived from the United States that October.

So it was that the 43rd Wessex Division and 8th Armoured Brigade moved south for the attack on Geilenkirchen. Horrocks specifically earmarked the Sherwood Rangers to work with the 84th 'Railsplitters'

Division after their successful cooperation with the 82nd Airborne. It was an awful journey. Winter had arrived early and with a vengeance; November was already proving a dreadful month with almost non-stop rain. Stanley Christopherson drove down with Frenchie Houghton in a jeep, and an extremely cold, wet and uncomfortable journey it was too. Eventually the regiment reached the coal-mining town of Palenberg, only a few miles south of Geilenkirchen but on the Dutch side of the border. With little to recommend it at the best of times, the town now lay wrecked and broken from recent shelling. None of the roads were tarmacadamed and all were thick with mud. Not a single building stood undamaged. It was hard to think of a more depressing place from which to launch a battle or worse conditions in which to do so. But it was through this sea of mud and destruction that the battle for Geilenkirchen was due to be launched on Saturday, 18 November 1944.

CHAPTER 24

Geilenkirchen

O NCE THE SHERWOOD RANGERS reached the Palenberg area, they had a week in which to get ready for the battle. It rained almost incessantly every single day. It was also cold, and the days were drawing in dramatically. Throughout history, warfare had always been so much harder in winter, which was why it had mostly happened during the 'campaigning season' of summer. Modern warfare was really no different, but the Allies were in a hurry to get on and finish the war. Shorter days, freezing cold, driving rain – no matter. They would fight on. But it made the misery of war even more miserable.

John Cropper had been rather pleased to have got hold of an American tank suit while they'd still been in the Nijmegen area, while Jack Holman had taken to wrapping himself up in a thick woollen duffel coat. Now, however, they were all issued with new tank oversuits, made of thick cotton, lined with Angora wool, each with an array of generous pockets and zips galore so that it could be easily put on over boots and battledress, and a belt around the middle to keep it all together. It also came with a lined collar and detachable zipped hood. These suits were warm and well designed, and although not entirely waterproof were a big improvement on the leather jerkins and woollen overcoats that had been available before their issue. None the less, they were inevitably bulky and restricted ease of movement a little.

Up to this point this area of the front had been very much the American part of the line. In fact, XIX Corps, part of US First Army, had actually reached the Westwall at Geilenkirchen by 17 September, the 2nd Armored Division capturing the village of Teveren, just a stone's throw to the west of the town. It had been the American intention to bulldoze straight on through and blow the German Westwall defences wide open – but then Bradley had taken one of the XIX Corps divisions and given it to Patton's Third Army instead; and a British thrust against the Ruhr on the First Army's northern flank, mooted by Montgomery early in September, did not materialize. Instead, there had been MARKET GARDEN, which hadn't worked out. All this had meant that a dangerous gap was emerging between the two US armies, leading directly to all thoughts of an assault on Geilenkirchen being abandoned for the time being. Then had come the battle for Aachen, First Army's fight a little way to the south: a brutal three-week slog before this became the first German city to fall to the Allies. During this time, a holding position had been adopted around Geilen-kirchen, and the town, the railway, the bunkers and the strongpoints had all been subjected to steady and relentless bombardment. On 8 November, fighter-bombers had flown over and napalmed the town. It was no wonder the place was such a wreck. By the middle of November 1944 there was a post-apocalyptic feel about the Geilenkirchen area – even though, in many ways, the apocalypse was still to come.

The Sherwood Rangers were billeted in the ruins of Palenberg. Arthur Reddish shared a cellar with his pal John Savage and the rest of Semken's tank crew, and also four American drivers who were members of a trans-port detachment. The house was pretty well smashed, but the ground floor rooms were just about habitable and had solid fuel fires. Below ground, in the cellar where they slept, it was dank, cold and dark; but it was fairly safe, which was just as well as most nights the Germans shelled the place. Reddish and Savage soon became firm friends with the Ameri-cans, who introduced the Sherwood Rangers boys to Frank Sinatra, had plenty of four-star brandy and loved playing poker, although the stakes were a little high for Reddish's limited means.

Meanwhile, Stanley Christopherson and the squadron leaders were spending their time poring over maps and attending endless conferences. Savage was worried about Semken's welfare, concerned that he was over-doing things. 'He isn't getting enough sleep,' he told Reddish. There was nothing that could be done about it, though. General Horrocks had come down to brief them all, and while he exuded his usual confidence, he made it quite clear they were going to have their work cut out. As usual, intelligence on the enemy was pretty good, and maps were issued with details of the Siegfried Line defences. A large swathe of land to the south-east of Geilenkirchen held a dense minefield – the thickest they had seen since Alamein – while the entire area east of the town and the River Wurm was protected by a mass of concrete bunkers. The town and the defences around it were held by the bulk of the 183. Volksgrenadier Division – hardly top drawer, but certainly strong in numbers. To their north was the 176. Division, while the bulk of XII. SS Korps artillery had been brought up to defend this strongpoint of the Westwall.

The regiment now had not only to work out a plan to get through these formidable defences in terrible wintry and rain-sodden conditions, but also create a working understanding with the 84th 'Railsplitters' Division, something of a challenge given their military and cultural differences, and the fact that the 84th had no combat experience whatsoever. The US Army had been tiny back in 1939, but had since grown exponentially. Entire divisions, each around 15,000 men, had been created and trained from scratch. The Railsplitters had been originally formed in 1917, then disbanded after the last war and reactivated as late as October 1942 – in Texas: a training ground that could hardly be more different from their new surroundings. Entire platoons, companies, battalions and regiments had been formed from scratch, mainly from conscripted soldiers; those showing promise were swiftly turned into NCOs, and those fresh from officer training units sent to command. Of course, some of their officers had seen action before, not least their commanding officer, Brigadier-General Alexander R. Bolling, the only one-star general in the US Army to be commanding a division at that time. He had served in France in the last war, had been twice wounded and had been awarded the Distinguished Service Cross, so he knew a thing or two about front-line experience.

None the less, the division had only arrived in England in October. Coming ashore on Omaha Beach between 1 and 4 November, from there they had been transported straight to Geilenkirchen, where they were now about to be hurled at one of the strongest points along the Siegfried Line. They were unquestionably thoroughly trained, and plenty of similarly fresh divisions had been plunged into combat and done incredibly well; yet experience counted for a very great deal, and the Sherwood Rangers were undeniably a little wary of their new partners. It was hardly surprising; time and again they'd struggled with infantry the first time they'd gone into combat together. The combination of appalling conditions and the heaviest defences they'd come up against since landing on 6 June created a thick layer of extra concern.

This was why the regiment's commander and senior officers were so determined to spend as much time as they possibly could before CLIPPER began getting to know their new brothers in arms and making sure they were all singing off the same hymn sheet. To this end, Stanley Christopherson asked his squadron leaders to move in with their respective battalion commanders in the run-up to the battle. For himself, he moved his HQ in with that of Colonel John H. Roosma, the commander of the 334th Regiment – who, as it happened, had been a basketball star back in the 1920s. An American infantry regiment was much the same size as a British brigade, consisting of three infantry battalions. It was those three battalions of the 334th who would be leading the charge for CLIPPER, supported by the men of the 333rd. Christopherson immediately struck up a good rapport with Colonel Roosma, but at the end of their first planning conference together was mildly frustrated that the American colonel appeared unwilling to make any decisions.

'I like the boys to have their say,' he told Christopherson, 'because the boys have to do the job.' Christopherson tried to suggest, tactfully but firmly, that it would save a lot of time and bother if instead they could agree a plan themselves, issue orders, then ask battalion and squadron leaders for comments.

None of the Sherwood Rangers could deny the extreme courtesy of their American partners. Peter Selerie moved to the HQ of Lieutenant-Colonel James H. Drum of the 2nd Battalion, and was both charmed and embarrassed by his insistence on giving him the only bed in the house. John Semken was sent to the 1st Battalion of the 334th, commanded by Lieutenant-Colonel Lloyd H. Gomes, and, like Selerie, warmed to his hosts immediately. Gomes and his staff became very agitated when they learned that General Horrocks was going to pay them a visit; none of them had seen a three-star general before, and Gomes wanted to know what Horrocks's hobbies were – his pet likes and pet hates. He was desperate they should make the right impression. 'Don't worry about all that,' Semken reassured him. 'He just wants to check everything's OK and then he'll be on his way.' Despite this, Gomes decided to get the cookhouse ready for inspection and ensured everyone on show had shaved and put on a tie and looked their smartest. 'Anyway,' said Semken, 'Horrocks showed up and was his usual charming self and sort of patted them on the head. And then went on his way.'

On Thursday, 16 November, First Army launched their drive towards the Roer river, just to the south of Geilenkirchen. This was Operation QUEEN, led by three divisions of XIX Corps and preceded by a massive heavy bombing raid, in which 1,239 bombers of the US Eighth Air Force and 1,188 heavies of RAF Bomber Command hit German communications lines along and behind the Roer. Some 9,400 tons of bombs were dropped in this raid alone, half the total amount of bombs dropped on London in the entire nine-month Blitz back in 1940–1. The towns of Heinsberg, Düren and Jülich were largely flattened; Düren, whose civilian population was still mostly living in the town, suffered 3,127 killed on that one day.

Although there were no bombers to support CLIPPER, there were tactical air forces on hand, plus the full weight of XXX Corps' artillery. Also brought up were a number of AVREs, including flail tanks to help clear the mines and anti-tank batteries. No one fancied getting sucked into a costly and difficult battle in the town itself, the Americans mindful of the brutal battle for Aachen suffered by First Army the previous month. Instead, they planned to envelop Geilenkirchen, attacking in a north-easterly direction, with the River Wurm acting as their axis of advance and with the Wessexmen on the western side and the Railsplitters to the east. The infantry and armour were to start early on the morning of Saturday, 18 November – in the dark, although searchlights were to be brought up to bounce off the low cloud and create artificial moonlight.

On the American side, flail tanks would clear two paths through the dense minefield south of an eastward-running spur of the railway that ran from the south-east of the town. These were to be code-named 'Red' and 'Blue'. The 1st Battalion of the 334th, with Semken's A Squadron, would head through Red and then push on to the village of Prummern, which stood on higher ground 2 miles east of Geilenkirchen, while the 2nd Battalion, with Selerie's B Squadron, would pass through Blue and try to drive a wedge between Prummern and the village of Süggerath, which was 2 miles north-east of Geilenkirchen in the Wurm valley. All around the town the countryside was largely low-lying, open farmland, flat to the south-east but otherwise gently undulating. The high ground really wasn't very high at all – perhaps 80–100 feet above the flat fields immediately to the south and east of the town; but just to the north-east, and running roughly north–south, there was a pronounced, wooded escarpment roughly three-quarters of a mile long.

On the 17th, a dress rehearsal of the breaching part of the operation was carried out to the south of Palenberg. It didn't go brilliantly well; there was heavy rain all day, and a number of the flails became bogged down. This didn't augur well; and there was more bad news at the final commanders' conference, when Brigadier Prior-Palmer announced, with spectacularly poor psychology, that they could expect to be fighting on throughout the winter, and that such were the manpower shortages now that home leave any time soon was out of the question. 'Which was somewhat depressing,' noted Stanley Christopherson with his customary understatement, 'before an operation that had every sign of being thoroughly unpleasant.'

H-Hour for the infantry was set for 7 a.m., by which time the Red and Blue paths through the minefield south of the railway embankment were to have been cleared. Arthur Reddish and the rest of Semken's crew were up early, awakened by the artillery barrage that let rip at 3 a.m. He and his mates were most touched that their American friends got themselves up to see them off, and to make sure they had a final swig of brandy to get them on their way.

Clambering into the tank in the dark, Johnny West, the driver, turned on the engine, the multibank whining wheezily before spluttering into life. In the turret, Henry Simons began the drill to net the squadron into the day's frequency on the radio. It was freezing cold, especially in the turret, until the engine warmed up as it was sucking in air through the open hatch. 'The draught on my back,' noted Reddish, 'wasn't funny.' Semken joined them, already a little frustrated. The previous day, he'd suggested to Colonel Gomes that they move down together to the start line the night before and the infantry bunk under the tanks, so they were all together and in the correct place. Gomes told him it was a great idea, but unfortunately would not be possible because Horrocks had told them to stay under cover until the last possible moment. Semken assured him that was not meant literally, but Gomes was having none of it. When a senior officer told him to do something, it was his duty to follow that to the letter. Perhaps it was just as well, as it was a cold, wet and miserable morning, but it meant there was some confusion trying to link everyone up in the dark at the start point.

The assembly area was about 800 yards south of the railway embankment, just to the south of a large farmhouse – a manor, really – known as Breil, which was already wrecked and surrounded by what a couple of months earlier would have been a lovely, lush orchard but was now desolate. Immediately north of the farm, running for around 400–500 yards, was the minefield; then came the railway embankment, with enemy troops dug in on the reverse slopes. A little further eastwards, towards the village of Immendorf, there were four concrete bunkers immediately south of the railway, with a further three just to the north of the

Geilenkirchen–Immendorf road 100 yards beyond the railway, and a further three immediately to the south of Prummern.

The searchlights, the noise of the armour and their own guns soon alerted the enemy, and as the Sherwood Rangers, with infantry behind them, began moving up through the orchard at Breil, so German shells started screaming over. It's hard to overstate the misery of the conditions: the cold, the dark, the rain – which inevitably worked its way into the tank, because it meant there was even more need to operate with the hatches open: periscopes were ineffective at the best of times, but especially when streaked with rain. Soon they were all starting to feel damp. The outside of the tank was slick with water, it was wet on the turret floor. It all added to the men's own personal feelings of growing nerves, that gnawing of the stomach that came before going into potentially life-threatening action.

Johnny West, Semken's driver, took them too close to a tree – easily done in the dark – and a branch hit the cupola on the top of the turret. This held the butterfly wing hatches and rotated, so that the open hatches could operate as moveable shields. Unfortunately, the blow knocked the hatches around so they were now jammed open forward and behind rather than on either side; Semken had been lucky not to be injured, but could now only see forward by pushing himself up and looking over the open half-hatch.

'See if you can fix the damned thing, Red,' he said to Reddish, who clambered out and tried to knock the hatches back into position with a sledgehammer. It didn't work. The cupola was wedged in its current position, and no banging with the hammer could budge it; Semken would just have to manage.

It was now 6 a.m. A troop of flails of the 1st Lothian and Borders Yeomanry were to clear the Red line, with American minesweeping engineers following behind, but one flail broke down in the mud before they even started, so that left only three. The wire entanglements laid by the enemy had been torn up by the shell-fire, but this had also churned up the ground, which had been made even worse by the incessant rain. The flails got going, their chains whipping round and round, mines occasionally detonating with a sharp blast and crack of fire, and spraying mud everywhere. Soon a second flail became bogged: this meant that a path that was supposed to be four tanks wide was now wide enough for just two.

Then a third flail became stuck and finally the fourth, some 50 yards or so short of the railway. It was still dark and still raining, the sky lit only dimly by the searchlights and by the flickering of exploding shells. Small arms crackled. Semken had a thankless decision to make: either reverse, or try to push forward through the mines. He switched to the B net and spoke to the squadron. They had a job to do: to get through the minefields and help the infantry. He was going to push on; if he hit a mine, then the next tank was to take over – and so on until they had crossed the minefield and the railway.

Semken gave the order to move off and Johnny West inched them carefully around the bogged-down flail. Everyone was tense, nerves taut, waiting for an explosion that would surely come. The engine working hard in that mud. The tank slithering. Grinding forward, a yard at a time. Ten yards gone, then another, and another. In the faint light, the railway stood within touching distance. Small-arms tracer stabbing through the air, clattering around the tank. Then a massive staccato explosion that lifted the tank in the air and whammed it back down into the mud. Although he was wearing headphones, Reddish reckoned it was the loudest explosion he'd ever heard. Semken: Was everyone all right? Yes. All answered. A miracle. Incredibly, they had just detonated four mines simultaneously and survived – possibly a unique distinction. Other tanks in the squadron pushed past. Through the periscope, Reddish saw them reach the railway – but the embankment was too steep, so they now ground their way east a little until the embankment dropped.

Semken and Reddish carefully clambered out of the turret. The tracks and wheels had all vanished and the tank now stood in a large crater, which at least offered a bit of cover.

'The job now,' said Semken, 'is to get out of the area and five is too large a group.' Their aim was to head back across the minefield to the assembly area by the farm, and to do so offering as small a target as possible. He decided he would head off with Henry Simons and Albert Ramsdale, and ordered Reddish to try his luck with Johnny West. 'OK, Red?' he said, turning to Reddish.

'OK,' Reddish replied, 'but I'd prefer you to go first.'

Semken agreed, they wished each other luck, and then Reddish and West clambered back into the tank.

'We'll give the others a few minutes before we go,' Reddish said. 'In the meantime, you keep watch and I'll make a brew.' With the sounds of battle still ringing in his ears, with shells crumping nearby, and with the bark and boom of their own tanks and artillery all around him, Reddish set up the Primus stove in the turret and made some tea. It would calm the nerves.

Once they'd got the life-saving nectar down them, Reddish felt better equipped to tackle the hazardous task of legging it back to Breil.

Unfortunately, as they clambered down, Johnny West fell awkwardly and badly hurt his hip. After giving him a shot of morphine, Reddish helped him stagger through the minefield, desperate to run for his life, even more so when mortars began chasing them; the only positive thing to be said for the mud was that it drastically reduced the effect of these normally highly deadly missiles. Once Reddish pushed West into an abandoned German trench and flung himself down beside him. Only after the barrage had stopped did they get up and keep going, eventually making it to the comparative safety of the farmhouse that was now the battalion and regiment CP.

David Render and his troop had already inched past Semken's knocked-out tank and cleared the railway embankment. By now dawn was creeping over the battlefield – but it was going to be one of those winter days that never properly grow light. A day of monochrome, of black, skeletal trees, the only vivid colour coming from explosions and the jets of flame from Crocodiles now reaching the far side of the minefield. A Squadron now quickly cleared the four pillboxes beyond the railway embankment. Most of the 183. Volksgrenadier Division were as new to battle as the 84th Railsplitters, but nothing like as well trained, and in the darkness of the early morning, the weight of Allied fire and determined attacks by the American infantry proved too much for most of them. Those not blasted out quickly appeared with hands held aloft. So far, despite the rain, mud and mines, the Allied advance was going better than many had privately expected.

Meanwhile, B Squadron had also been battling through the minefield – but not, as planned, using the Blue path to the railway. The flails simply hadn't been able to get through. Peter Selerie had never seen such terrible ground for a tank. There had been nothing for it but to use 'John's Gap', as he termed it, and push through two troops and the squadron HQ once A Squadron had made it across and over the other side. 'The going in this gap was appalling,' he wrote. 'People were becoming bellied everywhere and I had the misfortune to be compelled as a result to change my mount three times.' Making any progress required very careful driving – not too fast, but not too slow either; it was important to keep an even but high level of revs. At 6.55 a.m., the artillery opened up again with a concentrated stonk on the German defences beyond the railway; then the infantry moved up and, with the B Squadron tanks and also some Crocodiles, pushed on towards the hamlet of Loherhof on the tree-lined road from Geilenkirchen to Immendorf. It was as they were moving across this open ground that shells started falling all around. One landed close behind John Cropper's tank, and although his pack, hanging on the back of the turret, absorbed some of the shrapnel, he wasn't quite quick enough in taking cover and some shards hit him in the hand. Bleeding badly, he handed over command of the tank to his great pal Keith Cornish, then stumbled back towards their own lines. He'd not gone far when he met two American stretcher-bearers. 'Jump on, buddy,' they told him. He assured them he was all right to walk but they insisted.

The rest of B Squadron pushed on without him. From here, the flat farmland climbed very gently to an area of parkland around a large, late nineteenth-century sanatorium. Around that was a network of trenches, all of which were swiftly cleared with a number of prisoners taken. From here, the infantry and one troop pushed on up the road which cut through the escarpment running north, while another cut along the base of the ridge, blasting the bunkers and pillboxes there with HE. Crocodiles also moved up and fired their horrific jets of burning rubber and oil. 'German prisoners with their hands up began to emerge like rabbits from a warren,' noted Peter Selerie. 'There was a feeling of great satisfaction that after such a hard slog we were in the Siegfried Line.' In fact, this was the first battle fought by British troops on German soil since the Battle of Minden in 1759 – a bit of history appreciated by the B Squadron leader.

As nearly always the case in battle, it took time to cover ground. Tanks were inching forward, firing HE at any German position they could see and spraying them with machine-gun fire. Their own mortars were hammering away, too, and at the same time the American infantry were moving forward, squads and platoons and companies scurrying across the mud, hitting the deck, waiting for more suppressing fire, then getting up and moving again, the air heavy with rain and raining bullets, mortars and shells. It was painstakingly slow; but by mid-morning Company A and A Squadron had cleared the next set of bunkers near the road and were pressing on towards Prummern over wide, flat fields of mud – fields not so dense with mines as those they had crossed at the start, but still with enough to cause trouble.

Despite this encouraging start, Brigadier-General Bolling was aware of reports that panzers had moved up into the area the previous day; a counter-attack towards Geilenkirchen seemed likely, given the importance of this sector of the Westwall. He had duly warned Roosma and Christopherson accordingly. Also, a little after 11 a.m., aerial artillery observers reported having spotted an enemy column of an estimated 4,500 men in tanks and vehicles stretching as much as 3½ miles south from Heinsberg, just 8 miles or so to the north. The worry was that these were heading to Geilenkirchen; Roosma, with the intelligence about the panzers ringing in his mind, was understandably worried about pressing on to Prummern and overextending his forces. However, when by midday this enemy column had shown no sign of swinging down towards them, he ordered the assault on to Prummern to go ahead as strongly as possible. In fact, the enemy column was from the 15. Panzergrenadier Division, heading to reinforce German forces in the battle that was also raging to the south where Operation QUEEN was under way.

The Allied attack pushed on, the going somewhat easier now they were on slightly higher ground, although the endless mud was still causing problems and tanks continued to become bogged down. While the infantry and tanks were working impressively well together, there were also some Sherwood Rangers tanks operating quite independently – and successfully, too. Sergeant Charlie Webb had been providing fire support for a subsequent minefield breaching party; once this job was complete, he set off after the rest of A Squadron, but led his and two other tanks further east, along a route that unexpectedly kept them below the shallow ridgeline. Attacking from behind, he and his men blasted several pillboxes guarding the approach to Prummern, capturing thirty prisoners in the process, then pushed on, emerging on to the higher ground just to the east of the village where they paused and moved themselves into positions from where they could both watch the village and open fire if necessary.

By late afternoon, B Squadron with Company E had blasted the pillboxes and bunkers on the escarpment, taken the high ground above it and moved on to the highest part of the low ridge west of Prummern, Point 101. During a lull in the fighting, Peter Selerie now brought his tank alongside a captured German OP hastily set up as the 2nd Battalion CP. Clambering down, he went to speak to Drum, only to learn he had been wounded. Drum's XO – executive officer and second-in-command – had taken over, and while he was pleased with how his men had done so far, he was worried that his anti-tank guns and the half-tracks towing them had become bogged down. He wanted them up there on and around Point 101, ready for the next phase of their assault, and on hand should the enemy counter-attack; rumours had continued that the Germans were preparing to strike back, and enemy armour had been seen in and around Prummern. 'I immediately ordered one of my troops of Shermans to go to the rescue,' noted Selerie. 'This they managed to do successfully so that as the light failed every anti-tank gun had been towed into position.'

With the high ground secured, and both infantry and armour covering much of Prummern, the day's objectives had been taken; but
Brigadier-General Bolling now ordered the village to be overrun and for
his troops to finish the day on a line north of the village, overlooking Süggerath down in the Wurm valley on their left from a further high point,
code-named Mahogany Hill, to the north-east of Prummern.

Pausing at the edge of a field to the south of the village was Dick Holman's troop from A Squadron. From the turret of his Sherman, George
Dring had been watching the village very carefully for any movement or
sign of life. American infantry were all around them, digging in along the
hedge line. Dring reckoned the American boys had done pretty well that
day and rated them as among the best support troops he'd worked with –
they'd stuck to the task in hand and not hit the ground at the first sign of
trouble. Now an officer approached him and told him orders had just
come through that they were to attack Prummern that night. Dring told
him he'd been watching the place for a while and was pretty certain there
were at least no enemy troops on their side of the village.

It got him wondering, though, and so, while the rest of the crew brewed
up some tea, he set off on foot, as he was wont to do, to have a closer recce.
'I crept up dykes and hedgerows until I entered the village,' he wrote, 'where
I came across an abandoned Tiger tank and not wishing to push my luck
too far, I decided to return.' Instead of going back the way he'd come, however, he cut across the fields back towards their lines. He was out in the
open when, to his surprise and horror, he spotted a very well-camouflaged
Panther. Dring ran for it, but halfway across the next field, a shot rang out –
thankfully not very accurate – followed by four more. The last was close
enough. Flying shrapnel caught him on his left hand, badly cutting his
thumb and slicing off two fingers. Why the German commander hadn't
opened fire with his machine gun, Dring would never know. As it was, with
his hand bleeding profusely, he staggered on. 'I felt bad,' he wrote, 'but got
back to my tank, passed the information over the air then I'm sorry to say
I just passed out. I felt so bad.' He was then whisked off to the RAP.

Sergeant Charlie Webb, still operating without any infantry at all, had
meanwhile taken out an enemy 75mm anti-tank gun at the north-east
edge of Prummern. Then C Squadron arrived to take over and support the
334th's final push north of the day, while both A and B Squadrons pulled
back to rearm and refuel and leaguer for the night. Infantry often found it
hard to understand why tanks had to withdraw at night; but, as Peter
Selerie explained to Colonel Drum's successor, his tanks were almost

entirely dry of fuel and ammo – in spite of carrying extra pyramids of 75mm shells strapped under the gun, 'an entirely irregular custom'. He promised they would be back before first light the following morning.

It was still raining as they headed back to meet with the echelons, although now thankfully only drizzling rather than slashing down. Suddenly, Selerie saw a figure at the side of the road and realized it was a German infantryman.

'Kamerad!' he called out.

Selerie ordered his driver to halt. 'War no good,' added the German. Selerie motioned to him to climb up, and they headed back to the farm at Breil with their prisoner clutching the barrel at the front of the tank. There the man was handed over and taken off for interrogation. His war was over, and so too was George Dring's – his extraordinary wartime career finally at an end. He wouldn't get his fingers back but at least he was alive, which was more than could be said for Lieutenant Harry Crosbie and Trooper John Plowman, who had earlier been killed instantly when an AP round went through their turret. Peter Mellowes was devastated to learn of the death of his great friend 'Bing'. Corporal Murphy from the same tank was also badly wounded – as were Corporal Bill Tait and Trooper John Cameron. They'd been bringing back some POWs when one of the Germans stood on a mine. Several men were killed and others wounded, among them Tait and Cameron. A further two, one each from A and B Squadrons, had also been wounded that day. Even so, they'd been expecting worse.

Everyone, though, was very worried about John Semken. He had safely brought Simons and Ramsdale back to the farm at Breil, then had set off on his own on foot to try to get back to the squadron and resume command. No one had seen him since, or heard him over the net, as they would have done had he jumped into one of the squadron tanks. Eventually, Leslie Skinner decided to go and look for him, although where he might be was anyone's guess. Heading across the cleared paths through the minefields, Skinner began by looking in each of the pillboxes captured earlier in A Squadron's assault – and in one, to his huge relief, he found Semken, sitting with his back to the wall and quietly reading poetry. 'He was very bomb-happy,' wrote Skinner. 'We sat together for half an hour or more discussing poetry until we decided to walk out.' Back at the farmhouse, Semken was still in a state of some confusion. Shock, fatigue, the crushing burden of responsibility and four long years of brutally violent war were starting to take their toll on this still impossibly young man.

CHAPTER 25

Mud

ARTHUR REDDISH HAD BEEN on something of a wild goose chase since making it back to Breil and handing over Johnny West to the medics. Like Semken, he was in a state of shock and not thinking straight, and so first headed back to his billet where he found his American friends. 'What the hell has happened, Red?' they asked him. He told them, then tried to wash down his oversuit and his face and hands between liberal glugs of brandy. Then he put on his best battledress and greatcoat and announced he was heading back to Brussels. One of the boys slipped him a fifty-dollar note.

He'd not gone more than a mile, slithering around in the mud, when he was stopped by Corporal Gus Jacques, the post corporal from RHQ, who was in his jeep.

'What are you doing here, Red?' he asked.

'I'm on a special detail and am in a hurry.'

Corporal Jacques laughed. 'You're bloody drunk, mate!'

Reddish protested but Jacques told him to get in and that was an order. Reddish did as he was told, and for the rest of the day accompanied the corporal on his rounds, before eventually being dropped back at his billet where he found Ramsdale and Simons. By that time, he'd got over the shock of the morning's events – and sobered up.

The following morning, he and the crew were still exempt from further duty because there wasn't a tank for them, even though the recovery teams had been working tirelessly pulling back bogged-down and knocked-out tanks from the mud of the battlefield. While the crew twiddled their thumbs, John Semken, himself somewhat recovered after a bit of sleep, took over another tank and resumed command. That day, two troops of A Squadron were to accompany the 333rd Regiment as they pushed up from the south to clear the town.

That the Railsplitters now felt able to commit the 333rd was because not only had their sister regiment, the 334th, had a good first day, so too had the 43rd Wessex Division, supported by the other two regiments of 8th Armoured, on the western side of Geilenkirchen. During that first day they had taken several villages directly to the north of the town, advanced around 2 miles and then consolidated those gains. Moving this second American regiment into Geilenkirchen itself was part of the pre-battle plan.

None the less, on this second morning, there were signs that opposition was stiffening. In and around Prummern, it had certainly been a difficult night. Late on the 18th, with the searchlight company brought up to help, the infantry had pushed north of Point 101 as planned, while 1st Battalion had moved up into orchards to the south-west of the village. Sergeant Henry Douthwaite, who was commanding a troop in Jack Holman's C Squadron, had been ordered up to help them and given them support for the night, a role the tank men all hated. As the hours wore on, there had been increasing signs that something was brewing; around 2.30 a.m., a patrol from Company B, returning from a recce towards Mahogany Hill, reported at least six tanks north of the village and troops moving up.

While the 2nd Battalion's anti-tank guns had been brought up to Point 101 the previous afternoon, those of the 1st Battalion's heavy weapons company were still stuck and had not come up in line with the infantry. With enemy shelling now fairly constant it was even harder to bring them into position, which left Douthwaite's troop as the only close fire support. The village was built on a roughly square grid with roads leading off each of the corners. With only the milky artificial moonlight of the search-lights to see by, Douthwaite positioned his four tanks at each of the four corners, placing his own Sherman on a crossroads at the north-east of the village so that he could fire straight down two of the approach roads.

Sure enough, around 3 a.m. enemy shells started raining down on the village, followed by grenadiers of the 10. Panzergrenadier Regiment advancing on Prummern from the north-east along with half a dozen tanks of the 33. Panzer Regiment – both from the 9. Panzer Division. These units were a considerable cut above the poorly trained infantry of the 183. Division.

Although the approaching tanks could be clearly heard through the night air, it was panzerfaust-carrying infantry who first tried to infiltrate the village. Twice Douthwaite spotted them before they could get close enough, and twice he forced them back with a combination of HE and machine-gun fire. He also got his troop to lay a number of German anti-tank mines along each of the approach roads. Two approaching panzers were hit and knocked out, while a third detonated a mine and slewed to a halt. Douthwaite manoeuvred behind it, opened fire and brewed it up. Eventually, the remaining panzers pulled back, but by this time enemy infantry had crept into the northern half of the village. Despite Douthwaite's best efforts, it was clear as dawn broke at the end of a torrid night that both C Squadron and their American comrades were going to have a job on their hands to wrest back the northern half of the village.

As he'd promised, Peter Selerie was back with B Squadron to join the 2nd Battalion of the 334th Infantry before first light. The next phase of the battle was still to reach Mahogany Hill, and beyond it, to the north-east, the next village – called, confusingly for the SRY men, Beeck. A little further north of this small village, which nestled in a normally picturesque shallow hollow, was the outer extreme of the Siegfried Line defences. That was the objective this day.

Selerie found the CP of the 2nd Battalion somewhat agitated. The previous evening a company had been pushed forward along the undulating higher ground north-west of Prummern, but nothing had been heard from them since; all contact had been lost. Selerie immediately offered to go forward with his squadron and a platoon of infantry to try to restore the situation. Off they went, Selerie placing one troop of just three tanks up front, spaced apart as a vanguard across fairly wide, open country a few hundred yards to the north-west of Prummern. It had actually stopped raining and there was even a hint of sunshine, although the mud remained thick and deep, putting a strain on the tanks' engines and drives. Selerie himself was just to the rear of the first troop in his tank when he saw Lieutenant-Colonel Gomes' 1st Battalion also moving up around the western side of Prummern. The infantry platoon commander hurried alongside and signalled that he wanted to speak to him, so Selerie took off his headphones and called out to him to clamber up on to the rear of the tank so they could talk above the growl of the engine.

The major told him the lost company were now pulling back towards them. Selerie and his lead troop moved on and were approaching a slight crest when he spotted an enemy panzer, near a long farm building. Suddenly, this and a further enemy tank opened fire, shells whooshing across the open ground. In moments, two of the lead tanks had been knocked out; then the third went. An ambush. Panic. Crew bailing out. Other tanks frantically trying to move.

Immediately, Selerie gave the order to reverse slightly into a low dip on their side of the crest so they were no longer in plain sight of the enemy tanks. He then ordered up a stonk from the artillery. At this moment, Selerie's operator touched him on the left arm to get his attention. Leaning down to speak to him, Selerie had his right arm still on the cupola ring, when at that moment an anti-tank shell slammed into the turret, which must have been just still in plain sight. The blast knocked Selerie unconscious. He was quickly pushed up and out of the turret by his operator and gunner. When he came to again, HE rounds were bursting all around him, mud and grit spewing into the air then spattering down again. His brain told him his arm was still above his head when in reality it was lying shattered by his side. 'What was more alarming,' he wrote, 'was the fact that I had a bad wound in the upper part of my right leg from which I was losing copious quantities of blood.' With his good arm, he tried to push as much of his battle dress trousers as he could into the hole in his leg, but the blood kept flowing. With more shells crashing around him, and the tanks burning angrily, he tried to crawl away.

Suddenly, his driver, Lance-Corporal Lear, was over him and dragging him clear; then there was Lieutenant Bruce Charles beside him too, one of his troop leaders, and together they hoisted him on to the rear of his tank, which happened to be John Cropper's mount, *Blue Light Special*. Thick, oily smoke now covered the field and offered some cover. Hurriedly moving backwards out of the fray, they took him back to Drum's CP, from where he was transferred to a jeep. He then passed out again. By the time he reached the aid post his life hung precariously in the balance.

It was Lieutenant David Alderson who led the first troop of A Squadron into Geilenkirchen. There was fighting around the hospital but resistance was slight, all things considered. David Render's troop followed. 'Files of prisoners were soon emerging,' he noted, 'some waving white flags or approaching us with their arms raised.' David Alderson reckoned they took about 500 prisoners in clearing Geilenkirchen. Most of them were older men, emerging from cellars with dazed expressions on their faces. The town was a shattered wreck – buildings destroyed, rubble strewn across the streets, vehicles abandoned and burned, cables snaking across the roads. Dead left where they lay. David Render felt inured to it all and unhesitatingly used his guns on any building that looked like it might house snipers or machine-gun nests.

It was well into the afternoon when they pushed on up the Wurm valley. Some Crocodiles joined them, jetting long tongues of fire at a couple of bunkers near Süggerath. Resistance was continuing to strengthen, however, as it was on the higher ground to their right, and fighting continued around the northern part of Prummern. C Squadron knocked out several panzers during the day's fighting, but there was no further progress towards Mahogany Hill or Beeck. Later that day, Lieutenant Bruce Charles, who had helped rescue Peter Selerie, was killed when an AP round went through his turret, while Ernie Leppard's crew got their tank stuck in the mud. Corporal John Walsh in Jack Holman's C Squadron was also killed at Prummern when an AP round pierced the side of the tank. The rest of the crew hurriedly bailed out, but Walsh's body was still inside when the tank erupted into flames. Nor was it just the tank crews getting killed and wounded. A Squadron's fitters were trying to pull out a bogged-down tank in the minefield south of the railway line when Corporal Gavin Whitfeld stood on a mine. Several of the men were wounded by the blast, while Whitfeld completely disappeared. No one could find a trace of him.

Later, at an O group conference at RHQ, Sergeant James Small of the regimental recovery section told Colonel Christopherson they needed to abandon trying to recover bogged-down tanks for the time being; it was hopeless – the mud was too thick, too deep. He suggested they concentrate on recovering the wounded instead, which was quite difficult enough. Christopherson agreed; what else could he do? Sergeant Small had also been out with a search party to try to recover Corporal Whitfeld, but they'd found no sign of him either; clearly he'd been obliterated by the blast, body parts lost in the mud. He'd have known nothing about it, but it was horrible to think about and the padre was distraught to have another man unaccounted for. Skinner buried eight Sherwood Rangers together that day, and only afterwards realized he'd done so in a minefield. 'Frightening,' he noted, then added, '31 casualties to date.'

Sergeant Small's decision had a particular effect on Ernie Leppard and his fellow crew. 'At night time all our tanks disappeared out,' he said, 'but we couldn't get the armoured recovery vehicle to come and take us so we stayed in that position all night.' There was a lot of mortar and shell-fire coming over, so they all decided it was best if they stayed where they were, inside the tank. It made for a very long night.

*

When Peter Selerie had passed through the 2nd Battalion's CP, badly wounded, covered in blood and unconscious, it had been assumed he was already dead and so he had been immediately recommended for a posthumous Silver Star, an American award for gallantry. However, at the aid post a faint pulse had been discovered, and so he'd then been taken on to an American field hospital a few miles to the rear, where he was operated on and patched up and his life saved. On finally coming to, the first thing he saw was a bottle of blood and a tube.

'How are you doing?' said the doctor with a pronounced southern drawl.

'I'm doing all right,' Selerie mumbled, 'but is that a decent drop of blood you're giving me?'

'I'll have you know, Major,' the doctor replied, 'that is a rare old drop of rebel blood from way down south.' He would need it; his latest wounds were considerably worse than his last. A month after rejoining the regiment – and after so much effort to do so – he would soon be heading back to England again; the Silver Star, which would eventually reach him despite his not being dead after all, was the least he deserved for his troubles.

By nightfall on the 19th, the main objective of Operation CLIPPER had been met: Geilenkirchen was in Allied hands, and the infantry and armour advancing along the Wurm valley had linked up with the Wessexmen on their left. The ground rose more sharply to the north-west, but key villages were now in British hands. From here, the Westwall wound its way towards Waldenrath and then further north-west. Before the battle, both Brigadier-General Bolling and General Thomas had been concerned that the Germans might counter-attack from this direction. This now seemed unlikely; the main enemy threat now loomed from the north-east, from around Beeck towards Prummern and down the Wurm valley.

On the 20th some new tanks arrived for the Sherwood Rangers, but not enough to replace all those that had already got bogged down or been knocked out. And it rained again, heavily. In the Wurm valley, the 333rd Regiment, with A Squadron, once again led by John Semken, managed to bulldoze its way through Süggerath, but resistance was getting stronger. Around Prummern there was still fighting, not least because of a series of pillboxes just north-east of the village, but the biggest problem was that the mobility and flexibility of the British armour were sapped by the mud. Any kind of manoeuvring was next to impossible – and certainly any of the kind needed to deal with well dug-in panzers and anti-tank guns. The more shells the artillery flung over, the more the ground became churned up.

The rich clay soil was either slick and slippery or thick as treacle. Either way, it was hard to move. And when tanks couldn't move, they were in no position to put in an effective attack.

Stanley Christopherson spent most of the day with B Squadron at Prummern, where he was visited by Stephen Mitchell. Just before the battle had begun, Mitchell had been posted to 8th Armoured to take command of Brigade Headquarters Squadron. Mitchell thought Prummern the most desolate place of ruins and mud he'd ever seen, but even so had been relieved to see his old friend as cheery as ever. 'As always,' he wrote to Myrtle Kellett of Christopherson, 'he was at the top of his form, laughing and joking.' Christopherson had been especially tickled by one particular incident. At one point, a white flag was waved from a German slit-trench and he watched as Lieutenant Hubert Beddington jumped down from his tank and walked cautiously forward, his revolver at the ready. Beddington was suddenly confronted by an almost seven-foot-tall German. 'Hubert, who is only five foot four,' noted Christopherson, 'marched him back to his tank, but had to stand on it in order to search the German for arms, which presented a truly remarkable spectacle!'

That day, 20 November, the pillboxes at the north-east edge of Prummern were finally taken, with C Squadron Shermans supporting Crocodiles. Around 5.30 p.m. – and dusk – two Crocodiles clanked and shuffled their way forward through the mud. Small arms continued to rattle and crackle from the concrete emplacements; then, at about 75 yards' distance, the Crocodiles hissed and out spewed their jets of flame. 'The men who were lucky enough to see the spectacle momentarily forgot the mud and the danger and Mahogany Hill,' said one infantryman from Company I. 'It was one of those terrible and beautiful sights which the machines of war create . . . Once the Crocodiles had worked them over, those pillboxes were black, shrunken coffins.' The crossroads a couple of hundred yards north-east of Prummern was finally in Allied hands after three days' fighting – but Mahogany Hill still remained out of reach.

The German 15. Panzergrenadier and 10. Panzer Divisions were now closing in, both around Beeck and the villages to the north-east of Geilenkirchen and a little further to the south – in the US 2nd Armored and 102nd Infantry Divisions' sector, where the Operation QUEEN battle was still going on. From the German point of view, the static divisions like the 183. Volksgrenadier were expendable cannon fodder, there to delay the enemy until better mobile reserves could be brought forward. That moment had now arrived. Both the British and the Americans had superior numbers and resources, but not significantly so here, at this particularly strong part of the Westwall – not at the coal-face, at any rate, and especially not when the abysmal weather was working so brutally against any kind of attack. All day, the 43rd Wessexmen were heavily shelled, while around Prummern and towards Mahogany Hill both sides exchanged shell-fire, mortars and small-arms fire but got nowhere.

In the Wurm valley, A Squadron, still with the men of the 333rd, found themselves penned in. The road to Müllendorf, the next village along, and to Würm, their battle objective – just 2 miles further on – was heavily mined, and so Semken's crews tried to use the railway line instead; but debris at a demolished underpass in Süggerath blocked their path and stymied the plan entirely. From here, the terrain sloped gently up the high ground towards Prummern and Beeck, through lines of trees and ancient tracks. In summer, this was an idyllic spot: lush, green and fecund. In November, in the middle of battle, the landscape was one brutalized by shellholes, destruction and devastation. The slopes were marked by nests of pillboxes. Neither tank nor infantry could make any headway – not on the 20th, nor on the next day, Tuesday, 21 November 1944.

The following night, US engineers worked through the hours of darkness to clear the underpass at Süggerath, while XXX Corps' artillery prepared a rolling barrage behind which the 333rd might advance the next day. 'Sometimes the best-laid plans can go awry for the want of a single piece of equipment,' wrote the US official historian. 'That happened on 22 November when a bulldozer failed to arrive to complete the task of clearing the underpass in Süggerath so that the tanks might move.' Moving anything at all was problematic. However, the path was finally cleared by mid-afternoon, by which time the winter light was fading; how much easier fighting had been in the long days of high summer. There was, however, still enough time for both A Squadron's Shermans and the Crocodiles to get forward, and the pillboxes were rapidly destroyed. At long last the road to Müllendorf was open. This was the cause of so much mounting frustration: if Crocodiles and tanks could actually reach the pillboxes, they made short work of them; the issue was getting them there in the first place. As it was, immediately after they had cleared the pillboxes, the shortcomings of these terrifyingly effective beasts became clear: with the extra weight of the fuel trailers the Crocodiles had to tow, they now risked becoming bogged down in the rivers of mud along the valley, and so could go no further. By nightfall, the Americans were still half a mile short of the village. The advance that day could be measured in yards.

At Prummern, the 405th 'Ozarks' Regiment from the 102nd Division was brought up to help the depleted 334th, while B and C Squadrons were so reduced that Terry Leinster was told to take command of a composite squadron – the first time the Sherwood Rangers had had to take such a drastic course. A different approach to the village was made, from further south-east of Beeck and along a shallow valley from the small village of Apweiler. Artillery provided a smokescreen to cover the mile-long advance, but despite fierce fighting by both the infantry and the composite squadron's tanks, their assault on Beeck was once again repulsed. Operation CLIPPER was running out of steam.

That afternoon, Padre Leslie Skinner headed off in a jeep with the Baron to try to reach two C Squadron tanks that had been knocked out. On the way, they suffered a puncture and then lost the jack in the sea of mud. It took them twenty minutes to find it, by which time mud was oozing from the top of Skinner's wellington boots. Shell-fire then grew in intensity and they simply couldn't reach the tanks. It was frustrating, to put it mildly. 'Cold, wet, difficult and fruitless day,' he noted. Later that evening, he helped pick up more casualties before heading to a joint O group with neighbouring US divisions at Immendorf, driving past several more tanks abandoned in the mud. At 3.30 a.m., he was at another conference at Breil. 'At 03.30 drinking coffee and rum standing round truck,' he scribbled. 'Out again and back to Apweiler to pick up wounded man and brought him in. Bed at 05.30 and up again at 08.30.' The hours of daylight might have been much reduced, but not Skinner's working day.

Thursday, 23 November. The sixth day of battle. Terry Leinster had just five usable tanks left in his composite squadron. John Semken had a few more than that in A Squadron, and they were again to push forward to Müllendorf and then Würm. Having returned to his billet in the town the previous night, David Render was late for H-Hour that morning. Utterly spent, he had overslept, and woke only when he heard the engines starting up outside. Pulling his oversuit on over his pyjamas, he hurried out and clambered up on to *Aim*, the rest of the crew already in their positions. They sped after the rest of A Squadron, who were moving back down the Wurm valley to continue the attack on Müllendorf. They soon caught up, but Semken was not impressed and told him to push on, take the lead as planned, and support the leading American platoon. They hurried as fast as possible along the mud-soaked road, past ruined farm buildings and the spectral outline of the ruined Schloss

Leerodt away to their left on the far side of the river, then pulled off the road short of the village.

There were pillboxes to the south of Müllendorf and along the railway line. A squad of infantrymen were already flat on the ground in the middle of a field between the road and the railway as a machine gun spat bullets and stabs of flame from the slit of one of the concrete emplacements. Render urged his driver forward, anxious to get the tank in a good position from which to fire at the pillboxes and to make amends for his morning tardiness. His haste had made him careless, however, and he'd not taken enough care to watch the road ahead or the woods behind to the south of the village. Barely halfway across the field, he paused to paste the pillbox with several rounds of HE, which promptly shut it up, and then the tank suddenly rocked with a dramatic jolt and deafening crash, and a blinding flash engulfed them. Sparks spattered around the inside of the tank and moments later the hull was full of choking dust. 'And that,' noted Render, 'was the end of my tank, *Aim*.'

They had hit a Teller mine, and as they all bailed out – thankfully unhurt – the tell-tale whoosh of an anti-tank round screamed over their heads. Clearly, they needed to get out of there, and quickly. 'We were stonked to quite an extent,' wrote Render, 'but got back by nipping along in the crouched position.' Fortunately, 'good old' Sergeant Jackson had got himself into a cover position and fired back, making the most of the quick-firing 75mm to suppress the enemy anti-tank gun. After pausing to help a wounded American infantryman, Render and his crew were able to scurry to safety. His relationship with Jackson had improved as the long weeks and months had gone by, and there was now a level of mutual trust; certainly, Jackson's help that day very possibly saved Render's life, and those of his crew. They'd come a long way together since their first difficult meeting back in June.

The fighting continued that day, but no further progress was made. David Render and his crew had yet again got away with a close one, but Sergeant Joe Butler was killed when an AP round – possibly from the same gun that was firing at Render's tank – hit him in the turret. Butler was another stalwart of the Sherwood Rangers, a pre-war member and former hunt servant in Nottinghamshire. He'd served with Stanley Christopherson when the latter had been A Squadron leader in the desert. 'He was one of my most reliable and experienced tank commanders,' wrote Stanley, 'and I felt his loss most keenly.' Another fine fellow gone.

This was the Sherwood Rangers' last day of battle at Geilenkirchen. Six days of this kind of fighting was the upper end of what was sustainable; as it was, they were running out of tanks and men to keep the regiment going. 'Everybody was going through the motions,' noted Peter Mellowes, 'of living, fighting, and waiting for their time to die.'

That Thursday was also Thanksgiving Day for the Americans – not that many in the front line were able to do much by way of marking it. It was also the day the 84th Railsplitters were turned back over to XIII Corps and to Simpson's Ninth Army, their time with the British over. Across the river, to the north-west, the Wessexmen had suffered a bitter reverse, having attacked Hoven with the 5th DCLI but been forced back to their start line after suffering heavy casualties. The problem, as on the other side of the valley, was the lack of manoeuvrability in the sea of mud. Infantry, tanks and artillery could operate, but not together at the critical moments and only with the speed of manoeuvre drastically curtailed. But more than that, the Sherwood Rangers had evolved their tactics since D-Day; they'd learned how to use their Shermans by making the most of their speed of fire, mechanical reliability and agility. They could still fire just as quickly, but in the mud all speed and agility had gone. It was like fighting with two legs tied together.

That night the Railsplitters were told to go on to the defensive. There was no disgrace in this at all. They'd achieved their primary objectives, shown immense fortitude, and adapted to the atrocious conditions well and with extraordinary stoicism. The six days of battle had cost them more than 2,000 battlefield casualties and a further 500 from non-battle losses, mainly trench foot. Christopherson's men, meanwhile, had seen ten tanks destroyed, fifteen damaged but recoverable or already recovered, and a further twelve so hopelessly mired in the mud that they had been abandoned for good. The human cost was considerably worse: sixty-three in all, including sixteen killed in action and a further three who would later die of wounds. That made 326 casualties since D-Day, which was well over 100 per cent of the regiment's tank crews at any one time.

A stalemate of sorts had descended over this part of the line. In the faint evening light, the mud-covered tanks, with their exhausted and equally mud-spattered crews on board, pulled back over the war-torn and desolate landscape. Geilenkirchen had been one of their most brutal battles.

CHAPTER 26

The Red Badge of Courage

O N FRIDAY, 24 NOVEMBER, the regiment – those still standing – moved out of the front and headed to the town of Schinnen, some 15 miles to the west of Geilenkirchen in liberated Holland. It was a place that was familiar enough to most of them, as they had paused there en route to Palenberg before the last battle; now, on their return, the local inhabitants turned out to give them a warm welcome back. Stanley Christopherson, for one, was very touched by this, and by the genuine distress and tears of those who had housed men who had not survived the fighting.

His second-in-command, Major the Lord Leigh – 'the Baron' – once again set up Regimental Headquarters at an inn in the town, and both he and Christopherson got comfortable rooms with a shared bathroom. The bath, the Baron confided, cost him three bars of chocolate, but he considered this a worthwhile exchange. The colonel was not about to disagree.

Christopherson had been assured his men would be given a decent rest – but, as was so often the case, it wasn't to be quite the complete rest promised. Rather, he was to take command of a XXX Corps mobile force, known as 'Fox Force', which would include the 43rd Division Recce Regiment, one squadron of Horse Guards, armoured cars and a battery of anti-tank gunners in addition to the SRY. Two troops were to be constantly at four hours' notice, one squadron at 12 hours' notice, and the remaining two at twenty-four hours, and all in rotation. Fox Force had little to do, however. The Germans didn't try to counter-attack, and no one higher up the chain was in much of a mood to try any major new offensive just yet. The terrible, grinding battles of the Scheldt estuary had finally come to an end earlier in November, and the first Allied ship reached Antwerp – after a mammoth mine-clearing operation – on the 28th, four days after the Sherwood Rangers moved back to Schinnen. Millions of shells, more tanks, more trucks, more jeeps – more everything – would have to flow into Antwerp before the final phase of the war in Europe was launched.

All of which meant that, for the time being, while the Sherwood Rangers would remain on standby, they could at least afford to take things a little easier. At any rate, baths and entertainments were laid on, and the corps commander visited and told them all how well they'd done and assured them that as far as he was concerned, they were his most experienced armoured regiment. 'I suppose,' remarked Stanley Christopherson, 'corps commanders must say nice things about troops just out of action, but I do feel that he was sincere in what he said.' Horrocks's visibility, and the obvious effort he had repeatedly made with them since taking over XXX Corps, were certainly appreciated.

There was an investiture ceremony, too, at Brunssum, only a few miles from Schinnen, where Montgomery himself pinned a DSO on to Christopherson's chest, and gave MCs to Jack Holman, John Semken and Stuart Hills, and an MM to Sergeant Doug Nelson. Padre Skinner also attended and was a bit put out by the field marshal's appearance. 'Monty had turned up at Investiture in battle dress, with dirty cap and a long green pullover hanging out,' he observed. 'Poor show.' Photographs were taken, the SRY boys looking relaxed, cigarettes in hand, and still impossibly fresh-faced, despite the traumatic experiences they'd endured. John Semken, despite long years of war, appeared as young-looking as ever.

Perhaps it was because he knew he would soon be heading home. A repatriation scheme, known as 'Python', was being introduced. Those who had served abroad for four and a half years or more with less than six months' leave were eligible. This was potentially catastrophic for Stanley Christopherson, as throughout the regiment there were more than 100 men who fitted that bill. However, there was a caveat to the scheme. Those who took it might then be eligible for reposting at some point – but to a different theatre and with a different unit. The alternative was to opt for one month's leave with the promise of a return to the same regiment. Most, much to Christopherson's relief, opted for the latter option. John Semken was not among them, however. It seems that Christopherson, Young and Skinner had all agreed his nerves were just beginning to show signs of fraying. He had done enough.

He'd done more than enough. He had led his squadron from the front, shouldered gargantuan responsibilities, nurtured and guided fresh young officers, helped drive tactical innovations that had contributed to making the regiment one of the finest in the British Army, and had overseen some of the many triumphs it had experienced. He would be profoundly missed; but they needed to let him go. He knew it too. 'That was my last battle,' he said of Geilenkirchen. 'I lost my touch after that . . . After that I was finished. And I was invalided home.'

For those remaining, December proved a time to relax and catch up on sleep and rest – but also, as always, to reflect. Padre Skinner had held a church service soon after their arrival in Schinnen but he felt it hadn't gone well. 'Everyone too tired,' he scribbled in his diary. 'Too many casualties fresh in mind.'

For anyone, death was the great unknown – impossible to comprehend, the ultimate and terrible sacrifice. Most arrived at the front line apprehensive, not a little scared, but not believing they would be among those killed. After all, how could one think that when death was so final, so unimaginable? But exposure to the brutal realities of front-line combat soon changed everything. Blackened, charred corpses, mangled bodies, dead Germans repeatedly run over and flattened like dead rats on the road – it was grotesque, horrible, ugly. And brutally shocking. Everyone soon realized the same fate could befall them, that it could be their body burned to a crisp or mangled or atomized by a shell.

And so, for anyone joining the regiment, the prospect of being badly wounded, or killed, soon started to weigh heavily, like a dull ache or a grey fog that covered the world like a shroud. Some became fatalistic; others started to lose their nerve and become increasingly jumpy or bomb happy as the statistical realities became apparent. Quite simply, statistically, no tank man had a chance of surviving unscathed. Whether one was obliterated, badly wounded or lightly wounded was, to a very great extent, a question of chance: the turn of the head, a movement to the right, a momentary lack of concentration, happenstance. Or simply the relentlessness of what they were doing, which meant that, at some point, luck was bound to run out. There wasn't a single crew who had landed at D-Day that hadn't had their tank hit at some point. Knowing that at any moment it might be your turn inevitably preyed on the mind. And increasingly so as time went on.

'To advance into the unknown,' wrote Peter Mellowes, 'one can imagine an anti-tank gun or minefield every inch of the way.' Stuart Hills similarly found this aspect of tank warfare strained the nerves: the feeling that at any moment the fatal shot might come. It was easy initially to feel a sense of invulnerability once in a tank, but that quickly evaporated, replaced by a growing feeling that one's tank had become everyone's target. As Mellowes pointed out, the tank commander's field of vision was limited even with his head out of the turret.

'As you look out at the unfolding landscape,' he wrote, 'you feel as if a thousand eyes are looking at you from behind anti-tank guns, mortars and snipers' rifles, not to mention panzerfausts and mines strewn in your path. Advancing through a barrage of shells, mortar and machine-gun fire requires a considerable amount of concentration if one is to keep one's sense of direction.' And, of course, one had to keep watching the other tanks in the troop – and squadron – and issue orders. If one failed to read the ground properly, or wasn't watching keenly enough, or couldn't react with swiftness and clarity of mind, then one could well be knocked out. 'Unfortunately,' noted Mellowes, 'many of my friends were killed in this manner.'

Seeing men being killed or body parts strewn across the battlefield was traumatic, but for many the first dead man they saw was invariably the worst. 'The shock of death, is, I suppose,' noted Stuart Hills, 'something that every man in action soon gets hardened to and reactions are less painful than death under peaceful surroundings.' Losing friends was difficult, though, no matter how inured one had become to death in general. David Render had been devastated when Harry Heenan had been killed, just as John Semken had struggled to come to terms with seeing Ronnie Hill atomized before his eyes at Alamein back in October 1942. Render had become harder, less forgiving of the enemy or anyone who got in his way. Peter Mellowes was distraught that 'Bing' Crosbie had been killed, but he worked out early on that in order to survive mentally, he had to create a shell around himself and simply not allow any personal feelings or fears to affect him. 'So, on the face of it,' he wrote, 'one was not moved by fear, sorrow or compassion whatever the situation. If you failed to create this shield, you would crack up in the end and be of no use to anyone.'

Everyone understood that the chance of becoming a casualty was unspeakably high. The Sherman had a reputation for brewing up and incinerating its crews, and came with a number of black humour nicknames – like the 'Ronson', after the cigarette lighter whose slogan was 'lights every time', or 'Tommy cookers'. There was a perception that this was down to the engine and fuel, but in reality fires were usually started by ammunition igniting inside the tank, caused in turn either by the missile that hit it or by spawling – the spattering of white-hot bits of metal from the inside of the hull or turret. It was actually comparatively rare for a tank to brew up immediately – usually, a fire, if it was going to happen, took a few moments to catch as it was a secondary event to the initial hit. This gave crews a chance to get out, although it was obviously harder for those already injured to do so.

Furthermore, whether a tank was likely to burn was also down to how much ammunition was in the hull at the time it was hit. David Alderson's tank, for example, burned and the turret blew off near Nijmegen because they'd yet to fire and so the tank was full to bursting with ammunition. The same was true of Lieutenant Campbell's tank at La Bigne during BLUECOAT. A number of different studies were made of the causes of tank casualties. One, using a sample of 575 injured tank men, concluded there was no evidence to support the view that Shermans were more likely to brew up than, say, Churchills or Cromwells. Another, examining 333 AFVs and 769 personnel, showed that in cases where tanks were knocked out by AP or hollow charges, such as a panzerfaust, the chance of a major fire developing was 65 per cent for Shermans and 73 per cent for Fireflies, but only 36 per cent for Cromwells. Of course, these statistics did not specify whether the tanks surveyed had been hit with a lot, a little or some ammunition on board, and nor did they say at what stage the fires erupted.

One cause of the discrepancy might have been the fact that the independent armoured brigades, equipped with Shermans, were invariably in the vanguard of infantry-led battles and leading the way, whereas the Cromwells tended to be in armoured divisions, and were units of exploitation brought into the fray once the breakthrough had been made. There was a reason why the Sherwood Rangers had already got more battle honours than any other armoured unit, and that was because they had been in more battles. The greater the number of battles, the greater the number of casualties.

Interestingly, though, despite understandable fears of being burned alive, only 25 per cent of tank crew casualties suffered burns, and some 50 per cent of all of them occurred outside rather than inside the tank, a statistic agreed upon by both of the reports cited above. In other words, 75 per cent of tank crew casualties were not caused by fire. The reports also showed, as expected, that tank commanders were significantly more likely to be wounded or killed than other crew members. This, of course, was partly because they spent most of the time in combat with their heads, arms and shoulders exposed, but it was also because during an action they spent more time than others clambering down and talking to the infantry or other tank commanders. The lap-gunner was the least likely to be wounded inside the tank, while the operator, and then the gunner, had the most dangerous positions within the tank. It was also statistically more dangerous being in the turret than in the hull. Interestingly, the prime reason given for being outside a tank was 'making tea' – 22 per cent of cases – whereas escaping accounted for just 16 per cent. This was not quite as ridiculous as it might first appear. A Pavlovian response to a pause in activity among all British soldiers was to make tea. It was something to do, an energy boost, and a culturally ingrained morale booster. Yet, as the statistics showed, it was all too easy to be caught out by a sudden stonk while doing so. To that end, Arthur Reddish had been very sensible to brew his tea inside rather than outside the tank at Geilenkirchen – no matter how questionable an idea it was to use a Primus stove in a tank turret.

Statistics are all well and good, and make for interesting analysis, but the bottom line was this: being a member of a tank crew was an exceptionally hazardous occupation. So often in the war, technological advances in weaponry developed faster than man's effective means of operating it. Lancaster bombers could drop immense amounts of ordnance with increasing accuracy as the war progressed, yet the men flying in these tin cans were no better protected by the end of the war than they were when the Lancaster was first delivered to front-line squadrons in early 1942. By August 1944, Fireflies had been issued with a new kind of shell: an APDS – armour-piercing discarding sabot – which when fired had a velocity of over 4,000 feet per second. The dreaded German 88mm fired at around 2,900 feet per second. That was quite a difference. Yet Shermans remained underarmoured – and were deeply uncomfortable places to be, the hatches barely big enough to offer an escape route, and the concoction of fumes, dust and grit as noxious as when they first appeared on the battlefield in North Africa. Shermans were so effective because there were lots and lots of them, and they were reliable and quick-firing. The overall aim of the Allies was to win the war as quickly as they could with as few casualties of their own as possible. However, the speed part of the deal meant that casualties were still inevitable, and that there would be lots of them.

One way around this was for the Allies to use technology, mechanization and their huge global reach to limit the numbers of those directly in the firing line. On the whole, this strategy worked very effectively: in the British Second Army, for example, 43 per cent of all troops were service corps of varying kinds, while only 14 per cent were infantry and 8 per cent in armour. The rub, however, was that those in the infantry and the tanks were in for a disproportionately tough time. The chances of these men escaping unhurt were actually lower than for their equivalents in the 1914–18 war.

Much, then, was expected of these men, and much was expected of the Sherwood Rangers, as they were time and time again flung into the battle. It was the task of Stanley Christopherson, above all, to ensure they continued to function and operate effectively – an exceptionally difficult challenge that was all the harder now that Stephen Mitchell had left the regiment. Really, such was Mitchell's experience, he should have had his own regiment to command, and brigade continued to write to Christopherson asking him to recommend his friend for such a post. Mitchell, however, refused to let him do it.

Eventually, however, the decision had been taken out of their hands. The price of Rupert Leigh and his men and tanks from the Royal Gloucester Hussars was Stephen Mitchell. Christopherson had no choice in the matter. It seems the squadron leaders did not think a great deal of the Baron: his stature, the ever-red face, the quiet demeanour all made him a somewhat comical figure to them, and because of his lack of experience, he was not taken quite seriously enough. 'He was a joke,' said John Semken, flatly. This was possibly a bit harsh, and it seems Christopherson liked the Baron well enough, but they were certainly not bosom friends, let alone the soulmates, as Semken put it, that Stanley and Stephen Mitchell had been.

As a consequence, suddenly, at one of the most difficult moments in the regiment's journey since D-Day, Christopherson was at RHQ without any of his old mates. 'Nobody about Stanley had been in the regiment for any length of time,' said Semken of this moment in the regiment's journey across north-west Europe. 'They didn't know the men. The only shoulder he could weep on was either the doctor or the padre. So, Stanley lived through all this, completely isolated, coping with all these bloody infantry generals and brigadiers.'

He did at least have the padre and doctor, as Semken pointed out. 'Many times after an O group,' noted Skinner, 'I sat up with him while he talked the day over – worrying over what had happened. 'If he had done this or that differently would this man or that have not been killed or wounded.' Skinner found there was little he could say; he hoped, though, that by listening as the colonel got these worries off his chest, he was helping in some small way.

Christopherson did now have the companionship of a pet dog, however. The animal had been given to him by a Dutch couple with whom he'd been billeted during their stint near Nijmegen. It was only a puppy and he'd been told it was a pedigree Pinscher, although it seems Christopherson was the only one to believe this; everyone else thought its heritage considerably less pure-blooded. He named it Beek and trained the dog to sit and not move until he whistled, but was less assiduous in training him not to bark. Frenchie Houghton, the new adjutant, loathed the dog. Beek also had the habit of snapping at the heels of anyone he considered an enemy – and pointedly lacked the ability to discern who was German and who wasn't. None the less, Beek soon proved devotedly loyal to Christopherson and brought him considerable comfort – and no one was going to begrudge a man a rather noisy and only partially trained pet puppy when the CO had such an incredible burden on his shoulders.

Outwardly, at least, Christopherson was as cheery as ever, managing to strike the very difficult balance between authority, likeability and approachability. He continued to smile and laugh, to take pleasure in the ridiculous, and to fight tooth and nail for the well-being of his men. His compassionate treatment of John Semken, sending home possibly his most valued subordinate, was a case in point. And he also ensured that the men were rotated on leave, in Brussels and elsewhere.

This was good news for Arthur Reddish, who was finally allowed to head to the city legitimately. He was especially pleased about this because during his last time there, when he was AWOL, he had met a Belgian girl called Claire. She was married, it had been a brief fling, and he'd not expected ever to see her again. Yet on his return to Brussels, he looked her up and discovered her husband had been called up into the Belgian forces and was away. 'Those four days were the nearest I'd been to heaven,' noted Reddish. 'Me, I couldn't have enough of that girl.'

He got back to the regiment to discover John Semken was on his way home, although he arrived in time to wish him farewell and to thank him; Reddish reckoned Semken had taught him a lot, and told him so.

'And so has Trooper Savage,' Reddish added, grinning. Over the past few years, the three men had spent a lot of time together, one way or another. Semken might have been the officer and a troop and then squadron leader, but Savage had taught Reddish other, more worldly skills.

'Ah,' replied Semken, 'you'd learn far more from him than from me, Red.'

Preparations were under way for a new offensive to take the great forest of the Reichswald and push up towards the Rhine beyond Cleve and Goch – essentially the same operation they'd been preparing for when they'd been in the Nijmegen sector. This, however, was promptly cancelled when the Germans launched their shock counter-attack through the Ardennes in the early hours of 16 December. Operation WACHT AM RHEIN – Watch on the Rhine – was entirely Hitler's brainchild and was intended to drive on to Antwerp and split the Allies in two. It was no accident that it was launched through the Ardennes, the scene of the Führer's greatest victory back in May 1940. Preparations were made in the utmost secret, using four armies in all and two main striking forces, the Fifth and Sixth Panzerarmeen. More than 400,000 troops had been amassed for the attack, along with 550 panzers, 660 SPs and over 4,000 anti-tank guns and artillery pieces. December was chosen to limit the interference from Allied tactical air forces; but, as the Allies had discovered, attacking in such conditions – and it was now freezing cold and snowing – brought a host of other difficulties that would affect any fighting force.

That such forces could be assembled at this late stage of the war was extraordinary, and the scale of the operation certainly caught the Allies totally off guard. No one was expecting the Germans to counter-attack in such strength, not least because it made little sense militarily to do so, as the attacking force could not possibly hope to attain its objectives. Large though it was, it was not remotely big enough – and certainly not well fuelled enough – to reach Antwerp, which meant it could only end in failure, as Hitler's generals were well aware. Although the attack was launched at a quiet part of the American line and initially forced them back, the US Army was not the French army of 1940, and it was winter, not summer; very quickly, the German plan began to unravel.

At Schinnen, the Sherwood Rangers were as dumbfounded by the attack as everyone else when the news reached them two days later on 18 December. It was rumoured the whole of XXX Corps would be shifted south to help, and Frenchie Houghton, the adjutant, who had been in Paris, hurried back, convinced he would reach Schinnen only to find the regiment already packed and en route for the Ardennes. The regiment was not called upon, however; and, even better, the planned operations into the Reichswald were cancelled. So the Sherwood Rangers would not be imminently leaving Schinnen after all.

Even Padre Skinner had allowed himself some leave in Brussels, heading off on 5 December in the RHQ jeep with Frenchie Houghton and Dick Holman. There, they had decent dinners, went to an ENSA show and had a few drinks, although Skinner was feeling increasingly lousy; in truth, he'd been struggling with his ongoing ear problems and feeling under the weather for a while, and so spent a day undergoing tests at the 111th General Hospital and being poked, prodded and peered at. The medics didn't find anything sinister, though. 'Too much cold and wet, tiredness,' he noted, 'and overmuch noise of gunfire.' They were due to head back on the 8th – four days was the limit for every man – but when the time came there was no sign of Frenchie. Eventually he'd appeared at the hotel around nine that morning, swearing, with no money left and claiming to have been drugged. 'Silly ass might well have been,' added Skinner.

Leave and medical tests aside, Skinner had made several trips back up to Geilenkirchen searching for the missing men who'd been killed. At his final attempt, on 18 December, abandoned tanks still wallowed in the mud just as when he'd last been there, although they were now covered in snow and the ground had frozen solid. How different it all looked now the big chill had set in. First he went to the FDS, then to US XIX Corps Rear HQ, and then to the US Grave Registration Unit. Eventually, he was able to locate graves of three Sherwood Rangers who'd been missing and then that of an 'Unknown British'. Among the effects was a single envelope that had definitely belonged to Corporal Whitfeld – the fitter missing after detonating a mine on 19 November. 'Confirmed small part shattered body,' scribbled Skinner in his diary, 'seemingly something I had missed on the minefield but collected by Americans after show over, the minefield cleared.' The padre was much relieved; he really did hate to leave a single soul unaccounted for.

Back in England, Peter Selerie was making good progress, now in his third hospital: Park Prewett near Basingstoke in Hampshire, a former asylum converted for military use. His recovery, however, would be slow and often painful, and had already involved numerous operations, mostly to take grafts of skin from his good leg to be grafted on to his right leg and arm. Despite these ordeals and spending much of his first month or so in various plaster casts, he was aware he was more fortunate than some of his fellows in the hospital. There was 'Chips', a gunner captain who'd been blown up in his jeep and broken his spinal cord. He would never walk again. There was also a Polish officer who had lost an arm and a leg. Selerie wouldn't ever be able to write with his right hand again, but he vowed to teach himself to write with his left, and if his movement ended up being a little impaired – well, he had to remind himself it could have been worse.

Certainly his life was no longer in danger, which was more than could be said for the men of the Sherwood Rangers still out in Schinnen. They had still not been called upon to help stem the flow of the German offensive in the Ardennes, largely because the low cloud had started to disperse on 23 December, allowing Allied air forces to resume their hammering of enemy forces on the ground, and because the Americans, after the initial shock, were doing extremely well on their own, so that although some ground had been given initially, key nodal points had been held. By Christmas Eve the German attack had effectively been halted short of the River Meuse and was already something of a busted flush.

So, while American troops in the Ardennes were freezing in their foxholes, the Sherwood Rangers were able to enjoy some small Christmas comforts. There was a Christmas present of sorts for Stuart Hills. A letter arrived for him and his brother, Peter, from his father, written back in May 1942 in pencil on rice paper. What kind of journey it had been on since being written and how it finally found him were mysteries he was unable to fathom, but at the time of writing, at least, his parents had been alive and as well as could be expected considering they were prisoners of the Japanese. 'Hope you are both well and happy,' his father had written. 'Our house shelled and destroyed by fire with contents. I am interned in large prison camp since December 25. Suffering rather badly from gout, otherwise well, but very much thinner.' He'd been separated from their mother but he believed she was nursing. He signed off: 'Much love to you both and best of luck. Daddy.' Hills was shocked to receive it and unsure what to make of it. He had thought of his parents often, but while he was glad to have the letter and happy it had finally found him, he still had no idea what had become of them since it had been written. He could do nothing other than hope and pray for the best.

Padre Skinner held a number of services on Christmas Eve, which proved far better attended than those of Christmas Day itself. Even so, Stanley Christopherson joined twenty-one others from the regiment for Christmas communion at 9 a.m., heartily sang a number of carols and listened to a stirring address from the padre. Each squadron then held its own Christmas lunch with the officers waiting on the men, although A Squadron and the LAD joined RHQ, which made life a little simpler. They ate fresh pork, tinned turkey, vegetables and plum pudding, and each man was given a bottle of beer. Christopherson visited each of the squadrons in turn and wished the men a happy Christmas. By the time he reached C Squadron, he discovered Arthur Reddish's old crewmate, Sam Kirman, had somehow drunk six bottles of beer and stumbled towards him, clearly half-cut. 'During static periods,' recalled Christopherson, 'he always caused trouble and was a grouser of great magnitude.' But Kirman was also a brilliant wireless operator, and the Sherwood Rangers had always willingly tolerated awkward sods if they were able to make up for their oddities on the battlefield.

After the Christmas lunch, the regiment laid on a party for the children of Schinnen, who, after all, had not had much to cheer about during the past few years. A large Christmas tree was put up at the centre of the village; Neville Fearn dressed up as Father Christmas and George Culley, A Squadron's Essex Yeomanry FOO, as a clown, and together they rode down the main street on a sleigh towed by one of Recce Troop's Stuart tanks. Following behind were the children, laughing and trying to clamber on to the sleigh. 'It was a typical Christmas,' Stanley remembered, 'as the ground was white with frost and snow.' Every man had been asked to save up their sweet and chocolate rations so that each child might have a gift, handed out by two of the men from the tree. Culley then performed some acrobatics, at which he was impressively skilled; it wasn't just the children who enjoyed his show by the Christmas tree.

Finally, the officers had their own Christmas dinner. For the first time since leaving England back in June, the whole band of officers in the regiment sat down together as one. There was food, there was wine, and there was even a small gift for each of them – Christopherson's a packet of army biscuits. It was not much, perhaps, but it was the thought that counted. 'So ended my sixth and last wartime Christmas,' he wrote. 'I had spent two in England, two in the desert, one in Palestine and one in Holland.'

CHAPTER 27

Snow and Ice

THURSDAY, 28 DECEMBER, 1944. Trooper George Lait sat in his driver's seat in Sergeant Johnny Lanes's Firefly, frozen to the bone; it didn't pay to sit still in this cold, but they had little choice in the matter. A Squadron were on picquet duty, watching the front line from a small farming hamlet called Vinteln just inside the German border. A few houses, a larger farmhouse, a collection of barns and outbuildings – that was all. Around them, flat, open fields, covered in frozen snow. And ahead, due north and just under a mile away the far side of a tiny brook, were the German lines.

It was the early hours of the morning and almost pitch-black outside. Johnny Lanes had gone to talk to one of the other tank crews and all seemed icily still when suddenly Lait heard scrabbling and someone clambering on to the tank.

'Ich denke das ist ein Sherman,' a voice said. Lait held his breath, expecting the hatch to be lifted and a grenade dropped inside. Suddenly, shots rang out, the man jumped down, and Lait heard the sound of running and another burst of automatic fire. A moment later, Lanes was back in the turret. There were Germans everywhere, he said; he'd just shooed off the men around the tank but they could expect more.

The regiment had moved out of Schinnen the previous day, taking over positions of the 13/18th Hussars who had been supporting the 52nd Lowland Division, now holding this stretch of the line in the place of the 43rd Wessexmen. RHQ was at Schinveld, some 6 miles due west of Geilenkirchen on the German–Dutch border. Here, though, the frontier turned west–east before heading roughly northwards again, and the task of the Sherwood Rangers was to support the infantry in keeping a watch on the front line. It meant sending squadrons off to small outlying villages and hamlets just across the German border, such as Vinteln and, a few hundred yards to the west, Kievelberg. No one had expected much to be happening along this part of the front – not with the battle still raging in the Ardennes – but it seemed that on this night the Jerries were making a fairly large infiltration. Before long, small arms were chattering and mortars crashing around them. A new officer, Lieutenant George Cameron, the second with that surname to serve in the regiment, encountered some enemy troops and suddenly his tank was hit by a panzerfaust; he and all his crew were wounded. Despite this, the rest of the troop managed to hold off the attack and, with the help of the infantry, a considerable number of enemy were captured and the rest driven off.

As daylight crept over the front, A Squadron's HQ troop headed up to Vinteln to restore the situation, while David Render's troop was sent forward to nearby Kievelberg. Following HQ troop was Mike Howden in his Dingo scout car. Tony Gauntley had taken over command of A Squadron from John Semken, and Howden was now one of his captains. Driving the Dingo was Arthur Reddish in what was an entirely new role for him. The Dingo was lightly armoured, equipped with only a Bren light machine gun, and Reddish and Howden's own personal weapons. The HQ troop pushed on beyond Vinteln, making sure there were no enemy dug in ahead of their old positions, when suddenly a German soldier stood up and, armed with only a rifle, started taking pot-shots at the advancing tanks. Watching this, Reddish wasn't sure whether the man was stupid, very brave or fanatical – or all three. Over the net, Gauntley ordered the lead Sherman to wound the fellow and for Howden then to pick him up in the Dingo.

Shots rang out, the German fell and Reddish sped forward, not a little apprehensive that as they paused to pick up the wounded man others might stand up and blast them with a panzerfaust or cut them down as they got out.

They paused the Dingo a few yards short and then clambered out, leaving their weapons behind. Howden walked up and leaned over the man.

'It seems to me, Red,' said Howden, 'that he's copped it in the lower stomach region.'

'Poor bugger,' said Reddish. Stomach wounds were never good. Carefully, they picked him up and lifted him into the Dingo. No one fired. *Relief.* Then they drove off, Reddish going as carefully as he could.

Meanwhile, David Render and his troop stormed the farmstead at Kievelberg. Accompanied by infantry, they swiftly overwhelmed the enemy, killing a number and capturing more than thirty. Most were young boys. The German infiltration had achieved nothing, as Padre Skinner noted in his diary that day. 'Boche a loser on today's work,' he scribbled. 'We have got over a 100 POWs and our losses 4 wounded and 1 missing.'

The regiment was still in the line as the old year gave way to 1945. It was another freezing cold night, the air still. Arthur Reddish heard some singing, then one of them shouted, 'Hey, you Scottish bastards, come out and fight!' The British infantry did not rise to the bait, however. That night, Stanley Christopherson visited A Squadron and found Neville Fearn and George Culley in a cellar at Vinteln drinking champagne they had found out of German beer tankards. Seeing him, they found another beer mug, filled it and passed it to him. Happy New Year.

On the first day of 1945, the Germans launched two new offensives. The first, known as BODENPLATTE, involved a last-ditch strike by the Luftwaffe on Allied airfields in the Netherlands and Belgium. Although in this surprise attack they destroyed and damaged an astonishing 465 Allied aircraft, they lost 277 themselves – entailing an irreplaceable loss of aircrew, too. The second assault, Operation NORDWIND, was a major counterattack against the US Seventh Army north of Strasbourg, and was to be the last German offensive of the war in the west. Here Seventh Army, depleted after Eisenhower had sent reinforcements to the Ardennes, was forced to give ground.

Although these attacks were setbacks for the Allies, the losses to the Germans were both greater and more significant – a last-ditch roll of the dice in the endgame. BODENPLATTE fell well short of its objectives, although the Germans had created a long, narrow salient – or bulge – that now urgently needed to be reduced. General Patton had already sent troops from the south to help relieve the besieged town of Bastogne, and now launched a major drive northwards with his Third Army, while Montgomery ordered XXX Corps to thrust southwards. The plan was for them to meet up at the Ardennes town of Houflaize.

Yet although XXX Corps was involved in the Battle of the Bulge – as it was already being called – it did not involve the Sherwood Rangers or indeed any of 8th Armoured Brigade. Rather, on 6 January, Stanley Christopherson was summoned to a conference in Schinveld with his fellow commanders in 8th Armoured and also the 52nd Lowland Division to discuss their next operations. By this time, the bulge in the Ardennes was already being much reduced; the Germans had had to use their last reserves in an offensive that was rapidly becoming an expensive defeat. No matter how traumatic it had been for the Allied high command and those who had borne the brunt of the fighting, the task of driving across the Rhine and into Germany had been made easier as a consequence.

The port of Antwerp was now operating around the clock and depleted supplies were being built up once more. Manpower remained a persistent and critical problem for the British, but Montgomery was extremely mindful of the political pressure bearing on the question. Britain needed to continue to play an important and active role on the ground in north-west Europe; both prestige and post-war influence in Europe, and indeed on the wider world stage, necessitated this. There could be no taking a back seat, yet the two requirements – conserving manpower while playing a key part in the final battle for Germany – were not easy to reconcile. It meant, though, that inevitably Monty's most experienced units would have to continue playing their parts. Their past heroics made it essential.

All across the western front, the Allies were now readying themselves for the final strike into Germany. The Rhine remained, as it had done in early September when MARKET GARDEN was conceived, the biggest obstacle to final victory; but first the ground to the west of the great river needed to be cleared. Montgomery had been planning to drive across the Reichswald and beyond to the western side of the river since the end of September. Those plans had been abandoned once in October, again in November, then a third time in December when the Ardennes battle had more than upset the apple cart. It was hoped the Reichswald battle would finally get under way in early February; but first, a straightening of the line was needed a little further south.

The clearing of Geilenkirchen had left a triangular enemy salient jutting some 15 miles west at its deepest. Here, to the north of this border town, the front line turned westwards until it reached the River Maas, then north-east until the river joined the Roer at Roermond. Clearing this triangle, and with it the key town of Heinsberg, would both straighten and shorten the front, which in turn would allow more men to be thrust into the Reichswald battle. The operation to clear the Heinsberg triangle was code-named BLACKCOCK and had been first mooted the previous November, but like all the other Allied plans it had been scuppered by torrential rain, fog, freezing temperatures, snow and the German counter-attack in the Ardennes. It was still snowing and still freezing now, but

Montgomery could not wait any longer. There was a war to be won. BLACKCOCK was set for 15 January 1945.

As Christopherson learned at the BLACKCOCK planning conference, the 8th Armoured Brigade were to continue to support the 52nd Lowland Division; they were also both now part of General Neil Ritchie's XII Corps for this battle. Heinsberg was to be their main objective. Two German divisions manned this part of the Westwall, the defences of which had been substantially increased since the autumn – not so much with concrete as with extensive trenches, weapons pits, mines, tripwires and other horrors. The Germans had, for the most part, been on the defensive since July 1943. They had become rather adept at it.

Conference over, Christopherson returned to RHQ, scooped up his senior and squadron leaders, and on that snowy, icy cold afternoon took them back to their old haunts around Geilenkirchen. After the Sherwood Rangers had been pulled out on 23 November, the Americans had gradually inched forward a little further so that now, on 6 January, they could study the ground around Prummern and Beeck from the enemy perspective and learn how the Germans had used the terrain. Most of the battle debris was still there, too, which allowed them to examine the German tanks as well as their strongpoints and the way they connected. It made them all realize just how difficult their task had been.

Then something rather surreal occurred. 'While we were walking along a deserted street in Prummern,' noted Christopherson, 'a goat suddenly appeared with a pair of women's pants over its hindquarters and a straw hat perched on its head.' Much to their amusement, it then attached itself to George Culley and despite shouts and shoos would not be driven off and followed him devotedly for the rest of the battlefield tour. 'How the goat became so attired,' added Christopherson, 'we never discovered.'

The following day, Padre Skinner held a memorial service for the Geilenkirchen battle, and this time it was well attended with more than 250 of the men turning up. He also gave a stirring sermon on the nature of life, death and sacrifice, which seemed to strike a chord. 'Hylda' Young, who rarely attended his friend's services, told Skinner it was the best sermon he'd ever heard. Even Frenchie Houghton told him he'd been deeply moved, while Christopherson had also complimented him most warmly. 'Normally,' Skinner reflected, 'nobody comments.' He was pleased it had hit the spot. It was as though the ghosts of Geilenkirchen had somehow been laid to rest. Now they could face their next battle.

*

Once again, the regiment had a different look to it. A number of men had gone home for a month's leave – including Arthur Reddish, who decided to spend two weeks at home in Lancashire with his mother and two weeks in bed with his Belgian girlfriend, Claire, in Brussels. Jack Holman had also gone home on leave, while Stuart Hills had been sent back to England on a photo-intelligence reading course in Derbyshire for two weeks. This meant another large intake of new faces – but there were also some familiar ones back. Stuart Hills was still with the regiment in time to see his great friend Denis Elmore return, while Bill Wharton, whose daughter, Pam, had been born on 20 December, had rejoined B Squadron. It had been a terrible wrench for Wharton to drag himself back. 'Once again I am writing to you from "over there",' he wrote to his 'Darling Girl'. 'There's nothing new in that we have now been doing it for the best part of five years. But still I don't get used to it and again I feel blue at being cut off from you.' Marion had noticed a restlessness in him during his leave, but she did not need to worry. 'All my hopes are centred in looking forward to the time when we can live together in our own house.'

John Bethell-Fox was also back, as was Stan Perry, who had recovered from the wound sustained at Berjou and was once again commanding a troop in C Squadron. He was also now married – to a Danish girl called Anne-Lise. They'd met back in September, by which time he'd been making a good recovery and so was allowed out for the odd night from the hospital in Baguley. He and a fellow patient had headed into Manchester where, outside the Queen's Hotel, they had met a couple of girls and invited them for a drink. One of them was Anne-Lise. 'And,' said Perry, 'we became rather attached.' It had been very much a chance encounter; Lise's father ran a bed business in London and had only just moved up to Stockport to escape the V-1s and V-2s still terrorizing the capital. The new couple tried to see each other every single day, or at least, as often as they possibly could. After all, it was wartime, and there was no time like the present.

Then Perry had been posted down to Newmarket and while there had been summoned back to rejoin the SRY. 'I had got a letter from Stanley Christopherson,' said Perry, 'in which he wrote, "the return of this officer to his regiment at the earliest possible opportunity is requested". And then he struck out "requested" and wrote over the top of it, "demanded." ' This had been written during Christopherson's most anxious moments following the announcement of the Python scheme; Perry had received it in the first week of December.

No matter how urgently his return was demanded, however, he was still entitled to two weeks' embarkation leave; so he rang Lise and asked her if she would marry him. Lise wasn't sure her parents would agree – she was only eighteen. 'I said, "Will you marry me on Monday?"' recalled Perry. 'And she came back and said, "No, Mum says no. It's unlucky to get married on a Monday. If we get married it has to be on Saturday."' So that's what they did. They were married on Saturday, 16 December, at the Swedish Church in Harcourt Street in London, with a reception afterwards at the Danish Club above the Hyde Park Hotel. After one night's honeymoon in Finchley, of all places, Perry was on his way back. He rejoined the regiment at Schinveld on 5 January, along with Denis Elmore and John Bethell-Fox.

Stan Perry hardly recognized anyone in C Squadron, there were so many new faces. He had an entirely new crew in his own tank and an entirely new troop; and in Captain John Coleman, a new squadron leader too, since Jack Holman was on leave. 'He was a very nervous bloke,' said Perry. 'He was a nice chap, but he had a penchant for bloody O groups.' This was clearly a sign of Coleman's lack of self-confidence; not everyone had natural leadership skills, and the jump-up from troop to squadron leader could be a big one. This mattered less when they were out of the line and getting ready for BLACKCOCK, but Perry knew from experience that once the fighting began decisiveness was important; it was no good to be constantly asking for lots of different opinions.

The weather was still atrocious: the landscape white with snow, bleak and monochrome. With no sign of the snow abating, they were all ordered to give their tanks a coat of whitewash. The ground was frozen so hard that the flail tanks would not be able to churn many anti-tank mines, although it was hoped they might catch some of the anti-personnel ones. General Ritchie intended to launch BLACKCOCK on the night of 15 January with a heavy artillery barrage. His plan was to attack with three separate thrusts: 7th Armoured Division on the left, 52nd Lowland in the middle, driving towards Heinsberg, and 43rd Wessex on the right. The 7th Armoured, the Desert Rats, were to start first, with the Scots, supported by the Sherwood Rangers, getting going two days later.

In the event, thick fog meant BLACKCOCK didn't get under way until the morning of the 16th, by which time it was raining horizontally. The downpour soon turned the snow into slush, and just at the wrong moment the ground began to thaw, so that solid earth became thick mud. Approaches to the numerous streams and rivers that had to be bridged were rapidly transformed into quagmires. Here, across largely flat, open land, the conditions were akin to the Eastern Front in winter. It was utterly miserable.

The Sherwood Rangers went into action on the 18th, supporting the 4/5th Royal Scots Fusiliers, only to be scuppered by the tiny Saeffeler Beek, which ran roughly west–east across the axis of their advance. In summer, they would have simply driven straight over it; but now, in the deep midwinter, with the ground rapidly thawing and slushy mud and snow thick on the ground, the ground either side became a morass and utterly impassable. Three tanks got across the narrow stream, but then became bogged. As a result, the infantry had to cross and form a bridgehead on the far side on their own. The Sherwood Rangers eventually crossed through the shattered remains of Höngen, a market town where it would be possible to build a Bailey bridge across the stream, but not until the following day. The road north out of the town was mined, and a number of trees had been cut and laid across it as well. All these had to be patiently cleared, because the weather was forcing them to stick to the roads; conditions didn't favour any kind of mass movement cross-country.

The British Army was now more mechanized than ever before. Infantry were moving up in Kangaroos – a Canadian design, essentially the hull of a Sherman adapted to carry troops – and Weasels, which were new US-built tracked armoured personnel carriers. There were also flails and Crocodiles to help, plus the tanks, SPs, carriers and echelon vehicles. Traffic discipline was vital, and for the most part worked incredibly well on all three of the BLACKCOCK thrusts, but it was not at all easy making headway. The enemy infantry may not have been top drawer, but in addition to the mines and other obstacles, more German artillery was here than at other parts of the Westwall. Then the rain stopped, temperatures plunged again and the roads became slick with black ice. Tanks, half-tracks, trucks – all were skidding, causing yet more blocks and delays. The British were battling two enemies during BLACKCOCK: the Germans and the weather.

As a result, it wasn't until the 20th that the Sherwood Rangers finally played much of a part in the battle. They were supposed to be attacking a key village called Bocket early that morning, but the route up to it was mined and congestion once again caused hold-ups. Despite this, Bocket was taken comparatively easily, although B Squadron lost two tanks to mines. With the village in their hands, however, they now had a firm base from which to press on and capture a series of further villages, all of which were linked as an outlying series of defences around 3–4 miles south-west of Heinsberg. If they took these strongpoints, the door to Heinsberg itself would be blown wide open. With this in mind, the 52nd Lowland's commander, Major-General Edmund Hakewill-Smith, ordered his brigades – and the tank regiments of the 8th Armoured – to push home the advantage. One brigade of infantry plus the 13/18th Hussars was to take Waldfeucht to the north-west of Bocket, while the Sherwood Rangers were to support the 7th Cameronians and 1st Glasgow Highlanders to capture Frillinghoven and Hontem to the north of Bocket, and Selsten to the west.

Monday morning, 22 January. Freezing cold. Ice on the tanks, ice on the roads. Inside, the temperature of the tank was all right, but outside, the cold bit into any faces above the turrets, so they had the uncomfortable sensation of being warm enough in the toes but bitingly, numbingly cold around the head. B Squadron were attacking Frillinghoven and Hontem, with Ernie Leppard's troop heading to the former along with infantry from the 1st Glasgow Highlanders. 'The road went straight up into a village,' he said, 'but that was mined and Germans were holding the village and the road was under fire from anti-tank guns in the village.' They swung off the road and, despite the conditions, headed across a field and began moving towards Frillinghoven from the south-east.

As they paused, Leppard poked his head up out of the turret, joining Johnny Taylor to scan ahead with their field glasses. Suddenly, he saw three tracked vehicles heading southwards. 'And I said to Johnny,' added Leppard, 'I think they're German tanks come down.' Taylor told him to report them over the net, which he did, but his troop leader, Lieutenant Walsh, couldn't see anything. By this time, Bill Wharton was leading half the squadron as they attacked from the north-east tip of the village, brassing up the backs of the houses, and hadn't spotted the enemy armour heading south towards Waldfeucht and Frillinghoven. These were both Tiger tanks and SPs, survivors of the Ardennes battle and part of a significant counter-attack being launched by the enemy that day. Moments later, Wharton's tank was hit and he was struck by shrapnel in the chest. Having survived much of the war with barely a scratch, here he was, severely wounded in his first engagement back in the line. He needed expert care urgently; but getting him out and back to a hospital quickly was not going to be at all easy in these brutal conditions. Certainly, though, Bill Wharton's war was over. Yet another of the old guard felled.

Meanwhile, Leppard's troop was now being fired at in turn. They quickly went into reverse and pulled back. Fortunately for them, the panzers – some six Tigers and a further fifteen SPs in all – were headed primarily towards Waldfeucht, where the 13/18th Hussars were attacking.

Around the same time, C Squadron were attacking Selsten, a couple of miles across snow-covered fields from Bocket. Stan Perry was already without his troop sergeant, John Taubman, who had been killed the previous afternoon. Taubman had been standing up in the turret when the Firefly parked up behind had suffered a misfire and accidentally hit him at point-blank range; he'd been killed instantly. The rest of the crew, badly shaken, had bailed, and that morning Padre Skinner had hurried up alone to fetch Taubman back. 'Padre Skinner was absolutely wonderful,' said Perry. 'He took Taubman's body out and he got in and he cleaned the blood and guts from inside the tank.'

It was now early afternoon as they neared Selsten behind flails and Crocodiles beating a path across the wide, flat, open and once again frozen fields. As was so often the way, progress was staccato to say the least: inch forward, fire, stop, wait, peer through field glasses, move off again. At one such pause, Captain Coleman ordered yet another O group for his troop leaders. Cursing, Perry clambered down from his tank, hurried across, had the O group, then started scampering back again across the snow. Suddenly, he heard a whirr followed by a big crash. *Christ,* he thought, *a Nebelwerfer.* Another round screamed in. *Getting a bit close,* thought Perry, *better get my head down.* He was diving for cover when the third round moaned in and exploded and he was peppered down his left chest and arm, across his face and his right leg. Lying there, bleeding in the snow, Perry was in a critical condition. It was fortunate, however, that his new wife had given him a leather wallet and that he had kept it in his chest pocket. This absorbed just enough of the force of a piece of shrapnel that was horribly close to his heart. Without it, he'd have been dead; because of it, he had a chance of surviving – albeit on that freezing January day not an especially good one. 'Severe,' wrote Skinner in his casualty book of Perry's wound after he had eventually been evacuated to an American hospital.

Stan Perry was not the only C Squadron casualty – in all, four of their tanks were knocked out that day. Sergeant John Keen was killed as he and his crew bailed out of their Sherman – in fact yet again, most of the casualties that day had been hit outside, not inside, their tanks. None the less, by dusk, the German counter-attack had been flung back, at least three Tigers destroyed plus a number of SPs, and both Waldfeucht and the three villages allocated to the Sherwood Rangers and their accompanying infantry were secured. A captured German operation order showed their objective had been to retake Bocket. They'd never come close.

To ensure the 52nd Lowland held firmly on to their new gains, A and B Squadrons were ordered to leave one troop from either squadron in the villages throughout the night alongside the infantry. Ernie Leppard spent the night at Frillinghoven. It wasn't a big place, but having positioned their tanks the crews decamped to the village café where it was at least a bit warmer.

Meanwhile, Peter Mellowes' troop were holding Selsten, having been warned to expect a counter-attack. 'It was bitterly cold and many degrees below zero,' he noted. 'It was so cold that our tank tracks were frozen in the snow and mud.' The Germans were shelling them intermittently, but during a pause he decided to check on his crews and headed off on foot with his troop sergeant. The night was very dark except for moments of flickering light when a shell exploded. All around he could hear the cries of wounded infantry as stretcher-bearers moved around trying to find the stricken men. Suddenly, there was a loud whoosh and a shell landed not far away. Both Mellowes and his sergeant were lifted clean off their feet, flung into the air and hurled back down again on the hard frozen ground. By extraordinary luck, neither was hurt, save for a bit of bruising. 'We picked ourselves up,' wrote Mellowes, 'and continued our search and eventually found our tanks.'

Meanwhile, at around 1 a.m., Ernie Leppard and Johnny Taylor's crew were on 'prowler' duty in their tanks – each crew in the troop had agreed to take turns keeping watch while the rest got their heads down in the café. Suddenly their driver, Bill Kendrick, spotted something up ahead. Kendrick was older than most and considered himself a non-combatant; he was prepared to drive but wouldn't go near a weapon himself. Now he switched on the tank's lights, and up ahead they saw two Germans coming towards them, their hands up, surrendering. 'So we took them in the café,' said Leppard, 'and everybody was asleep going, "Why the bloody hell don't you shut up, give them a cup of tea and tell them to doss down in the corner."'

Leppard's crew were back in the café and fast asleep themselves when at around 6 a.m. one of the other crew men came in to tell them to get up and come outside and have a look. They hurried out to see a tiny Scottish soldier, just 5 feet tall, marching in with over forty prisoners.

'Got anything to drink?' the Scot asked them. They offered him some schnapps. 'Just what I bloody well wanted,' he replied. 'It's been freezing cold all night.' The SRY men then handed over their two prisoners and after the Jock had searched them for wallets and watches, he went on his way. 'He marched them off,' said Leppard, 'with half a bottle of schnapps in him. He was singing, "I Belong to Glasgow" as he marched those Germans out of the village.'

At Selsten, Peter Mellowes had barely slept, but at least there had been no counter-attack. He was, however, horrified by the scene that greeted him as the pale winter light spread slowly across the battlefield. It seemed there were men who'd not been found by the stretcher-bearers during the night, and he now saw a number lying half out of their foxholes and slit-trenches. 'They were frozen to death,' wrote Mellowes, 'with their arms frozen as they had tried to attract attention to no avail. A sight which I will never forget.'

Also on 22 January, A Squadron had helped take the next village, Laffeld, and by the 23rd they were at the edge of Heinsberg itself. At dawn the following day, Wednesday, 24 January, A Squadron were ordered to attack the town along with the 4th King's Own Scottish Borderers. Opposition was not expected to be heavy, but the final advance on the town still meant 3 and 4 Troops had to cross some 800 yards of open ground. In the process, three of 3 Troop's tanks were hit and knocked out in quick succession by enemy SP guns. The driver of one of these was Trooper George Knight. Although both he and Trooper Hargreaves, the lap-gunner beside him, were wounded, Knight kept driving the tank until he'd got it behind some kind of cover. By this time, it was on fire, so he and the rest of the crew bailed out. As they did so, a machine gun opened fire on them – but as they dived for safety, Knight noticed his mate was struggling to get out of his hatch and so he dashed back, despite his own wounds, and helped Hargreaves get clear.

Soon afterwards Peter Mellowes, pressing forward with his 4 Troop, spotted Knight staggering back and, seeing he was badly wounded, paused to pick him up. After strapping him on to the back they rumbled on through the snow as Heinsberg loomed up ahead – a shattered, ruined hell-hole after the pounding it had received the previous November by the heavy bombers. They'd not gone far, however, when Mellowes' tank was hit too, an AP round smashing into the engine from the left-hand side and stopping the tank dead in its tracks. Immediately, Mellowes ordered his crew to bail out; and no sooner had they done so than the

Sherman began to burn. Just a short distance away was a large potato clamp, which offered some small protection.

They had only just dived behind it when mortars started crashing around them. Suddenly, Mellowes remembered that George Knight, now unconscious after the morphine shot they'd given him, was still strapped to the back of the tank, so it was now his turn to perform a rescue act. Shouting for someone to help, he dashed over, climbed on to the back of the burning Sherman and tried to pull Knight clear. But the wounded man was stuck – the belt of his oversuit had caught on something. Desperately, Mellowes looked around for help, but he was on his own and the Germans were now using him for target practice. Mortar shells crashed all too close and bullets fizzed and whipped by. In the nick of time, he managed to free Knight's belt, haul him off the back and carry him back to the potato pile as a clatter of machine-gun bullets spat up spurts of snow just behind him.

Eventually, the firing died down and two stretcher-bearers appeared to pick up Knight, who by this time was in a very bad way, and together they all set off back to their own lines, Mellowes half-expecting to be gunned down at any moment. 'I shall never forget trudging through the snow,' he wrote, 'my legs feeling like jelly.' Thanks to his bravery, however, Knight would live.

Heinsberg fell that morning, thanks not least to Johnny Lanes, who took over as lead tank after Mellowes' had been hit. 'With a bit of smoke,' Lanes noted, 'myself and the corporal dashed across the open ground and made it. This seemed to give the infantry a lift and we moved forward taking prisoners.' Light shelling and mortaring continued as the last of the enemy troops in the town were mopped up, but a stonk by the Essex Yeomanry brought an end to the German fire. Heinsberg had been taken – and that night, reports reached the division that the enemy were pulling back across the River Roer. Both the 7th Armoured and the Wessexmen had had similar success. The Heinsberg triangle had been eliminated, and on 27 January the Sherwood Rangers were pulled back. Operation BLACKCOCK was over.

A few days later, fresh orders arrived. They were to move back north to the Nijmegen sector. At long last, the attack on the Reichswald was about to be launched. This was to be Operation VERITABLE – the biggest assault by 21st Army Group since D-Day itself.

CHAPTER 28

Cleve

Peter Selerie was still in hospital near Basingstoke when, at the beginning of February, a letter arrived telling him that as he had been wounded, his temporary rank of major had been terminated, that he was now a captain once more, and that as a result his army pay had been adjusted accordingly. The bean-counters at the Paymaster General's department of the War Office had never been known for their generosity, compassion or tact. Otherwise, he was recovering well.

George Dring was also making steady, albeit clearly painful, progress. He had written to Stanley Christopherson from St James's Hospital in Leeds to congratulate him on his award of the DSO. 'Pleased to say I am going on fairly well,' he wrote, 'I have got my hand growing in my stomach now. They have put a flap out and sewn my hand in it I haven't lost it all I have two fingers left that work and one that doesn't.' They were, he told him, trying to make a kind of web from the remains of his shot-away fingers; it meant the end of his army career. 'It was hard to have to leave the regiment,' he added, 'it was a great fighting unit. I have had some wonderful times and one couldn't wish to meet a better crowd of officers, NCOs and men.' Apologizing for his 'scrawl', he sent his best wishes to all and signed off. He might have lost precious use of one hand, but he had survived.

Bill Wharton and Stan Perry, meanwhile, both of whom had been taken straight to an American field hospital, were in a bad state. News of Wharton's wounding reached his wife by telegram. 'CAPT E WHARTON ROYAL ARMOURED CORPS WAS PLACED ON THE SERIOUSLY ILL LIST ON 22 ND JANUARY 1945 SUFFERING FROM SHELL

WOUND LEFT CHEST STOP THE ARMY COUNCIL EXPRESS SYM-
PATHY LETTER FOLLOWS SHORTLY STOP.' Horribly worrying days
followed for Marion. Wharton had arrived at the hospital in a pitiful condition. Telegrams were always brutally stark and inevitably prompted
more questions than they answered. This one reached her on 27 January;
four days later a further wire arrived with better news: he was now off the
seriously ill list.

Perry, initially placed in a bed neighbouring Wharton's, was in an even
more serious state. When he first awoke it was to discover a Purple Heart
on the locker next to his bed. This was a medal issued to US troops who
had received a combat wound. In due course, a clerk came around and
asked him some questions. 'Oh, you're a Limey,' he said. 'You can't have
that then.' And his Purple Heart was taken away. In another of his more
lucid moments, an American serviceman called on him and asked him
whether there was anything he wanted. 'Any last wishes?' he asked. Perry
was conscious enough to be a little shocked by this, but said he understood the American PX – the US equivalent of the NAAFI – had pineapple
juice, and if it wasn't too much trouble, he'd really like a glass of that. The
next day, a couple of dozen cans of the stuff appeared by his bedside.

On 26 January, Padre Skinner visited them both at the American field
hospital and was assured they would be all right. For both men, however,
it had been touch and go.

While the war was over for Perry and Wharton, for the rest of the regiment there was another big battle to fight. By 25 January, the bulge in the
Ardennes had been entirely eradicated and the front line was back where
it had been before the enemy counter-offensive. Seventh Army's front
had also been stabilized north of Strasbourg. All along the lengthy Allied
line, preparations were under way to get back on the offensive themselves
and finally get across the River Rhine.

The Sherwood Rangers' route back up to the Nijmegen area was a long
and circuitous one, during which they broke the journey at the Belgian
town of Mol, a stone's throw from Bourg-Léopold. Here, at the site of a
colliery, they were all packed off to some pithead showers, which were
ideal places to clean up filthy soldiers from the front. Ernie Leppard reckoned he hadn't washed for at least two weeks; most had not even changed
their underwear in that time, let alone their battledress and oversuits. It
had been too cold to strip down.

At the showers there was a strict and efficient system: they stripped off, chucked their old clothes in a pile, had a good shower and soaped themselves down, then ran down the corridor, threw their towels on a heap and headed, naked but clean, to a bench where new clean clothes were issued. 'And we gets there,' said Leppard, 'and then suddenly it's a big long bench manned by Belgian women. And we're all dashing in there naked.' Leppard found it rather embarrassing. 'You had to go to a different person each time,' he explained, 'for a pair of socks, undershirt, pants, shirt.' It turned out these women had not only seen all of 8th Armoured Brigade in the buff, but also all of 43rd Wessex Division and the Desert Rats too.

Apart from his blushes, Leppard enjoyed the trip back to Nijmegen. They all knew they were out of the line for a week or so and they'd survived the last battle. 'Everybody was in a good mood,' he said, 'and everybody cracking jokes.' They even tuned in the radio and listened to the latest songs from America on the US AFN radio network.

By the evening of 2 February they were back near Nijmegen, and here, as ever during these pauses, the revolving door of personnel turned. The Irishman Ronnie Hutton had begged to be allowed to return to a sabre squadron, and so was put in temporary charge of A Squadron since Tony Gauntley was now on leave. Mike Howden, who had been in A Squadron since Tunisia, was given Hutton's old job of running B Echelon behind the line – a reward for his considerable front-line service, although few ever saw it that way. Again, this was down to Christopherson, Young and the padre deciding he needed a break.

Back with B Squadron was John Cropper, who, like Stan Perry before him, had got himself married between leaving the Geilenkirchen battlefield wounded and arriving back with the regiment. That had been on 13 January, and he had been due back on the 16th; but his mother was seriously ill and so he asked for an extra four days so he could visit her. When this was refused he'd absconded, been to see her anyway, and only reported back to the transit camp on the 20th – at which point he'd been promptly arrested – though in truth, this was an 'arrest' in only the loosest sense of the word and he was allowed to report back to the regiment just as he would have done normally. Immediately, he was marched in to see Stanley Christopherson; Cropper explained about his mother, and the colonel dismissed the charge there and then. Only once he was back outside did the RSM chide him, not for going AWOL but for not contacting him to begin with. 'He said that if I ever got in that situation again, I was to contact the Regiment and they would sort everything out.' 'You see,' Cropper added, 'the Regiment was like a big family – they looked after their own.'

He was now given command of a Firefly in Lieutenant Dick Hyde's troop, and with it an entirely new crew. He immediately had *Blue Light Special II* painted on it, although most crews had long ago given up naming their tanks; they were getting through too many to bother. To begin with, he was rather reluctant to have the four-crew 17-pounder, not least because the tank was a little more sluggish than the normal Sherman. Fortunately his new driver, Frank Milner, who was a dab hand mechanically, got tinkering with the engine and managed to improve its performance by around 15 miles per hour. Cropper was happy about that, and even happier that his new tank had a gun that generally destroyed whatever was in its way with one single shot.

Arthur Reddish also arrived back from leave, and with much to think about, as his married girlfriend, Claire, was pregnant. They agreed she should keep the baby and that if Reddish survived the war she would get a divorce and marry him instead. 'That leave,' he noted, 'was too short.' Now, he was back and hurried to find Captain Howden.

'We've both been posted to the echelon, Red,' Howden told him. So it was farewell to A Squadron – but Reddish felt that it had changed with Semken gone, and George Dring, and others. Even his mate John Savage was back in England on the Python scheme. 'The squadron,' Reddish wrote, 'didn't look quite the same.'

David Render, too, was told he was soon to be given a break. For the moment he was to remain in A Squadron, but for Operation VERITABLE he would be Stanley Christopherson's liaison officer with brigade, his task to follow the colonel around and run whatever errands were needed. For this, he was to be given his own Dingo scout car. Render increasingly felt his luck could not last. Clearly, Christopherson had recognized that this indefatigable troop leader – a young man John Semken referred to as the 'Inevitable Mr Render' because he inevitably survived each battle – needed a break, just as Mike Howden needed a change.

Render accepted the posting without grumbling, although he would miss his dog, Fritz, who he agreed should remain with the crew. Fritz was an Alsatian, and had almost certainly been trained as a mine-sniffing dog. One morning in early January, when they'd been watching the border north of Schinnen, the dog had come bounding towards them across the snow. It had stopped a few yards from the tank and Render had jumped down, given it a tickle and fed it a biscuit. The two became instantly devoted to one another, and when the tank had pulled back to leaguer, the dog had readily jumped up on to the back of it and quite happily followed Render into the turret, using the breech of the 75mm main gun as a stepping stone. Instinctively, Fritz, as they renamed him, made himself a bed in one of the storage areas running along the hull under the turret ring. He had been with them in the turret throughout BLACK-COCK, and was still with them now back at Nijmegen. No one seemed to mind. A number of crews had pet rabbits and even chickens in their tanks. And Stanley Christopherson, of course, had his 'Pinscher', Beek.

Although Render was only twenty years old and Peter Mellowes twenty-one, it was experience that counted above all, and by now both of them were hardy veterans compared with the latest crop of young officers who had just joined the squadron. Most had come straight from Sandhurst, and both Render and Mellowes did their best to pass on the lessons that John Semken had given them when they'd first joined, from the vital importance of reading the lie of the land in order to keep tanks off the skyline, to how best to enter a village or town. Ideally, you'd arrange for a troop to fire on either side of the road. 'The rear tank to cover your rear, in case there were infantry hiding in ditches and upstairs windows, who would fire at you from behind as you passed,' noted Mellowes. 'Another lesson was never to turn your tank broadside on the enemy, as our side armour was not as thick as the front armour.' The trouble was, while these fresh-faced young officers arrived fit, could read maps, and knew all the features of the tank and how to aim and fire a gun, they were totally unprepared for the confusion of battle and the challenges of working with infantry. There was no inbuilt sixth sense; and there was so much for a troop leader to think about and do when in action that almost inevitably the new leader would miss something, maybe scanning for a hidden enemy gun, or find his brain scrambled when it needed to be crystal clear. A young fighter pilot, for example, could join a squadron, be sent up for some training with a veteran, learn the ropes a bit and be sent on a 'milk-run' for his first operational mission, and so ease his way into combat flying. There was no such path for new troop leaders: a day under instruction and that was it. They had to sink or swim – or rather, pray for a big slice of luck and hope they absorbed the lessons of combat in very short order.

Stanley Christopherson was summoned to a conference held by 'Von Thoma' on 3 February. It was as if normal service had resumed now they were back in XXX Corps and working in tandem with the 43rd

Wessexmen once again, although Christopherson hardly relished a further round of serving under General Thomas. Maps were hung up and the battle plan explained. Monty's 21st Army Group now contained three armies: British Second, Canadian First and US Ninth. The Canadians were going to be in charge for VERITABLE, although XXX Corps had been attached for the operation and swollen to five divisions: all in all, there would be some 200,000 men, including attached artillery and corps service troops. These five divisions would jump off on 8 February, advancing through the great border forest of the Reichswald to capture Cleve and Goch. The Canadian II Corps would then join in. In the next phase of VERITABLE, they would all push on together and clear the western part of the Rhineland. Montgomery viewed the operation as a two-fisted punch, however, and a little after VERITABLE had been launched, General Bill Simpson would begin Operation GRENADE slightly to the south, pushing his US Ninth Army across the River Roer and then converging with the British and Canadian forces around Wesel on the Rhine. The First Canadian Army had 470,000 troops in total and the US Ninth 300,000, which meant 21st Army Group's February offensive would involve more than three-quarters of a million men. It was an immense force; and yet the battle was expected to be a difficult one. The Siegfried Line, or Westwall, had three belts of defences, each between 500 and 1,000 yards in depth. Forest fighting was horrible, as the Americans had discovered in the Hürtgen forest to the south – a brutal, vicious battle that had lasted from September to December. Then there were the flat flood plains of the Rhine, whose waters were controlled by sluices; the Germans would almost certainly flood these areas the moment the Allies reached them. Days were still short, it was still bitterly cold, and the tens of thousands of vehicles upon which the Allies were so dependent were likely to struggle in these extreme conditions and over this very troublesome terrain.

At the conference, Christopherson learned that the Sherwood Rangers and 43rd Wessex Division would be attacking on the northern flank, not through the Reichswald itself but across the edge of the flood plain, along a road that ran through the border towns of Kranenburg and Nütterden, following a day after the 15th Scottish, whose immediate objective was the city of Cleve on the far side of the Reichswald. In the middle of the assault, the 53rd Welsh were to clear the mass of the Reichswald, while 51st Highland were to take the higher ground to the south-west of the forest and then push on to the town of Goch, 10 miles south of Cleve.

The Canadians were then to attack on the northern flank south of the Rhine, while the Wessexmen, with the Sherwood Rangers supporting them, would reach Cleve, go through the 15th Scottish and sweep down to meet the 51st Highland at Goch.

A pretty clear intelligence picture of the enemy had been prepared, drawn from a combination of intercepted radio traffic, decrypts of cipher messages and the superb work of photo-reconnaissance – both the high-definition photographs themselves and the subsequent analysis. This part of the front was defended by the 1. Fallschirmjäger Armee, and specifi-cally the 84. Infanterie Division, destroyed at Falaise but re-formed the previous September. Also in the line was the 2. Fallschirmjäger Regiment, along with around 100 field guns and a number of 88mm dual-purpose anti-aircraft and anti-tank guns. The whole front was strewn with tens of thousands of mines. Roads were all particularly well laid and defended. Plus there were Nebelwerfers, mortars, machine-gun nests, and a substan-tial anti-tank ditch west of the Reichswald. Annotated Allied maps marked up all the known enemy defences. There was a soberingly large number of them.

Fire-power was the foundation upon which any new Allied offensive was launched, and VERITABLE was to be no exception. General Hor-rocks had been fretting over whether to call upon the heavy bombers, but in the end decided the destruction of Cleve and Goch was a price that had to be paid if it meant saving the lives of his front-line troops. An oil depot at Emmerich, to the north of Cleve, was bombed by the tactical air forces on 6 February; then, on the night of the 7th–8th, before D-Day for VERITABLE, 287 heavies of Bomber Command came over and flattened the medieval city of Cleve, a further 153 doing a similarly efficient job on Goch. Ninety-five more bombers hit other targets in the area. Allied heavy bombers could strike with considerable accuracy by this stage of the war – they were only a week away from destroying Dresden – and by the time they were on their way home, barely a building was left standing in either town. Cleve would claim to be the most completely destroyed town of its size in all of Germany.

That same night of 7–8 February, the Sherwood Rangers had moved up to the far side of the Groesbeek Heights ready for an early-morning bombardment of the forward German lines. Tanks were not designed to be used in an artillery role, and Stanley Christopherson wasn't particu-larly happy about it, but orders were orders. The previous evening, they'd moved down either side of a farm and barns on the slopes overlooking the Groesbeek–Wyler road; in fact, it was only a few hundred yards east of the wood from which Stuart Hills and his troop had been ordered to rescue the isolated American paratroopers the previous September; they were now on the ground that had then been occupied by the Germans. Each tank was given 220 rounds of HE, although the Fireflies were initially issued with AP by mistake. Only with the urgent help of the 12th KRRC and their vehicles were they able to get back to the ammo dumps and collect the right shells for the 17-pounders.

It was pitch-black when they began, opening fire along with the artillery at 5 a.m. A thousand guns suddenly ripping apart the air. David Render was still commanding his troop until the end of Operation PEPPERPOT, as this part of the battle plan was code-named. Barrels elevated to the maximum. Targets marked on maps. Each tank firing in turn, two rounds a minute. The air thick with smoke and sharp with the stench of cordite that stuck in the back of the throat and made eyes smart. Later, as dawn crept over the scene, an official photographer recorded the sight: tank after tank lined up, hazy in the misty morning drizzle, empty shell cases piled on the ground. David Render was captured standing on the back of a Firefly, coordinating the firing of his tanks. He reckoned his troop alone had fired 9 tons of shells at the enemy.

The only tank having trouble was that of John Cropper and his crew, who had a misfire with their first round. This was potentially incredibly dangerous. 'The fear was that if we had to open the breech then the shell might explode,' said Cropper, 'which meant the end of us.' They recocked the firing mechanism, which was the standard drill, but it still didn't fire. They did it again: same result. By now everyone was getting a little frantic. Eventually they agreed that Ted King, the operator, would open the breech, and immediately Cropper would catch the shell and throw it straight out of the turret. It was a heart-stopping moment, but there was no explosion and in the end they realized the problem was with the firing pin, not the shells. Jack Snedker, the gunner, soon replaced this and they were then able to join in the stonk of the enemy positions.

They fired for an hour and a half, shell after shell. At 7.30 a.m. they stopped, watching the smoke build up over the German lines as the shells continued to scream over – then, for ten minutes between 7.40 and 7.50 a.m., there was quiet. At this point the hope was that the enemy would open up with counter-battery fire and in so doing provide the XXX Corps artillery with the opportunity for sound-ranging and flash-spotting; and sure enough they did, although somewhat half-heartedly. Then, at 7.50 a.m., the

British and Canadian artillery opened up again, all 1,000 guns plus tanks. Finally, at 9.20 a.m., smoke shells and HE were fired over the first line of defences. And at 10.30 a.m. the infantry got going, pushing out across the open ground towards the Reichswald, into the smoke, into confusion, into battle. Into no-man's-land.

'We then packed up,' said Ernie Leppard, 'cleared our tank out, cleaned our guns and got ready to move off and link up with echelon to refuel with ammunition, fuel and have a meal.'

The first day of VERITABLE went well. By around 5 p.m., the 15th Scottish were in Kranenburg, only a few miles west of Cleve. In the forest, the 53rd Welsh had met hideous numbers of mines, and tracks were soon chewed up, but even so they made steady progress. So too did the 51st Highland. To the north of the Nijmegen–Cleve road, though, the Germans had opened the sluice gates, and the flat land south of the Rhine was rapidly flooding.

The Sherwood Rangers spent most of the day after PEPPERPOT was over at Nijmegen, and the following morning, Friday, 9 February, linked up with 129th Brigade from the Wessex Division: A Squadron with the 4th Somersets, B with the 4th Wiltshires, C Squadron with the 5th Wiltshires. In the afternoon, pine logs were brought up and strapped to the sides of the tanks, not so much for extra protection as for use if they became bogged down and for crossing slit-trenches. Loud-hailers were handed out for communicating with the infantry. Then, at 7 p.m., they got moving. The route: Beek–Kranenburg–Nütterden–Cleve.

It was dark and raining as they trundled forward, nose to tail, for about 5 miles. Then they stopped. No one knew what was causing the hold-up; then word came back that 15th Scottish had only got one brigade forward, and two other brigades were strung out along the same road they were now on. To Ernie Leppard it looked like one hell of a traffic jam. Stop, start. Move a little forward. Stop again. By 11.30 p.m., they'd reached Nütterden. 'Then it was hopeless,' said Leppard. 'It was completely blocked. And during the route, the Germans were shelling the road, it was drizzle, icy cold, infantry on the backs of our tank.' They brewed tea in the turret and smoked and waited. Then, at around two in the morning, they were lead tank and lead troop in B Squadron, so they decided to turn off the main road to Cleve and instead try to pass through a firebreak in the narrow neck of the Reichswald, with Lieutenant Ray Gaiger, the troop leader, leading them on foot on the track through the trees.

'And then we come to this defended position, just towards the edge of the Reichswald,' said Leppard. 'It was all pitch dark, and then suddenly illuminated with gun flashes.' Leppard thought it looked like a gamekeeper's house or a forester's place. 'Germans were firing back,' he added, 'and so we just blasted the place out of existence.' A little way behind them was a Sherman bulldozer, so they brought him up and once he'd cleared away the rubble they rumbled on through. Leppard must have dozed off, because when he awoke it was light and they were at the edge of Cleve. It was now the morning of Saturday, 10 February 1945.

Cleve was desolate. Once a beautiful, thriving medieval town, home of King Henry VIII's fourth wife, Anne of Cleves, it now stood utterly ruined, an island of destruction almost entirely surrounded by flooding. B Squadron drove on into the town, all in a line, and over the radio they learned that 15th Scottish had taken the city. They were to pause before pushing on with the Wessexmen to start clearing the outlying villages to the south and south-east. They were to be ready to move again at nine.

Leppard jumped down from the tank. It was his turn to make some breakfast, but the box on the back of the Firefly that contained their plates had gone – probably the infantry had assumed it was a box of mortar rounds and chucked it away – at any rate, they had gone: both the infantry and their plates. There were empty and broken houses on the street, so he wandered into one and found a camera, some plates, knives and forks – and, even better, a live chicken out the back, which he grabbed. 'Just coming out and then all hell let loose,' he said. 'We were mortared, machine-gunned and fired at, and it was apparent we'd broken through into the town of Cleve and it was still being defended.'

He dashed to the back of the tank where the rest of the crew were taking cover, the dixie full of tea still boiling on the back above them. The others asked him where the hell he'd been. Just getting breakfast sorted, he told them. Suddenly, the tank lurched back about 2 feet as it was hit by the shell of an 88. The gunner, Trooper Fred Davis, had still been asleep and was killed immediately. A second shot hit the tank and went straight through where Leppard would have been sitting. He and the rest of the crew dived clear and eventually took shelter in the basement of a house on the street. Cleve was most emphatically not yet in British hands.

Meanwhile, Regimental HQ were following close behind with the headquarters of 129th Brigade, also strung out on the same road into the city centre. David Render had spent the entire night following *Robin Hood* in his Dingo, getting wet and cold and feeling vulnerable without a tank. As they all paused, Frenchie Houghton, the adjutant, told him to find a house where they could set up shop and get some tea going. Then he heard mortar fire comparatively close by and, hurrying back to his Dingo, watched as his own troop in A Squadron moved on past. He felt a bit helpless.

Immediately ahead was 129th Brigade HQ, who were hit by an SP gun moving about the place and also being shot at by enemy snipers. One sniper tried to hit the Baron, the bullet fizzing past his head and missing him by a whisker. Fortunately, he spotted smoke at the window from which the bullet had been fired and immediately traversed his own tank, *Maid Marion*, and fired back with a mix of AP and then HE that caused the entire corner of the building to collapse. As the house crumbled it revealed a Jagdpanther, which had been hidden behind it.

David Render, still sitting in his Dingo, now found himself literally staring down the barrel of the Jagdpanther's big 88mm gun. There was no time to move before it fired; the shell whooshed a foot above his head. The Dingo, only 4 feet 11 inches off the ground, was so close that the Jagdpanther had not been able to depress its gun far enough.

The Baron's gunner, Corporal Newton, now fired several shots, but missed. Fortunately, the Jagdpanther reversed and moved away. The Baron, however, was irate at the lack of support and immediately went on the radio to berate Frenchie Houghton.

'Couldn't you see that I have been engaging a bloody SP gun?' he said. 'You might have given me support. Out.'

'Can't you see that a bloody SP gun is about to emerge from the street to your right rear,' Houghton impatiently replied, 'for whom your bottom will be a perfect target when he does appear? Off.'

The angry exchange was swiftly forgotten as the Baron hurriedly manoeuvred his tank to deal with this latest threat. This, too, was driven off, but the situation in Cleve was difficult, to say the least. Because of the lack of sufficient roads, the flooding, the turning to quagmire of any road not asphalted, there were just not enough troops in the town; these circumstances had conspired to scupper the chances of a swift lightning-bolt charge by XXX Corps. Kranenburg, for example, was now completely flooded. It was passable along the main road – just – but any other routes were out of the question. And one road through the neck of the Reichswald was not enough. Had it been dry, and had it been summer, VERITABLE would have been a cake-walk. But it wasn't. It was winter, it was raining, and the ground was flooded. Already, plans were afoot to start using amphibious vehicles and craft to bring supplies forward.

The consequence of all this was a dramatic slowing of the advance. So, while the first day had gone really very well, the second hadn't – and nor, now, had the third. Traffic congestion had slowed the 15th Scottish's advance so that instead of rushing into Cleve and taking it before the disintegrating German forces could occupy and hold it themselves, the enemy had had enough time to move up troops. It seemed the 15th Scottish had probably missed their chance to bounce the enemy out of Cleve by a matter of hours. By the end of that day, elements of three reserve German divisions had been identified, including units from the 6. and 7. Fallschirmjäger Divisionen as well as piecemeal units from 15. Panzergrenadier and 116. Panzer Divisionen reported to be moving into the area.

Nor was progress helped by the ruins of Cleve. 'From the infantryman's point of view,' wrote the author of a terse post-battle report, 'heavy bombing has every disadvantage and no advantage.' Air photographs lost considerable value; craters and rubble not only created obstacles but also made clearing casualties more difficult; and ruins made the enemy's task of hiding and camouflaging himself that much easier. 'From our experience in clearing a town not bombed, to one that has been heavily bombed, there is little doubt the infantryman would ask the airman to go elsewhere.'

The British Army had learned so much during the long years of war, yet it was incredible how often generals continued to misuse strategic air power. Time and again, the heavy bombers had been called in and had flattened towns, with the net result of not only the destruction of centuries of history but the creation of a mass of craters and piles of rubble that made the task of advancing harder, not easier. Cassino, Caen, Saint-Lô and now Cleve. It was astonishing how they simply had not learned.

Throughout the day the Sherwood Rangers helped clear the town, supporting infantry as they swept through the ruins clearing houses and streets, one at a time. Peter Mellowes thought it was like playing a deadly game of hide and seek with German SPs and snipers. 'They would climb up over the rubble,' he noted, 'and we would poop away at them.' It was miserable, tense work and nerves were soon strung taut. Lurking SPs, men with panzerfausts, snipers; at any moment one of these might suddenly jump out and fire a fatal shot. Ranges were short among the ruins. The Sherwood Rangers lost six tanks that day, for three SPs, which was not a good return. Captain Coleman was wounded and Lieutenant Rhys Thomas killed when an HE round exploded beside their tanks. Thomas had been one of those fresh-faced young subalterns who had arrived just after BLACKCOCK. This was his first action, and he was just nineteen years old. Four other men were killed and four wounded.

Meanwhile, quite a party of Sherwood Rangers was building up in the cellar where Ernie Leppard was sheltering, as two more crews had had their tanks knocked out and had joined them. As night fell, they could still hear firing going on somewhere outside. Then, at around four in the morning, they heard a tracked vehicle rattling and squeaking and imagined it was a panzer and German troops coming to get them. In fact, it was a Sherman bulldozer trying to clear the streets. 'We stayed 'til morning,' said Leppard. 'It was a bit distressing, one of our chaps had gone completely bomb happy, off his rocker, and we had a job to keep him quiet. He was crying and screaming and – his tank had got hit, and I think he was slightly wounded. But he had gone off his head.' They eventually emerged and were all told by the squadron sergeant-major to head back to Nijmegen and the FDS to pick up new tanks. Since the flooding was now so bad, they were taken back in DUKW amphibious vehicles which had been hurriedly brought up.

On 12 February, with Cleve finally secured, they continued their advance with the Wessexmen. The River Rhine ran to the north of Cleve but then curved southwards, around 10 miles to the east of the town as the crow flies. The aim of VERITABLE was to clear this stretch of the Rhineland as far south as Issum, around 25 miles away, and in line with Wesel on the eastern bank of the river. At this point, it was hoped they would converge with the Americans of Ninth Army, who would soon be launching GRENADE. The Sherwood Rangers' immediate task, though, was to press on towards Goch and Udem to the south and south-east of Cleve and clear the villages round about.

Padre Skinner, meanwhile, was struggling to get between Nijmegen, where the regiment's echelons were still based, and Cleve. Canadian lumberjacks were building a log-road through the Reichswald, while vehicles now had to drive through some 2½ feet of water in Wyler and Kranenburg. 'Floods deeper,' noted Skinner on 13 February. 'Huge bow waves in village street and here and there the odd tank or gun more than belly down in the water.' The following day, he travelled through the Reichswald in a convoy of the 13/18th Hussars, although they were held up on the way. At one point a German jet aircraft roared over; the world was evolving rapidly, but getting through the Reichswald was no easier in February 1945 than it had been three centuries earlier in the Thirty Years War.

Meanwhile, on the 11th, A Squadron moved south-east out of Cleve. That night, they billeted themselves in a large building that seemed to be completely empty. Only once they started looking around did they realize it was a mortuary and that in the basement were a number of bodies that had been abandoned. 'They were,' wrote Peter Mellowes, 'quite high.' Understandably, the Rangers beat a hasty retreat and the next morning, with men of the 4th Wiltshires riding shotgun, they moved further southeast and took Louisendorf, a model village built around a church at the heart of a perfect tree-lined square. Stanley Christopherson, who was not far behind, heard Ronnie Hutton come over the net to tell him they had captured an asylum at the edge of the village and with it three doctors, thirty nurses and 1,300 lunatics. Christopherson replied that he should keep the doctors and patients where they were, but could he please send the nurses to RHQ. Not long after, Stanley reached the village himself, where he spotted a small white flower. 'I found a snowdrop,' he noted, 'the first I had seen for such a long time.' Spring was coming.

PART IV

Spring – Germany

CHAPTER 29

The Rhineland

THE SHERWOOD RANGERS HAD two days of scrappy, difficult fighting in the countryside and villages south and south-east of Cleve as enemy resistance stiffened. On 13 February the Germans, now reinforced by the newly arrived 116. Panzer and 15. Panzergrenadier Divisionen, counter-attacked. 'Four tanks were lost,' noted Denis Elmore, now the intelligence officer. 'Lt. Wheeler and Lt. Knapp were wounded, 3 ORs killed and 5 wounded, 1 missing.' The following day, 14 February, there was a further enemy counter-attack along the roads that ran north-west towards Cleve and a platoon of the 4th Wiltshires was overrun. C Squadron were supposed to attack at midday, but the enemy were too strong. Later, around 5 p.m., C Squadron tried again with a troop from B Squadron but still got nowhere. They were only 5 miles or so south-east of Cleve, in a flat, wide and open landscape – a patchwork of fields dotted with farmsteads and either side, a mile or two away, thick, deep forest. It was hard here for tanks to move forward to take on hidden anti-tank guns and SPs because they could always be seen. A night-time attack was planned, with A Squadron brought up – but then was cancelled at the last moment. Two more men were killed that day and another two wounded.

Instead, they were pulled back, and although B and C Squadrons were given a holding role the following day, by the evening of the 15th the entire regiment was back in the ruins of Cleve, the men distributed among the wreckage. Even better, the A1 Echelon had managed to get through. Among those appearing in a 3-ton Bedford lorry was Arthur Reddish, who was pretty happy to be out of a tank and spending most of his time a way to the rear. He was certainly living better, with plentiful supplies of rations but also more time and opportunities to scrounge food locally. His driver was a fellow called Jim, who'd been driving the same truck since Normandy, and the two of them had struck up an unofficial partnership with two others, Cliff and Taffy, when it came to meals and cooking. Both Cliff and Taffy were 'inveterate rascals', always on the scrounge for loot, but Reddish liked them enormously, and since he wasn't shy about bending the rules either, he felt quite at home in this new environment.

The echelon sergeant led their column of trucks in his Dingo. Near Cleve, they halted by a crossroads and the sergeant waved them on. 'The tanks are about a mile ahead,' he told them as they rumbled on past. The further they drove on, however, the less Reddish liked it.

'Stop this lorry, for Christ's sake, Jim!' he suddenly said.

'Why, what's the trouble?'

'I don't know,' Reddish replied, 'but everything's too bloody still for my liking.' Absolutely nothing stirred. Soon after, the Dingo raced down and overtook them then stopped.

'Don't panic,' the sergeant told them, 'we're down the wrong bloody road. Just turn around quietly and retire.' They did so and all was well. That sixth sense, built up over years of front-line combat, had served Reddish well.

Padre Skinner spent much of the 15th out and about collecting casualties. 'Total now over 30,' he noted. 'Shelled once and machine-gunned several times in area.' This was another significant number of losses: six entire Sherman crews' worth, and it meant that once the regiment was out of the line again yet more changes would need to be made. Really, it was relentless, and yet somehow Stanley Christopherson, overseeing the entire Sherwood Rangers show, had to ensure that morale remained strong, that his officers, especially, were not being overburdened, and that new faces were swiftly absorbed – and, more importantly, that the regiment were ready for the next round of fighting when it was thrust upon them.

He also had some difficult decisions to make. Bill Enderby, wounded in the arm on D-Day, had been medically downgraded as a result, but had persuaded a medical board to allow him to go back to active service and specifically to let him rejoin the Sherwood Rangers. Major Enderby was a near-contemporary of Christopherson's, was an old friend, and had had command of a squadron. On the other hand, he'd not seen action yet in Europe – he'd been wounded in the landing craft – and it was hard on

Ronnie Hutton, who had done a good job. Still, his seniority warranted a squadron, and so he got the posting.

Christopherson also needed a new second-in-command, as Robin Leigh was returning to his old regiment now the Royal Gloucester Hussars were about to be deployed. This choice was made easier by the news that Basil Ringrose wanted to rejoin. A pre-war member of the Sherwood Rangers, he had gone with them to Palestine but had quarrelled with Flash Kellett and been posted to work with Emperor Haile Selassie in Ethiopia. He had then returned to the SRY as Christopherson's second-in-command in A Squadron for the Battle of Alamein. At the end of the North Africa campaign, Ringrose had ended up in a succession of staff jobs but now wanted to return to active service. 'Such applications always created certain ill-feeling among those who had fought continuously in the Regiment,' wrote Christopherson. 'Although he had been with the Regiment before the war, his return would block promotion.' He had been wondering how he could bring Ringrose back when suddenly the Baron's departure created the ideal solution: he could be his replacement second-in-command. And it was also important that Christopherson was looked after too; an old friend was just the ticket.

Stuart Hills, now back from leave, was immediately called to see Christopherson at the latest RHQ building on the edge of Cleve. For some time, Hills had coveted a post in the Recce Troop and had several times asked if he could become second-in-command under Ian McKay. The latter, however, had taken over B Squadron for VERITABLE, leaving the Recce Troop without a commander. Christopherson now offered the post to Hills, who was thrilled – and also very relieved to discover that both Denis Elmore and Dick Holman were out of sabre squadrons and at RHQ instead. During their time out of the line at Cleve, the three of them were able to share a billet together. They were such great friends, and yet because they'd been in different squadrons and because of Elmore getting wounded, this was the first chance they'd had to spend any time together since before D-Day. Fortunately, they got on as well as they ever did. 'I was never happier than when I was in their company,' noted Hills, 'and we were certainly a very happy trio.'

He had his work cut out, though, with the Recce Troop. 'Both men and tanks were in a deplorable condition,' he wrote. 'They were, I suppose, the dirtiest and most undisciplined bunch of men in the regiment.' Determined to lick them into shape, he immediately interviewed every single man – all thirty-five of them – and fortunately struck up a rapport with the Hinitt brothers, who in many ways were the beating heart of the Recce Troop. Nev Hinitt was the troop sergeant, a pre-war regular who had served in India along the North-West Frontier, and who was from the old SRY stomping ground of Retford. His younger brother, Arthur, had been with the regiment in North Africa; now he drove Hills's own Stuart tank and also acted as his batman. 'He was a joy to be with,' wrote Hills, 'as he was invariably smiling and enjoyed a good joke. I never heard him grumble.' Although there was a touch of roguishness about both of them, they were also utterly imperturbable; Hills warmed to them from the outset.

David Render was less happy, however. He'd taken back command of 5 Troop after only a brief stint at RHQ, and now had a new troop sergeant as Leslie Jackson had finally gone home on the Python scheme. While he had no concerns with Sergeant Dennis Webb, Render was unhappy that Bill Enderby was now squadron leader instead of Ronnie Hutton. Render knew Enderby's background as a regular cavalry officer and was instinctively prejudiced against such men. He'd been against Geoffrey Makins taking John Semken's position back at the end of June and he was against Enderby coming in now; as far as Render was concerned, Enderby was just thinking about his post-war career and, as a regular, wasn't a proper Sherwood Rangers type.

So Render's hackles were already up a little when he then discovered he'd been given an A57 Chrysler multibank petrol-engined Sherman Mk V rather than a diesel-fuelled Mk III, as *Aim* had been. The crew weren't happy either, as all of them were convinced that the multibank-engine Shermans were more flammable and likely to brew up. They were also equally certain they had a tendency to stall; the A57's multibank consisted of five Chrysler six-cylinder engines welded together around a single drive shaft. They had concluded that because some of the engines were effectively upside down, gravity would make the fuel drain out when idle. Even worse, they thought the Mk V lacked the torque of their old diesel Mk III.

These perceptions mattered, because men like Render and his crew were being asked to put themselves in incredibly dangerous situations and it was important they had faith in their tanks. But all these views were just that: perceptions rather than reality. Almost all Shermans in the British Army were now what the Americans called the M4A4 and the British the Mk V, with the A57 multibank. The old M4A2 – or Mk III – diesels were no longer being supplied; and this was because logistically, operating with two types of fuel was inefficient. In any case, what type of

Sherman was issued to the regiment was entirely out of their hands. They had to accept what they were given and get on with it.

In any case, the Mk V multibank was, in many ways, a better machine than the diesel Mk III. Nor was there any statistical evidence to suggest that the petrol engine was more likely to brew up than a diesel. Nor was it more likely to stall; that was a figment of the men's imagination. In fact, the A57 multibank was incredibly robust and could still move with up to 12 of its 30 cylinders not working; that kind of hardiness was worth a lot. It also had greater torque than the Mk III, not less, and was a substantially smoother tank to drive.

Still, Render and Webb had got it into their heads they'd been given a dud, and had worked themselves up into a lather of indignation. They weren't happy, and Render took his complaint to his new squadron leader. Although he'd accrued a huge amount of experience since June the previous year, Render was still only twenty, still only a lieutenant and still only a troop leader, while Enderby was two ranks and twelve years his senior. So being berated by Render about the type of tank he'd been given on almost their first meeting did not go down at all well with the new squadron leader. Render felt he wasn't being listened to; Enderby thought Render was sounding like a spoiled schoolboy who needed to remember who he was talking to. Enderby gave him short shrift, and Render returned to his troop absolutely fuming. In truth, Render missed Semken, he missed his great mate Harry Heenan, and he probably needed a bit longer out of the sabre squadrons than he'd been given; in many ways, he was aping the attitude of Sergeant Jackson the previous June: just as Jackson had been chary of Render, Render was now wary and resentful of Enderby. Perhaps, though, Render could have done with a little more patience and understanding. Enderby might have been his senior, but he was playing catch-up with his more experienced subordinates and it was important to win them over – especially given that he was following in the wake of John Semken.

On the other hand, Ernie Leppard was rather pleased with his crew's new tank. They had been given a four-man Firefly. Arthur Falconer had left the regiment, too, which Leppard was pleased about, as had Bill Kendrick, their old driver. Bert Tye was the new driver, Bill Ashton the gunner and Corporal Johnny Taylor still the commander. Leppard was well aware that the Germans tended to target the Firefly whenever they saw one, but he reckoned the ordinary Sherman was always the devil to escape from for the operator, whereas the turret of his new tank had a different configuration, which included a generously sized hatch on the left-hand side above his position as operator. 'So, my head was outside of the tank seeing what was going on more than it was inside,' said Leppard. 'And, you know, the tank commander is watching the action in front and if you've got another one out of the turret looking around the area as well, it's a bonus when you're going into action.' The breech block of the 17-pounder was so enormous, however, that it did make the turret a lot more cramped. A rectangular hollow block extended from the back of the turret, housing a big lump of lead as a counterweight as well as the radio, and this allowed a little more wiggle room for loading the larger 17-pounder shells. There was also no coaxial machine gun. Rather, the Firefly's machine gun was to the left of the main gun, poking through the turret, and was manned by the loader/operator. So Ernie Leppard had rather a lot to do: he had to man the radio, load the 17-pounder and fire the Browning.

Peter Mellowes seemed to have a more phlegmatic approach than Render to the changes in A Squadron. He and the other officers had set themselves up in a partially ruined house a couple of hundred yards from a crossroads which was repeatedly shelled by the Germans. They soon realized that this shelling happened fairly regularly, so worked out when they could expect the next salvo. This was important not least because of the calls of nature. Because Cleve was in ruins there was no running water in their house, and so they had built a latrine a short way away from it. This took the form of a hole dug in the ground with an old wooden ammo box placed over it with a hole cut out to sit on, and a wooden frame covered in canvas around it for some kind of privacy. Once finished doing their business, they would pour petrol over it and throw in a match.

Mellowes found this latrine was a good place in which to retreat with letters from home, and so he used to sit there, trousers down, and read them in peace. One day, though, he was in the latrine when he heard the tell-tale shriek of an incoming shell. It sounded close; and, sure enough, it landed only 20 or so yards away. 'The blast blew our loo cover away,' he noted, 'leaving me feeling very vulnerable.' Even out of the line, it seemed, danger lurked at every corner; a few days later, Padre Skinner had to bury an Essex Yeomanry sergeant who'd been killed on a motorcycle. As the man had tried to pass a number of tanks and half-tracks, he'd skidded and fallen under the tracks. 'What can one say to the family?' scribbled Skinner in his diary.

*

The Sherwood Rangers spent the last few days of February on standby waiting to rejoin the battle. VERITABLE was taking longer than had been expected, but really, in the conditions, this was not surprising. The sticking point had not been Cleve, after all, but Goch, the town 10 miles to its south which had become the focus of German resistance. Feldmarschall Gerd von Rundstedt, the commander of all German forces in the west, had wanted to retreat to the far side of the Rhine, but Hitler, as was his way, insisted on fighting for every yard. Over this flooded and waterlogged ground, that ensured a slugging match, a slow, remorseless drive by the Allied infantry and armour behind immense fire-power and supported by increasingly ingenious logistics. Speed and mobility, however, were unavoidably lost in the thick treacle of the Reichswald and Rhineland, which were still not free of winter.

Goch finally fell on 22 February, and the following day the US Ninth Army launched GRENADE, their attack across the Roer river. The Allies were inextricably grinding their way closer to the Rhine, but it was proving a painfully slow process – and costly, too. The Canadians, for example, were pushing towards Calcar, east of Cleve and Goch, but suffered 25 per cent casualties among their 8th Infantry Brigade and lost seventeen tanks knocked out.

'Colonel attended conference at 53 Div at 1400 hrs,' recorded Denis Elmore on 26 February. 'Result: no immediate move.' The next day, he wrote: 'Still no move. Regiment expecting orders at any moment.' Not until 5 a.m. the following morning, 28 February, were they suddenly moved south to Goch and from there told to support the 53rd Welsh in an attack on the next town to the south, Weeze.

This town stood on the western banks of the narrow River Niers, just 10 yards wide, which snaked southwards. Here, the land undulated softly. Large woods lay amid farmland to the west and more heavily covered the eastern side of the river. Basil Ringrose, the new regimental second-in-command, was put in command of a battlegroup of C Squadron, A Company of the KRRC and a squadron of the 53rd Division's recce regiment. They had moved south on the eastern side of the Niers but then had to cross a stream that joined the river from the east. This they managed to do early, and then attacked eastwards, taking a farm and capturing over forty prisoners. A Squadron, meanwhile, had also crossed the stream and found themselves heading down the road that ran straight over the river into Weeze with Peter Mellowes' troop in the lead. Up ahead, either side of the road, were pine woods. 'The road through the woods was narrow,' he wrote, 'and an ideal place for the Germans to concentrate their anti-tank guns and any other nasties.' Their job was to get to the far side of this wood and then hurry down into Weeze before the enemy could blow the bridges.

Mellowes paused and had a good look around. In one of the woods the pine trees seemed young, and he reckoned his Shermans could simply bulldoze a path through them and so avoid heading directly down the road. After giving his orders, they set off. The ruse worked, and they reached the far side of the wood unscathed. The edge of Weeze now stood only around 500 yards away. Mellowes reported his position to Bill Enderby.

'Four troop will charge,' Enderby replied.

Mellowes wondered what on earth he was talking about; after all, the regiment had long ago handed over its horses and sabres. But when he queried the command over the net, Enderby merely repeated it.

'In view of this,' wrote Mellowes, 'I had no option but to obey the order.' This was exactly the kind of Balaclava charge John Semken had so detested, and Mellowes feared it might well be the last act of his short life. He was about to give the order to 'charge' when there was a huge explosion as the Germans blew the bridges. They then heard the sound of lorries and armoured vehicles moving off. The race to reach Weeze had failed; but the charge order was not rescinded, so the German action had very possibly saved the lives of the men of 4 Troop.

Around midday, B Squadron were ordered into the fray. They were to push southwards, still on the eastern side of the River Niers, and capture the last bridge still standing in the area, which was about a mile south of Weeze near the grounds of Schloss Wissen, a country house on the eastern side of the river, set in parkland but surrounded by yet more thick woods. These woods were a problem because they were hard to navigate through and potentially full of enemy. So the plan was to move southwards to the east of the woods. No one was entirely sure what enemy troops they might find. It was known that the Panzer-Lehr-Division, their old enemy from the first days in Normandy, was in the area, along with other panzers and SPs; there was a huge range in the quality of the enemy troops and they too were operating over entirely unfamiliar ground. Here, to the east of Weeze, the ground rose gently to a shallow crest before dropping away again, which meant B Squadron, and the infantry of the 1st East Lancashires they were supporting, would have to cross the skyline of this higher ground before moving on southwards with the forest on their right.

'So, we were all lined up,' said Ernie Leppard, 'and we were to go over the brow of this hill and down towards this farmhouse.' John Cropper was in his own Firefly. 'Usually when we worked with infantry,' he said, 'they would walk behind. This time they formed four or five rows across our front and we lined up right behind their back rank.' As they cleared the rise, however, German machine guns opened fire and the infantry immediately went to ground. Away across the open ground to the east was a farmhouse, so 5 Troop were ordered to hurry towards it and take out the machine-gun nests. Off they moved, out across the fields. Suddenly a Panther appeared and began firing at them. Shells screamed over, most careering into the ground. The infantry were up again, scampering forward as Brens chattered behind them. Tank guns booming, the bright muzzle flash of the Fireflies. Smoke. One Sherman reached the farmhouse, sprayed it with HE and machine-gun fire, but was then hit by a panzerfaust. A second Panther appeared, but a B Squadron shell drilled it in the engine and the crew bailed. Two other Shermans were hit. Confusion and mayhem: shells whooshing and crashing, bullets streaming through the air, swirling smoke. Infantry running forward again. In Taylor's tank Bert Tye, the new driver, trying to dodge the shells and speed southwards as quickly as he could, turned the Firefly towards the wood on their right. The ground, though, was saturated, slick and slippery. They slid and hit a tree. 'Everything come down with a clatter,' said Leppard. 'Bert had knocked himself out, the gun skewed round, and everything went dead.' Engine stopped, electrics down. Smoke filling the turret. Out they jumped – but machine-gun bullets were fizzing and zipping past them and mortars crashing nearby. So they got back in.

More B Squadron tanks were knocked out, but the second Panther appeared to have been silenced too. That was two down, and they didn't appear to have any more. Leppard and his crew tentatively clambered out of their Firefly again, cranked the gun into position and fired off a few rounds. The farmhouse was captured and the fighting moved on, further south, the tanks and infantry disappearing amid the smoke and haze of battle. 'Everybody had disappeared and just left us,' said Leppard, 'and we was completely dead, no radio, and it was getting dark.'

Although B Squadron had had five tanks knocked out that afternoon, by dusk they had reached the road leading to the bridge at Schloss Wissen. On the far side of the river, infantry and armour had been trying to break into Weeze from the north and north-west and, as the light began to fade, the 4/7th Dragoons unleashed a 'Pepperpot' – a barrage with their tanks' guns – to try to catch the retreating Germans, then pushed on into the town.

In the meantime, Ernie Leppard and his crew had decided they should sleep in the tank and then get help the following day once it was light. Suddenly, at around two in the morning, they heard knocking outside and then heard the word 'surrender'. At first, they thought it must be German troops wanting them to surrender, but then they realized it was the enemy troops who'd had enough and wanted to give themselves up. But Johnny Taylor didn't want any prisoners to look after – none of them did – so they pointed back up the rise and told the Germans to give themselves up to the infantry. Only after they'd shuffled off did Leppard and his mates twig they'd been wearing black panzer uniforms; they had probably been the crew of one of the knocked-out Panthers.

Early the next morning, the Germans blew the bridge and abandoned both Weeze and the entire area either side of the River Niers, which meant the Welshmen had to bring up bridging engineers. The Sherwood Rangers remained where they were, recovering knocked-out tanks and waiting for orders for the next stride, while the 4/7th Dragoon Guards leapfrogged them and helped the infantry clear the road south to the next two towns, Kevelaer and Geldern. Ernie Leppard, meanwhile, had scrounged some rations from one of the knocked-out tanks and, so fortified, then worked out that when they'd hit the tree, they'd moved a piece of metal underneath the turret that was now brushing the battery terminals, shorting the electrics. They cleared the offending bit of metal, straightened the turret, then fetched a battery from one of the other tanks and used it to charge their own. They'd just got the Firefly going again when the ARV finally turned up – and was not best pleased to have had a wasted trip; but now they'd got the Firefly running again, that meant four of the six tanks knocked out the day before had been recovered. Really, the ability of the technical teams and LADs to follow so soon after the fighting and recover as many tanks and vehicles as they did was extremely impressive.

In fact, only one of the B Squadron tanks had been destroyed by the Panthers; panzerfausts, bogging, other damage and, of course, driving into a tree had done for the others. Two men had been killed, but all things considered they had got off lightly. Back in their Firefly, Johnny Taylor and his crew gently trundled over to the farmhouse to look at the Panthers only to discover they were, in fact, Jagdpanthers. That did a lot to explain why these beasts had not knocked out more of B Squadron's tanks; with no turret, they had only a very limited traverse, which made hitting a moving target very difficult indeed. 'They was hidden behind a gate that led into a sunken lane,' said Leppard. 'One had lost its track. And behind it was the other one, completely intact. Nothing wrong with it.' They spent half an hour looking all over it, fascinated to be able to see it so close – and inert. Leppard reckoned it must have run out of fuel.

Of the two men killed, Corporal Ken Turner was discovered a short distance away from the fighting. He'd been horrifically wounded in the legs when his tank had been hit by a panzerfaust. The Germans had picked him up and taken him to their own RAP where his shattered leg had been amputated. He'd not survived, however, and he'd been left, abandoned by the Germans when they fled the RAP. It took the padre a while to find him, but when he did, he carefully buried him and marked his grave, which was near a crossroads to the south of the farmhouse where he'd been hit.

Refreshed after his leave and thrilled to be commanding the Recce Troop, Stuart Hills had actually been feeling rather excited about the prospect of a return to action after three months out of the front line. However, the ground had been too wet and too muddy around Weeze for his lighter and smaller Stuart tanks, and so they had been left on the sidelines for much of the battle. Three days later, however, on 4 March, the Sherwood Rangers were closing in on Issum, only a few miles west of the River Rhine.

C Squadron tanks were in the lead ahead of Hills in his Stuart. Suddenly, the tank in front paused, swung its turret around to the right and fired several shots. Wondering what they were firing at, Hills peered through his binoculars only to realize, to his horror, they were American armoured cars. Ordering the tank to cease fire immediately, he then told the tank commander to hurry over and apologize profusely. Fortunately, no harm had been done. Later, they met in the town; the American commander took a great shine to the British oversuits, already nicknamed 'Pixie' suits, and asked for a couple. 'In view of our shooting error,' wrote Stanley Christopherson, 'I readily agreed.' A call was put through to the quartermaster and two Pixie suits were brought up and handed over.

The small town of Issum was bisected by a narrow river, but the bridges across had all been blown by the retreating Germans, so they were forced to pause until the stream was bridged; while it wasn't wide, it was several feet deep and totally impassable to vehicles. A mile out of town towards the Rhine was another blown bridge. Here, the brook was completely dry in summer; but after the snow and excessive rain of the past few months it was running fast and the surrounding flat countryside was saturated, so this too would have to be bridged. It meant a hold-up in progress.

While they waited, Hills set up RHQ in an abandoned German house near the river in the centre of Issum, and was soon joined here by his friend Denis Elmore. Desultory enemy shelling was now directed at the town, and at one point, while he and Elmore were talking out in the street, a shell whistled past them, straight through a window and into the house, where it exploded. It had been another close shave. As dusk fell, Corporal Evans arrived with a bulldozer and began shunting the rubble from a destroyed house into the stream to make a temporary bridge by filling in a narrow stretch of the river.

With nothing much to do until the rubble bridge was complete, Hills and Elmore decided to turn in; after all, it wasn't every day they got to sleep on a proper bed. Hills had been asleep for just an hour when he was woken up by the adjutant, Frenchie Houghton.

'The Colonel wants one of your tanks up at the next bridge,' he told him, 'to give the engineers some protection if they're counter-attacked.'

Hills decided it was something he should do himself, and for a companion chose Corporal Morris, who was ever-cheerful, ever-calm and ever-competent. Clambering into their Stuart in the dark, with just Hills in the turret and Morris driving, they headed over the new rubble bridge and continued along the dead-straight road out of Issum until, a mile or so further on, they reached the engineers. A scissor bridge – an AVLB or armoured vehicle launched bridge – had been brought up; this was a Valentine tank chassis from early in the war with a folded bridge on top of it, which was pulleyed up into position and carefully lowered as a comparatively quick and straightforward means of creating a temporary bridge. However, sporadic mortars were falling nearby and the engineers were not attacking their work with the kind of gusto Hills had expected. When more mortars suddenly began crashing all too close by, the engineers suddenly began hurrying back down the road along with the AVLB. Hills quickly ordered Morris to pull back too, although only a short distance, and after ten minutes or so, realized there was no counter-attack taking place and absolutely no reason why the engineers shouldn't get on with the job. The problem was, there was now no sign of them.

Reluctantly, Hills went back to RHQ where he found Stanley Christopherson and Brigadier Prior-Palmer and explained the situation. The sapper officer was summoned and given a roasting. 'I was sorry for him,' admitted Hills, 'and felt I had been telling tales out of school.' Now turning to Hills, the brigadier put him in command of the bridging operation and told him he wanted it completed by first light and that they were not to leave until it had been done even if they were counter-attacked by two panzer divisions.

So off they all went again. By this time the mortaring had lessened, and they were able to finish the bridge in short order and before first light as instructed. Job done, Hills radioed in to RHQ and was told to stay where he was to act as a guide as B Squadron were now moving up. Not long afterwards he heard their low rumble and the squeaking of tracks, and then they were drawing up alongside. It was normal practice for the troop leader to head up his troop, followed by the troop sergeant and then the corporals, but on this occasion Johnny Taylor in his Firefly had been ordered to take the lead. Over they went, pushing on another 100 yards or so towards a slight rise, lined either side by woods. It was the perfect place to site an anti-tank gun – and sure enough, a round now smacked into them, knocking off one of their tracks. Frantic panic to get out. Ernie Leppard pushed himself up and out as a second round whooshed just above their heads. They'd all only just got on to the road when a third shell hit the turret with an enormous crash and cascade of sparks.

The rest of the tanks furiously fired back and hurriedly pulled off to the side of the road, while Hills got permission to pull back to RHQ, his task complete. Back at his billet he got into bed and went straight to sleep – only for Arthur Hinitt to wake him and Elmore half an hour later. 'What a smashing night,' said Elmore, who had been asleep the entire time and had no idea what antics his friend had been through.

Meanwhile, Ernie Leppard and his crew had taken shelter in a German bunker beside the bridge. A number of infantry had also tried to shelter there, and mortars were raining down around them. One landed close to the bunker, killing and wounding a number of the men. Leppard tried to help by carrying one of the wounded into the bunker, but as he did so the man's head fell off. 'Very disturbing,' he said, 'to see his bloody head come off in your hand.'

Beyond the bridge, the tanks had fanned out so they were out of the direct line of the enemy guns, but the ground was too sodden for them to operate. Infantry, however, were pushing into the woods either side of the road. Johnny Taylor's crew, meanwhile, hungry and fed up, had made a dash for their tank and clambered back inside. There they found some rations and, once fortified, began using the gun to blast enemy machine-gun nests with their 17-pounder. 'There was nothing wrong with our tank,' said Leppard, 'except for the track off and a gouge in the turret.' It was after midday, however, following a heavy stonk on the German positions, that A Squadron, now supporting 158th Brigade, and accompanied by a substantial smokescreen, were able to secure the road and the ridge ahead.

The day's fighting was long done and darkness had fallen before the ARV arrived to help fix the shattered track on Johnny Taylor's Firefly. 'You bloody lot again,' the fitter grumbled. 'Don't you ever sort yourselves out?' At least this time they really did need him. It didn't take too long; tracks were kept in place by a series of bolts, and with the right tools and equipment it was straightforward enough to remove one section and replace it with another. Once repaired, they turned around and headed back to Issum.

This was the end of VERITABLE for the Sherwood Rangers. That night, Leppard heard a massive explosion away to the east: it was the Germans blowing a bridge across the Rhine. The war would not be over until the Allies had finally got across that mighty barrier.

CHAPTER 30

Crossing the Rhine

T HE REGIMENT REMAINED IN Issum for a few days in case they were
needed for further operations. They were not, however, and instead
moved north back to Goch where they were to remain out of the line for
the next fortnight as 21st Army Group prepared for Operation PLUN-
DER, the crossing of the Rhine at Wesel and Rees. The entire area west of
the Rhine had now been cleared. Some 51,000 POWs had been taken
during the twin operations of VERITABLE and GRENADE, and more
than 38,000 enemy troops killed or wounded. The cost had been almost
16,000 dead or wounded to Canadian First Army, which included XXX
Corps and, of course, the Sherwood Rangers. Everyone knew the war
against Nazi Germany was nearing its endgame, yet the Germans insisted
on fighting to the bitter end – despite irreversible defeat, despite millions
dead, despite the reduction of the Reich's cities to rubble; it wasn't just
Cleve and Goch that had been pulverized in recent weeks but Dresden
and Pforzheim as well. Some 20,000 people were killed in Dresden; in
Pforzheim the death toll was over 17,600 – which amounted to 25 per
cent of the population – and it was estimated that 86 per cent of the town
was completely destroyed. The Ruhr cities and Cologne had been hammered yet again too. It was all so pointless. And soon enough the men of
the Sherwood Rangers would have to dust themselves down, take a deep
breath and head back into battle, each man hoping he would be spared
and somehow make it through to the very end. Those like Stanley Christopherson or Stuart Hills or Neville Fearn or SSM Henry Hutchinson,
who had been there on D-Day and were still standing, just had to hope
that with the finishing post in sight, their luck would hold.

Montgomery planned for the crossing of the Rhine to be the last major set-piece operation of the war. As such, the planning of PLUNDER – the ground force's crossing – and its companion airborne piece, VARSITY, was an immense undertaking. Risk was to be reduced as far as possible, which meant overwhelming force, as few casualties as possible and planning for every conceivable scenario. Perhaps this was a little overcautious, especially as the Americans to the south had unexpectedly managed to capture the Ludendorff bridge across the Rhine at Remagen on 7 March. On the other hand, much had been learned since D-Day and the Normandy campaign, the Allies had such huge resources at their command, and British – indeed, Allied – strategy had always been to use technology and mechanization as much as possible; 'steel not flesh' was the mantra. Stacking the odds in their favour and trying to reduce casualties was a laudable aim, especially since there was the prospect of the ongoing war against Japan to confront once Hitler and the Nazis had been vanquished. This was not the time to be cavalier with manpower.

It did mean, however, that there was not a lot for the front-line troops to do for a few weeks until PLUNDER and VARSITY were launched. Certainly, after slogging their way through the Reichswald and across the Rhineland, the Canadians and XXX Corps needed the rest. At any rate, it meant Stanley Christopherson could take his first leave since D-Day and head back to England for a fortnight, although he intended to use part of the time to see old comrades and catch up with Myrtle Kellett on various regimental welfare issues.

For the rest, however, there was the chance to take a few days' break in Brussels in between maintenance, conferences to discuss recent operations and further training. Stuart Hills managed to get away with Dick Holman, Denis Elmore and Mike Howden. Like all British officers, they stayed at the Plaza Hotel, which had been specially requisitioned for them. They had three whole days and nights there, and established a very enjoyable routine. Get up around 10 a.m. Go across the road to the Tile Room above the W. H. Smith shop for waffles and treacle and coffee. Shopping from 11 a.m. to noon; first drinks of the day, followed by lunch and a trip to the cinema. More drinks from 6 to 8 p.m., then dinner. Then off to a nightclub until, maybe, five in the morning. Back to the Plaza. One night, Stuart Hills had dinner with a Wren friend he'd met, and invited her to join him, Dick and Denis at the movies the following day. 'Dick's language during the film was simply appalling,' he wrote, 'and I gave him hell about it afterwards.'

Peter Mellowes followed them a day or two later. His mother's birthday fell on 16 March, while he was in Brussels, and she'd written asking for a photograph of him. He'd felt it was the least he could do, so he went to a studio, had it done properly and posted it back to England. On his first night there, he'd had a good soak in the bath and had just put on clean underwear when the loudspeaker system announced that the debutantes of Brussels were down in the lounge and would like to meet British Army officers for drinks.

Mellowes was naturally a rather shy fellow and had barely spoken to a girl in two years. He was, however, introduced to a beautiful young woman called Simone Guillaume; they got chatting, hit it off, and she invited him to meet her parents. He readily agreed and the following night duly turned up at her home, suddenly very self-conscious about the state of his battledress; they were given fresh underwear every two weeks, but he hadn't had his battledress cleaned or changed in eons. Only now, standing outside the Guillaumes' very grand house in one of the smartest corners of Brussels, was he acutely aware of how much he smelled of fuel, oil and grime. Nerves gripped him, but Simone put him at his ease and her parents were charming. When he eventually left, she promised to come and see him off the following morning. And, at the appointed hour, there she was – the most beautiful girl he had ever laid his eyes on. 'She gave me a very chaste kiss on the cheek,' he noted, 'and I went on my way on cloud nine.'

In Goch, meanwhile, Ernie Leppard and his crew were billeted in an old mews house at the edge of town. Where the owners were was not really much of a cause for concern. Leppard was just glad to find a house that still had a roof and, even better, a range in the kitchen. He liked cooking, and managed to scrounge some flour and make himself and the lads a few pies. But, like Peter Mellowes, he was also starting to feel a bit self-conscious about the state of his personal hygiene. He found an old tin bath and took it up to the second floor where there was a half-decent drawing room, albeit one which had had its windows blown in. He heated up a load of water on the range, then took it up to the bath, got himself undressed and stepped in. Just as he lay back, he suddenly realized two German women had come into the room. 'And that was the first time I'd come into contact with German civilians,' he said. 'You know, the sudden shock of it.' He reached for his revolver and was about to ask them what the bloody hell they were doing there when they ran off. He never saw them again.

*

Stanley Christopherson arrived back at RHQ on 22 March just in time for the flurry of final planning conferences for PLUNDER. 'I have just got back to find a great deal of activity,' he wrote to Myrtle Kellett the next day, 'which I suppose is just as well; I don't know at all where we will be when you get this letter.' The weather had much improved since he'd been away. Spring was on its way, the hedgerow now flecked with green, the grass growing once more, buds appearing on the trees. She had asked him what more she could do for the regiment; he replied asking her for a consignment of socks – that was the one item, above all, of which they could never have too many. Christopherson had been rather smitten by Myrtle, and it was easy to see why: she was strikingly beautiful, supremely self-assured and glamorously well-connected. 'It was lovely seeing you again,' he added, 'and I only wish that it could have been for longer.' He signed off, 'So much love, Stanley.'

That same day, he attended the final planning conference. Passwords were issued, exploitation plans were agreed, and Montgomery's message to the troops was handed out on simple one-sided slips of paper. The Sherwood Rangers were not to be in the first wave of crossings; timings for them would be confirmed later, depending on how the operation went. PLUNDER was launched at nine o'clock that night, Friday 23 March, sup-ported by more than 3,500 guns in an opening barrage at three crossing points: XXX Corps at Rees, XII Corps near Wesel, and the US XVI Corps from Ninth Army at Dinslaken to the south. Some 32,000 vehicles had been amassed for the operation, along with some 118,000 tons of supplies. To put this in perspective, the Sicilian campaign in the summer of 1943 had required 6,000 tons of supplies per day. Yet again, the heavy bombers were brought in: 195 Lancasters and 23 Mosquitoes hit Wesel, a town that had been hit throughout the war ever since 1940, although only heavily for the first time back on 16 February. After this final raid, however, some 97 per cent of the town was destroyed. Cleve had been ruined but Wesel was obliterated.

Both British crossing points were supported by 79th Armoured Div-ision 'funnies': DD tanks, Buffalo amphibious tracked vehicles for boggy and flooded ground, and 8,000 engineers just in XXX Corps alone. All German civilians had been evacuated 6 miles west of the river; Winston Churchill, the prime minister, had insisted on coming over to watch, along with Field Marshal Sir Alan Brooke, the British Chief of the Imper-ial General Staff, and security was extra tight.

All three crossings were easier than had been feared, although at Rees,

General Tom Rennie, the commander of the 51st Highland Division, was killed by mortar fire having made it to the far shore. At 10 a.m. on the 24th, some 16,900 paratroopers from the US 17th and British 6th Airborne Divisions began falling on targets to the east of Wesel in what was unquestionably the most accurate and successful airborne drop of the entire war. Even so, casualties were still around 20 per cent; airborne operations were costly.

The Sherwood Rangers received their orders at 10 p.m. on 25 March. They were to move across the river at Rees at 3 a.m., in the order: B Squadron–RHQ–C–A. Almost inevitably, there were delays, however, and it wasn't until around 7 a.m. that John Cropper inched *Blue Light Special II* on to the raft at the crossing point TILBURY. Several such points had been established using barrage balloon winches and steel hawsers to pull the ferries back and forth; a pontoon bridge, code-named LAMBETH, was being constructed across this 400-yard wide stretch of the Rhine, but was not yet completed, so the Sherwood Rangers went across by raft. Getting a tank on to one of these was not easy. 'If it was not in line,' said Cropper, 'the first track to touch would lift one side of the raft and you had to start again.' Cropper decided the best way to ensure the Firefly got on swiftly and safely was to stand at the far end of the raft and personally direct the driver. This worked, and they were soon on their way. It was a hazy spring morning. Gunfire and other sounds of battle could be heard from the far side. They all sat on top of the tank so that if it went in, they might have a chance of swimming clear. Halfway across a few salvoes whistled in and hit the water some 50 yards away, but they got across without mishap.

So too did Ernie Leppard and his crew, although on the flood plain on the far side the ground had already become so churned up they got stuck, and they had to be towed across it for 250 yards and up the bank of the dyke. Forming up on the far side was understandably a piecemeal process, although as they were the reserve armoured regiment – the Staffordshire Yeomanry had gone across first in DD Shermans, alongside the leading infantry of the 51st Highland Division – they had the rest of the day to get across, set up RHQ and push inland to rendezvous with 154th Brigade, whom they were due to support the following day, 27 March. Their objective was the town of Isselburg, around 6 miles to the north-east of the crossing.

Late in the afternoon, B Squadron were forming up to the north of Rees when the enemy sent over some shells. No one was hit, but a shard of shrapnel struck the bedding strapped to the back of Johnny Taylor's tank and it caught fire. Ernie Leppard was on the radio when someone said, 'Would you like to look behind you, 4 Baker? You're brewing up nicely.' Both Leppard and Taylor looked behind and with panic now saw flames starting to lick up from their stowage.

'Get out of the bloody line before you blow somebody up,' Ian McKay, the squadron leader, now told them over the net. Bert Tye, the driver, sped off across the fields, while Taylor and Leppard flung their fuel cans clear of the back of the tank as quickly as they could. Fortunately, no lasting damage was done to the tank, although much of their bedding and stowage was lost. After learning they were all safe, McKay told them to wait to refuel and then catch up with the rest of the squadron towards Isselburg. 'So,' said Leppard, 'we was stuck in a field for the night and we rescued a chicken and had a chicken supper.'

Early the following morning, B Squadron caught up with the 1st Black Watch, their objective the village of Vehlingen. An autobahn was marked on their maps running roughly east–west to the south of the village; and there were woods between the autobahn and the village. Attacking both the woods and the village meant crossing open ground. Mortars and artillery shells were exploding around them, but the squadron managed to get through unscathed and began clearing the woods with the infantry. 'We fired belt after belt of Browning at spots where we thought Jerry would be,' recalled John Cropper. After a brief lull, between twenty and thirty enemy troops suddenly cut and ran, and although Cropper's operator, Ted King, tried to cut them down, his Browning machine gun jammed.

'For Christ's sake,' said Frank Milner, the driver, over the intercom, 'shoot 'em, you're letting them go.' By the time the jam had been cleared, however, the enemy had disappeared into the darkness. Even so, at 5 a.m. the B Squadron tanks managed to cross the bridge over the autobahn and, after a pause to clear the inevitable mines, helped take the village soon after.

A little way to the east, A Squadron had been helping to clear the ground north of Rees. The going had been slow, thanks to the usual mass of mines and soggy, flat and low-lying ground, but by mid-afternoon they were nearing the autobahn and the infantry they were supporting, the 1st Gordons, had established a command post in a farmhouse to the south. It was now C Squadron's turn to take over the lead and capture the autobahn. This was marked clearly on the map, and ahead was a high embankment which Jack Holman rightly identified as the autobahn itself. Certainly it was an obvious defensive position.

First, though, he needed to liaise with the infantry – but there was only one road heading north to the farmhouse, and it was overlooked by the autobahn embankment pretty much all the way. He decided that he and his four troop leaders should make a dash for it in a Dingo and so off they set, mortars crashing worryingly close by; they made it across the 600-yard stretch of open ground in what Holman reckoned had to be a record time. 'Little did the Jerry mortar men realise,' he reflected, 'that by aiming off a little, they might have collected a good bag.' By the time they had begun a second salvo, however, Holman and his troop leaders were all safely in the farmhouse with colour once more returning to their cheeks.

A plan was made. Rather than attacking down the main road across the autobahn and on to Isselburg, they decided to move cross-country either side of the road and then attack the autobahn where it was hoped the enemy defences might not be so strong and where perhaps they wouldn't encounter so many mines. Around 5 p.m., tanks and infantry moved out together, the tanks offering suppressing fire, pounding the embankment with HE and spraying it with their Brownings.

Now was the moment for the final dash, Lieutenant Tom Morris leading with his troop. Jack Holman was anxiously listening in on the net, and as dusk was falling heard Morris say, 'I am certain I must have passed the autobahn.' Holman was sceptical but following up realized Morris had been right after all; they'd inadvertently crossed an incomplete section where there was yet to be any embankment built.

Johnny Taylor's crew had not yet caught up with the rest of B Squadron. Earlier that morning, having refuelled and being about to head north towards Isselburg, they were commandeered by a Canadian major from the Nova Scotia Highlanders. The Canadians, having crossed at the same place as the Sherwood Rangers, were fanning out north on the left flank of the Highlanders, and it seemed his men had run into some trouble. He told them he needed the fire-power of their Firefly to blast a farmhouse from which the enemy were causing trouble. Taylor knew they were expected back with B Squadron, but he was a corporal and the Canadian was a major and they were all supposed to be allies, so they did as they were bidden.

When they joined the infantry, the farmhouse was pointed out, around 500 yards away. They reckoned there were around five machine-gun nests plus mortars, but the ground all around was wide open and flat. The infantry couldn't get near it. 'We spent an hour or so wandering around it,' said Leppard, 'putting shells through the windows of the farmhouse. And we knocked them all out.' Then the Canadians stormed the place and swiftly overran it. On this occasion, armour–infantry cooperation had worked very effectively.

As ever, though, time had been sucked up by the assault, and it was once again getting dark. Taylor knew they should be getting going, but the Canadians were having none of it. 'They said, "We'll do you a slap-up meal tonight,"' Leppard recalled, 'because the farmhouse was well stocked with pigs and poultry and sides of bacon and homemade wine. So, we had a party until about 12 o'clock at night.'

The following morning, A Squadron pushed up towards Isselburg at first light, with one troop accompanying the 5th Cameronians into the town. It was in their hands by 6 a.m. This, however, was because the Germans had pulled back during the night, and were holding a series of woods and farmhouses between Isselburg and the Aa river/canal just north of the town. Actually, the Aa marked the border between Germany and north-west Holland; this was the back-door northern corridor into Germany that Montgomery had hoped to exploit had MARKET GARDEN been a success the previous September. The next challenge for the Highlanders and the Sherwood Rangers was how to get across the Aa and take the next significant town, Dinxperlo, on the Dutch border.

Spring might now definitely be in the air, but the flat flood plains of the Rhine remained saturated. This was canalizing the British armour, especially, down narrow raised roads liberally laid with mines – roads that inevitably led them to one river or canal after another only to find that, by the time they reached them, their bridges had been blown. That morning, 28 March, an OP tank from the Essex Yeomanry hit a mine, and the blast and shrapnel hit the tank behind, which was Neville Fearn's. He was hit in the head, and while the wound did not appear to be life-threatening, he was swiftly evacuated, his long war finally over.

With the roads so heavily mined, there was a strong temptation to try and chance it and get the tanks across open fields instead, because although there were mines here too, they were fewer than on the roads; on the other hand, they could only be navigated by someone taking the plunge and walking ahead, looking carefully for both anti-tank mines and firm enough ground. Anti-tank mines were usually fairly easy to spot, either because they'd not been properly buried or because they had only recently been laid and there was fresh soil around them. Henry Hutchinson had dismounted for precisely this role when he stood on a mine and was killed. Everyone in A Squadron and all the old-timers in the regiment were devastated by his loss. Hutchinson was revered and loved by everyone, his bravery legendary, his status within the regiment second to none. After fighting through such long years in the desert and right across north-west Europe, he had appeared indestructible, and yet he too had now been struck down. He left a young wife and children, and an unfillable hole in the Sherwood Rangers.

Yet no matter who was killed, whether the CO or a revered NCO, the show went on. There was still a war to be fought and won. Dick Holman's tank also struck a mine, although he was able to dismount, after which he cleared the road himself – by hand. The rest of the day was spent clearing as much of the ground to the north of Isselburg as possible. Then, that evening, A Squadron were put on notice to support the 5th Seaforths at dawn on the 29th, following their night-time attempt to cross the Aa. Peter Mellowes was in the lead troop that morning as they pushed forward as planned. They were due to be at the Aa by just after 4 a.m., but ran into a thickly laid minefield still to be cleared along the track they were taking and came to a halt. Time passed. Mine-clearing was a laborious process at the best of times, but especially difficult in the dark. Up ahead were the sounds of fierce fighting and this, combined with a ticking clock that told them they were getting horribly late for their rendezvous, persuaded Mellowes, like Hutchinson the previous day, that he had little choice but to try to find an alternative path. 'I left my tank,' he wrote, 'and walked through the minefield very carefully and guided my tanks through safely by giving them hand signals to avoid the mines.' With only the pale light of dawn to guide him and, of course, knowing exactly what had happened to Hutchinson a day earlier, it took some nerve.

Clear of the minefield, they then made a dash across some exposed fields with mortars and artillery shells crashing around them. Fortune was smiling on them that morning in a way it had not on Fearn and Hutchinson the day before, and they were able to reach the forward infantry near the river. It was now 7.05 a.m., so nearly three hours behind their planned meeting time, and Mellowes found the Seaforths in a bad way. There were two bridges, one over the Aa and a second almost immediately beyond over a tributary that joined a little further west. They had captured the first bridge as planned early in the morning, but the second had been blown and was no longer passable to vehicles, though it could be crossed by infantry. Then, just after 5.30 a.m., several hundred *Fallschirmjäger* had counter-attacked not from Dinxperlo but from Anholt, a mile and a half to the west. They had pushed through the forward platoons and swamped the Seaforths' battalion HQ, which at the time had been protected only by their carrier platoon. The commanding officer, adjutant, intelligence and signal officers, and others had all been captured and led off. The rest of the battalion had fought back and were awaiting the long-promised tanks before launching a counter-attack of their own.

Now, at long last, here they were. Having been shown the farmhouses along the river where the Germans were holed up, Mellowes led his troop in to attack, blasting the buildings and overrunning them swiftly, taking more than 250 prisoners in the process. To his amazement, among those who emerged once they had the farm was Lieutenant-Colonel James Sym and all his staff; their captivity had lasted less than an hour and a half.

With the 5th Seaforths' position now restored, Mellowes radioed to Bill Enderby and asked him to send up a scissor bridge and armoured bulldozer. By now, their positions were being shelled, but the bridge and dozer arrived and, after ordering a smokescreen to be laid down, Mellowes personally oversaw the laying of the scissor bridge a short distance from the wrecked one. This completed, he then brought his troop across and, along with the Seaforths, set up a defensive position between a row of houses at the edge of Dinxperlo and reported back that a bridgehead had been successfully established. 'I was ordered to hold the position until reinforcements and anti-tank guns could be brought up.' That, however, was not for another eight hours, and in the meantime they were shelled almost incessantly. 'Eventually we were relieved and returned to rejoin our squadron,' noted Mellowes. 'It had been quite a busy day.'

Johnny Taylor's crew had finally caught up with the rest of B Squadron, although they had nearly been blasted by their own side as they'd approached them from the west of the bridgehead – where they'd been with the Canadians, but also broadly the same direction from which the German counter-attack had come earlier that morning. Ian McKay was not happy, and threatened to put them on a charge for having been absent nearly two days and a night. 'And then we give him a couple of sides of bacon and some homemade wine,' recalled Leppard, 'and he was completely different then.'

They rejoined their troop and B Squadron to the south of Dinxperlo, but that evening Johnny Taylor suddenly and unexpectedly left them. It seemed he had earlier got his mother to write to Stanley Christopherson asking him to be sent home on compassionate leave. It's unlikely Christopherson fell for this, but Dr Young was obviously persuaded that Taylor was suffering from combat fatigue. In such circumstances, it did not pay to keep men in the regiment. That night, he departed the crew and the squadron, leaving Leppard temporarily in command of the tank and with no replacement crewman. It was a sad end to a successful partnership between the two men.

As it happened, it was C Squadron and the Recce Troop that had been given the job of supporting 154th Brigade's attack on Dinxperlo, which meant Leppard did not have to go back into action straight away. Rather, it was Stuart Hills who found himself attending an O group with Jack Holman and others later that night. Divisional artillery had been pounding Dinxperlo all day, something about which Stanley Christopherson felt deeply uncomfortable; after all, the town was Dutch and they were supposed to be liberating them, not destroying their homes. Collateral damage over and above the lives of Allied soldiers had always been accepted, however, and that wasn't about to change in these final days of the European war. As Stuart Hills stood in the dim candlelight, listening to Jack Holman explain the plan, he was actually rather glad that artillery shells were limiting the places where snipers and machine-gun nests might lurk.

Holman wanted Hills's troop to recce into the town first. How far should he go? Hills wanted to know. As far as possible, Holman told him. In other words, until one of his tanks was knocked out. It was the kind of order that put a dull ache in the stomach. The war was still going on out there in the darkness. Desultory shelling from the enemy: the dull boom of the guns, the scream of the passing shell, the crash of explosion and the pulse through the ground. Ahead, the town; patrols reported it empty of Germans, but there might well be lurking fanatics with panzerfausts, snipers, mines and other horrors.

At 3 a.m., it was time to move. It was Good Friday: 30 March 1945. Not much sleep that night. Hills led the troop into Dinxperlo himself, the only light the occasional flicker of shells throbbing in the sky. Even their smaller Stuart tanks seemed impossibly loud in the quiet still of the shattered town in the witching hours, the rumble of their engines and grinding and squeaking tracks reverberating down the streets. But not a soul stirred and they made it to the far side without incident. From here, the northern edge of town, they were to push on and recce two roads heading north, which forked like the top half of a giant 'Y'. The number of houses quickly thinned along both roads, but especially the one leading north-east. He sent Corporal Robert Slater down this one, and Corporal George Morris down the left, north-western, fork. Hills, meanwhile, remained at the junction with Sergeants John Pothecary and Neville Hinitt and the rest of the troop. If either Morris or Slater needed help, they could then readily head back down either fork.

Not long after, Corporal Slater came on over the net saying that he'd been hit by a panzerfaust at close range. They were a man light in any case, so operating only a three-man crew, but while he and one other had got out, Trooper Southam, the driver, was still in the tank. Slater didn't know whether he was wounded or dead. Hills sent Nev Hinitt and one other tank to investigate and the Dingo to pick up Slater. When his sergeant returned he reported the knocked-out Stuart was sitting right in the middle of the road blocking the way completely. Opposition was heavy: the enemy had prepared a substantial road-blocking position with machine guns and several 20mm light anti-aircraft guns being used in a ground role. Hinitt reckoned it was impossible for them to get close in their Stuarts.

Hills now got on the A net to speak with Jack Holman and asked for some infantry and some C Squadron tanks to plaster the place with HE. 'He seemed very annoyed about the whole thing,' recalled Hills, 'but he said he'd do what he could and we waited.' Commanding in a battle like this was hardly conducive to good humour, of course. Even so, a little while later, Holman himself arrived with a company of 7th Argyll and Sutherland Highlanders and two troops of tanks. A quick conflab at the junction followed. After the situation had been explained, the Argylls' company commander seemed rather dubious as to the level of enemy threat. Both he and his second-in-command were armed only with swagger sticks. Hills noticed the CO had the ribbon of a DSO and MC and his second-in-command an MC and bar.

'Well,' said the major wearily, 'come on, show us where this opposition is.' They set off on foot.

'This is too bloody silly for words,' Hills whispered to Holman. 'As soon as we get round this next corner we're all going to be shot to pieces.'

Sure enough, as they turned a right-hand bend, they were greeted by a volley of machine-gun fire and all four men ended up diving for a ditch at the side of the road. They crawled back, then once clear, hurried back to the junction. 'At this point,' commented Holman, 'things appeared most tricky.' Holman radioed to Arthur Warburton of the Essex Yeomanry and asked him to put a stonk down on the German positions either side of the road, while his tanks fired smoke shells. A Sherman moved forward, advancing round the bend with the stricken Stuart, the thick smoke providing cover. Hills and Nev Hinitt also moved up on foot to oversee the operation; but although a tow rope was hitched up to Slater's tank, it twice slipped, and by then the smoke was starting to thin. Hills and Hinitt suddenly found themselves caught out in the open and so, seeing a large shed-like building on the left-hand side of the road, made a dash for it in the hope of finding some cover. As they reached the door machine guns and 20mm cannons opened fire; as they now discovered, the building was a milk-processing plant attached to a dairy, and glass now began shattering all around them. The noise was incredible; Hills and Hinitt were terrified.

Eventually the firing died down and they tried to make good their escape – but every time they opened the door, more bullets rattled and pinged around them and they scuttled back inside. However, Jack Holman had ordered both troops to fire everything they had on every bush, tree and wood, and every building too. This temporarily silenced the enemy and allowed a second and successful attempt to rescue the knocked-out Stuart. It also gave Hills and Hinitt a chance to escape the bottling plant, first scampering to the ditch at the side of the road. 'I was beginning to feel really desperate', noted Hills. By now, though, more C Squadron tanks had moved up, and one now laid down a series of 2-inch smoke grenades just in front of them. 'Sgt Hinitt and I took our chance', Hills added, 'and jumping out of the ditch, raced for safety.' As they hurried back, he passed the Argylls' company commander lying wounded on a stretcher with a 20mm cannon shell through his foot.

Back at the junction, he discovered that Trooper Sid Southam had been tragically killed when the tank had been first hit; the panzerfaust had shot away most of his head. Trooper Ernie Duckworth had also been severely wounded during the rescue of Southam – and did not pull through.

Fighting continued for much of the day. Eventually, C Squadron worked their way off the road and, although several tanks became bogged down in the process, first one 20mm gun was knocked out, then a second. Opposition gradually lessened and in the end the Germans pulled back altogether. Another messy, difficult and frustrating day's fighting was over – and with it, the battle of the Rhine bridgehead was almost over too. The second great Allied pursuit was about to begin.

CHAPTER 31

Pursuit

'THE ENEMY LINE IS broken,' wrote Stanley Christopherson on 30 March in his report for Myrtle Kellett's RWA, 'and once again, we formed up a Regimental Group with our old friends, C Coy of the 12/60th and our own battery from the Essex Yeomanry in support. We are going to support 130 Brigade, and our next objective is Bremen.' Since the end of the Normandy battle, the Sherwood Rangers, along with the 12th KRRC and Essex Yeomanry, had become very adept at swiftly forming themselves into an all-arms mobile battlegroup, capable of rapid gains and swift movement. It also helped enormously that the practice in 8th Armoured Brigade was that each of the three tank regiments would always be supported by the same battery of the Essex Yeomanry and the same company of the 12th KRRC, so they were not just old friends but also permanent partners throughout the campaign.

Yet before Christopherson's regimental group were unleashed this time, they had to let the Guards Armoured Brigade burst through the gap they had painstakingly punched on the eastern side of the Rhine. Christopherson was not alone in thinking they rather got the rough end of the deal, carrying much of the hard yards while the armoured divisions then hoovered up the accolades 'for the more pleasant swanning part of the operation'. Just after Dinxperlo had fallen, Christopherson and others in the regiment watched as a column from the Guards Armoured moved past them.

'Mind your paint, sir, as you go through,' called out one of the SRY tank commanders.

A little galling it might have been, but in truth, most in the regiment would have been happy to take a back seat and have an easier ride for the rest of the war. There was no chance of that, however. Now back with the 43rd Wessex Division, they had been treated to a visit by General Thomas, who was keen to ensure that once the Guards Armoured had pushed through the gap, the Sherwood Rangers also pressed on with all urgency. 'Scheme sounds OK,' noted Leslie Skinner, 'but in fact is asking an awful lot of SRY.' There was certainly still plenty of fighting for them to do yet.

On Sunday, 1 April – Easter Day – A Squadron and Regimental Head-quarters set off early, at 4.30 a.m., with a company of the 4th Wiltshires mounted in Kangaroos, and reached Ruurlo, 20 miles north of Dinx-perlo, without any hold-ups at all. The town was empty of enemy and they pushed on through, heading towards Lochem, some 6 miles further along. The town was protected by woods to the south and a canal to the north, so the ideal place for the Germans to set up ambushes and make some kind of stand. Bill Enderby decided the squadron, which was still in the lead, should split up and try to encircle Lochem from a number of different approaches. David Render thought this a terrible idea, arguing for concentration of force. He had a point; but with German resistance thinning, the enemy could not be everywhere, and the orders from von Thoma were clear: they were to get a move on – and, as General Thomas had repeatedly shown, anyone who didn't tended to get sacked. Render knew little of this; what he did know, however, was that he didn't like Bill Enderby, and he certainly didn't respect him as a squadron leader. The two men, in fact, were starting to get badly on each other's nerves. As they folded away their maps, Peter Mellowes told Render that he was his own worst enemy when it came to dealing with their new squadron leader. He was quite right.

While Render went back to his own troop, chuntering and muttering, Peter Mellowes set off along the road that led directly to Lochem and made contact with the infantry. Up ahead, the lead platoon of the Wilt-shires had run into a roadblock, so Mellowes was ordered to try to outflank the position. Thick woods flanked the road to either side, but there was a track that led off to the right and into the trees, so Mellowes decided to follow this; according to his map, the woods emerged into fields that then ran all the way up to the southern edge of the town.

Without infantry, Mellowes decided he'd better perform their role himself, and so he clambered down from the tank and, together with his troop sergeant, carried out a recce on foot. They carefully made their way through the wood and on the far side, around 700 yards further on, they paused to scan the ground ahead. Just to their left, nestling at the edge of the wood, was an elegant turn-of-the-century house with 'De Enk' painted on the walls just below the roof. Ahead, ploughed fields sloped gently towards Lochem, a little more than half a mile away and looking peaceful enough. No obvious defences, no SPs or panzers or anti-tank guns that he could see, either at the town's edge or anywhere on the ground in between. Hurrying back to his tank, he reported to Enderby, who told him to press ahead towards Lochem.

One of Mellowes' tanks had broken down, so there were just three of them – his own Sherman plus those of Sergeant Alf O'Pray and Corporal Tommy Spoors. They rumbled along the track in the wood in a line; then, as they emerged from the treeline, O'Pray pulled up alongside Mellowes and they moved out across the open field.

Suddenly, *Fallschirmjäger* troops emerged from well-hidden trenches in the field and fired a volley of panzerfausts; from the edge of the wood, Mellowes had simply not seen them at all. Thinking quickly, Taffy Williams, Mellowes' driver, swiftly put their tank into reverse, the Sherman jolting backwards, engine growling, exhaust belching, dust kicking up. A charge fizzed towards them but exploded just ahead.

'Reverse another hundred yards,' Mellowes told Williams urgently.

Get out of panzerfaust range. More than that: get to a position where their own guns could be sufficiently depressed. A sudden, jolting explosion away to their right. O'Pray's tank hit by a panzerfaust. Thick, oily smoke and flames – angry fire almost instantly. Men jumping out, on fire – one, then another. Four in all, and all flaming. A burst of machine-gun fire and the crew cut down. A fifth crew member escaping through the smoke – and running, running towards the enemy. Revolver in hand, now standing at the edge of a slit-trench and firing before diving for cover.

It was Tommy Potts, O'Pray's driver – now waving at Mellowes, who in reply frantically indicated for him to duck back down. Potts understood, his head disappeared and Mellowes ordered his gunners to fire, the main gun with HE, the Brownings raking the positions with bullets. Enemy mortars now exploding. Corporal Tommy Spoors' crew on the net – their turret hit, getting Spoors in the eye. Mellowes ordered him to pull back and get medical help. This left him alone, but still he continued firing along the entire length of the enemy position, raking it with the Brownings. An order to his operator: two-second delays on the fuses of the HE. And to his gunner: bounce the shells short so they detonate as air bursts above the trenches. Now on the A net to Enderby. Assistance needed, urgently. Suddenly, bullets were raking the back of his tank. Frantically turning, he realized he was being fired on by a Sherman 500 yards behind – not Sherwood Rangers but men of the 4/7th Dragoon Guards. A tirade from Mellowes over the net. The firing stopped, but not before his bedding on the back of the tank had been riddled.

Soon after, ahead: a white handkerchief.

'Hände hoch, Schweinhund!' Mellowes shouted. More white handkerchiefs, and men cautiously emerging from their trenches out in the field. About sixty in all, hands raised. Mellowes now rumbled forward, picked up Tommy Potts and then, together, they hoisted the bullet-riddled and burned bodies of O'Pray and his crew and put them on the back of the tank. He then drove back through the woods and met up with Enderby and squadron HQ.

Mellowes felt numb with shock. Both Potts and Spoors were wounded; he thanked them for their loyalty and friendship, and wished them good luck before heading over to the bodies of the dead – men who had been alive and well earlier that day but were now no more. Bill Enderby came up to him and put an arm on his shoulder. After muttering a few words of sympathy, he told Mellowes that reinforcements were arriving and asked him to lead the next attack as well.

'All I could say,' recalled Mellowes, 'was "right". I then went and sat down by myself for a minute or two.'

Stuart Hills had been listening to this engagement on a loudspeaker at the mobile RHQ. Because Bill Enderby's troops were so spread out, Mellowes had been talking to him on the A net. It was common practice for the RHQ signals sergeant to fix this up to a loudspeaker so that the regimental command could all hear what was going on. And Hills had also heard Bill Enderby asking for help, initially in terms of support for Mellowes but then to sort out the prisoners.

'Get your section,' Hills told Sergeant Pothecary, 'we're going up.' Everyone enjoyed the opportunity to frisk prisoners for loot. By the time they got there, however, his friends Dick Holman and Denis Elmore were already at De Enk. 'I was damned annoyed,' admitted Hills, 'especially as Denis and Dick of all people had got there first!'

Meanwhile, David Render and his troop had taken the road to Zwiep and, skirting around the eastern edge of the same large wood, approached Lochem from the south-east. All was well until they emerged from the edge of the wood into open fields, with the River Berkel, which flowed into Lochem, on their right. Keen to get clear of the open ground as quickly as possible, he told his driver to speed up; but as he did so, the tracks started to slide and lose grip on the wet and soggy ground, and he stalled. Cursing, Render frantically scanned around for signs of any enemy anti-tank guns lurking behind hedgerows or buildings or trees. He could see nothing but the tank was stuck and wouldn't restart – and he wasn't going to hang around waiting to be shot up. So he gave the order for them to bail out.

They ran towards the woods, Fritz the dog bounding along with them. A machine gun opened fire from the far side of the river, then a shell screamed over, followed by several more. As they reached the edge of the woods, a further shell hit the tank in the turret, knocking off the cupola and hatches. The destruction of the tank certainly vindicated Render's decision to bail – but as they caught their breath, they realized that Fritz was no longer with them. 'He disappeared into the trees,' wrote Render, 'and didn't come back.'

When they eventually rejoined the rest of the squadron, Bill Enderby was seething and threatened to have Render court-martialled for needlessly abandoning his tank. Fortunately, at this point Ronnie Hutton intervened and managed to calm both men down, but although there was no more talk of charges, Render had been badly stung by the accusation. Later, once Lochem had been secured, they returned to the tank to try to salvage some of their kit, and from the damage they saw realized they wouldn't have stood a chance had they stayed inside. They also went looking for Fritz; but there was no sign of him. Their dog, who had brought so much companionship and solace, had gone. It was the end of a bad day for Render.

At least Peter Mellowes had not been needed again that day. With Lochem taken, new orders arrived for an early-morning attack on the Twente canal at Hengelo, a further 20 miles to the north-east and close to the German border once more. Off they set at 3.30 a.m. and in pitch darkness, in their battlegroup formation but with Hills's Recce Troop in the lead. There was no opposition at all on the way, but on reaching the canal they discovered the bridges had been blown, so Stanley Christopherson now asked Hills to recce the Delden lock, which was marked on their maps a couple of miles to the west, suggesting there might be a bridge there. Hills took the Dingo along with Sergeant John Pothecary and Corporal George Morris in their Stuarts.

Having found the right spot, they halted. The canal was banked by a raised dyke, and so Hills got out and walked across the open ground. A lone German soldier appeared silhouetted, then vanished. Cautiously, Hills clambered up the dyke and peered over, praying he would not be fired upon. There was no reaction at all. And there was the lock, with an island in the middle and a bridge spanning the canal. It was certainly wide enough for a vehicle, but appeared to have been partly blown a little over halfway across.

Hills knew he needed to find out more. Back at RHQ, they would want to know how wide the blown gap was, whether the bridge was capable of taking a tank, whether it was covered by enemy fire, whether it was mined. Hills thought for a moment and realized there was only one way to find out the answers to these questions: he would have to walk across it himself. 'My greatest fear throughout the whole of the campaign was that on some occasion I might be thought yellow by the men I commanded,' he wrote. 'I can honestly say from my heart that I would sooner die than let this happen and I knew that this was one of the occasions when I had to take the risk.' That didn't make the task any easier, however. There was no point in being overly cautious, he told himself. He just had to get on with it: get up, walk down to the bridge and head straight over it. He would be silhouetted against the dawn sky, and a clear target, but it couldn't be helped.

A deep breath, heart pounding. Down the bank he went. On to the bridge. When would the fatal shot ring out? He reached the gap. No sign of any mines, but the bridge was not remotely suitable for tanks; that much was obvious. The gap could probably be planked and used by infantry. He glanced around and saw Morris and Pothecary approaching, having followed him down.

'Have you looked at the opposite bank, sir?' whispered Morris. 'Because about two hundred yards away in the line of those trees, there are about two or three hundred Boche.' And so there were. How had the Germans not spotted them?

'Come on,' said Hills, 'we're getting out of this.' And then they ran for their lives, a few intermittent shots ringing out behind them.

They got back to their vehicles, panting and rather hot in their oversuits, then headed back to RHQ. Bill White, the colonel of the 12th KRRC, was there with Christopherson and wanted to go back and recce the bridge again. So off Hills went a second time, with White and one of the KRRC company commanders. This time, they didn't even reach the dyke before they were fired upon and had to make a dash for a farmhouse to shelter. Shots continued to ring out, but Hills was able to explain the lie of the land and relevant features.

'Well, come on,' said Colonel White eventually, 'we'll go one at a time and run like hell.' As they made a dash for it, a few inaccurate shots pinged and zipped nearby, and the company commander got caught on a barbed-wire fence. Trying to free himself, he tore his oversuit to shreds, but they all made it away unscathed and headed back to plan the attack.

Despite the enemy they'd seen, opposition was not expected to be heavy. The attack was to go in at 1 p.m.: B Company of the 12th KRRC leading, supported by two troops of Jack Holman's C Squadron. A fifteen-minute artillery stonk beforehand and liberal use of 4.2-inch mortars would also be laid on. It was hoped this would do the trick.

Sadly, it did not. Enemy machine guns, as well as artillery and mortars, stopped B Company's attack in its tracks. Over thirty casualties were suffered by the lead platoons, including two officers killed. With the crossing point so effectively covered, throwing more men into the attack would simply cause yet more casualties, so instead they withdrew and prepared to attack again at night. This, however, was later cancelled. Rather, the battlegroup would push east, take the town of Enschede from the south early the following morning, and from there capture Hengelo from the south-east.

It poured with rain on Tuesday, 3 April, but Enschede was swiftly taken. Padre Skinner found RHQ in the town later that morning. '*Robin Hood* in a factory yard trying to command a bit of battle somewhere in the town,' he noted in his diary, 'or at least keep in touch, while excited youngsters let off their high spirits at being liberated by swarming all over the tank.' Despite these distractions, they safely crossed over the troublesome Twente canal and moved on towards Hengelo, just a couple of miles to the north-west; by five that afternoon they had the town in their hands. 'Billeted in houses,' added Skinner, 'and in bed by 23.00. Slept like a log in a comfortable bed and woke feeling marvellous about 08.30.'

After a bit of mopping up north of the town, the regiment was given a few days' rest. 'News excellent,' wrote Skinner on Wednesday, 4 April. 'End will not be long now.' The regiment had passed through many newly liberated cities, but this was the first time they had entered a town and then remained there, and so were now for the first time witnessing scenes that had been, and were being, repeated throughout western Europe. A few houses down from where Skinner was billeted, for example, a sixteen-year-old Jewish girl emerged from an attic where she had been hidden for four years. 'This was the girl's first time out of the house in all that time,' he scribbled. 'The lads were almost awe-struck trying to realise what it meant, though they quite naturally showered the family with sweets and food.'

Yet there were ugly scenes, too. Jack Holman had been living in a large house that belonged to a collaborator who was subsequently imprisoned. He had a beautiful daughter, which Stanley Christopherson suspected was precisely why Holman had chosen this particular house. Then one morning, some local Dutch men turned up at the house, grabbed her and took her away. She returned a few hours later, her head shaved. Holman was horrified. Ernie Leppard witnessed such head-shaving scenes as he had first entered the town. 'We picked them up on our tank and drove them to the end of the road and let them go,' he said, ' 'cos they was being a bit, well – there's always a vicious element to anything like that.' He and his crew were billeted with a Dutch family and were invited to join them for dinner. 'All they had was one big pile of spuds,' he said, 'and that's all they'd lived on, potatoes, for weeks on end.'

It was Stuart Hills's twenty-first birthday on 5 April. What a year he had had as a twenty-year-old. Quite a fuss was made of him; a party was laid on at RHQ and a band brought in to play 'Happy Birthday'. They all had a sit-down meal and he was presented with a cheque for £10 to which the officers had contributed. The fitters also made him a beautifully crafted model rocket in recognition of all the 'rockets' he had been given from his superiors ever since joining the regiment. 'Altogether,' he remembered, 'it was a wonderful evening and I felt indeed that life was very good.'

They were not out of the woods, yet, however. Their next orders were to move out early on 9 April, heading across the border in their battle-group on an axis of advance that led directly to Bremen. Once again, the regiment had been bolstered by another intake of officers and men, including Peter Kent, a German Jew who had fled Nazi Germany before the war. Although interned at the start of the war, he was soon released; naturalized, he changed his name and eventually was sent to Sandhurst and commissioned. Kent took over as intelligence officer from Denis Elmore, now moved, at his request, to B Squadron; Christopherson rather dreaded the thought that Kent might be captured, and so decided to keep him at RHQ where he would be less exposed than others. After all, that Kent was serving with them at all was testimony to his courage.

On they went into Germany and to Lingen, a pretty Pied Piper German town of timber-framed houses and narrow streets, largely untouched. Then on to Planknorth and up behind the 4/7th Dragoon Guards at the next town, Herzlake. Through Herzlake early on 11 April, supporting the Wessexmen of 130th Brigade once more and now in the lead, pressing deep into northern Germany. Here the countryside was vast and flat and wide, field after field, farmsteads dotting the landscape between small villages and one town after another on the road to Bremen. But there were also large forests, dark with pine – the forests of Wagner and the Brothers Grimm – through which the road passed. German resistance was crumbling, but there were pockets still holding out: men with machine guns and submachine guns and grenades, and, worst of all for any British troops moving along this road, men with panzerfausts. The Germans had spent the war designing, building and operating an array of incredibly complex and sophisticated weaponry, but this simple, mass-produced tube of metal was ensuring there was no easy ride for the Sherwood Rangers or any other Allied troops advancing deep into Germany.

That day, B Squadron were leading, the rest of the regiment and infantry following, so they were first in line for any ambushes or roadblocks. The Germans were now resorting to guerrilla tactics. Usually, a tree would be felled across the road, and often booby-trapped. This meant the column had to stop, check it, defuse any device and then move it out of the way. As they set about doing so, enemy troops would attack from the dark of the forest either side. Most of these enemy troops would be killed or captured for their pains, but by then the damage was done: another tank left smouldering, more crew dead and wounded.

Ernie Leppard now had a new tank commander, Sergeant Freddie Jones, and also a new troop leader, Lieutenant Ken Hunt, straight out of Sandhurst. On that morning, however, it was Lieutenant Hubert Beddington's 4 Troop in the lead – or rather, it was until they were ambushed at a road block and mortared, leaving Beddington and three of his crew wounded. Lieutenant Hunt's troop now took the lead instead, although because he was new and inexperienced, Freddie Jones was asked to be point. Or rather: 'Wasn't asked,' said Ernie Leppard, 'bloody ordered to! And it's a single road, and you're leading and the whole bloody army's behind you.' Leading was a terrible job; it was almost certain that at some point they would be hit. It was the waiting, the tension, the wondering whether the next moment would be their last. The raw fear.

Immediately behind them were men of the 12th KRRC in Kangaroos. In the turret, Jones had his Sten at the ready while Leppard was also half out, grenades in his hand and clipped into his belt. Everyone scanning, searching, watching the forest. It was all right while they were out in the open, but west of the next town, Löningen, they entered another forest. Here they slowed right down so they could better see any danger. Then word came over the net for them to hurry up and stop crawling. Push on. Lieutenant Hunt was told to take over the lead. He acknowledged the order and sped past. Barely 100 yards further on, a German fired a panzerfaust from the side of the road, hitting the turret. It was always a shock to see: the explosion of sparks, the smoke, the knowledge that men were dead or badly wounded. Leppard saw only one man get out – his friend Charlie Stamp, the driver, who jumped down and dived to the side of the road.

The entire column now ground to a halt; never had the phrase 'more haste less speed' been more appropriate. An AVRE Churchill clanked forward and fired petards into the forest, then asked for some help getting the men out of the knocked-out Sherman up ahead. Jones ordered Leppard to go. But Leppard didn't fancy sitting exposed on the back of a Churchill, so jumped down on to the road and, half-crouching, hurried forward, straining his eyes into the woods. Suddenly, 50 yards on, he spotted a young German kid with a stick grenade. For a moment, they looked at each other and then the boy threw it. 'He just chucked it,' said Leppard, 'but he hadn't armed it.' It landed inert and Leppard dashed back to his own tank to tell them to brass up the woods. While HE and machine-gun fire were blasting the left-hand side of the wood, Leppard ran on up to the stricken Sherman. The Churchill was already alongside by the time he reached Hunt's smoking tank, the air cloying and thick with the stench of smoke and explosive, but he clambered up on to the back and looked inside the turret. It was a mess. Hunt was dead, so too his gunner, Trooper Alfred Tyler. The operator had lost both legs but was still alive. Somehow they pulled him out, amid the blood and the shattered bodies. 'And I think at that point,' admitted Leppard, 'I'd lost my nerve. I'd been all right up to then, but getting them out . . .'

While the dead and wounded were sent back down the line, Leppard went to look for his mate, Charlie Stamp. He moved round to the front of the tank and then saw a slit-trench at the side of the road and realized, to his shock, that there were still Germans in there, trying to keep hidden. Leppard pointed his revolver at them, then remembered to his horror that the chamber was empty. This did not do his nerves much good. The game was clearly up, however, and the Germans got to their feet and put their hands in the air. Leppard searched them, took some money and a wristwatch, and began marching them back. Hugh McDonald, a big Scot and a heavyweight boxer, made a lunge for them and would have knocked them down, but was restrained by Lieutenant Gaiger, his troop leader. McDonald's anger was more than understandable. Just what the hell were these Germans doing? Why were they still fighting? Why were men in the Sherwood Rangers still being killed when everyone knew the war was all but over?

Leppard had not found Stamp; he hoped his friend was all right. By now it was getting late. They pressed on and reached Löningen, leaguering up for the night in a field at the edge of town. It had been a dull, sullen, overcast day and it was a dull, sullen, overcast evening. Padre Skinner buried Tyler and Hunt beside the road at the edge of the wood; goodness, he'd dug some graves since landing on D-Day more than ten months earlier. Suddenly, two Germans appeared, fully armed but wanting to surrender. Then a couple more, and before he knew it, there were fourteen of them. 'All I could do was order them to carry their arms at the trail,' he noted, 'except for the leading two men who kept their hands high above their heads, lest some enterprising British soldier started shooting.' Some fitters, seeing this small column, came running over and immediately disarmed them.

Later that evening, Ernie Leppard finally caught up with his friend Charlie Stamp, who had managed to get clear of the enemy and scamper back to safety. He was in a bit of a state, though. Lieutenant Hunt had been the fifth of his troop leaders who'd been killed. 'I've had enough,' he told Leppard. 'The fifth is enough. I can't go on any more.' He had badly grazed his leg escaping and so he now grabbed some cow dung and rubbed it into the wound. 'That'll go septic soon,' he told Leppard, 'and I'll get sent back.'

The following day, it was C Squadron's turn to take the lead. The next town to sweep through was Lastrup, and intelligence reports suggested it was clear. It was not, however. The first tank sped through but was shot at. Following behind was Harry Budner, another stalwart sergeant of the regiment; his tank was hit by a panzerfaust and he and Trooper Arthur Young were killed. Every day on this run through Germany a few more Sherwood Rangers were losing their lives. The attack on Budner's tank led to a more methodical clearing of the town, and while this was going on Regimental Headquarters and a company of the 12th KRRC took a detour around the north of the town. They soon became hopelessly lost. Stanley Christopherson blamed the quality of the maps, which had been hastily produced on the basis of inadequate information, but in fact they had clearly simply taken a wrong turn. Christopherson's go-to person when it came to matters of orientation was his friend Chris Sedgwick of the Essex Yeomanry; Stanley believed that, as a gunner, he would have a greater appreciation of the lie of the land and map-reading. On this occasion, however, Sedgwick became rather irritated by the endless appeals as to where they were and how they could get back to the main road. 'For all I know,' he said eventually, 'we may be in Burma.' Needless to say, they eventually righted themselves, and continued on their way towards the next town – Cloppenburg.

This unremarkable place was just 40-odd miles from Bremen. The town was not big, but was more substantial than any they'd yet encountered since crossing over the German border, and an important road and railway hub. It was now Friday, 13 April – not an auspicious date. A Squadron were leading as they reached the town at around six-thirty in the morning. One tank was knocked out by an SP at the edge of town; then B Squadron went past them and on into the town with a battalion of infantry. Cloppenburg was defended by *Fallschirmjäger*, who had destroyed most of the bridges over the narrow River Soeste and seemed determined to fight on for the northern half of the town. Fortunately, one bridge had not been sufficiently blown and so one troop was able to get across.

Street fighting was never easy, and especially not against men hiding with panzerfausts, machine guns and sniper rifles. Terry Leinster, now second-in-command of B Squadron, couldn't help laughing as he heard Corporal Hugh McDonald cursing on the net. 'Every time I put my loaf out for a shufti,' said McDonald, 'some fucker draws a bead on me. I'm getting right fed up with it.'

Freddie Jones, meanwhile, had led a troop south around the town and on to a very low hill that overlooked the road heading out of Cloppenburg towards Bremen. There were two large hayricks on this rise which offered an ideal place from which to watch the road and also provided a bit of cover. As they approached, however, they discovered a number of German paratroopers had had the same idea. Ernie Leppard was manning the Browning in the turret and sprayed the haystacks, but German troops kept popping up and taking pot-shots and trying to fire panzerfausts. Leppard had loosed off an entire box of ammunition – but the Browning jammed on the last bullet. 'Then some silly bugger stepped out with a panzerfaust straight at us,' he said. 'So, we fired the 17-pounder at him. He was only twenty yards in front – blew him to smithereens and then at that, the whole lot surrendered.'

Difficult fighting continued in the town late into the afternoon, although the B Squadron crews, increasingly impatient, took to blasting anything that moved. Some Churchill III AVREs with their flying dustbins also helped, demolishing buildings suspected of housing snipers. No one was in a particularly compassionate mood. Lieutenant Dick Hyde's troop got caught up in fighting at the eastern end of the town. Sergeant Harry Sage had his tank brewed up by a panzerfaust, killing him along with Trooper George Fletcher. Sage had been with the regiment since before the war. He'd been through the whole damned thing – Middle East, North Africa, D-Day and north-west Europe. Two more men, Ernie Holland and Jack Snedker from John Cropper's crew, were also killed, cut down by machine-gun fire while foolishly trying to get some loot from a dead German on the road.

Freddie Jones's troop had been called in to help Dick Hyde's tanks clear the town from the east. They trundled down and over the net were ordered to knock out a particular building. Only once they'd blown apart the back wall did they realize it was a bank. Clambering down and picking their way through the wreckage, they discovered a vault with a safe. They couldn't angle a tank gun on to it, though; on the other hand, nor could they simply leave a safe standing there before them untouched. Then someone remembered there was a stash of captured panzerfausts back at the haystacks. One was duly fetched and brought down to the vault, along with a German prisoner who was ordered to fire the weapon at the safe. 'Of course,' said Leppard, 'it makes a nice round hole and everything inside's destroyed. So, our bank job come to nothing.'

CHAPTER 32

War's End

NAZI GERMANY WAS COLLAPSING. By 6 April, Red Army troops were in the suburbs of Vienna, while to the north Königsberg, once the jewel of the Baltic and the capital of East Prussia, was captured by the Soviets on 9 April. The final battle for Berlin was launched 30 miles to the east of the city on the 16th. As British bombers continued to pound the capital, British forces were sweeping into northern Germany. At the same time, the US armies – Simpson's Ninth and Hodges's First – began encircling the Ruhr, the industrial heartland of Germany; by the time their troops met on 14 April, the German Army Group B had completely collapsed and a staggering 317,000 men had been captured. On the 15th, its commander, Feldmarschall Walter Model, took himself to a quiet wood and blew his brains out. Allied advances also overran several of the Nazi horror camps, US forces reaching Buchenwald on 12 April and British troops Bergen-Belsen three days later. To the south, meanwhile, in Italy, General Mark Clark launched his final Allied offensive on the 10th.

Hitler had promised a thousand-year Reich or Armageddon, and it was the latter that Germany now faced. He had no intention of surrendering; rather, Germany was to fight to the very end, and still, at this moment of total collapse, there were troops prepared to fulfil his wish and fight on. Some were fanatics, others believed they had no choice; and so now, in mid-April 1945, as the noose was drawn ever tighter around the Third Reich, Germany was aflame and total defeat lay around the corner, still, ridiculously, the fighting continued, with all the terrible loss of life that came with it.

And the Sherwood Rangers were not exempt from that fighting. Their target now remained the northern city of Bremen, although after two days' pause following the capture of Cloppenburg, on 16 April they moved to the town of Bassum, 20 miles south of Bremen, where they came under command of 3rd Division. This had been Montgomery's division back in France in 1940, and had landed at Sword Beach on D-Day; the Sherwood Rangers had now supported every single infantry division in Second Army and three American divisions since the previous June, and travelled thousands of miles in so doing. They had also all seen many changes, not least technologically. New, bigger battle tanks such as the British Comet and American Pershing had entered service in these final stages of the war, while on 16 April the Sherwood Rangers were given a demonstration of new tank rockets. These were fixed to the turret and could be fired straight ahead; the idea was to have the destructive capability of a Churchill AVRE without the need for the Churchill itself.

Such new gizmos were not to be part of their arsenal in the battle for Bremen, however, and on the next day, Tuesday, 17 April, the regiment headed north. By nightfall the following day they had secured Sturh, a village at the south-west edge of Bremen, and then, early on Thursday 19th, C Squadron and the 2nd Lincolns pushed on broadly northwards towards the suburb of Mittelschuchting; frustratingly, it was impossible to avoid either the outlying villages or the main roads, because on their right flank was the low-lying flood plain of the River Weser. Like so much of this vast, flat swathe of north-west Europe, the ground here was saturated and impassable to vehicles. As C Squadron and the Lincolns advanced, they shot up a number of poorly trained German troops and captured around seventy prisoners, while A Squadron with the 2nd Royal Ulster Rifles also pushed north. Both the quality and the determination of resistance were markedly diminishing.

There was now a palpable sense that the end was near, and neither tank men nor infantry were taking too many chances. The tanks, with infantry on foot beside them, blasted houses and sprayed anything that moved with machine guns as they pushed slowly, cautiously, on. Peter Mellowes was once again in the lead tank of the lead troop, advancing north down a fairly narrow road. The infantry were walking on either side of them, with another platoon a couple of hundred yards ahead acting as an advance guard. Orders reached him to turn left, to the west. Suddenly, a platoon commander came running back and Mellowes realized he wanted to speak to him, so he ordered his driver to stop and the lieutenant clambered up on to the tank. Up ahead, he told Mellowes, about 400 yards further on, was a crossroads, and on it was a large house heavily defended by Germans, who were clearly expecting an attack from the west and certainly not the east. The infantry lieutenant reckoned there was a great chance of getting behind them before the enemy even realized they were there.

As Mellowes drew nearer the crossroads, he saw an orchard on his right, so moved into it. 'I found I was about fifty yards directly behind them,' he wrote. 'They were dug into the road embankment with anti-tank guns, machine-guns and mortars.' This position stretched all along the road facing westwards either side of the crossroads, and as the panicked enemy troops began to realize what was happening, Mellowes immediately gave orders to his troop to open fire, smashing the German guns with their 75s and 17-pounders and hosing the infantry with the Brownings. It was a massacre – a short, sharp explosion of carnage in which hundreds of enemy troops were cut down. When there appeared to be no one else to shoot, Mellowes ordered a ceasefire. As suddenly as they had opened fire, their guns were now silent. An eerie quiet descended on the scene.

With the infantry, they picked their way forward to see if there were any survivors, but found none. Mellowes was horrified to discover most of the dead were merely boys, perhaps sixteen or seventeen. This was what it had come to: boys being pushed into the firing line, with next to no training, and then slaughtered. Returning to his tank, Mellowes reported in over the radio and was told to remain where he was and consolidate. Several hours later, a troop from B Squadron arrived, led by Denis Elmore. It was now around four-thirty that Thursday afternoon. Mellowes went over to talk to him, explained what had happened at the crossroads, and Elmore told him he had been ordered to push on northwards to cut the road between Deldenhorst and Mittelschuchting that led directly to the eastern part of Bremen.

Elmore had fixed a small model aeroplane on to the front of his Sherman. There was a breeze that day, so the propeller was whirring; Mellowes was rather struck by the toy. Moments later, Elmore and his troop were on their way. The road north stretched straight for perhaps 300 yards then turned on a right-hand bend. Mellowes watched them head off and saw Elmore's tank disappear around the corner out of sight. And then he heard a loud explosion.

Stuart Hills had been at Regimental HQ all day, which at this point was based alongside 9th Brigade Headquarters near Seckenhausen, a few miles to the south. There was not much for him or his Recce Troop to do, so he had been smoking, drinking tea and listening in on the RHQ radio. Later in the afternoon, however, he decided to head off in his Dingo and visit the forward troops to see how things were going. He was racing along the road north towards Sturh and fast approaching Peter Mellowes' crossroads when he saw Frenchie Houghton.

'I'm afraid Richard Hyde has just had it up the road,' Houghton told him. 'His vehicle's been completely brewed up.'

Immediately, Hills felt his heart quicken. 'What was the code sign?' he asked.

'A1,' Houghton replied.

'That's not Richard Hyde,' said Hills. 'It's Denis.'

Hills told his driver to keep going; he felt a growing emptiness inside him and his mouth becoming drier. A tank was coming towards him with wounded on the back. Hills flagged it down.

'What happened?' he asked. 'Is it Mr Elmore's tank?'

'We were hit by an eighty-eight, sir, right through the turret,' one of the wounded men told him. 'Mr Elmore's had it.'

Hills's stomach felt as though it were completely turning over.

'Can anyone get near the tank?' he asked.

'No, sir,' came the reply. 'It's burning like hell and all the rounds are exploding all over the place.'

'There's positively no chance of him having got out?'

'None whatever, sir.'

At this, Hills ordered his driver to turn around and drop him back at RHQ. Once there, he took himself off to spend the next few hours alone. He felt utterly bereft, grief-stricken by the violent loss of his oldest and greatest friend, a loss somehow made worse because the war was so nearly over. 'My troop were wonderful to me,' Hills recorded, 'and I have never experienced such kindness. So were the officers in RHQ. But I really felt as though I never wanted to speak again.'

At RHQ everyone was stunned by Elmore's death; he'd been a hugely popular man and a much-valued intelligence officer. It was a hard blow for Stanley Christopherson, too; Elmore had been a first-class IO and there was absolutely no need for him to move to a sabre squadron. Yet Denis had pleaded with him to be given a troop to command before it was all over, and Christopherson had not felt it was his right to stop him. In any case, they badly needed a few more men with experience in the squadrons. The colonel said a few words that night, then congratulated the padre on being mentioned in dispatches for the second time. A bottle of champagne was produced and opened for them all to have a drink – a toast to both Denis and Skinner.

Elmore was not the only member of the crew killed in this attack; both the gunner and the operator, Troopers Charlie Harkness and Denis Miles, also lost their lives. Thankfully, at least theirs were the last deaths for a few days. On the 20th the squadrons pushed further northwards, cut the road into Bremen and reached the railway that ran west–east into the city, taking a further 200 prisoners including the commander of the SS Lehr Bataillon. More prisoners of war kept coming in throughout the night. Then the regiment was out of the line for a couple of days, their time with 3rd Division over. Plans were afoot for Bomber Command to plaster Bremen and then to demand the city's surrender; if the bombing failed to do the trick, however, the regiment would be going in with the 43rd Wessexmen again.

On the 21st, once Denis Elmore's tank had sufficiently cooled, Padre Skinner managed to recover the bodies and bury them. The following day, with the regiment still at rest, he was asked by the Senior Chaplain of 43rd Division to find a suitable location for a divisional cemetery to serve the Bremen area. Having found this and marked it out, he then had to go off and exhume the bodies from Elmore's tank and rebury them. 'Went into outskirts of Bremen seeking wood for crosses,' he noted. 'German civilians and many slave workers of different nationalities looting quite a bit.'

That same day, having been in a state of numb shock since the loss of his friend, Stuart Hills sat down to write to Elmore's mother. 'I loved him better than anyone else in the world,' he told her, his raw grief bursting off the page, 'so I know just how you feel, and the bottom has been knocked out of my world. His popularity in the regiment both with officers and the men was so great, that a sort of shadow seems to have beset us all – in spite of the fact that we have all become hardened to death.' He told her that Denis had every quality that was best in a man. He was so very sorry and sent his deepest sympathy. If there was anything at all he could do for her, he would. 'The supreme sacrifice, as Denis and I always remarked to each other,' he added, 'was "the luck of the game", and Denis had made it 'very, very nobly; he will never be forgotten'.

How hard it was to bear, all these terrible losses. Stanley Christopherson wrote to Mrs Elmore too, as did Padre Skinner, and as did Myrtle Kellett, just as they had every time a man had been killed. They did the

same for Troopers Miles and Harkness too, although it made a big difference when they knew the men personally, as Christopherson and Skinner
had known Elmore. Christopherson acknowledged just how inseparably
linked Denis had been with Hills and Dick Holman, and how hard his
loss had hit them both. 'But as I told them,' he wrote to her, 'Denis had so
much good in him that such goodness simply can't just end – it must go
on in some form.'

Some 767 aircraft were sent by Bomber Command to hammer Bremen,
although because of heavy cloud and because it was known that XXX
Corps were south of the city ready to attack, the raid was stopped after 195
bombers dropped their loads lest they hit their own troops. The Sherwood
Rangers were 15 miles to the south, but close enough to witness the bombardment for themselves. Peter Mellowes clearly heard the air raid sirens
and saw searchlights criss-crossing the sky. He heard the bombers, too,
thundering over, then the bombs exploding and the anti-aircraft guns firing. 'It seemed very strange,' he wrote, 'to have a grandstand view of what
was going on.' Despite the curtailing of the raid, 3,664 houses were
destroyed or damaged and 172 civilians killed; even at this late stage in the
war, city officials were still studiously keeping records.

Predictably, the German garrison did not surrender, and so the attack
went in the next day with 3rd Division and the 52nd Lowland taking the
lead. Not until the 26th were the Sherwood Rangers called upon, supporting the Wessexmen once more as they attacked from the south-east of the
city. Opposition was light, much to everyone's relief; it was the first time in
action where Peter Mellowes' troop did not suffer a single casualty. Progress was still slow, however; Stuart Hills reckoned it was because most of
the troops on the ground and in the tanks realized the war was all but over
and were no longer willing to take unnecessary risks. 'The civilians seemed
very subdued and abnormally frightened of us,' noted Hills. 'They seemed
very surprised when we didn't shoot them on the spot.' It was no wonder
they were frightened. Their city lay in ruins, so did the entire country.
They were the vanquished, their world destroyed, the future – if they had
one – unknowably grim.

Ernie Leppard was in action – as was his pal, Charlie Stamp, whose leg
had healed unexpectedly and unwantedly quickly, thanks to the cow dung.
'I've never known a cure like it,' he admitted sheepishly to Leppard. That
day, they and the rest of B Squadron helped capture General Fritz Becker,
the commander of the Bremen garrison. Holed up in a big command

bunker, Becker found himself completely surrounded. 'All our tanks lined up round it,' said Leppard, 'all pointed at the command post, and then the little white flag come out.' Soon afterwards General Becker and his staff emerged, although he refused to surrender to Lieutenant Talbot, Leppard's latest troop leader, so they had to fetch Ian McKay, the squadron leader and a major. When McKay demanded the general's binoculars, Becker smashed the lenses before handing them over. 'Most unsporting,' said Leppard, 'but they were led off and then it was a free for all in looting this German high command blockhouse.' Leppard scrounged 10,000 Turkish cigarettes and 2,000 cigars; he wasn't a smoker himself, but he reckoned he could make a bob or two from them.

Bremen had finally fallen, and for no losses at all to the Sherwood Rangers, although the following day, as they cleared the last pockets of resistance, Trooper Arthur Harris was tragically killed when a shell exploded in the breech; such accidents did very occasionally happen. It was 27 April, and the end was very near; yet a palpably sinister, violent atmosphere remained in the city even after its capture. Stanley Christopherson saw Soviet slave workers running amok, and the Allied troops also found a number of large mansions in the suburbs, largely untouched, where entire families, children included, had committed suicide – or rather, the parents had murdered their sons and daughters and then taken their own lives.

On the 29th, they pushed on north-eastwards into the countryside between Bremen and Hamburg. A patchwork of fields, small, pleasant woods and quiet villages. In Buchholz, they were told a German officer had executed nine of his men for wanting to surrender. The locals had tried to lynch him, but he had escaped and fled. What madness it all was. On they went, tanks and infantry together, through villages such as Harpstedt, Tamstedt, Bedhamm and Hanstedt, all captured with little resistance.

But not entirely without opposition. Peter Mellowes was leading his troop with infantry behind when a mine suddenly went off, blowing to pieces the Kangaroo and with it the KRRC men inside, and creating a huge crater. The mine had been fashioned from a large Luftwaffe bomb and designed to detonate only after a number of vehicles had passed over it. At any rate, the road was now impassable and the ground either side too soft, so the engineers were called up to bridge the hole. Stanley Christopherson now came on the radio asking what the situation was. Mellowes explained and was told to press on with his troop alone. 'We now knew that these mines had been laid and there was no means of knowing where the next one would be,' noted Mellowes. 'Not a very happy thought.' He made it, though, and the next day, along with the 4th Dorsets, they captured Rhade, more than 30 miles from Bremen. It was now 1 May 1945. The day before, in Berlin, with Red Army soldiers swarming around the capital, Hitler had shot himself in his bunker beneath the Reichskanzlei.

The following day, Wednesday, 2 May, the Sherwood Rangers suffered their last death of the war. The area round about them now was again low-lying and sodden, much of it boggy, peaty ground. Roads had been blown and booby-traps and mines laid. Progress was slow as engineers tried to pick a way through or fill in and bridge craters. Trooper Lawrence Carter was in A1 Echelon, but along with a military policeman was trying to direct traffic around a crater when they were both shot and killed by a sniper. 'Buried both by roadside,' recorded the indefatigable Skinner.

The next day, the regiment crossed the Hame–Ooste canal and took the pretty village of Karlshöfen without opposition. It was a small farming community with a number of large, brick-built eighteenth- and nineteenth-century houses and barns, as well as a church and war memorial to those from the village killed in the previous war. Its houses and plentiful barns and yards made it an ideal place to set up RHQ. What's more, just 6 miles to the north-east, men from the 8th Armoured Brigade had discovered Stalag X-B, a German POW camp, at Sandbostel. The camp had been divided, and while the 15,000 POWs found there were in a pitiful enough condition, a further 8,000 inmates of the section designated a concentration camp were in an utterly horrifying state – emaciated, disease-ridden, lying in their own excrement. The liberators began referring to Sandbostel as 'Little Belsen'. A huge relief operation began, and Stanley Christopherson was able to contribute to the lorries and medical teams now doing their frantic best to save as many lives as possible. The horrors discovered at Sandbostel were a reminder, if any were needed, of why they had needed to fight the war.

At Karlshöfen, however, the sun was shining. Summer was on its way. The three large oak trees at the mouth of the farm's entrance were just starting to come into leaf. There was dust amid the cobbled stones that led to the large old farmhouse Christopherson had chosen as his own billet. Jeeps, Dingos and lorries were parked up in the yard, as were *Robin Hood* and *Maid Marion* and the other RHQ tanks. The village had a touch of Englishness about it – an architectural style and leafy ambience reminiscent of Lincolnshire and parts of Norfolk – and it was blissfully intact. Really, there was little sign of the war at all, and nothing whatever to suggest the horrors of Sandbostel just a few miles across the fields.

Brigadier Prior-Palmer called in for tea that afternoon to brief Christopherson on the next operation, which was an assault on the coastal port of Bremerhaven. Once again, the brigade was to be supporting the 43rd Wessex Division. After Prior-Palmer had left, the rest of the afternoon and evening was spent making plans. Around 8.30 p.m. Christopherson was summoned from the farmhouse to *Robin Hood*, where he was told an important message had arrived for him from Brigade HQ. Sergeant William Pick was waiting for him and handed over a scrap of paper torn from an exercise book.

'This message has just come over the air from Brigade Headquarters,' Pick told him. He looked flushed and a little agitated.

Christopherson's first thought was one of slight irritation at the scrap of paper and badly handwritten scrawl. Then he read the words that had been written down. '*No advance beyond present positions. Stop. No further harassing fire. Stop. No further tactical move unless ordered. Stop. BBC News Flash confirmed. Stop. German Army on 21 Army Group front surrenders WEF 08.00 hrs 5 May 1945. Stop. Details as to procedure later. Stop.*'

The war was over.

'My first reaction,' he noted, 'was a feeling of profound relief, followed by indescribable exhilaration, and finally a sorrowful longing for those special friends, no longer with us, with whom I wished to share this moment.' It was, none the less, a moment for celebration. A large stock of captured champagne had been given to them by the 51st Highland Division after crossing the Rhine, and this was now brought up and many bottles opened – and drunk.

Stuart Hills had been out with his troop that afternoon and it was getting dark as he headed back to RHQ in his Dingo. Suddenly, hundreds of brightly coloured Very lights were shooting up into the air like fireworks.

'That's either a signal for a night attack,' he said to his driver, Bert Crowhurst, 'or else peace has been declared. Step on it and we'll find out.'

At RHQ, it was mayhem, the party already in full swing. Hills felt stunned with relief and overwhelming joy – but then, after about half an hour or so, he missed Denis more than at any other moment and so he left the celebrations and went to bed.

David Render was also feeling a little subdued after the initial euphoria.

He had survived; he'd made it through, against all the odds, and despite so many very close shaves with death. Before joining the others, he remained a while out in the cool night air and thought of Sergeant-Major Henry Hutchinson and so many others who had not survived and who now lay under a thin layer of soil in makeshift cemeteries from Normandy to northern Germany. And he thought especially of Harry Heenan, his great friend, who had saved his life back in September, then been killed himself just after.

B Echelon was leaguered in the same village. 'The euphoria was tremendous,' noted Arthur Reddish. Like David Render, he was a survivor, although having joined up back in 1940, he'd been in the game a lot longer. Five years later, it was all over and he was still alive to celebrate. 'It was a great feeling,' he added. He certainly drank his fill that night.

Stuart Hills woke the next day in a bed with sheets and with the sun pouring through the windows and birdsong filling the air. They had all been waiting so long for this morning. 'No more death, shooting or loud explosions,' he noted. 'We could rise from our beds and go to breakfast without fear of being blown to bits. Everything that for so long had held us down and ruled our lives had now been shattered in an instant and we were free – we were at peace.'

Namen	Vornamen	Wohnort	Wohnung	Geburts-datum bzw. Alter	Das wie-vielte Kind	Eheftands-darlehen benötigt (ja) versagt (nein)

53 A H GB. CP. JK. — Location.

Helop 16 a min repair to obtacle will be ready in 15 mn. Mafis repair ready by 1900 hrs. for vehicles like ourselves.

OP Mess. 041500 B

act VEF

AQ28 ⊙ Sh card 1.550 ⊙ AF CN AQ CE BF DF JA AN FK HM HM FD⊙ To report to Molar minor less HQ at 1000 hrs tomorrow to be interviewed by Pro to JN D1 HP FG.

Sgt Hughs ll   30 Corps

            XSS to goal

041500 B   AF CN JA LH D CO BF DF F1 EB AL HM BN HP admitted hospital yesterday. LH 7 HAMs 4 DORs. Remedy to obstacle now OK. HKQ and XQZ are over complete. your location order children's locations. No advance on before present forces No further removing fire No practical move outlet further orders BBC news confirmed, German army in front Surrender at 0800, details of procedure will follow. 988170

tr. 179
arel. Herm. Bümmann, Bremervörde.

The last "War" Message from Brigade Head Quarters received over the wireless in my Tank "Robin Hood" announcing the end of the war in Europe.

Men of C Squadron: *centre*, with accordion, is John Bennett

Postscript

THE WAR IN EUROPE was over; but the Sherwood Rangers were not going home any time soon. A victory parade in Bremerhaven before General Horrocks was followed by a posting to Hanover; Germany was wrecked, and British troops were needed to guard the hundreds of thousands of prisoners and also the many 'displaced persons' camps, as well as to keep order in a country that had suddenly and dramatically been liberated from twelve years of totalitarian rule. In June they moved again, this time to Magdeburg and then in July to Einbeck. In between, there were trips through the ruins of the Reich; Stanley Christopherson, for example, visited the horror camp at Belsen and also made a trip to Berlin, where he saw the wreckage of the Reichskanzlei and Hitler's bunker.

The wider war had not yet ended, moreover, and Christopherson volunteered the regiment to head to Burma. Allied concerns about the ongoing fight against Imperial Japan had clouded the great victory against Nazi Germany, not least because the closer the Americans got to the Japanese home islands, the harder the enemy had been fighting. Peleliu, Iwo Jima and Okinawa had become bywords for brutal slaughter; Okinawa had been the bloodiest battle yet in the war, which was saying something. Allied planners were expecting an invasion of Japan to cost millions of lives and take the war into 1946.

Yet in the end it did not come to that. A top-secret project to build an atomic bomb had been completed at the end of July, and the two bombs subsequently dropped on Hiroshima and Nagasaki finally brought about a Japanese surrender on 15 August. The Sherwood Rangers were not needed in the Far East after all. Instead, in September, they were dismounted for a second time, losing their tanks. The writing was on the wall for the future of the regiment, and on 2 February 1946 Field Marshal Montgomery personally wrote to Christopherson to tell him the Sherwood Rangers were to be broken up and 'dispersed'. On 1 March 1946 the regiment ceased to exist.

Theirs had been an astonishing journey. They had begun the war as weekend part-time soldiers, then had been sent overseas on their horses, had performed cavalry charges with sabres drawn, had been converted to artillery, had survived the Siege of Tobruk, had been mechanized and had turned themselves into one of the finest armoured regiments in the British Army. During the war, they amassed an astonishing thirty battle honours, sixteen of them since D-Day: more than any other single unit ever in the entire British Army. Stanley Christopherson, who had commanded the regiment since that dark day on 11 June, had taken part in every single one of those thirty battles. For a man who had never had any burning desire to be a full-time soldier, he'd done rather well, winning a DSO, two Military Crosses and an American Silver Star as well as being mentioned in dispatches four times.

On one occasion during the war in north-west Europe, he'd been sheltering in a slit-trench, trying to make himself as small as possible, and feeling wet, cold and frightened as shells rained down. 'I made three resolutions,' he later wrote, 'which I was determined to keep after the war – should I survive. First, never to be bored; second, never to be frightened again; and third, when slowly submerging into a steaming hot bath, to say, "Thank God for this Hot Bath – Amen."'

After the Sherwood Rangers were disbanded, many of the men were posted to other regiments. Arthur Reddish ended up in the 11th Hussars until he was finally sent back to England in July 1946. He was eventually demobbed in October that year, but not before the Sherwood Rangers were granted the Freedom of the City of Nottingham in a grand parade in September. There was a full muster of survivors, and Reddish found himself marching between his old friend John Savage and Major John Semken. 'The reunion that followed was marvellous,' he wrote. 'But there were some terrible gaps in the ranks.'

In all, the Sherwood Rangers lost 148 men killed and 299 wounded just in the eleven months since D-Day, a tally of casualties which amounted to some 40 per cent of the entire regiment and 150 per cent of the total serving in tanks at any one time. It was a hideously large number. Now those who had survived had to come to terms with civilian life. Stanley Christopherson was at rather a loss to start off with. It was hard, having had so many people to look after and so much to think about, suddenly to have neither. Nor was there to be any future life with Myrtle Kellett, no matter how brightly and briefly a flame had burned in those final months of the war. She remarried in February 1946, continuing to play a very full part in the Regimental Welfare Association, which went on supporting veterans and their families for years to come. She even led a tour of the battlefields and cemeteries to pay her respects to fallen men of the regiment. Thousands of letters survive from Myrtle and those who helped with the association. Forces charities continue to play a vital role, but in the immediate post-war years the welfare state was only just coming into being, and for many the transition to peacetime life was difficult and painful. Myrtle offered help to George Dring, for example, who spent too long trying to claim from the War Office the pension he was due for his second Military Medal.

Others survived only to face tragedy back at home. Corporal John Sadler, for example, had been wounded in early October 1944. At the time, his wife had been frantic with worry about him and the lack of news following the usual stark telegram. She had appealed to the Welfare Association, who had swiftly discovered where he was being tended and details of the extent of his wound. Sadler recovered and was reunited with his wife; but in September 1945 she became ill and tragically died. 'She has been a grand mate and mother,' he wrote, 'and I can only repeat that I will miss her very much, as half my life is her too.' Life could be very cruel.

It was also very tough for Henry Hutchinson's widow, who had only her inadequate war widow's pension to fall back upon, with two children to bring up and look after. Once again, the Welfare Association was able to help, finding her son a place at a prep school in Grantham for which they paid the fees. In a world in which both veterans and bereaved families were largely left to fend for themselves, the Welfare Association and the wider Sherwood Rangers community provided much-needed support.

Recognizing this, many of the officers' families, especially, made donations and continued to do so after the war. At Christmas 1945, for example, Peter Selerie sent Myrtle Kellett a cheque for £3 10s, the proceeds from a raffle his mother had held. He was still recovering from his wounds, but making good progress and now able to write with his left hand instead of his right. 'I have been fortunate in being granted Xmas leave,' he told her.

'As a matter of fact, this is the only Xmas – with the exception of 1943 – that I have spent with my people since 1938.'

Selerie recovered sufficiently to be able to enjoy a full life. Invalided out of the army in 1946, he worked for a company that owned a number of pubs, hotels and restaurants; here he gradually built up an expert knowledge of wine, and spent the rest of his working life as a wine and spirits dealer. He became managing director or chief executive of various concerns, including Hedges & Butler and the Hampstead Wine Company, the latter growing to some sixty outlets. He married and had three children, his eldest, Gavin, becoming an acclaimed poet. Selerie kept in touch with Stanley Christopherson and others from the regiment, and remained rightly proud of his time in the Sherwood Rangers and of his war service. He passed away in July 1989 aged seventy-two; his funeral service was conducted by Leslie Skinner.

Bill Wharton also recovered from his wounds and, reunited with his wife and daughter, never had any cause to part from them again. He took on the family printing business started by his father, and he and Marion had two more children, a son and a daughter. He died in 1986, still with bits of shrapnel inside him. Stan Perry also recovered, briefly rejoined the Sherwood Rangers in Germany, then stayed in the army and ended up as the adjutant of a POW camp for German prisoners near Weston-super-Mare in the West Country – with two senior officers above him who rarely showed up for work, which left him in effective charge. 'I had 3,000 German prisoners under command,' he said, 'and there I had a whale of a time. I lived like a king.' He later worked for a printing firm in Copenhagen in Denmark; after that, he and his wife returned to England and he worked for Unilever. He kept up with a number of old comrades, not least George Dring, whom he used to meet in a pub for lunch every month after they both retired. Dring had not found life easy – and not just because of the loss of his fingers; he was also haunted by his experiences, and for years afterwards refused to talk about the war. Having been so used to stalking Panthers and Tigers, he later became scared of walking alone at night. Immediately after the war, Dring worked with POWs, learning German and French in the process, and later for the immigration service. Cancer got him in the end. 'His last month was very sad,' said Perry. 'I was very pleased I was able to go and visit him every day.'

Arthur Reddish badly missed the camaraderie he'd experienced during the war and struggled to settle down. After the war, he briefly rekindled a relationship with Claire but, perhaps inevitably, it didn't work out, and she eventually drifted back to her husband. Then, in 1949, he saw an advertisement inviting unmarried building tradesmen to apply for emigration to New Zealand. Having trained as a bricklayer, he applied immediately, was accepted and headed off to start a new life, settling in Wanganui in the North Island where he lived out the rest of his days.

Ernie Leppard remained in the army for a further couple of years, living off the large cache of cigarettes and cigars he had liberated in Bremen, so that by the time he was finally demobbed he'd saved two years' army pay. This helped him settle back into civilian life and set up his own business as a plasterer. He married and had children, and when he finally retired began getting back in touch with some of his old comrades as well as becoming an avid stamp collector and a fellow of the Royal Philatelic Society. He died in 2007 aged eighty-one.

David Render was transferred to the Derbyshire Yeomanry and posted to Egypt, where he had a happy time guarding POWs and cruising the desert in armoured cars. He was demobilized in 1947 and went into the building business. He made enough money to indulge a passion for motor racing for the rest of his life, becoming British sprint champion in 1983 and 1986. Even in his nineties, he was visiting his old battlefields in Normandy in a Jaguar E-type. He married and had a daughter, and was a lifelong and very generous philanthropist. He passed away in 2017, aged ninety-two.

Micky Gold left the army and went back into the City. He was one of the officers who rejoined the SRY when it was re-formed as a territorial regiment in 1947, serving as Squadron Leader of C Squadron at Retford. He married and had children late, but remained the life and soul of any party. His children remember a family holiday in Normandy when they stopped suddenly in Bayeux at the same house he had visited many times during the war – and by all accounts the family made as much of a fuss over him as they had in 1944. He died, aged seventy-four, in 1992.

Peter Mellowes was transferred to the Royal Scots Greys when the SRY were disbanded and offered a permanent commission, but instead chose to take up a place as an articled clerk in a London law firm. He arrived back in England in January 1947. 'I left my smart army uniform behind and became a nobody,' he wrote. 'It was quite a culture shock to adjust to civilian life.' He studied hard for a law degree and eventually qualified as a lawyer in 1950. Soon after that he met Gillian Hill, who he initially thought must be the sister of Simone Guillaume, the beauty he'd met in Brussels; she was not, but he and Gillian married in 1953. They settled in Bournemouth and had three children. Peter died in 2003, aged seventy-nine.

Stuart Hills was demobilized in 1946 and briefly joined Stanley Christopherson in South Africa before joining the Malayan civil service. After the Malayan Emergency of 1948–60, he returned to England and joined Associated Octel, a part of Shell, spending much of his subsequent career travelling in the Far East, especially Japan. He married, had three daughters and eventually retired to Tonbridge, where he had spent his schooldays, and spent a lot of time watching cricket and rugby. He died in 2004.

Leslie Skinner was demobilized in July 1946. The following year he was invited to join the newly reconstituted Territorial Army and served for another fifteen years, retiring as chief TA Chaplain of London District with the rank of lieutenant-colonel, the highest that could be held by a TA chaplain in peacetime. In civilian life he became a parish priest, serving in a number of places across England including Altrincham, Stockwell in south London, Chessington and Corby, before 'retiring' in 1977 – after which he continued as a supernumerary priest in Epsom for another twenty years. He and his wife Etta had two sons and a daughter, and he lived to see six of his grandchildren. Retaining close links with the men of the Sherwood Rangers, he performed the wedding – and funeral – ceremonies of many of those with whom he had served in north-west Europe. He died, aged eighty-nine, in 2001.

John Semken was demobilized in 1946 and went up to Pembroke College, Oxford, to read jurisprudence; after graduating, he joined the Legal Advisers Branch of the Home Office, becoming its head in 1977 and a member of the Criminal Law Revision Committee in 1980. He married, had three sons, and later retired to Aldeburgh on the Suffolk coast. He died in 2016, aged ninety-five.

Stanley Christopherson moved back to South Africa, where he returned to work for Consolidated Gold Fields. He stayed there for ten years before heading back to London and joining the stockbrokers Hoare & Co. Christopherson married comparatively late, in 1959 – his wedding was conducted by Leslie Skinner – and then, with his wife, Cynthia, bought a large house in Kent called Spring Grove, which in 1965 they turned into a prep school. Their son David was the school's first pupil. It continues to this day.

Christopherson died, as charming and humorous as ever, in 1990, aged just seventy-seven – his two children only vaguely aware of the scale of what he'd achieved in the war. Like so many of his generation, he rarely talked about it. 'He was so much fun,' says his son, David, 'and we always laughed a great deal.' Years later, I travelled with David to talk to some of the surviving Sherwood Rangers, including David Render and John Sem-ken. 'The Colonel, Stanley,' said Render, 'was always laughing. And that permeates through.' John Semken was still rather in awe of him. 'I don't know how he did it,' he told us. 'I don't know how he kept going, always cheerful. He was a lovely man. A very great man. A very great gentleman.'

Yet there were dark moments, when Stanley would retreat. David and his sister, Sara Jane, did not understand why, but knew to leave him alone at such times; few emerged from the war without any scars. 'Every com-mander does feel the casualties,' admitted John Semken. 'You did suffer very deeply. The Regiment had a very, very rough passage.' The conversa-tion David Christopherson and I had with John Semken was one of the most profoundly moving I have ever conducted with a veteran of the war – and I have met and talked with hundreds over the years. He was an old man then, but it was clear that the war had had a very profound effect on him; a dull ache he'd never quite been able to get rid of. The scars clearly ran very deep. He thought Stanley was a great man, but Semken was also truly remarkable. He might never have understood how Stanley managed to keep everyone going, himself included, but it is hard not to be in awe of what John achieved as A Squadron leader – at so young an age, and after what he had already experienced. I am profoundly glad we had the opportunity to talk to him at such length before it was too late.

Some years later, sitting talking to Stan Perry in his garden in the June sunshine, I asked him whether he thought much about the war and the terrible losses the regiment had suffered. He was, by this time, the last sur-viving troop leader from the Sherwood Rangers. 'Thinking back over the years, you don't forget,' he told me. He reckoned he bore three types of scars from the war. 'There's the first, your conscience, that you actually killed some young chap who was probably not very different from you.' The second was what he called the conscience of the mind. 'The mind worry. The memory. Had you been a better soldier, had you deployed differently on a certain occasion, would that have saved the life of some of your men?' It bothered him that the orders he had given had resulted in some of his men losing their lives. 'That hangs about,' he said. 'And then the other scars you have, of course, are the physical scars from wounding.'

These words stayed with me as I delved deeper into the experiences of the regiment over those last eleven months of the war. Walking over their old battlefields, it was possible to picture them back in 1944 and 1945, struggling with the terrain, with the enormous weight of expectation, with the huge responsibility on their shoulders. At Berjou, Lieutenant

Galvin's tank had been shunted off the road; and although it has since gone, trees grew up around it to the side of the road so that its imprint remains. There are other imprints, too: scarring on the walls of the farm where RHQ was shelled on 11 June 1944. Rusting metal in the woods near Geilenkirchen. Shrapnel marks on the church in the market square in Gheel.

In October 2020 David Christopherson and I journeyed through Germany, following the route the Sherwood Rangers had taken in the last winter of the war. We tramped over the Geilenkirchen battlefield, working out where the minefield had once been, wondering which crossroads Sergeant Douthwaite had valiantly held in Prummern, and coming to understand how the terrain so favoured the defenders and must have been so miserable for the attackers. We also stood on the rise near Groesbeek where the Sherwood Rangers had lined up and fired towards the Reichswald at the start of Operation VERITABLE; and we paused by the grave of Lieutenant Rhys Thomas, the nineteen-year-old killed at Cleve in his first action. Passing through the forests near Löningen and Cloppenburg, it was all too easy to picture the Sherwood Rangers meeting roadblocks and being pounced on by Germans with panzerfausts. As we travelled their old routes and delved deeper into the battles they had fought, both of us were struck by the relentlessness of their experiences – the grinding, debilitating violence, the endless casualties and deaths. And it was such a largely unknown, unappreciated sacrifice, too, a brutal, horrible business; and yet these men somehow, in some way, managed to keep their humanity – enough to notice a first snowdrop, or to lay on a Christmas spectacle for the children of a small Dutch town. They were a remarkable lot of young men.

Our tour ended in Karlshöfen, on a beautiful, sun-dappled autumn afternoon. The big oaks were still in leaf, the sky above a deep blue, the village quiet, peaceful and rather lovely. We walked about, imagining the Sherwood Rangers there in early May 1945. It wasn't hard to do. Half close your eyes, and there in the farmyard were the 3-tonners, and *Robin Hood*, the CO's tank. A smell of cigarette smoke and pipe tobacco, a clang of a spanner, chatter drifting on the early summer air. I could almost see Stanley in his battledress, black tanker's beret on the back of his head, American jump boots on his feet, clutching that scrap of an old German exercise book on which news of the German surrender had been hastily written. Ghosts from the past and a moment in time. It gave me quite a lump in my throat.

Glossary of Terms and Abbreviations

ABCA	Army Bureau of Current Affairs
AFN	American Forces Network
AP	armour-piercing
APDS	armour-piercing discarding sabot
ARV	armoured recovery vehicle
AVLB	armoured vehicle launched bridge
AVRE	Armoured Vehicle, Royal Engineers
AWOL	absent without leave
BLA	British Liberation Army
CO	commanding officer
CP	command post
DCLI	Duke of Cornwall's Light Infantry
DG	Dragoon Guards
DLI	Durham Light Infantry
DSO	Distinguished Service Order
DUKW	(pronounced 'duck') modified amphibious truck by General Motors using the company's nomenclature: D = designed in 1942; U = utility; K = all-wheel drive; W = dual-tandem rear axles
DWR	Duke of Wellington's Regiment
ENSA	Entertainments National Service Association
FDS	Forward Delivery Squadron
FOO	forward observation officer
GIR	Glider Infantry Regiment
HE	high explosive
IO	intelligence officer
KOYLI	King's Own Yorkshire Light Infantry
KRRC	King's Royal Rifle Corps
LAD	light aid detachment

LCA	landing craft, assault
LCG	landing craft, gun
LCT	landing craft, tank
LST	landing ship, tank
MC	Military Cross, awarded only to officers
MDS	main dressing station
MG	machine gun
MM	Military Medal, awarded to non-commissioned officers and other ranks
MO	medical officer
NAAFI	Navy, Army and Air Force Institutes
NCO	non-commissioned officer
OP	observation post
PIAT	projectile, infantry, anti-tank
PIR	Parachute Infantry Regiment (US)
POW	prisoner of war
RAChD	Royal Army Chaplains' Department
RAP	regimental aid post
RASC	Royal Army Service Corps
REME	Royal Electrical and Mechanical Engineers
RHQ	Regimental Headquarters
RWA	Regimental Welfare Association
sabre squadron	the three fighting squadrons, A, B or C
serial	group of four LCTs
SLI	Somerset Light Infantry
SOAG	senior officer, assault group
SP	self-propelled (gun)
SRY	Sherwood Rangers Yeomanry
StuG	Sturmgeschütz, low-profile self-propelled gun on Panzer Mk III chassis
TA	Territorial Army
TD	Territorial Decoration
VHF	very high frequency
WN	*Widerstandsneste* (Ger: strongpoint)
Wren	member of the Women's Royal Naval Service
XO	executive officer (second-in-command): US

Appendix 1

Make-up of an Armoured Regiment

Armour massed for the launch of Operation VERITABLE, 8 February 1945

British Armoured Regiment

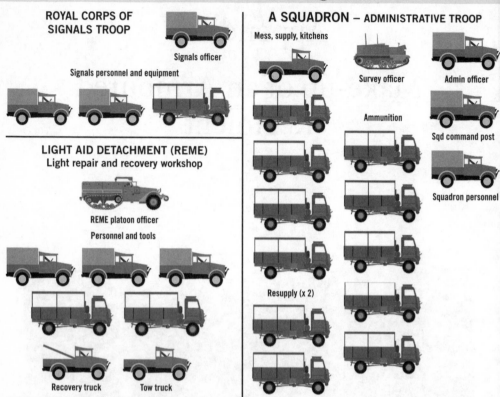

ROYAL CORPS OF SIGNALS TROOP

Signals officer

Signals personnel and equipment

LIGHT AID DETACHMENT (REME)
Light repair and recovery workshop

REME platoon officer

Personnel and tools

Recovery truck

Tow truck

A SQUADRON – ADMINISTRATIVE TROOP

Mess, supply, kitchens

Survey officer

Admin officer

Ammunition

Sqd command post

Squadron personnel

Resupply (x 2)

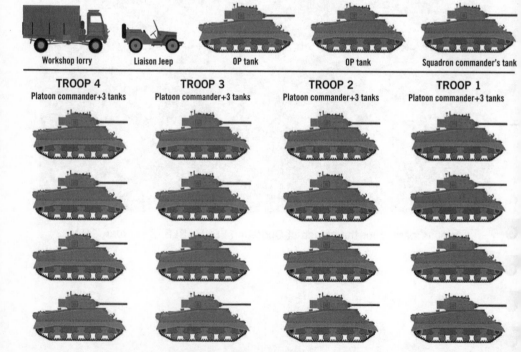

COMMAND POST SQUADRON   3 squadrons (A, B, C)

Workshop lorry

Liaison Jeep

OP tank

OP tank

Squadron commander's tank

TROOP 4
Platoon commander+3 tanks

TROOP 3
Platoon commander+3 tanks

TROOP 2
Platoon commander+3 tanks

TROOP 1
Platoon commander+3 tanks

Command Post personnel

Regimental HQ light vehicle

REGIMENTAL HQ
CORPS COMMANDER'S COMMAND POST

4th tank

OP tank (Forward observation)

OP tank (Forward observation)

Regimental commander's tank

AA PLATOON
Platoon commander +7 tanks

RECON. PLATOON
Platoon commander +10 tanks

ADMINISTRATION PLATOON (Includes 8 motorbikes)

Liaison

Second-in-command

Liaison

Workshop

Survey officer

Medical evacuation

Signals officer

Quartermaster

Officers' mess

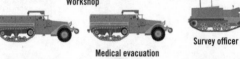

Ammunition trucks

Mess water tankers

LIAISON PLATOON
Platoon commander + 8 Scout cars

Mess trucks

Transport trucks

Workshop

Appendix 2

Commanders within the Sherwood Rangers Yeomanry, D-Day to VE-Day

Commanding Officer

Lt-Col. John D'Arcy Anderson	Wounded in action 6 June 1944
Major Mike Laycock	Killed in action 11 June 1944
Lt-Col. Stanley Christopherson	Acting 11 June 1944; formally 15 June 1944

Second-in-Command

Major Mike Laycock	Until 6 June 1944
Major Stephen Mitchell	6 June to 19 Aug. 1944
Major Lord Robin Leigh	19 Aug. 1944 to 20 Feb. 1945
Major Basil Ringrose	From 21 Feb. 1945

Adjutant

Captain George Jones	Killed in action 11 June 1944
Captain Terry Leinster	15 June 1944 to March 1945

Headquarters Squadron (inc. A Echelon)

Major Roger Sutton-Nelthorpe	From 6 June 1944

B Echelon

Captain Ronnie Hutton	6 June 1944 to Feb. 1945
Captain Mike Howden	From Feb. 1945

A Squadron

Major Stanley Christopherson	Until 11 June 1944
Major John Semken	15 June to early July 1944
Major Geoffrey Makins	6–11 July 1944
Major John Semken	11 July to Dec. 1944
Major Tony Gauntley	Dec. 1944 to 2 Feb. 1945
Captain Ronnie Hutton	2–18 Feb. 1945
Major Bill Enderby	From 18 Feb. 1945

B Squadron

Major John Hanson-Lawson	Wounded in action 27 June 1944
Captain Colin Thomson	27 June to 6 July 1944
Major Micky Gold	6 July to 11 Sept. 1944
Captain Tony Gauntley	12 Sept. to 25 Oct. 1944
Major Peter Selerie	25 Oct. to 19 Nov. 1944
Major Tony Gauntley	19 Nov. 1944 to Dec. 1944
Major Ian McKay	Dec. 1944 to 1 March 1946

C Squadron

Major Stephen Mitchell	Until 15 June 1944
Major Peter Selerie	15 June until wounded in action 2 Aug. 1944
Major Jack Holman	2–20 Aug. 1944
Major Stephen Mitchell	20 Aug. to Sept. 1944
Major Jack Holman	From Sept. 1944

Appendix 3

Medals Won by the Men of the Sherwood Rangers, D-Day to VE-Day

Distinguished Service Order (DSO)

Lt-Col. Stanley Christopherson
For actions and outstanding leadership at Gheel, 10–12 Sept. 1944. Passed 25 Sept. 1944.

Capt. Neville Fearn
For consistent outstanding leadership and bravery, but especially at Point 103 on 11 June 1944, for temporarily leading A Squadron on the German border on 26 Dec. 1944, and for actions and leadership during BLACKCOCK, Jan. 1945. Passed 20 July 1945.

Military Cross (MC)

Lt Fred 'Jimmy' Cagney
For actions near Issum, 6 March 1945. Passed 6 April 1945.

Lt Geoffrey Coleman
For actions with C Squadron at Beeck, 22 Nov. 1944. Passed 26 Nov. 1944.

Capt. Tony Gauntley
For actions at Prummern, 18 Nov. 1944. Passed 2 Dec. 1944.

Major Michael Gold
For actions at the Noireau and Berjou, 16 Aug. 1944. Passed 7 Oct. 1944.

Lt Ian Greenaway
For actions on D-Day, and at St Pierre, 11 June 1944. Passed 22 Aug. 1944.

Capt. (then Lt) Stuart Hills
For actions at Gheel, 11 Sept. 1944. Passed 7 Oct. 1944.

Lt Dick Holman
For actions near Isselburg, 27–8 March 1945. Passed 22 April 1945.

Major (then Capt.) Jack Holman
For actions at the Noireau, 17 Aug. 1944. Passed 17 Oct. 1944.

Lt Dick Hyde
For actions near Issum, 6 March 1945. Passed 30 May 1945.

Capt. Ian McKay
For actions at Beek and Wyler, 21 Sept. 1944. Passed 4 Dec. 1944.

Capt. John Mann
For actions near Fontenay, 25 June 1944. Passed 22 Aug. 1944.

Lt Peter Mellowes
For actions near Dinxperlo, 29 March 1945. Passed 15 May 1945.

Lt Reginald Reed
For actions at Cloppenburg, 13 April 1945. Passed 5 May 1945.

Major John Semken
For actions at Rauray, 26 June 1944. Passed 22 Aug. 1944.

Lt Reginald Smith
For actions near Weeze, 1 March 1945. Passed 9 April 1945.

Capt. Colin Thomson
For actions on D-Day (passed 14 June 1944) and at Fontenay, 25 June 1944 (passed 17 Sept. 1944).

Capt. (then Lt) Eric 'Bill' Wharton
For actions near Gheel, 11 Sept. 1944. Passed 16 Nov. 1944.

DCM (Distinguished Conduct Medal)
RSM Arthur Barlow
For outstanding service, courage and devotion to duty as Regimental Sergeant-Major during the entire period, and for fighting through every single one of the regiment's battles. Passed 15 Aug. 1945. (Award later upgraded to MC.)

S/Sgt Sidney Collis

For consistent outstanding service, but particularly on D-Day and at Geilen-kirchen. Passed 30 July 1945.

Sgt Stanley Nesling

For actions at Gheel, 10–11 Sept. 1944. Passed 16 Nov. 1944.

L/Sgt Robert Wheeler

For actions near Bremen and Hucting, 19 April 1945. Passed 20 June 1945.

Military Medal (MM)

Sgt Edward Birch

B Squadron, for knocking out a Tiger tank at Rauray, 27 June 1944. Passed 16 July 1944.

Sgt William Bracegirdle

For actions with B Squadron at Le Hamel on D-Day. Passed 14 June 1944.

L/Sgt Harold Budner

For actions supporting US 405th Regiment at Beeck, 22 Nov. 1944. Passed 2 Dec. 1944.

S/Sgt Joseph Butler

For actions throughout June 1944, but especially at the Bois de Boislonde, 18 June, and at Hottot, 11 July. Passed 18 Aug. 1944.

L/Sgt Leslie Cribben

For actions near the River Noireau on 14 Aug. 1944. Passed 25 Aug. 1944.

S/Sgt Henry Douthwaite

For actions at Prummern, 19 Nov. 1944. Passed 2 Dec. 1944.

Sgt George Dring

Bar to MM for actions near Rauray, 27 June 1944. Passed 16 July 1944.

L/Sgt Leslie Jackson

For actions at Doullens, 4 Sept. 1944. Passed 16 Nov. 1944.

L/Sgt John Kirman

For actions on D-Day. Passed 20 Aug. 1944.

Tpr George Knight

For actions at Heinsberg, 24 Jan. 1945. Passed 14 Feb. 1945.

Sgt John Lanes

For actions at Heinsberg, 25 Jan. 1945. Passed 14 Feb. 1945.

Sgt Harold Markham

For consistent courage and dedication as mechanist sergeant with A Squadron, but especially for actions at Rhada on 2 May 1945. Passed 13 June 1945.

Sgt Doug Nelson

For actions in June 1944, and then south of Rauray, 2 July 1944. Passed 22 Aug. 1944.

Sgt William Pick

For consistent courage in action and then for outstanding work as Regimental Signals Sergeant. Passed 20 Aug. 1945.

L/Sgt William Pollard

For actions at Hontem and Heinsberg during BLACKCOCK, Jan. 1945. Passed 14 Feb. 1945.

Tpr Thomas Potts

For actions south of Lochem, 8 April 1945. Passed 9 May 1945.

Cpl Irvine Powell

For actions at Bremen, April 1945. Passed 20 June 1945.

Cpl James Redfern

For actions at Vintelen, 28 Dec. 1944. Passed 21 Jan. 1945.

Cpl Fred Roberts

For actions near Gheel, 11 Sept. 1944. Passed 3 Nov. 1944.

L/Sgt Jack Robinson

For actions with C Squadron at Gheel, 11 Sept. 1944. Passed 16 Nov. 1944.

SSM William Robson

For actions near Gheel, 11 Sept. 1944. Passed 4 Dec. 1944.

Sgt James Small

For actions near Beeck, 23 Nov. 1944. Passed 16 Dec. 1944.

Sgt George Stanton
For actions with C Squadron near Gheel, 11 Sept. 1944. Passed 16 Nov. 1944.

Sgt Dennis Webb
For actions near Prummern, 18 Nov. 1944. Passed 16 Dec. 1944.

Silver Star (awarded by the United States)
Lt-Col. Stanley Christopherson
For actions at Geilenkirchen, 18–20 Nov. 1944.

Major Jack Holman
For actions at Geilenkirchen, 18–20 Nov. 1944.

Sgt J. Moffett
For actions at Geilenkirchen, 18–20 Nov. 1944.

Cpl William Pollard
For actions at Beeck, 22 Nov. 1944, including destruction of two Tiger tanks.

Major Peter Selerie
For actions at Geilenkirchen, 18–20 Nov. 1944.

Major John Semken
For actions at Geilenkirchen, 18–20 Nov. 1944.

Member of the British Empire (MBE)
Major Roger Sutton-Nelthorpe
For two and a half years running HQ Squadron and especially for his work while under command US 84th Division.

Above: Lieutenant David Alderson's troop from A Squadron with troops of 333rd Infantry Regiment near the hospital in Geilenkirchen

Below: Sherwood Rangers tanks near Prummern during the Geilenkirchen battle

Appendix 4

The Tanks: The Sherman and the Firefly

Tanks of the Sherwood Rangers lined up for Operation PEPPERPOT, 8 February 1945

SHERMAN V

AXE CHOPPING J L B.

MATTOCK.

2 SMOKE DISCHARGERS C W
2 GENERATORS & 2 COVERS
MUZZLE & 2 COVERS BREECH.
HAMMER. SLEDGE

SHOVEL. GS.

HANDLE. MATTOCK

CROWBAR 4. 9.

EXTINGUISHER. FIRE.
METHYL BROMIDE TYPE

BOX. FIRST-AID SMALL

'B' AERIAL

'A' AERIAL

LOCKER CONTAINING
15. BLANKETS.
5. GROUNDSHEETS.
COVER. MUZZLE, 2-IN. BOMB
THROWER (IF CARRIED)
MATCHET

13. GROUSERS UNDER EACH LOUVRE

CONTENTS OF BIN
TANK CLEANING. KIT
TOOLS. TRACK
TRACK ADJUSTING TOOL
BAG, SPARE TRACK PARTS
5 GREATCOATS

NOTE.
PADLOCKS CARRIED
AS NECESSARY.

SHERMAN V
STOWAGE SKETCH
EXTERIOR-REAR & R/H

SKETCH BY TEULON	CHECKED BY	FOR D.I.D.	SHEETS	SHEET No. 2.
	7.			T.D. 11695

| 9. | 3. | 43. | 19. | 10. | 43 |

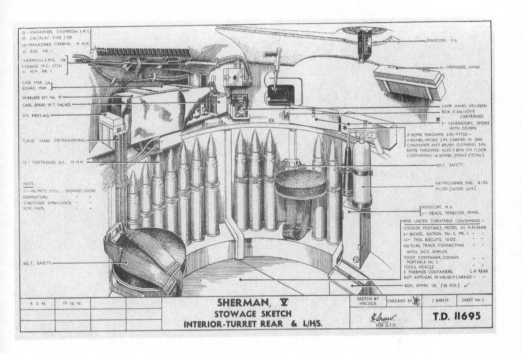

SHERMAN, V
STOWAGE SKETCH
INTERIOR-TURRET REAR & L/H/S.

T.D. 11695

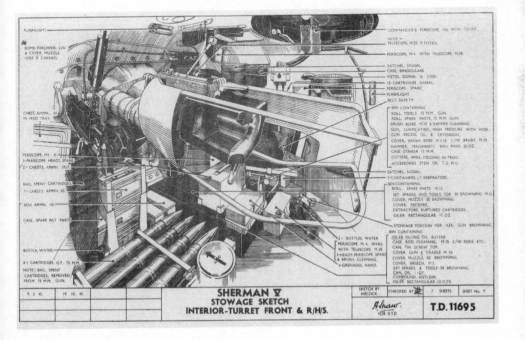

SHERMAN V
STOWAGE SKETCH
INTERIOR-TURRET FRONT & R/H/S.

T.D. 11695

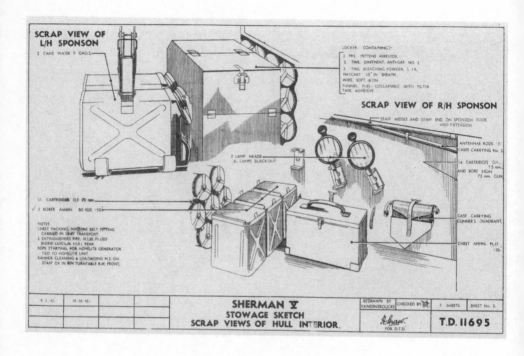

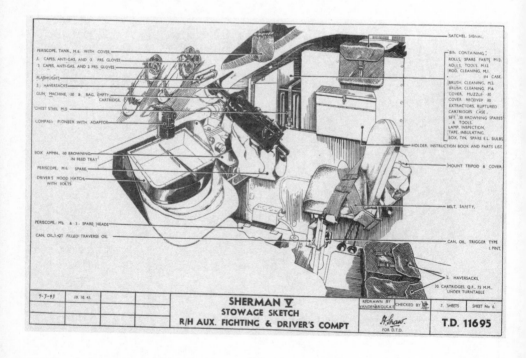

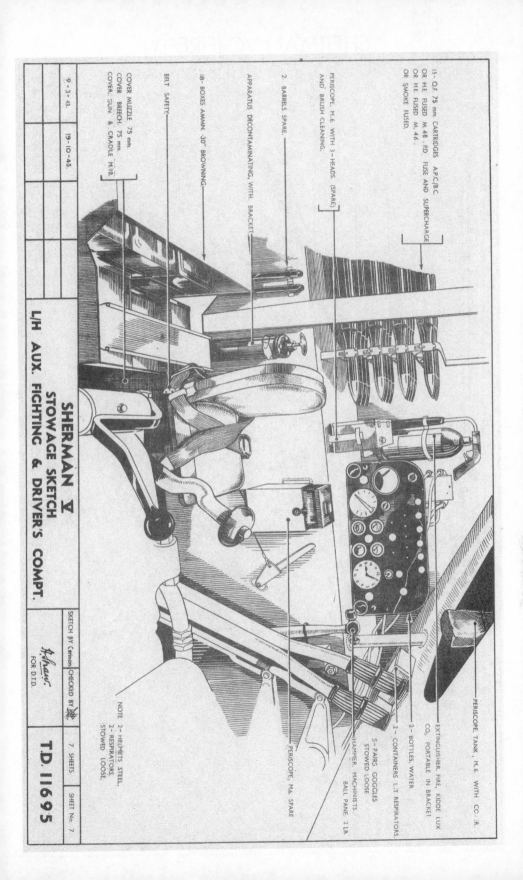

15- Q.F. 75 mm. CARTRIDGES A.P.C./B.C.
OR H.E. FUSED M.48. P.D. FUSE AND SUPERCHARGE
OR H.E. FUSED M.46.
OR SMOKE FUSED.

PERISCOPE, M.6. WITH 3- HEADS. (SPARE)
AND BRUSH CLEANING.

2- BARRELS SPARE.

APPARATUS DECONTAMINATING, WITH BRACKET.

18- BOXES AMMN. ·30" BROWNING.

BELT SAFETY.

COVER MUZZLE 75 mm.
COVER BREECH. 75 mm.
COVER, GUN & CRADLE M.10.

PERISCOPE, TANK , M. 6. WITH CO . R.

EXTINGUISHER, FIRE, KIDDE LUX
CO₂ PORTABLE IN BRACKET

2- BOTTLES WATER

2- CONTAINERS L.T. RESPIRATORS.

5- PAIRS GOGGLES
STOWED LOOSE

HAMMER, MACHINISTS
BALL PANE, 2 LB.

PERISCOPE, M.6 SPARE

NOTE 2- HELMETS STEEL,
2- RESPIRATORS,
STOWED LOOSE.

SHERMAN V
STOWAGE SKETCH
L/H AUX. FIGHTING & DRIVER'S COMPT.

6 - 3 - 43.		
19 - 10 - 43.		
SKETCH BY Cannon	CHECKED BY	T.D. 11695
FOR D.T.D.	7 SHEETS	SHEET No. 7

SHERMAN VC (FIREFLY)

BROWNING, M.G., CAL. .50

'AMP SPOT

BROWNING, M.G., CAL. .30

6 TRACK LINKS, SPARE

ORDNANCE, Q.F., 3-IN. 17 PDR. MK. IV

NOTE
2 DISCHARGERS SMOKE
GENERATOR
2 GENERATOR SMOKE
2 COVERS, MUZZLE,
CARRIED WHEN 2-IN.
BOMB THROWER, IS NOT FITTED.]

AXE CHOPPING 5 LB.
EXTINGUISHER, FIRE,]
METHYL BROMIDE
MATTOCK HEAD
SHOVEL 'D' HEAD
MATTOCK HANDLE
CROWBAR

MIRROR, DRIVING

24. 3. 44.	13. 5. 44.		

SKETCH BY,
S.W. TEUTON.

CHECKED BY

7' SHEETS

SHEET No. 1.

SHERMAN V. C.
STOWAGE SKETCH
EXTERIOR—FRONT & R/H/S

R. Shaw.
FOR D.T.D.

T.D.24635

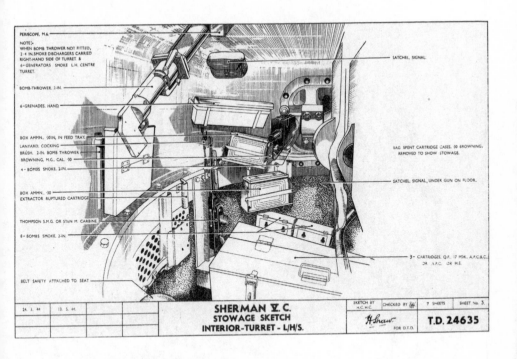

PERISCOPE, M.6.

NOTE:-
WHEN BOMB THROWER NOT FITTED,
2-4 IN.SMOKE DISCHARGERS CARRIED
RIGHT-HAND SIDE OF TURRET &
6-GENERATORS SMOKE L.H. CENTRE
TURRET.

BOMB-THROWER, 2-IN.

6-GRENADES, HAND.

BOX AMMN., 30IN, IN FEED TRAY.
LANYARD, COCKING
BRUSH, 2-IN. BOMB THROWER
BROWNING, M.G. CAL. .30

4-BOMBS SMOKE, 2-IN.

BOX AMMN., .30
EXTRACTOR RUPTURED CARTRIDGE

THOMPSON S.M.G. OR STEN M. CARBINE.

8-BOMBS SMOKE, 2-IN.

BELT SAFETY ATTACHED TO SEAT

SATCHEL, SIGNAL

BAG SPENT CARTRIDGE CASES, 30 BROWNING.
REMOVED TO SHOW STOWAGE.

SATCHEL, SIGNAL, UNDER GUN ON FLOOR.

3-CARTRIDGES, Q.F. 17 POR., A.P.C.B.C.
OR A.P.C. OR H.E.

24. 3. 44	13. 5. 44.		SHERMAN V C. STOWAGE SKETCH INTERIOR-TURRET - L/H/S.	SKETCH BY H.C.H.C.	CHECKED BY	7 SHEETS	SHEET No. 3.
				H.Shaw FOR D.T.D.		T.D. 24635	

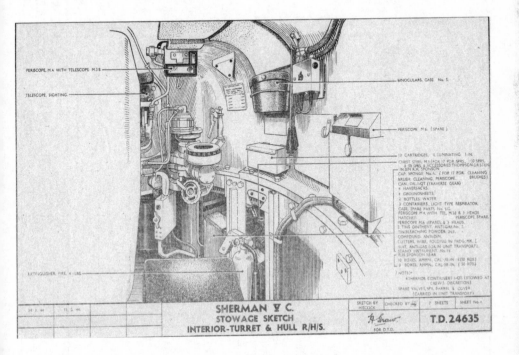

PERISCOPE, M.4 WITH TELESCOPE M.38

TELESCOPE, SIGHTING.

EXTINGUISHER, FIRE, 4-LBS.

BINOCULARS, CASE No. 5.

PERISCOPE, M.6. (SPARE.)

13 CARTRIDGES, ILLUMINATING, 1-IN.
CHEST, STEEL, M.S.(FOR 17 SPRS. .10 SPRS. 1.50 SPRS. & ACCESSORIES THOMPSON OR STEN IN.R.H. SPONSON
CAP, SPONGE No.6. (FOR 17 POR. CLEANING
BRUSH, CLEANING, PERISCOPE.   BRUSHES)
CAN, OIL, 1-QT (TRAVERSE GEAR)
4 HAVERSACKS.
6 GROUNDSHEETS.
2 BOTTLES, WATER
3 CONTAINERS, LIGHT TYPE RESPIRATOR.
CASE, SPARE PARTS No.1G.
PERISCOPE M.4 WITH TEL. M.38 & 3 HEADS
HATCHET.   PERISCOPE, SPARE.
PERISCOPE M.6 (SPARE) & 3 HEADS.
3 TINS OINTMENT, ANTIGAS No. 2.
TIN BLEACHING POWDER, 2LB.
COMPOUND, ANTIDIM.
CUTTERS, WIRE, FOLDING IN FROG, MK. I
SUIT, ANTIGAS (OIL IN UNIT TRANSPORT)
STAND INSTRUMENT, No.14.
R.H SPONSON GEAR
10 BOXES, AMMN., CAL.30-IN. (250 RDS)
3 BOXES, AMMN, CAL.50-IN. (50 RDS)

NOTE:-
4 THERMOS CONTAINERS 1-QT. (STOWED AT CREWS DISCRETION)
SPARE VALVES, SPL. BARREL & COVER
(CARRIED IN UNIT TRANSPORT)

24. 3. 44	13. 5. 44.		SHERMAN V C. STOWAGE SKETCH INTERIOR-TURRET & HULL R/H/S.	SKETCH BY. HISCOCK	CHECKED BY	7 SHEETS	SHEET No. 4
				H.Shaw FOR D.T.D.		T.D. 24635	

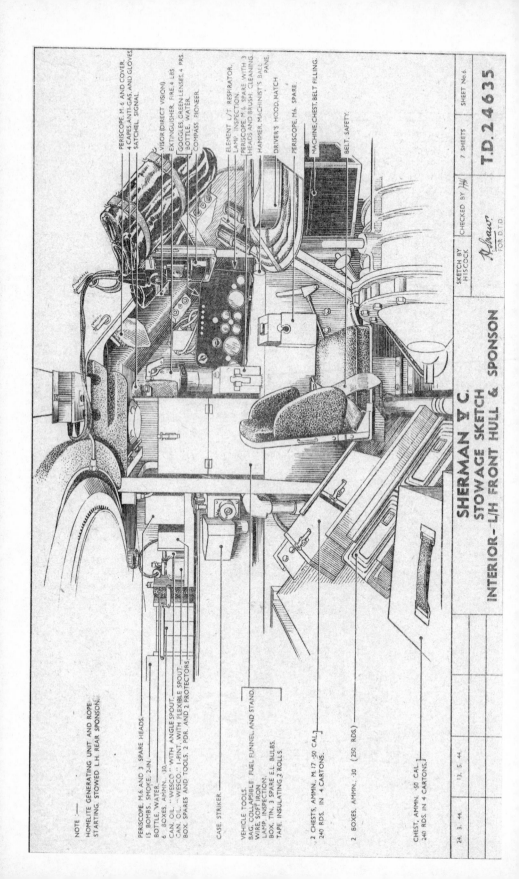

NOTE :—
HOMELITE GENERATING UNIT AND ROPE
STARTING. STOWED L.H. REAR SPONSON.

PERISCOPE. M.6. AND 3 SPARE HEADS.
15 BOMBS. SMOKE. 2-IN.
BOTTLE. WATER.
6 BOXES. AMMN. .30.
CAN. OIL. "WESCO" WITH ANGLE SPOUT.
CAN. OIL. "WESCO." 1-PINT. WITH FLEXIBLE SPOUT.
BOX. SPARES AND TOOLS. 2 PDR. AND 2 PROTECTORS.

CASE. STRIKER.

VEHICLE TOOLS.
BAG, COLLAPSIBLE. FUEL FUNNEL AND STAND.
WIRE, SOFT IRON
LAMP INSPECTION.
BOX, TIN. 3 SPARE E.L. BULBS.
TAPE, INSULATING. 2 ROLLS

2 CHESTS, AMMN. M.17. .50 CAL.
240 RDS. IN 4 CARTONS.

2 BOXES, AMMN. .30 (250 RDS)

CHEST, AMMN. .50 CAL.
240 RDS. IN 4 CARTONS.

PERISCOPE. M. 6 AND COVER.
4 CAPES. ANTI-GAS. AND GLOVES.
SATCHEL. SIGNAL.

VISOR (DIRECT VISION)

EXTINGUISHER, FIRE. 4 LBS.
GOGGLES, GREEN. LENSES, 4 PRS.
BOTTLE. WATER.
COMPASS PIONEER.

ELEMENT. L/T RESPIRATOR.
LAMP. INSPECTION.
PERISCOPE. M.6. SPARE WITH 3
HEADS AND BRUSH. CLEANING.
HAMMER, MACHINIST'S BALL.
PANE.
DRIVER'S HOOD. HATCH

PERISCOPE, M.6. SPARE,

MACHINE. CHEST. BELT FILLING.

BELT. SAFETY.

SHERMAN V.C.
STOWAGE SKETCH
INTERIOR—L/H FRONT HULL & SPONSON

24. 3. 44.	13. 5. 44		SKETCH BY HISCOCK	CHECKED BY	SHEET No.6.
			Achaur FOR D.T.D	7 SHEETS	T.D.24635

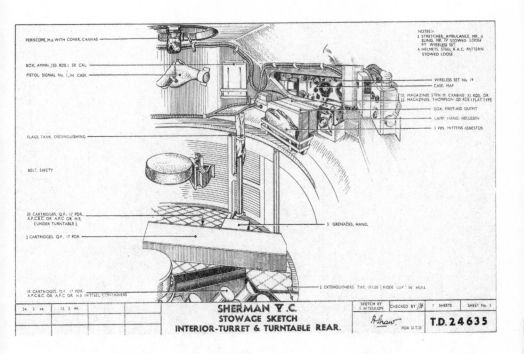

PERISCOPE, M.6 WITH COVER, CANVAS

BOX, AMMN. (50 RDS.) 50 CAL.

PISTOL, SIGNAL No. I, IN CASE.

FLAGS, TANK, DISTINGUISHING

BELT, SAFETY

20 CARTRIDGES, Q.F. 17 PDR.
A.P.C.B.C. OR A.P.C. OR H.E.
(UNDER TURNTABLE)

2 CARTRIDGES, Q.F. 17 PDR.

18 CARTRIDGES, Q.F. 17 PDR.
A.P.C.B.C. OR A.P.C. OR H.E. IN STEEL CONTAINERS

NOTES:-
2 STRETCHER, AMBULANCE, MK. II
SLING, MK. IV STOWED LOOSE
BY WIRELESS SET
4. HELMETS, STEEL, R.A.C. PATTERN
STOWED LOOSE

WIRELESS SET No. 19
CASE, MAP
10. MAGAZINE STEN M. CARBINE 32 RDS. OR
22 MAGAZINES, THOMPSON (20 RDS.) FLAT TYPE
BOX, FIRST-AID OUTFIT
LAMP, HAND, HELLESEN
2 PRS. MITTENS ASBESTOS

3 GRENADES, HAND.

2 EXTINGUISHERS, FIRE, 10 LBS. (RIDDE LOX') IN HULL

24. 3. 44.	13. 3. 44.			SHERMAN V.C. STOWAGE SKETCH INTERIOR-TURRET & TURNTABLE REAR.	SKETCH BY S. W. TEULON	CHECKED BY	7 SHEETS	SHEET No. 5
					A. Shaw FOR D.T.O.		**T.D. 24635**	

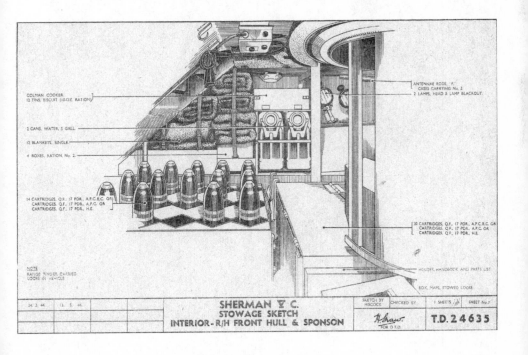

COLMAN COOKER
12 TINS, BISCUIT (10-OZ. RATION)

2 CANS, WATER, 2 GALL.

12 BLANKETS, SINGLE

4 BOXES, RATION No. 2.

14 CARTRIDGES, Q.F. 17 PDR., A.P.C.B.C. OR
CARTRIDGES, Q.F. 17 PDR., A.P.C. OR
CARTRIDGES, Q.F. 17 PDR., H.E.

NOTE
RANGE FINDER, CARRIED
LOOSE IN VEHICLE

ANTENNAE RODS, 'F'.
CASES CARRYING No. 2
2 LAMPS, HEAD & LAMP BLACKOUT.

30 CARTRIDGES, Q.F. 17 PDR., A.P.C.B.C. OR
CARTRIDGES, Q.F. 17 PDR., A.P.C. OR
CARTRIDGES, Q.F. 17 PDR., H.E.

HOLDER, HANDBOOK AND PARTS LIST

BOX, MAPS, STOWED LOOSE

24. 3. 44.	13. 3. 44.			SHERMAN V.C. STOWAGE SKETCH INTERIOR- R/H FRONT HULL & SPONSON	SKETCH BY HISCOCK	CHECKED BY	7 SHEETS	SHEET No. 7
					A. Shaw FOR D.T.O.		**T.D. 24635**	

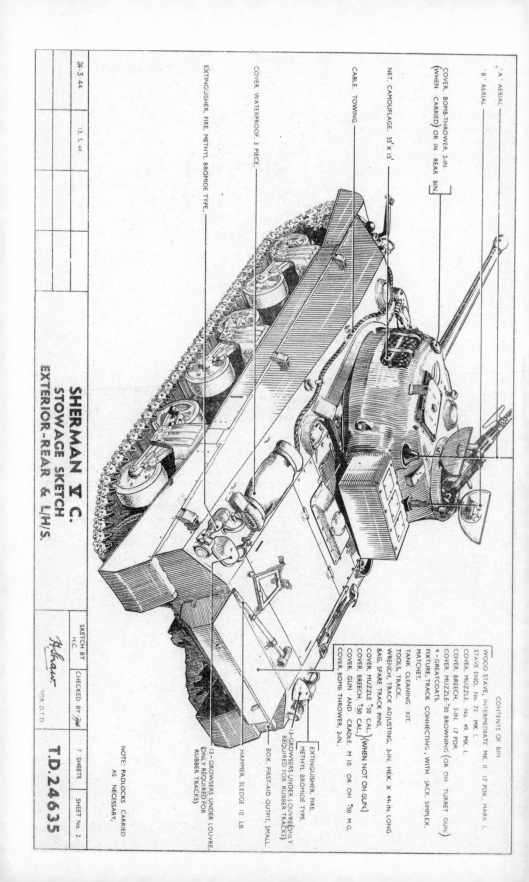

'A' AERIAL.

'B' AERIAL.

COVER, BOMB-THROWER, 2-IN.
(WHEN CARRIED, OR IN REAR BIN.)

NET, CAMOUFLAGE, 35' X 15'.

CABLE, TOWING.

COVER, WATERPROOF, 3 PIECE.

EXTINGUISHER, FIRE, METHYL BROMIDE TYPE.

CONTENTS OF BIN

WOOD STAVE, INTERMEDIATE MK. II. 17 PDR., MARK I.
STAVE END, No. 72, MK. I.
COVER, MUZZLE, No. 49, MK. I.
COVER, BREECH, 3-IN. 17 PDR.
COVER, MUZZLE, '30 BROWNING (OR ON TURRET GUN.)
4 - GREATCOATS.
FIXTURE, TRACK CONNECTING, WITH JACK, SIMPLEX.
MATCHET.
TANK CLEANING KIT.
TOOLS, TRACK.
WRENCH, TRACK ADJUSTING, 3-IN. HEX. X 44-IN. LONG.
BAG, SPARE TRACK PINS.
COVER, MUZZLE '50 CAL. } (WHEN NOT ON GUN.)
COVER, BREECH '50 CAL. }
COVER, GUN AND CRADLE, M 10. OR ON '50 M.G.
COVER, BOMB THROWER, 2-IN.

13-GROWSERS UNDER LOUVRE.(ONLY
REQUIRED FOR RUBBER TRACKS)

EXTINGUISHER, FIRE,
METHYL BROMIDE TYPE.

BOX, FIRST-AID OUTFIT, SMALL.

HAMMER, SLEDGE 10 LB.

13 -GROWSERS UNDER LOUVRE.
(ONLY REQUIRED FOR
RUBBER TRACKS)

NOTE: PADLOCKS CARRIED
AS NECESSARY.

SHERMAN V C.
STOWAGE SKETCH
EXTERIOR-REAR & L/H/S.

24. 3. 44.

13. 5. 44.

SKETCH BY
H.C.

CHECKED BY
FOR D.T.D

T.D.24635

7 SHEETS

SHEET No. 2.

B Squadron tanks moving forward near Cleve during Operation VERITABLE

Appendix 5

Letter from Major John Semken to Mr Heenan

Major John Semken
Notts S. R. Yeo
B.L.A.

29th September 1944

Dear Mr Heenan,

Harry's passing has been a bitter blow to us all. Since he joined us long ago the days have run into weeks and weeks into months and together the officers of the squadron have formed a happy family indeed, and together have seen very much hard fighting. The loss of Harry is a bitter blow indeed and we who are left can at least realise your grief to some tiny extent and are sorry.

I have no hesitation in saying that no finer officer ever led a troop in this regiment – he was universally loved and respected throughout the squadron – particularly by the few hard-headed old warriors who remain. Of his exploits I cannot hope to tell you all, but perhaps an inadequate amount of two will serve to give some indication of the manner of man he was.

About four days before he was killed, Harry was told to take his troop in order to guard a certain road, and since he knew the area, it was left to him where he wished to place it. Knowing that there were some infantry insecurely placed on a high hill beside the road out in front of all the main positions, Harry chose to take his troop through the morning mist, over two miles of open road up to them, within shouting distance of the enemy. He knew when the mist cleared he would not be able to return until darkness covered his route, and that no support could be sent him along this road during daylight. But there he went and he fought off attacks all that day under vile shell fire. How grateful those infantry were. He finally massacred a German force which attempted to cut the road in his rear and returned safe and sound by nightfall. I have never known Harry at any time in action or out, before an attack or during it, to give the least indication of nervousness or alarm. Unfortunately, he cannot posthumously receive the Military Cross, which he so richly deserves.

The day he was killed his troop was a mile to the north of a sister troop which was getting into an increasingly desperate condition in the south. The troop leader of the southern troop had got into a position before the rain came. It then came down in torrents and he could not get his tank back until the ground had an opportunity of drying. Just then an 88mm, firing shells and armour-piercing shot alternately, opened upon him.

Things were a bit critical. Some infantry with Harry spotted the gun. He whistled his tank round the corner and down the road and knocked it out with its crew, its ammunition lorry and all. It was after returning after a reconnaissance on foot to see the damage he had done, that he was shot, at about six in the evening. He died peacefully about a quarter of an hour later and a disconsolate squadron returned from a highly successful day.

I cannot say how sorry I am at his loss. He was buried next day on Dutch soil, a mile from the German Frontier and Father Fondy attended his grave.

This letter is at the best grossly inadequate I fear, but I wish to offer my condolences and convey the sympathy of all my squadron at the loss of your son for whom we had the greatest respect as a man and affection as a friend.

Yours very sincerely,
John Semken

Notes

Abbreviations used in notes

IWM   Imperial War Museum, London
SRY   Sherwood Rangers Yeomanry
TTM   The Tank Museum, Bovington

Prologue

5   'It was a night of hell': John Semken, 'Journal'.
6   'really clean': ibid
6   'You would never . . .': cited ibid
7   'I have never known . . .': ibid
7   'The enemy line was crumbling': ibid

1 Passage

14   'It has rained a little this evening . . .': Wharton letter, 1 June 1944
17   'It was a lovely . . .': Hills, 'My Experiences with the Notts Sherwood Rangers', ch. 1
19   'The next morning . . .': Christopherson, 'Journal 1944–1945', part IV, ch. 1
24   'We spent an uneventful . . .': ibid, ch. 2
25   'I reduced him . . .': Selerie, 'The Second Front', part 1, p. 15
25   'Yes, sir, I will . . .': ibid
26   'If you knew . . .': ibid, p. 6
26   'There followed a period . . .': ibid

2 Rough Landings

29   'Get off the fucking air . . .': Hills, 'The Assault on the Beaches of Normandy', p. 2
30   'Go, go, go!': Hills, *By Tank into Normandy*, p. 79
30   'We're taking on water . . .': cited in Reddish, *Normandy 1944*, p. 23
31   'The relief we felt . . .': Holman, 'D-Day'
31   'It was goodbye . . .': ibid

33   'only one wished . . .': ibid
34   'The damned sea . . .': Jenkins, interview with author
34   *'Christ, we're going to be fried in here'*: ibid
34   'I ducked to the ground . . .': ibid
35   'There was not a thing . . .': ibid

3 Off the Beaches
39   'Opposition was remarkably light': Holman, 'D-Day'
40   'Shellfire pretty hot . . .': Skinner, *The Man Who Worked on Sundays*, 6 June 1944
41   'Heavy work . . .': ibid
41   'He certainly appeared . . .': Christopherson, 'Journal 1944–1945', part IV, ch. 2
42   'splendid Nelson touch': Selerie, 'The Second Front', part 1, p. 7
45   'And it was not altogether pleasant': Christopherson, 'Journal 1944–1945', part IV, ch. 2
46   'If you want . . .': Evers, 'The Early Years', p. 29
47   'It wasn't until later . . .': Jenkins, interview with author
47   'And I was given . . .': ibid
48   'The dinghy proved . . .': Reddish, *Normandy 1944*, p. 24
49   'Never in my wildest . . .': Christopherson, 'Journal 1944–1945', part IV, ch. 1
51   'Bed on ground about 01.30': Skinner, *The Man Who Worked on Sundays*, 6 June 1944

4 Point 103
52   'It was heartening': Selerie, 'The Second Front', p. 9
53   'Regardless of the . . .': Christopherson, 'Journal 1944–1945', part IV, ch. 3
54   'intermediate': TTM, 8th Armoured Brigade, 355.486.5
56   'Give them a burst . . .': Cox, interview with author
56   'B-b-b-bugger . . .': ibid
59   'Wretched tank country . . .': Skinner, *The Man Who Worked on Sundays*, 8 June 1944
60   'Journey back in dark nightmare . . .': ibid
62   'I'll haunt you forever . . .': cited in Gray, ed., *This is War!*, p. 160
63   'It's always the bloody same . . .': ibid
63   'Yeah, waiting for some . . .': ibid
64   'But with this blasted . . .': Bethell-Fox, 'Green Beach', p. 103, BL 99807/7/3
64   'I considered myself . . .': Christopherson, 'Journal 1944–1945', part IV, ch. 3
65   'With common accord . . .': Bethell-Fox, 'Green Beach', p. 104

5 Felled in the Field
68   'I think we'd better . . .': cited by Cox, interview with author
68   'I stopped to . . .': Cox, interview with author
68   'A burning tank . . .': Bethell-Fox, 'Green Beach', p. 106
68   'Mike's stammer . . .': Christopherson, 'Journal 1944–1945', part IV, ch. 3

69   'I am glad to say . . .': Bethell-Fox, 'Green Beach', p. 107
69   'John, I have some bad news . . .': ibid, p. 108
69   'I stared at him . . .': ibid
71   'I came from . . .': Perry, interview with author
71   'He used to take us . . .': ibid
71   'I joined up to drive a tank . . .': ibid
72   'He said . . .': ibid
72   'In the end . . .': Selerie, 'The Second Front', part 1, p. 11
73   'He was not morbid about it': Skinner, *The Man Who Worked on Sundays*, 9 June 1944
73   'Bed by 0300 . . .': ibid
73   'To all purposes . . .': John Bethell-Fox, BL

6 Tragedy at Tilly

75   'I was queen bee . . .': John Semken, IWM 21050
75   'For five months . . .': ibid
76   'The result was complete chaos . . .': ibid
78   'This was indeed . . .' Christopherson, 'Journal 1944–1945', part IV, ch. 3
79   'Hanson-Lawson only scratched . . .' Skinner, *The Man Who Worked on Sundays*, 11 June 1944
80   'We all tried to knock it out . . .': Mitchell, 'St Pierre'
81   'I suggested that we . . .': Christopherson, 'Journal 1944–1945', part IV, ch. 3
82   'Did I leave my map . . .' ibid
465   'RAP still busy . . .' Skinner, *The Man Who Worked on Sundays*, 11 June 1944

7 A Brief Discourse on How the Regiment Worked

83   'Right. Waterproof them . . .': Render, interview with author
84   'We never knew . . .': ibid
85   'Get those fucking things . . .': cited ibid
85   'I'd just been talking to them . . .': ibid
86   'It suddenly dawned on me . . .': ibid
89   'You can piss off . . .': ibid
89   'Don't get out . . .': cited in Render, 'Into Action', SRY Archives
90   'The German snipers often think . . .': cited ibid
90   'Don't *ever* raise . . .': ibid
90   'The first thing . . .': Perry, interview with author
91   'And then I spoke . . .': ibid
91   'Well, chaps . . .': cited in Semken, interview with author
91   'Everybody was asleep . . .': ibid
92   'Nightmare drive in the dark . . .': Skinner, *The Man Who Worked on Sundays*, 12 June 1944
98   'The tank colonel . . .': Christopherson, 'Journal 1944–1945', part IV, ch. 2

8 Into the Woods

99   'It brought it home . . .': Hills, *By Tank into Normandy*, p. 91

99   'You'll get a shock . . .': Reddish, *Normandy 1944*, p. 9

100   'One of the worst . . .': Wharton letter, 14 June 1944

100   'There is nothing like . . .': Wharton letter, 15 June 1944

100   'Now, whenever we hand round the fags . . .': ibid

101   'I do look forward to the time . . .': ibid

106   'Behind them strolled the infantrymen openly across the terrain . . .':
        Meyer, *The 12th SS*, Vol. 1, p. 291

106   'If you see me . . .': Reddish, *Normandy 1944*, p. 31

107   'Be aware at all . . .': ibid

107   'But infantry . . .': ibid, p. 34

107   'Follow the tank . . .': ibid

108   'What do you reckon?': ibid, p. 35

109   'Hullo, 5 Able . . .': Render, 'Into Action'

109   'I got away with . . .': ibid

110   'Perhaps that salved . . .': Perry, interview with author

110   'Thou fookin' boogers!' cited in Render, *Tank Action*, p. 97

110   'Every passing group . . .': cited in Hills, *By Tank into Normandy*, p. 95

110   'Being shelled . . .': cited ibid, p. 94

111   'A handcart stood . . .': ibid

111   'Because I was ignorant . . .': Hills, 'My Experiences with the Notts
        Sherwood Rangers', ch. 3

111   'Christopherson brought . . .': Render, *Tank Action*, p. 99

112   'Aren't you under a misapprehension . . .': Lindsay, *Sherwood Rangers*,
        p. 109

9 On the Hoof

113   'Apart from one . . .': Skinner, *The Man Who Worked on Sundays*, 18 June
        1944

113   'We called him . . .': Christopherson, 'Journal 1944–1945', part IV, ch. 3

114   'CO and Sqn Ldrs . . .': SRY War Diary, TTM

116   'I had a few words with Michael . . .': Christopherson, 'Journal 1944–1945',
        part IV, ch. 3

116   'The first we heard . . .': Mitchell letter, 22 June 1944, SRY Archives

117   'It was grand . . .': Wharton letter, 22 June 1944

117   'There are hundreds . . .': Heenan letter, 23 June 1944

118   'It was absolutely . . .': Semken, IWM 21050

119   'I found they were being used as a squadron leader's bodyguard . . .':
        Semken, interview with author

119   'You'd have to be . . .': Semken IWM 21050

119   'The tank commander . . .': Semken, interview with author

120   'Hearing him talking . . .': Render, *Tank Action*, p. 92

120   'Of course, you didn't . . .': Semken, IWM 21050

122   'Scrounged some blankets and started to tie them up . . .': Skinner, *The Man Who Worked on Sundays*, 22 June 1944
122   'I hate posting . . .': ibid
125   'I don't think . . .': Mitchell letter, 22 June 1944
125   'Most of the fighting . . .': ibid

10 Fontenay
126   'He was a creditably . . .': Gray, ed., *This is War!*, p. 167
128   'There are German . . .': ibid, pp. 168–9
128   'We came to a halt . . .': ibid, p. 170
128   'Funny to think . . .': ibid
129   'Remember, in a few hours . . .': ibid, p. 171
129   'Not just one noise . . .': ibid, p. 173
129   'X-ray nine for Christ's sake . . .': ibid, p. 173
130   'Hello, X-ray eleven . . .': ibid
130   'X-ray two . . .': ibid
131   'Load H.E. . . .': ibid, p. 175
131   'Wait a minute . . .': ibid
131   'Bring him down again . . .': ibid
131   'Larwood did it . . .': ibid, p. 176
133   'He smiled his usual . . .': Skinner, *The Man Who Worked on Sundays*, 26 June 1944
133   'It shook me . . .': ibid
133   'I operated my Browning . . .': Gray, ed., *This is War!*, p. 178
134   'Hallo, X-ray . . .': ibid, p. 179
135   'Prepare for action . . .': cited in Reddish, *Normandy 1944*, p. 42
136   'Get behind us!': ibid, p. 43
136   'It all seemed . . .': ibid
136   'It's impossible country . . .': cited in Gray, ed., *This is War!*, p. 184
137   'Indeed, in this country . . .': ibid

11 Tiger, Tiger, Burning Bright
139   'nest of Spandaus': Barclay, *The History of the Duke of Wellington's Regiment*, p. 229
139   'D'y'see what . . .': Gray, ed., *This is War!*, p. 185
139   'I reckon they are . . .': ibid
140   'Sitting there . . .': ibid, p. 186
140   'Can you see . . .': ibid
142   'The Inf had had . . .': SRY War Diary, TTM, 26 June 1944
143   'Where's the fire . . .': Reddish, *Normandy 1944*, p. 44
143   'I knew it was . . .': ibid
144   'Enemy hornet!': ibid, p. 45
145   'Shit! It's a bloody Jerry!': Render, interview with author
145   'Fire, it's a Hun!': ibid

145   'And the road was filled with smoke from the tracer . . .': Semken, interview with author
145   'The smoke slowly . . .': Semken, IWM 21050
146   'All stations . . .': cited in Render, *Tank Action*, p. 119
147   'He laughed at those . . .': ibid, p. 121
149   'AP. Traverse right . . .': ibid, p. 123
149   'Next thing was . . .': Semken, IWM 21050
149   'We knocked out . . .': ibid
150   'You don't see . . .': TTM, 21st Army Group AFV Technical Issues, 355.48.5/MH.5
151   'As a result . . .': Christopherson, 'Journal 1944–1945', part IV, ch. 3
151   'To the east of Rauray . . .': TTM, 21st Army Group AFV Technical Issues, 355.48.5/MH.5

12 Faces Gone, Faces New
152   'After another long . . .': Wharton letter, 28 June 1944
153   'Sgt Crookes was . . .': Christopherson, 'Journal 1944–1945', part IV, ch. 3
153   'My spirits reach zero . . .': Wharton letter, 29 June 1944
153   'We got them going . . .': John Semken, IWM 21050
154   'sheer misery': Wharton letter, 28 June 1944
154   'We did receive . . .': ibid
154   'I must say that good old Catholic . . .': Heenan letter, 8 July 1944
155   'It was impossible . . .': Meyer, *Grenadiers*, p. 252
157   'The large number . . .': Render, *Tank Action*, p. 126
158   'Red, you bloody fool!': Reddish, *Normandy 1944*, p. 49
158   'Who's that chap?': ibid
158   'And it was returned . . .': ibid, p. 50
159   'Obviously, he was dog-tired . . .': Christopherson, 'Journal 1944–1945', part IV, ch. 3
159   'In fifteen seconds . . .': ibid
159   'Shook me a bit': Skinner, *The Man Who Worked on Sundays*, 4 July 1944
159   'The relief was enormous . . .': Reddish, *Normandy 1944*, p. 50
160   'Yesterday, we pulled out . . .': Wharton letter, 5 July 1944
160   'I just wish . . .': ibid
160   'Stan is doing very well as C.O . . .': Mitchell letter, 28 June 1944
160   'The sun is shining . . .': Mitchell letter, 6 July 1944
161   'We were all close . . .': cited in SRY Welfare Association Report, Sept. 1944
162   'There was the effort against Villers Bocage . . .': ibid
162   'The whole thing . . .': Heenan letter, 8 July 1944
163   'A quelle heure dit M. le Cure le Masse?': ibid
163   'Another conference at 231 Bde HQ': SRY War Diary, TTM, 8 July 1944
164   'The country is . . .': ibid
164   'Not for me . . .': Reddish, *Normandy 1944*, p. 56

164   'We shook hands . . .': ibid
164   'The awful day came,': ibid, p. 60
164   'I'm not looking forward . . .': ibid

13 Exhaustion

167   'With that bloody . . .': Render, interview with author
167   'Redfern's job . . .': Render, *Tank Action*, p. 133
167   'He was windy . . .': Render, interview with author
168   'It was a horrible . . .': Heenan letter, 22 July 1944
168   'The entire scene . . .': Reddish, *Normandy 1944*, p. 59
169   'It was really very sad . . .': cited in Hills, *By Tank into Normandy*, p. 116
169   'Hottot was one of those . . .': Heenan letter, 22 July 1944
169   'Both these brigades . . .': Christopherson, 'Journal 1944–1945',
         part IV, ch. 3
171   'The high silhouette . . .': Peter Selerie, conversation with Gavin Selerie
171   'It was a marvellous thing . . .': Semken, IWM 21050
171   'Which is very . . .': ibid
172   'The driver suffers . . .': TTM, 21st Army Group AFV Technical Issues,
         355.48.5
173   'The tank commander spends at least twelve hours a day standing . . .':
         Semken, interview with author
173   'As soon as the troop . . .': Perry, interview with author
173   'And I thought it was important . . .': ibid
174   'There was a bit of a classical theme going on . . .': ibid
174   'George had never . . .': ibid
175   'No matter how . . .': Wharton letter, 16 July 1944
175   'But M is trying . . .': ibid
176   'I feel like a millionaire!': ibid
176   'And all the people . . .': Heenan letter, undated [July 1944]
177   'to give it moral support . . .': Christopherson, 'Journal 1944–1945',
         part IV, ch. 4
177   'However, in position . . .': Wharton letter, 19 July 1944
177   'Yesterday was a sunny day . . .': ibid

14 Back into Action

179   'A quiet day . . .': SRY War Diary, TTM, 31A, 31B
179   'I have my ears . . .': Wharton letter, 21 July 1944
180   'She was a beautiful . . .': Reddish, *Normandy 1944*, p. 62
180   'This chap looks after him . . .': Wharton letter, 21 July 1944
181   'Another quiet day . . .': SRY War Diary, TTM
181   'People like us don't.': Holderness, *The Ritz and the Ditch*, p. 45
181   'He knew I was pulling a fast one . . .': Skinner, *The Man Who Worked on
         Sundays*, 21 July 1944
182   'Long list of casualties in my absence . . .': ibid, 27 July 1944
184   'all caution to be . . .': Montgomery diary, 28 July 1944, IWM LMD 60/1

185 'An hour ago . . .': Wharton letter, 29 July 1944
185 'Darling, we have come . . .': ibid
186 'They sailed over us . . .': Heenan letter, 22 Aug. 1944
186 'We felt the earth shake . . .': Reddish, *Normandy 1944*, p. 66
186 'When the bombs hit . . .': Render, 'Briquessard, 1944'
187 'Very unhealthy . . .': ibid

15 Bloody Ridge

189 'News that 24th Lancers . . .': Skinner, *The Man Who Worked on Sundays*, 30 July 1944
191 'Cahagnes was a terrible mess . . .': Hills, *By Tank into Normandy*, p. 121
191 'But it was a bit of a close run': Perry, interview with author
192 'So we pulled off . . .': Heenan letter, 8 Sept. 1944
192 'Finally departed as . . .': Heenan letter, 18 Sept. 1944
192 'We felt quite naked . . .': Hills, 'My Experiences with the Notts Sherwood Rangers', ch. 3
192 'Towards evening . . .': Skinner, *The Man Who Worked on Sundays*, 1 Aug. 1944
193 'The place had been . . .': Reddish, *Normandy 1944*, p. 68
195 'Gunner, traverse . . .': ibid p. 67
196 'There followed . . .': Selerie, 'The Second Front', p. 20
196 'Some five years . . .': ibid
196 'What's wrong with everybody . . .': cited in Reddish, *Normandy 1944*, p. 68
198 'To say we were tired . . .': Reddish, *Normandy 1944*, p. 69
199 'I think I went . . .': Render, *Tank Action*, p. 161
199 'As a consequence . . .': ibid
199 'What the fuck . . .': ibid, p. 167
200 'Right fifty . . .': ibid
200 'We must be on . . .': Reddish, *Normandy 1944*, p. 71
201 'Why don't we . . .': ibid, p. 72
201 'There's a German . . .': ibid

16 Letters Home

202 'There was a big . . .': Perry, interview with author
203 'I am a bit vague . . .': Wharton letter, 5 Aug. 1944
203 'We have great fun . . .': ibid
203 'The thing is . . .': ibid
203 'It was marvellous . . .': Reddish, *Normandy 1944*, p. 74
205 'Nothing ever got Peter down . . .': Christopherson, 'Journal 1944–1945', part IV, ch. 3
205 'He was inclined . . .': ibid
206 'Dorsets MO says . . .': Skinner, *The Man Who Worked on Sundays*, 4 Aug. 1944
206 'Managed with difficulty . . .': ibid

206   'Awful business . . .': ibid, 7 Aug. 1944
206   'His completely unflappable . . .': Hills, *By Tank into Normandy*, p. 122
207   'The main thing . . .': Cropper, *Dad's War*, p. 34
207   'The occasional rests are very highly organized . . .': Heenan letter, undated [probably 9 Aug. 1944]
208   'It is plain . . .': Heenan letter, undated [second week July 1944]
208   'bloody marvellous bloke': ibid
208   'When a tank . . .': ibid
209   'Personal ablutions . . .': Perry, notes given to author
209   'I was extremely lucky . . .': ibid
210   'Peeing wasn't too much . . .': Cropper, *Dad's War*, p. 58
210   'In extremis . . .': Perry, notes given to author
210   'The big snag . . .': Perry, interview with author
210   'He's become armour conscious . . .': Reddish, *Normandy 1944*, p. 76
211   'He has not been . . .': Wharton letter, 13 Aug. 1944
211   'Michael, speaking French . . .': Christopherson, 'Journal 1944–1945', part IV, ch. 5

17 The Noireau

213   'General Thomas was . . .': Semken, interview with author
213   'I felt sorry . . .': Christopherson, 'Journal 1944–1945', part IV, ch. 3
213   'All the brigade . . .': ibid
213   'And quite often . . .': Perry, interview with author
213   'And then he would mix . . .': ibid
214   'I was a bit flash . . .': ibid
213   'I think every . . .': ibid
214   'You're used to doing a little night job . . .': ibid
215   'And with a bit of careful listening . . .': ibid
215   'And I want you over the river by dawn . . .': ibid
215   'Oh, you won't be able to get over here . . .': ibid
215   'We were the only . . .': Perry, notes given to author
216   'This chap threatened . . .': Perry, interview with author
217   'I drew the line . . .': ibid
217   'It was getting . . .': ibid
218   'And the first one . . .': ibid
218   'But I had a . . .': ibid
218   'We went back cross-country again . . .': ibid
221   'The next five minutes . . .': Reddish, *Normandy 1944*, p. 79
222   'Those taking part . . .': Hills, 'My Experiences with the Notts Sherwood Rangers', ch. 4
222   'I frantically spun . . .': Cropper, *Dad's War*, p. 38
222   'Our nerves were shot . . .': ibid
222   'All they had . . .': Reddish, *Normandy 1944*, p. 80

18 The Chase

227   'From there I could . . .': Christopherson, 'Journal 1944–1945', part IV, ch. 3

228   'Fearful job . . .': Skinner, *The Man Who Worked on Sundays*, 17 Aug. 1944

228   'This was more than normally . . .': ibid

228   'The sight of the heroic . . .': ibid

228   'Horribly sick . . .': ibid

229   'And all of a sudden . . .': Perry, interview with author

230   'The shock of death . . .': Hills, 'My Experiences with the Notts Sherwood Rangers', ch. 3

230   'The casualty levels . . .': Semken, interview with author

230   'The finger was opened . . .': Reddish, *Normandy 1944*, p. 82

231   'He spoke very little . . .': Christopherson, 'Journal 1944–1945', part IV, ch. 4

231   'The sight is horrible . . .': Heenan letter, 24 Aug. 1944

232   'A bit of a mess . . .': Christopherson, 'Journal 1944–1945', part IV, ch. 4

232   'Whenever we came out . . .': Stuart Hills, 'My Experiences with the Notts Sherwood Rangers', ch. 4

233   'We were by the grace of God . . .': Heenan letter, 28 Aug. 1944

233   'The farmhouse is more . . .': Wharton letter, 27 Aug. 1944

234   'Which, of course . . .': ibid

234   'The end never seemed far off . . .': Hills, 'My Experiences with the Notts Sherwood Rangers', ch. 4

235   'I don't think . . .': Render, *Tank Action*, p. 177

236   'When Michael reported . . .': Christopherson, 'Journal 1944–1945', part IV, ch. 4

237   'We can't start . . .': Heenan letter, 30 Aug. 1944

238   'We did a lot of truck bashing on that trip': Cropper, *Dad's War*, p. 41

239   'I had a lucky escape . . .': Heenan letter, 15 Sept. 1944

19 Talking with the Enemy

241   'With rifle at the ready . . .': Skinner, *The Man Who Worked on Sundays*, 2 Sept. 1944

241   'I saw the Great War . . .': Heenan letter, 15 Sept. 1944

241   'I cannot begin to describe . . .': Wharton letter, 7 Sept. 1944

241   'The tanks get covered in flowers . . .': Heenan letter, 30 Aug. 1944

241   'so no shy . . .': Wharton letter, 7 Sept. 1944

241   'In fact, in recent . . .': ibid

242   'One chap was trying . . .': Cropper, *Dad's War*, p. 44

242   'So the stove . . .': ibid, p. 45

244   'Not surprisingly . . .': Christopherson, 'Journal 1944–1945', part IV, ch. 4

244   'I shall never forget . . .': ibid

244   'I told the orderly . . .': ibid

245   'I am Colonel Christopherson . . .': ibid

245   'I should be obliged . . .': ibid

245   'Stephen scowled . . .': ibid

245   'His adjutant . . .': cited in Hills, 'My Experiences with the Notts Sherwood Rangers', ch. 4

245   'No organized German . . .': Christopherson, 'Journal 1944–1945', part IV, ch. 4

246   'But I have under . . .': ibid

247   'I forthwith . . .': ibid

248   'The colonel then turned to me': ibid

248   'But in the haste of the moment . . .': ibid

248   'Once again the majority . . .': Wharton letter, 9 Sept. 1944

248   'I must have eaten . . .': Heenan letter, 8 Sept. 1944

248   'We also have . . .': ibid

249   'The food was superb . . .': Christopherson, 'Journal 1944–1945', part IV, ch. 4

249   'It took him . . .': ibid

249   'I reckon that is just about too old . . .': Wharton letter, 10 Sept. 1944

20 Surrounded

251   'They always think I am terribly young . . .': Heenan letter, undated [approx. 9 Sept. 1944]

252   'I am afraid . . .': ibid

255   'Information was extraordinarily . . .': Holman, 'Gheel'

256   'But the Boche continued . . .': Hills, 'My Experiences with the Notts Sherwood Rangers', ch. 6

257   'Needless to say . . .': ibid

257   'Everything had gone so rapidly . . .': Holman, 'Gheel'

260   'I think I should tell you . . .': Christopherson, 'Journal 1944–1945', part IV, ch. 4

260   'For God's sake . . .': ibid

260   'Night was falling . . .': Hills, 'My Experiences with the Notts Sherwood Rangers', ch. 6

261   'The flashes of guns . . .': Cropper, *Dad's War*, p. 47

262   'Hold it, Ritchie . . .': ibid, p. 48

262   'Listen lads . . .': ibid, p. 49

262   'Oh, my God, a Jerry!': ibid, p. 50

263   'It was like . . .': ibid

263   'Baker Four . . .': ibid

264   'He looked so . . .': Wharton letter, 14 Sept. 1944

21 Gheel and Garden

267   'If you can . . .': Cropper, *Dad's War*, p. 52

267   'I was going . . .': ibid, p. 53

267   'I touched him . . .': ibid, p. 54

268   'I should just like to . . .': Christopherson, 'Journal 1944–1945', part IV, ch. 4

268   'Reload. Drop fifty': ibid

270   'The tank was covered . . .': Hills, 'My Experiences with the Notts Sherwood Rangers', ch. 6

270   'It was a wicked moment . . .': ibid

271   'Jimmy seemed . . .': ibid

271   'The first withdrawal . . .': ibid

272   'Fearful job . . .': Skinner, *The Man Who Worked on Sundays*, 12 Sept. 1944

272   'It is lovely here . . .': Wharton letter, 16 Sept. 1944

272   'I am sitting . . .': Heenan letter, 15 Sept. 1944

273   'The idea of it!' ibid

273   'We drank a mixture . . .': Wharton letter, 16 Sept. 1944

273   'All so thoroughly . . .': Christopherson, 'Journal 1944–1945', part IV, ch. 5

273   'Life is full . . .': Heenan letter, 19 Sept. 1944

274   'The subsequent awakening . . .': Hills, *By Tank into Normandy*, p. 171

274   'Again, I have had . . .': Wharton letter, 14 Sept. 1944

274   'the lucky guys': ibid

274   'A new young . . .': ibid

275   'I think in twelve . . .': Leppard, IWM 19075

275   'I was there twenty-four hours . . .': ibid

275   'Our major, John Semken . . .': Heenan letter, 16 Sept. 1944

276   'We worshipped him . . .': Render, *Tank Action*, p. 243

276   'We travelled . . .': SRY War Diary, TTM, 19 Sept. 1944

22 Luck

281   'I was perfectly all right . . .': Report by 312861 Lieut Alderson, D. G., Christopherson Papers

281   'He showed great . . .': ibid

282   'But I will not . . .': ibid

282   'Not very exciting . . .': Skinner, *The Man Who Worked on Sundays*, 22 Sept. 1944

282   'I have two P.T. vests . . .': Heenan letter, 9 Sept. 1944

282   'They were the most tremendous . . .': Semken, IWM 21050

283   'We used to give them . . .': Render, interview with author

283   'It meant that if we were fired on . . .': Hills, 'My Experiences with the Notts Sherwood Rangers', ch. 7

284   'It was just . . .': ibid

285   'But nothing near us . . .': Skinner, *The Man Who Worked on Sundays*, 24 Sept. 1944

285   'The most cheerful . . .': Cutting, Christopherson Papers

285   'Well, it is several . . .': Heenan letter, 24 Sept. 1944

286   'Wait a minute . . .': Render, interview with author

287   'Christ! I'm blind!': ibid

287   'Oh, Christ!': ibid

287   'Wallop!': ibid

287   'Hello 5 . . .': ibid

288   'What are you talking about?': ibid

288   'I have to live . . .': ibid
288   'He was universally loved . . .': Semken letter, 29 Sept. 1944
289   'As I walked back . . .': Hills, 'My Experiences with the Notts Sherwood Rangers', ch. 7
290   'The 82nd . . .': ibid
290   'I had never quite realized . . .': Christopherson, 'Journal 1944–1945', part IV, ch. 5
291   'When all was quiet . . .': ibid

23 Revolving Doors

297   'I don't know . . .': Reddish, *Normandy 1944*, p. 20
297   'Look, Trooper . . .': ibid, p. 21
298   'They were a grand lot . . .': Peter Mellowes, 'Peter's Wanderings'
298   'Sunday evening . . .': Wharton letter, 9 Oct. 1944
299   'You can imagine . . .': ibid
299   'Damn them . . .': ibid
299   'I am inclined . . .': ibid
300   'Though not actually . . .': Hills, 'My Experiences with the Notts Sherwood Rangers', ch. 7
300   'A few more shells . . .': ibid
300   'Hylda as usual . . .': ibid
302   'I want the inside of this tank as clean as a surgery . . .': SRY War Diary, TTM, 19 Sept. 1944
302   'He wouldn't pull his weight . . .': Ernie Leppard, IWM 19057
302   'You had to be nimble with what you were doing . . .': ibid
303   'It is just so hard . . .': Wharton letter, 25 Oct. 1944
304   'To my great dismay . . .': Selerie letter, 28 Sept. 1944
304   'Sir, you being . . .': Selerie, 'The Second Front', part 2, p. 2
305   'The Colonel and Major . . .': SRY War Diary, 1 Nov. 1944
305   'I think you should dance . . .': Christopherson, 'Journal 1944–1945', part IV, ch. 6
306   'We unanimously agreed . . .': ibid, ch. 5
306   'I shall never forget . . .': ibid
307   'Well, Jorrocks . . .': cited in Ford, *Assault on Germany*, p. 17

24 Geilenkirchen

310   'He isn't getting enough . . .': Reddish, *Normandy 1944*, p. 37
312   'I like the boys . . .': Christopherson, 'Journal 1944–1945', part IV, ch. 7
000   'Don't worry about all that . . .': Semken, interview with author; IWM 21050
314   'Which was somewhat depressing . . .': Christopherson, 'Journal 1944–1945', part IV, ch. 8
314   'The draught . . .': Reddish, *Normandy 1944*, pp. 39–40
315   'See if you can . . .': ibid, p. 40
316   'The job now . . .': ibid, p. 41
317   'The going in this gap . . .': Selerie letter, 14 Dec. 1944

317   'Jump on, buddy': Cropper, *Dad's War*, p. 66
318   'German prisoners . . .': Selerie, 'The Second Front', part 2, p. 7
319   'I immediately ordered . . .': ibid
320   'I crept up dykes . . .': Dring letter, 8 Aug. 1982, Christopherson Papers
320   'I felt bad . . .': Dring letter, 13 Dec. 1944, Christopherson Papers
321   'an entirely irregular custom': Selerie, 'The Second Front', part 2, p. 7
321   'Kamerad!': ibid, p. 8
321   'He was very bomb-happy . . .': Skinner, *The Man Who Worked on Sundays*, 18 Nov. 1944

25 Mud

322   'What the hell has happened . . .': Reddish, *Normandy 1944*, p. 43
322   'You're bloody drunk, mate!': ibid, p. 44
325   'What was more alarming . . .': Selerie, 'The Second Front', part 2, p. 9
325   'Files of prisoners . . .': Render, *Tank Action*, p. 233
326   'Frightening . . .': Skinner, *The Man Who Worked on Sundays*, 19 Nov. 1944
326   'At night time . . .': Leppard, IWM 19057
327   'How are you doing?': Selerie, 'The Second Front', part 2, p. 9
328   'As always . . .': Mitchell letter, 21 Nov. 1944
328   'Hubert, who is . . .': Christopherson, 'Journal 1944–1945', part IV, ch. 7
328   'The men who . . .': Extract from Draper, *The 84th Infantry Division in the Battle of Germany*, n.p.
329   'Sometimes the best-laid plans . . .': MacDonald, *The Siegfried Line Campaign*, p. 555
330   'Cold, wet, difficult . . .': Skinner, *The Man Who Worked on Sundays*, 22 Nov. 1944
330   'Out again and back . . .': ibid
331   'And that was the end . . .': Render letter, 17 Nov. 1982, Christopherson Papers
331   'We were stonked . . .': ibid
331   'He was one of my . . .': Christopherson, 'Journal 1944–1945', part IV, ch. 7
332   'Everybody was going . . .': Mellowes, 'Peter's Wanderings'

26 The Red Badge of Courage

334   'I suppose . . .': Christopherson, 'Journal 1944–1945', part IV, ch. 7
334   'Monty had turned up . . .': Skinner, *The Man Who Worked on Sundays*, 30 Nov. 1944
335   'That was my last battle . . .': Semken, interview with author
335   'Everyone too tired . . .': Skinner, *The Man Who Worked on Sundays*, 26 Nov. 1944
335   'To advance into the unknown . . .': Mellowes, 'Peter's Wanderings'
336   'As you look . . .': ibid
336   'Unfortunately, many . . .': ibid
336   'The shock of death . . .': Hills, 'My Experiences with the Notts Sherwood Rangers', ch. 4

336   'So, on the face . . .': Mellowes, 'Peter's Wanderings'
336   'lights every time': Advertisement, *Saturday Evening Post*, 1938
337   'One, using a sample . . .': This first report is Mayon-White, 'Tank Crew Casualties'; the second, Wright and Harkness, 'A Survey of Casualties'
338   'making tea . . .': Mayon-White, 'Tank Crew Casualties', p. 60 and fig. VII
339   'He was a joke': Semken, interview with author
339   'Nobody about Stanley . . .': ibid
339   'Many times after an O group': Skinner, *The Man Who Worked on Sundays*, 4 Oct. 1944
340   'Those four days . . .': Reddish, *Normandy 1944*, pp. 47–8
340   'And so has Trooper Savage . . .': ibid, p. 49
342   'Too much cold . . .': Skinner, *The Man Who Worked on Sundays*, 7 Dec. 1944
342   'Silly ass . . .': ibid
342   'Confirmed small part . . .': ibid, 18 Dec. 1944
343   'Hope you are both . . .': cited in Hills, *By Tank into Normandy*, p. 205
344   'During static periods . . .': Christopherson, 'Journal 1944–1945', part IV, ch. 7
344   'It was a typical Christmas . . .': ibid
344   'So ended my sixth and last wartime Christmas . . .': ibid

27 Snow and Ice
346   'It seems to me, Red . . .': Reddish, *Sherwood Rangers Yeomanry*, p. 50
347   'Boche a loser . . .': Skinner, *The Man Who Worked on Sundays*, 28 Dec. 1944
349   'While we were walking . . .': Christopherson, 'Journal 1944–1945', part IV, ch. 8
349   'Normally . . .': Skinner, *The Man Who Worked on Sundays*, 7 Jan. 1945
350   'Once again I am writing . . .': Wharton letter, 10 Jan. 1945
350   'And we became . . .': Perry, interview with author
350   'I had got a letter . . .': ibid
351   'I said . . .': ibid
351   'He was a very nervous . . .': ibid
353   'The road went straight . . .': Leppard, IWM 19057
353   'And I said to Johnny . . .': ibid
354   'Padre Skinner . . .': Perry, interview with author
354   '*Christ, a Nebelwerfer . . .*': ibid
354   'Severe': Skinner, 'Casualty Book 1944–1945', IWM
355   'It was bitterly cold . . .': Mellowes, 'Peter's Wanderings'
355   'We picked ourselves . . .': ibid
355   'So we took them . . .': Leppard, IWM 19057
355   'Got anything to drink?': ibid
356   'They were frozen . . .': Mellowes, 'Peter's Wanderings'
357   'I shall never forget . . .': ibid
357   'With a bit of smoke . . .': Lanes, '556020 Sgt J. R. Lanes'

28 Cleve

358 'Pleased to say I am going on fairly well . . .': Dring letter, 13 Dec. 1944, Christopherson Papers

358 'CAPT E WHARTON': Telegram, 25 Jan. 1945, Wharton Papers

359 'Oh, you're a Limey . . .': Perry, interview with author

360 'And we gets there . . .': Leppard, IWM 19057

360 'Everybody was in a good mood . . .': ibid

360 'He said that . . .': Cropper, *Dad's War*, p. 70

361 'That leave . . .': Reddish, *Normandy 1944*, p. 54

361 'We've both been posted . . .': ibid, p. 55

362 'The rear tank . . .': Mellowes, 'Peter's Wanderings'

365 'The fear was . . .': Cropper, *Dad's War*, p. 72

366 'We then packed up . . .': Leppard, IWM 19057

366 'Then it was hopeless . . .': ibid

467 'And then we come to this defended position . . .': ibid

367 'Just coming out and then all hell let loose . . .': ibid

368 'Couldn't you see . . .': Christopherson 'Journal 1944–1945', part IV, ch. 9

369 'From the infantryman's . . .': Report on Operation 'Veritable', Ike Skelton Combined Arms Research Library

369 'They would climb . . .': Mellowes, 'Peter's Wanderings'

370 'We stayed 'til morning . . .': Leppard, IWM 19057

370 'Floods deeper . . .': Skinner, *The Man Who Worked on Sundays*, 12 Feb. 1945

371 'They were quite high . . .': Mellowes, 'Peter's Wanderings'

371 'I found a snowdrop . . .': Christopherson, 'Journal 1944–1945', part IV, ch. 9

29 The Rhineland

375 'Four tanks were lost . . .': SRY War Diary, TTM, 13 Feb. 1945

376 'inveterate rascals': Reddish, *Normandy 1944*, p. 56

376 'The tanks are . . .': ibid, p. 57

376 'Total now over 30 . . .': Skinner, *The Man Who Worked on Sundays*, 15 Feb. 1945

377 'Such applications always created certain ill-feeling': Christopherson, 'Journal 1944–1945', part IV, ch. 9

377 'I was never happier . . .': Hills, 'My Experiences with the Notts Sherwood Rangers', ch. 9

377 'Both men and tanks . . .': ibid

378 'He was a joy . . .': Hills, *By Tank into Normandy*, p. 215

380 'So, my head . . .': Leppard, IWM 19057

380 'The blast blew . . .': Mellowes, 'Peter's Wanderings'

380 'What can one say . . .': Skinner, *The Man Who Worked on Sundays*, 3 March 1945

381 'Colonel attended . . .': SRY War Diary, TTM, 26 Feb. 1945

381 'Still no move . . .': ibid, 27 Feb. 1945

381   'The road through . . .': Mellowes, 'Peter's Wanderings'
383   'So, we were all . . .': Leppard, IWM 19057
383   'Usually when we . . .': Cropper, *Dad's War*, p. 75
383   'Everything come down with a clatter . . .': Leppard, IWM 19057
383   'Everybody had disappeared . . .': ibid
385   'They was hidden . . .': ibid
385   'In view of our shooting error': Christopherson, 'Journal 1944–1945', part IV, ch. 9
386   'The Colonel wants . . .': Hills, 'My Experiences with the Notts Sherwood Rangers', ch. 10
387   'I was sorry for him . . .': ibid
387   'What a smashing night . . .': ibid
387   'Very disturbing . . .': Leppard, IWM 19057
388   'There was nothing wrong with our tank . . .': ibid
388   'You bloody lot . . .': ibid

30 Crossing the Rhine

456   'Dick's language . . .': Hills, 'My Experiences with the Notts Sherwood Rangers', ch. 10
391   'She gave me . . .': Mellowes, 'Peter's Wanderings'
391   'And that was . . .': Leppard, IWM 19057
392   'I have just got back . . .': Christopherson letter, 23 March 1945
393   'If it was not in line . . .': Cropper, *Dad's War*, p. 80
394   'Would you like . . .': Leppard, IWM 19057
394   'Get out of the bloody line . . .': ibid
394   'So we was stuck . . .': ibid
394   'We fired belt . . .': Cropper, *Dad's War*, p. 80
394   'For Christ's sake . . .': ibid
395   'Little did the Jerry . . .': Holman, 'Operation Plunder'
395   'I am certain I must have passed the autobahn': ibid
395   'We spent an hour or so': Leppard, IWM 19057
396   'They said . . .': ibid
397   'I left my tank . . .': Mellowes, 'Peter's Wanderings'
398   'I was ordered . . .': ibid
398   'And then we give him . . .': Leppard, IWM 19057
400   'He seemed very annoyed . . .': Hills, 'My Experiences with the Notts Sherwood Rangers', ch. 11
400   'At this point . . .': Holman, 'Operation Plunder'
401   'I was beginning to feel really desperate': Hills, 'My Experiences with the Notts Sherwood Rangers', ch. 11

31 Pursuit

402   'The enemy line is broken . . .': SRY Welfare Association Report, Dec. 1945
402   'for the more pleasant swanning part of the operation': ibid
402   'Mind your paint, sir . . .': Holland, ed., *An Englishman at War*, p. 495

403   'Scheme sounds OK . . .': Skinner, *The Man Who Worked on Sundays*, 30 March 1945
404   'Reverse another hundred . . .': Mellowes, 'Peter's Wanderings'
405   'All I could say . . .': ibid
405   'Get your section . . .': Hills, 'My Experiences with the Notts Sherwood Rangers', ch. 11
405   'I was damned annoyed . . .': ibid
406   'He disappeared . . .': Render, *Tank Action*, p. 271
407   'My greatest fear . . .': Hills, 'My Experiences with the Notts Sherwood Rangers', ch. 10
407   'Have you looked . . .': ibid
407   'Come on . . .': ibid
408   '*Robin Hood* in a factory . . .': Skinner, *The Man Who Worked on Sundays*, 3 April 1945
408   'Billeted in houses': ibid, 3 April 1945
408   'News excellent . . .': ibid, 4 April 1945
408   'This was the girl's first time . . .': ibid, 4 April 1945
409   'We picked them up . . .': Leppard, IWM 19057
409   'All they had was . . .': ibid
409   'Altogether, it was a wonderful . . .': Hills, 'My Experiences with the Notts Sherwood Rangers', ch. 11
410   'Wasn't asked, . . .': Leppard, IWM 19057
411   'He just chucked it . . .': ibid
411   'And I think . . .': ibid
412   'All I could do . . .': Skinner, *The Man Who Worked on Sundays*, 11 April 1945
412   'I've had enough . . .': Leppard, IWM 19057
413   'For all I know . . .': Christopherson, 'Journal 1944–1945', part IV, ch. 10
413   'Every time I put . . .': cited by Terry Leinster, Christopherson Papers
413   'Then some silly . . .': Leppard, IWM 19057
414   'Of course, it makes . . .': ibid

32 War's End

417   'I found I was about . . .': Mellowes, 'Peter's Wanderings'
418   'I'm afraid Richard . . .': Hills, 'My Experiences with the Notts Sherwood Rangers', ch. 12
418   'My troop were wonderful . . .': ibid
419   'Went into outskirts . . .': Skinner, *The Man Who Worked on Sundays*, 22 April 1945
419   'I loved him better . . .': Hills letter, 22 April 1945
420   'But as I told them . . .': Christopherson letter, 24 April 1945
420   'It seemed very strange, . . .': Mellowes, 'Peter's Wanderings'
420   'The civilians seemed very subdued . . .': Hills, 'My Experiences with the Notts Sherwood Rangers', ch. 12
420   'I've never known . . .': : cited in Leppard, IWM 19057

421   'All our tanks lined up round it . . .': ibid

421   'We now knew . . .': Mellowes, 'Peter's Wanderings'

422   'Buried both by roadside': Skinner, *The Man Who Worked on Sundays*, 2 May 1945

423   'This message . . .': Christopherson, 'Journal 1944–1945', part IV, ch. 10

423   'No advance beyond . . .': ibid

423   'My first reaction . . .': ibid

423   'That's either a signal for a night attack . . .': Hills, 'My Experiences with the Notts Sherwood Rangers', ch. 12

424   'The euphoria was tremendous': Reddish, *Sherwood Rangers Yeomanry*, p. 65

424   'No more death . . .': Hills, 'My Experiences with the Notts Sherwood Rangers', ch. 12

Postscript

428   'dispersed': Montgomery letter to Christopherson, in Holland, ed., *An Englishman at War*, p. 511

428   'I made three resolutions . . .': ibid, p. 513

428   'The reunion that followed . . .': Reddish, *Sherwood Rangers Yeomanry*, p. 85

429   'She has been a grand . . .': Sadler letter, 10 Sept. 1945

429   'I have been fortunate . . .': Selerie letter, 26 Dec. 1945

430   'I had 3,000 . . .': Perry, interview with author

430   'His last month . . .': ibid

431   'I left my smart army uniform . . .': Mellowes, 'Peter's Wanderings'

432   'He was so much fun . . .': David Christopherson, interview with author

432   'The Colonel, Stanley, . . .': Render, interview with author

432   'I don't know how he did it . . .': Semken, interview with author

433   'Every commander does feel the casualties . . .': ibid

433   'Thinking back over the years . . .': Perry, interview with author

Selected Sources

PERSONAL TESTIMONIES

Interviews by the Author

Cox, Stan
Jenkins, Bert
Perry, Stan
Render, David

Semken, John
Tout, Ken
Watson, Stuart

Oral Histories, Sound Archives, Imperial War Museum, London

Clough, Bill, IWM 22602
Ewing, Kenneth, IWM 21589
Lanes, John, IWM 22115

Leppard, Ernest, IWM 19057
Semken, John, IWM 21050

UNPUBLISHED REPORTS, MEMOIRS, PAPERS, ETC.

The British Library, London

Bethell-Fox, John: BL ADD 60587
Douglas, Keith: Papers

Ike Skelton Combined Arms Research Library (CARL), Fort Leavenworth, Kansas

Report on Operation 'Veritable'

The Imperial War Museum, London

Jenkins, Bert: Papers
Montgomery, Field Marshal Sir Bernard Law: Diary, IWM LMD 60/1
Skinner, Leslie: 'Casualty Book 1944–1945'

The National Archives, Kew, London

Unit War Diaries

1st Gordon Highlanders
1st Hampshire Regiment
1st Worcestershire Regiment
2nd Devonshire Regiment
2nd Lincolnshire Regiment
2nd Royal Ulster Rifles
4th Dorsetshire Regiment
4th King's Own Scottish Borderers
4th Somerset Light Infantry
4th Wiltshire Regiment
4/5th Royal Scottish Fusiliers
4/7th Dragoon Guards
5th Black Watch
5th Dorsetshire Regiment
5th Duke of Cornwall's Light Infantry

5th Highland Light Infantry
5th Seaforth Highlanders
5/7th Gordon Highlanders
6th Durham Light Infantry
7th Duke of Wellington's Regiment
7th Somerset Light Infantry
8th Armoured Brigade
8th Durham Light Infantry
9th Durham Light Infantry
10th Durham Light Infantry
12th King's Royal Rifle Corps
13/18th Hussars
24th Lancers
61st Reconnaissance Regiment

Documents

Miles Dempsey Papers
Diary
Intelligence Reports

The National Collection of Aerial Photography, Glasgow

Asnelles, Lower Normandy, NCAP-000-000-023-295
Asnelles, Lower Normandy, NCAP-000-000-347-042
Asnelles, Lower Normandy, NCAP-000-000-022-760
Asnelles, Lower Normandy, NCAP-000-000-022-761
Asnelles, Lower Normandy, NCAP-000-000-347-333
Audrieu, Lower Normandy, NCAP-000-000-382-398
Caumont, Lower Normandy, NCAP-000-000-021-106
Dinxperlo, Gemeente, NCAP-000-001-116-667
Fontenay-le-Pesnel, NCAP-000-000-021-077
Fontenay-le-Pesnel, NCAP-000-000-021-584

Gold Beach, Lower Normandy, NCAP-000-000-071-364
Gold Beach, Lower Normandy, NCAP-000-000-071-280
Groesbeek, Gelderland, NCAP-000-000-385-42
Issum, Düsseldorf, NCAP-000-001-050-310
Jurques, Lower Normandy, NCAP-000-000-021-961
Moordeich, Hanover, NCAP-000-001-117-126
Tilly, Lower Normandy, NCAP-000-000-021-497

Sherwood Rangers Yeomanry Archives, The Sherwood Rangers Association, Carlton Barracks, Nottingham

Personal Testimonies

Bethell-Fox, John, 'Green Beach', BL 99807/7/3, excerpts
Christopherson, Stanley, Letter to Myrtle Kellett, 16 Sept. 1944
Cox, Stan, 'My War'
Evers, Owen, 'The Early Years of Owen Evers'
Ewing, Ken, 'The Second Front: Memories of 50 Years Ago'
Hawkins, Ernest, 'Corporal E. J. Hawkins H.Q. Squadron'
Hills, Stuart, 'The Assault on the Beaches of Normandy on "D" Day 6th June 1944'
Holman, Jack, 'D-Day'
—'Gheel'
—'Operation Plunder'
Houghton, Frenchie, 'RHQ Enters Cleve 10 Feb. 1945'
Howden, Mike, 'A Report of the Entry into Bayeux, 7th June 1944'
Lanes, Johnny, '556020 Sgt J. R. Lanes'
Leppard, Ernie, 'Crossing the Rhine'
—'Operation Veritable: Cleve to Goch February 1945'
—Photographs with notes
Mellowes, Peter, 'Peter's Wanderings 1923–1958'
Mitchell, Stephen, 'Report, Period 5th July'
—'St Pierre'
Reddish, Arthur, 'The Gale 19th to 22nd June'
Render, David, 'Briquessard, 1944'
—'Into Action'
Upton, Percy, 'The Windmill Boys: The Story of the 1680 Artillery Platoon Royal Army Service Corps (Light)'

Photographs

McDonald, J. A. Personal album

Sherwood Rangers Yeomanry Medal Citations

Barlow, Arthur
Birch, Edward
Bracegirdle, William
Budner, Harold
Butler, Joseph
Cagney, Frederick
Christopherson, Stanley
Collis, Sidney
Fearn, Neville
Gauntley, John
Gold, Michael
Greenaway, Ian
Hills, Stuart
Holman, Jack
Holman, Richard
Hyde, Richard
Jackson, Leslie
Kirman, John
Knight, Stanley
Lanes, John
Lindsay, Thomas
McKay, Ian
Mann, John
Markham, Harold

Mellowes, Peter
Nelson, William
Nesling, Stanley
Pick, William
Pollard, William
Potts, Thomas
Powell, Irvine
Redfern, James
Reed, Reginald
Roberts, Frederick
Robinson, Jack
Robson, William
Sandars, John
Sanders, John
Semken, John
Small, James
Smith, Reginald
Stanton, George
Sutton-Nelthorpe, Roger
Tandy, George
Thomson, Colin
Webb, Charles
Wharton, Eric
Wheeler, Robert

Welfare Association Correspondence

Carter, W.
Christopherson, Stanley, Letter to Denis Elmore's mother, 24 April 1945
Douthwaite, Henry
Dring, George
Hills, Stuart, Letter to Denis Elmore's mother, 23 April 1945
Holman, Jack
Horley, Monty
Hutchinson, Henry
Kellett, Myrtle, Letter to Denis Elmore's mother, 30 April 1945
Mellowes, Peter
Sadler, G.
Sage, A.
Selerie, Peter
Skinner, Leslie, Letter to Denis Elmore's mother, 24 April 1945
Symes, Ben

Other Papers, Documents, etc.

'Sergeant George Dring'
'The Battle of Geilenkirchen 18th to 23rd November 1944'
'The Seine Crossing at Vernon 25th to 28th August 1944'
'The Noireau Crossings'

The Tank Museum, Bovington, Dorset

21st Army Group Administrative Statistics
21st Army Group AFV Technical Issues, 355.48.5
21st Army Group AFV Technical Reports, 355.486.1
8th Armoured Brigade, 355.486.5/RH 5 8AB
Mayon-White, R. M., 'Tank Crew Casualties', Dec. 1948
Miscellaneous maps
Nottinghamshire Sherwood Rangers Yeomanry Welfare Association Report,
    Sept. 1944, RH, 85 SHE
Nottinghamshire Sherwood Rangers Yeomanry Welfare Association Report,
    April 1945, RH, 85 SHE
Nottinghamshire Sherwood Rangers Yeomanry Welfare Association Report,
    Dec. 1945, RH, 85 SHE
Nottinghamshire Yeomanry (Sherwood Rangers) Miscellaneous Papers, RH.85
    SHE MH.5
Nottinghamshire Yeomanry (Sherwood Rangers) War Diary Original (31A, 31B;
    35A, 35B)
RAC Half-Yearly Report No. 10, 355.29 (41)
Wright, Captain H. B., and Harkness, Captain R. D., 'A Survey of Casualties
    Amongst Armoured Units in North West Europe', January 1946, 355.29 (41)

The US Army Heritage and Education Center, Carlisle, Pennsylvania

Gavin, General James, Diary and Papers

Other Unpublished Memoirs, Papers, Photographs, etc.

Christopherson, Stanley, Journals, Letters, Photographs, Artefacts
Heenan, Harry, Letters
Hills, Stuart, 'My Experiences With the Notts Sherwood Rangers in North West
    Europe, June 1944 – May 1945'
Neave, Julius, 'The War Diary of Julius Neave'
Selerie, Peter, 'The Second Front'
—Recorded Family History
Semken, John, 'Journal'
Wharton, Bill, Letters and Papers

PUBLISHED SOURCES

Official Histories

Barclay, Brigadier C. N., *The History of the Duke of Wellington's Regiment, 1912–1952*, Clowes, 1953

Blumenson, Martin, *United States Army in World War II: Breakout AND Pursuit*, Historical Division Department of the Army, 1970

Craven, Wesley Frank, and Cate, James Lea, *The Army Air Forces in World War II, Volume II: Europe: Torch to Pointblank*, University of Chicago Press, 1947

—*The Army Air Forces in World War II*, Vol. 3, *Europe: Argument to VE Day, January 1944 to May 1945*, University of Chicago Press, 1983

Duncan Hall, H., and Wrigley, C. C., *Studies of Overseas Supply*, HMSO, 1956

Echternkamp, Jörg, ed., *Germany and the Second World War*, Vol. 9/1, *German Wartime Society 1939–1945: Politicization, Disintegration, and the Struggle for Survival*, Clarendon, 2008

Eisenhower, Dwight D., *Report by the Supreme Commander to the Combined Chiefs of Staff on the Operations in Europe of the Allied Expeditionary Force, 6 June 1944 – 8 May 1945*, HMSO, 1946

Ellis, L. F., *Victory in the West*, Vol. 1, *The Battle for Normandy*, HMSO, 1962

—*Victory in the West*, Vol. 2, *The Defeat of Germany*, HMSO, 1968

Essame, Major-General H., *The 43rd Wessex Division at War 1944–1945*, Clowes, 1952

Fergusson, Bernard, *The Black Watch and the King's Enemies*, Collins, 1950

Harrison, G. A., *United States Army in World War II: Cross Channel Attack*, Historical Division Department of the Army, 1951

Howard, Michael, *Grand Strategy*, Vol. 4, *August 1942 – September 1943*, HMSO, 1972

The Institution of the Royal Army Service Corps, *The Story of the Royal Army Service Corps 1939–1945*, Bell, 1955

Kennett, B. B., and Tatman, J. A., *Craftsmen of the Army: The Story of the Royal Electrical and Mechanical Engineers*, Cooper, 1970

Lindsay, T. M., *Sherwood Rangers*, Burrup, Mathieson, 1952

MacDonald, Charles B., *The United States Army in World War II: The Siegfried Line Campaign*, Department of the Army, 1963

Meyer, Hubert, *The 12th SS: The History of the Hitler Youth Panzer Division*, Vol. 1, Stackpole, 2005

Militärgeschichtliches Forschungsampt, *Germany and the Second World War*, Vol. 6, *The Global War*, Clarendon, 2001

Miller, C. B., *History of the 13th/18th Royal Hussars (Queen Mary's Own) 1922–1947*, Bradshaw, 1949

Parker, H. M. D., *Manpower: A Study of War-Time Policy and Administration*, HMSO, 1957

Pogue, Forrest, *United States Army in World War II: The Supreme Command*, Historical Division Department of the Army, 1954

Postan, M. M., *British War Production*, HMSO, 1952

—Hay, D., and Scott, J. D., *Design and Development of Weapons*, HMSO, 1964

Rapport, Leonard, and Northwood, Arthur, *Rendezvous with Destiny: A History of the 101st Airborne Division*, 101st Airborne Association, 1948

Rissik, David, *The D.L.I. at War: The History of the Durham Light Infantry 1939–1945*, The Depot, Durham Light Infantry, n.d.

Scott Daniel, David, *Regimental History of the Royal Hampshire Regiment*, Vol. 3, *1918–1954*, Gale & Polden, 1955

Scott, J. D., and Hughes, Richard, *The Administration of War Production*, HMSO, 1955

Stirling, Major J. P. D., *The First and the Last: The Story of the 4th/7th Royal Dragoon Guards 1939–1945*, Art & Educational Publishers, 1946

Warren, John C., *Airborne Operations in World War II, European Theater*, USAF Historical Division, 1956

Equipment, Weapons and Technical Books

Barker, A. J., *British and American Infantry Weapons of World War 2*, Arms and Armour Press, 1969

Bidwell, Shelford, and Graham, Dominick, *Fire-Power: British Army Weapons and Theories of War 1904–1945*, Allen & Unwin, 1982

Bouchery, Jean, *The British Soldier*, Vol. 1, *Uniforms, Insignia, Equipment*, Histoire & Collections, n.d.

—*The British Soldier*, Vol. 2, *Organisation, Armament, Tanks and Vehicles*, Histoire & Collections, n.d.

Chamberlain, Peter, and Ellis, Chris, *Tanks of the World*, Cassell, 2002

Falconer, Jonathan, *D-Day Operations Manual*, Haynes, 2013

Farrar-Hockley, Anthony, *Infantry Tactics 1939–1945*, Almark, 1976

Fleischer, Wolfgang, *The Illustrated Guide to German Panzers*, Schiffer, 2002

Forty, George, and Livesey, Jack, *The Complete Guide to Tanks and Armoured Fighting Vehicles*, Southwater, 2012

Gander, Terry, and Chamberlain, Peter, *Small Arms, Artillery and Special Weapons of the Third Reich*, Macdonald & Jane's, 1978

Gordon, David B., *Equipment of the WWII Tommy*, Pictorial Histories, 2004

—*Uniforms of the WWII Tommy*, Pictorial Histories, 2005

—*Weapons of the WWII Tommy*, Pictorial Histories, 2004

Hogg, Ian V., intr., *The American Arsenal: The World War II Official Standard Ordnance Catalog of Small Arms, Tanks, Armored Cars, Artillery, Antiaircraft Guns, Ammunition, Grenades, Mines, Etcetera*, Greenhill, 1996

Lepage, Jean-Denis G. G., *German Military Vehicles*, McFarland, 2007

Lüdeke, Alexander, *Weapons of World War II*, Parragon, 2007

Suermondt, Jan, *World War II Wehrmacht Vehicles*, Crowood, 2003

Sutherland, Jonathan, *World War II Tanks and AFVs*, Airlife, 2002

Vanderveen, Bart, *Historic Military Vehicles Directory*, After the Battle, 1989

Ware, Pat, *Sherman Tank 1941 Onwards: Owners' Workshop Manual*, Haynes, 2012

Wise, Terence, *World War 2 Military Vehicle Markings*, Stephens, 1981

Zaloga, Steven, *Armored Attack 1944*, Stackpole, 2011

—*Armored Thunderbolt: The US Army Sherman in World War II*, Stackpole, 2008

—*D-Day Fortifications in Normandy*, Osprey, 2010

Memoirs, Biographies, etc.

Blunt, Roscoe C., *Foot Soldier: A Combat Infantryman's War in Europe*, Da Capo, 2001

Caddick-Adams, Peter, *Monty and Rommel: Parallel Lives*, Preface, 2011

Cropper, Andy, *Dad's War*, Anmas, 1994

Douglas, Keith, *Alamein to Zem Zem*, Faber, 1992

—*The Letters*, Carcanet, 2000

Edwards, Donald A., *A Private's Diary*, self-published, 1994

Graham, Desmond, *Keith Douglas 1920–1944: A Biography*, Oxford University Press, 1974

Gray, Jennie, ed., *This is War! The Diaries and Journalism of Anthony Cotterell, 1940–1944*, Spellmount, 2013

Hills, Stuart, *By Tank into Normandy*, Cassell, 2002

Holderness, Diana, *The Ritz and the Ditch: A Memoir*, Stone Trough, 2018

Holland, James, ed., *An Englishman at War: The Wartime Diaries of Stanley Christopherson, DSO, MC, TD, 1939–1945*, Bantam, 2014

Horrocks, Brian, *A Full Life*, Collins, 1960

Jary, Sydney, *18 Platoon*, self-published, 1987

Jones, Keith, *Sixty-Four Days of a Normandy Summer: With a Tank Unit after D-Day*, Hale, 1990

Leinbaugh, Harold P., and Campbell, John D., *The Men of Company K*, Morrow, 1985

Meyer, Kurt, *Grenadiers: The Story of Waffen SS General Kurt 'Panzer' Meyer*, Stackpole, 2005

Moorehead, Alan, *Eclipse*, Hamilton, 1945

Picot, Geoffrey, *Accidental Warrior: In the Front Line from Normandy till Victory*, Book Guild, 1993

Reddish, Arthur, *Normandy 1944*, Sherwood Rangers Association, n.d.

—*Sherwood Rangers Yeomanry: The Final Advance*, Sherwood Rangers Association, n.d.

Render, David, with Tootal, Stuart, *Tank Action: An Armoured Troop Commander's War 1944–45*, Weidenfeld & Nicolson, 2016

Skinner, Leslie, *Sherwood Rangers Casualty Book 1944–1945*, self-published, 1996

—*The Man Who Worked on Sundays: The Personal War Diary June 2nd 1944 to May 17th 1945 of Revd. Leslie Skinner*, self-published, n.d.

Tout, Ken, *By Tank: D to VE Days*, Hale, 2007

White, Peter, *With the Jocks: A Soldier's Struggle for Europe, 1944–45*, History Press, 2011

General

Addison, Paul, and Calder, Angus, eds, *Time to Kill: The Soldier's Experience of War in the West 1939–1945*, Pimlico, 1997

Allport, Alan, *Browned Off and Bloody-Minded: The British Soldier Goes to War 1939–1945*, Yale, 2017

Ambrose, Stephen E., *Band of Brothers*, Pocket, 1992

Beevor, Antony, *Arnhem: The Battle for the Bridges*, Penguin Viking, 2018

Buckley, John, *British Armour in the Normandy Campaign 1944*, Cass, 2004

—*Monty's Men: The British Army and the Liberation of Europe*, Yale University Press, 2013

—, and Preston-Hough, Peter, eds, *Operation Market Garden*, Helion, 2018

Citino, Robert M., *The German of War*, University of Kansas, 2005

Delaforce, Patrick, *Monty's Marauders: The 4th and 8th Armoured Brigades in the Second World War*, Pen & Sword, 2008

Draper, Theodore, *The 84th Infantry Division in the Battle of Germany, November 1944–May 1945*, Eumenes, 2019 (e-book; first publ. 1946)

Edgerton, David, *Britain's War Machine*, Allen Lane, 2011

Ellis, John, *The Sharp End: The Fighting Man in World War II*, Pimlico, 1990

Fennell, Jonathan, *Fighting the People's War: The British and Commonwealth Armies and the Second World War*, Cambridge University Press, 2019

Ford, Ken, *Assault on Germany: The Battle for Geilenkirchen*, David & Charles, 1989

Gardiner, Juliet, *Wartime: Britain 1939–1945*, Review, 2005

Geerings, Gil, *September helden, 7–22 September 1944*, Verbroedering Vaderlandslievende Groepering, 2019

Gilbert, Martin, *The Day the War Ended*, HarperCollins, 1995

Hastings, Max, *All Hell Let Loose*, Harper, 2011

—*Armageddon*, Pan, 2015

Holland, James, *Normandy '44: D-Day and the Battle for France*, Bantam, 2019

Hunt, Jonathan, *Hard Fighting: A History of the Sherwood Rangers Yeomanry 1900–1946*, Pen & Sword, 2016

Jary, Christopher, *D-Day Spearhead Brigade: The Hampshires, Dorsets and Devons on 6th June 1944*, Semper Fidelis, 2019

—*They Couldn't Have Done Better: The Story of the Dorset Regiment in War and Peace 1939–67*, Semper Fidelis, 2014

Jarymowycz, Roman, *Tank Tactics: From Normandy to Lorraine*, Stackpole, 2009

Jeanne, Frederick, *The Bear and the Fox, Ready for the Fray: Fontenay–Rauray*, Maranes, 2020

Kite, Ben, *Stout Hearts: The British and Canadians in Normandy 1944*, Helion, 2014

LoFaro, Guy, *The Sword of St Michael: The 82nd Airborne Division in World War II*, Da Capo, 2011

Lopez, Jean, et al., *World War II Infographics*, Thames & Hudson, 2019

Lowe, Keith, *Savage Continent: Europe in the Aftermath of World War II*, Penguin Viking, 2012

Meredith, Captain J. L. J., *The Story of the Seventh Battalion The Somerset Light Infantry (Prince Albert's)*, Naval & Military Press, print on demand

Middlebrook, Martin, *Arnhem 1944: The Airborne Battle*, Penguin, 1995

Murray, Williamson, and Millett, Allan R., *A War to Be Won: Fighting the Second World War*, Belknap, 2001

O'Brien, Phillips Payson, *How the War Was Won*, Cambridge University Press, 2015

Smith, John A., *British Armoured Formations 1939–1945: A Bibliography*, Tank Factory, 2014

Stephenson, Michael, *The Last Full Measure: How Soldiers Die in Battle*, Crown, 2012

Todman, Daniel, *Britain's War: A New World 1942–1947*, Allen Lane, 2020

Townend, Will, and Baldwin, Frank, *Gunners in Normandy*, History Press, 2020

Trew, Simon, *Battle Zone Normandy: Gold Beach*, Sutton, 2004

Willis, Leonard, *None Had Lances: The Story of the 24th Lancers*, 24th Lancers Old Comrades Association, 1985

Zetterling, Niklas, *Normandy 1944: German Military Organization, Combat Power and Organizational Effectiveness*, Fedorowicz, 2000

Poetry and Fiction

Baron, Alexander, *From the City, From the Plough*, Pan, 1953

Douglas, Keith, *Complete Poems*, Faber, 2000

Elstob, Peter, *Warriors for the Working Day*, Imperial War Museum Wartime Classics, 2020

Halsey, Alan, and Selerie, Gavin, *Days of '49*, West House, 1999

Pamphlets, Magazines, Journals, etc.

Baume, Eric, *Five Graves at Nijmegen*, Batsford, 1945

Film Footage, DVDs, TV, etc.

British Pathé, *British Troops Cross German Frontiers*, 1944

—*Liberation Scenes in Paris*, 1944

Imperial War Museum, *Artillery and Armoured Units Participate in 43rd (Wessex) Division's Assault on Bricquessard*, A70 105-4

—*British Armour Advances South of Caumont*, A70 107-5

—*British Troops Enter Germany*, A70 172-4

—*Field and Medium Artillery Goes into Action on 30th Corps' Front South of Caumont*, A70 105-5

—*Operation Epsom – Capture of Rauray Spur (Part 1)*, A70 59-6

—*Preparations for the Assault on Hottot, Part 1*, A70 77-11

—*Preparations for the Assault on Hottot, Part 3*, A70 78-2

—*Preparations for the Assault on Hottot, Part 4*, A70 77-4

—*Scenes in Geldern and Issum, Germany, after British and US Soldiers Had Linked up*, A70 258-2

—*Scenes on 43rd (Wessex) Division's Sector of 30th Corps' Front*, A70 126-3

—*30th Corps Follows up the German Retreat beyond the Noireau Valley*, A70 128-2

—*30th Corps Goes Onto the Offensive in the 'Bocage' Region of Normandy*, A70 107-7

—*30th Corps in Action in the 'Bocage'*, A70 105-3

—*30th Corps in Action South of Caumont*, A70 107-8

Murray, Al, *Road to Berlin*, ITN Factual, 2004

Potter, Justin, and Holmes, Ian, *The Fighting Wessex Wyverns: Their Legacy*, 2012

Acknowledgements

I have been following the fortunes of the Sherwood Rangers Yeomanry since 2004, when I first visited Normandy; since then I have made plenty of friends along the way, including a very dear friend, had the opportunity to meet some wonderful and truly inspiring veterans, and been gradually introduced to the really rather extensive wider Sherwood Rangers fraternity.

So, to begin with, I'd like to pay sincere thanks, respect and even homage to all the Sherwood Ranger veterans who served with such astonishing courage and fortitude during the period I have covered in this book. I am, of course, eternally grateful that I had the opportunity to talk at length to Stan Cox and Bert Jenkins, and especially to David Render and John Semken. David was such a live wire and incredibly young for his age when we first met, and his death came as a great shock. The conversation David Christopherson and I had with John Semken was among the most deeply thought-provoking and moving I have ever had with a veteran of the Second World War, and I remain profoundly grateful that I had the chance to meet him and talk to him in such detail before it was too late.

I am also extremely glad I've had the opportunity to get to know Stan Perry and his wonderful daughter, Kat. Both have been immensely kind and incredibly helpful, never minding that I have pestered them at odd times. It has been lovely meeting them both and a privilege to write about Stan's wartime exploits with the Sherwood Rangers. Thank you, both.

Writing about others, some more recently passed, others long gone, has been a fascinating experience, but one tinged with deep wistfulness. I feel as though I knew Bill Wharton, Peter Selerie, Leslie Skinner, Stanley Christopherson, Stuart Hills, Harry Heenan, the inimitable Ernie Leppard and Arthur Reddish and others, although I never did – I just got to know something of them. I have, however, got to know a number of their families. I am very grateful to Martin Galea and his family for letting me look at his uncle Harry Heenan's letters. They have not shared them before, and it was an act of faith and trust to do so with me. Telling Harry's story has, I am sure, greatly enhanced the book. Thank you, Martin.

Gavin Selerie – an acclaimed poet – and his sister Clare have also been very kind and helpful, sending me material, helping me with facts about their father and reading the manuscript. Angus Gold and his sister Charmian have also been very supportive, and Angus, especially, particularly helped with a lot of background detail about his father as well as hilarious memories of Micky. Michael Wharton has been utterly wonderful – sending me a transcript of his father's letters in the first place and bending over backwards to help at every turn. It has also been lovely to be in touch with Nikki Lewis, Peter Mellowes' daughter, and Annette Conway, whose father was the extraordinary Padre Leslie Skinner. Huge thanks also to David Walsh, a great friend of Stuart Hills, with whom Stuart collaborated for his memoir, *By Tank into Normandy*. David has been incredibly generous with his own archive of Stuart's papers and I am enormously grateful. My thanks, too, to Margaret Hutchinson, Henry Hutchinson's daughter, for getting in touch. I am also hugely grateful to Rob Miles, whose father, Ben Symes, served with both the 24th Lancers and the Sherwood Rangers. Rob lent me a number of his father's letters and has answered innumerable questions from me. Thank you, Rob.

Diana Holderness, daughter of Myrtle Kellett, has also been immensely kind and helpful, as has Stanley Christopherson's daughter, Sara Jane Grace. Thank you, both of you.

Those currently serving in A Squadron (Sherwood Rangers) of the Royal Yeomanry have also been very supportive, especially Captain Karl Stone, whose enthusiasm and passion for the heritage of the unit with which he now serves is second to none. Karl, I am hugely grateful. At Carlton Barracks in Nottingham, Steve Cox and his small band of volunteers who manage the museum and Sherwood Rangers archive have bent over backwards to accommodate me during a testing time. Like many others, Steve has gone the extra mile and has dug out extra material from the depths of the archive, patiently answered questions, given me unfettered access to an extensive body of material and helped at every turn. I am also grateful to Steve's wife, Rita, for her help – and for plying me with tea and refreshments during my visits.

Michael Elliott is a mine of information and contacts and a long-standing pillar of the Sherwood Rangers community, and has also been helpful at every turn. So too has Jonathan Hunt, former colonel of the post-war Sherwood Rangers, historian of the regiment, and not only a source of considerable amounts of information but also a terrific facilitator. Jonathan and his wife Sue have kindly hosted me at their house, and Jonathan has given me a mass of material, talked through a wide range of issues, and produced extensive and incredibly helpful notes on the first draft of this book. Jonathan, I am indebted to you for all your immense help and huge support.

Others in the Sherwood Rangers fraternity to whom I owe thanks include my old mate Mick Haltby at Thoresby, Mark Wilson, Adrian Charman, Alan Brooks, Wayne Birch, Murray Colville and Mark Smith.

There is, however, one person who has gone above and beyond in helping me with the minutiae of Sherwood Rangers details, and that is my new friend in Dublin, Karl McDermott. Karl's grandfather, William Reid, was killed at Gheel, and an urge to learn more about this man he sadly never knew has led him to collate a vast archive on the Sherwood Rangers. His collection of photographs, writings, letters and details about the men who served in the SRY is extraordinary. So too is Karl's generosity. He has been holding my hand since the outset, and this book simply would not have been possible in its current form without his enormous input and willingness to help at every turn. Karl, I truly am utterly indebted to you and I thank you from the bottom of my heart. I have absolutely no doubt that your grandfather would be immensely proud of the work you have done to preserve the heritage of him and his colleagues.

I have made other new friends along the way. Christopher Jary, son of the legendary Sydney Jary of *18 Platoon* fame, is a trustee at The Keep Museum in Dorchester, and has been an enormous help as I have tried to make sense of just exactly what happened on D-Day on Jig Gold Beach. Stephen Fisher, an archaeologist and the man responsible for piecing together the wartime career of LCT 7074 at the D-Day Story Museum in Portsmouth, has been incredibly helpful. We've shared photos; he's passed on documents, sent annotated photographs back, sat through Zoom calls in which we've discussed whether a tiny dot on a photo is a Churchill or an AVRE, and done more than any other person to help me piece together the Sherwood Rangers' part in D-Day – a task more complicated and time-consuming than I had ever imagined before I began work on the book. Steve, huge thanks – and it's been great fun too.

My old friend Paul Woodadge has also been a considerable help. Woody lives in Normandy, and he and fellow historian Colin Taylor went on a recce on my behalf to the Noireau valley and to Berjou – a place I was unable to visit in person because of the pandemic. Woody and Colin tramped the ground, pieced together what had happened, where Stan Perry and Frank Galvin et al. had been – and also those German troops – and sent me back a film plus annotated Google maps. As with D-Day, this was tricky to piece together, so Woody and Colin's recce proved invaluable. Thank you, both of you, and *merci beaucoup* also to Louis Bon, curator and owner of the museum in Berjou, who opened up especially for Woody and Colin.

In Geel, Gil Geerings has also been incredibly helpful, sending maps, photographs and his book, while in Normandy, Frederick Jeanne, another friend I have made in recent years, also sent me maps and photographs and talked me through some of the details of the battles around Tilly, Fontenay and Rauray. To Gil and Frederick – thank you both.

A number of others have helped along the way in some shape or form: Doug Banks, Marcus Budgen, Keith Brigstock, Andrew Edwards, Rob Glennie, John Murphy, James Senior, Trevor Sheehan, Stuart Tootal and a number of other friends and colleagues with whom I've been able to chew the cud. Peter Caddick-Adams is not only a great mate but also a sounding board on so many matters; the same must be said for Stephen Prince, the Head of the Naval Historical Branch and a fount of all wisdom. Ditto Seb Cox at the Air Historical Branch. Nicholas Moran is one of the most knowledgeable people in the world on the subject of armoured warfare in the Second World War and I owe him thanks for sharing his knowledge. I also owe enormous thanks to John Buckley, one of the finest historians of the Second World War we have here in this country, who has also been an incredibly helpful sounding board.

Thanks are also due to those of a more mechanical mind. To Tobin Jones and Tom Crawford, to Adrian Barrell and especially to Jim Clark, whose own Sherman is in Sherwood Rangers markings and who with Jamie Meachin allowed me to spend a day thundering across Holland in this beast, and who has let me spend numerous other times with *Lily Marlene*. You've become great mates and have helped me with this book enormously.

Many thanks to the staff at The National Archives in Kew but especially to Joseph Quinn, and also to Kevin Asplin, Jane O'Hara and Tina Hampson, who helped gather numerous battalion war diaries during a time of severe restrictions on access to the archives.

An obvious first port of call when researching this book was the Tank

Museum at Bovington. It's a fabulous place full of wonderful, dedicated and extremely friendly people, and I am very grateful to David Willey and Stuart Wheeler for their help; also to Richard Smith, Roz Skellhorn and all the team there for allowing me to clamber over and inside their tanks, for helping source diagrams and pictures, and for allowing me to plunder their archives.

The National Army Museum have been incredibly helpful and are putting on an exhibition about the Sherwood Rangers. To Justin Miesjewski, a friend and also the Director of the Museum, thank you. Huge thanks also to Peter Johnstone, Nicola Ayrton, Jane Holmes, Jenni Fewery, Iain Maine and all the staff there. Huge thanks also to Andrew Whitmarsh of the D-Day Story, who has been helping to curate the 'Brothers in Arms' Exhibition.

I am also eternally thankful to John Orloff, screenwriter of two episodes of the iconic *Band of Brothers* TV series, for unwittingly planting the idea of this book in my mind. Huge thanks, too, to the team behind *We Have Ways of Making You Talk* – Harry Lineker, Jon Gill and Joey McCarthy, and to all the afflicted of the Independent Company, but especially to two great mates, Tony Pastor and Al Murray, who have lived this book with me as I've been writing it and allowed me to waffle on about it on the podcast. Al, thank you for all the incredible amount of chatting we've done and for being such a brilliant sounding board and fellow cudchewer. And finally, thank you for reading this book so beautifully too.

Putting together a book like this does involve quite a number of people. To Lalla Hitchings and Laura Bailey my thanks, as always. To all the brilliant team at Bantam Press and Penguin Random House – thank you: Phil Lord, Eloisa Clegg, Tom Hill, Sophie Bruce and Tony Maddock, you have all put so much care, effort and attention into this and previous books, and I really am immensely grateful. To Gillian Somerscales, thank you so much for your brilliant and sensitive copy-editing and for your endless patience – you have made a very real difference to this book. To Bill Scott-Kerr, thank you, as ever, for your friendship, guidance and unceasing support – it is enormously valued and appreciated, I assure you. At Grove Atlantic, my enormous thanks are due to all the team, but especially Morgan Entrekin, for your backing and support, to Justina Batchelor, and particularly to George Gibson, for your greatly valued friendship, guidance, patience and backing. I feel very lucky to be in such very capable hands. The same goes for the team at PEW Literary – to John Ash, Rebecca Sandell and Margaret Halton, thank you so much for all that you do on my behalf. And thank you, as always, to Patrick Walsh, dear friend, and a guiding hand with all my books and not least this one.

I am more grateful than I can say to my family – my parents, my brother Tom and his gang, and, of course, to Rachel, Ned and Daisy, who are always there for me and give me so much. But lastly, I want to thank David Christopherson, son of Stanley, with whom this adventure with the Sherwood Rangers really began, first at Le Hamel on Gold Beach in June 2004 and then, a day later, as we walked up on to Point 103. A seed was sown – of enduring friendship, of adventures together and a journey into the wartime past of the Sherwood Rangers Yeomanry that has been immeasurably rewarding and a great source of joy. David, I'm very happy we've walked so much of this path together. Thank you so very much.

Picture Acknowledgements

All photographs have been kindly supplied by the author except those listed below. Every effort has been made to trace copyright holders; any who have been overlooked are invited to get in touch with the publishers.

Section 1

Page 2, bottom left
Shermans lined up in southern England before loading for D-Day: © Imperial War Museum CNA 902.

Page 3, top right
An A Squadron Sherman driving off an LCT on to Jig Red on D-Day: The Tank Museum, Bovington.

Page 4, top left
Dead cattle around Point 103, Saint-Pierre and Fontenay: © Imperial War Museum B 5938.

Page 4, top right
A knocked-out Pak 40 anti-tank gun and Panther: © Imperial War Museum B 5939.

Page 4, middle
Charles Renney's knocked-out B Squadron Sherman: © Imperial War Museum B 6043.

Page 4, bottom left
A 24th Lancers Sherman heads south towards Rauray: © Imperial War Museum B 6266.

Page 4, bottom right
Stanley Christopherson sits beside the 88mm gun of a Tiger: Stanley Christopherson Papers.

Page 5, top left
John Hanson-Lawson, commander of B Squadron: Karl McDermott.

Page 5, top right
B Troop of the Essex Yeomanry with their Sexton: Stanley Christopherson Papers.

Page 5, bottom left
Tommies clamber over a captured Jagdpanther: © Imperial War Museum STT 3583A.

Page 7, top left
John Semken during a pause in the charge through France and Belgium: Karl McDermott.

Page 7, middle left
Cpl Cyril Burnet and his Firefly crew: Karl McDermott.

Page 7, middle
Lt Ted Cooke's troop was wiped out at Gheel by hidden Jagdpanthers: Gil Geerings.

Page 7, middle right
A Jagdpanther was destroyed by Cyril Burnet's Firefly: © Imperial War Museum BU 868.

Page 7, bottom
Jagdpanther knocked out near the edge of Gheel: Gil Geerings.

Page 8, top left
Johnny Mann, killed at Gheel: Karl McDermott.

Page 8, middle right
Stanley Christopherson and Jack Holman consult astride Bramley: Stanley Christopherson Papers.

Page 8, bottom
Sgt Nelson and his crew pose with their Stuart: © Imperial War Museum NA 4491.

Section 2

Page 9, middle
American transport under command of XXX Corps badly bogged in a muddy track: © Imperial War Museum B 12034.

Page 9, bottom right
Major Jack Holman (in the turret) and his Sherman tank crew of the Nottinghamshire Yeomanry: © Imperial War Museum B 12253.

Page 10, top left
Jack Holman and Jimmy McWilliam: Stanley Christopherson Papers.

Page 10, top right
Dick Holman, David Render, Ronnie Hutton and John Semken: Stanley Christopherson Papers.

Page 10, middle left
Investiture: Lt-Col. Stanley Christopherson MC, CO of the Sherwood Rangers Yeomanry, receives the DSO from Field Marshal Montgomery: © Imperial War Museum B 12511.

Page 10, bottom
Stanley Christopherson with fellow officers at Brunssum following investiture: Stanley Christopherson Papers.

Page 11, top
Stanley Christopherson stands alongside fellow senior officers before BLACK-COCK: Karl McDermott.

Page 11, lower middle left
BLACKCOCK was briefly threatened by yet more rain – and mud – before the freeze returned: Karl McDermott.

Page 11, bottom left
Johnny Lanes' Firefly, hull down near Heinsberg: Karl McDermott.

Page 12, top
Lt-Gen. Horrocks, FM Montgomery and Gen. Thomas study a map of the front: © Imperial War Museum B 14871.

Page 12, bottom left
Flooding of the Rhine during VERITABLE: Stanley Christopherson Papers.

Page 12, bottom right
Flooding of the Rhine during VERITABLE – dead cattle: Stanley Christopherson Papers.

Page 13, top left
British transport passing through the flooded roads of Kranenburg: © Imperial War Museum B 14536.

Page 13, top right
Following the capture of Cleve, Sherwood Rangers tanks move forward with infantry south of Kranenburg: Sherwood Rangers Archives.

Page 13, upper middle right
The regiment moved back to Cleve and RHQ managed to find a house still intact: Stanley Christopherson Papers.

Page 14, top left
Stanley Christopherson with an American soldier in Issum: © Imperial War Museum B 15232.

Page 14, top right
Issum was badly knocked about: Stanley Christopherson Papers.

Page 14, middle left
The Sherwood Rangers crossed the mighty Rhine on 26 March: Stanley Christopherson Papers.

Page 14, middle right
Tanks waiting to be ferried over the Rhine: Stanley Christopherson Papers.

Integrated Pictures

Page x
Jig Gold Beach: James Holland.

Page xii
Stanley Christopherson (right) leans on the bonnet of a jeep: © Imperial War Museum B 6219.

Page xxxix, top
An anti-tank platoon of the 11th DLI: © Imperial War Museum B 6045.

Page xxxix, bottom
A Sherman of the 24th Lancers near Rauray: James Holland.

Page xliii, top
Two Sherwood Rangers crewmen preparing food beside their tank: James Holland.

Page xliii, bottom
A five-man Sherman crew from A Squadron: James Holland.

Page xlix
The whitewash has already started to streak and wash away as this Sherwood Ranger Sherman struggles in the snow during BLACKCOCK: © Imperial War Museum B 13970.

Page lv
Sherman Rangers in Issum, 6 March 1945: © Imperial War Museum B 15233.

Page lxi
Ernie Leppard's Firefly crew in Issum: © Imperial War Museum B 15229.

Pages lxiv–lxv
Principal personalities: supplied by the author from various sources.

Pages 10–11
Part I opener: © Imperial War Museum B 5258.

Pages 224–5
Part II opener, Sherman tanks crossing a Bailey bridge over the Seine at Vernon: © Imperial War Museum B 9750.

Pages 292–3
Part III opener, Sherman tanks of 8th Armoured Brigade advance through the snow: © Imperial War Museum B 13971.

Pages 372–3
Part IV opener, Sherman tanks, carriers and other vehicles in Geldern: © Imperial War Museum B 15230.

Page 426
Men of C Squadron, John Bennett playing accordion: James Holland.

Page 448, top
A Squadron in Geilenkirchen: James Holland.

Page 448, bottom
Sherman tanks advancing near Geilenkirchen: © Imperial War Museum BU 1411.

Page 449
Appendix 4 opener, Tanks of the Sherwood Rangers lined up for Operation PEPPERPOT: © Imperial War Museum BU 1732.

Pages 450–8
Tank drawings: The Tank Museum, Bovington.

Index

Page numbers in *italics* refer to illustrations.